H.G.M. Williamson

Studies in Persian Period History and Historiography

WIPF & STOCK · Eugene, Oregon

HUGH G. M. WILLIAMSON, born 1947; Graduate of Cambridge University; 1975–1992 Lecturer in Hebrew and Aramaic at Cambridge; since 1992 Regius Professor of Hebrew, University of Oxford and Student of Christ Church, Fellow of the British Academy.

Wipf and Stock Publishers
199 W 8th Ave, Suite 3
Eugene, OR 97401

Studies in Persian Period History and Historiography
By Williamson, H. G. M.
Copyright©2004 Mohr Siebeck
ISBN 13: 978-1-60899-417-5
Publication date 2/11/2010
Previously published by Mohr Sieback, 2004

This edition reprinted 2010 by Wipf and Stock through special arrangement with Mohr Siebeck Gmbh & Co. KG.
Copyright © 2004 Mohr Siebeck.

*Dedicated to my colleagues in the
Society for Old Testament Study
in gratitude for the honour of being
elected as President for the year 2004*

Preface

It was a great honour to be invited by the editors of the series *Forschungen zum Alten Testament* to submit a collection of articles for publication. As they left the selection entirely to me, I decided that I could most helpfully include most of the articles and other studies which related to the lengthy period during which I focused my research and writing on the books of Chronicles, Ezra and Nehemiah. This is intended to lend the collection a certain coherence, and also fills in a good deal of the background work which related to my preparation of commentaries on these books.

The question which always arises in these circumstances is whether or not to revise the articles to take account of more recent work. I have decided against undertaking revision for one simple reason. Research on any particular topic is inevitably undertaken within the framework of the state of knowledge and the questions which are being raised at the time. If they then have any effect on the course of the subsequent discussion (which is not always the case!), within a decade or two the framework is altered and new questions have arisen. To tack on a little additional bibliography, or to make a few remarks in response to particular points of criticism, skews the presentation and leaves a misleading impression. The earliest pieces included here were written nearly thirty years ago. Inevitably, new material has come to light in the meantime, opinions have been modified and the course of the discussion has moved on. Although I am in no way ashamed of anything republished here, it would be equally surprising if I still agreed with every word that I wrote then. But it is as they were that they made their contribution, and I prefer that they be preserved within their own context rather than turned into something that they were never intended to be. New situations call for fresh work, not the reworking of old, and in fact the final article in this collection is precisely an attempt to revisit a problem with which I had dealt long before in an attempt to bring the discussion up to date.

The exceptions to this self-imposed rule should be mentioned for the sake of accuracy. First, for aesthetic reasons the attempt has been made to adopt a unified style for references and the like, not to reproduce the several different systems that characterize the different journals and *Festschriften* in our field. In some cases, this has meant providing footnotes to include the references which in the original publication were provided only in collected bibliographies at the end of the article, and there is no article which has not had to receive some modification to conform to the style adopted for this book. Since in addition most of the collection was written before the days when the use of word-processors was common, the whole was at the same time put on disk for the convenience of the publisher. For undertaking this monumental task, I should like to express my sincere thanks to Dr Francesca Stavrakopoulou of Worcester College, Oxford; whatever is pleasing about the text's appearance is due to her dedicated labours.

Secondly, the nature of chapter 12 should be explained. At its base lies an article of the same name that was published in the *Tyndale Bulletin*. At about the same time, I was also preparing an article for a *Festschrift* for Professor Seeligmann of Jerusalem. The topics overlapped in one particular, but some detail included in the latter was not reproduced in the former. For the present book, therefore, I have incorporated the material from the Seeligmann volume which did not find inclusion in the other (about two pages in all). The details of the original article which has here been plundered are 'The Dynastic Oracle in the Books of Chronicles', in A. Rofé and Y. Zakovitch (eds.), *Essays on the Bible and the Ancient Near East: Isac Leo Seeligmann Volume*, 3 (Jerusalem, 1983), 305–18.

Finally, the first chapter has not been previously published. It was written many years ago for a composite volume which in the end never appeared. Although again it is something of a child of its time, it also sets out some of my thinking about the problems and possible solutions relating to the whole enterprise of history writing in connection with the province of Judah in the Persian period, and I find that on this I have not changed my mind in major ways. It therefore serves rather well in place of an introduction to the whole.

Since not everything could be included in this volume, I have added a list of my other publications on the material relevant to its concerns after the list of acknowledgments.

It remains for me only to thank the editors of this series once again for inviting me to make this selection, and to the editorial staff at Mohr Siebeck for their helpfulness in bringing the project to fruition.

Christ Church, Oxford   H.G.M. Williamson

Table of Contents

Preface VII
Acknowledgments XI
Other Publications on Persian Period History and Historiography XIII

Historical Studies

1. Early Post-Exilic Judaean History 3
   A. The Nature of the Sources 3
   B. Procedure 7
   C. The Early Years 11
   D. From Zerubbabel to Nehemiah 16
   E. Nehemiah 19
   F. The Last Century of Achaemenid Rule 21
2. Judah and the Jews 25
3. The Governors of Judah under the Persians 46
4. Nehemiah's Walls Revisited 64
5. The Historical Value of Josephus' *Jewish Antiquities* xi. 297–301 ... 74
   A. Evidence for the Use of a Source 75
   B. The Value of Josephus' Source 79
   C. Josephus' Handling of his Source 80
   D. Conclusions 88

Chronicles

6. Introduction to M. Noth, *The Chronicler's History* 93
7. Sources and Redaction in the Chronicler's Genealogy of Judah 106
8. 'We are Yours, O David': The Setting and Purpose of
   1 Chronicles 12:1–23 115
9. The Origins of the Twenty-Four Priestly Courses:
   A Study of 1 Chronicles 23–27 126
10. The Accession of Solomon in the Books of Chronicles 141
11. The Temple in the Books of Chronicles 150

12. Eschatology in Chronicles 162
    A. The Present Position 163
    B. Alternative Viewpoints: Survey and Critique 166
    C. The Dynastic Oracle 176
    D. Later development 186
    E. The Significance of 2 Chronicles 7:12–22 191
    F. Conclusions 194

Ezra-Nehemiah

13. Post-Exilic Historiography 199
14. Ezra and Nehemiah in the Light of the Texts from Persepolis 212
    A. Language 216
    B. Support of Local Cults 220
    C. Travel and Transportation 224
    D. Conclusion 230
15. Scripture Citing Scripture: *The Historical Books* 232
    A. The Law 232
    B. Narrative 239
    C. The Prophets 242
16. The Composition of Ezra 1–6 244
    A. Ezra 2 245
    B. Ezra 1 250
    C. Ezra 4:6–6:22 257
    D. Ezra 3:1–4:5 264
    E. Provenance and Purpose 267
    F. Concluding Summary 270
17. The Belief System of the Book of Nehemiah 271
    A. The Nehemiah Memoir 273
    B. Other Material in the Book of Nehemiah 277
    C. The Final Redactor 279
18. Structure and Historiography in Nehemiah 9 282
19. The Problem with First Esdras 294

Indexes 307
  Biblical Passages 307
  Modern Authors 318
  Subjects 324

Acknowledgments

Thanks are due as indicated below for permission to republish the following articles:

To the Nederlands Instituut voor het Nabije Oosten for **2**. 'Judah and the Jews', in M. Brosius and A. Kuhrt (eds.), *Studies in Persian History: Essays in Memory of David M. Lewis* (Achaemenid History 11; Leiden, 1998), 145–63.

To the editor of the *Tyndale Bulletin* for **3**. 'The Governors of Judah under the Persians', *TynB* 39 (1988) 59–82, and **12**. 'Eschatology in Chronicles', *TynB* 28 (1977), 115–54.

To the editor of the *Palestine Exploration Quarterly* for **4**. 'Nehemiah's Walls Revisited', *PEQ* 116 (1984), 81–88.

To Oxford University Press for **5**. 'The Historical Value of Josephus' *Jewish Antiquities* xi.297–301', *JTS* ns 28 (1977), 49–66, and **16**. 'The Composition of Ezra i–vi', *JTS* ns 34 (1983), 1–30.

To Continuum (incorporating the former Sheffield Academic Press) for **6**. 'Introduction' to the English translation of M. Noth, *The Chronicler's History* (JSOTSup 50; Sheffield, 1987), 11–26, and **11**. 'The Temple in the Books of Chronicles', in W. Horbury (ed.), *Templum Amicitiae: Essays on the Second Temple Presented to Ernst Bammel* (JSNTSup 48; Sheffield, 1991), 15–31.

To the Society of Biblical Literature for **7**. 'Sources and Redaction in the Chronicler's Genealogy of Judah', *JBL* 98 (1979), 351–59, and **13**. 'Post-Exilic Historiography', in R. E. Friedman and H. G. M. Williamson (eds.), *The Future of Biblical Studies: The Hebrew Scriptures* (Semeia Studies, 1987), 189–207.

To Brill Academic Publishers for **8**. '"We are Yours, O David": The Setting and Purpose of 1 Chronicles xii 1–23', in A. S. van der Woude (ed.), *'Remembering all the Way ...' (OTS* 21; Leiden, 1981), 164–76; **9**. 'The Origins of the Twenty-Four Priestly Courses: A Study of 1 Chronicles xxiii–xxvii', in J. A. Emerton (ed.), *Studies in the Historical Books of the Old Testament* (VTSup 30; Leiden, 1979), 251–68; **10**. 'The Accession of Solomon in the Books of Chronicles', *VT* 26 (1976), 351–61, and **17**. 'The Belief System of the Book of Nehemiah', in B. Becking and M. C. A. Korpel (eds.), *The Crisis of Israelite Religion: Transformation of Israelite Tradition in Exilic and Post-Exilic Times* (OTS 42; Leiden, 1999), 276–87.

To Eisenbrauns for **14.** 'Ezra and Nehemiah in the Light of the Texts from Persepolis', *Bulletin for Biblical Research* 1 (1991), 41–61.

To Cambridge University Press for **15.** 'History', in D.A. Carson and H.G.M. Williamson (eds.), *It is Written: Scripture Citing Scripture. Essays in Honour of Barnabas Lindars* (Cambridge, 1988), 25–38.

To the World Union of Jewish Studies for **18.** 'Structure and Historiography in Nehemiah 9', in M. Goshen-Gottstein and D. Assaf (eds.), *Proceedings of the Ninth World Congress of Jewish Studies. Panel Sessions: Bible Studies and Ancient Near East* (Jerusalem, 1988), 117–31.

To Mercer University Press for **19.** 'The Problem with First Esdras', in J. Barton and D. Reimer (eds.), *After the Exile: Essays in Honour of Rex Mason* (Macon, 1996), 201–16.

Other Publications on Persian Period History and Historiography

Israel in the Books of Chronicles (Cambridge, 1977)
1 and 2 Chronicles (NCB; Grand Rapids and London, 1982)
Ezra, Nehemiah (WBC, 16; Waco, 1985)
Ezra and Nehemiah (OTG; Sheffield, 1987)
'A Note on 1 Chr. vii 12', VT 23 (1973), 375-9
'"The Sure Mercies of David": Subjective or Objective Genitive?', JSS 23 (1978), 31-49
'The Death of Josiah and the Continuing Development of the Deuteronomic History', VT 32 (1982), 242-8
'A Reconsideration of 'zb II in Biblical Hebrew', ZAW 97 (1985), 74-85
'Reliving the Death of Josiah: a reply to C.T. Begg', VT 37 (1987), 9-15
'Clutching at Catchlines', Bible Review 3 (1987), 56-9
'The Concept of Israel in Transition', in R.E. Clements (ed.), The World of Ancient Israel (Cambridge, 1989), 141-61
'Isaiah 63,7-64,11. Exilic Lament or Post-Exilic Protest?', ZAW 102 (1990), 48-58
''eben gĕlāl (Ezra 5:8; 6:4) Again', BASOR 280 (1990), 83-8
'Laments at the Destroyed Temple', Bible Review 6 (1990), 12-17
'Palestine, Persian Administration of' and 'Sanballat', in Anchor Bible Dictionary 5, 81-6 and 973-5
(with K.D. Tollefson) 'Nehemiah as Cultural Revitalization: An Anthropological Perspective', JSOT 56 (1992), 41-68 (reprinted in J.C. Exum [ed.], The Historical Books: A Sheffield Reader [Sheffield, 1997], 322-48)
'Ezra and Nehemiah', in D.A. Carson et al. (eds.), New Bible Commentary: 21st Century Edition (Leicester, 1994), 420-41
'Chronicles 1, 2: Theology of' and 'Persia', in W.A. VanGemeren (ed.), New International Dictionary of Old Testament Theology and Exegesis 4 (Carlisle, 1997), 466-74 and 1046-48
'Ezra and Nehemiah, Books of', in J.H. Hayes (ed.), Dictionary of Biblical Interpretation (Nashville, 1999), 1.375-82
'Exile and After: Historical Study', in D.W. Baker and B.T. Arnold (eds.), The Face of Old Testament Studies: A Survey of Contemporary Approaches (Grand Rapids and Leicester, 1999), 236-65

'The Family in Persian Period Judah: Some Textual Reflections', in W. G. Dever and S. Gitin (eds.), Symbiosis, Symbolism, and the Power of the Past: Canaan, Ancient Israel, and Their Neighbors – from the Late Bronze Age through Roman Palestina (Winona Lake, 2003), 469–85

Historical Studies

1. Early Post-Exilic Judaean History

The historian of the province of Judah during the Achaemenid period (538–333 BCE) appears at first sight to be unusually well provided with detailed and reliable sources. First, within the Bible the books of Ezra and Nehemiah are paramount, but further light is shed, to a greater or lesser extent, from such prophetic books as Haggai, Zechariah, Malachi, Isaiah 56–66, Joel, and possibly others. Second, the evidence from archaeological discoveries, whether architectural, artifactual, or epigraphic, has been brought together in a magisterial synthesis by Ephraim Stern[1] that must be the envy of those working in other periods, whether earlier or later. Third, there is no shortage of written material from the regions beyond Judah: the corpus of Old Persian texts may be modest, but it has been well studied and has the merit of taking us to the very heart of the empire.[2] Complementary points of view are expressed in the Greek historians, supremely Herodotus, with whose writings historiography is generally thought to have come of age. No less valuable for our purpose are the papyri from Elephantine in Egypt[3] and from Wâdī ed-Dâliyeh in Palestine itself. Finally, though from a much later period, Josephus includes material in his account of this period[4] which most scholars believe to be of some value.

A. The Nature of the Sources

As so often proves to be the case, closer examination reveals that the historian is not left without difficulties in exploiting this apparent abundance of material. First, despite the progress that recent years have seen in the study of the Achaemenid empire, there is still an almost total silence about Palestine in Persian and Greek sources. Thus even if we understood fully Herodotus's

---

[1] E. STERN, Material Culture of the Land of the Bible in the Persian Period 538–332 BC (Warminster and Jerusalem, 1982).

[2] R.G. KENT, Old Persian: Grammar, Texts, Lexicon (AOS, 33; 2nd edn; New Haven, 1953).

[3] See A. COWLEY, Aramaic Papyri of the Fifth Century BC (Oxford, 1923); B. PORTEN, Archives from Elephantine: The Life of an Ancient Jewish Military Colony (Berkeley and Los Angeles, 1968); P. GRELOT, Documents Araméens d'Égypte (Paris, 1972).

[4] *Ant.* 11.

account of the organization of the satrapies, we should still know nothing from that quarter about the constitutional status of Judah. This may come as something of a surprise to those who are used to relying on the now classic *History of the Persian Empire* by A.T. Olmstead;[5] do not considerable portions of his work deal explicitly with Judah and her relations with the central imperial power? It needs to be realized, however, that for those sections Olmstead depends wholly, and sometimes none too critically, upon the biblical record. Its integration with the wider history of the empire was a matter of (perhaps almost unconscious) hypothesis – not to be rejected for that reason alone, as we shall see below, but equally not to be accorded the status of objectivity. Similarly, the importance of Judah to the Achaemenids is probably exaggerated in the minds of Olmstead's readers simply because of his particular interest in the subject. By contrast, it comes as something of a shock to the biblical scholar when perusal of the three modern syntheses of the history of this period – by the classicist J.M. Cook,[6] the Iranian scholar R.N. Frye,[7] and in the recent massive volume devoted to this period in the *Cambridge History of Iran* series[8] – reveals that scarcely any attention whatsoever is paid to characters and events which he or she had always considered fundamental. The somewhat parochial nature of the present chapter needs therefore to be borne in mind.

Second, for all their apparent fullness, the biblical sources suffer from certain defects from the point of view of the historian. Chief among these is the lack of any overall chronological framework. In the pre-exilic period, when Judah was still an independent monarchy, state records (presumably) furnished the Deuteronomistic Historian with such basic information as the order of the kings and the length of their reigns. For whatever reason, no such records have survived from the post-exilic period. Their nearest equivalents, the lists of high priests, are not necessarily complete and in any case are not generally synchronized with our other sources of information. The problems that this circumstance poses are compounded by the fact that there were three Persian kings named Artaxerxes, three named Darius, and two named Xerxes, and that these are not satisfactorily distinguished from each other in the majority of our sources. Consequently, even where there are cross-references to these kings in the biblical texts, there remains uncertainty as to which king is being referred to.

Before the full horror of this situation can be appreciated, it is necessary also to take into account the true nature of our primary source, the books of Ezra and Nehemiah. Despite the evident attempts of editors to weld them together into a literary and theological unity, it is becoming increasingly apparent that these

---

[5] A.T. OLMSTEAD, History of the Persian Empire (Chicago and London, 1948).

[6] J.M. COOK, The Persian Empire (London, 1983).

[7] R.N. FRYE, The History of Ancient Iran (Handbuch der Altertumswissenschaft, III.7; Munich, 1984).

[8] I. GERSHEVITCH (ed.), The Cambridge History of Iran, 2: The Median and Achaemenian Periods (Cambridge, 1985).

books were assembled from originally completely discrete sources. This is not the place to undertake a full literary analysis, but the results of such a study may be usefully, if somewhat cavalierly, stated.

The account of the return of the Jews from their Babylonian exile to Judah and their restoration of the temple in Ezra 1–6 was built up from first-hand official records by an editor working long after the events in question.[9] These records, which are mostly cited *in extenso*, are of outstanding value as raw materials for a history, but their narrative conjoining is only what the editor could deduce from the sources themselves, and so is devoid of independent historical value. Where there are references to the kings in these documents, the historical contexts are for the most part reasonably secure; but not all are so dated.

The account of Ezra's journey to Jerusalem and his reform (Ezra 7–10; Nehemiah 8) is also to be regarded as a once quite independent source. At least, that is the best that can be said about it, for many scholars are extremely skeptical about its historical value.[10] I have tried to argue elsewhere[11] that such skepticism may not be warranted, but even if that be granted, we must still accept that only one year's activity is described, with no antecedent cause or subsequent effect alluded to. In other words, the material may be detailed, but it remains isolated, the reference to 'the seventh year of Artaxerxes' in Ezra 7:7 being notoriously slippery.

The situation is not dissimilar in the case of Nehemiah. The importance of his so-called memoir is celebrated on all sides, and rightly so when it is taken on its own terms. In their enthusiasm, however, scholars seem generally to overlook the fact that the events recorded here fall into two groups. The first is focused almost entirely on the wall-building and its immediate aftermath, and so again spans no more than a year at most. The remainder comprises a number of brief paragraphs describing various social and religious reforms, not themselves dated for the most part, but possibly belonging together as a record of some of the activities of Nehemiah's 'second term' as governor. Once again, therefore, isolated moments of Judah's history are brilliantly illuminated, but nothing connects them firmly to anything recorded in our other sources.

Finally, the rest of the material in the book of Nehemiah is a motley collection of once separate sources, many, perhaps, drawn from the temple archives, if their somewhat priestly bias is to be taken at face value. Only here do we approach the possibility of bridging our historical gaps by way of lists of high priests in Nehemiah 12. Unfortunately, however, many believe that these lists are defective. They seem too short to cover the period in question, so that

---

[9] See H.G.M. WILLIAMSON, 'The Composition of Ezra i–vi', JTS ns 34 (1983), 1–30 (below, 244–70).

[10] C.C. TORREY, The Composition and Historical Value of Ezra-Nehemiah (BZAW, 2; Giessen, 1896); cf. W. TH. IN DER SMITTEN, Esra: Quellen, Überlieferung und Geschichte (SSN, 15; Assen, 1973), for a more recent bibliography.

[11] H.G.M. WILLIAMSON, Ezra, Nehemiah (WBC, 16; Waco, 1985).

whether by haplography of repeated names or some other reason it is not impossible that some names have dropped out. This at once casts doubt on any attempt confidently to locate chronologically the high priests mentioned in our other sources on the basis of these lists. Furthermore, as presented to us now, the lists' own chronological indicators are apparently governed more by ideological than by historical concerns. The reference to 'Darius the Persian' in Neh. 12:22 is a case in point,[12] and the summarizing dates in v. 26, which should in any case be ascribed to the very latest level of redaction in these books, seem more concerned to conflate than to order the material in hand.

The outcome of these considerations is that even though by comparison with other eras the history of Judah in the Achaemenid period seems to many to be a precious necklace, it turns out on examination to be rather an assortment of isolated gems which have lost the chain that ought to be keeping them in shapely order. In scholarly writing characters and events are slid up and down the scale of absolute chronology in a totally bewildering variety of permutations.

There is one further introductory point concerning our sources that ought not to need saying but that in fact needs to be emphatically underlined. These works were not written with historical interests primarily in view. It is therefore very frustrating to find that there are several issues in addition to chronology that seem fundamental to us in the historical enterprise, which they pass over as of no significance. The best-known example concerns an issue that we have already seen is not resolved to everyone's satisfaction by extra-biblical sources either, namely the constitutional status of Judah and the position of its leaders. In one of his now classic essays, Alt[13] was able to exploit this situation in order to argue that before Nehemiah's time Judah was administered as part of the province of Samaria within the satrapy of 'Beyond the River'. Only with the appointment of Nehemiah did Judah gain the status of a separate province with its own governor. Since Alt wrote, the discussion of his theory has been prolonged and shows no sign of resolution yet. To re-examination of the texts[14] have been added considerations from epigraphical sources.[15] But whereas we might have hoped (and some have claimed) that these would settle the matter, we find in fact that they come up against chronological problems of their own. In brief, the clearest evidence ought to come from the references to 'governor' on bullae and seals, but sadly the experts disagree over whether they come before or after Nehemiah.[16]

---

[12] See WILLIAMSON, Ezra, Nehemiah, 364–65.

[13] A. ALT, 'Die Rolle Samarias bei der Entstehung des Judentums', in A. ALT (ed.), Festschrift Otto Procksch (Leipzig, 1934), 5–28; reprinted in Kleine Schriften zur Geschichte des Volkes Israel, 2 (Munich, 1953), 316–37.

[14] M. SMITH, Palestinian Parties and Politics that Shaped the Old Testament (New York and London, 1971), 193–201; S. E. MCEVENUE, 'The Political Structure in Judah from Cyrus to Nehemiah', CBQ 43 (1981), 353–64.

[15] N. AVIGAD, Bullae and Seals from a Post-Exilic Judean Archive (Qedem, 4; Jerusalem, 1976).

[16] See STERN, Material Culture of the Land of the Bible, 199–209.

If the later date is upheld, then clearly their evidence, however valuable in other respects, is mute with specific regard to Alt's theory. But Alt in turn, it needs to be said, based his argument very much on silence, and as ought to be clear by now, such arguments need to be treated with the very greatest caution in the present context. Japhet[17] has done well to show the extent to which ideological concerns may account for the lack of attention to political issues in Ezra in particular. Although this cannot wholly account for the ambivalent attitude of the official records included in Ezra 1–6, it serves at any rate as a warning not to expect clear answers to most of the questions which we pose today almost as a matter of course.

B. Procedure

Our discussion thus far leaves us with the difficult problem of how best to proceed. One possibility is to become an academic sniper, picking off all hypotheses without necessarily having anything very positive to propose in their place. For the reasons we have noted, this approach is extremely easy for the period under consideration; for every date or connection proposed, to go no further, it is always possible to intone the response that there is an alternative, so that nothing should be considered certain. The present book is hardly the place for such self-indulgence, however.

Second, we may proceed to retell the biblical story, more or less modified according to critical predilections, and with extra-biblical tidbits thrown in where possible. This is the standard procedure in history textbooks, but ultimately it is not satisfying. The reason is that it tries to make a single narrative thread out of what are, generally speaking, historically unrelated subjects. It was the genius of the biblical authors to do this for their theological purposes, and of course that was, and remains, a legitimate exercise. But it is not the same enterprise as historiography as generally understood. Thus the endless debate about the relative chronology of Ezra and Nehemiah becomes less pressing if the need to relate them to one another is dropped: their purposes, status, and spheres of authority are clearly shown in the texts to be distinct, and it is better to treat them as such. The same can be said for the tensions between official documents and their later theologically-motivated editors, and so on.

I propose, then, that at this stage the most fruitful advance may be made by tracing two distinct histories: of political institutions and of religious thought and practice. The advantage of my proposal is that it allows us to compare like with like. In this way, despite all the gaps in our knowledge, there is the potential for a relative chronology within each of the categories concerned. I am not

---

[17] S. JAPHET, 'Sheshbazzar and Zerubbabel', ZAW 94 (1982), 66–98.

unaware of the objection that political and religious history cannot be separated in the biblical world. I accept that objection to a limited extent, if by it is meant that political leaders may sometimes have acted out of religious motives and convictions and vice versa. But I should still maintain that there is a sufficient distinction to enable us to proceed. After all, Judah was by now part of a large and totally non-Jewish empire. In Judah as much as in Babylon the Jews were having to learn how to live both by 'the law of your God and the law of the king' (Ezra 7:26).

Again, the opinion is frequently advanced that increasingly through the Persian period political power was bifurcated between the secular governor, with his responsibility for taxation on behalf of the central authorities of the satrapy and the empire, and the high priest, who raised internal revenue by way of a temple tax necessary for the administration of what some regard as a temple-state. Powerful support for this view will no doubt be claimed from the newly-published coin[18] bearing the inscription 'Johanan the priest' alongside coins of a similar type inscribed with the name of the province, *yhd*. Furthermore, Meyers[19] has recently argued that this situation prevailed already from the sixth century BCE on. Yet even if this were so (and the evidence, it has to be said, remains very slight; one wonders to what extent earlier scholars assumed it on the basis of the situation later in the Hellenistic period and more recent writers have merely perpetuated the idea), it would still not invalidate my proposal: the political role of the high priest would still need to be kept distinct from a history of religious thought.

In the bulk of this chapter, therefore, attention will be concentrated on the political history of Judah in the Achaemenid period, with developments in religious thought referred to only where they impinge upon this particular area. One consequence of this procedure is that comparatively little notice will be taken of Ezra. This may seem strange to some readers who are familiar with his dominant position within biblical and post-biblical tradition. The fact is, however, that his political impact appears to have been minimal, and readers will have to judge whether our presentation is the poorer without him.

I have stated that as far as possible two branches of history – political and religious – need to be kept distinct. Ideally, a third area of study should be included, namely what may be broadly classified as social history. Whitelam[20] has recently entered a powerful plea to the effect that this should be taken far more seriously than is customary in the research of historians of ancient Israel, and indeed he implies that it should take precedence over what he calls text-based reconstructions. Among the disciplines whose importance he urges, he

---

[18] D. BARAG, 'Some Notes on a Silver Coin of Johanan the High Priest', BA 48 (1985), 166–68.

[19] E.M. MEYERS, 'The Shelomith Seal and the Judean Restoration: Some Additional Considerations', ErIsr 18 (1985), 33*–38*.

[20] K.W. WHITELAM, 'Recreating the History of Israel', JSOT 35 (1986), 45–70.

refers to social scientific methods, new archaeology, settlement patterns, demographic studies, the effects of climate, disease, shifting trade patterns, and so on. For many, recent literary study has eroded confidence in the biblical texts for the early history of Israel, at least until the founding of the monarchy,[21] and Whitelam claims that this erosion is likely to continue into even later periods. As a result, one plank of what he regards as a nineteenth-century western approach to historiography is removed. The other plank is the view that 'men make history', with its consequence that history is the study of leading personalities. But, urges Whitelam, this is just a reflection of the bias of our literary sources. In fact, 'the novel can only be understood in terms of the recurrent and regular', and to ignore the primacy of the latter, for which literary sources are not at all best suited as evidence, is to court the danger of encouraging 'the reduction of complex historical reality to simplistic categories'.

With specific reference to the period under discussion here, he deserves to be cited in full:

What kind of history is it that devotes its attention to the precise chronological sequence of Ezra and Nehemiah, or how many Elyashibs and Sanballats may have figured in the history of Israel and is able to say little, if anything, about the wider social reality?[22]

Standard treatments of Ezra and Nehemiah, for instance, concentrate upon the personalities and the politics of the biblical narratives and the perplexing problem of their chronological relationship. There is little time left to investigate the situation of Palestine vis-à-vis the Persian empire, particularly changing trade patterns, or to outline changes in settlement patterns in Palestine as a result of the change in political hegemony. It is only when such questions are seen to be significant that strategies will be devised to investigate these complex problems.[23]

There is much in Whitelam's criticisms of current writing on Israel's history that is justified, and indeed most of his points have already been made by others, even if in less concentrated form. Nevertheless, it is difficult to avoid the impression that he has somewhat exaggerated his case in order to make his point more forcefully, and he himself recognizes that text-based history retains some validity. Although it would be inappropriate to take up the issues fully here, some remarks are in order to justify the more conservative approach adopted in the present chapter.

First, the methods that Whitelam advocates have been largely developed as tools for historical research in the context of what is misleadingly termed prehistory, that is to say the history of non- or pre-literate societies. It would be churlish, however, to deny the value of written historical sources where they are available. They give us access, albeit partial and one-sided, to a wealth of

---

[21] See J.A. SOGGIN, A History of Israel: from the Beginnings to the Bar Kochba Revolt, AD 135 (London, 1984).
[22] WHITELAM, 'Recreating the History of Israel', 53.
[23] WHITELAM, 'Recreating the History of Israel', 54.

information that is simply unobtainable in any other form, and it is only the consequence of natural human interest that gives them particular prominence in the work of many historians.

Second, although it is true that few, if any, of the biblical texts are free of major critical problems, Whitelam has overstated the negative consequences of these difficulties, at least so far as the later biblical period is concerned. If historians pay much attention to the detailing and, where possible, unravelling of these problems, that is because they hope to move towards their resolution, and not to their being ruled out altogether as primary evidence. This is certainly the case with our review of the sources available for the history of Achaemenid Judah.

Third, it needs to be remembered that the types of evidence that Whitelam favours are also highly ambiguous, material remains being in themselves largely mute and the subject of hypothesis and controversy among the experts.

Fourth, Whitelam's article is a call for a new research strategy, not an exposition of work accomplished. As he candidly recognizes, many of the necessary data are not yet available, and those that are have yet to be collected and organized. We may thus heartily endorse his appeal for work to be done in this area and at the same time recognize that in a chapter such as the present one it will not be possible at this stage to include such material.

Fifth, this conclusion is more particularly the case with regard to our period where, despite a few pioneering efforts,[24] such a programme lies way in the future. Since all such work is more than usually inter-disciplinarian, the historian is at the moment left waiting for his colleagues in cognate disciplines to advance along the lines of their own expertise before seeing what can be made of their results.

Finally, although acknowledging that the unique or unusual stands out only by contrast with what is normal, it would be wrong to deny that those who were present at the time had a less clear idea of this contrast than we do today. Such considerations will sometimes have determined what was recorded. Of course, such perceptions entail value judgements, but it is precisely because many historians of Israel share some of the values of those whom they study that the latter retain an interest which other data do not. If all historical writing reflects the bias of its writers, then a more traditional approach should not be dismissed as totally illegitimate. The history of ideas or institutions or religion may not be the interest of a social historian, and the latter may well have far more to say about these subjects than we have yet imagined. But that does not amount to a

---

[24] E.g. H.G. KIPPENBERG, Religion und Klassenbildung im antiken Judäa: Eine religionssoziologische Studie zum Verhältnis von Tradition und gesellschaftlicher Entwicklung (SUNT, 14; Göttingen, 1978); W. SCHOTTROFF, 'Arbeit und sozialer Konflikt im nachexilischen Zeit', in L. and W. SCHOTTROFF (eds.), Mitarbeiter der Schöpfung: Bibel und Arbeitswelt (Munich, 1983), 104–48.

denial of the intrinsic value of attempting a reconstruction of political or religious history, for which in our period the literary evidence, so it seems to me, remains paramount.

C. The Early Years

For the early part of our period, the major issue to be resolved concerns the disagreement already described about whether Judah was an autonomous province within the satrapy of 'Beyond the River' or whether until Nehemiah's time it was part of the larger province of Samaria. According to the biblical sources, from the days of the first return Judah was referred to as a $m^e dînâ$ (Ezra 2:1), and two officials, Sheshbazzar and Zerubbabel, are termed $pehâ$ (Ezra 5:14; Hag. 1:1). *Prima facie*, therefore, one would suppose that Judah was a separate province from the very earliest days of Persian rule.[25]

Alt and those who have followed him, however, have maintained that the title $pehâ$ is sufficiently flexible to allow that these two officials were merely individuals commissioned with specific tasks, while Fensham[26] has argued, not very convincingly, that $m^e dînâ$ refers to Babylon, whence the exiles came, rather than to Judah, whither they were bound. It is doubtful, however, that he would have attempted this explanation had he not already been persuaded by Alt's overall view.

Potentially important new evidence has been added to the debate by Avigad's publication of a number of bullae and seals.[27] Many of these bear the name of the province, $yh(w)d$, and some also include personal names. With good reason the following two points are now generally agreed:

(a) The bullae and seals should be interpreted in the light of one another, the whole horde thus deriving originally from some official archive. Although their provenance is unknown, they were apparently discovered together. As well as those with the name of the province only, some combine the name of the province with the name of an individual, and others link personal names with official titles (e.g., phw' see below, and $hspr$). It is thus probable that those with personal names only should also be regarded as officials of some kind.

(b) The reading phw', 'the governor', is also to be regarded as assured, despite its linguistic irregularity.[28] When this word was first read alongside some per-

---

[25] See G. WIDENGREN, 'The Persian Period', in J.H. HAYES and J.M. MILLER (eds.), Israelite and Judaean History (London, 1977), 509–11.
[26] F.C. FENSHAM, 'Mĕdînâ in Ezra and Nehemiah', VT 25 (1975), 795–97.
[27] AVIGAD, Bullae and Seals.
[28] For a suggested explanation of this linguistic irregularity see E.Y. KUTSCHER, 'Phw' and its Cognates' Tarbiz 30 (1960–61), 112–19 (Hebrew).

sonal names on some stamped jar handles from Ramat Raḥel,[29] it was challenged by Cross.[30] He observed that after about 500 BCE the letter *wāw* was no longer written with a 'peaked right shoulder' and that even before that it was becoming rare. Since there was no reason to date these stamps earlier than the fifth century BCE, Cross affirmed that the letter in question must be a *rēš*, and that the word should thus be read as *phr'*, 'the potter'. This was a not unreasonable conclusion in the light of the evidence available at that time. The material published by Avigad, however, confirms the reading *pḥw'* for the following reasons: (i) in the context of the horde as a whole, we expect an official title; (ii) although a potter's name is conceivable on a jar, it is highly improbable on a seal; (iii) one of the seals (no. 14) is inscribed 'Belonging to Shelomith, the maidservant of Elnathan the governor'. (The last word is damaged, but the restoration appears certain by comparison with bulla no. 5.) To read 'potter' in this context (and hence also in bulla no. 5) would be ridiculous; (iv) elsewhere in the horde there are several clear examples of the letter *wāw* written with the 'peaked right shoulder' (e. g., in *yhwd* at plate 5(d); in some examples of *lbrwk* at plate 8, etc.).

What remains in dispute is the date to be ascribed to these bullae and seals. On the basis of palaeography Avigad dated them to the sixth century BCE. Some of the letters display early, and even archaic, features which had certainly disappeared by the fifth century BCE. Although some have rejected Avigad's conclusion (see below), I am not aware of any attempt to present alternative evidence which would refute his specifically palaeographical discussion. It is, of course, recognized on all sides that such evidence cannot be finally decisive, but in the absence of better arguments it deserves to be taken seriously and the attempt made to see whether it can be supported on other grounds.

One such possibility has been advanced (apparently independently) by Lemaire[31] and Meyers.[32] They note that Avigad had drawn attention to the coincidence of names between the Shelomith of the seal referred to above (no. 14) and the Shelomith of 1 Chron. 3:19, who was a daughter of Zerubbabel. In favour of identifying the two, they point out that both in biblical genealogies and on seals the names of women are comparatively rare; that the curiosity of having a woman mentioned in the Davidic genealogy is best explained if she held some official position; and that the dates of the two named may be plausibly held to have coincided. These arguments seem reasonable, and if we adopt their conclusion we should note that this would also fit well with the most natural understanding of Neh. 5:15, which speaks of governors prior to Nehemiah's time

---

[29] Y. AHARONI, Excavations at Ramat Raḥel: Seasons 1959 and 1960 (Rome, 1962); Excavations at Ramat Raḥel: Seasons 1961 and 1962 (Rome, 1964).
[30] F. M. CROSS, 'Judean Stamps', ErIsr 9 (1969), 20–27.
[31] A. LEMAIRE, Review of Avigad, in Syria 54 (1977), 129–31.
[32] MEYERS, 'The Shelomith Seal'.

who, one should assume with Smith[33] and others, were governors of Judah rather than Samaria. We shall be able later to suggest alternative reasons why there may have been some changes in the situation when Nehemiah came to Jerusalem, without having to go to the lengths of adopting Alt's theory.

According to Ezra 1:1, within a year of his entering Babylon in October 539 BCE, Cyrus had authorized the return of the Jews to Jerusalem and the rebuilding of the temple. Although the authenticity of the decree that follows (Ezra 1:2–4) has often been disputed,[34] its general tenor is confirmed by the Aramaic version in Ezra 6:3–5, whose reliability is widely, and rightly, accepted.

The first return was led by Sheshbazzar, about whom all that is known is that he was appointed governor (Ezra 5:14), that he brought some of the temple vessels back from Babylon (1:7–11), and that he was responsible for an unsuccessful start on the rebuilding of the temple (5:16). There is no evidence to link him with the Davidic family,[35] and the probability must be that he was a leading member of the community of the exiles.[36]

Sheshbazzar was apparently succeeded as governor by Zerubbabel, but our sources remain silent about the transition. First, the date of Zerubbabel's journey to Jerusalem is uncertain. Although Ezra 2:1–2 appears to suggest that it was at the very start of the period of Persian rule, the list in Ezra 2 was only dated so by the late editor of Ezra 1–6 when he took it over from Nehemiah 7. The list itself shows signs of being a compilation, and it has been frequently assumed that it summarizes a number of different returns during the first twenty years or so of Achaemenid rule. On that assumption, Zerubbabel could have come at any time up until the year 520 BCE (the second year of Darius I), when he was certainly active in Jerusalem (see Hag. 1:1; Ezra 5–6). Those who adopt this latest possible date point in support to the accounts in 1 Esdr. 3:1–5:6, which have Zerubbabel initially serving as a guardsman in the court of Darius. But for various reasons it seems unlikely that we should lay any weight at all on this.

Alternatively, Ezra 3:1–6 seems to suggest that Zerubbabel was present in Jerusalem from the very first. Although much of Ezra 3 relates to the later rebuilding under Darius I, and of the remainder of Ezra 3 most is written for other than historical purposes, I have suggested,[37] admittedly on the basis of only tenuous evidence, that this particular aspect of the chapter may rest on

---

[33] SMITH, Palestinian Parties and Politics.

[34] R. DE VAUX, 'Les décrets de Cyrus et de Darius sur la reconstruction du temple', RB 46 (1937), 29–57 (English translation in The Bible and the Ancient Near East [London, 1971], 63–96); but cf. E.J. BICKERMAN, 'The Edict of Cyrus in Ezra 1', JBL 65 (1946), 249–75 (revised and reprinted in Studies in Jewish and Christian History. Part One [Leiden, 1976], 72–108).

[35] See P.-R. BERGER, 'Zu den Namen ששבצר und שנאצר', ZAW 83 (1971), 98–100.

[36] There is no positive evidence to support the suggestion of J.M. MILLER and J.H. HAYES, A History of Ancient Israel and Judah (London, 1986), 445–46, that he was the 'incumbent ruler of the Judaean province at the time of Cyrus' triumph'.

[37] WILLIAMSON, Ezra, Nehemiah, 44–45.

authentic tradition. If so, we must assume that Zerubbabel accompanied Sheshbazzar back to Jerusalem and worked at first under his authority. In what circumstances he replaced him as governor can only be the subject of speculation, but in view of Zerubbabel's Davidic descent it would seem that there was a desire on the part of the Persians to strengthen their ties with the province. It would be reasonable, then, to link Zerubbabel's promotion with Cambyses' preparations for the conquest of Egypt in 525 BCE. Though such a campaign had been an ambition of Cyrus, he never had the opportunity to fulfil it. It must therefore remain an open question to what extent he concerned himself in detail with the affairs of the Levant. Cambyses' invasion of Egypt, however, both brought him personally to the region and is likely to have meant that he would have been anxious to ensure the loyalty of those provinces through or by which his lines of communication lay.[38] Moreover, if Zerubbabel had already been given such authority, the excitement that centred on his Davidic connections during the troubled early years of Darius I's reign (Hag. 2:20-23) becomes more intelligible than if he was appointed only then precisely in order to guarantee Judah's quiescence. But when all is said and done, it has to be remembered that Zerubbabel may simply have succeeded Sheshbazzar at any time through natural causes, such as death, or because Sheshbazzar's term and commission were limited to the initial return.

As with Sheshbazzar, so with Zerubbabel little can be said for certain of his achievements beyond the vital fact that the temple was rebuilt. Suggestions that he was removed from office or even executed because of seditious activity early in Darius I's reign are to be emphatically rejected,[39] a conclusion now reinforced if, as we have argued above, he was succeeded by his son-in-law Elnathan, the husband of Shelomith. Nor do we have any evidence to suggest that Judah was particularly concerned in Darius's reorganization of the satrapies.[40] Although the province would now have come under the jurisdiction of the smaller satrapy of 'Beyond the River' (and so perhaps more liable to closer inspection and supervision; cf. Ezra 5), its constitutional position apparently remained unchanged.

Evidence for the size of the province and its sub-division into districts comes only later, from Nehemiah's day. On the basis of the information in Nehemiah 3, it has been possible to conclude that the province was considerably smaller than the pre-exilic kingdom of Judah, though it perhaps conformed more closely to the reduced boundaries established by Nebuchadnezzar. We should then note in

---

[38] There are some parallels with what is known of the Egyptian collaborator Udjaḥorresnet, on whom see most recently A. B. LLOYD, 'The Inscription of Udjaḥorresnet, a Collaborator's Testament', JEA 68 (1982), 166–80, with bibliography; note also MILLER AND HAYES, History of Ancient Israel and Judah, 454.

[39] H. G. M. WILLIAMSON, 'Eschatology in Chronicles', TynB 28 (1977), 115–54 (see 162–95 below).

[40] See A. RAINEY, 'The Satrapy "Beyond the River"', AJBA 1 (1969), 51–78; J. M. COOK, 'The Rise of the Achaemenids and Establishment of their Empire', in I. GERSHEVITCH (ed.), The Cambridge History of Iran, Vol. 2, 244–77.

1. Early Post-Exilic Judaean History 15

particular that in the south the border apparently ran to the south of Beth-zur and Keilah but to the north of Hebron, Lachish, and Mareshah, cities which were thus excluded from the province at this time. The main discrepancy between Nehemiah 3 and Ezra 2 concerns the former's omission of the trio of cities in the north-west of the province, Lod, Hadid, and Ono. Since Neh. 6:2 implies that Ono was close to the border in Nehemiah's time, it is clear that this omission is not significant and that these cities should be included. The list of Nehemiah 3 is incomplete, as other evidence suggests, and it is not difficult to see why few if any would have come from so remote a region to help with the wall-building.

Five sub-divisions of the province are referred to by way of their administrative centres: Jerusalem, Beth-hakkerem, Mizpah, Beth-zur, and Keilah. This may not represent a complete picture, however. The north-western sector, whose absence from the list we have already noted, may have had a separate centre,[41] and it would also make geographical sense if Jericho and its environs were a separate district. This brings the total to seven, though Stern reduces the number to six by linking Beth-hakkerem with Jerusalem. Clearly there can be no certainty about such matters, but the overall size and approximate divisions of the province are clear. Since the differences between the lists can be explained, it would seem that this picture remained broadly constant throughout our period.

A final point regarding this early period concerns the population. Clearly Judah was not entirely deserted during the exile, and it is not improbable that alongside the indigenous Judaean population new settlers, such as Edomites, moved in behind the departing exiles. The Jews who first returned were thus obliged to resettle in an area of mixed population. Despite the picture that develops later in the period, it is possible that early on a reasonable degree of accommodation was achieved. The evidence for this comes from Japhet's attractive suggestion[42] that the list of Ezra 2 reflects a combination of returning exiles, registered by families, and those who had remained in the land, registered by domicile. If, then, the list was compiled in response to Tattenai's enquiry about who was involved in the temple-building (Ezra 5:4, 10), as suggested by Galling[43] and others, it would seem that many of the tensions of later times were not a necessary consequence of resettlement. In line with this, the rejection of the northern offer of help in rebuilding (Ezra 4:1–3) is not unintelligible if Judah was a separate province and if the motive was to abide close to the terms of Cyrus's authorization for sound political reasons.[44]

---

[41] STERN (Material Culture, 248) suggests Gezer.

[42] S. JAPHET, 'People and Land in the Restoration Period', in G. STRECKER (ed.), Das Land Israel in biblischer Zeit (Göttingen, 1983), 103–25.

[43] K. GALLING, Studien zur Geschichte Israels im persischen Zeitalter (Tübingen, 1964), 89–108.

[44] See C. SCHULTZ, 'The Political Tensions Reflected in Ezra-Nehemiah', in C. D. EVANS, W. W. HALLO, and J. B. WHITE (eds.), Scripture in Context: Essays on the Comparative Method (Pittsburgh, 1980), 221–44.

D. From Zerubbabel to Nehemiah

Little is known about the period following the dedication of the second temple. We have argued above that Zerubbabel was succeeded as governor by his son-in-law Elnathan, but we have no other evidence to suppose that the succession was regularly a family affair, as it apparently was later in Samaria. On the basis of the stamped jar handles from Ramat Raḥel, Avigad[45] also includes Yehoʿezer and Ahzai as governors prior to Nehemiah, but this is much less certain both because of the lack of any corroborative evidence and because the palaeography of these stamps is more mixed: it is just as possible in material of this kind to argue that the early features are conservative archaisms as that the later features are recent innovations.

As the approach determined for this chapter requires, we shall say nothing about Ezra at this point (regardless of his date) because his strictly political significance is minimal. Instead, we come to the period just prior to Nehemiah's appointment where again there are sufficient circumstantial pointers in our sources to allow for the hypothetical reconstruction of a further step in Judah's development.

The international stage was set by the Egyptian revolt of 460 BCE, which took several years to put down.[46] It was eventually the Syrian satrap Megabyzos who restored Persian hegemony over Egypt, assisted by the newly-appointed Egyptian satrap Arsames.[47] What happened next is related only by Ctesias, the detail of whose account is not generally considered reliable.[48] Five years after the conquest of Egypt, Megabyzos himself led a revolt of the western satrapies: having concluded an agreement with the Athenians, who had been implicated in the Egyptian revolt, Megabyzos found his work cast aside through the machinations of Amestris, the Queen Mother. This personal slight is said to have provoked him to rebel. This development takes us to the year 449 BCE, which Cook[49] defends as being approximately correct on independent grounds. The revolt did not last long, and Megabyzos was restored (temporarily) to favour, but it means that there was a period of very considerable unrest, to say the least, shortly before Nehemiah's appointment in 445 BCE.

It is to this period, secondly, that we should date the fiasco of Ezra 4:8–23. This passage presents the text of an exchange of correspondence between

---

[45] AVIGAD, Bullae and Seals, 35.

[46] There had been an earlier revolt at the beginning of the reign of Xerxes I in 486–485 BCE, but although it brought Xerxes to Palestine in person, we have no direct evidence of Judah's involvement, despite some speculative suggestions to the contrary. Ezra 4:6 may relate to these events, but no details are given.

[47] FRYE, History of Ancient Iran, 127–28.

[48] A.R. BURN, 'Persia and the Greeks', in GERSHEVITCH (ed.), The Cambridge History of Iran, Vol. 2, 292–391 (336).

[49] COOK, The Persian Empire, 169.

Artaxerxes and some local officials of 'Beyond the River', the outcome of which was to put a halt to an attempt to rebuild the walls of Jerusalem. It is thus out of place chronologically in its present setting, but must be dated prior to Nehemiah, who saw the wall-building through to a successful conclusion with imperial support. It is perhaps significant that the letter accusing the Jews of sedition (vv. 8-16) is not said to have been sent by governors or satraps but rather by an odd assortment of officials and others who had originally been resettled in the area by the Assyrians. It then becomes attractive to date this correspondence to the time of Megabyzos' rebellion and to see the accusation as coming from a local group who remained loyal to the Persian court. It need not be supposed that the wall-building necessarily attests Judah's involvement in the revolt (and if Ezra 4:12 refers to Ezra and his caravan, such an accusation would seem more than ever out of place), but in such troubled times even innocent measures were open to misrepresentation, and in the circumstances Artaxerxes' harsh reply (vv. 17-22) is fully intelligible.

Third, the evidence from Samaria suggests that there was a change in the style of administration at about this time. When Nehemiah came to Jerusalem, the governor of Samaria was Sanballat.[50] As we now know from both the Elephantine and the Wâdī ed-Dâliyeh papyri,[51] Sanballat was succeeded as governor by his direct descendants through four further generations until the beginning of Hellenistic rule. It is implied by his description as 'the Horonite', however, that he was the first in this line of succession. Perhaps, then, in the wake of the revolt, there was a need for new office-holders in the region, and Sanballat may have been appointed as one on whom Artaxerxes could rely for support; it is difficult to see otherwise how his 'dynasty' would have lasted so long.

Fourth, the appointment of Nehemiah fits well into this setting. From the Achaemenid point of view, it will again have been seen as a means of ensuring loyal leadership in a troubled but strategically important corner of the empire. This circumstance, it may be suggested, is sufficient to explain the evidence which Stern adduces in favour of Alt's view that Nehemiah was in fact the first governor of the newly-independent province of Judah.[52] He argued that after this time the use of anepigraphic official seals with imitations of Achaemenid motifs gave way to the use of *yhwd* stamps, suggesting greater independence for the province. In response, it may be noted that the use of Achaemenid motifs in the earlier period cannot be used as evidence that Judah was administered as part of Samaria at that time (if anything, it would be more suggestive of 'direct rule'); that some of the *yhwd* stamps may come from as early as the sixth

---

[50] Sanballat is never actually given this title in Nehemiah, but see COWLEY, Aramaic Papyri, 30:29.
[51] F.M. CROSS, 'A Reconstruction of the Judean Restoration', JBL 94 (1975), 4-18.
[52] E. STERN, 'Seal Impressions in the Achaemenid Style in the Province of Judah', BASOR 202 (1971), 6-16; Material Culture of the Land of the Bible, 209-13.

century, in which case they would have been used contemporaneously with the anepigraphic seals for a while; and that if Nehemiah's appointment was part of an overall policy towards 'Beyond the River', as suggested here, a change in style need not indicate a change in constitutional status.

Finally, there remains the question of what happened between Artaxerxes' letter ordering the cessation of the wall-building (Ezra 4:17–22) and the appointment of Nehemiah. Again, a reconstruction is possible only on the basis of circumstantial evidence, no direct evidence being available. One of those who was allied with Sanballat in his opposition to Nehemiah was 'Tobiah the Ammonite servant' (Neh. 2:10). The common view that he was a member of the influential Transjordanian Tobiad family as known from later times[53] and that he was therefore the governor of Ammon is improbable. If that were the case, we should have expected ʿebed to be used in the construct state before 'Ammon', rather than with the adjective 'Ammonite'. Second, Neh. 3:35 (ET 4:3) shows that the adjective is indeed intended to describe his origin, and not his sphere of activity. Third, we do not know for certain that Ammon was a separate province, and even if it were, it would be difficult to explain why its governor had such close ties with certain circles in Jerusalem. Finally, Mazar's attempt to link Tobiah with the one whose name is carved twice in the scarp of the rock facade of a cave tomb at ʿAraq el-Emir in Transjordan must be discounted on palaeographical grounds.[54]

It seems preferable, therefore, to regard Tobiah as a junior colleague to Sanballat, of Ammonite origin (perhaps emphasized by Nehemiah with pejorative overtones based on Deut. 23:4 [ET 3]), but active in the Samarian administration. How, then, should we explain the fact that he had so many close contacts, supporters, and even relatives in Jerusalem (Neh. 6:17–19; 13:4–8)? It may be suggested that he had been appointed to temporary authority over Judah following the debacle of Ezra 4. As Kellermann has observed,[55] one of those who wrote in accusation of the Jews on another unspecified occasion was Tabeel (Ezra 4:7), the Aramaic equivalent of Tobiah. The name is too common categorically to assert an identification, but the possibility is attractive: as a loyal junior official in the region, he was rewarded with the role of 'caretaker governor' over the supposedly unruly province of Judah until its affairs could be more permanently settled. His close ties with Jerusalem are thus explained, as is the obvious pique which he felt when his temporary duties were brought to an end by the arrival of Nehemiah. In any event, it is likely that this latter event marked something of a turning point in the history of the province, just as Sanballat's appointment had done not long before in the north.

---

[53] So, for instance, C. C. McCown, 'The ʿAraq el-Emir and the Tobiads', BA 20 (1957), 63–76; B. Mazar, 'The Tobiads', IEJ 7 (1957), 137–45 and 229–38.

[54] See J. Naveh, The Development of the Aramaic Script (Jerusalem, 1970), 62–64.

[55] U. Kellermann, Nehemia: Quellen, Überlieferung und Geschichte (BZAW, 102; Berlin, 1967).

E. Nehemiah

Our sources leave us in no doubt that Nehemiah came to Jerusalem with the full support of the king himself. This is apparent not only from his previously close personal contacts in his role as 'cupbearer' and the measure of practical assistance that he was granted, but also from the fact that the permission given to him to build the walls of Jerusalem overturned a previous decree of the same king to the contrary effect (Ezra 4:21). We are not explicitly told that he was appointed governor from the start. Although this appears to be the implication of Neh. 5:14, it is not impossible that he was promoted to this position only after the successful completion of the initial task that he came to undertake, since Neh. 2:6 implies that this was expected to take a limited time. He served a first term of twelve years and then had an indeterminate period of leave before returning to Jerusalem; we are not told that this was for a second term as governor, but it is usually assumed that it was.[56] The well-attested leave of absence enjoyed by Arsames, the satrap of Egypt,[57] provides an apt parallel. Indeed, it raises the question whether Nehemiah did not also have personal estates to administer. There are sufficient hints in Nehemiah 2 and 5 to suppose that he did, and if so, they may have provided a more mundane motivation for his initial concern for the situation in Jerusalem than our present text suggests. This does not, however, allow us to suppose that Nehemiah was also a member of the Davidic family.[58]

Despite the detailed description of a few of Nehemiah's activities, we actually know surprisingly little about his achievements as a whole. To generalize from the particular, however, it appears that he pursued a rigorously isolationist policy as regards external affairs and was concerned to strengthen the social cohesion of the province internally. The first point emerges clearly from his activities as wall-builder and his related treatment of the leaders of the potentially more powerful surrounding provinces.[59] The second point, of course, is the almost inevitable corollary of the first. External adversity demands a united internal front. The disturbed period prior to his appointment had opened the way

---

[56] Against the contrary opinions of S. MOWINCKEL, Studien zu dem Buche Ezra-Nehemia. II. Die Nehemia-Denkschrift (Oslo, 1964), 35–37, and KELLERMANN, Nehemia, 48–51, see WILLIAMSON, Ezra, Nehemiah, 382–83, 387.

[57] See G.R. DRIVER, Aramaic Documents of the Fifth Century BC (corrected edition; Oxford, 1965).

[58] See J.A. EMERTON, Review of KELLERMANN, JTS ns 23 (1972), 171–85, and W. TH. IN DER SMITTEN, 'Erwägungen zu Nehemias Davididzität', JSJ 5 (1974), 41–48; contra KELLERMANN, Nehemia, 156–59.

[59] On which see A. ALT, 'Judas Nachbarn zur Zeit Nehemias', PJB 27 (1931), 66–74, reprinted in Kleine Schriften zur Geschichte des Volkes Israel, 2 (Munich, 1953), 338–45; I. RABINOWITZ, 'Aramaic Inscriptions of the Fifth Century BCE from a North-Arab Shrine', JNES 15 (1956), 1–9; KELLERMANN, Nehemia, 166–73; W.J. DUMBRELL, 'The Tell el-Maskhuṭa Bowls and the "Kingdom" of Qedar in the Persian Period', BASOR 203 (1971), 33–44.

for the personal concerns of a number of Judaeans to override what Nehemiah regarded as their broader priorities. Economically, the better-off members of society had pressed their advantages to the severe detriment of the poorer classes; politically, a number developed stronger ties with their peers in Samaria than with their own people; socially, assimilation in family life and language appeared an easier option than the discomforts of particularity; and religiously, many of the establishment clearly favoured what today would be labelled an ecumenical stance. No doubt for most of these positions attractive and plausible arguments could be advanced, but they could not be tolerated alongside Nehemiah's ideal of a strong and independent Judah. The reforms to which he refers, as well as the background that other parts of his narrative presuppose, all seem to have in common a concern to solidify Judaean society, if not in egalitarian terms then at least along the lines of working towards a common objective (see Neh. 2:16–18; 4:15–17 [ET 21–23]; 5; 6:17–19; 7:4–6; 13). It is probable that these moves were popular with the lower class majority and that Nehemiah was able to mobilize their numerical strength in order to force through his reforms. The comparisons that have been drawn between Nehemiah and Solon of Athens a century earlier are thus much to the point.[60]

Despite all this, it is uncertain whether Nehemiah's measures succeeded in effecting lasting change. If the evidence of Nehemiah 13 may be taken at face value, many of the older attitudes resurfaced as soon as his back was turned. Although his personal wealth may have enabled him to introduce a few 'tax cuts' (Neh. 5:14–15), these cannot have lasted longer than his own period in office, and we have no reason to suppose that they affected 'the royal tribute' (5:4) due from the province as part of the revenue exacted from the satrapy of Beyond the River as a whole. Furthermore, such little evidence as we have from the fourth century does not suggest that either religious or social cohesion was maintained for long.

In sum, the biblical presentation is probably nearer the mark. It sees the real significance of this period to lie elsewhere, and so sets Nehemiah's activity within a framework provided by the work of Ezra (whenever he should be dated). Within the context of developing an approach to the *tôrâ* which afforded its laws and narrative a timeless authority and applicability for Judaism as a religious community, Nehemiah came to Jerusalem at an opportune moment. His policies gave the heartland of Judaism a breathing space and a secure framework within which to work through the implications of the new position. This task could best be done without the distractions of external interference; a measure of independence and self-confidence was necessary if Judaism was not to emerge with a soft centre, and this Nehemiah accomplished with outstanding

---

[60] E.M. YAMAUCHI, 'Two Reformers Compared: Solon of Athens and Nehemiah of Jerusalem', in G. RENDSBURG *et al* (eds.), The Bible World: Essays in Honor of Cyrus H. Gordon (New York, 1980), 269–92.

success. But in the long term, the political fortunes of a minor province in the Achaemenid empire were of only temporary significance by comparison with the shape of the religious faith that emerged from it.

F. *The Last Century of Achaemenid Rule*

It is not possible even to attempt to write a consecutive history of Judah from the end of Nehemiah's term as governor to the close of the period of Achaemenid rule (or even for some while after). As John Bright has correctly stated, 'As regards the community in Judah, one can say little more than it was *there*'.[61] If we assume that the province's constitutional status remained largely unchanged, the few further facts available to fill out the picture may be briefly stated.

We know from the Elephantine Papyri[62] that in the year 408 BCE a certain Bagohi was governor. His name is Persian, but that does not necessarily mean that he was not Jewish; there is a Bigvai, for instance, among the list of those who returned from exile in Ezra 2:2. Since every other governor of Judah that we know about in the Persian period, both before and after 408 BCE, was Jewish, there must be a strong presumption in favour of the view that Bagohi was as well. There is certainly not enough evidence to link him with the Persian Bagoses mentioned by Josephus, even though this has been asserted by many.[63]

From Ramat Raḥel come the names of two further governors, Yeho'ezer and Ahzai. Scholars disagree about their date, but most put them later than Nehemiah.[64] Nothing more of them is known.

The name of a final governor, Yeḥezqiyah, is known from coins that date from the very end of our period.[65] As with the case of seal impressions, other coins carry simply the name of the province, *yhd*.[66] Most recently, Barag has claimed to read 'Johanan the priest' on another coin of the same general type.[67]

All this is tantalizing in the extreme. Does the right to strike local coins reflect a further administrative shift in the province towards greater independence in

---

[61] J. BRIGHT, A History of Israel (3rd edn; London, 1981), 409.
[62] COWLEY, Aramaic Papyri, text 30:1.
[63] See further below.
[64] See STERN, Material Culture, 202–6.
[65] L.Y. RAHMANI, 'Silver Coins of the Fourth Century BC from Tel Gamma', IEJ 21 (1971), 158–60.
[66] For surveys with further bibliography, see L. MILDENBERG, 'Yehud: A Preliminary Study of the Provincial Coinage of Judaea', in O. MØRKHOLM and N.M. WAGGONER (eds.), Greek Numismatics and Archaeology: Essays in Honor of Margaret Thompson (Wetteren, 1979), 183–96; and STERN, Material Culture, 224–27.
[67] D. BARAG, 'Some Notes on a Silver Coin of Johanan the High Priest', BA 48 (1985), 166–68.

the fourth century BCE, or is it to be regarded as no more than an inevitable development within a generally static situation? What should we make of the occurrence of a priest's name on a coin? It has often been assumed, in view of what we know from later times, that during the Persian period the high priesthood rose to a situation of increasing dominance in administrative affairs. In the question of taxation, for instance, the governor is thought to have been responsible for levying revenue from the province for the empire, while the high priest raised what income was necessary for the temple and its services. The evidence we have noted is compatible with these suggestions, and recently Meyers[68] has argued that this was the situation from more or less the start of the period. However, when direct evidence is lacking, it is difficult to make a firm decision on such a matter.

It would be attractive to link the name on the coin with that of one of the protagonists in an incident referred to by Josephus (*Ant.* 11.7.1 § 297–301). Here we are told that a high priest Joannes murdered his brother Jesus in the temple. This Jesus had been promised the high priesthood by Bagoses, a general of Artaxerxes; but Joannes resisted this move. As a consequence, Bagoses imposed a tax on the daily sacrifices. Because of the coincidence of names, many scholars have linked the Bagoses and Joannes of this incident with the Bagohi and Johanan of the papyrus from Elephantine referred to above. They thus place the incident in the reign of Artaxerxes II. I have argued elsewhere, however, that the evidence is better satisfied if the king is Artaxerxes III.[69] Bagoses need not then be a governor of Judah (he is not so named in the text) but the well-known general of Artaxerxes III, who, among other things, played a significant part in the recapture of Egypt (344–343 BCE). That there was a high priest named Johanan late in the Persian period in addition to one in 408 BCE has been argued by some,[70] and it appears now to be confirmed by the coin already mentioned. In that case, we clearly have intense rivalry within the priesthood late in our period. But why?

One possibility is to take seriously the involvement of Bagoses and to argue that the incident must thus be linked with wider political concerns. Barag[71] has argued that references in much later literature to an exile of Jews to Hyrcania by Artaxerxes III Ochus may indicate that Judah along with other provinces in Palestine was caught up in the revolt of Phoenicia against Persia, led by the Sidonian king, Tennes. In support, he adduces archaeological evidence for a mid-fourth century destruction or abandonment of a number of Palestinian sites.

---

[68] MEYERS, 'The Shelomith Seal and the Judean Restoration'.

[69] H.G.M. WILLIAMSON, 'The Historical Value of Josephus' Jewish Antiquities xi.297–301', JTS ns 28 (1977), 49–66 (see below, 74–89).

[70] Moreover, it is perfectly reasonable to hold to it without necessarily accepting all the other names that CROSS, 'A Reconstruction of the Judean Restoration', JBL 94 (1975), 4–18, restores to the list of high priests; cf. WIDENGREN, 'Persian Period', 506–9.

[71] D. BARAG, 'The Effects of the Tennes Rebellion on Palestine', BASOR 183 (1966), 6–12.

It must be noted in reply, however, that the only Judaean site that he mentions is Jericho, where the relevant strata were excavated as early as the beginning of this century. The evidence there amounts only to an argument from silence and, as is well known, such evidence has to be treated with the very greatest caution in view of the low standards of early excavation when compared with modern techniques. Furthermore, the literary sources, whose late date must be emphasized, generally associate the exile of Jews to Hyrcania with the Persian campaign against Egypt, and not with the Tennes revolt. The involvement of Judah in the revolt thus remains very questionable. Finally, should the attempt be made to link this revolt with the story in Josephus (a link that Barag does not himself make), then it must be asked what connection could have existed between the two events. It looks more probable that we should seek an explanation in terms of a power struggle within Judah itself.

Here, too, our sources provide no direct or unambiguous data; but there are a number of converging lines of circumstantial evidence that are sufficient for the construction of a reasonable hypothesis. First, it is clear beyond a shadow of doubt that throughout the Persian period there continued to be fundamental differences of opinion within Judah concerning the attitude which should be adopted towards the descendants of the former northern kingdom of Israel. It is true that not infrequently in the past this issue has been confused with the personal animosities between Nehemiah and his like and their political counterparts in the north. At the same time, however, the radical isolationism of Ezra (whenever he should be dated) went much further, and the accounts of his reform point to a more widespread popular movement that by practice, if not by carefully thought-out conviction, saw no harm in fostering relationships on a broad and conciliatory basis. That a number of leading priests were involved in this practice is explicitly stated, and the relationship by marriage between the high priestly family and Sanballat (Neh. 13:28) should be regarded as symptomatic. According to Josephus (*Ant.* 11.7.2 § 312), these ties continued throughout the fourth century, despite the earlier opposition of both Ezra and Nehemiah, and there is no good reason to doubt his testimony on this matter.

Second, I have suggested elsewhere[72] that there is evidence for a radical reorganization of the Jerusalem priesthood late in the Persian period. A revision of the work of the Chronicler testifies to a radical disjuncture between the earlier genealogically-based presentation of the priestly and Levitical families and a new system based upon the twenty-four courses familiar from later times. And it seems to me significant that very few of the names coincide, even though the gap between them is no more than a generation.

Third, there is a developing consensus that the Samaritan community became established for the first time in Shechem at about this period, and that their temple

---

[72] H.G.M. WILLIAMSON, 'The Origins of the Twenty-Four Priestly Courses', VTSup 30 (1979), 251–68 (see 126–40 below).

was founded there not too long after, in the late fourth or early third century.[73] Furthermore, Kippenberg[74] has made a case for detecting a convergence in later Samaritan tradition of lay northern interests with those of a priestly group with a good claim to legitimacy.

Each of these three points can and should be substantiated with much fuller detail than space allows here. Taken together, they point to a heightening of tensions within the priesthood until they reached breaking point. A number of the most open-minded group then left Jerusalem in order to establish a new community at the venerated site of Shechem in conjunction with some from the province of Samaria with whom they were most closely allied. And this, it may be suggested with all due reserve, may also give the necessary background to the incident recounted by Josephus under discussion. Bagoses, it need not be doubted, would have been anxious to foster good relations between neighbouring petty provinces on the western extremities of the empire. Like many another since, he would have had difficulty understanding the rigid isolationism of some of the Jewish leaders, and he may have found a more 'reasonable' ally in Jesus, to whom in consequence he promised the high priesthood. It seems inconceivable that he should have done this had he not believed that his candidate had a wider measure of support. When the plan was brutally overturned, however, he reacted with acrimonious disdain: the Jews could keep their system – but at a price! Meanwhile, however, the situation for Jesus' supporters became finally untenable in Jerusalem, with the consequences that we have already outlined.

That this reconstruction is hypothetical cannot be denied, and it will doubtless be rejected by some for that very reason. It is not inappropriate, however, that our survey should draw to a close on that note. We have no other material available with which to fill out the final decades of Persian rule in Judah. The period closes as it began – with flashes of light 'amidst encircling gloom'. The historian once again is reduced to sketching what connections he or she can and submitting the conclusions to the judgement of any who can advance more effective suggestions with which to draw together the isolated threads of evidence at our disposal.

---

[73] R. J. BULL AND G. E. WRIGHT, 'Newly Discovered Temples on Mt. Gerizim in Jordan', HTR 58 (1965), 234–37; R. J. BULL, 'The Excavation of Tell er-Ras on Mt. Gerizim', BA 31 (1968), 58–72; for a broader introductory discussion, see R. J. COGGINS, Samaritans and Jews: The Origins of Samaritanism Reconsidered (Oxford, 1975).

[74] H. G. KIPPENBERG, Garizim und Synagoge (RVV, 30; Berlin, 1971).

2. Judah and the Jews

The study of Jewish history in the sixth to fourth centuries BC has both benefitted by, and contributed to, the recent upsurge of interest in the sources of knowledge available to historians of the Achaemenid empire. Although Judah was a small and relatively insignificant province in the satrapy of Transeuphrates, its affairs are better documented than many others, both in terms of literary sources – primarily, of course, the Old Testament – and in terms of the steadily accumulating mass of archaeological and epigraphical data.

Despite this apparently privileged position, biblical scholars are often the despair of their ancient Near Eastern counterparts. Their interests, it is charged, are narrow and blinkered, their agenda being determined too rigidly by the particular concerns of their sources rather than by the broader social, economic and political issues which ought to concern the historian of a major world empire; they have developed hugely sophisticated methods for the analysis of the biblical sources which leaves them critical of other historians who try to make use of this material at its face value, and yet at the same time they disagree with each other so much on such basic matters as chronology and the historical authenticity of the material, to say nothing of individual topics, that they are unable to provide their colleagues with even a minimum of agreed data with which to work.

Although there seems to be little prospect of change on this latter front,[1] there are now signs that Judah's situation within the wider empire is being taken more seriously,[2] that there is a greater attempt to integrate 'biblical' concerns with those of scholars working in other disciplines,[3] and that there is more willingness to experiment with methods other than those which have traditionally characterised biblical studies.[4]

---

[1] For a recent, useful survey, which makes the difficulties clear, see L.L. GRABBE, Judaism from Cyrus to Hadrian (London, 1992), 27–145.

[2] See, for instance, K.G. HOGLUND, Achaemenid Imperial Administration in Syria-Palestine and the Missions of Ezra and Nehemiah (SBLDS, 125; Atlanta, 1992 [in the context of the present volume, it may be of interest to note that in a letter to me, dated 9.iv.1993, David Lewis observed that this book is 'well above average', but then expressed a number of criticisms which, if justified, would severely undercut several of HOGLUND's central theses]); H.G.M. WILLIAMSON, 'Ezra and Nehemiah in the Light of the Texts from Persepolis', BBR 1 (1991), 41–61 (see below, 212–31).

[3] See in particular the participation in the activities of the Association pour la recherche sur la Syrie-Palestine à l'époque perse and its journal Transeuphratène.

[4] Mention here should be made in particular of the Society of Biblical Literature's

In this context, it is not surprising that interest has begun to focus on the work of the Latvian scholar J.P. Weinberg. Based on his earlier dissertation, Weinberg published a number of articles in Russian and German during the 1970s, which at first received little more than passing mention.[5] Now, however, many more scholars of this period are appealing to his theories in the context of their own work, and this is likely to increase in the wake of a helpful translation into English of a number of these articles, together with a new essay in which Weinberg summarises and updates his position, at the same time responding to some early criticisms of his work.[6] Because his theory concerns the very nature of the Jewish community in Judah during the Achaemenid period, and because, moreover, he appeals to what he regards as comparable constitutional organisations elsewhere in the empire, while insisting that the Judean example is the best documented, so that it may serve as 'a model for the reconstruction of this sociopolitical organization',[7] it seems appropriate to examine the evidence to which he appeals in the present volume.[8]

The essence of Weinberg's theory may be summarised as follows. He accepts the theory of Alt and others that, when the Persians inherited the former Babylonian empire, they initially maintained the administrative structure in Palestine

---

ongoing 'Sociology of the Second Temple Consultation', which has so far given rise to two publications: P.R. DAVIES, Second Temple Studies, 1. Persian Period (JSOTSup, 117; Sheffield, 1991), and T.C. ESKENAZI and K.H. RICHARDS (eds.), Second Temple Studies, 2. Temple and Community in the Persian Period (JSOTSup, 175; Sheffield, 1994). Note too K.D. TOLLEFSON and H.G.M. WILLIAMSON, 'Nehemiah as Cultural Revitalization: an Anthropological Perspective', JSOT 56 (1992), 41–68, which struggles to integrate the results of a socio-anthropological approach with those of more traditional source and redaction criticism.

[5] See, however, the brief critical appraisal by H. KREISSIG, 'Eine beachtenswerte Theorie zur Organisation altvorderorientalischer Tempelgemeinden im Achämenidenreich: zu J.P. Weinbergs "Bürger-Tempel-Gemeinde" in Juda', Klio 66 (1984), 35–9, and the more positive evaluation of P.E. DION, 'The Civic-and-Temple Community of Persian Period Judaea: neglected insights from eastern Europe', JNES 50 (1991), 281–7.

[6] J.P. WEINBERG, The Citizen-Temple Community (JSOTSup, 151; Sheffield, 1992); the new essay, 'The Postexilic Citizen-Temple Community: Theory and Reality', is on pp. 127–38. The translator, D.L. SMITH-CHRISTOPHER, worked in collaboration with WEINBERG, who introduced a number of changes in the text of his previous articles; the new translation will, therefore, be used as the basis for the following analysis. It may further be noted that, in his 'Translator's Foreword', 10–16, SMITH-CHRISTOPHER helpfully locates WEINBERG'S research in the broader school of Soviet ancient historiography and pays a handsome tribute to his 'life of heroic scholarship' in the face of considerable opposition and obstruction. For SMITH's own use of WEINBERG's work, see D.L. SMITH, The Religion of the Landless: The Social Context of the Babylonian Exile (Bloomington, 1989), 106–20.

[7] Citizen-Temple Community, 26, and cf. 106.

[8] For other analyses, see especially the essays of J. BLENKINSOPP ('Temple and Society in Achaemenid Judah', in DAVIES, Second Temple Studies. 1, 22–53), P.R. BEDFORD ('On Models and Texts', in DAVIES, Second Temple Studies, 1, 154–62), and R.A. HORSLEY ('Empire, Temple and Community – but no Bourgeoisie!', in DAVIES, Second Temple Studies, 1, 163–74), of which BLENKINSOPP's is the fullest. There remain many areas to examine, however.

whereby, it is maintained, Judah was governed as part of the larger province of Samaria. The proclamation of Cyrus (Ezra 1:2–4), permitting the Jewish exiles to return to Jerusalem and to rebuild the temple, was motivated by his desire to secure a loyal element in the population of this province as part of his strategic preparations for the planned conquest of Egypt; no alteration in political authority was envisaged, however, so that the group of those who returned, together with some of those in the land who joined with them, comprised only a minority of some 20% or less[9] of the population of Judah, living in three isolated enclaves in the coastal area, Jerusalem and its surrounding towns, and the southern part of the Jordan valley (Ezra 2 = Nehemiah 7). After 458/457 BC (the date at which Weinberg believes Ezra came to Jerusalem), this expanded to about 70% (p. 43) or 50–60% (p. 133), and the territorial extent of the community had similarly expanded, including now some population centres outside the borders of Judah (Nehemiah 11). At this crucial turning point in the community's development, it was accorded more substantial powers of internal administrative control and its members were granted tax exemption by Artaxerxes I (Ezra 7:12–26). At the same time the ratio of clergy to laity increased significantly. It is from this period, therefore, that Weinberg dates the start of the 'citizen-temple community' in Judah in its full form as a separate socio-political unit with its own self-administration; prior to this it 'was still not a defined citizen-temple community, but an organism in an emerging status ... Nevertheless, this amorphous structure carried in itself the seeds of the later citizen-temple community and local power' (p. 115; cf. pp. 28, 43, 59, 64 and 71–2). Throughout this period, therefore, three separate sectors of administrative power must be clearly distinguished: the central imperial power, the local provincial authority in Samaria, and the developing internal jurisdiction of the citizen-temple community.

Not long after the watershed date of 458/457, Judah (*yehud*) was granted autonomy from Samaria, but the threefold structure remained in place. Nehemiah, who according to Alt was the first governor (*peḥâ*) of Judah, was only the head of the self-regulating citizen-temple community in Weinberg's opinion. Nevertheless, as the community grew in size and so became the dominant element in Judah, it was inevitable that eventually the high priest should also, in the manner of a personal union, become the governor of the province as a whole, and this is thought to have happened at some point during the fourth century BC, though a full and formal merger did not come about before the Hellenistic period.

An important element in Weinberg's reconstruction is the social and economic structure of this community. He stresses the degree of disruption which

---

[9] In WEINBERG, 'Demographische Notizen zur Geschichte der nachexilischen Gemeinde in Juda', Klio 54 (1972), 45–59 = Citizen-Temple Community, 34–48, and elsewhere, WEINBERG puts the figure at 20%. In his recent essay (132), this is reduced without explanation to 13–15%.

was caused by the exile to Babylon, and finds that by the time of the return the Jews had organised themselves in quasi-agnatic groups known as the *bêt 'ābôt*, the 'fathers' house'. With an average male membership of 1,000, these are somewhat larger than the ancient Iranian agnatic groups, which consisted of 600 mature men, according to A. G. Perichanian, but sociologically they are nevertheless comparable. Linking back to the ideology of earlier Israel, these 'fathers' houses' controlled the community's land as inalienable property (*'ªḥuzzâ/naḥªlâ*), dividing it into smaller parcels for the use of the separate constituent families. This resulted in a noteworthy degree of social homogeneity, a fact reflected also in the relatively limited number of slaves.

It is clear that one of the essential features of Weinberg's understanding of the post-exilic Judaean community is the radical dichotomy, which his model seeks to explain, between the imperial/provincial authorities and the separate, and to a large extent self-regulating, citizen-temple community with which the biblical sources are principally concerned. As he repeatedly stresses, one should not speak about the post-exilic community of Judah as though they were identical, but rather of the post-exilic community *in* Judaea (and later in *yehud*). And, without doubt, this understanding can be used heuristically to explain such features of our texts as the opposition to the temple building by 'the people of the land' (Ezra 4) and the prominence of the topic of mixed marriages in the time of both Ezra (Ezra 9–10) and Nehemiah (Neh. 13:23–8).[10] Nevertheless, before such advantages are pressed to justify the theory in the first place, it is important to step back and examine the extent to which justice is done to all the evidence at our disposal.

In order to lay the basis for the analysis, it is necessary to clarify the position on the contentious matter of the reliability of the biblical sources. Weinberg generally takes them at face value, though, as will be seen, his dating at a few crucial points is idiosyncratic. In general, I share Weinberg's confidence about the authenticity of the documents incorporated into our primary source, the books of Ezra and Nehemiah. At the same time, it is necessary to be aware of the fact that these first-hand sources have been incorporated into the later compositions which are our present books, so that it is imperative to be sensitive to the concerns of the later redactors, and so to distinguish carefully for strictly historical purposes between primary source and secondary redaction.[11] Of course, those who take a radically sceptical view on this issue leave themselves with

---

[10] See, for example, H. C. WASHINGTON, 'The Strange Woman (אשה נדה/נכריה) of Proverbs 1–9 and Post-Exilic Judaean Society', in ESKENAZI and RICHARDS, Second Temple Studies, 2, 217–42.

[11] For justification and explanation, see H. G. M. WILLIAMSON, 'The Composition of Ezra i–vi', JTS n. s. 34 (1983), 1–30 (see below, 244–70); Ezra, Nehemiah (Waco, 1985); cf. B. HALPERN, 'A Historiographic Commentary on Ezra 1–6: a Chronological Narrative and Dual Chronology in Israelite Historiography', in W. H. PROPP et al (eds.), The Hebrew Bible and Its Interpreters (Winona Lake, 1990), 81–142.

virtually no common ground on which to debate with Weinberg, but this remains a minority view (if currently a somewhat vocal one). In principle, I shall not attempt to fault Weinberg at this point. Nor do I disagree with him on the other constantly debated topic – the date of Ezra. Weinberg locates Ezra in the seventh year of Artaxerxes I, as an initial reading of Ezra 7:7 implies, but as is all too well known, many other scholars (though not so many now as a generation ago) favour a later date, usually the seventh year of Artaxerxes II, 398 BC.[12] As Dion[13] has suggested, however, it would not be impossible to modify Weinberg's thesis to take account of this alternative date. In the interests of clarity, I shall work with Weinberg's chronology on this matter.

1. As is clear from the fact that Weinberg repeatedly comes back to the matter,[14] a cornerstone in his theory is his conviction that the list in Ezra 2 = Nehemiah 7, purporting to record the number of those who returned to Judah from the Babylonian exile in the days of Cyrus, in fact reflects the membership of the community at the crucial turning point some eighty years later, 458 BC.

It is generally agreed that this list represents an amalgam of those who returned over a longer period of time than the text initially suggests, not least because it includes some elements which indicate a standpoint of those already settled back in the land. A number of those listed are grouped according to the place of their residence, for instance, while the 'Tirshatha', evidently a leader of some sort, is presupposed to be already active in his work (Ezra 2:63; cf. Neh. 7:69). Because of this, two possible dates for the list have generally been canvassed. A minority of scholars relates it to the later time of Nehemiah, who claims to have found it as a 'genealogical record of those who had come up at the first (בראשונה)' (7:5).[15] Most, however, take this claim more seriously, and so relate it in some way to the time of temple building (520–515 BC) during the reign of Darius I.

If, as Weinberg does, we take even the details of the text as reliable, the following factors would seem to support this second position: (i) In Ezra 2:61 the family of Hakkoz is excluded from the priesthood because they could not prove their genealogical pedigree. By 8:33 (the time of Ezra), however, they appear to have been reinstated, and this remained the case under Nehemiah (Neh. 3:4 and 21). (ii) The registration of those without genealogical record

---

[12] See most recently A. LEMAIRE, 'La fin de la première période perse en Egypte et la chronologie judéenne vers 400 av. J.C.', Trans 9 (1995), 51–61. I have summarised the main points in the debate and presented my own opinion in H.G.M. WILLIAMSON, Ezra and Nehemiah (Sheffield, 1987), 55–69.

[13] DION, 'Civic-and-Temple-Community', 283.

[14] Cf., for example, WEINBERG, Citizen-Temple Community, 27, 41–2, 53, 64ff., 80 and 132.

[15] See most recently, J. BLENKINSOPP, Ezra-Nehemiah: A Commentary (London, 1988), 83.

according to the (obscure) Babylonian places from which they came (Ezra 2:59) only makes sense within a period shortly after their return. (iii) The list presupposes a date when there was as yet no 'priest with Urim and Thummim' (Ezra 2:63). In the post-exilic period this is clearly a reference to the high priest (cf. Exod. 28:30; Lev. 8:8; Num. 27:21), in which role Jeshua was certainly active from 520 BC onwards. (iv) The presentation of the minor cultic officials in the second half of the list reflects an earlier situation in the development of their position than elsewhere in these books and in Chronicles: here, neither singers nor gatekeepers are yet classified as Levites, whereas later they invariably were.[16] (v) The use of the gold drachma (Ezra 2:69) probably antedates the introduction of the daric by Darius.[17] (vi) The distribution of the population is not what we should have expected had the list been drawn up only in Nehemiah's time.[18]

The original purpose for which the list was drawn up remains uncertain, though some suggestions are less probable than others. For instance, had it been for the purposes of taxation,[19] we should not have expected the cultic officials to be included, while the form of the list as a whole does not seem suited to the purpose of determining land rights.[20] In view of the list's likely date, perhaps the most attractive proposal is that of Galling,[21] who pointed to the need posed by Tattenai's inquiry at the time of the building of the temple (Ezra 5:10) for a list of all who were covered by Cyrus' permission to return from exile and to build.[22] This, at any rate, is concrete evidence of the need for such a list at this time, but more cannot be said with certainty.

In the light of the importance of this matter for Weinberg's thesis, it is surprising that he offers no evidence whatsoever for his novel suggestion that the list gives 'an indication of the collectives belonging to the "citizen-temple community" until the year 458/457 BCE' (p. 42). After briefly noting some of the alternative possibilities, he merely introduces his proposal with the words

---

[16] For further detail, see H. GESE, 'Zur Geschichte der Kultsänger am zweiten Tempel', in Vom Sinai zum Zion (München, 1974), 147–58, and H.G.M. WILLIAMSON, 'The Origins of the Twenty-Four Priestly Courses: A Study of 1 Chronicles xxiii–xxvii', VTSup 30 (1979), 251–68 (see below, 126–40).

[17] Cf. H.G.M. WILLIAMSON, 'Eschatology in Chronicles', TynB 28 (1977), 115–54 (123–5) (see below, 162–95).

[18] E. SELLIN, Geschichte des israelitisch-jüdischen Volkes, 2 (Leipzig, 1932), 89.

[19] G. HÖLSCHER, 'Die Bücher Esra und Nehemia', in E. KAUTZSCH (Hsg), Die heilige Schrift des Alten Testaments, 2 (Tübingen, 1910), 449–92 (478).

[20] A. ALT, 'Die Rolle Samarias bei der Entstehung des Judentums', in Kleine Schriften zur Geschichte des Volkes Israel, 2 (München, 1953), 316–37 (334–5) = Festschrift Otto Procksch zum 60. Geburtstag (Leipzig, 1934), 6–28.

[21] K. GALLING, 'Die Liste der aus dem Exil Heimgekehrten', in Studien zur Geschichte Israels im persischen Zeitalter (Tübingen, 1964), 89–108.

[22] See too C. SCHULTZ, 'The Political Tensions Reflected in Ezra-Nehemiah', in C.D. EVANS et al. (eds.), Scripture in Context: Essays on the Comparative Method (Pittsburgh, 1980), 221–44.

'in my view'. Without firm evidence for the proposed date, or a plausible suggestion as to how such a list was drawn up at that time and why it should have been necessary, Weinberg seems to imply that this conclusion is of such heuristic value for the purpose of the overall thesis being argued that it becomes *ipso facto* compelling. This, however, is a totally circular argument, and, insofar as it presupposes the thesis in the first place, it is further undermined by the other considerations treated below.

2. Both with regard to this list and with some others,[23] Weinberg treats the numbers mentioned as strictly accurate.[24] He then compares this with his estimate of the total population of Judah at the time in order to arrive at his proportions which are thought to show the separate nature of the citizen-temple community and its growth through time. Needless to say, however, both steps in this argument are highly contentious, especially the latter. To arrive at his figure, Weinberg estimates the population of pre-exilic Judah at 220,000–250,000, on the basis of the likely population of towns and villages at that time and by treating the town-lists in the second half of the book of Joshua as a full and accurate reflection of the situation in the late pre-exilic period, and by then subtracting his estimate of the number of those deported in the exile. Apart from the fact that post-exilic Judah was not co-extensive with the pre-exilic state of the same name, there are so many uncertainties in this calculation that it is difficult to treat it seriously as a basis for discussion; by way of illustration, it may be noted that on the basis of a not dissimilar line of argument, Albright[25] proposed a figure as low as 20,000, a mere 10% of Weinberg's figure.

Research on this uncertain topic has recently been advanced and put on a more secure footing by Carter[26] who has been able to benefit by the recent

---

[23] I shall not deal at length with WEINBERG's use of Neh. 11:25–36, on which he bases his evidence for the territorial expansion of the community in the fifth century (Citizen-Temple Community, 44–5). As I have attempted to show elsewhere (Ezra, Nehemiah, 341–54), the list is probably a later addition to its context and completely utopian in nature. There is absolutely no evidence that the Persian province of Judah extended as far south as this passage indicates, while if it is 'diaspora' members of the community who are in view, it is not clear why they should be limited to the towns mentioned in this list and relatively few others (Citizen-Temple Community, 46–8) alone.

[24] There are minor difficulties of a textual nature with regard to Ezra 2 = Nehemiah 7, in that the two forms of the list do not always agree with each other on these matters, nor do the totals given agree with the sum of the parts. WEINBERG's proposal, that this is because the total number includes women and children who are not included in the individual entries, is possible but, of course, conjectural. For a more convincing textual explanation, see H.L. ALLRIK, 'The Lists of Zerubbabel (Nehemiah 7 and Ezra 2) and the Hebrew Numeral Notation', BASOR 136 (1954), 21–7.

[25] W.F. ALBRIGHT, The Biblical Period from Abraham to Ezra (repr.; New York, 1965), 87.

[26] C.E. CARTER, 'The Province of Yehud in the Post-Exilic Period: Soundings in Site Distribution and Demography', in ESKENAZI and RICHARDS, Second Temple Studies, 2,

surface surveys of Judah and Benjamin by Israeli archaeologists as well as by the methodological advances of the so-called 'new archaeology' in the process of population estimates. The results of his analysis are that 'the population of Yehud ranged from a low of 11,000 in the late-sixth/early-fifth centuries BCE to a high of 17,000 in the late-fifth/early-fourth centuries BCE'. These are, clearly, substantially lower figures than any previous estimate. Part of the explanation for this is that Carter excludes the relatively fertile region of the valley of Ono in the Shephelah (Lod, Hadid and Ono), which the literary sources suggest was part of the province at this time. The matter remains debated.[27] Even if we make adjustments to take account of this, however, it is clear that Weinberg's total estimate now appears to be far too high, that the figures in Ezra 2/Nehemiah 7 are unlikely to be as reliable as he assumes, and that his calculation of the proportions in question is, therefore, questionable.

To this conclusion may be joined a point concerning a further consideration regarding the make-up of the basic list in Ezra 2/Nehemiah 7. As already indicated, the lay families are grouped in two main ways, by 'fathers' house' and by place of residence. Although this variation is not explained, the most probable reason is that it represents a combination of those who returned from Babylon, where, we may agree, the agnatic organisation of the exiles developed, and those who remained in the land but who still felt themselves to be sufficiently related by ties of blood, social orientation and religion to join (and be accepted by) those returning to rebuild the temple.[28] In his most recent essay (p. 132), Weinberg accepts this analysis, and refers for support to an article of his in Russian (and therefore unfortunately not accessible to me) which deals with the same topic.[29] He calculates (p. 42) that this second group comprised some 28–29% of the total community, but does not, apparently, pause to consider its implications for his theory as a whole. It is obvious, however, that if the total population of Judah was much smaller than Weinberg originally thought, and if a considerable proportion of those who had remained in the land were part of his 'community' from early Achaemenid times, then the proposal that this community was but a small element in the total population of the province, such that it makes sense to discuss its constitution in separation from that of the province as a whole, is seriously undermined.

106-45. Part of this article is based on his 1991 Duke University PhD dissertation, which I have not been able to consult. [It has subsequently been published in revised form as JSOTSup, 294; Sheffield, 1999.]

[27] See recently, for instance, J. SAPIN, 'Sur le statut politique du secteur de Ono à l'époque perse', in T. RÖMER (ed.), Mélanges Françoise Smyth, Lectio Difficilior Probabilior (Heidelberg, 1991), 31–43.

[28] S. JAPHET, 'People and Land in the Restoration Period', in G. STRECKER (ed.), Das Land Israel in biblischer Zeit (Göttingen, 1983), 103–25.

[29] J.P. WEINBERG, 'Collectives, named by Toponyms in Achaemenid Judea', ArOr 42 (1974), 321–53 [Russian].

3. There is another, separate matter which also has an important bearing on this matter of demographic proportions within the province. When Weinberg first wrote, he accepted the then quite widely adopted view of Alt[30] that, for at least the first century of Achaemenid rule, Judah was not a separate province within the satrapy of Transeuphrates but that it was administratively part of the province of Samaria. Only under Nehemiah did it gain its independence, so to speak. In his most recent essay (p. 135), Weinberg has again reaffirmed this opinion, as will be noted further below. If that were true, then, of course, those returning from exile, even with the addition of a considerable number of those who had remained in the land, would still have been only a small minority within the extensive province of Samaria as a whole. The question of their constitutional position within this larger entity might then legitimately be raised.

In the years since Alt first wrote, however, new data have accumulated which have caused most scholars to re-evaluate the literary evidence on which Alt perforce based the weight of his case and so, by and large, to reject his principal conclusion.[31] I have discussed the issues fully elsewhere,[32] and in view of their complexity will offer only a brief summary of the salient points here.

(i) A hoard of bullae and seals published by Avigad[33] most probably refers to a governor of the province of Yehud in the late sixth century BC.[34] (ii) The

---

[30] ALT, 'Die Rolle Samarias'.

[31] Two major exceptions are S.E. McEVENUE, 'The Political Structure in Judah from Cyrus to Nehemiah', CBQ 43 (1981), 353–64, who, however, amongst other unsatisfactory arguments, appeals to completely discredited readings to get round the new epigraphical evidence, and E. STERN, 'Seal-Impressions in the Achaemenid Style in the Province of Judah', BASOR 202 (1971), 6–16; it should be noted that STERN has since found himself obliged to modify his conclusions in the light of the more recent evidence, so effectively undermining the force of his own position; see, for instance, E. STERN, 'The Persian Empire and the Political and Social History of Palestine in the Persian Period', CHJ I (1984), 70–87 (82–3).

[32] H.G.M. WILLIAMSON, 'The Governors of Judah under the Persians', TynB 39 (1988), 59–82 (below, 46–63); see too M. SMITH, Palestinian Parties and Politics that Shaped the Old Testament (2nd edn; London, 1987), 147–53; G. WIDENGREN, 'The Persian Period', in J.H. HAYES and J.M. MILLER (eds.), Israelite and Judaean History (London, 1977), 489–538; A. LEMAIRE, 'Populations et territoires de la Palestine à l'époque perse', Trans 3 (1990), 31–74; HOGLUND, Achaemenid Imperial Administration, 69–86.

[33] N. AVIGAD, Bullae and Seals from a Post-Exilic Judean Archive (Qedem, 4; Jerusalem, 1976).

[34] The date is deduced from palaeographical evidence and the likely identification of 'Shelomith the אמה (wife/official?) of Elnathan the governor' with the Shelomith of 1 Chron. 3:19 (the post-exilic genealogy of the Davidic family); the rarity of women named in genealogies or on seals, both of which could be explained if she held some official position, suggests this identification; cf. A. LEMAIRE, Review, Syria 54 (1977), 129–31; E.M. MEYERS, 'The Shelomith Seal and the Judean Restoration: Some Additional Considerations', ErIsr 18 (1985), 33*–38*; 'The Persian Period and the Judean Restoration: From Zerubbabel to Nehemiah', in P.D. MILLER et al (eds.), Ancient Israelite Religion: Essays in Honor of Frank Moore Cross (Philadelphia, 1987), 509–21. There are some other governors named on seal impressions from Ramat Rahel, but it remains uncertain whether any should be dated before

references to Sheshbazzar (Ezra 5:14) and Zerubbabel (Hag. 1:1, 14; 2:2, 21) as governor should therefore also be taken at face value. (iii) Nehemiah's reference to 'the governors who were before me' (Neh. 5:15) makes best sense in context if he is referring to those who held the same position as he did himself. (iv) The correspondence in Ezra 4:7–23 clearly presupposes that Judah enjoyed a measure of autonomy; if Judah had been under Samarian rule, there would have been no need for officials from there to act in the manner here described. Similarly, in Ezra 5 we should have expected Tattenai to approach the Samarian officials with his enquiry, not the Jews directly. (v) There is a complete lack of direct evidence for Judah's incorporation into Samaria after the fall of Jerusalem in the first place. Indeed, according to Hoglund,[35] such an incorporation 'would constitute a major departure from what seems to have been a prevailing pattern in Neo-Babylonian practice'. Alt offers none, but merely states it as a suggestion to get his discussion of the later situation off the ground.

In his most recent essay, Weinberg maintains (135) that it is premature to conclude on the basis of this evidence that Alt's case has collapsed. He repeats his earlier argument (113–15) that Sheshbazzar and Zerubbabel generally occur without titles in the official documents included in Ezra 1–6 and that the use of the title *peḥâ* in Haggai for Zerubbabel is merely 'a demonstration of the wishes and hopes of the returnees in regard to the status of their leaders'. This overlooks several crucial factors, however. First, Sheshbazzar is explicitly stated to have been appointed as *peḥâ* by Cyrus at Ezra 5:14 (in an 'official document'). Secondly, in the present form of the Aramaic text, there is another reference to the governor of the Jews (יהודי פחת) in an 'official document' at Ezra 6:7, and in the context it is clearly Zerubbabel who is intended. The text is not entirely smooth at this point, however, so that some have wished to delete this reference. Even if that were so (and the evidence is by no means clear cut either way), the addition would still attest a glossator's later understanding of the situation. Thirdly, there is, as we have seen, a reference to 'the tirshatha' at Ezra 2:63. Although the etymology of this word remains uncertain,[36] it is consistently used in the biblical texts (and hence should be understood here) as an alternative title for governor (see especially Neh. 8:9; 10:2). Fourthly, it is improbable that the use of a Persian title in Haggai expresses the wishes and hopes of the returnees for Zerubbabel. Haggai envisages the imminent overthrow of the present world order and the protection of Zerubbabel in that day so that he may assume some new but vaguely worded position in the future (2:20–23). Far from an expression of hope, the title governor is thus one which Haggai anticipates will soon be

---

Nehemiah. It may be noted here that WEINBERG's dating (123–6) of some other stamps, particularly the *yršlm* group, to the late Persian period, as part of his evidence for the increased official role of Jerusalem and of the high priests, is almost certainly too high; cf. WILLIAMSON, 'Governors of Judah', 66–8 (below, 51–53).

[35] HOGLUND, Achaemenid Imperial Administration, 84–5.
[36] WILLIAMSON, Ezra, Nehemiah, 27.

left far behind. Finally, Weinberg errs in stating that these officials occur with titles in the narrative parts of Ezra 1–6; the position is, in fact, precisely the reverse. Here, the distinction between sources and redaction noted above is crucial, for it has been shown that it is the work of the later redactor to have decreased the emphasis on titles for ideological reasons of his own, and that his treatment of titles is consistent with other features of his composition, influenced in part by the different circumstances which prevailed at his time of writing.[37]

It may be concluded, therefore, that there is no evidence for the supposition that, in the first part of the Achaemenid period, Judah was not administered as an autonomous province. Once again, the consequence is that there is far less reason than Weinberg implies for regarding the Persian treatment of the Jewish community as something completely separate from their normal provincial administration.

4. So far, I have dealt with matters which relate primarily to the first half of the Achaemenid period. In the next two points, I turn to matters relating to what Weinberg regards as the major turning point in the development of the citizen-temple community, and both points are crucial for his hypothesis.

First, he argues that, at the time of Ezra's mission to Jerusalem, the whole of the community was granted a special tax exemption by Artaxerxes, 'by means of which the citizen-temple community was separated from the surrounding socio-political structure' (p. 117). This he argues on the basis of his controversial exegesis of Ezra 7:24.

Before that verse is examined more closely, however, note should be taken of Neh. 5:4. Nehemiah 5 describes a crisis which arose in the Jewish community, ostensibly at the time when Nehemiah was building the walls of Jerusalem. In verses 2–5, three groups[38] bring a complaint against their fellow Jews regarding the desperate economic measures to which they are being reduced because of a variety of misfortunes. One of these is that 'we have had to borrow money on our fields and vineyards for the royal tribute (מדת המלך)'. This word does not occur elsewhere in Hebrew in the Old Testament, but its Aramaic equivalent is found at Ezra 4:13, 20, and, most significantly, Ezra 7:24 (and cf. Akkadian *maddattu*), where there can be no doubt that the reference is to a contribution to the imperial tax which was levied on each satrapy. Although Weinberg does not

---

[37] S. JAPHET, 'Sheshbazzar and Zerubbabel – Against the Background of the Historical and Religious Tendencies of Ezra-Nehemiah', ZAW 94 (1982), 66–98.

[38] H.G. KIPPENBERG, Religion und Klassenbildung im antiken Judäa: Eine Religionssoziologische Studie zum Verhältnis von Tradition und gesellschaftlicher Entwicklung (Göttingen, 1978), 56–7, thinks rather of three steps in a downward spiral on the path to debt-slavery. Though this would not affect the point at issue here, it seems less likely than the usual view; see H. KREISSIG, Die sozialökonomische Situation in Juda zur Achämenidenzeit (Berlin, 1973), 78–9, and WILLIAMSON, Ezra, Nehemiah, 237–8.

appear to discuss our particular verse, he makes use of Nehemiah 5 in other contexts[39] as important evidence for the social composition of the citizen-temple community (note especially the use of אח, 'brother', in vv. 1, 5, 7, 8), and indeed the whole process which Nehemiah here initiates is predicated on the basis that all involved are of the same community over against their 'gentile enemies' (v. 9; cf. v. 8). Here, then, is apparently clear-cut evidence that lay members of the community were still subject to secular taxation[40] even after the time of Ezra.

As already mentioned, Weinberg arrives at his contrary opinion on the basis of Ezra 7:24. This verse forms part of the (Aramaic) edict of Artaxerxes to Ezra, incorporated into which, as the text now stands,[41] there are instructions to the treasurers of Transeuphrates (vv. 21–4) to the effect that they are to make certain stipulated provisions for the Jerusalem temple. The edict then continues, 'Be it further known to you that you have no authority to impose tribute, tax or dues upon any of the priests and Levites, the musicians, gatekeepers, temple servants or (other) servants of this house of God' (v. 24). As usually interpreted, this gives tax exemption only to the Jerusalem cult officials, something not unprecedented in Achaemenid policy.[42] No reference is made to the laity.

Weinberg's interpretation is radically different in two respects.[43] First, he maintains that the *nethinim* (translated above as 'temple servants') were not cultic officials at all, but rather the descendants of those who (under the same title) were, in the pre-exilic period, 'hand workers, craftsmen in royal service and/or royal servants who were deported together with other residents of Jerusalem'. In the post-exilic period, this group were at the bottom of the social pyramid, and virtually disappeared after the fifth century. Secondly, he maintains that the 'servants of this house of God' is a reference to the non-priestly members of the community (87–8).

Unfortunately, neither of these proposals seems convincing. Whatever the function of the *nethinim* may have been in the pre-exilic period, Ezra 8:20 demonstrates clearly that their function was cultic in our period, for they are there described as those 'whom David and the princes had appointed to serve the Levites'. The probability that this is an anachronistic rationalisation does not, of course, deflect the force of this evidence for the way things were understood in the post-exilic period, but if anything strengthens it. Furthermore, the position

---

[39] E.g. 102, 133.

[40] No reference is made in this context to the contributions to the temple which were also expected; cf. Neh. 10 and 13.

[41] Like WEINBERG, I here assume the authenticity of this document. Naturally, for those who question it, the issue of the community's tax status does not arise; see recently, for example, L. L. GRABBE, 'What was Ezra's Mission?', in ESKENAZI and RICHARDS, Second Temple Studies, 2, 286–99.

[42] Cf. WILLIAMSON, 'Ezra and Nehemiah in the Light of the Texts from Persepolis', 50–54 (below, 220–24).

[43] See especially 75–91.

of the *nethinim* in the list of Ezra 2 (with other cult officials, following the laity in the first half of the list), as well as the order in Neh. 10:29 (ET 28) accords with this understanding.⁴⁴

What, then, of 'the servants of this house of God (פלחי בית אלהא דנה)' in Ezra 7:24? This phrase is not attested elsewhere. If the list of officials in this verse is compared with the order in which they are listed in Ezra 2/Nehemiah 7, it will be seen at once that they come in the place where we should have expected to find 'the sons of Solomon's servants' (Ezra 2:55/Neh. 7:57). This may, therefore, be simply another way of referring to the same group. Alternatively, since the *nethinim* and the sons of Solomon's servants were closely associated with each other by this time (cf. Ezra 2:58/Neh. 7:60), it is also possible that the *wāw* before *pāleḥê* should be construed epexegetically, so that the phrase would be a summary description of the whole of the preceding list ('that is to say, the servants...'). Either way, the laity would not be mentioned. Weinberg (87) responds that *plḥ* is not always used with a religious meaning. This, of course, is perfectly true (compare English 'service'), but the context strongly indicates that it is so used here: the same root occurs with cultic significance in verse 19, it is qualified by a reference to the temple in our verse, and all the preceding officials are cultic. Had the laity been intended, we should have expected them either to come first in the list (as in Ezra 2/Nehemiah 7) or to have been referred to in some unambiguous way. And since, according to Neh. 5:4, precisely one of the forms of tax mentioned in Ezra 7:24 is expected of the laity, there can be no justification for contending that the whole community was here granted tax exemption. We may, therefore, conclude that there was no distinction between the Jewish community as a whole and other inhabitants of the province of Judah on the basis of their tax status.

5. The second issue relating to this central period of Persian rule concerns the status of Nehemiah. Believing that shortly before his time the citizen-temple community had been definitively established as a constitutionally separate entity within the (now autonomous) province of Judah, Weinberg is more or less obliged to argue that Nehemiah was not the provincial governor, but rather only the leader of the community.⁴⁵ This proposal has already been briefly criticised by others,⁴⁶ but the matter is so important that further discussion is required: if

---

⁴⁴ WEINBERG's appeal (86) to the order of the summary in Neh. 7:72 (ET 73) is vitiated by the obvious textual confusion which this verse has suffered; see the parallel Ezra 2:70 and, for discussion, WILLIAMSON, Ezra, Nehemiah, 271–3.

⁴⁵ It is ironic to note that WEINBERG continues to follow ALT's historical reconstruction, as we have seen, when the whole basis of ALT's contention that Judah became an independent province at this time was based on his understanding of Nehemiah as the first provincial governor.

⁴⁶ KREISSIG, 'Eine beachtenswerte Theorie zur Organisation', 37; BEDFORD, 'On Models and Texts', 157–8.

Nehemiah was the provincial governor, as has always been assumed, his evident involvement in the specifically Jewish community would seem to leave little room for a separate level of official administration.

Even allowing for the one-sided nature of Nehemiah's account,[47] the following points relating to Nehemiah's role are suggestive of a provincial governor.

(i) Nehemiah's carrying through of his plan to rebuild the walls of Jerusalem seems certainly to have stirred up the opposition of the leaders of the neighbouring provinces. Indeed, in Nehemiah 4 they are portrayed as threatening armed force to prevent it, and Nehemiah is obliged to take defensive counter-measures. It is scarcely credible that such a situation could have developed without some intervention by the provincial governor, if there had been one apart from Nehemiah, but the text offers no hint of such a possibility. Even Dion,[48] who is generally sympathetic, concedes this point. He finds Weinberg's view 'hard to believe; in our sources, Nehemiah is on an equal footing with Sin-uballiṭ, the governor of Samaria; and there is never any hint that Nehemiah seeks the permission or enjoys the support of any governor of *yehūd* placed over him'.

(ii) In Neh. 2:7-8, Nehemiah requests letters to the governors of Transeuphrates 'so that they may grant me a safe conduct until I reach Judah', as well as a letter to the keeper of the king's park for the supply of timber. It seems more than curious that he should not also have asked for a letter to the governor of Judah itself to explain the nature of his mission, since *ex hypothesi* it would have affected affairs under his jurisdiction very considerably.

(iii) *Pace* Weinberg, it is by no means obvious that the refortification of Jerusalem involved 'only the community and not the province of Yehud'. Are we to suppose that the province had a separate capital?

(iv) In Neh. 5:14, Nehemiah speaks of the time when he was appointed to be 'their governor in the land of Judah'. Weinberg argues that the pronominal suffix indicates that Nehemiah was not governor of Judah (he would have expected פחת יהוד if that were the case) but rather governor of (probably) the Jews. In view of the following verses (see below), however, it seems more probable that the suffix should be taken as loosely anticipatory, so that Nehemiah's governorship would be more closely associated with 'the land of Judah' than Weinberg supposes.

(v) In 5:14-18, Nehemiah boasts that he did not draw the salary to which he was entitled as governor and he contrasts this with his predecessors: 'The earlier governors who came before me laid a heavy burden on the people and exacted from them for their daily ration forty shekels of silver. Their retainers too used to lord it over the people'. This seems to imply the level of jurisdiction which we

---

[47] See especially D.J.A. CLINES, 'The Nehemiah Memoir: the Perils of Autobiography', in What Does Eve Do to Help? And Other Readerly Questions to the Old Testament (JSOTSup, 94; Sheffield, 1990), 124-64.

[48] DION, 'Civic-and-Temple Community', 284, n. 33.

should associate with a provincial governor,[49] not just a community leader, and for Nehemiah's claim to have any sense, he must be comparing like with like.

(vi) In his dealings with the king, with the officials of neighbouring provinces and with his own people, Nehemiah consistently acts on his own authority; never once is there any indication of another official with what must have been to a limited extent an overlapping sphere of jurisdiction. Although this is an argument from silence, and although allowance must be made for Nehemiah's confident personal style, it still seems to present a difficulty for Weinberg's view.[50]

In sum, I can see no justification from the Nehemiah account for the assumption that he was not the provincial governor, in which case it becomes impossible to isolate a separate citizen-temple community within Judah at that time.

6. Although I can claim no expert knowledge of the nature of the citizen-temple communities elsewhere in the ancient Near East to which Weinberg appeals,[51] there emerges a clear distinction which he himself acknowledges and which sets the Jerusalem temple apart in a category all of its own. As he presents his conclusions (29 and 104), there are two main types of citizen-temple community, of which the first can be further subdivided. The criteria for these divisions are: existence or non-existence of temple land; and existence or non-existence of a temple economy. He sets out the resulting distinctions as follows:

> Group A-1 includes the communities whose temple was *de facto* the owner of land and whose land was divided among the members of the community, but partly self-managed – for example, the communities in Uruk, Sippara, Comana, Zela, Akilisene.
>
> Group A-2 contains the communities whose temples were *de facto* owners of lands, but did not run their own economy. All temple lands were in use by the community members, for example, the community in Mylasa-Olymos.
>
> Group B is composed of those citizen-temple communities whose temples owned no land nor maintained their own economy, for example, the Palestinian community (p. 29).

It is striking that neither here nor elsewhere, so far as I can see, does Weinberg cite any other example in Group B. Yet the distinction is surely critical. If, uniquely in this case, the temple played no constitutional role in the social and economic life of the community, what justification can there be for positing a 'citizen-temple community' in the first place? And here it should be remembered that Weinberg regards the Palestinian example as the best documented and the one which can therefore serve as a model for all others (26 and 106).

---

[49] WEINBERG more or less concedes this point on p. 21, though without relating his discussion there to the issue of Nehemiah's role.

[50] The suggestion that the Pethahiah of 11:24 was the provincial governor (136) seems unlikely, since ליד המלך implies residence at the court, and the verse is in any case part of a series of later additions to the chapter, of uncertain date; cf. WILLIAMSON, Ezra, Nehemiah, 349 and 352–3.

[51] See, too, the helpful presentation of some of the relevant data in BLENKINSOPP, 'Temple and Society'.

Such evidence as we have suggests that the community in Judah adopted a somewhat ambivalent attitude towards the temple. Their delay in getting round to build it in the first place is castigated by the prophet Haggai as demonstrating a reprehensible selfishness on their part, and even after the supposed watershed date of 458 BC the leaders continued to experience considerable difficulties in getting in enough of the dues that were necessary to support the cult and its functionaries (Nehemiah 10 and 13). The book of Malachi, whose precise date is uncertain but which cannot be far removed from this period, paints a comparable picture. This hardly sounds like the attitude of a group whose very social cohesion and economic well-being depended upon the temple in physical terms. The temple neither owned any land, so far as we know, nor exercised any form of control over title to property by way of membership of its community.[52] It would seem that community membership and status were determined by other means in Achaemenid Judah. But if the temple is elsewhere the centre, indeed, the *raison d'être*, of the type of community being cited as a parallel, whereas here the temple plays no constitutional role whatsoever, so far as our evidence goes, then in what sense is there a parallel at all?

The rather obvious conclusion of this lengthy examination is that there was a considerably closer overlap between the Jewish community and the Persian province of Judah in terms of both population and administration than the model of the citizen-temple community suggests, and nowhere (as, for instance, in the matter of taxation) have we found any evidence that the Jewish community was treated differently from others who may have lived within the province. The Jerusalem temple was undoubtedly singled out for special consideration by the Persian authorities, but in strictly circumscribed terms.

It would go beyond the confines of this limited discussion to enter fully into the alternative understanding of the position of the Jews in the Achaemenid empire which this negative conclusion clearly calls for. There is space for only a few summary remarks, on the basis of research which has been published elsewhere.

First, as has already been indicated, there need not have been such a stark division between returning exiles and those who had remained in the land in the first years of Achaemenid rule as has often been supposed.[53] It would appear that the returnees were primarily 'a dominant elite of proven loyalty',[54] who

---

[52] BEDFORD, 'On Models and Texts'.

[53] H. G. M. WILLIAMSON, 'The Concept of Israel in Transition', in R. E. CLEMENTS (ed.), The World of Ancient Israel: Sociological, Anthropological and Political Perspectives (Cambridge, 1989), 141–61.

[54] BLENKINSOPP, 'Temple and Society', 50. Indeed, according to A. LEMAIRE, 'Zorobabel et la Judée à la lumière de l'épigraphie (fin du VIe s. av. n.è)', RB 103 (1996), 48–57, it is even possible that, at the start of the Persian period, Judah was governed as a royal vassal, whereby the Persian governor (*peḥâ*) could legitimately be regarded as king (*melek*) by the local population; see too F. BIANCHI, 'Le role de Zorobabel et de la dynastie davidique en Judée du VIe siècle au IIe siècle av. J.-C.', Trans 7 (1994), 153–65.

provided the administrative class for the whole province. Even the issue of land rights may not have been as severe as might at first be thought: summarising the results of archaeological surveys of the region, Hoglund[55] has shown that, in contrast with the neighbouring territories, Judah saw a marked increase in the number of settlements at the start of the Persian period and that some 65% of the total number of settlements had not been occupied during the Iron II period. He explains this as part of an imperial domain policy of ruralisation, which would have affected the local population as much as those returning, and concludes that 'there would be no land claims by any group rooted in the notion of familial or tribal possession. *The presumption of a class struggle between exiles and "remainees" over land rights does not fit the evidence of the pattern of these Persian period villages*' (59–60, emphasis his).

The textual evidence for discord should not be related to internal disputes. Ezra 4:1–3 is part of the much later redactor's composition, but may well be based on authentic source material.[56] The reference to Esarhaddon has no Old Testament precedent (though cf. the gloss in Isa. 7:8, where his name itself does not occur), but the action attributed to him here fits with what is known of his policies. This paragraph, then, clearly speaks of inhabitants of the old Northern Kingdom of Israel, now the province of Samaria, approaching the temple builders and being rebuffed. Writing as much as two centuries later, and following a long history of disputes between the provincial officials, our redactor understandably labels this group 'the enemies of Judah and Benjamin' (verse 1), and subsequently refers to them as עַם הָאָרֶץ, 'the people of the land'.[57] This fact must determine our interpretation of his use of the same term in 3:3 (of which part of 4:4–5 is a 'summary notation'), which is equally certainly part of the redactor's composition and for which there is less evidence of an underlying source. The phrase is there used in the plural, 'the peoples of the lands' preventing the immediate building of the temple by intimidation. This, then, is part of a much later rationale for the delay in temple building, something which the contemporary Haggai explains very differently and without appeal to external opposition.

The first period for which we have sources, then, concludes with the temple eventually built to the joy of an apparently united population (cf. Ezra 6:21). We know nothing of the inhabitants of Judah who were not participants in this cult – they are simply not our narrator's concern. Other sources, such as Isaiah 56–66,[58] give indications of ideological differences of opinion amongst the commu-

---

[55] K.G. HOGLUND, 'The Achaemenid Imperial Context', in DAVIES, Second Temple Studies, 1, 54–72.
[56] WILLIAMSON, Ezra, Nehemiah, 49–50.
[57] Note that, in contrast, the contemporary prophets Haggai and Zechariah still use this term for members of the community, closer to pre-exilic usage; cf. Hag. 2:4; Zech. 7:5.
[58] See most recently B. SCHRAMM, The Opponents of Third Isaiah: Reconstructing the Cultic History of the Restoration (JSOTSup, 193; Sheffield, 1995); P.A. SMITH, Rhetoric

nity members, but these have no bearing on the questions of administration and constitution. At this point, the narrative jumps a period of more than half a century. This is not because 'there was nothing worthy of reflection', so that 'the silence of sources can be very eloquent',[59] but is simply the result of the lack of documentary sources available to the later redactor. Admittedly, he makes a theological virtue of this necessity here and elsewhere,[60] but that should not lead us to assume that we are confronted with a 'silence of history'. We simply do not know, and must therefore be alert to the possibility of change by the time we reach Ezra himself.[61]

Ezra did not come to Judah as governor, and yet, according to the copy of the edict of Artaxerxes, he was given extensive powers in the pursuance of his mission (7:26). Even if this indicates that the civil governor was to support him rather than that he had the authority to carry out these penalties himself, this still constitutes our first firm evidence for a sphere of jurisdiction which is not coterminous with the civil power. Of the four tasks assigned to him, two are straightforward: to lead a return from Babylon to Judah and to transport various gifts and grants for the temple. The following narrative recounts in some detail how this was carried out.

The third task is less clear: 'to conduct an inquiry into the situation in Judah and Jerusalem on the basis of the law of your God' (7:14). This is not directly explained, so that caution is demanded, but there are two clues to help us. First, the continuation of the edict shows great concern for the conduct of worship at the Jerusalem temple. This suggests that the inquiry was to determine the extent to which the temple cult conformed to its officially sanctioned constitution, 'the law of your God', which must, therefore, be close to, if not identical with, the Mosaic law (the Pentateuch). The impression is that the renewal of the recurrent grants and concessions (7:17 and 21–4) depended upon a satisfactory outcome. In his support of the cult, the Persian king required some formally agreed basis for his patronage, but this does not go so far as the suggestion, which has sometimes been voiced, that this law was therefore expected to become the civil law of the province. We may assume that, as a leader of the diaspora community in Babylon, Ezra had managed to work out a *modus vivendi* in regard to the delicate balance between loyalty to 'the law of your God' and 'the law of the king' (7:26), and it seems that this was what, as his fourth task, he was expected to teach to Jews in the Levant living outside the province of Judah itself (7:25–6).[62] There is no historical possibility here of any expectation that the whole

---

and Redaction in Trito-Isaiah: The Structure, Growth and Authorship of Isaiah 56–66 (VTSup, 62; Leiden, 1995).

[59] WEINBERG, Citizen-Temple Community, 128.
[60] WILLIAMSON, Ezra, Nehemiah, xlviii–xlix.
[61] Cf. G.W. AHLSTRÖM, Who Were the Israelites? (Winona Lake, 1986), 114–17.
[62] לכל in v. 25 has resumptive force, 'even all', as regularly in late Biblical Hebrew, e.g. 1:5; cf. BDB, 514B, and GK § 143*e*. It therefore clearly qualifies those who are to be taught

population of Transeuphrates should come under Jewish law; rather, as a new development, the Persians gave official sanction to the notion that religious allegiance should be allowed some recognition alongside civil responsibility. 'There was a dual system of laws in the empire, the "king's law" applicable everywhere, and local laws which were codified by order of the king',[63] and there is ample evidence that this applied to religious communities as much as political authorities.[64]

The second clue to the interpretation of 7:14 comes from the observation that the carrying out of the first two points in Ezra's commission is fully described in the following narrative. There is no possible further reference to the fourth point, just discussed. If this sets a pattern, then perhaps this third point may be linked with 10:16, where we read that, at Ezra's instigation, a commission was established to 'inquire'[65] into the matter of mixed marriages. Whether or not this coincided with the king's intention,[66] it is possible to see how this could be fitted into the general scope of Ezra's work as defined above: the ordering of the cult on the basis of an agreed law in a way that should satisfy the authorities and so enable them to continue their concessions would quickly run up against the problem of these 'mixed' cases, especially when, as interpreted by Ezra (9:1–2), the constitutional basis for membership was primarily ethnic. The interests of the Persian administration in its treatment of an officially recognised cult may here have coincided with the private and more ideologically determined agenda of Ezra and his party.

Two important consequences for our purpose follow from this analysis. First, the lines of community membership of the Jerusalem cult within the province of Judah indeed begin to be more tightly drawn with Ezra, but this is to be understood as a separate issue from the wider provincial administration. It is in no way comparable with the concept of the citizen-temple community. Secondly, and in part as a corollary of this, we find here the first indications of an official sanction for the Jerusalem temple as the centre of the wider diaspora. The two points go together in suggesting that we should maintain the clear distinction of the edict itself between 'the law of your God' and 'the law of the king'.[67]

---

as Jews. By extension, 'any who do not acknowledge them [the laws]' will mean 'any who do not acknowledge these laws but who ought to on account of their background'.

[63] R.N. FRYE, The History of Ancient Iran (München, 1984), 119.

[64] E.g. the 'Passover Papyrus' from Elephantine; A.E. COWLEY, Aramaic Papyri of the Fifth Century B.C. (Oxford, 1923), 60–5. For the oft-cited parallel with Udjahorresnet, see most recently J. BLENKINSOPP, 'The Mission of Udjahorresnet and those of Ezra and Nehemiah', JBL 106 (1987), 409–21.

[65] This is, of course, in Hebrew, so that we cannot be sure that it is a direct reference to the wording of the Aramaic edict.

[66] For an alternative suggestion, see HOGLUND, Achaemenid Imperial Administration, 226–40.

[67] For fuller justification of this approach to Ezra's mission, see WILLIAMSON, Ezra, Nehemiah, xlvi–xlviii; Ezra and Nehemiah, 69–76; and 'The Concept of Israel in Transition'.

Nehemiah's term as governor does not seem to indicate any development from our point of view. As a Jewish governor of the province with an evident personal concern for his fellow-countrymen, he claims to have involved himself in all areas of their life, religious as well as civil, but in the book which bears his name every significant move for which he gives himself credit is paralleled by accounts of the same actions and decisions taken by the people as a whole under priestly direction and preserved in separate (third-person) sources, perhaps in the temple archives.[68] It would be hazardous, therefore, to argue that his role is indicative of any change in the constitutional position of the governor with regard to the cult. His policy (influenced by Ezra?), especially with regard to external relations, may well have differed considerably from that of his immediate predecessors,[69] but that, of course, is a very different matter.

At this point, our primary sources come to an end. For the last century of Persian rule we have only tatters of information which it is extremely difficult to contextualise historically. With more than usual uncertainty, therefore, we might seek to construct a case for the coalescing of the roles of high priest and governor on the following grounds: (i) The inscription on a small silver coin of the mid-fourth century has recently been read as יוחנן הכנה, 'Yohanan the priest'.[70] Since the coin is of identical type with another which reads 'Yeḥizqiyah the governor [הפחה]', it is probable that this indicates that Yohanan held the same office. It is not known, however, whether this was under exceptional, even emergency circumstances, whether it was in the form of a 'personal union', or whether it indicates a general change in constitution, such as became normal in Hellenistic times.[71] (ii) A story in Josephus, *Jewish Antiquities* xi §§ 297–301, recounts the murder of Jesus by his brother Joannes, the high priest, in the temple, and the consequent imposition of a tax on the daily sacrifices by a Persian official, Bagoses. I have argued elsewhere that the core of this story is historically reliable, and that it should be dated to the reign of Artaxerxes III.[72] The first conclusion is widely accepted, but the second has been disputed.[73] If

---

[68] Cf. WILLIAMSON, Ezra, Nehemiah, xxxii–xxxiii.

[69] See, for instance, GRABBE, Judaism, 131–6. This would be all the more so if, as I have speculated, Tobiah had been installed as a caretaker governor shortly before Nehemiah, following the debacle recorded out of chronological sequence in Ezra 4:8–23; cf. WILLIAMSON, Ezra, Nehemiah, 183–4.

[70] D. BARAG, 'Some Notes on a Silver Coin of Yohanan the High Priest', BA 48 (1985), 166–8; 'A Siver Coin of Yohanan the High Priest and the Coinage of Judea in the Fourth century B.C.', INJ 9 (1986–7), 4–21.

[71] See the different opinions on this matter in BARAG, 'A Silver Coin'; I. EPH'AL, 'Syria-Palestine under Achaemenid Rule', CAH IV (1988), 139–64 (152); H. TADMOR, 'Judah', CAH VI (1994), 261–96 (285–86), and cf. J.W. BETLYON, 'The Provincial Government of Persian Period Judea and the Yehud Coins', JBL 105 (1986), 633–42, for a different dating of the coin.

[72] H.G.M. WILLIAMSON, 'The Historical Value of Josephus' *Jewish Antiquities* xi.297–301', JTS ns 28 (1977), 49–66 (see below, 74–89).

[73] E.g. D.R. SCHWARTZ, 'On Some Papyri and Josephus' Sources and Chronology for the Persian Period', JSJ 21 (1990), 175–99; J.C. VANDERKAM, 'Jewish High Priests of the

the later date is nevertheless correct, it might be possible to associate Joannes with the Yohanan of the coin and to see here further evidence for the involvement of the high priest in wider administration.[74] (iii) There are some other names on coins and official stamps from the late Persian period who, it has occasionally been suggested, were also priests. (iv) Both on coins and official seals of this period, Hebrew language and script tended to replace the use of Aramaic.[75] This too could be interpreted as indicating a move in administration in a more nationalist direction; the temple would be an obvious focus for this development.

It hardly needs to be said that this is speculative in the extreme. The only justification for raising the possibility here is that, if there is any truth in it, it would suggest a move by the priesthood in the direction of secular power, and not a move in a 'Jewish' direction by the secular authorities in response to the growth of the phantom citizen-temple community.

Persian Period: Is the List Complete?', in G.A. ANDERSON and S.M. OLYAN (eds.), Priesthood and Cult in Ancient Israel (Sheffield, 1991), 67–91; L.L. GRABBE, 'Who was the Bagoses of Josephus (Ant. 11.7.1, §§ 297–301)?', Trans 5 (1992), 49–55.

[74] D. BARAG, 'Bagoas and the Coinage of Judea', in T. HACKENS and G. MOUCHARTE (eds.), Proceedings of the XIth International Numismatic Congress (Louvain, 1993), 261–5.

[75] J. NAVEH and J. GREENFIELD, 'Hebrew and Aramaic in the Persian Period', CHJ 1 (1984), 115–29; A. LEMAIRE, 'Les inscriptions palestiniennes d'époque perse: un bilan provisoire', Trans 1 (1989), 87–104.

3. The Governors of Judah under the Persians

In 1934 Albrecht Alt published an essay on the history of the political status of Judah in the post-exilic period which, like so many others of his writings, set the agenda for scholarly discussion in the ensuing half-century.[1] A major conclusion of this study, and one which has been adopted by many scholars since, was that the arrival of Nehemiah in Jerusalem was accompanied by a major change in Judah's constitutional position. Previously, the Persians had taken over from the Babylonians a system whereby Judah was subsumed within the province of Samaria. Those such as Sheshbazzar and Zerubbabel who preceded Nehemiah and who are designated *peḥâ*, usually translated 'governor', should be understood rather as special commissioners whose role was restricted to specific and chronologically limited tasks in connection with the Jerusalem cult. Under Nehemiah, however, Judah was granted limited independence with its own governor – limited because, of course, it was still a part of the Persian empire. It now became, in effect, a province alongside that of Samaria within the Satrapy of 'Beyond the River'.[2] It was this new development, Alt suggested, which provoked the vigorous opposition which Nehemiah at first encountered.

Alt's essay was largely based upon a careful, if sometimes speculative, examination of the Biblical texts. In 1934 there was little enough light of any sort that archaeological research could shed on the often obscure history of the Levant during the Persian period, and of course with regard to so specific a proposal as that which Alt was advancing it would not have been surprising if no trace of it whatever had survived in the archaeological record.[3] Nevertheless, with characteristic thoroughness, Alt marshalled in a dozen lines and two footnotes what evidence he could from that quarter, namely the evidence from the

---

[1] A. ALT, 'Die Rolle Samarias bei der Entstehung des Judentums', Festschrift Otto Procksch zum 60. Geburstag (Leipzig, 1934), 5–28 = A. ALT, Kleine Schriften zur Geschichte des Volkes Israel, II (Munich, 1953), 316–37.

[2] At the start of Persian rule, Beyond the River was linked with Babylon. Perhaps as part of Darius I's organization of the empire into 20 satrapies (though this is far from certain) it became a separate province in its own right; cf. O. LEUZE, Die Satrapieneinteilung in Syrien und im Zweistromlande von 520–320 (Halle, 1935); A. F. RAINEY, 'The Satrapy "Beyond the River"', AJBA 1 (1969), 51–78; J. M. COOK in I. GERSHEVITCH (ed.), The Cambridge History of Iran. II: The Median and Achaemenian Periods (Cambridge, 1985), 261.

[3] It is not my intention to become embroiled in the debate as to whether it is proper for archaeology to look for evidence of specific events; it is enough to observe that many Palestinian archaeologists of the 1930s did.

3. The Governors of Judah under the Persians

Elephantine Papyri that by the year 408 BC, at any rate, Judah was a separate province with its own governor alongside Samaria, and, more significantly, the evidence as known at that time from seal impressions and coins that it was from this period on that the official title of the province – *yhd* – came into common use.

During the half century since Alt wrote, there have been a number of further discoveries of similar material whose relevance to the topic in hand has been contested. My purpose in the present lecture is to explain the main points at issue in the interpretation of this newer data and then to see what bearing they may have on Alt's theory as well as on a wider consideration of the administration of Judah under the Persians.

We may conveniently look first at the work of Ephraim Stern, because he has marshalled some of the evidence from seals in favour of a modified form of Alt's hypothesis.[4] Whereas most interest has traditionally been focussed on inscribed seals, Stern for the first time examined anepigraphic seal impressions of this period on which are depicted various animals, in particular, lions. All come from the Jerusalem region, with the single exception of one from Shechem.

Various considerations led Stern to conclude that these impressions are to be dated to the earlier part of the Persian period: there is a close typological relationship between them and the jar-handles from the end of the Iron Age; the impression from Shechem is to be dated no later than 475 BC on the basis of associated finds within the same stratum; Gibeon, where two of these seals were found, was destroyed at the beginning of the fifth century BC;[5] and in Jerusalem, Duncan found this type of seal impression at a lower level than those of the *yhwd* type.

Turning then to the motifs which occur on these impressions, Stern succeeded in elucidating one group in the light of known Achaemenid imperial scenes in which a Persian king is in combat with a roaring lion who stands upright on his hind legs because of his pain on being wounded. Those found in Judah represent only part of the motif, and without the find of the whole scene from hoards of

---

[4] E. STERN, 'Seal-Impressions in the Achaemenid Style in the Province of Judah', BASOR 202 (1971), 6–16; cf. Material Culture in the Land of the Bible in the Persian Period 538–332 B.C. (Warminster and Jerusalem, 1982), 209–13.

[5] J.B. PRITCHARD dated the destruction of Gibeon to the start of the Babylonian exile; cf. Gibeon – Where the Sun Stood Still: The Discovery of the Biblical City (Princeton, 1962), 163 (though to be fair it should be added that Pritchard reckoned with some subsequent habitation precisely on the basis of the *mṣh* seal impressions, a fact generally ignored by his critics). However, this date has not generally been accepted; cf. the reviews of the two original reports by W.F. ALBRIGHT, BASOR 159 (1960), 37, and by G.E. WRIGHT, JNES 22 (1963), 210–11. The suggestion these reviewers advanced to lower the date of Gibeon's destruction to at least the end of the sixth century has received palaeographical support from F.M. CROSS, 'Epigraphical Notes on Hebrew Documents from the Eighth-Sixth Centuries B.C.: III. The Inscribed Jar Handles from Gibeon', BASOR 168 (1962), 18–23, and support from the character of a number of other finds from STERN, Material Culture, 33.

Achaemenid seal impressions they would have remained obscure.[6] Furthermore, a previously unexplained object can best be interpreted as the stylized representation of an Achaemenid fire-altar. Stern concludes not unreasonably in view of this rather clear evidence that the depictions on the other two groups of related seal impressions also show Achaemenid influence, and parallels for them from this quarter are not lacking. Further, it thus becomes plausible to suppose that in Judah as elsewhere such seals were used by officials serving in the administration of the Persian empire.

In his original study, Stern let his case rest at this point. 'The difference between these [anepigraphic] impressions and those bearing the name *yhwd* ("Judah") is outstanding. The latter, in my opinion, also belonged to officials serving the administration of the province, but much later in the Persian period' (15). He linked this change with the radical reform in administration proposed by Alt. A later restatement of the theory has slightly complicated the issue.[7] Not wishing to discount the Biblical evidence that Sheshbazzar and Zerubbabel were governors, he now suggests that only after Zerubbabel was removed from office – perhaps under suspicion of plotting an uprising – was authority over Judah transferred to Samaria, returning to Jerusalem with the arrival of Nehemiah some seventy years later.

In examining Stern's theory, it should be emphasized that there is no intention of criticizing his handling of archaeological data as such, for regarding the archaeology of Palestine under the Persians Stern is a leading authority; his elucidation of the motifs in question, which had baffled those who first discovered and published them, stands up quite apart from the historical consequences which he draws from it. As regards the latter, however, we should note the following points:

(i) Whilst arguing for a change in the style of administration of Judah, Stern has not produced any evidence whatsoever which supports the more significant aspect of Alt's theory, namely that in the earlier period Judah was administered from Samaria. Indeed, the brief remarks he makes about the situation in Samaria might be held to point in exactly the opposite direction. He writes

We know of three additional seal-impressions from the satrapy [he must mean 'province'] of Samaria, two from the site of Samaria and one from Shechem. All three are in a pure Achaemenid style, but they differ from those found in Judah in their workmanship. Samaria apparently used imported seals, not local imitations as in Judah (15).

---

[6] Stern overlooked, however, Avigad's publication of a Judaean seal which depicts a comparable motif; cf. N. AVIGAD, 'Three Ornamented Hebrew Seals', IEJ 4 (1954), 236–8.

[7] E. STERN, 'The Persian empire and the political and social history of Palestine in the Persian period', in W.D. DAVIES and L. FINKELSTEIN (eds), The Cambridge History of Judaism. I: Introduction; The Persian Period (Cambridge, 1984), 70–87 (cf. especially 72 and 82–8).

That there was a general material and cultural similarity between the hill-country of Judah and Samaria in the Persian period (in continuity with the late Iron Age) in contrast to the situation along the coastal plain, for instance, is now well established. In such a situation, it is the differences that stand out as more significant. Stern has not been able to explain why, if the whole area was administered as a single province at this time, there should be any distinction of the kind he has described between Judah and Samaria. In the matter of official seals above all, we should have expected there to be no difference whatever.

(ii) The use of Achaemenid motifs in Judah cannot be used as evidence that Judah was administered as part of Samaria at that time. If anything, it would be more suggestive of 'direct rule', except that the use of such motifs elsewhere shows that this cannot be so.

(iii) Stern in fact presupposes Alt's theory before supporting it. A change in the style of administration – if that is what his evidence suggests – may be the consequence of any number of possibilities, and I have elsewhere suggested an alternative which I regard as more probable.[8] Without going into detail again here, we should remember that when Nehemiah came to Jerusalem the western provinces of the empire were only just emerging from nearly fifteen years of turbulence – the Egyptian revolt which lasted for several years from 460 BC on, and then the revolt of the western satrapies under the leadership of Megabyzos in about 449 BC.[9] Now in these circumstances, a 'shake-up' of political power in the west would not be at all surprising, and independent evidence of this may come from Samaria itself. It is known from the Elephantine papyri that when Nehemiah came to Jerusalem, his arch-foe Sanballat was the governor of Samaria.[10] We also know from the same source and from the Wâdī ed-Dâliyeh papyri[11] that he was succeeded in this office by his direct descendants through four generations until the beginning of Hellenistic rule. His description as 'the Horonite' (Neh. 2:10), however, implies that he was the first in this line of succession. If so, then it becomes attractive to see in his appointment part of a larger attempt by Artaxerxes to reassert control over the region, and Nehemiah's mission a little later might reflect the same policy. This, I suggest, could explain the evidence Stern has adduced without resorting to the hypothesis of a period of Samarian rule over Judah.

(iv) An important plank in Stern's platform is his claim that no stamps of the *yhwd* type should be dated earlier than the second half of the fifth century BC. When he wrote his initial study, this was a reasonable, though unproved, assumption. It was based largely on the absence of such material from Gibeon, and

---

[8] 'Early Post-Exilic Judaean History', above, 16–18.
[9] Cf. J.M. COOK, The Persian Empire (London, 1983), 168–9; R.N. FRYE, The History of Ancient Iran (Handbuch der Altertumswissenschaft, III/7; Munich, 1984), 127–8.
[10] A. COWLEY, Aramaic Papyri of the Fifth Century B.C. (Oxford, 1923), 30:29.
[11] Cf. F.M. CROSS, 'A Reconstruction of the Judean Restoration', JBL 94 (1975), 4–18.

supported by the fact that no other really reliable stratigraphical data lay to hand. Absence of evidence, however, can hardly be said to constitute proof, and when in his later study[12] Stern dismisses new and potentially damaging contrary evidence from Avigad without, so far as I can see, discussing a single one of Avigad's and others' arguments, it is hard to resist the impression that he has already decided the issue on other grounds, which, as we have seen, include Alt's theory itself.[13]

We may conclude this first part of our discussion by affirming that Stern's attempt to uphold Alt's theory on archaeological grounds has not succeeded, despite the value of his discussion in other, perhaps more important, respects. If Alt were right, his suggestions might provide one possible explanation of the data Stern has advanced, but conversely these data cannot be used to support the theory in the first place.

It has already begun to emerge from our discussion that an important part of the evidence to be considered focuses on the so-called *yhwd* seals, and so these may be appropriately considered next. By 1976, the year in which Avigad published his important collection of bullae and seals to be discussed later, an element of consensus had been reached about these seals following decades of controversy. First, the reading *yehud* in various spellings, sometimes also including a *ṭêt*-symbol, is generally agreed for seals which had previously been variously read as עדיה,[14] יהו[15] and העיר.[16] Sukenik was the first to introduce the correct reading of יהד for יהו by analogy with the *yhd* coins,[17] and Albright was quick to develop the suggestion to arrive independently from, but simultaneously with, Sukenik's revised reading of the העיר stamps as יהד + monogram.[18] This was still not universally accepted,[19] however, until 1960, when Avigad,

---

[12] STERN, *Material Culture*, 206.

[13] Stern's attempt to link the evidence from coins with the proposed reform is questionable, since there is no reason to suppose that coins would have been minted or widely used in Judah in any case until the second half of the Persian period, regardless of the province's constitutional status. On this matter, though not on a number of others, I should agree with J. W. BETLYON, 'The Provincial Government of Persian Period Judah and the Yehud Coins', *JBL* 105 (1986), 633–42

[14] E.g. W. F. ALBRIGHT, 'Notes on Early Hebrew and Aramaic Epigraphy', *JPOS* 6 (1926), 75–102.

[15] E. SELLIN and C. WATZINGER, *Jericho: Die Ergebnisse der Ausgrabungen* (Leipzig, 1913), 158–9 and 188–9.

[16] E. L. SUKENIK, 'The "Jerusalem" and "the city" Stamps on Jar Handles', *JPOS* 13 (1933), 226–31.

[17] E. L. SUKENIK, 'Paralipomena Palaestinensia', *JPOS* 14 (1934), 178–84.

[18] W. F. ALBRIGHT 'Light on the Jewish State in Persian Times', *BASOR* 53 (1934), 20–22; SUKENIK, *JPOS* 14 (1934), 183, n. 4.

[19] Cf. L.-H. VINCENT, 'Les Épigraphes Judéo-Araméennes Postexiliques', *RB* 56 (1949), 274–94, followed by S. J. SALLER, 'Stamped Impressions on the Pottery of Bethany', *LASBF* 3 (1952–53), 5–36. Saller's main argument is that the proposed *ṭêt* symbol raised difficulties which the reading *h'yr* does not. However, the *five*-letter stamps *ṭ* + *yhwd* discussed by Avigad (see next note) completely invalidates this objection.

3. The Governors of Judah under the Persians

developing his insight into the correct way of reading the *mwṣh* seal impressions (namely in horizontal lines of two letters each), established that those stamps which it had still been possible to read as *h'yr* should now be read as *ṭêt + yhd*,[20] or even in one case *ṭêt + yhwd* (with *plene* spelling, a spelling which Avigad had earlier established for a seal from Jericho[21]), and which confirms beyond doubt the correctness of his interpretation of the *h'yr* stamps.

Secondly, a measure of agreement was also reached by 1976 over the general dates to which these and other post-exilic seal impressions should be assigned. The *yhd* + symbol together with the *yršlm*[22] impressions are to be dated last on several grounds. Ceramically, they have close parallels as to both form and ware with pottery from Shechem of the third quarter of the third century BC.[23] Palaeographically, they fall together in the Hellenistic period as being inscribed in Palaeo-Hebrew rather than the lapidary Aramaic of the other impressions.[24] Archaeologically, the evidence from Jerusalem,[25] Bethany (where only these two types of impression were found, and that in association with typically Hellenistic pottery) and from Ramat Raḥel agrees in this later dating.[26] Finally, these two classes of stamp combine against those of the others (except those of the *pḥw'* type yet to be considered) in having their impression near the top of the handle.[27]

At the upper end of our period, it is also generally believed that the *mwṣh* impressions should be dated earliest,[28] primarily because they alone were found at Gibeon, which was destroyed at the beginning of the fifth century BC.[29] This leaves the various Aramaic *yhd* impressions which a majority of scholars assigned to the second half of the Persian period, though not on particularly strong grounds, as we shall see.

---

[20] N. AVIGAD, 'Yehûd or Ha'îr?', BASOR 158 (1960), 23–7.

[21] N. AVIGAD, 'A New Class of Yehud Stamps', IEJ 7 (1957), 146–53; cf. W. F. ALBRIGHT, 'The Seal Impression from Jericho and the Treasurers of the Second Temple', BASOR 148 (1957), 28–30.

[22] This group of seals has the letters of *yršlm* written between the points of a star. Although this reading was suggested early, it was established definitively by SUKENIK, JPOS 13 (1933), 226–31.

[23] P. W. LAPP, 'Ptolemaic Stamped Handles from Judah', BASOR 172 (1963), 22–35 (see especially 22–5), and cf. H. N. RICHARDSON, 'A Stamped Handle from Khirbet Yarmuk', BASOR 192 (1968), 12–16.

[24] F. M. CROSS, 'Judean Stamps', ErIsr 9 (1969), 20–7 (and *apud* LAPP, 26, n. 20).

[25] N. AVIGAD, 'More Evidence on the Judean Post-Exilic Stamps', IEJ 24 (1974), 52–8.

[26] G. GARBINI, 'The Dating of Post-Exilic Stamps', in Y. Aharoni, Excavations at Ramat Raḥel: Seasons 1959 and 1960 (Rome, 1962), 61–8; cf. AHARONI, *ibid.*, 29–30, and Excavations at Ramat Raḥel: Seasons 1961 and 1962 (Rome, 1964), 20 and 43.

[27] LAPP, BASOR 172 (1963), 30.

[28] So STERN, Material Culture, 207–9, *contra* J. NAVEH, The Development of the Aramaic Script (Jerusalem; The Israel Academy of Sciences and Humanities, Proceedings, V, 1 [1970]), 61–2. For a summary of previous discussions of this class of stamp, cf. N. AVIGAD, 'New Light on the MṢH Seal Impressions', IEJ 8 (1958), 113–19.

[29] See above, n. 5.

Finally, when we turn to enquire after the significance of these seal impressions, we find less agreement. Cross assigned them very little direct historical significance, seeing in them no more than formulae for inscribing wine bottles of official measure. This conclusion he based primarily upon some jars from Shiqmona, whose inscriptions read, for example:

1. Ben Mattōn 25 royal measures (=*lmlk*)
2. wine of Gat Karmel
3. *ṭêt* symbol[30]

According to Cross, the use of a number before *lmlk* shows that it is an indication of units according to the royal standard, and the *ṭêt* symbol, here together with *lmlk*, came in time to replace it altogether. Of particular importance is line 2 which, being written here in full, shows that the place name signifies the location of the vineyards from which the wine came. By analogy, this then is also the explanation of the name *yhd* in our post-exilic seal impressions.[31]

Cross's theory is not without its difficulties, however. (i) Whilst the names of towns such as Moṣah may be explained in the way Cross suggests, the various forms of the provincial name cannot be classed in the same category. The whole force of Cross's argument is that it is the precise locality of the origin of the wine that is significant, and for this purpose the name *yhd* is far too general. (ii) The letters *yhd* also occur on some coins of the Persian period.[32] In this case, the association with the administration of the province is clear. Since often on the jar handles *yhd* occurs alone, without any indication of capacity and so on, the analogy with the coins may be considered quite as close as the Shiqmona jar inscriptions. (iii) Cross does not apparently try to explain the later *yršlm* stamps by his theory, and in fact they pose problems for it, both because it is implausible to suppose that Jerusalem only entered the wine trade at a very late stage and because the way the letters of *yršlm* are written between the points of a star seems to single it out from other place names on jar inscriptions. It is clear, then, that we must seek an alternative explanation for the occurrence of *yhd* (and *yršlm*).

Though other possibilities have been proposed,[33] the majority opinion is that these stamps were used in connection with the collection of taxes, a view that can be subdivided into two possibilities: (i) that the jars were used for the

---

[30] F.M. CROSS, 'Jar Inscriptions from Shiqmona', IEJ 18 (1968), 226–33, and cf. ErIsr 9 (1969), 21–2.

[31] 'The place names on wine jars have the same sense: wine of *Gib'eon*, *Moṣah*, *Yehūd*, Thasos, Rhodes, and indeed on the old Judahite stamps, wine of *mmšt*, *ḥbrn*, *z(y)p*, and *swkh*', IEJ 18 (1968), 232.

[32] They now also occur on a number of bullae (see below), though CROSS could not have known that when he wrote.

[33] NAVEH, Development, 61, for instance, has suggested that the name indicated a standard quantity as agreed by the provincial administration.

collection of secular taxes for the governor, and (ii) that they were used for contributions to the temple alone (cf. Neh. 10:32-9; 13:10-13). When in the later period these needed to be distinguished from the secular taxes, the new *yršlm* impression was adopted for this temple tax. This second suggestion is not very likely, however; to propose that in the Ptolemaic period jars formerly marked *yhd* were replaced by jars marked *yršlm* whilst *yhd* came to be used for something else is unconvincing. The former suggestion, that these jars were used throughout for the collection of general taxation is clearly more plausible and enables the name to carry the same significance as it does on the coins, that is to say, a reference to the official administration of the province.[34]

While the various points I have just outlined represented the consensus of opinion a decade or so ago, it is apparent that these data have only a very limited bearing on our topic. The date in the second half of the Persian period assumed for the *yhd* impressions meant that they could contribute directly to the issue of Judah's status earlier on.

In 1976 the matter was taken a dramatic step further with the publication of N. Avigad's *Bullae and Seals from a Post-Exilic Judean Archive*.[35] In this volume, Avigad published two seals and more than seventy bullae (that is to say, small lumps of clay which had been used to seal letters or documents and which were then stamped with a seal). The find-spot of this material is unknown, but its homogeneity as a collection seems to be assured by the facts that a number of the bullae were impressed with the same seal and that 'one of the seals (No. 14) is directly connected by its legend to one of the bullae types (No. 5)' (p. 1). Many of the bullae and one of the seals are inscribed with the name of the province, *yh(w)d*; some additionally have a personal name, whilst others have only a personal name with or without an official title.

Before proceeding to discuss the date of this material, it will be helpful first to take note of some of the names and titles, for these relate to a further controversy which was far from resolved in 1976. Amongst a large number of seal impressions previously found by Aharoni at Ramat Raḥel, a few bore the names of individuals as well as that of the province, others had a name plus title, and uniquely several impressions of a single type had *yhwd* + personal name +

---

[34] This fits well with LAPP's view regarding the situation later in the Ptolemaic period, and suggests that secular and religious authority were kept distinct throughout the post-exilic period. It means that for the Persian period we do not have (or have not recognized) direct evidence for the collection of revenue in kind for the temple. It is not difficult to think of reasons why this might be so. The situation may appear to have been complicated by D. BARAG's proposal (cf. 'Some Notes on a Silver Coin of Johanan the High Priest', BA 48 [1985], 166-8) to read *yḥn[n] hkhn*, 'Johanan the priest', on a coin of similar type to those inscribed *yḥzqyh hpḥh* (see below). Does this indicate that by the late Persian period secular and religious authority had become completely fused? Not necessarily; since there is no evidence that this situation continued, it seems likely at present that this was simply a 'one-off' case in circumstances about which we are completely in the dark.

[35] Qedem, 4 (Jerusalem, 1976).

title.³⁶ The most controversial aspect of these finds was the title. Aharoni read it as פחוא, 'the governor', an apparently anomalous form linguistically (see further below), but one which Kutscher had endeavoured to explain as a backformation from the plural פחותא, פחון.³⁷ Cross, however, observed that after about 500 BC the letter *wāw* was no longer written with a 'peaked right shoulder' and that even before that it was becoming rare. Since there was no reason to date the Ramat Raḥel material earlier than the fifth century BC, Cross affirmed that the letter in question must be a *rēš*, and that the word should thus be read as פחרא, 'the potter'. This was not an unreasonable conclusion in the light of the evidence which was available at that time, and Naveh in particular lent it his support.³⁸

The material which Avigad has published, however, confirms that *pḥw'* was the correct reading after all. The word occurs on one bulla (No. 5) following the personal name Elnathan. It is also almost certainly to be restored through comparison with No. 5 as the damaged last word on one of the two seals (No. 14), which reads in full:

Belonging to Shelomith	לשלמית
maidservant of Elna-	אמת אלנ
than *pḥ* . .	תן פח . .

The reasons for favouring the reading *pḥw'* include the following: (i) The horde as a whole seems clearly to have come originally from some kind of official archive. This is suggested not only by the number of documents which must have been included but also by the presence of an actual seal (No. 13) inscribed *yhd* as well as a large number of impressions which bear the name of *yh(w)d* and the use of a title such as *hspr* (cf. No. 6 – ten bullae all with an identical inscription). In such a context we expect an official title. (ii) Whilst a potter's name is conceivable on a jar, it is highly improbable on a bulla used for sealing a document. (iii) In the case of seal No. 14, quoted just above, the reading 'potter' would be ridiculous. By extension, therefore, it is equally inconceivable in the case of bulla No. 5. (iv) Elsewhere in the horde there are a number of clear examples of the letter *wāw* written with the 'peaked right shoulder', for instance in *yhwd* at plate 5, nos. a, b, and d, and in *lbrwk* at plate 8. There can thus be no palaeographical objection to what is contextually so obviously a superior reading.

If this reading has found a widespread measure of agreement in recent years, the same cannot be said for its precise significance. It has long been known that

---

[36] Cf. AHARONI, Ramat Raḥel Seasons 1959 and 1960, 7–10 and 32–4; Ramat Raḥel Seasons 1961 and 1962, 21–2 and 44–5.

[37] E. Y. KUTSCHER, 'פחוא and its Cognates', Tarbiẓ 30 (1960–61), 112–19 (Hebrew). He cites as an identical parallel the development in Syriac of *mḥw'* from *mḥ'*.

[38] CROSS, ErIsr 9 (1969), 24–6; NAVEH, Development, 61; see also S. A. KAUFMAN, The Akkadian Influences on Aramaic (Assyriological Studies, 19; Chicago and London, 1974), 82.

the Hebrew and Aramaic word *pḥh* (from Akkadian [*bēl*] *pīḫātu*) has a broad range of meaning; within Biblical texts referring to the Achaemenid period alone it can refer to a satrap (Ezra 5:3) as well as a provincial governor (e.g. Neh. 5:14b), whilst as we have noted Alt maintained that it could also be used for those commissioned to a specific task, such as Sheshbazzar and Zerubbabel. Further afield, the occurrence of the plural form פחותא in the Migdol Papyrus I 4 appears to refer to junior officials acting in a judicial capacity.[39] This ambiguity is exploited in a general way by McEvenue[40] and rather specifically by Naveh and Greenfield to cast doubt on the translation 'the governor' as a title for Elnathan in the Avigad collection and for Yehoezer and Ahzai in the seal impressions from Ramat Raḥel.[41] Their argument is that the Aramaic word for governor is *peḥâ*, which in the emphatic state should be *paḥtā'*. Our *paḥwā'*, therefore, they take to be a backformation specifically from the plural *paḥwātā'* of the Migdol Papyrus and therefore to mean not a governor but a lower governmental official. They conclude:

These texts were clearly from an archive which belonged to Shlomit who was the maidservant/concubine of Elnathan. The sealings belonged either to the participants in the affairs recorded in the papyri or to the witnesses. The *yhwd* sealings reflect the interest of the government in these procedings and therefore we find among the participants Elnathan 'the official'. There is no need to assume that this was an official archive (123f.).

In the course of a recent publication of some Hebrew pre-exilic bullae, Avigad has made a partial response to these arguments by emphasizing again the evidence that this was indeed an official archive, and adding the further considerations that it is unlikely that the 'maidservant' of a low-ranking official would have a formal seal or be the owner of so large an archive.[42] Furthermore, in his

---

[39] E. BRESCIANI, 'Papiri aramaici egiziani di epoca persiana presso il Museo Civico di Padova', RSO 35 (1960), 11–24; J.A. FITZMYER, 'The Padua Aramaic Papyrus Letters', JNES 21 (1962), 15–24, revised in A Wandering Aramean: Collected Aramaic Essays (SBLMS, 25; Missoula, 1979), 219–30; J. NAVEH, 'Old Aramaic Inscriptions (1960–64)', AION ns 16 (1966), 19–36; J.C.L. GIBSON, Textbook of Syrian Semitic Inscriptions. II: Aramaic Inscriptions (Oxford, 1975), 143–7.

[40] S.E. MCEVENUE, 'The Political Structure in Judah from Cyrus to Nehemiah', CBQ 43 (1981), 353–64. In this article, MCEVENUE seeks to defend ALT's thesis against the criticisms of SMITH (below, n. 59) and of G. WIDENGREN, 'The Persian Period', in J.H. HAYES and J.M. MILLER (eds.), Israelite and Judaean History (London, 1977), 489–538. A number of the matters discussed above are intended to suggest a different evaluation of the evidence from that offered by MCEVENUE. Here, however, we should note in particular that he fails to discuss the relevant coins, that his treatment of AVIGAD is less than fair (as we have already noted, the damaged seal No. 14 needs to be read in association with bulla No. 5) and that his appeal to CROSS's reading *pḥr'* is no longer acceptable.

[41] J. NAVEH and J.C. GREENFIELD, 'Hebrew and Aramaic in the Persian Period', CHJ I (above, n. 7), 115–29.

[42] N. AVIGAD, Hebrew Bullae from the time of Jeremiah: Remnants of a Burnt Archive (Jerusalem, 1986), 122, n. 149.

original publication he had sought to dismiss the relevance of the Migdol Papyrus by suggesting that the word in question should not be vocalized as the emphatic plural of *pḥh*, but rather as an otherwise unattested abstract noun *paḥûtā'* meaning 'prefecture'.[43] This is quite unconvincing, however, for the word occurs in a well-attested fixed legal formula in which in every other case a personal title is to be expected at this point.[44] There can be no serious doubt that in this case, at least, the plural of *pḥh* is used for officials lower than the rank of governor.

Acceptance of this point, however, by no means involves agreement with Naveh and Greenfield over the meaning of *pḥw'*. First, for their argument to work, they would have to establish that the plural *paḥwātā'* was only ever used of junior officials so that a backformation from it to the singular *paḥwā'* could be used somewhat artificially to mean 'the (junior) official' in distinction to the regular emphatic *paḥtā'* meaning 'the governor'.[45] This, however, is manifestly not the case; the Aramaic plural *paḥᵃwātā'* at Dan. 3:2, 3 and 27 must refer to senior officials on the basis of their position in the list, and the same is probably true for Dan. 6:8. The Hebrew plural forms *paḥôt* and *paḥᵃwôt* are of relevance as showing that in a closely related language the plural form with the meaning 'governors' was well-known; cf. especially Ezra 8:36 and Neh. 2:7, 9 (and further Est. 3:12; 8:9; 9:3). There can thus be no objection in principle to *pḥw'* being a backformation from the plural with the meaning governor.

Secondly, therefore, we need to ask which is the more probable meaning in the context. Here, three factors tip the balance in favour of 'governor'. One is Avigad's point that we should not expect the wife or female subordinate of a junior official to have a seal which, in addition, was in use in the context of an official archive. The second factor which in my opinion emphatically endorses Avigad's position is the analogy which cries out to be drawn with a small group of coins which have only recently been definitively read. Alongside the fourth century BC silver coins stamped simply *yhd*, there are three which are inscribed instead *yḥzqyh hpḥh* (= *yeḥezqîyâ happeḥâ*), 'Hezekiah the governor'.[46] Though

---

[43] AVIGAD, Bullae and Seals, 6, n. 5.
[44] For references, cf. FITZMYER, Wandering Aramean, 223.
[45] There is, in fact, no evidence at all that *paḥtā'* was the 'regular' emphatic form in Judah. So far as I can see, the form is only attested anywhere once – namely in the Aramaic version of the Behistun inscription (line 31 = line 18 of COWLEY's edition) found at Elephantine. This text is so badly preserved that one might be inclined to query the reading, but the most recent photographs quite clearly show a *t*; cf. J.C. GREENFIELD and B. PORTEN, The Bisitun Inscription of Darius the Great: Aramaic Version (Corpus Inscriptionum Iranicarum I. v.l; London, 1982), plate ix; note also A. YARDENI's reconstruction, plate iv, and the text of the new edition, 34.
[46] L. MILDENBERG, 'Yehud: a Preliminary Study of the Provincial Coinage of Judaea', in O. MØRKHOLM and N.M. WAGGONER (eds.), Greek Numismatics and Archaeology: Essays in Honor of Margaret Thompson (Wetteren, 1979), 183–96; cf. L.Y. RAHMANI, 'Silver Coins of the Fourth Century B.C. from Tel Gamma', IEJ 21 (1971), 158–60; STERN, Material

these inscriptions are in Hebrew, the parallel with our Aramaic material is exact, and since it cannot be supposed that anyone other than the provincial governor is being referred to on the coins, the same is likely to be true in the case of the earlier seal impressions.[47] A third factor which deserves consideration is the parallel which may be drawn with the practice in Samaria. Like the coins just mentioned, the evidence comes from late in the Persian period, but it is striking nonetheless. One of the clay seals discovered in the Wâdī ed-Dâliyeh is inscribed:

[ ]yhw bn [sn']
blṭ pḥt šmr[n]

[Belonging to Yĕšaʻ]yahū, son of [San]ballat, governor of Samaria[48]

This seal is written in Hebrew (and in palaeo-Hebrew rather than Aramaic script) and the force of pḥh here is therefore not in doubt. The reference to Sanballat further underscores the word's significance. The fact that a seal of this sort could be affixed to a contract relating to the sale of a vineyard shows that seals even of the governor were used in the course of regular transactions. This fits extremely well with the material published by Avigad and makes it attractive to understand it in similar terms.

We have arrived at the probable conclusion that Elnathan was indeed a hitherto unknown governor of Judah. The question which was previously held over, but which can now no longer be avoided, is that of date.

In his original publication, Avigad argued that the bullae should be dated in the sixth century BC. In the absence of any archaeological context or the identification (as he thought) of any of the persons named with characters known from elsewhere, he was obliged to base his conclusions entirely on palaeography. On the one hand he finds evidence of a number of 'classical' or 'archaic' forms which cannot be later than the sixth century and on the other of

---

Culture, 224–27 (with discussion of earlier opinions); BETLYON (above, n. 13), JBL 105 (1986), 633–42.

[47] E. LIPIŃSKI, BiOr 42 (1985), 164, has attempted to press NAVEH's and GREENFIELD's suggestion even further. He writes, 'There is little doubt, however, that pḥw is not the same word as pḥh. Pḥw occurs above all in legends of stamps impressed on jars. This indicates... that the official called pḥw' should be identified with the pēḫû ša karpati, mentioned in the lexical series Aa A = nâqu II/3, Section B (MSL XIV, 277, B, 8`), after the "locksman", sēkeru ša mê... he is no "governor", but the official "who seals" the jars'. My colleague, J. N. POSTGATE observes, however, that these words should be taken as infinitives, not as participles (pēḫû and sekēru), and that the only example of the process in question relates to the smearing of bitumen on ships. This is hardly appropriate to the context in hand, and it would leave Elnathan as a very junior workman, not an 'official' at all – and certainly not one whose 'mh we should expect to have a seal of her own.

[48] F. M. CROSS in P. W. and N. L. LAPP (eds.), Discoveries in the Wâdī ed-Dâliyeh (ASOR Annual, 41; Cambridge, Mass., 1974), 18.

several letters which in lapidary script had not developed the forms which they take here before the sixth century BC. The kind of arguments involved have already been noted above in connection with the letter *wāw*. Avigad's conclusions have since been upheld by Herr's independent (though not always completely accurate) study of *The Scripts of Ancient Northwest Semitic Seals*.[49]

So far as I am aware, no one has refuted Avigad's palaeographical analysis, although some have rejected his conclusions without further discussion. The problem is that in material of this kind it is difficult to escape the impression that the palaeographer's date, which may well be typologically correct, can never be more than a *terminus post quem* in absolute terms. The retention of older forms of script should cause no surprise in the case of official seals, and seems in fact to be certain in the case of the *wāw* of *pḥw'* from Ramat Raḥel already discussed. Indeed, on palaeographic grounds, Herr states that there would be nothing to prevent us dating a few of Avigad's seals to the seventh or eighth centuries if we did not know better – a further indication of the conservatism of official and perhaps provincial seals. Thus although we may be inclined towards Avigad's sixth century date, we are not obliged to accept it.

Perhaps, however, his date can be supported – though again not decisively established – on other grounds. Apparently independently, both Lemaire and Meyers have proposed identifying the Shelomith of Seal No. 14 with the Shelomith of 1 Chron. 3:19, a daughter of Zerubbabel.[50] (Avigad had observed the coincidence of names, but no more.) In favour of this identification, they point out that both in Biblical genealogies and on seals the names of women are comparatively rare. In the case of the Biblical genealogy, the curiosity of having a woman mentioned might be explained if in fact she held some official position. And the dates of the two named may plausibly be held to have coincided.

It is not clear quite what significance we should ascribe to Shelomith's title *'mt 'lntn*. On the one hand it has been suggested that this means no more than 'wife' as the counterpart to *b'l* in the sense of husband.[51] There are a few Ammonite seals which use the same word, whilst in earlier Hebrew seals we find the more prosaic *'št*.[52] On the other hand, we might suppose a little more adventurously that *'mh* here is in some way the counterpart of *'bd*[53] which

---

[49] L.G. Herr, The Scripts of Ancient Northwest Semitic Seals (HSM, 18; Missoula, 1978), 24–9, dates the collection to the late sixth-early fifth centuries.

[50] A. Lemaire, Syria 54 (1977), 129–31; E.M. Meyers, 'The Shelomith Seal and the Judean Restoration: Some Additional Considerations', Erlsr 18 (1985), 33*–38*. Lemaire goes on to propose two further identifications (*ḥnnh*, cf. 1 Chron. 3:19; and *šm'y*, cf. 1 Chron. 3:19) but then rightly admits that 'ces deux identifications restent assez hypothetiques'.

[51] E. g. Lipiński, BiOr 42 (1985), 165; Lemaire, Syria 54 (1977), 130.

[52] For examples (not exhaustive), see conveniently Herr, Scripts, 63 and 98. This has caused G.I. Davies to speculate privately with me on the outside possibility that Elnathan might have been a governor of Ammon.

[53] This suggestion seems first to have been advanced in connection with other seals by W.F. Albright, 'Notes on Ammonite History', in R.M. Díaz (ed.), Miscellanea Biblica B.

occurs on a number of pre-exilic seals either in the title '*bd hmlk* or with a personal name of someone who was in fact a king. This title, it is agreed, was a high ranking official in the circle close to the king,[54] so that if '*mh* were its female counterpart it would again point to the importance of Elnathan's status. Either way, the translation 'maidservant/concubine' is misleading.[55] Whether by marriage or in her own right, Shelomith was a woman to be reckoned with, and it is by no means unreasonable to identify her with the daughter of Zerubbabel of the Davidic family.

It should be emphasized at this point that in order to affirm that Elnathan was a governor of Judah a generation or so after Zerubbabel, we have to rely either upon palaeographical dating or upon the identification of a name on a seal with one in a Biblical genealogy or on both points. In the nature of the case, neither argument can be regarded as absolutely compelling, but the balance of probability seems to me to lie in favour of the position I have been arguing for. If this is accepted, then the likelihood that the ascription of the title *pḥh* to Sheshbazzar and Zerubbabel is to be taken in the same way becomes irresistible, and with at least three governors of Judah prior to Nehemiah,[56] Alt's case with which we started this lecture collapses. That is not to say that the arrival of Nehemiah in Jerusalem did not herald any change in the administration of Judah; I have argued elsewhere[57] (and therefore shall not set out the evidence again here) that between the abortive wall-building effort recorded out of chronological order in Ezra 4 and the appointment of Nehemiah it may well have been that Tobiah acted as a caretaker governor under the supervision of Samaria, and when discussing Stern's theory above we noted hints that in fact there may have been some administrative reforms at about this time throughout the Levant. But that is a far cry from asserting that prior to Nehemiah Judah was but another district within the province of Samaria.[58]

Ubach (Scripta et Documenta, 1; Montserrat, 1953), 131–6, and it has been tentatively applied to our seal by AVIGAD, Bullae and Seals, 11–13, and MEYERS, EI 18 (1985), 35*.

[54] Cf. R. DE VAUX, Les Institutions de l'Ancien Testament (Paris, 1958), 184–5 (ET Ancient Israel: Its Life and Institutions [2nd edn; London, 1965], 120).

[55] In this connection it is worth emphasizing the distinction between the use of this word on a seal and in literary texts or funerary inscriptions (for an example of the latter, cf. N. AVIGAD, 'The Epitaph of a Royal Steward from Siloam Village', IEJ 3 [1953], 137–52).

[56] AVIGAD, Bullae and Seals, 35, would also include Yeho'ezer and Ahzai, known from Ramat Raḥel, as governors before Nehemiah. Because the Ramat Raḥel stamps come from a refuse dump, however (cf. AHARONI, Ramat Raḥel: Seasons 1959 and 1960, 28, and Ramat Raḥel: Seasons 1961 and 1962, 19 and 43), the date of this material is even less certain than in the case of Elnathan, and so cannot be used as evidence at this point.

[57] Cf. note 8 above.

[58] There are, of course, literary and historical arguments leading towards the same conclusion, but they lie beyond the scope of the present lecture. In particular we might ask how the situation in Ezra 4:7-23 could have developed if Jerusalem were under Samarian control; the whole exchange of correspondence seems clearly to presuppose Judah's relative autonomy.

Before concluding, we may profitably glance briefly at Neh. 5:14–19, a passage which comes closer than any other to addressing directly the issues with which we have been concerned. Indeed, it was from verse 15 that Morton Smith derived his most telling literary argument against Alt, namely that Nehemiah's whole apologia in this paragraph would collapse if he were not comparing like with like.[59] Thus, when Nehemiah compares himself favourably with 'the earlier governors who came before me', he ought to be referring to governors of Judah, whereas Alt, of course, was obliged to suppose less plausibly that governors of Samaria were in view. So far as it goes, our discussion and Smith's are heading in the same direction.

There is, however, a prior textual issue to be resolved, one on which the material we have examined may possibly shed some light, but one which North has exploited in developing his case that Nehemiah was never governor of Judah at all, but rather a 'charismatic building-contractor'.[60] The MT of 5:14a as it stands reads

גַּם מִיּוֹם אֲשֶׁר־צִוָּה אֹתִי לִהְיוֹת פֶּחָם בְּאֶרֶץ יְהוּדָה

which the Revised Version renders, 'Moreover, from the time that I was appointed[61] to be their governor in the land of Judah'. The principal difficulty here, of course, is the word *peḥām*, on which North comments, 'even strong defenders of the governorship like Rudolph admit that the reading *peḥām* is impossible. It is taken by the Septuagint to mean "their governor", which would require emendation to *peḥātām*. But in the absence of any antecedent for the plural pronoun, Rudolph like Gesenius-Brown accepts rather the emendation *peḥā'* (393). North's counter-proposal is to read בָּהֶם, and thus to eliminate all reference to Nehemiah as governor;[62] he translates, 'Even from the day when it was commanded me to be among them in the land of Judah' (394).

It seems likely to me on other grounds that the normal emendation is more probable than North's, but is it in fact necessary? We have argued at length in favour of the view that in Judah at about this time there was an Aramaic singular emphatic formation *pḥw'* beside what is assumed to be the regular *pḥt'* (but cf. note 45 above); it may hesitantly be proposed that a similar situation prevailed

---

[59] M. SMITH, Palestinian Parties and Politics that Shaped the Old Testament (New York, 1971), 193–201.

[60] R. NORTH, 'Civil Authority in Ezra', in Studi in Onore di Edoardo Volterra, VI (Milan, 1971), 377–404 (380).

[61] A more literal translation would be 'from the day that one/he appointed me...', either an impersonal construction, which would be unusual in the singular, or with 'the king' understood as subject. Alternatively, many run the words *ṣwh* and *'ty* together to give *ṣw'ty* = *ṣwyty* (pual) = 'I was appointed'; cf. W. RUDOLPH, Esra und Nehemia (HAT; Tübingen, 1949), 132. The meaning is not greatly affected either way.

[62] He appears to overlook Neh. 12:26, however. He would presumably minimise its impact on the ground that it is not from Nehemiah's first person account but only from a subsequent editor who might not have been aware of the true situation.

in Hebrew, or at least in Hebrew that was so heavily influenced by Aramaic as was Nehemiah's and as was the language of official administration.[63] Whether to avoid the feminine overtones of the grammatically anticipated form[64] or whether for some other reason, analogy with the seal impressions suggests the possibility of a form *pḥm* beside the regular *pḥtm*. The suffix which bothered North will, of course, be anticipatory – a standard construction in Aramaic and so possibly another hint of influence from that quarter.

Further on in this same verse, Nehemiah boasts that neither he nor his brothers have eaten the *leḥem happeḥâ*, 'the bread of the governor'. Unlike earlier governors who burdened the people in this way, Nehemiah provided generously out of his own resources not only for himself and 150 of his officials, but also for visiting foreign delegations. The fare was rich, but, Nehemiah re-emphasizes in v. 18, 'for all this I did not claim "the bread of the governor"'.

For North, this is no more than a comment on Nehemiah's life-style; he 'lived like a lord', as we might say. To those familiar with the Persepolis fortification and treasury texts, however, almost every phrase of this paragraph is heavy with the overtones of Persian bureaucracy. These texts, well over two thousand of which have been published,[65] record receipts and payments in cash or kind at one of the Achaemenid capitals during the years 509–494 and 492–458 BC. Being written in Elamite, they are by no means perfectly understood, but their number, together with the fact that there are often only small variations between one text and another, means that there is reasonable certainty about the general situation. So far as I can see, Biblical scholars have almost completely ignored this material. In my view, however, there are a great many points of contact with the administrative procedures underlying not a few passages in the books of

---

[63] It should be noted that from a linguistic point of view the material published by AVIGAD is mixed. Of the four words used which allow certain diagnosis, two are Hebrew (*hspr*, No. 6; *bn*, Nos. 7, 8, 9 and 10) and two are Aramaic (*pḥw'*, Nos. 5 and 14; *yh(w)d*, Nos. 1,2,3,4, 11 and 13). However, there are seals known from elsewhere which have *yhwd* written in Hebrew letters (cf. STERN, Material Culture, 202–3) and so comparable influence from Aramaic on the Hebrew *pḥh* would not be at all surprising.

[64] For use of masculine forms where feminine are expected, cf. GK §§ 110k, 135o, 144a, 145p, t, u; R. POLZIN, Late Biblical Hebrew: Toward An Historical Typology of Biblical Hebrew Prose (HSM, 12; Missoula, 1976), 52–4. The reasons seem to vary from case to case.

[65] The principal publication of the Fortification Tablets is R.T. HALLOCK, Persepolis Fortification Tablets (University of Chicago Oriental Institute Publications, 92; Chicago, 1969), but see also R.T. HALLOCK, 'Selected Fortification Texts', Cahiers de la Délégation Archéologique Française en Iran 8 (1978), 109–36. It appears that a considerable number remain unpublished. Most of the Treasury Tablets have been published by G.G. CAMERON, Persepolis Treasury Tablets (University of Chicago Oriental Institute Publications, 65; Chicago, 1948); 'Persepolis Treasury Tablets Old and New', JNES 17 (1958), 161–76; 'New Tablets from the Persepolis Treasury', JNES 24 (1965), 167–92. For a helpful introductory discussion, cf. R.T. HALLOCK, 'The Evidence of the Persepolis Tablets', CHI II (above, n. 2), 588–609.

Ezra and Nehemiah and I hope to be able to explore these more fully elsewhere. Let me therefore here simply list the major comparative points with this paragraph in Nehemiah 5 in order to press the case that *leḥem happeḥâ* should be taken more literally than in North's reconstruction.

(i) Payment of officials at all levels, from artisans to satraps, was generally reckoned in kind, the quantities, of course, varying according to the individual's status. The most regular commodity for salaries was grain or flour, the amounts of which in the cases of senior officials far exceeded what even a large family could consume. Seen in such a context, 'the bread of the governor' is therefore quite simply the governor's salary.

(ii) In the treasury texts, which are the later of the two collections and which stop only shortly before Nehemiah's ministry, we have records of cash payments in lieu of part of the regular payment in kind. This may well help clarify the textually obscure first half of v. 15, rendered in RSV as 'The former governors who were before me laid heavy burdens upon the people, and took from them food and wine, besides forty shekels of silver'.

(iii) Many of the texts record payments of goods to officials not only for themselves but also for those working with or under them. I cite here part of one illuminating example relating to Parnaka, a well-known senior official: 'Daily (by) Parnaka together with his boys 48 *BAR* is received. (By) Parnaka himself 18 *BAR* is received. (By) his 300 boys 1 *QA* each is received' (PFa 4, lines 8–16).[66] 'Boys' in this context, as the editor of the texts recognizes,[67] does not refer to age, but to rank; they occur frequently elsewhere and it is clear from the evidence as a whole that they are close assistants of (in this case) Parnaka, and that they are dependent upon him for their salary. The case is similar with the use of *na'ar* in Neh. 5:15, and if they were also directly dependent on the governor's salary for their own sustenance, we can understand why it is said of the former governors that 'their retainers (*na'ᵃrêhem*) too used to lord it over the people'.

(iv) When Nehemiah speaks of 150 Jewish officials being 'at my table' (v. 17) it is tempting to read this in the same light.

(v) In verse 18, Nehemiah states what was prepared each day at his own expense: 'one ox, six choice sheep, and some poultry, and, at ten day intervals, wine of every kind in abundance.' As a menu this is somewhat restricted; it is clearly not meant to be exhaustive, but rather to indicate the scale of provision. It is thus illuminated by the fact that Parnaka and others of his rank were in receipt of two sheep per day, but that ox and poultry feature almost exclusively in texts recording specifically royal provisions, e.g. *PFT* 692, 1–5: '1 ox, supplied by Rumada, (at) the storehouse (?), (was) paid to the king (at) Anzama-

---

[66] 10 *QA* = 1 *BAR*, whatever that may mean in absolute terms. A daily ration of 1–1.5 *QA* of flour for workmen seems to have been quite normal, so that Parnaka's payment was up to 180 times as great.

[67] Cf. HALLOCK, *PFT*, 30 and 39.

nakka', or *PFT* 698, 1–9, '432 fowls, (included) in them (being): 6 *ippur*, 15 *basbas*, 65 *šudaba*, 346 *kuktukka* fowls, supplied by Iršena, were dispersed in behalf of the king'. Through the texts as a whole it emerges that the quantities used for royal provision were, not unexpectedly, far higher than those for any single official. On this scale, Nehemiah's 'menu' is closer to the range of that of an official in terms of quantity, but its quality was clearly superior.

(vi) The apparently strange statement that whereas provisions were supplied daily wine was supplied at ten day intervals again fits well with our suggested background, where the texts generally specify the time that each commodity should cover, whether monthly salary, daily provision or something in between. As an example of a close parallel to our particular situation we may cite *PFT* 675, 1–8, '24 *marriš* (of) wine, entrusted to Ušaya, Ziššawiš received for rations. For a period of 8 days, in the intercalary (?) twelfth month, 22nd year, (at) Parmadan ...'.

As I have suggested, these remarks only begin to touch on the kind of illumination which we may expect to come from this largely neglected quarter. As regards Nehemiah 5, however, they leave little room to doubt that Nehemiah voluntarily forewent an allowance or salary to which he was entitled as governor. As such, he takes his place alongside his predecessors of similar status in Judah, even if the evidence from the *yhd* jars is that they were not so generous as he when it came to exacting their dues.[68]

---

[68] Cf. AVIGAD, Bullae and Seals, 35.

4. Nehemiah's Walls Revisited

Controversy about the size of the city of Jerusalem in ancient times has continued to be the subject of lively scholarly debate over many years. At the beginning of the twentieth century it was generally assumed that by Nehemiah's time, at any rate, the Western hill had been enclosed within the city. While this view continued to be held by many, as the survey of opinions in Simons[1] shows, others then began to argue that this westward expansion came only very much later. Alt,[2] in particular, maintained that during both the monarchy and the post-exilic period Jerusalem remained confined to the Eastern hill, Ophel. This conclusion appeared to be confirmed by Kenyon's[3] excavations.

Almost immediately after the conclusion of her work, however, the controversy was dramatically reopened by Avigad's discovery in the present Jewish Quarter of the Old City of Jerusalem of a massive city wall from (probably) the eighth century BC.[4] This was proof of a westward expansion in the period of the monarchy. To this, evidence of other material remains was added, although doubt has remained about how much of the Western hill was enclosed.[5]

Because of the impossibility of investigating this problem by major archaeological excavations, other sources of information are naturally sought and exploited. Prominent amongst these is material found in the book of Nehemiah, and in particular the description of his night inspection (2:13-15), of the rebuilding of the walls (3:1-32) and of their subsequent dedication (12:31-39). While there are many points of detail which these passages can contribute to our knowledge of Jerusalem in ancient times, the following remarks will be confined to what light they shed on the major point of dispute outlined above. Needless to say, this is undertaken in full recognition of the difficulties of working from text to topography. Should subsequent excavation throw up new

---

[1] J. SIMONS, Jerusalem in the Old Testament (Leiden, 1952).

[2] A. ALT, 'Das Taltor von Jerusalem', PJB 24 (1928), 74-98 = Kleine Schriften zur Geschichte des Volkes Israel, III (Munich, 1959), 326-347.

[3] 1961-67, summarized in K. KENYON, Digging Up Jerusalem (London and Tonbridge, 1974).

[4] Cf. N. AVIGAD, 'Excavations in the Jewish Quarter of the Old City of Jerusalem, 1970 (Second Preliminary Report)', IEJ 20 (1970), 129-140.

[5] For varying opinions on this, cf. KENYON, Digging Up Jerusalem, 144-65; H. GEVA, 'The Western Boundary of Jerusalem at the End of the Monarchy', IEJ 29 (1979), 84-91; and A.D. TUSHINGHAM, 'The Western Hill under the Monarchy', ZDPV 95 (1979), 39-55.

and contrary data, it would, of course, be necessary to rework the arguments here presented. Nevertheless, in view of the practical difficulties already alluded to, it seems worthwhile to see what contribution these texts can make that is consonant with our knowledge from other sources.

Almost without exception, scholars have assumed that Nehemiah inspected and rebuilt the line of the pre-exilic city wall; only so, it is believed, could he have accomplished the task so quickly (in fifty-two days, according to Neh. 6:15). Consequently, some have used the evidence from Nehemiah to help settle the controversy about the line of the wall in pre-exilic times.[6] It will now be suggested, first, that such a direct correlation is not justified on the basis of the available evidence and, second, that the texts themselves in fact allude to an alternative solution.

A.

First, then, for a considerable number of reasons, it should not be assumed that Nehemiah necessarily followed the line of the pre-exilic walls of Jerusalem.

1. In Ezra 4:7–24 reference is made to building work in Jerusalem, including the walls, during the reign of Artaxerxes. The chronology of Ezra 4 as a whole is, of course, unclear. Nevertheless, it is widely accepted that this was Artaxerxes I. At all events, it is difficult to see how the incidents related could come at any time after Nehemiah. Accepting for the moment the traditional date for Nehemiah's activity later on in the reign of Artaxerxes I, it becomes attractive to adopt the following hypothesis. Shortly before Nehemiah's journey to Jerusalem, an attempt was made to build a wall round Jerusalem. It is likely that substantial progress had been made with this, since time must be allowed for news of the work to have reached Rehum and his colleagues (Ezra 4:8–10), for their letter to have gone to Artaxerxes (4:11), and for his reply to be received (4:17–22) before the work was stopped. When news of this setback reached Nehemiah (Neh. 1:1–3), it stirred him to seek permission from the king to return to Jerusalem. In favour of this view (which is far from novel, but accepted by many commentators and historians) it may be observed, first, that the description of the wall which Nehemiah inspected in Neh. 2:13 and 17 echoes that in 1:3, and, second, that this in turn is unlikely to refer to the fall of Jerusalem in 587 BC since the context is suggestive of news of recent events sufficient to spark Nehemiah's concern.

Should the broad outline of this hypothesis be agreed, then we may move on to observe that commentators have generally failed to reckon with the likeli-

---

[6] Cf. most explicitly M. AVI-YONAH, 'The Walls of Nehemiah: A Minimalist View', IEJ 4 (1954), 239–248.

hood that it was this later wall which Nehemiah inspected and repaired, and, moreover, that there is no reason to suppose that this wall necessarily followed the pre-exilic line at every point. Parts may have been damaged beyond repair; other sections may have been dismantled during the intervening 140 years or so in order to re-use the stones for separate and more urgent building projects. Finally, the substantially reduced population of Jerusalem may well not have required a city as extensive as Jerusalem appears to have become late in the period of the monarchy.

To this general argument, many specific points, both literary and archaeological, should be added. Not all are of equal weight, it is true, but it may be suggested that they carry a certain cumulative weight. Objections to this conclusion will be considered afterwards.

2. On the eastern side of Ophel it is now known that Nehemiah gave up the attempt to follow the earlier line which ran half-way down the steep slope. Instead, he followed a new and easier line along the ridge, thus reducing the size of the city at that point.[7]

3. Where limited evidence is available on the Western hill, it has been argued that the later Hasmonaean wall 'was founded over the outer face of its Israelite predecessor'.[8] The evidence on which this conclusion is based may not be accepted by all. Nevertheless, at those points which have been discussed there appears to be neither trace of nor space for a wall of the Achaemenid period. The same holds true for other building remains also.[9]

4. This conclusion is corroborated by the complete lack of any evidence of building on the Western hill during this period. The latest summarizing survey puts the total finds there for the period in question at a few sherds and one Yehud stamp of the fourth century BC.[10] While this is admittedly negative evidence, it is in striking contrast with the situation of the earlier Iron Age and later Hellenistic periods.

5. At Neh. 3:8 there appears to be a statement to the effect that part of Jerusalem was abandoned by those who were building the new wall: *wayya'az^{e}bû y^{e}rûšālaim 'ad haḥômāh hār^{a}ḥābāh*, 'and they abandoned [i.e. left out part of] Jerusalem as far as the broad wall'. This interpretation of *'zb* is not accepted by all translators and commentators by any means; they favour the view that there is a second root *'zb* in biblical Hebrew meaning 'to repair, restore', on the basis of post-biblical Hebrew *ma'^{a}zîbāh*, 'restoration, erection', and the cognate root *'db* in the Sabaean dialect of Epigraphic South Arabian.[11] The existence of this

---

[7] Cf. KENYON, Digging Up Jerusalem, 183–187.
[8] GEVA, 'The Western Boundary of Jerusalem', 91.
[9] Cf. M. AVI-YONAH, 'The Newly-Found Wall of Jerusalem and its Topographical Significance', IEJ 21 (1971), 168–169 (168).
[10] N. AVIGAD, The Upper City of Jerusalem (Hebrew. Jerusalem, 1980), 62.
[11] See the recent Lexicons of A.F.L. BEESTON, M.A. GHUL, W.W. MÜLLER, and J. RYCKMANS, Sabaic Dictionary (English-French-Arabic), (Louvain-la-Neuve and Beirut,

root in biblical Hebrew is uncertain, however. It is postulated on the basis of the present verse only. It has been suggested that it occurs also at 3:34 (EVV 4:2), but the text there is difficult and, as I hope to show elsewhere, that verse can be better understood if ʿzb retains its common meaning; at the very least the difficulties of that verse are of such a kind that it cannot support the existence of the second root. The second root could only be used in an explanation of Neh. 3:34 if its existence were firmly established elsewhere. This, therefore, throws the whole burden of the case on to our present verse, Neh. 3:8, and here such a meaning is quite inappropriate since the object of the verb is Jerusalem. The context, however, refers clearly to the rebuilding of the walls, not of the city as such. In addition, no explanation is given for a supposed reference to a wider building activity at this point, while none of the ancient versions recognized the existence of this second root. By contrast, within the overall picture being developed here, the common and usual meaning of ʿzb makes excellent sense and, as translated above, has no difficulty in accommodating 'Jerusalem' as its object. Moreover, it will be possible below to offer an explanation for the introduction of such a reference at this point in the description.

6. In the description of the dedication of the walls at Neh. 12:31-39, we are told that one procession went 'layyāmîn upon the wall toward the Dung Gate' (12:31). Since this particular procession went in a counter-clockwise direction, it is evident that on coming out of the city it must have actually turned to the left. layyāmîn cannot, therefore, mean 'to the right' in this context, but 'southwards'. Now the Dung Gate, it is universally agreed, lay in the south-east corner of the city.[12] Further, comparison of the first point which each procession passed with their location in the list of Neh. 3, together with the lack of reference to the Valley Gate in Neh. 12, shows clearly that it was from the Valley Gate that the processions set out, and this conclusion too is universally accepted.[13] If the Valley Gate (which was 1,000 cubits from the Dung Gate; Neh. 3:13) was located on the western wall, half-way up the Tyropoeon, as on the 'minimalist' view,[14] then indeed the procession would have moved southwards from it towards the Dung Gate. On the 'maximalist' view, by contrast, the Valley Gate has to be sited on the southern wall, towards its south-western corner. In that case, however, it would then be inexact to describe the direction taken by the first procession as 'southwards'; it should, rather, be 'eastwards'. This argument

---

1982), 12, and of J.C. BIELLA, Dictionary of Old South Arabic, Sabaean Dialect (Harvard, 1982), 354-355. More recently, Ugaritic ʿdb 'to make, prepare' (cf. J. AISTLEITNER, Wörterbuch der ugaritischen Sprache, zweite Auflage, hrsg. von O. Eissfeldt [Berlin, 1965], 227), has also been compared; cf. J.M. MYERS, Ezra, Nehemiah (AB, 14; Garden City, 1965), 110. MYERS is mistaken, however, in adducing the Vulgate in his support.

[12] See most recently W.S. LASOR, 'Jerusalem', in G.W. BROMILEY et al. (eds.), The International Standard Bible Encyclopedia, II (Grand Rapids, 1982), 998-1032.

[13] Cf. the commentaries and M. BURROWS, 'The Topography of Nehemiah 12.31-43', JBL 54 (1935), 29-39.

tells strongly against plotting the line of Nehemiah's wall along the course presupposed by the 'maximalist' position.

7. At Neh. 3:6 and 12:39 there is reference to a gate called in the MT ša'ar hayšānāh. This cannot be 'the old gate' (RV), because ša'ar is a masculine noun, whereas y^{e}šānāh is a feminine form of the adjective.[15] It must, therefore, be in the construct state. Consequently, some understand y^{e}šānāh as a proper name, Jeshanah being a town in the neighbourhood of Bethel. The definite article remains unexplained on this view, however, as does the curious feature of having a city gate in Jerusalem named after a relatively obscure town. It is probable, therefore, that we should follow the quite widely adopted proposal of emending the y to an m and so reading ša'ar hammišneh, 'the Mishneh Gate'. If, however, it is considered unlikely that the same textual error should have arisen twice, then we may prefer to adopt an alternative solution which comes, topographically, to the same thing, namely to assume an ellipse of hā'îr, 'the city', a feminine noun, and so to translate 'the gate of the old city'.[16]

The Mishneh is generally thought to be the name of the area of habitation to the west of the original city which gradually developed during the period of the monarchy but which was walled only late in that period.[17] Since gates are usually named after places or areas towards which they lead from inside the city, the Mishneh Gate presumably led out into this developing area. It was therefore not part of the more extensive wall which was later built to enclose the Mishneh. It follows that Nehemiah would not have rebuilt it at all had he been following the line of that later wall.

8. While it is probable that the list of builders in Neh. 3 is not complete,[18] a full circuit of the walls is nevertheless described. It is therefore likely that only fragments here and there have been lost in the course of transmission rather than that substantial sections are lacking. Comparison of the numbers working on each section of the wall has therefore been considered instructive. Our lack of knowledge concerning many of the details involved in the operation suggests that we should not put too much weight on this argument, but Tuland's calculations[19]

---

[14] A gate at about this spot was found by CROWFOOT in 1927; cf. J. W. CROWFOOT AND G. M. FITZGERALD, Excavations in the Tyropoeon Valley, Jerusalem, 1927 (Annual of the PEF for 1927; London, 1929), 12-23. Its date is uncertain, but it could come from Nehemiah's time; cf. KENYON, Digging Up Jerusalem, 194-195. Even if it does not, it is at least evidence that this was considered a reasonable site for a gate.

[15] In addition, ša'ar lacks the definite article, so that the word following need not be an adjective in agreement with it, though it could be; cf. GK § 126w.

[16] Cf. A. B. EHRLICH, Randglossen zur Hebräischen Bibel, VII (Leipzig, 1914), etc.

[17] Cf. 2 Kgs 22:14; 2 Chron. 34:22; Zeph. 1:10.

[18] W. RUDOLPH, Esra und Nehemia samt 3. Esra (HAT, 20; Tübingen, 1949), 113; U. KELLERMANN, Nehemia – Quellen, Überlieferung und Geschichte (BZAW, 102; Berlin, 1967), 15.

[19] C. G. TULAND, "zb in Nehemiah 3:8. A Reconsideration of Maximalist and Minimalist Views', AUSS 5 (1967), 158-180 (178).

may be cited as supporting evidence, at least: 'The length of the whole city wall in minimalist terms was approximately 3,000 meters, the north and west wall with *ca.* 1,650 meters covered by 20 labor gangs as against 1,350 meters on the east with 22 groups.' This variation in ratio is, of course, to be explained by the greater difficulty facing the workers on the eastern wall. Tuland then goes on to suggest, however, that this difference in ratio becomes unacceptably large on the maximalist view, for that theory 'would require more than 2,500 to 2,800 meters for the western section alone, to be divided between only 20 groups of laborers'.

9. Outside of Nehemiah, the Valley Gate is mentioned only at 2 Chron. 26:9, where it is said that Uzziah fortified it with towers. If the Chronicler's account is historically sound (and most commentators believe that it is for the varied notices in verses 6–15;[20] others date some of them to the reign of Jehoshaphat, which does not affect the argument being advanced here[21]), then it would appear to have been in existence before the circumvallation of the Western hill, which on literary, historical, and archaeological grounds has reasonably been ascribed to the time of Hezekiah at the earliest.[22] In that case, the Valley Gate cannot have been part of this new wall. Because of the measurements in Neh. 3:13, however, the maximalist position has to hold that it was, but the minimalists do not.

B.

It remains in this part of our discussion to look briefly at the main recent arguments which have been raised against the view that Nehemiah's Jerusalem did not include the Western hill, principally by Michaeli[23] and LaSor.[24]

1. Greatest weight is laid on the fact that, when referring to a valley in the vicinity of Jerusalem, *haggay'* always means the Hinnom Valley. It is therefore argued that this gate must have overlooked that valley, and so have been located along the southern part of the Western hill.

In reply, it must be stated that the conclusion does not follow from the facts. The name of a gate need not be taken from the feature to which it immediately

---

[20] An important exception here is P. WELTEN, Geschichte und Geschichtsdarstellung in den Chronikbüchern (WMANT, 42; Neukirchen-Vluyn, 1973), 63–66, whose arguments deserve very careful consideration. WELTEN himself, however, locates the Valley Gate in the Tyropoeon, and so agrees at this point with the position maintained here.

[21] Cf. H.G.M. WILLIAMSON, 1 and 2 Chronicles (Grand Rapids and London, 1982), 333–338.

[22] Cf. M. BROSHI, 'The Expansion of Jerusalem in the Reigns of Hezekiah and Manasseh', IEJ 24 (1974), 21–26.

[23] F. MICHAELI, Les Livres des Chroniques, d'Esdras et de Néhémie (CAT, 16; Neuchâtel, 1967).

[24] LaSor, 'Jerusalem'.

leads (e.g. the Ephraim Gate). It is sufficient that this was the gate which one would use when going to the Hinnom Valley. Moreover, Alt[25] has given good reasons to explain why, on a minimalist view, it was located where it was, rather than somewhat further south.

2. Michaeli argues from the use of '*br*, 'to cross, pass over', in Neh. 2:14 that Nehemiah must have passed from one hill to the next during his inspection. However, it should be noted that the word occurs only after Nehemiah had already reached the Dung Gate, whose location on the Eastern hill is agreed by all. In this context it probably means that, in rounding the southern tip of the city, Nehemiah crossed over the slight ridge at that point between the Tyropoeon and Kidron Valleys.

3. It is argued by some[26] that Nehemiah's description in 7:4 as 'wide and large' does not fit the smaller size of the city, and that Nehemiah need not have been so concerned about the limited population if the city were confined to the Eastern hill. However, to call any place 'wide and large' is a relative judgement. If the population of Jerusalem had grown small by comparison with the size of the city, then Nehemiah's description would be understandable enough. After all, he was hoping for some action in response to his words, so that it would be an unimaginative exegesis indeed which did not make allowance for some rhetorical flourish.

We may therefore conclude this main part of our discussion by reaffirming that Nehemiah occupied himself with a Jerusalem that was restricted to Ophel and the Temple area to the north, even though in earlier, pre-exilic times it had already expanded to cover part, at least, of the Western hill.

C.

Having reached this point, it seems worthwhile in conclusion to ask whether the evidence presented above does not also contain a possible clue to the course of the pre-exilic western wall. This issue too has been much debated since Avigad's initial discovery, and several suggestions have been advanced which cannot all be reviewed here. Our contention is rather that there is one piece of relevant textual evidence which has so far been overlooked.

The evidence comes in Neh. 3:8b, whose translation was discussed above: 'and they abandoned Jerusalem as far as the broad wall'. Scholars have already sought to identify 'the broad wall' with the late pre-exilic wall on one of two possible grounds: it has been maintained that it was a thick, massive wall – a

---

[25] ALT, 'Das Taltor von Jerusalem'.
[26] E.g. MICHAELI, Les Livres des Chroniques, d'Esdras et de Néhémie; AVIGAD, The Upper City of Jerusalem, 62.

proposal which finds some support from the remains unearthed by Avigad[27] – whilst Grafman[28] has argued on the basis of the use of *rḥb* elsewhere in the Bible that it means 'extensive', 'large' or 'widespread'.

These proposals have, however, been coupled with the suggestion that this wall enclosed the whole of the Western hill, rejoining the line of the earlier wall at the south of Ophel.[29] This view runs into insurmountable difficulties, however. It fails to explain why the reference to 'the broad wall' is included at 3:8, at a point in the description of the circuit of the wall which does not coincide with any part of the broad wall whatsoever. More seriously, it falls down completely as an explanation for Neh. 12:38, for there the procession evidently made physical contact with 'the broad wall' at a point between the Gate of Ephraim to its north and the Tower of the Furnaces to its south. This second landmark is mentioned also in Neh. 3:11 at a point between the Valley Gate further south (3:13) and the reference to 'the broad wall' in 3:8. The Gate of Ephraim is not mentioned in Neh. 3, but it is clear from 12:39 that it came somewhat south of the Mishneh Gate, which is referred to also in 3:6. It is therefore evident that the reference to the broad wall in Neh. 3:8 and 12:38 is to a point somewhere along the line of Nehemiah's wall, that that point is the same in both cases, and that it was located north of the Valley Gate but south of the Ephraim Gate (and, *a fortiori*, of the Mishneh Gate). Grafman cannot, therefore, make use of 3:8 to support his reconstruction of its course.

Instead, a more plausible interpretation of 3:8 may be advanced, namely that it describes the point at which the late pre-exilic wall ('the broad wall') rejoined the older western wall which, we have argued, Nehemiah was following at this point. The plural subject of the verb, 'they abandoned', will then refer in a general and summarizing way to a number of the preceding sections in the list of Neh. 3. The northern point at which the walls diverged is not explicitly mentioned, but on the argument presented above it was clearly to the north of the Mishneh Gate (3:6), and scholars generally think, as common sense would suggest, in terms of a location near the Fish Gate, close to, if not at, the northwest corner of the city. 2 Chron. 33:14 is sometimes cited in support of this conclusion, though its interpretation and relevance are far from certain.

A review of the proposals for the line of the wall enclosing the Western hill in pre-exilic times shows that the evidence advanced here coincides very closely with the conjecture of Kenyon.[30] Of course, it relates only to where the two walls joined, and cannot contribute to a discussion of the further course of 'the broad wall'. Kenyon's proposal accommodates the segment of wall unearthed by Avigad. What is more, even if Geva[31] has correctly identified elements of the

---

[27] AVIGAD, 'Excavations in the Jewish Quarter', 133.
[28] R. GRAFMAN, 'Nehemiah's "Broad Wall"', IEJ 24 (1974), 50–51.
[29] See especially GRAFMAN's discussion and map.
[30] KENYON, Digging Up Jerusalem, 146, Fig. 26.
[31] H. GEVA, 'The Western Boundary of Jerusalem'.

pre-exilic wall to the west of the line proposed by Kenyon (and, as was mentioned above, this is not entirely certain), that would require only a modification to Kenyon's basic position. Although Geva plots a line for the wall enclosing the whole of the Western hill, his evidence relates only to the northern half: he presents no evidence from material remains for the southern part of the wall, so that there is nothing in his findings to rule out the possibility that the wall cut back approximately along the line of the present southern wall of the Old City of Jerusalem to rejoin Ophel at the point we are suggesting.

It should be emphasized that this proposal does not rule out the possibility of habitation further to the south on the Western hill, or even the possibility that that area too may have been subsequently walled in late pre-exilic times. The problems posed by the location of the Pool of Siloam are well known, but cannot, without further specific evidence, determine the issue under discussion.[32]

To summarize: all we are suggesting is that, *prima facie*, Neh. 3:8, when coupled with 12:38, points to the remains of a pre-exilic wall which once enclosed the Mishneh and rejoined the original western wall at a point north of the Valley Gate, but that this wall was not rebuilt by Nehemiah who here, as on the east, reduced the size of the city by comparison with its pre-exilic extent. The likelihood that this was also the line followed by the builders in Ezra 4 was also suggested.

---

[32] Cf. N. SHAHEEN, 'The Siloam End of Hezekiah's Tunnel', PEQ 109 (1977), 107–112.

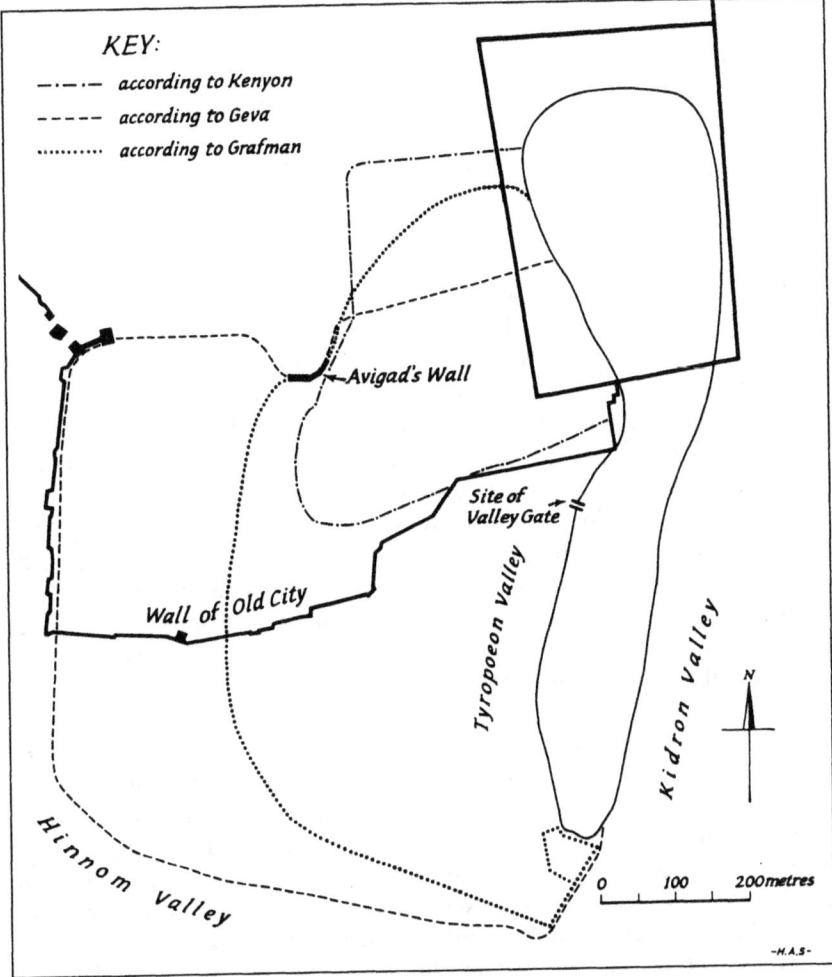

Fig. 1: Some suggestions for the line of the pre-exilic western wall.[33]

---

[33] The meticulously careful preparation of this map by Mr H. A. SHELLEY of the Department of Geography in the University of Cambridge revealed a disturbing discrepancy in those published hitherto. None of the three so far plotted agrees either with any other or with AVIGAD himself over the precise siting and direction of the one piece of the Western wall which has been excavated. In this map, using the present walls of the Old City and the Temple site as fixed points, it is shown according to AVIGAD's latest published plan, and GEVA's and GRAFMAN's proposals have been adjusted slightly in consequence. It is, nevertheless, regrettable that the one piece of objective evidence to hand has been treated in so cavalier a fashion in previous discussions. Fortunately, the arguments of the present article are not affected by this discrepancy, since they concern primarily the point at which the southern line of the westward expansion rejoined the original walls, and not the line of the wall in its northern sector.

5. The Historical Value of Josephus' Jewish Antiquities xi. 297–301

In his *Jewish Antiquities,* Book xi. 297–301,[1] Josephus recounts the murder of Jesus by his brother Joannes, the high priest, in the temple, and the consequent imposition of a tax on the daily sacrifices by Bagoses, the governor. Since our knowledge of the history of Jerusalem during the fourth century BC is so notoriously limited, it is only natural that scholars should have been anxious to derive the maximum amount of information possible from this account. Despite this, however, discussion of it has generally been rather uncritical, with no real attempt made to distinguish between the material that Josephus may have derived from an earlier source and the manner in which he himself has then used it. It is this necessary first step that is to be discussed in the present article.

We may start by observing that, despite the half millennium which separates Josephus from the Persian period, there is nothing inherently improbable in supposing that he may have had sources that preserved reliable material, but which have not come down to us. Such a supposition, indeed, has received remarkable confirmation from an even earlier period, the closing years of the Judean monarchy, for which comparison with the Babylonian Chronicle suggests that he had two, and possibly three, such pieces of information.[2] Secondly, it is clear that on one matter of Persian history, Josephus did in fact have independent knowledge, namely the order of the first Persian kings (Cyrus-Cambyses-Darius-Xerxes-Artaxerxes).[3] Indeed, on the basis of this knowledge, he sought to 'correct' the Biblical chronology, notably in the problematic Ezra 4 (1 Esdras 2) at *Ant.* xi. 21 ff., but also in Ezra 7:1 (1 Esdras 8:1) at *Ant.* xi. 120. Josephus only needed to do this, however, because he believed that his source was attempting to present a narrative in direct chronological sequence. At Ezra

---

[1] Text and translation of all Josephus' works are cited throughout from the edition in The Loeb Classical Library, edited by H. St. J. Thackeray, R. Marcus, A. Wikgren, and L. H. Feldman (Cambridge, Mass., 1926–65).

[2] Cf. C. J. Gadd, The Fall of Nineveh: The Newly Discovered Babylonian Chronicle, No. 21,901, in the British Museum (London, 1923), 7 and 16; M. Noth, Überlieferungsgeschichtliche Studien I (Halle, 1943), 140; A. Malamat, 'The Last Wars of the Kingdom of Judah', JNES 9 (1950), 220, n. 14, and 'A New Record of Nebuchadrezzar's Palestinian Campaigns', IEJ 6 (1956), 250 f.; D. J. Wiseman, Chronicles of Chaldaean Kings (626–556 B.C.) in the British Museum (London, 1956), 24–7; H. Tadmor, 'Chronology of the Last Kings of Judah', JNES 15 (1956), 228.

[3] Cf. the comments of R. Marcus on *Ant.* xi. 21.

4, however, it seems likely that the author has grouped by theme rather than by chronology. Josephus' corrections, therefore, which rest from one point of view on accurate historical knowledge, result in the end in unhistorical confusion.[4] From this instance where we have Josephus' source in front of us and can see how he has handled it, we learn to realize that even allowing for the fact that he may have had good sources at his disposal, that in itself is no guarantee for the accuracy of his representation of them, especially in matters of chronology.

A. Evidence for the Use of a Source

In the light of these opening remarks, it is clear that an attempt must first be made to establish whether or not there is firm evidence that Josephus was using a source in this passage and not simply amplifying his account in the way he is known to have done elsewhere. Whilst on general grounds it would be surprising if he had merely invented a story so unfavourable to his own people and the priesthood in particular, yet it seems possible in this instance to come to a positive answer on the basis of more certain evidence than mere probability. Moreover, a precise delimitation of the source, which has never before been attempted, will be found to be helpful in the assessment of Josephus' use of it. As far as the present writer is aware, the form in which the story is cast has never been examined: a study of it has proved instructive, however. The introduction (297a) on the succession of the high priests cannot help us, since it might have been drawn from Neh. 12:22.[5] In the narrative proper, however, the result of the affair is given first (297b), namely that when Joannes was high priest, Bagoses 'defiled the sanctuary, and imposed tribute on the Jews'. The incident which led to this result is then recounted (298–301a), whilst a conclusion explicitly links the cause and its effect ('This, then, being the pretext which he used, Bagoses made the Jews suffer seven years for the death of Jesus', 301b). Finally, and of special interest, we must point out the phrase by which the transition is made between the two main parts of the narrative: 'The reason for this was the following happening' (τούτου δὲ τὴν αἰτίαν τοιαύτην συνέβη γενέσθαι – 298a).

A survey of the whole of the *Antiquities*[6] shows that this form is not unique to our passage. Of more significance is the observation that in every case where we

---

[4] Cf. C.G. TULAND, 'Josephus, *Antiquities*, Book XI. Correction or Confirmation of Biblical Post-exilic Records?', AUSS 4 (1966), 176–92.

[5] This is more likely than Neh. 12:10f., in view of Josephus' inclusion of Joannes rather than Jonathan; see further section C below.

[6] Discussion is restricted to the *Antiquities* because, with roughly half of it running parallel to the Biblical account, which Josephus explicitly follows (cf. *Ant.* i. 17 and *passim*), we can most easily see here his procedure in handling sources. Moreover, we cannot be sure

have the means for checking his use against his sources, Josephus uses a similar connecting formula to introduce a close paraphrase of his source. This makes it highly probable that in a situation such as that under discussion, but for which we do not have the means for checking, he has adopted a similar procedure. Examples of this form may now be given:

i. *Ant.* x. 17f. tells of the failure of Sennacherib's siege of Jerusalem. The result is given first: 'A little while after this the king of Assyria failed in his attack upon the Egyptians and returned home without accomplishing anything.' Then comes the connection – 'for the following reason' (δι' αἰτίαν τοιαύτην), after which Josephus tells the story from his source (2 Kings 19:8f.)[7] and finally draws the whole together in a summary: 'And so ... King Senacheirimos left Pelusium and withdrew, as I said, without accomplishing anything.' We should note that, as so often, the final result is in fact that Josephus' account differs somewhat from that in 2 Kings 19 (cf. especially verses 35f.), but that does not affect our argument at present concerning Josephus' introduction of material from his sources.

ii. *Ant.* x. 18f. Our second example comes in the very next paragraph, and concerns the same event. The striking point here is that, whilst the result is to give a quite different reason for Sennacherib's withdrawal, Josephus' method of narration is identical. Once more, the result – the abandoning of the siege at Pelusium – comes first, with the connecting link immediately following – 'for the following reason' (ἐξ αἰτίας τοιαύτης). The narrative is then cited from his source (Herodotus, *Histories* ii. 141), and the result repeated: 'he withdrew his army from Pelusium. This then is the account which Herodotus gives.'

iii. *Ant.* ii. 1–3 tells how Esau came to be called Adom (Edom) and his country Idumaea in consequence. The context (continuing from Book i and after in ii. 4ff.) is Gen. 35–36, but an explanation is required for this name. This, then, is the result of the incident which is to follow: 'he bore the surname Adom', and the familiar form of connection is given next: 'which he had obtained under the following circumstances' (κατὰ τοιαύτην αἰτίαν). The narrative of Esau's sale of his birthright is then extracted from Gen. 25:27–34, which, we may note in passing, is thus separated from its Biblical context and intrudes in a slightly strained manner in its present setting. As in the instances already analysed, a summary concludes the section (3b).

iv. *Ant.* ii. 8ff. introduces the Joseph narrative. The introduction, however, looks right forward to the time of the Exodus: God 'made even events that seemed to him [Jacob] deplorable become the source of the utmost felicity and brought about the departure of our ancestors from Egypt by means of Jacob and his offspring' *(Ant.* ii. 8). The time span that this outline introduces would not

---

that in other books he adopted an identical method, and thirdly sufficient evidence is furnished by the *Antiquities* alone to establish our case.

[7] 'Pelusium is substituted by Josephus for Bibl. Libnah from the text of Herodotus who is quoted directly below', R. Marcus, ad loc.

lead us to expect the short narrative and concluding summary that we have noted up till now. Nevertheless, *Ant.* ii. 198–200 shows clearly that even so the form in this respect has not broken down completely, for it serves as both a retrospective and prospective editorial link on the same theme, whilst *Ant.* ii. 318f. picks up the same thought in summarizing form, and explicitly completes the cycle of Jacob to the Exodus. Of importance for us is the observation that at *Ant.* ii. 9, Josephus picks up his source to narrate the history, introduced by the familiar words: ὑπὸ τοιαύτης αἰτίας.

v. *Ant.* iv. 150ff., the death of Zambrias. The form, by now familiar, is apparent here once more: the summarizing introduction (151b), the connecting formula (ἐκ τοιαύτης αἰτίας) introducing the paraphrase of a source (Num. 25:7ff. in 152–5), and the final conclusion.

vi. It is unnecessary, having now established this pattern, to analyse every example in detail. We may here simply list the other passages where the form occurs and where the source is certainly known to us. The reference in each case is to the paragraph in which the connecting formula (using the word αἰτία) occurs, and the source which this introduces is then indicated in brackets: *Ant.* i. 139 (Gen. 9:20–7); ii. 13 (Num. 16:1[8]); iv. 101 (Num. 22); v. 135 (Judg. 19); v. 175 (Judg. 1:18 with 34 and 18:1ff.); v. 338 (1 Sam. 2:12–17 with 22ff.); vii. 162 (2 Sam. 12); viii. 199 (1 Kgs 11:14ff.); x. 212 (Dan. 3); and xii. 11 (Letter of Aristeas, para. 9).

This makes a total of fifteen examples where we have in front of us the source that Josephus was using. There are, however, a number of additional occurrences of this form, where the section which we expect to be cited from a source in fact coincides with a passage that has been attributed to Josephus' sources, since lost to us, on quite other grounds. These are:

vii. *Ant.* i. 53. The account of the murder of Abel by Cain which follows (54ff.), though obviously based on Gen. 4, is amplified by so many details which find parallels in later Jewish tradition[9] that it seems quite likely that Josephus was here making use of a midrashic expansion of the Biblical narrative.

viii. *Ant.* x. 73, the death of Josiah. Most scholars[10] agree that Josephus had, in addition to the Biblical narrative, a separate, reliable source for the Battle of Megiddo.

ix. *Ant.* xvi. 271. It is generally accepted that the account of the war between Herod and the Arabs which follows is taken from a source, though there is no agreement as to whether this is the history by Nicolas of Damascus or not.[11]

---

[8] Some of the details of the story which are not found in Num. are not Josephus' own invention, but are taken by him from later Jewish tradition: cf. H. BLOCH, Die Quellen des Flavius Josephus in seiner Archäologie (Leipzig, 1879), 42.

[9] Cf. H. BLOCH, Quellen, 26f. and the comments of H. ST. J. THACKERAY ad loc.

[10] See above, n. 2.

[11] MARCUS and WIKGREN, ad loc., for instance, imply that it was. G. HÖLSCHER, however (Die Quellen des Josephus für die Zeit vom Exil bis zum jüdischen Kriege [Leipzig, 1904],

x. *Ant.* xviii. 39. For the item of Parthian history which follows this introduction, we again do not have Josephus' source for ourselves. However, the confirmation of his account in a general way from other sources,[12] together with the evidence (cf. xi below) that he did have written sources for part of this material, combine to make it highly probable that here too his account is based on a written source.

xi. *Ant.* xviii. 310, 340, 343, 373 and xx. 17. The form of narrative which we are tracing is associated with each of these five references. Inasmuch as they deal with aspects of Parthian history, the general considerations listed above apply here also. However, even more compelling evidence has been adduced by Schalit,[13] who argues, primarily on the basis of an Aramaism within the Greek text at *Ant.* xviii. 343,[14] that *Ant.* xviii. 310–79 and xx. 17–96 are extracts of a source that was originally written in Aramaic. This, then, lends strong support to the case we are seeking to develop here.

xii. For the remaining passages of the *Antiquities* where our form occurs, we do not have immediate evidence that Josephus was introducing a source in this way. General probabilities, however, often suggest that he is, and on this basis alone most of the passages have been included in the various sources traced by scholars through the second half of the work.[15] To cite these passages directly as evidence, however, would be to argue in a circle, and therefore we can only list

---

30 and 55), argues that it belongs rather to a source which he names the *Vita Herodis*. A clearer statement of HÖLSCHER's views may be found in his article 'Josephus' in PAULY-WISSOWA-KROLL, Real-Encyclopädie der classischen Altertumswissenschaft (Stuttgart, 1916), vol. ix, especially cols. 1977 ff. A brief reply to HÖLSCHER is made by R. J. H. SHUTT, Studies in Josephus (London, 1961), 88–90.

[12] E. TÄUBLER, Die Parthernachrichten bei Josephus (Berlin, 1904). N. C. DEBEVOISE, A Political History of Parthia (Chicago, 1938), xxix, speaks highly of Josephus' reliability for Parthian history: 'Time after time from numismatic or written sources Josephus can be proved correct.' On pages 143 ff., DEBEVOISE gives the story as found here in Josephus, with references for aspects of it to other classical writers, though none that we know of now seems to have served as an exact source for Josephus. ZIEGLER also, within the context of his wider study, uses the narrative of Josephus at this point, along with other classical writers, as a reliable, historical source; cf. K.-H. ZIEGLER, Die Beziehungen zwischen Rom und dem Partherreich: Ein Beitrag zur Geschichte des Völkerrechts (Wiesbaden, 1964), 50–3.

[13] A. SCHALIT, 'Evidence of an Aramaic Source in Josephus' "Antiquities of the Jews"', ASTI 4 (1965), 163–88.

[14] His conclusions have been accepted by L. H. FELDMAN in his translation at this point. J. NEUSNER, 'The Conversion of Adiabene to Judaism: A New Perspective', JBL 83 (1964), 60–6, also thinks that *Ant.* xx. 17–96 rests on reliable sources.

[15] Works that attempt a detailed *Quellenkritik* of these books include H. BLOCH, Quellen; J. VON DESTINON, Die Quellen des Josephus in der Jüd. Arch. Buch XII–XVII = Jüd. Krieg Buch I (Kiel, 1882); F. A. C. SCHEMANN, Die Quellen des Flavius Josephus in der jüdischen Archaeologie Buch XVIII–XX = Polemos II, Cap. VII–XIV, 3 (Hagen, 1887); G. HÖLSCHER, Quellen, and his article 'Josephus', cols. 1950–94. Particular mention should be made of the detailed studies of individual passages by E. BICKERMANN and A. SCHALIT listed in H. SCHRECKENBERG, Bibliographie zu Flavius Josephus (Arbeiten zur Literatur und Geschichte des hellenistischen Judentums, I; Leiden, 1968).

the references for the sake of completeness: *Ant.* xii. 42, 187; xiv. 268; xv. 252, 343; xvi. 300; xvii. 166, 299; xviii. 91, 109, 152; xix. 19; xx. 105 and 118.

In some of these passages, not every element of the form is found. As we saw earlier, the final conclusion is the weakest element and most liable to drop out, but that does not alter the general conclusions we have reached.

xiii. It remains finally to mention a number of passages where the form is found, but where the connecting formula is expressed in a way that does not include the word αἰτία. The general situation apart from this, however, is identical: *Ant.* ii. 10 (Gen. 37:5ff.); ii. 74 (Gen. 41); ii. 209;[16] v. 187 (Judg. 3:15); v. 275 (Judg. 13) and xi. 184f. (Esth. 1).

On the basis of all this evidence, we conclude that Josephus was drawing on an independent source for his narrative in *Ant.* xi. 298–301.

B. *The Value of Josephus' Source*

Since the events recorded in *Ant.* xi. 298–301 are unknown to us from any other source, we have no direct evidence upon which to base a judgment as to their accuracy. It is striking, however, that every indirect consideration favours the view that we have here reliable information.

The four names included in the passage are appropriate. Artaxerxes requires no comment. Bagoses was a common Persian name, Justi listing six different people in ancient sources who bore it,[17] and that before the discovery of the Elephantine Papyri. Though attested in several different forms (בגוי,[18] בגוהי,[19]

---

[16] This introduces the (unscriptural) account of Amram's prayer to God and God's answer in a dream foretelling the birth of the saviour Moses. In both the Mechilta and the Midrash Rabba we find a tradition in which Miriam prophesies to the same effect; cf. I. H. WEISS, Mechilta: Der älteste halachische und hagadische Commentar zum zweiten Buche Moses (Hebrew: Wien, 1865), 52a. Whilst this tradition is thus not identical with that found in Josephus, it again makes it probable that he is citing a tradition known to him at this point; cf. H. BLOCH, Quellen, 35. J. WEILL, in the first volume of Œuvres complètes de Flavius Josèphe, traduites en français sous la direction de Théodore Reinach (Paris, 1900), 117 n. 3, cites the passage in WEISS to support the view that 'le sage d'Amram est connu cependant de la tradition'. This, as we have seen, is mistaken, however, though it may have been suggested by a misunderstanding of a footnote by WEISS in which he (misleadingly) says that the prophecy of Miriam is alluded to by Josephus. THACKERAY (comments ad loc.) is then in turn misled by WEILL when he says that 'Amram's dream... is mentioned in the oldest Rabbinic commentary on Exodus, known as *Mechilta*'.

[17] F. JUSTI, Iranisches Namenbuch (Marburg, 1895), 59f.; cf. M. NOTH, Die israelitischen Personennamen im Rahmen der gemeinsemitischen Namengebung (BWANT, 3/10; Stuttgart, 1928), 64.

[18] Ezra 2:2, 14; 8:14; Neh. 7:7, 19; 10:17.

[19] A. COWLEY, Aramaic Papyri of the Fifth Century B.C. (Oxford, 1923; henceforth cited as AP), 30.1; 32.1.

Βαγώας, Βαγουιαί, Βαγοεί, etc.[20]), the common first element (meaning 'God') argues that the name is in each case the same. 'Ιωάννης is known from Neh. 12:32 and 33 as the name of a high priest in the Persian period, whilst 'Ιησοῦς (hellenized form of י[הו]שע) is also a common Jewish name.

Secondly, it may be argued on general grounds that the incident shows up the Jerusalem priesthood in such a bad light that fabrication is unlikely. There is no polemical purpose apparent such as might explain it away, whereas its result (defilement of the temple and probable cessation of sacrifice for a while) is of sufficient moment for it to have been recorded.

Finally, preservation of the story in some temple or priestly chronicle may be plausibly conjectured on the basis of the place and people involved. Though the suggestion inevitably lacks proof, it is not surprising that such a source has often been proposed or implied by scholars for both this and other similar passages.[21]

Up to this point, it is to be hoped that our study has been a quite uncontroversial examination of Josephus' editorial method. The discussion which follows, however, enters an area where there has been much disagreement amongst eminent scholars, and it attempts furthermore to suggest that there may be grounds for re-examining a consensus that has grown up over the dating of this incident. It is in consequence worth pointing out that the results achieved thus far are not in any way dependent upon what follows, but may be assessed independently and in their own right. Nevertheless, since our form-critical analysis enables us to distinguish more precisely than heretofore between Josephus' source and the context with which he himself has provided it, it is necessary to take the further step of investigating whether this conclusion has any bearing upon the use to which Josephus and many others since his day have put this material. The need for caution in this regard is heightened by what has already been said about Josephus' handling of the Scriptural narrative.

C. *Josephus' Handling of his Source*

According to Josephus *(Ant.* xi. 297), the Joannes of this incident is to be identified with Johanan the second high priest following Eliashib (Neh. 12:22). He is further identified as Eliashib's grandson, although, as we shall see, this is not stated in any of our other extant sources.

---

[20] For these and other Greek forms, cf. E. HATCH and H. A. REDPATH, A Concordance to the Septuagint and Other Greek Versions of the Old Testament (including the Apocryphal Books), Supplement (Oxford, 1906), 31. The form usually found in classical sources is Βαγώας, in the passage of Josephus under consideration: Βαγώσης (variant: Βαγώας).

[21] E. g. H. BLOCH, Quellen, 147–50; R. MARCUS, Antiquities IX–XI, 499f.; C. G. TULAND, 'Josephus, *Antiquities*, Book XI', 182f.

Since this same Johanan is known from the Elephantine Papyri to have been high priest whilst Bagohi was governor (פחת יהוד[22]), it is not surprising that most scholars have accepted Josephus' identification. Consequently, utilizing both Josephus and the Elephantine Papyri, a number of reconstructions of the background to this story have been put forward.[23] Whilst disagreements about the high priestly genealogy and the dating of Ezra's mission to Jerusalem lead to differences in the detail of these reconstructions, they all have certain elements in common, in particular that Johanan continued the 'particularist' policies of Nehemiah whilst Jesus and Bagohi favoured closer contacts with both Samaria and Elephantine. It is further generally held that the two brothers were but representatives of larger communities within Jerusalem.[24]

It should at once be admitted that some such reconstruction as this is possible; but the paucity of our knowledge of the period forbids dogmatism. On the other hand, this very fact should also lead to a more rigorously critical appraisal of what evidence there is, without accepting too readily identification of all characters bearing the same name. The following factors highlight precisely this problem:

i. In the source itself, the king, Artaxerxes, is not more closely defined. In the introduction to the account, however, Bagoses is called ὁ στρατηγὸς τοῦ ἄλλου Ἀρταξέρξου. Our analysis above has shown that this is not part of the source, but a free composition on the basis of the source by Josephus. In other words, even if the phrase means to indicate a particular Artaxerxes, that indication does not have the value of contemporary evidence, but has to be judged in the light of Josephus' understanding of the chronology of the Persian period as a whole (see section iv below). For this reason, the comments of R. Marcus (ad loc.) are rather beside the point. He argues first in favour of retaining the word ἄλλου against those such as Niese who think it is an interpolation, and then identifies the king as Artaxerxes II Mnemon (404–359 BC). His concluding remark is significant: 'If ἄλλου is removed as spurious, Bagoses is probably to be identified with the Persian general of Artaxerxes III, mentioned in Diodorus xvi. 47.' We have already seen, however, that ἄλλου is spurious, not because it is a textual interpolation, but because it represents an 'interpolation' into his source by Josephus. It thus remains possible that Artaxerxes III Ochus (358–338 BC) is intended.

---

[22] Cf. AP, 30.1.

[23] Cf. R. MARCUS, op. cit., Appendix B; J. MORGENSTERN, 'A Chapter in the History of the High-Priesthood', AJSL 55 (1938), 1–24, 183–97 and (especially) 360–77; A. SCHALIT, 'A Chapter in the History of the Party Disputes in Jerusalem at the End of the Fifth Century and the Beginning of the Fourth Century B.C.', Commentationes in memoriam Johannes Levy (Hebrew: Jerusalem, 1949), 252–72; K. GALLING, 'Bagoas und Esra', Studien zur Geschichte Israels im persischen Zeitalter (Tübingen, 1964), 149–84; M. SMITH, Palestinian Parties and Politics that Shaped the Old Testament (New York and London, 1971), 171 ff.

[24] Cf. especially A. SCHALIT, 'A Chapter in the History of the Party Disputes', 267 and M. SMITH, Palestinian Parties and Politics, ch. 7.

It must be further urged against relying on Josephus' identification here that ἄλλος does not, of course, mean 'second', as Marcus translates, but 'another, i.e. one beside what has been mentioned'.²⁵ The previous section of *Ant.* xi has dealt with the story of Esther, which Josephus places in the reign of Artaxerxes I (465–424 BC), so that the use of the word ἄλλος would imply that he did not distinguish between Artaxerxes II and III.²⁶ Thus not only is his reference ambiguous, but it is more likely to be misleading.

ii. There are also grounds for questioning whether Bagoses should be identified with the Bagohi of the Elephantine Papyri. According to our source, he was the στρατηγός of Artaxerxes, and it is implied that he was a Persian *(Ant.* xi. 300). This title clearly refers to military rank.²⁷ It is so used elsewhere by Josephus, for instance of the Rabshakeh, the commander of the Assyrian army at *Ant.* x. 6, 8, and 11. Moreover, in the LXX²⁸ it is never used to translate פחה, but rather such words as שר in contexts like 1 Sam. 29:3; 1 Chron. 11:6; 2 Chron. 32:21, where the military reference is evident. By contrast, פחה is generally rendered by words such as σατράπης,²⁹ τοπάρχης, and ἔπαρχος. In the Elephantine Papyri, however, Bagohi is titled פחת יהוד. Both this and his functions as they may be gleaned from the Papyri set him clearly in the same office as that held by Nehemiah (cf. Neh. 5:14).

On the basis of this evidence, it seems most unlikely that the Bagoses of our source is the same man as the governor of Judah known from the Elephantine Papyri. On the one hand, there is no reason to suppose that Josephus' source would not have applied to Bagoses the obvious title of governor (σατράπης) had that in fact been his position; on the other hand we know of a Bagoses who precisely fits the description as reconstructed from Josephus' source, namely the Persian general of Artaxerxes III. His role as a military officer fits the title στρατηγός of *Ant.* xi. 300, whilst the fact that he is also known to have been involved in civil administration (cf. Diodorus Siculus XVI.1.8) suggests that he could well have imposed a tax on the Jews as recounted in this narrative.

This proposed identification is not, of course, by any means new.³⁰ Our purpose in reviving it here is primarily negative, namely to suggest that the

---

²⁵ H. G. LIDDELL and R. SCOTT, A Greek-English Lexicon (7th edn; Oxford, 1890), 66a.

²⁶ So also S. MOWINCKEL, Studien zu dem Buche Ezra-Nehemia, I: Die nachchronistische Redaktion des Buches: Die Listen (Skrifter utgitt av det Norske Videnskaps-Akademi i Oslo. II. Hist.-Filos. Klasse. Ny Serie. No. 3. Oslo, 1964), 162.

²⁷ Cf. generally LIDDELL and SCOTT, 1437a. For the later, Hellenistic development of the title to include also civil administration, cf. H. BENGTSON, Die Strategie in der hellenistischen Zeit: Ein Beitrag zum antiken Staatsrecht (Münchener Beiträge zur Papyrusforschung und antiken Rechtsgeschichte, 26., 32. und 36. Heft. 2nd edn; München, 1964).

²⁸ Cf. HATCH and REDPATH, 1295.

²⁹ Josephus, too, uses this word for the ruler of Samaria, which we may assume to be the equivalent of the governor in Jerusalem *(Ant.* xi. 302).

³⁰ Cf. C. C. TORREY, 'The Two Persian Officers Named Bagoas', AJSL 56 (1939), 300f.

dating of this incident now so widely adopted does not in fact rest upon the most probable identification of the characters involved.

Along different lines, Porten has tended towards the same conclusion,[31] for he thinks that the Bagohi of the Elephantine Papyri was a Jew. He accepts Aharoni's evidence[32] for a considerable succession of Jewish governors of Judah during the fifth and fourth centuries, and thus quite reasonably argues that Bagohi too is likely to have been a Jew. No difficulty need be felt from his Persian name, since we know of other Jews with such names, e.g. Ostanes, the brother of 'Anani (AP 30.18f.), and indeed one bearing the very name בגוי itself (Ezra 2:2, 14; Neh. 7:7, 19; 10:17). However, if Bagohi were a Jew, he could not be identified with the Persian Bagoses of Josephus' account.

Whilst there are now serious grounds for questioning the evidence for the series of governors postulated by Aharoni,[33] that does not in itself demand that Porten's suggestion be rejected. Other considerations still point in the same direction: firstly, in the neighbouring and parallel province of Samaria, it seems to have been the Persian policy to keep the governorship even within the same family, as the Samaria Papyri show.[34] This fact argues against sudden shifts in Persian policy in this regard.[35] Secondly, though we may not have the impressive list of governors of Judah that Porten assumes, yet it is significant that all those of whom we do hear, from whatever period, certainly are Jews: Zerubbabel (Hag. 2:21[36] with 1 Chron. 3:19), Nehemiah (Neh. 5:14), and יחזקיו.[37] To these

---

[31] B. PORTEN, 'שיבת ציון' באור כתבי יב', Beth Mikra 16 (1963), 66–79 (especially 71f.) and Archives from Elephantine: The Life of an Ancient Jewish Colony (Berkeley and Los Angeles, 1968), 290.

[32] Y. AHARONI, Excavations at Ramat Rahel: Seasons 1959 and 1960 (Rome, 1962), 56–9.

[33] Cf. F.M. CROSS, 'Judean Stamps', ErIsr 9 (1969), 20–7; J. NAVEH, The Development of the Aramaic Script (The Israel Academy of Sciences and Humanities Proceedings, vol. V, no. 1. Preprint: Jerusalem, 1970), 61.

[34] F.M. CROSS, 'The Discovery of the Samaria Papyri', BA 26 (1963), 110–21; 'Aspects of Samaritan and Jewish History in Late Persian and Hellenistic Times', HTR 59 (1966), 201–11 and 'Papyri of the Fourth Century B.C. from Dâliyeh: A Preliminary Report on their Discovery and Significance', New Directions in Biblical Archaeology, ed. by D.N. FREEDMAN and J.C. GREENFIELD (Garden City, 1969), 41–62. It is immaterial for these purposes whether or not the original Sanballat was of local origin, though if he were (so, for instance, H.H. ROWLEY, 'Sanballat and the Samaritan Temple', Men of God [London and Edinburgh, 1963], 246f.), his position would parallel Bagohi's still more closely.

[35] Contra K. GALLING, 'Bagoas und Esra', 162.

[36] This first-hand testimony, repeated in slightly different form also at Hag. 1:1, 14 and 2:2, seems stronger than W. RUDOLPH's inference from Ezra 4:2 that because Zerubbabel appears there only as a primus inter pares, he cannot have been governor; cf. Esra und Nehemia samt 3. Esra (HAT; Tübingen, 1949), 49.

[37] L.Y. RAHMANI was able to read the legend יחזקיו הפחה on two of a set of five silver coins found at Tel Gamma; cf. 'Silver Coins of the Fourth Century B.C. from Tel Gamma', IEJ 21 (1971), 158–60. He further proposed a similar reading (יחזקיה/ו [ה]פ[חה]) for the much discussed coin from Beth-Zur, initially published in O.R. SELLERS, The Citadel of Beth-Zur (Philadelphia, 1933), 73f.

should also probably be added Sheshbazzar[38] and possibly Hananiah.[39] What evidence we have, therefore, would suggest that Bagohi too was Jewish, rendering his identity with Bagoses the Persian of Josephus' narrative improbable.

It should finally be observed that the evidence from Elephantine allows us to be certain only that Bagohi was governor in 408 BC during the reign of Darius II, whereas the Bagoses of Josephus is linked with Artaxerxes. It is not, of course, at all difficult to postulate that Bagohi continued in office for the four or five years necessary to date him also within the reign of Artaxerxes II, but in view of the difficulties already seen to this theory, it should also be pointed out that it does rest in the first place upon conjecture alone.

iii. Thus far, an attempt has been made to show that the characters mentioned by Josephus' source incline us, against current opinion, to date the incident related to the reign of Artaxerxes III. Attention must now be directed towards the two members of the high-priestly family involved, Joannes and Jesus. Since, as we shall see below, there certainly was a high priest named Johanan in 408 BC, it seems *a priori* reasonable to assume that this automatically involves us in identifying him with the Joannes of Josephus' source, thus favouring the earlier dating of that incident. Our purpose in this section, therefore, is not to build the case for the later dating on the evidence from the high priestly family, but rather to show that an alternative approach is possible and indeed, in view of the paucity of evidence for this period, quite as reasonable as that normally proposed. If this can be achieved, the other considerations which bear upon the question of dating may be allowed their full weight at face value.

---

[38] Sheshbazzar was certainly the first governor of Judah after the return from exile (cf. Ezra 5:14), but there is considerable doubt as to his identity. A few have thought that he was either a Babylonian or Persian, e.g. L. H. BROCKINGTON, Ezra, Nehemiah and Esther (NCB; London, 1969), 16. However, since it is known that some Jews adopted foreign names, there is no direct evidence to support this view. Against it is his designation in Ezra 1:8 as 'the Prince of Judah'. This has led other scholars to see in him a member of an upper-class Jewish family, e.g. P. R. ACKROYD, Exile and Restoration: A Study of Hebrew Thought of the Sixth Century B.C. (OTL; London, 1968), 142–4; K-M. BEYSE, Serubbabel und die Königserwartungen der Propheten Haggai und Sacharja: Eine historische und traditionsgeschichtliche Untersuchung (Arbeiten zur Theologie, 1/48; Stuttgart, 1972), 23–8. Most, however, seem to take a further step in identifying him with the Davidic descendant Shenazzar (1 Chron. 3:18), e.g. W. F. ALBRIGHT, 'The Date and Personality of the Chronicler', JBL 40 (1921), 104–24, especially 108–10; L. W. BATTEN, A Critical and Exegetical Commentary on the Books of Ezra and Nehemiah (ICC; Edinburgh, 1913), 34, 37f., and 137; J. BRIGHT, A History of Israel (OTL; 2nd edn; London, 1972), 362; J. S. WRIGHT, The Building of the Second Temple (London, 1958), 10–12; J. M. MYERS, Ezra. Nehemiah. Introduction, Translation and Notes (AB; Garden City, 1965), 9. However, this view has been opposed on linguistic grounds by P.-R. BERGER, 'Zu den Namen שֵׁשְׁבַּצַּר und שֶׁנְאַצַּר', ZAW 83 (1971), 98–100. W. RUDOLPH, Esra und Nehemia, 4 and 7, is undecided, but states that Sheshbazzar was a Jew (page xxvi); K. GALLING appears to adopt a similar position (Studien, 81 and 132).

[39] Hananiah, Nehemiah's brother, was, of course, Jewish; it has been suggested that he may have succeeded his brother as governor; cf. C. G. TULAND, 'Hanani-Hananiah', JBL 77 (1959), 157–61.

5. The Historical Value of Josephus' Jewish Antiquities xi. 297–301

The question of who Jesus was can be quickly dealt with, since he is not mentioned by name in any other source for the period. Galling,[40] nevertheless, has suggested that he is the priest whom Nehemiah expelled from Jerusalem because he married Sanballat's daughter (Neh. 13:28). On this view, Bagoas sought to procure the office of high priest for Jesus as part of his policy of reconciliation between Jerusalem and Samaria. It is hard to believe, however, that any governor could have been quite so insensitive as to reintroduce to the Jerusalem temple one whom Nehemiah had so ignominiously expelled. We conclude, therefore, that the mention of Jesus cannot help us in dating the story.

The identity of Joannes is more difficult, however. There is a Johanan mentioned twice in Nehemiah in a context that suggests strongly that he was high priest (Neh. 12:22, 23). Since his father (or grandfather, as some conjecture), Eliashib, was high priest at the time of Nehemiah's first arrival in Jerusalem (cf. Neh. 3:1), it is virtually certain that this must be the Jehohanan the high priest of the letter from Elephantine, to be dated in 408 BC (AP 30.18). It is thus often plausibly assumed that this is the Joannes of Josephus' account. As emphasized above, however, in view of the doubts already expressed about associating the story with this precise period at all, we must inquire whether such an identification is the only one demanded by the evidence.

The obstacles in the way of reconstructing satisfactorily the high priestly succession and family tree for the Persian period are insurmountable. The sources are simply insufficient. In view of this, it can only be urged once more that greater attention must be paid both to the detail and to the silences of these sources if we are to proceed on firm ground. Harmonizing arguments should only be invoked at the end of a discussion, not made its initial starting point.

For these reasons, it is precarious to start, as many seem to do,[41] by equating the Jonathan of Neh. 12:11 with the Johanan of Neh. 12:22, 23. Rather, we should follow Mowinckel[42] in observing that not only are the names different, but that their positions within the family are different: according to the explicit statements of Neh. 12:10f., Jonathan was the grandson of Eliashib; Johanan, however, is said in verse 23 to be the son of Eliashib, and there are no valid grounds for taking this statement other than at its face value in the first instance.[43] This is not to say that בן can never mean 'grandson', but rather that, since in this case there is no direct evidence to demand such a meaning, sound method suggests that we should start by understanding it as 'son', revising our

---

[40] K. GALLING, 'Bagoas und Esra', 164f. This view is also taken by N.H. SNAITH, Studies in the Psalter (London, 1934), 13f. and F.M. CROSS, 'Aspects of Samaritan and Jewish History', 202.

[41] E.g. R. MARCUS, 456, note e; A. SCHALIT, 'A Chapter in the History of the Party Disputes', 254; W. RUDOLPH, Esra und Nehemia, 190; J.M. MYERS, Ezra. Nehemiah, 195.

[42] S. MOWINCKEL, Studien, I, 158–60.

[43] Impressive support for MOWINCKEL's argument here, though without explicit reference to this chapter, comes from J.R. PORTER, 'Son or Grandson (Ezra x. 6)?', JTS n.s. 17 (1966), 54–67.

conclusion only if obliged to do so in the light of further considerations. From this, we have to conclude that the lists we have are fragmentary, Neh. 12:10f., for instance, giving only the line of direct descent without reference to brothers who may have acted as high priest, whilst Neh. 12:22 neither purports to give a complete list nor to associate them genealogically.

Other considerations bear out this conclusion: Joshua was active as high priest at the time of Zerubbabel (c. 520 BC) when the temple was restored (Ezra 5:2; Hag. 1:1, 14; 2:2, 4; Zech. 3:1–10; 6:11), and Eliashib during Nehemiah's governorship (starting 445 BC). It is unlikely that only one high priest (Joiakim, Neh. 12:10) should have filled the whole of the extensive period between these two dates,[44] a problem that may be eased on the supposition that again our list is incomplete.

According to Josephus (Ant. xi. 302ff.), the high priest at the time of Alexander the Great's closest contact with Jerusalem (c. 333 BC) was Jaddua, whom he clearly identifies with the Jaddua of our lists in Neh. 12. Again, however, this identification seems improbable. According to Neh. 12:11, Jaddua was the son of Jonathan. Since both Jonathan's father (Joiada) and his uncle (Johanan) were high priests before him, Jonathan is unlikely to have been young when he assumed the office. Johanan's term of office is fixed in part at 408 BC (see above), so that Joiada, who was in the direct line of succession, was high priest before that (cf. Neh. 12:10f. and 22). To postulate only two generations (Jonathan and Jaddua) between him (pre 408 BC) and 333 BC would be to presuppose an abnormal situation.[45] Thus, whether Josephus is right or not in linking a Jaddua with Alexander, it seems probable that we should include other high priests within the Persian period after the Jaddua of Neh. 12:11.[46]

If these arguments are sound, then the identification of the Joannes of Josephus' source with the Johanan of Neh. 12 must at least be open to question.

---

[44] S. MOWINCKEL, Studien, I, 158.

[45] Cf. J. MORGENSTERN, 'A Chapter in the History of the High-Priesthood', 362 (footnote), who has to postulate several long living high priests who all had sons late in life. MORGENSTERN concedes, on this basis, that a name may have been lost from our list. Others who postulate a lacuna in the text include W. F. ALBRIGHT, 'The Date and Personality of the Chronicler', 112 n. 18 and 122, who fills it with a Jaddua II immediately after Jaddua I; P. LAPP, 'Ptolemaic Stamped Handles from Judah', BASOR 172 (1963), 22–35; cf. 33 n. 54: 'There is a gap in our knowledge of the names of high priests at least from the early fourth century to the time of Alexander, but the principle of papponymy would tend to minimize this gap', and F. M. CROSS, 'Aspects of Samaritan and Jewish History', 205, who says, 'it seems highly probable that we must insert a Johanan (?) and a Jaddua III in the series of high priests'. CROSS has further developed his views in a paper published only after the present article had been drafted – 'A Reconstruction of the Judean Restoration', JBL 94 (1975), 4–18.

[46] We cannot, of course, rule out the possibility that we are dealing here with an exceptional occurrence in which so few generations did in fact cover such an extensive period. Indeed, Dr. Caird has kindly drawn my attention to examples that would parallel this very situation. My point, however, is not to deny such a possibility, but precisely to suggest that it would be exceptional and that it thus remains under suspicion in any weighing of probabilities. This suspicion will in turn be increased by the other difficulties already noted to the earlier dating.

Johanan, it goes without saying, was a common name in the period,[47] and with the increasing evidence for the practice of papponymy in the leading families for this period,[48] it would be unwise indeed to rule out the possibility that there was a high priest named Johanan in the later part of the Persian period. We may thus conclude that the appearance of Joannes and Jesus in Josephus' source is not in itself sufficient to settle the issue of dating one way or the other.

iv. It remains finally to consider the evidence which Josephus himself supplies on the dating of this incident. The source itself, we should emphasize, gives no direct evidence on this matter. We have already established that *Ant.* xi. 297 is Josephus' own composition, whose purpose is to introduce the subsequent narrative. It starts with the high priestly genealogy which shows that Josephus dated the incident in the time of the Johanan of Neh. 12. This list, however, has no independent value, but is clearly taken by Josephus from Neh. 12:22, and misunderstands that verse as reflecting a line of direct descent. This confirms the suspicions raised earlier that not only did Josephus have no external and reliable chronological data for this period, but that he even misrepresented what sources he did have at this point.

We have seen furthermore that there are strong grounds for believing that Josephus 'reduced' the Persian period by at least as much as two generations.[49] Firstly, we noted that his use of ἄλλος at *Ant.* xi. 297 shows that he did not distinguish between Artaxerxes II and III. Secondly, it is clear that he identified the Sanballat of the Nehemiah Memoir with the Sanballat of Alexander's time nearly a century later. This is demonstrated by his comment at *Ant.* xi. 302 that Sanballat 'had been sent to Samaria as satrap by Darius the last king'. This can only refer to the first of the Sanballat's whom we now know to have held

---

[47] This will be accentuated if we accept the strong evidence for disassociating the Jehohanan the son of Eliashib of Ezra 10:6 from the Johanan of Neh. 12. He is there shown to have a link with a room in the temple, and this points us also to the Eliashib of Neh. 13:4. He is there defined as 'the priest, who was appointed over the chambers of the house of our God'. This definition seems intended to identify Eliashib, and is presumably, therefore, to *distinguish* him from Eliashib the high priest, who could have been satisfactorily designated by his title alone, as at Neh. 3:1. Moreover, we would not expect the high priest to function as a caretaker (cf. W. RUDOLPH, Esra und Nehemia, 203f.; J. M. MYERS, Ezra. Nehemiah, 214; L. H. BROCKINGTON, Ezra, Nehemiah and Esther, 208; C. G. TULAND, 'Ezra-Nehemiah or Nehemiah-Ezra?', AUSS 12 [1974], 47–62). Such similarity of names within the priestly families only accentuates the possibilities of confusion where our sources are so fragmentary.

[48] For the Tobiad family, cf. B. MAZAR, 'The Tobiads', IEJ 7 (1957), 137–45 and 229–38; for the Sanballat family, cf. F. M. CROSS, 'Aspects of Samaritan and Jewish History', who refers in addition to the alternation over five generations of the names Onias and Simon in the high priestly family of Hellenistic times. He further suggests (p. 205) that Jaddua itself is 'caritative form of his grandfather's name, Joiada', which would show that papponymy was practised in the high priestly family too.

[49] Cf. S. MOWINCKEL, Studien zu dem Buche Ezra-Nehemia, II: Die Nehemia-Denkschrift (Skrifter Utgitt av det Norske Videnskaps-Akademi i Oslo. II. Hist.-Filos. Klasse. Ny Serie. No. 5. Oslo, 1964), 116.

office.⁵⁰ Thirdly, however, it is probable by the same token that Josephus did not distinguish between Darius II and III, for whilst admittedly this cannot be proved, his arrangement of material in *Ant.* xi. 302f. is such as to link 'Darius the last king' both with the period of Alexander the Great following (cf. 304: 'Now it was just about this time that Philip, king of Macedon, died...') and with the incident under consideration preceding (cf. 302: 'When Joannes departed this life...'), which we have seen he himself dates in the reign of Artaxerxes II. Since Josephus nowhere else mentions Darius II, whilst at the same time he confused Artaxerxes II and III, it appears that he may have identified Darius II and III, placed their reign immediately after Artaxerxes II, and therewith closed his account of the Persian period. Finally, we have argued that he may have misunderstood the list of high priests in Neh. 12:22 as extending to the time of Alexander.⁵¹ These observations can best be explained on the supposition that Josephus foreshortened the Persian period. Such an error is readily intelligible in view of the fact that the names of the kings of Persia in the fourth century (Artaxerxes and Darius) were the same as the kings at the end of the preceding century, and that Josephus had hardly any material at his disposal which could have led him to realize the gap of nearly a century which intervened between the time of Nehemiah and the fall of the Persian empire. It then becomes quite understandable that he should have identified the Joannes of his source with the Johanan of Neh. 12. At the same time, however, his identification loses any worth for an accurate dating of the incident related in his source.

D. Conclusions

In the first part of this article, we attempted to show, on the basis of an examination of Josephus' editorial method, that *Ant.* xi. 297–301 contains the account of an incident drawn from an apparently reliable source. 297 is not part of that

---

⁵⁰ Cf. H.H. ROWLEY, 'Sanballat and the Samaritan Temple', 256.

⁵¹ It is likely that the reference at the end of the verse to 'the reign of Darius the Persian' influenced Josephus at this point. Unfortunately, there are too many difficulties surrounding the second half of the verse to enable us to use it intelligently in our discussion: (i) the text seems to be corrupt, the preposition על being unsuitable in the context; consequently, any conclusions drawn from this verse must be hypothetical; (ii) the identity of Darius is disputed. For instance, amongst modern commentators, Darius I is favoured by MYERS, Darius II by RUDOLPH, and Darius III by BROCKINGTON; (iii) the verse is very disjointed in its present condition, such that even if the identity of Darius were agreed, it would still be very uncertain to whom such a date refers. The immediate antecedent is 'and the priests', which seems to be a counterpart to 'the Levites' at the start of the verse, and 'the sons of Levi' at the start of the next. This suggests that they were ordinary priests, to be distinguished from the high priests in the first half of the verse, as most commentators agree; but who they were, and how the second half of the verse as a whole relates to the first half, remains uncertain.

source, however, but represents Josephus' own introduction, composed partly on the basis of the source, and partly on the basis of the list of high priests in Neh. 12. Since this introduction by Josephus has led many scholars to link the incident related with the situation underlying the letter from Elephantine (AP 30), it was considered worthwhile then to examine whether our conclusions in any way affected this consensus. It was suggested that no evidence contained in Josephus' source compelled an early date, whilst some even tended to favour a later date. Such a confusion was found to be readily intelligible in view of the limited material available to Josephus for a historical reconstruction of this period and the consequently reduced chronological outline which he appears to follow. It would still be possible to hold to the earlier date if Bagoses were some Persian official otherwise unknown to us, but we incline towards the later date as satisfying the evidence as a whole more easily.[52]

We may thus conclude that the sharp divisions in the Jerusalem community, and the priesthood in particular, with which we are familiar from the times of Ezra and Nehemiah, were not restricted to the fifth century BC, but continued much longer. The background to the incident is not known to us, and even the widely accepted supposition that it reflects more than a purely personal feud is only conjectural. Those who date it in the reign of Artaxerxes II generally agree that it reflects a sharp difference of opinion over what attitude should be adopted towards the inhabitants of the old Northern Kingdom. There are good reasons, however, for believing that this dispute continued through much of the fourth century also,[53] such that this still remains the most probable explanation.

Alternatively, however, if in fact Bagoses were to be identified with the well-known general of Artaxerxes III, an entirely different situation might possibly lie behind the incident. This Bagoas played a prominent part in the recapture of Egypt in 344–343 BC.[54] It has been reasonably conjectured that the Tennes revolt which preceded this campaign must have split Jerusalem into pro-Egyptian and pro-Persian parties.[55] Nothing is known of Judah's involvement in this revolt, despite evidence of its having been widespread.[56] Several ancient writers do mention a deportation of Jews to Hyrcania at this time,[57] and it is not impossible that the two events are connected. The possibility cannot, therefore, be ruled out that the incident recorded in Josephus has this, rather than north-south differences, as its background.[58]

---

[52] 338 BC, the end of the reign of Artaxerxes III, provides a *terminus ante quem*.

[53] Cf. H. G. KIPPENBERG, Garizim und Synagoge: Traditionsgeschichtliche Untersuchungen zur samaritanischen Religion der aramäischen Periode (RVV, 30; Berlin, 1971), 48–59.

[54] A. T. OLMSTEAD, History of the Persian Empire (Chicago, 1948), 437–41.

[55] M. SMITH, Palestinian Parties and Politics, 156.

[56] D. BARAG, 'The Effects of the Tennes Rebellion on Palestine', BASOR 183 (1966), 6–12.

[57] Cf. ibid., 8f., and L. E. BROWNE, Early Judaism (Cambridge, 1929), 202–5.

[58] I am grateful to Dr. G. B. Caird for his comments on an earlier draft of this article, which have helped me to clarify my argument at a number of points.

Chronicles

6. Introduction to M. Noth, The Chronicler's History

Noth's work on the books of Chronicles, Ezra and Nehemiah might appear at first sight to have been less influential or significant than his celebrated theory of a Deuteronomistic History. This initial impression is not altogether justified, however. Of course, in the generation after the appearance of Noth's book in 1943, the post-exilic historical works suffered a period of quite exceptional and wholly unjustified neglect which the last fifteen years have only begun to restore. It is thus no surprise that in scholarly literature as a whole Noth's work on the Chronicler received less mention and in consequence his views did not become so readily identified as was the case in regard to the earlier historical work.

There is, however, a far more significant factor than this to consider. For whatever reason, there was a long gap after Noth's work before commentaries in any language appeared which treated his theory of a Deuteronomistic History with sustained consideration. This is especially true of the books of Kings, on which Noth himself left a major unfinished commentary at his untimely death in 1968.[1] For this reason, scholarly monographs and articles were obliged to work directly from Noth's own statement of his theory, and since for a considerable period his principal conclusions largely went unchallenged his achievements in research on this literature stood out as unrivalled.

The situation with regard to Chronicles, Ezra and Nehemiah is quite different. Here, in the wake of Noth's treatment, W. Rudolph produced two superb commentaries, one on *Esra und Nehemia* in 1949 in the Tübingen 'Handbuch zum Alten Testament' series, and the other in 1955 on *Chronikbücher* in the same series. So outstanding were these commentaries and so clear their lines of argument and modes of expression that in a period when little first-hand research was being undertaken on the books in question a whole generation of scholars appears not to have felt the need to consult further than them. In a situation quite unlike that of the Deuteronomistic History, therefore, the name of Rudolph became closely associated with the work of the Chronicler.

Now, there is no intention whatever to detract from Rudolph's achievement if we observe at this point how indebted he frequently was to Noth's earlier publication. Of course they did not agree in all details, and indeed as we shall see later they diverged quite markedly on some important matters. Furthermore,

---

[1] M. Noth, Könige, I. Teilband (BKAT; Neukirchen-Vluyn, 1968).

precisely because Rudolph was writing commentaries there is much in his work which is fresh and independent. My point here, rather, is to observe the extent to which a comparable method pervades their approach to literary and historical criticism so that their works stand out as the products not just of the same period but of the same school of scholarship. It thus came about that Noth's profound influence was not so readily perceived as such in this area, since it was refracted through the prism of Rudolph's commentaries.

This influence can best be seen by contrasting the approach of Noth and Rudolph with the state of research on Chronicles prior to Noth's work. During the nineteenth century from de Wette to Wellhausen[2] the books of Chronicles featured prominently in research on the Old Testament. Broadly speaking, however, interest was less in the books themselves than in two other areas for which the books of Chronicles were adduced merely as evidence. The first such area was the history of Israelite religion, which itself was integrally bound up with the development of theories of Pentateuchal origins. The second area, which developed by way of conservative reaction to the first, was the testimony of Chronicles to earlier historical 'sources'[3] which might then be used in the enterprise of constructing a critical history of Israel from the national and political points of view.

With the general acceptance of a critical approach to the Old Testament this second area of interest fell away as a serious focus for research during the early decades of the present century. Naturally, historians continued to pay lip-service to Chronicles,[4] but little fresh or creative work resulted.[5] The first area of interest, however, continued to attract a certain amount of attention, but in a manner which tended to suggest that the method was beginning to go to seed. Instead of Chronicles serving as part of the backdrop against which to unravel the composition-history of the Pentateuch, the documentary hypothesis came itself to influence the framing of theories about how Chronicles was written. It

---

[2] Cf. T. WILLI, Die Chronik als Auslegung (FRLANT, 106; Göttingen, 1972), 33–45. WILLI says of DE WETTE that his 'Stellungnahme ... zur Chronik ist zwar nur ein Nebenprodukt der Beschäftigung mit der pentateuchischen Frage – genau wie später das Chronik-Kapitel in J. Wellhausens Prolegomena' (33); J. W. ROGERSON, Old Testament Criticism in the Nineteenth Century: England and Germany (London, 1984).

[3] Cf. especially C. F. KEIL, Apologetischer Versuch über die Bücher der Chronik und über die Integrität des Buches Esra (Berlin, 1833).

[4] E. g. the brief commentary of R. KITTEL, Die Bücher der Chronik (HAT; Göttingen, 1902). Typical of the period is T. H. ROBINSON's judgement when discussing the sources available for the history of the Israelite Monarchy in the standard textbook on the subject in English, W. O. E. OESTERLEY and T. H. ROBINSON, A History of Israel, I (Oxford, 1932), 177: 'Our Biblical evidence is contained in the books of *Samuel* and *Kings*, with some doubtful additions from *Chronicles*. But the extent to which this latter compilation can be used as an authority independent of *Samuel* and *Kings* is very uncertain.'

[5] These remarks naturally apply only to the books of Chronicles. Ezra and Nehemiah, which constitute our main source for the history of the post-exilic period, will be discussed separately below.

would seem that it was impossible to move forward in research on Chronicles without relating one's results to the results of Pentateuchal criticism. Furthermore, it is a notorious fact that during these decades the literary analysis of the Pentateuch became excessively elaborate, some scholars apparently feeling no qualms about confidently postulating multiple layers of both sources and redaction,[6] and this too had an impact on the study of Chronicles.

The most obvious example of these trends was the massive commentary *Das erste Buch der Chronik* (KAT; Leipzig, 1927) by J.W. Rothstein and J. Hänel.[7] Here it was suggested that 1 Chronicles had as its basis a narrative which continued the Pentateuchal source P – still known as a separate document – and that this then went through an elaborate series of subsequent redactions which gradually accommodated it more closely to the Pentateuch as a whole, including, as of particular importance, Deuteronomy. Very different in tone, but apparently still sensing the need to justify its proposals in terms of the documentary hypothesis, was the monograph of A.C. Welch, *The Work of the Chronicler* (London, 1939). Welch believed that the 'original' Chronicler's work was to be dated before the post-exilic restoration and that it was written by a member of the community who had never been in exile. It 'must be set alongside the proposals in Ezekiel as one of the programmes which were put forward, before the final settlement was reached'.[8] Thus not only did Welch inevitably regard 1 Chron. 1-9 as secondary, but also all passages which betray the influence of P. He therefore devoted much of his monograph to the task of isolating the work of a later reviser who shard the outlook of P. The original Chronicler, he argued, compiled his book within a community which still accepted D as its authoritative law-code.

The one work of this period to make a sustained effort to break this impasse was G. von Rad's *Das Geschichtsbild des chronistischen Werkes* (BWANT, 54; Stuttgart, 1930), a contribution whose value Noth himself acknowledged.[9] In seeking to penetrate the historical, religious and theological framework of the Chronicler's mental horizons, von Rad naturally paid considerable attention to the law which the Chronicler presupposed. In direct response to the theory of Rothstein and Hänel, he succeeded in demonstrating that the Chronicler drew on both P and D, and indeed that in certain important respects the latter was especially important for him. In this regard, von Rad's work has been widely accepted (though Welch is an obvious exception) and Noth clearly believed that there was no need to add anything further on that score.

---

[6] See, for instance, the introductory survey in O. EISSFELDT, The Old Testament: an Introduction (Oxford, 1965; ET of the 3rd edn, 1964, of Einleitung in das Alte Testament), 168-70.

[7] See also J. HÄNEL, 'Das Recht des Opferschlachtens in der chronistischen Literatur', ZAW 55 (1937), 46-67.

[8] WELCH, The Work of the Chronicler, 156.

[9] NOTH, The Chronicler's History, 97 ff.

Despite the welcome fact that von Rad's monograph evidenced interest in the Chronicler himself and not just a desire to consult him for evidence on some other matter, it nevertheless left a number of important issues unresolved. First, it made no pretence of dealing with the questions raised by historical criticism. Second, perhaps by way of reaction to the excesses of Rothstein and Hänel's commentary, it paid little attention to literary-critical issues either. Only in his treatment of the Levitical singers was von Rad obliged by the results which his traditio-historical method produced to isolate a small number of short passages as having been added secondarily to the work of the Chronicler. On the whole, however, von Rad seems to have assumed that his conclusions would stand regardless of the results of literary analysis.[10] Third, von Rad paid little attention to such standard introductory questions as date and setting, despite the fact that he regarded a good deal of the Chronicler's work as arising directly out of the concerns of the writer's own day. In short, therefore, whilst von Rad marked the path for a return to an interest in the Chronicler for his own sake, he pursued this in only one area of study, and one which is generally taken to be the conclusion, not the starting point, of Old Testament research. There thus remained an all-too-obvious need for a thoroughgoing and comprehensive analysis of these books on their own terms, that is to say, with methods of study that were appropriate to them as opposed to being imposed upon them from the very different situation presented in the Pentateuch. It was this requirement that Noth was the first to fulfil.

It is not necessary to give a full summary and appreciation of Noth's study at this point. It may, nevertheless, be helpful to point out a few of the areas where his work may be seen to have had a lasting effect. First of all, he injected a healthy dose of realism and common sense into the literary-critical study of Chronicles. Whether or not one agrees with Noth's conclusions, it is difficult to read his first chapter on this subject without appreciating the clarity and logic of his argument. Freed from the constraints of external sources, Noth looked simply for internal narrative coherence as the key that should reveal secondary insertions. Thus, for instance, the narrative connection between 1 Chron. 23:1–2 and 28:1 suggested to him, as it already had to others, that the intervening chapters (23–27) were all added later, and should not, therefore, be included in a consideration of the Chronicler's own thought and purposes.

This straightforward approach to the literary-critical enterprise was taken up by Rudolph in his commentary, and though he did not agree with Noth in every detail, much of his analysis is broadly comparable. The outline of their conclusions then came to be adopted in most of the textbooks of the following decades. Furthermore, of the monographs which attest to the recent revival of interest in

---

[10] See VON RAD, Das Geschichtsbild des chronistischen Werkes, 133, where he appears to concede Rothstein's analysis of 'two Chroniclers' but goes on to assert that this is irrelevant to his investigation.

6. Introduction to M. Noth, The Chronicler's History

Chronicles, several accept these conclusions at points which are of fundamental importance for their own hypotheses. It would have been difficult, for instance, for Willi to pursue his theory that the books of Chronicles are intended to be an 'exegesis' of their authoritative counterparts in the former prophets had he not been able to follow Noth in regarding as secondary a good deal of that material which has no parallel in earlier Biblical books, material which had often been thought to serve the very different purpose of pro-Levitical propaganda.[11]

A comparable influence may be traced with regard to Noth's treatment of extra-Biblical sources available to the Chronicler[12] and hence of the historical value of those parts of his work for which no other source has survived for us. For a long time discussions of this topic had revolved around the Chronicler's apparent citation of sources at the end of the reign of each king. Indeed, this approach is still often repeated today. Even if it were valid, however, it would still only allow us to speak in the most general terms about the historical value of the Chronicler's special material because there would be no means of knowing which parts of it were drawn from these hypothetical sources.

Noth responded negatively to this 'method' by arguing that these source citation formulae were a purely literary device based on the practice of the books of Kings and so devoid of all value as testimony to the existence or otherwise of sources behind Chronicles. His own approach, whilst unable, in the present state of our knowledge, to be so comprehensive, is far more satisfactory and convincing from the point of view of method. He endeavoured first to isolate those two or three items which the Chronicler alone recorded for which there was sufficient reasonable evidence from other sources to uphold their authenticity. Since the Chronicler could not have fabricated them, he must in these few cases have been dependent on other sources. The principal examples which Noth adduced in this regard were the construction of Hezekiah's tunnel (2 Chron. 32:30) and the account of the death of Josiah (2 Chron. 35:20-24). From these two certain cases, Noth believed that it was reasonable to proceed to other examples of royal building projects and of military matters similarly recorded only in Chronicles. In many of these cases, though authenticity could not be proved, there were nevertheless reasons which made it seem likely. This likelihood would be strengthened if these passages were drawn into relationship with the undoubtedly authentic passages already noted by postulating on the basis of similarity of subject matter that they all came from the same source.

---

[11] T. WILLI, Die Chronik als Auslegung, 194-204.

[12] It is also worth observing that NOTH cut through another area of earlier speculation by affirming in the case of passages which have a Biblical parallel that the Chronicler worked directly from the texts as we know them and not from the sources which may have lain behind them. This view, which has not been seriously challenged since (though cf. A.G. AULD, 'Prophets through the Looking Glass: Between Writings and Moses', JSOT 27 [1983], 2-23), is not materially affected by more recent textual discoveries (see below).

In this field of research, too, it has been Noth's approach that has largely dominated more recent work. The search for 'certain' or 'probable' items of reliable information in Chronicles is to be found in all the commentaries as well as in a number of specialized articles. Generally speaking this has been in the direction of expanding Noth's list in the light of archaeological and other historical research.[13] However, in 1973 the whole issue was drawn together in a fresh examination by P. Welten,[14] who adopted a method which may be regarded as a direct development of the procedure outlined by Noth. Welten groups the relevant material into categories that he labels *topoi*, such as building or details about the army. He then studies each text belonging to that *topos* in turn, looking for both literary and historical evidence by which to evaluate it. He also, however, considers each *topos* as a whole in relation to the Chronicler's literary methods and purposes. On the whole, Welten's conclusions are closer to Noth's than most others who have written on this subject. He regards as most certainly historical the information included in 2 Chron. 11:5b, 6a–10aβ; 26:6a and 10; 32:30a; next in order of probability come 2 Chron. 11:22f.; 21:1–4; and 35:20–25 (cf. pp. 192–93). The important point here, however, is not so much to compare the detailed results with those of Noth as to observe the compatibility of the methods which each scholar has pursued. It is to be hoped that these examples will be sufficient to illustrate the extent to which Noth's study of the books of Chronicles set the agenda for subsequent research right down to the present day. It would be a mistake to imply, however, that new approaches have not also intervened during the past forty years; they have, and it would be idle to pretend that anyone can simply put the clock back to Noth's day. In order further to appreciate his position within the history of scholarship in this field we may conclude this part of our introduction with an indication of those areas which have been developed since Noth's time, those which are still being actively exploited, and those in which some of the positions he maintained are, inevitably, being modified.

First, the discovery of the Dead Sea Scrolls has had a significant impact on the study of Chronicles. When Noth was working, he was able to assume that the Masoretic text of Samuel and Kings represented quite closely the *Vorlage* which the Chronicler followed. In consequence, any differences between the texts in parallel passages could be taken without further ado as evidence of the Chronicler's *Tendenz*. Such an assumption cannot be so simply made today. With regard to the books of Samuel in particular, the discovery of 4QSam^a has shown[15] that

---

[13] An extreme exception is R. NORTH, 'Does Archeology Prove Chronicle Sources?', in H.N. BREAM, R. D. HEIM, and C. A. MOORE (eds.), A Light Unto My Path: Old Testament Studies in Honor of Jacob M. Myers (Philadelphia, 1974), 375–401.

[14] P. WELTEN, Geschichte und Geschichtsdarstellung in den Chronikbüchern (WMANT, 42; Neukirchen-Vluyn, 1973).

[15] This text has still not been published, and studies based upon it by the pupils of F. M. CROSS, in whose care it is, do not always agree in every detail over readings. However, from

there once existed a Hebrew text which differed to a sometimes significant extent from the MT and that it was from this that the LXX was translated.[16] Whilst it is theoretically possible that this text has in places been influenced by parallel passages in Chronicles, it is usually believed with good reason that in fact it existed before Chronicles was written and that it was this text, or something very like it, which the Chronicler followed rather than the MT. If so, not every difference between the MT of Samuel-Kings and Chronicles need inevitably reflect the Chronicler's *Tendenz* or bias.

There can be little doubt that some exaggerated conclusions were drawn from this state of affairs when first it became widely known.[17] Comparison of synoptic passages is still important for the study of Chronicles, even though now it must be conducted with greater attention to witnesses to the text of Samuel other than the MT and in full recognition of the dangers of placing too much weight on a single deviation. Nonetheless, scholars can never move in this area with quite the same confidence that Noth did, and for future research the possibility is opened up that in some cases there may have been even more substantial differences between Samuel-Kings and the *Vorlage* of the Chronicler than has hitherto been suspected.[18]

Second, and to some extent as a consequence of this first point, a number of recent studies of Chronicles have tended to draw their conclusions about the Chronicler's views and aims from a much broader appreciation of his overall narrative structure. If detailed differences in synoptic passages are a less reliable guide, it seems reasonable to concentrate instead on the general shape of the work, for this at least must have been due to the Chronicler himself. Thus the exegete needs to give due attention to the type of material which the Chronicler chose to include and to omit, the major themes to which he gave emphasis by his

---

the publications of those who have had access to photographs of the manuscript we can learn enough to substantiate the points made above; cf. W.E. LEMKE, 'The Synoptic Problem in the Chronicler's History', HTR 58 (1965), 349–63; E.C. ULRICH, The Qumran Text of Samuel and Josephus (HSM, 19; Missoula, 1978); P.K. MCCARTER, I Samuel (AB; Garden City, 1980); II Samuel (AB; Garden City, 1984). Of the numerous secondary discussions, it is necessary to mention here only E. Tov, 'The Textual Affiliations of 4QSam^a', JSOT 14 (1979), 37–53.

[16] The peculiar importance of the LXX for the textual criticism of the books of Samuel has long been recognized; cf. in particular J. WELLHAUSEN, Der Text der Bücher Samuelis (Göttingen, 1872), and S.R. DRIVER, Notes on the Hebrew Text and the Topography of Samuel (2nd edn, Oxford, 1913). For the significance of the Greek versions for synoptic studies, cf. M. REHM, Textkritische Untersuchungen zu den Parallelstellen der Samuel-Königsbücher und der Chronik (Münster, 1937), and G. GERLEMAN, Synoptic Studies in the Old Testament (Lund, 1948). Note also L.C. ALLEN, The Greek Chronicles (2 vols., VTSup, 25 and 27; Leiden, 1974).

[17] For a single example of how such exaggeration is now being modified, cf. P.E. DION, 'The Angel with the Drawn Sword (II [sic!] Chr. 21, 16): An Exercise in Restoring the Balance of Text Criticism and Attention to Context', ZAW 97 (1985), 114–17.

[18] Cf. my 'The Death of Josiah and the Continuing Development of the Deuteronomic History', VT 32 (1982), 242–48.

own additions and the arrangement of all this material in one order rather than another, if he is to do justice to the Chronicler's composition. Thus, to give but a few examples, R. Mosis,[19] to some extent both anticipated and followed by P.R. Ackroyd,[20] has argued that the Chronicler presents the history of Israel in terms of a recurring cycle of 'exile' and 'restoration', with the age of Solomon depicted as a third potential situation, that of ultimate, even eschatological, blessing. Words such as 'paradigm' characterize this fruitful approach as they seek to do justice both to the Chronicler's evident dependence on the earlier history and his ability to work creatively with it. Again, I have myself suggested that appreciation of narrative patterns spanning more than a single passage can advance our understanding of such disputed questions as the Chronicler's attitude towards the northern kingdom of Israel and towards the future of the Davidic dynasty.[21] Finally, in addition to a number of useful articles in similar vein by R.L. Braun and others,[22] mention must be made of the magisterial volume of S. Japhet, *The Ideology of the Book of Chronicles and its Place in Biblical Thought* (in Hebrew; Jerusalem, 1977), in which, not uncontroversially, the full range of material in these books is drawn together in a sustained attempt to present a synthesis of their outlook. The result of all these studies has been (so far as one may justifiably speak of a consensus) to modify some of Noth's cardinal points in his evaluation of the Chronicler's thought and purpose, especially his emphasis on the anti-Samaritan *Tendenz* which he believed he could detect in the Chronicler's work.

Third, whereas the significance of Noth's contribution to the development of literary-critical method with regard to the books of Chronicles has been emphasized above, there are signs of unease about the manner in which he pursued it in isolation from other considerations. To be sure, Noth's conclusions were broadly followed by Rudolph; Myers was unwilling to commit himself in detail, but on occasion, at least, indicated his general acceptance of Noth's position.[23] The same is true of the monographs of Willi,[24] Mosis (who generally follows Noth's and Rudolph's literary-critical judgments, though without full discussion) and Welten, in so far as the latter's position on this issue can be determined.

---

[19] Untersuchungen zur Theologie des chronistischen Geschichtswerkes (Freiburg, 1973).

[20] Cf. especially out of numerous publications on these books, The Age of the Chronicler (Auckland, 1970); I & II Chronicles, Ezra, Nehemiah (London, 1973); and 'The Chronicler as Exegete', JSOT 2 (1977), 2–32.

[21] Cf. Israel in the Books of Chronicles (Cambridge, 1977), 87–131; 'The Accession of Solomon in the Books of Chronicles', VT 26 (1976), 351–61 (below, 141–49); and 'Eschatology in Chronicles', TynB 28 (1977), 115–54 (below, 162–95).

[22] R.L. BRAUN, 'Solomonic Apologetic in Chronicles', JBL 92 (1973), 502–14; 'Solomon, the Chosen Temple Builder', JBL 95 (1976), 581–90; 'A Reconsideration of the Chronicler's Attitude toward the North', JBL 96 (1977), 59–62; R.B. DILLARD, 'The Chronicler's Solomon', WTJ 43 (1980), 289–300; 'The Literary Structure of the Chronicler's Solomon Narrative', JSOT 30 (1984), 85–93.

[23] See, for instance, J.M. MYERS, I Chronicles (AB; Garden City, 1965), 12 and 110.

[24] 194–204.

In the modern climate of opinion, however, it is somewhat disquieting that Noth never stopped to ask who was responsible for the multifarious additions to Chronicles which he had detected and what was the rationale for their inclusion.[25] In addition, Noth showed no interest in literary structure and patterning. This has become a fashionable subject of study in modern scholarship and is undoubtedly open to the abuses of excess; nevertheless, there are cases where it has provided convincing examples of planned literary composition which cut across some of the results of earlier critical work. Along with these modern studies there have also been attempts to establish some of the literary devices which authors of antiquity used. Without access to the facilities of modern book production and the flexibility afforded by such devices as the footnote and appendix, Biblical authors were obliged to use other conventions. Admittedly the use of these cannot be proved any more than can the results of any other form of literary-critical analysis, but for some, such as the device known as 'repetitive resumption', there is impressive evidence, and their identification invites modifications of Noth's conclusions. Next, it is difficult to see how the literary-critical exercise can be pursued in total isolation from the consideration of sources. In the genealogies of 1 Chron. 1–9 in particular, modern research has adduced analogies for some of the types of material which suggest that they may have belonged together from the start and so should not be broken up in the manner Noth suggests. Finally, whilst it is to Noth's credit that his proposals were detailed and explicit and his reasons for them stated quite clearly, it also means that his proposals are open to modification or refutation as new evidence is brought to bear.[26] Thus, whilst it is clear that there can be no going back to 'pre-Nothian' approaches, it is also the case that he did not speak the last word on the issue of determining the precise shape of the work which left the Chronicler's hands.

There is one final matter which has affected the study of Chronicles since Noth's time but which has not been referred to in the foregoing. Readers will have noticed that so far nothing has been said about Ezra-Nehemiah. In setting

---

[25] This is an appropriate point at which to refer to the attempt by K. GALLING, Die Bücher der Chronik, Esra, Nehemia (ATD; Göttingen, 1954), to distinguish two 'Chroniclers' throughout the work, each with an identifiable individuality. In regard to 1 Chronicles, GALLING's second Chronicler coincides to a considerable extent with the material which NOTH simply characterized as 'secondary'. In 2 Chronicles, however, matters change dramatically because here, unlike GALLING, NOTH detected only a few brief and isolated additions. Probably because of the publication of RUDOLPH's commentary the following year, GALLING's proposals received very little attention, critical or otherwise, from other scholars. So far as I know, apart from reviews of the commentary, only WELTEN, himself a pupil of GALLING, has given his theory considered attention (189–91), and then only to reject it.

[26] For illustration and justification of all the points made in the foregoing paragraph, I would refer to my 1 and 2 Chronicles (NCB; Grand Rapids and London, 1982) on the passages discussed by NOTH in chapter 14 and to the modern literature which is cited there.

about his work, Noth shared in the almost complete consensus of his time that the Chronicler's history originally included these two books. So confident was he about this that his opening paragraph concludes with the sentence: 'In this case, therefore, in contrast with our analysis of the Deuteronomic History, there is no need to start with a demonstration of the work's literary unity'.

Credit is due to Japhet for reopening this issue in so forceful a way as to draw others after her.[27] Previously, those such as Welch who had adopted the minority opinion of treating Ezra and Nehemiah separately from Chronicles had been almost completely ignored. Following Japhet's work, however, a number of scholars turned their attention to this issue, albeit embarking from quite varied critical starting-points. One group, for instance, finds a setting for the core of Chronicles in the earliest days of the post-exilic restoration and so postulates a series of redactions of the work which embrace Ezra and Nehemiah at only a secondary stage of the work.[28] Others, such as Willi and Welten, find it incompatible with their understanding of the purpose of Chronicles as a whole to accept Ezra and Nehemiah as part of the work, although they nevertheless allow the possibility that they may be two quite separate works of the same author. Yet a third group follow Japhet more closely in examining the two works and concluding that the differences between them preclude unity of authorship on the one hand whilst on the other hand the traditional arguments for unity are flawed.[29]

Of course, not all scholars by any means have been persuaded that Chronicles should be separated from Ezra-Nehemiah;[30] however, that the question is genuinely open may be judged from the fact that the newer view has found favour in several recent textbooks.[31] The important point to stress here, however, is that

---

[27] S. JAPHET, 'The Supposed Common Authorship of Chronicles and Ezra-Nehemiah Investigated Anew', VT 18 (1968), 330–71.

[28] Cf. F.M. CROSS, 'A Reconstruction of the Judean Restoration', JBL 94 (1975), 4–18; J.D. NEWSOME, 'Toward a New Understanding of the Chronicler and his Purposes', JBL 94 (1975), 201–17; D.L. PETERSEN, Late Israelite Prophecy: Studies in Deutero-Prophetic Literature and in Chronicles (SBLMS, 23; Missoula, 1977); J.R. PORTER, 'Old Testament Historiography', in G.W. ANDERSON (ed.), Tradition and Interpretation (Oxford, 1979), 125–62; M.A. THRONTVEIT, When Kings Speak: Royal Speech and Royal Prayer in Chronicles (SBLDS, 93; Atlanta, 1987); and note the brief, but in many ways programmatic, essay by D.N. FREEDMAN, 'The Chronicler's Purpose', CBQ 23 (1961), 436–42.

[29] Cf. H.G.M. WILLIAMSON, Israel in the Books of Chronicles, 5–70; R.L. BRAUN, 'Chronicles, Ezra, and Nehemiah: Theology and Literary History', VTSup 30 (1979), 52–64.

[30] Of those who have discussed the issue in any detail, note H. CAZELLES, VT 29 (1979), 375–80; S.J.L. CROFT, JSOT 14 (1979), 68–72; A.H.J. GUNNEWEG, 'Zur Interpretation der Bücher Esra-Nehemia – zugleich ein Beitrag zur Methode der Exegese', VTSup 32 (1981), 146–61 (and cf. the Bonn dissertation of GUNNEWEG's pupil T.-S. IM, Das Davidbild in den Chronikbüchern [Frankfurt am Main, 1984]); D.J.A. CLINES, Ezra, Nehemiah, Esther (NCB; Grand Rapids and London, 1984), 9–12 and 25–31; M. HARAN, 'Book-Size and the Device of Catch-Lines in the Biblical Canon', JJS 36 (1985), 1–11.

[31] E.g. M. SAEBØ, 'Chronistische Theologie/Chronistisches Geschichtswerk', TRE 8 (1981), 74–87; O. KAISER, Einleitung in das Alte Testament (5th edn; Gütersloh, 1984), 192–94; and J.R. PORTER (above, n. 28).

6. Introduction to M. Noth, The Chronicler's History

this obviously makes a difference to an appraisal of the Chronicler's 'Central Theological Ideas' (Chapter 20). As I have tried to show elsewhere,[32] one of the major features which Noth expounded, the Chronicler's supposed anti-Samaritan polemic, was based entirely on a prior analysis of Ezra-Nehemiah. Once that plank is removed, a completely different picture comes into view, as several of the recent monographs have recognized from their different angles. Thus, just as Noth correctly perceived the need to modify von Rad's characterization of the Chronicler's theology in the light of his literary-critical conclusions, so Noth's own sketch is open to modification as further preliminary critical work develops.

These remarks serve as a useful bridge to a consideration of the significance of Noth's work on Ezra and Nehemiah, and here it will be possible to be brief. Because these books are our major witness for Jewish history in the Persian period, they have inevitably been studied with greater intensity than Chronicles. Moreover, they have not been bedevilled by some of the problems which we noted in connection with Chronicles in the period before Noth; and some aspects, at least, of their literary history have received a general degree of assent amongst scholars. Finally, since Noth recognized the extensive use of sources in Ezra-Nehemiah whereas his own interest was primarily in the work of the Chronicler, he did not touch on several of the major issues in the study of the books. A particularly noteworthy example of this concerns the Nehemiah Memoir. Noth was happy to accept the usual view of its extent and authenticity and, in contrast with his thorough treatment of pre-exilic sources in Chronicles, he showed little interest in it thereafter, even though its genre and purpose are widely debated and far from agreed.[33] In addition, he quietly dismissed[34] the relevance of the apocryphal Greek work 1 Esdras, even though a number of scholars both before and since have argued that its ending (roughly Ezra + Nehemiah 8) represents the 'original' ending of the Chronicler's work.[35] For these reasons amongst others Noth's work was bound to have less influence on subsequent scholarship than was the case with regard to Chronicles.

---

[32] Israel in the Books of Chronicles, 2–4.
[33] Cf. U. KELLERMANN, Nehemia: Quellen, Überlieferung und Geschichte (BZAW, 102; Berlin, 1967).
[34] Cf. NOTH, Chronicler's History, 153f., n. 62.
[35] Cf. K-F. POHLMANN, Studien zum dritten Esra: Ein Beitrag zur Frage nach dem ursprünglichen Schluss des chronistischen Geschichtswerkes (FRLANT, 104; Göttingen, 1970), with a full and helpful survey of earlier discussions. Of these, we would mention only two here as being of particular influence: G. HÖLSCHER, 'Die Bücher Esra und Nehemia', in E. KAUTZSCH and A. BERTHOLET (eds.), Die heilige Schrift des Alten Testaments (4th edn, Tübingen, 1923), and S. MOWINCKEL, Studien zu dem Buche Ezra-Nehemia I (Oslo, 1964), 1–28. Significant work which has been influenced by POHLMANN includes that of MOSIS, ACKROYD and CROSS (see above, notes 19, 20 and 28). In my opinion, however, NOTH's opinion on this matter was sound; cf. Israel, 12–36 and JTS n. s. 34 (1983), 2–8 (below, 245–50).

In fact, there is only one major subject on which he advanced a fresh suggestion which has had a significant impact on subsequent study, and that concerns the nature of the so-called 'Ezra Memoir'. The account of Ezra's activities is found in Ezra 7–10 and Nehemiah 8 (with which Neh. 9–10 are frequently associated). Many questions are raised by this material: why is it split into two parts? Why is some transmitted as third-person and some as first-person narrative? Why is its Hebrew style apparently so similar to that of the Chronicler? How reliable is the Aramaic edict of Artaxerxes in Ezra 7:12–26? To these questions, scholars have suggested several answers encompassing the whole range of possibilities between the fully conservative view which takes the narrative at face value as Ezra's own account of his mission (apart from the editorial recasting of some first-person material as third-person narrative) through to the radical view of C. C. Torrey[36] to the effect that Ezra never existed and that the whole account was a fabrication by the Chronicler.

Noth's proposed solution to this dilemma was characteristically straightforward in its essential details. He accepted that the Aramaic edict in Ezra 7:12–26 and the list of those who returned to Jerusalem with Ezra in 8:1–14 were sources antecedent to the Chronicler. (This in itself, Noth hastened to affirm, did not settle the question of their historical authenticity.) The Chronicler also knew the Nehemiah Memoir. On the basis of this material, the Chronicler himself wrote the whole of the Ezra account, for Noth could find nothing in this material which demanded other independent knowledge. He was thus able to explain why the style of writing so closely resembled that of the Chronicler, why Nehemiah 8 was not included with Ezra 7–10 (the Chronicler wrote it from the first for its present setting for theological reasons), and why part of the account was in the first person (imitation of the Nehemiah Memoir, but characteristically not pursued consistently by the Chronicler). The influence of Noth's views on this matter may be gauged by the fact that they have been adopted with only minor changes by both Kellermann[37] and In der Smitten.[38]

On this occasion in particular, Noth was not followed by Rudolph. In his commentary, Rudolph went to considerable lengths carefully to justify a more conservative position. The result has been that in recent decades scholars have found that their agenda for discussion of the Ezra material has again largely been set by these two scholars.[39] Whilst this is not the place to set out the reasons why Rudolph's approach may be preferred to that of Noth,[40] it is clear that such a

---

[36] C.C. TORREY, The Composition and Historical Value of Ezra-Nehemiah (BZAW, 2; Giessen, 1896); Ezra Studies (Chicago, 1910).

[37] See above, n. 33.

[38] W.TH. IN DER SMITTEN, Esra: Quellen, Überlieferung und Geschichte (Assen, 1973).

[39] The only major alternative proposal in the meantime has been that of S. MOWINCKEL, Studien zu dem Buche Ezra-Nehemia III: Die Ezrageschichte und das Gesetz Moses (Oslo, 1965), but on the whole he has not attracted much scholarly support.

[40] See my Ezra-Nehemiah (WBC, 16; Waco, 1985).

preference cannot be expressed without the most careful attention to the pioneering work of Noth on this topic and the supporting arguments which those who have followed him have adduced.

In drawing this introduction to a close, it should perhaps be emphasized that there has been no intention of providing a comprehensive survey of work on Chronicles, Ezra and Nehemiah. My aim has been rather to set Noth's contribution into its context in the history of scholarship and to outline something of his influence and of how matters have since developed in those particular areas. We may conclude, in the light of this discussion, by venturing the opinion that despite all the advances and changes that have taken place since he wrote, it is nevertheless to Noth's contribution here presented in translation that the modern era of Chronicles studies may be traced.

7. Sources and Redaction
in the Chronicler's Genealogy of Judah

Students of the Chronicler's genealogies (1 Chron. 1-9) may approach their subject with a wide variety of questions. Nearly all are in agreement that much ancient and valuable material has been retained in these chapters, so that not surprisingly they have most often been examined as a unique source of historico-geographical information. Not least is this so for 1 Chron. 2:3–4:23, which deals with the genealogy of Judah. Clan and tribal movements,[1] information about ancient guilds in Israel (4:21–23)[2] and details of the postexilic Davidic line (3:19–24)[3] are but the main topics which have received attention since the rise of critical scholarship.

It is unlikely, however, that the Chronicler himself included this material for the sake of such considerations. That he had a particular interest in the tribe of Judah is clear from his explanation of its position at the head of the tribal genealogies in his presentation of them at 1 Chron. 5:1-2:[4] 'Judah became strong among his brothers and a prince was from him.' Our concern here, however, is to go beyond the broader outline of the Chronicler's genealogies to his internal structuring of the Judah material. In general terms, this has, of course, been attempted before.[5] It is hoped nevertheless that a more accurate

---

[1] In addition to the major commentaries, cf. J. WELLHAUSEN, De Gentibus et Familiis Judaeis, quae 1 Chr 2. 4 enumerantur (Göttingen, 1870); M. NOTH, 'Eine siedlungsgeographische Liste in 1. Chr. 2 und 4', ZDPV 55 (1932), 97–124; idem., 'Die Ansiedlung des Stammes Juda auf dem Boden Palästinas', PJ 30 (1934), 31–47 = Aufsätze zur biblischen Landes- und Altertumskunde (ed. H.W. Wolff; Neukirchen-Vluyn, 1971) 1, 183–96; R. DE VAUX, 'The Settlement of the Israelites in Southern Palestine and the Origins of the Tribe of Judah', in H.T. FRANK and W.L. REED (eds.), Translating and Understanding the Old Testament: Essays in Honor of Herbert Gordon May (Nashville, 1970), 108–34; W. BELTZ, Die Kaleb-Traditionen im Alten Testament (BWANT, 98; Stuttgart, 1974); V. FRITZ, 'Erwägungen zur Siedlungsgeschichte desh Negeb in der Eisen I – Zeit (1200–1000 v. Chr.) im Lichte der Ausgrabungen auf der Ḥirbet el-Mšāš', ZDPV 91 (1975), 30–45, esp. 42–43.
[2] I. MENDELSOHN, 'Guilds in Ancient Palestine', BASOR 80 (1940), 17–21; A. DEMSKY, 'The Houses of Achzib', IEJ 16 (1966), 211–15.
[3] In addition to the histories of the period, see especially the speculations of J.W. ROTHSTEIN, Die Genealogie des Königs Jojachin und seiner Nachkommen (Berlin, 1902).
[4] Cf. H.G.M. WILLIAMSON, Israel in the Books of Chronicles (Cambridge, 1977), 89–95.
[5] E.L. CURTIS and A.A. MADSEN, A Critical and Exegetical Commentary on the Books of Chronicles (ICC; Edinburgh, 1910), 82–84; F. MICHAELI, Les livres des Chroniques, d'Esdras et de Néhémie (CAT, 16; Neuchâtel, 1967), 47–49.

delimitation of the sources on which the Chronicler drew in these chapters and consequent awareness of his contribution to their arrangement will establish these attempts on a firmer basis, advance them in certain particulars and defend the integrity of the structure against those who find here a haphazard accumulation of later expansions of an original brief core.[6]

Clearly, an accurate source analysis is of supreme importance. Four blocks of material may be distinguished. First, a good deal seems to have been derived from earlier biblical texts or their near equivalents. Though of interest in its own right, discussion of the precise text-form that was available to the Chronicler is not significant for our present purposes.[7] Suffice it here to say that in nearly every passage which has a biblical parallel (namely 2:2–8, 10–17, 20; 3:1–16) there are quite noteworthy departures from or additions to the MT in the Chronicler's version which are unlikely to have been simple fabrication on his part since nothing of apparent importance hangs upon them (e. g. the addition of 2:8, 'and Ethan's son was Azariah').

Secondly, it is widely agreed that 2:25–33 and 42–50a stand out as a related unit by their exactly parallel opening and closing formulae:

2:25a The sons of Jerahmeel, the first-born of Hezron:
2:33b These were the descendants of Jerahmeel.
2:42a The sons of Caleb, the brother of Jerahmeel:
2:50a These were the descendants of Caleb.

Since nowhere else in the OT are Jerahmeel and Caleb called brothers or made the sons of Hezron, this pattern was probably already found in the Chronicler's source.

A third block of material, again structured in an orderly fashion in its original form, appears to have been overlooked in previous studies, probably because it has been more radically broken up by the Chronicler, and because it has suffered corruption at two places. It therefore requires more detailed attention here.

In his initial study of these chapters,[8] Noth correctly observed one element of the source. In 2:50b, we find a genealogical opening, 'The sons[9] of Hur the first-born of Ephrathah', whose conclusion comes only at 4:4b, 'These were the sons of Hur, the first-born of Ephrathah, the father of Bethlehem.' It is clear, however, that this list has been interrupted; furthermore, the break is still visible: 'Haroeh' (= 'the seer'; 2:52), improbable as a proper name, has been corrupted from Reaiah (4:2). Thus at one time 2:50b–52 and 4:2–4 formed a continuous section

---

[6] This approach finds its clearest and most thorough exposition in W. RUDOLPH, Chronikbücher (HAT, 21; Tübingen, 1955), 10–37.

[7] For a general introduction to the subject, see W. E. LEMKE, 'The Synoptic Problem in the Chronicler's History', HTR 58 (1965), 349–63.

[8] M. NOTH, 'Eine siedlungsgeographische Liste', 101.

[9] RSV here correctly restores the plural with LXX and Vg; cf. BHS. To retain the singular, thus making Hur the father of Caleb, would both contradict 2:19 and ignore the parallel with 4:4b observed above.

(though it will be suggested later that it had already been disrupted before it reached the Chronicler).

We notice next that 4:5-7 deals with the family of 'Ashhur, the father of Tekoa', who, according to 2:24, was the second son of Caleb by Ephrathah. It is thus very probable that these verses represent the direct continuation of the same source.

These considerations now lead us back to examine the much disputed section in 2:18-24. We would suggest that, interspersed with other material, they contain the original heading of the list just isolated. Verses 18-19 start this off in a straightforward enough manner. After the children of Caleb by Azubah have been listed (v 18),[10] we then learn (v 19) of Caleb's marriage to Ephrath, and the birth of the first son treated in the later list, Hur. Verse 20, however, comes as a complete surprise. Although ostensibly continuing the line of Hur, the list does not tie up at all with the genealogy of 2:50b-52, even though the latter, with its definition of Hur as 'the first-born of Ephrathah', must, so far as family connections are concerned, be the direct continuation of 2:19. In fact, however, 2:20 is to be compared rather with Exod. 31:2: 'See, I have called by name Bezalel the son of Uri, son of Hur, of the tribe of Judah' (and cf. Exod. 35:30; 2 Chron. 1:5). Using the name of Hur in the context of the genealogy of Judah as a peg, the Chronicler has here woven in a reference to the builder of the tabernacle. Since the preceding section of his genealogy (2:10-17) had dealt with David, it may be suggested that he has thus characteristically juxtaposed the themes of king and temple, so closely associated in his subsequent narrative.

In the paragraph under discussion, we next come to a further disjointed fragment in vv 21-23. This conclusion is indicated first by the summary in v 23b, 'All these were descendants of Machir, the father of Gilead', which suggests that the preceding verses probably once had a more extensive setting. Secondly, to revert to the family affairs of Hezron (cf. v 9) in the middle of a treatment of the genealogy of one of his sons, Caleb, is evidently out of order. What, then, is this fragment doing here? Many scholars[11] argue that it was composed by the Chronicler himself, and that vv 10-17 were its intended continuation. Moreover, in Hebrew narrative the word 'afterward' (*'aḥar*) is a stereotyped literary formula of transition, and is by no means always so precise as to demand an immediate and specific antecedent.[12] It is therefore more probable that the Chronicler felt that the reference in v 24 to the death of Hezron could best be given a context by the inclusion of this otherwise admittedly rather out-of-place fragment concerning Hezron's second marriage.

---

[10] There is a textual problem concerning whether Jerioth was a daughter or a second wife to Caleb. However, as it does not affect the present argument, it will not be discussed here.

[11] E. g. I. BENZINGER, Die Bücher der Chronik (Kurzer Hand-Commentar zum AT; Tübingen and Leipzig, 1901), 9; W. RUDOLPH, Chronikbücher, 17.

[12] Cf. U. CASSUTO, Biblical and Oriental Studies (Jerusalem, 1975), 2, 23.

7. Sources and Redaction in the Chronicler's Genealogy of Judah   109

With v 24, as already indicated, we return to the source broken off after v 19. Considerable difficulty surrounds the verse in detail, however; it seems to be corrupt, and several explanations of it have been advanced in consequence. The MT reads:

ואחר מות חצרון בכלב אפרתה ואשת חצרון אביה
ותלד לו את אשחור אבי תקוע

The closest attempt to render this in English is that of AV, RV: 'And after that Hezron was dead in Caleb-ephrathah, then Abijah Hezron's wife bare him Ashhur the father of Tekoa.' In fact, however, this skates over the *wāw* of *wattēled*, and is itself obscure, as even those who attempt to defend it acknowledge.[13] Most, therefore, follow the proposals of Wellhausen[14] in reading *bā' kālēb* for *bĕkālēb*, deleting the *wāw* before *'ēshet* and reading *'ăbîhû* for *'ăbiyyâ*. This is adopted by RSV, which translates in consequence: 'After the death of Hezron, Caleb went in to Ephrathah, the wife of Hezron his father, and she bore him Ashhur, the father of Tekoa.'

The first alteration makes excellent sense and is supported by both LXX and Vg. It involves so slight and so common a textual change[15] that everything seems to speak in favour of accepting it. Used with this particular nuance, *bô'* is usually followed by *'el* or *'al* to introduce the woman concerned. However, at Prov. 2:19 it is used with an object suffix (*kol-bā'ệhā* – 'all who come in to her'), which might provide a parallel in support of Wellhausen's conjecture at this point if 'Ephrathah' as a whole is to be construed as a proper name. Alternatively, however, it may represent the name 'Ephrath' (see v 19) followed by directive *hē* instead of the more regular preposition. This unusual construction could further help to account for the error. We know that 'Ephrathah' was indeed used as a proper name in other contexts (cf. Mic. 5:1; Ruth 4:11), and this may have influenced a scribe, who misunderstood the construction in consequence, to read *bĕ* for *bā'*.

The second two alterations suggested by Wellhausen, however, are totally conjectural, having no versional support whatever. Moreover, they suffer from the disadvantage of creating two unnecessary difficulties. First, they suggest that Ephrath(ah) was married twice, which is mentioned nowhere else, and, second, they lead to confusion with v 19 which in context implies that Caleb had married Ephrath before Hezron's death.

An alternative solution to the problem may therefore be advanced, namely to retain the MT of v 24b exactly but to understand the difficult words *wĕ'ēshet ḥeṣrôn 'ăbiyyâ* ('and the wife of Hezron [was] Abijah') as a misplaced gloss on

---

[13] E.g. C.F. KEIL, *The Books of Chronicles* (Edinburgh, no date; German original, 1870), 66.

[14] J. WELLHAUSEN, *De Gentibus*, 14 n. 1.

[15] Cf. F. DELITZSCH, *Die Lese- und Schreibfehler im alten Testament* (Berlin and Leipzig, 1920), § 14c.

v 21. We noted above that that verse was part of a disjointed fragment concerning the marriage of Hezron to the daughter of Machir. Perhaps precisely because of the verses' fragmentary nature, this wife is not named. If our conjecture is correct, the glossator aimed to remedy this deficiency. Further in favour of the proposal, we may note that the phrase is absent from the Peshitta and that a *wāw* followed by a nominal clause of this nature is a familiar form for a gloss.[16] Though normally a man's name, 'Abijah' is used for a woman at 2 Chron. 29:1. Finally, we may suppose that after the initial error had arisen in v 24, the gloss was attracted thither by the mention of Hezron and mistakenly incorporated there in an attempt to salvage some sort of sense. The verse in its original state would then have run: 'After the death of Hezron, Caleb went in to Ephrath, and she bore him Ashhur, the father of Tekoa.' This follows on quite naturally from v 19, from which it was separated by the Chronicler's insertion of the two fragments already noted, and the whole forms an ideal introduction to 2:50b–52, 4:2–4 and 5–7.

In concluding the discussion of this third source available to the Chronicler on Judah, we should observe against Noth and Rudolph that the present order of the verses, though now separated from one another, is probably original. They would prefer[17] to place 2:24 between 4:4 and 5, but this leads to the unnecessary

---

[16] Cf. G.R. DRIVER, 'Glosses in the Hebrew Text of the Old Testament', Orientalia et Biblica Lovaniensia 1 (1957), 123–61, esp. 128, and G. FOHRER, Studien zur alttestamentlichen Prophetie (1949–1965) (BZAW, 99; Berlin, 1967), 220. A slight difficulty for the view advanced here might be raised by asking whether a gloss on v 21 could have been incorporated as much as three verses later. Because the isolation of glosses in the text of the OT is itself inevitably hypothetical, it is not easy to provide analogies that would be universally accepted. One approach, however, which can claim a measure of external support has been advanced by L.C. ALLEN, 'Cuckoos in the Textual Nest at 2 Kings xx.13; Isa. xlii.10; xlix.24; Ps. xxii.17; 2 Chron. v.9', JTS ns 22 (1971), 143–50, and 'More Cuckoos in the Textual Nest: At 2 Kings xxiii.5; Jeremiah xvii.3,4; Micah iii.3; vi.16 (LXX); 2 Chronicles xx.25 (LXX)', 24 (1973), 69–73. Allen's treatment of Isa. 49:9 and 11 on pp. 144–45 of his earlier article would suggest that such displacement did sometimes occur. As shown above, several factors combined in the passage under study to make such an occurrence probable.

[17] NOTH, 'Eine siedlungsgeographische Liste,' 102; RUDOLPH, Chronikbücher, 11. In fairness, it should be noted that although both scholars adopt WELLHAUSEN's emendations of 2:24 rejected above, there are other substantial differences between their respective positions. Briefly, NOTH (101–104) argued that 20:50b implied the birth of a second son to Ephrathah by another, unnamed husband, and this he then linked with (the emended form of) v 24. On this view, then, Ashhur was the son of Kaleb-Ephrath; Hur, however, was the son of Hezron-Ephrath. This is in direct contradiction to 2:19, which, NOTH said, comes from another source. RUDOLPH (14) rejects NOTH's interpretation of 2:50b as 'quite unnatural', postulating instead (10–14) a somewhat complicated history of gradual accumulation of additions to the Chronicler's original core. He concludes that these additions in 1 Chron. 2 and 4 are *disjecta membra* of diverse origin. Without attempting to deal with his arguments in detail here, it may be observed first that RUDOLPH's whole discussion starts from the emended form of 2:24, and second that he seems to find difficulty in accepting that elements from the Chronicler's sources which may have stood in some tension with one another may nevertheless have been allowed to stand side by side by the Chronicler who, if he even noticed them, was prepared to sacrifice fully systematic unity in the interests of his wider presentation analyzed above.

repetition of 'Ashhur, the father of Tekoa,' whereas if 2:18-19 and 24 are taken together as an introduction to the more detailed genealogy following, the situation becomes at once more intelligible.

The fourth block of material available to the Chronicler for these chapters does not constitute a unified source, but for convenience of classification it must just be labelled as an assortment of miscellaneous fragments. That such material should have been available to a post-exilic writer is not implausible in the case of Judah and finds support from the observation that for the other two tribes which formed the core of the community, Levi and Benjamin, he seems similarly to have had more extensive sources than for the other tribes (cf. 1 Chron. 6:1-81; 7:6-12; 8:1-40). Some may well have been composed out of living memory (e.g. 3:19-24), while the remainder (principally 2:21-23, 34-41; 4:8-23) could well have been handed down within the families that survived the exile.

Having now established in general outline the main blocks of material available to the Chronicler, we may move towards the question of his arrangement of it by asking first whether he was responsible for interrupting the third source analyzed after 2:52, for this will affect appreciation of the positioning of chap. 3. The answer seems certainly to be that he was not responsible, but that the interruption was already present in the source as it reached him. The main argument in favour of this conclusion comes from 4:1. This verse is a clear editorial note to remind the reader where he was, so to speak, before the interruption. The names mentioned quickly trace the line again (father to son) from Judah to Shobal, the father of Reaiah, and hence to the very point at which the interruption had occurred. It is most unlikely, however, that 4:1 was composed by the Chronicler, first because it does not trace quite the same line as he himself did from Judah,[18] and second because when the Chronicler uses the expression 'the sons of x', he never introduces a bare list of names going from father to son, as is done here, but rather a list of brothers who are all equally sons of the father mentioned (see, for example, the closing verses of chap. 3 immediately preceding). It follows from these considerations that once chap. 3 is removed, the surrounding material will represent substantially the shape that the source had acquired before it reached the Chronicler.[19] It may be noted in addition that, although 2:53-55 (the original intrusive verses) are very difficult to understand in detail, their presence at this point is intelligible as an expansion on the family of Kiriath-jearim (compare vv 52a and 53a).[20]

---

[18] Contrast 2:3-8, noting in particular the occurrence of Carmi where we might have expected Caleb. Perhaps at an earlier stage there was confusion with Gen 46:9.

[19] That the Chronicler, wishing to add the material of chap. 3 at approximately this point (see below), should have spotted the resumptive nature of 4:1 and so inserted chap. 3 immediately before it is both intelligible and logical.

[20] 2:55 constitutes a separate problem and must to some extent remain a mystery. As translated by RSV, it appears to deal with the guilds of scribes and so to fit better at 4:21-23

In connection with this postulation of layers of material within the pre-chronistic sources, it is worth recalling the starting point of Noth's discussion in his article already referred to. Despite the broad agreement with his views by Myers,[21] his detailed literary reconstruction is not acceptable, as shown above. Nevertheless, his initial observation remains valid: there is in these chapters a large number of genealogical formulae on the pattern 'X (was) the father of Y', where Y is a place name, a pattern which hardly ever occurs elsewhere in the OT, and certainly not with the frequency apparent here. Noth's suggestion that this is to be explained as the characteristic of an earlier source is thus attractive, but its distribution through the more immediate sources analyzed here points to its break-up at a stage even earlier than their composition.

Turning now to the earlier part of chap. 2, we find that v 9 stands out as important because it introduces the following substantial section. Three factors suggest that it is the Chronicler's own editorial composition, whereby he combined for the first time the genealogies of Jerahmeel and Caleb with that of Ram. First, the genealogy of Ram, which immediately follows, is constructed on the linear principle,[22] whereas those of Jerahmeel and Caleb (vv 25–33, 42–50a) take rather the form of a 'segmented genealogy'. These latter two, we have argued, were already combined in the Chronicler's source, while vv 10–17 have close affinities with other biblical passages. Thus the Chronicler was probably himself responsible for combining these two types of material, with v 9 as the introductory link. His source (cf. vv 25 and 42) together with Ruth 4:19 would have suggested to him that Jerahmeel, Ram and Caleb were brothers. Secondly, since Caleb is here called Chelubai (kĕlûbāy), this verse probably did not stand in the same source as v 42, where his name is spelled in its more usual manner (kālēb).[23] Thirdly, the expression 'that were born to him' (ʾăšer nôlad-lô) is

---

than in its present context. However, the word translated 'scribes' (sōpĕrîm) has no article in the MT, and, unlike other professional guilds, they would probably not have been restricted to a particular locality. We therefore expect a proper name, perhaps (with repointing only) 'Siphrites' (i.e. men of [Kiriath-] Sefer); so BHS, following a suggestion first made by an anonymous Jewish commentator cited by S. KLEIN, 'Die Schreiberfamilien: I Chronik 2, 55', MGWJ 70 (1926), 410–16. If this is correct, the verse can more easily stand as part of the pre-chronistic insertion.

[21] J.M. MYERS, I Chronicles: Introduction, Translation, and Notes (AB; Garden City, 1965), 12–16, 27–29.

[22] For the use of such terminology in genealogical analysis, cf. R.R. WILSON, Genealogy and History in the Biblical World (Yale Near Eastern Researches, 7; New Haven and London, 1977), 9.

[23] It is less easy to explain why the spelling Chelubai occurs here. It is not found otherwise in the OT, though it is attested elsewhere, for instance in Ugaritic (cf. F. GRÖNDAHL, Die Personennamen der Texte aus Ugarit [Studia Pohl, 1; Rome, 1967], 395, and the comments of W.F. ALBRIGHT, 'Two Letters from Ugarit (Ras Shamrah)', BASOR 82 [1941], 47), in Palmyrene (cf. J.K. STARK, Personal Names in Palmyrene Inscriptions [Oxford, 1971], 29) and in Phoenician (cf. KAI 1, no. 8 with discussion at 2, 10). It appears to be a familiar form (cf. F. PRAETORIUS, 'Fuʿail im Hebräischen und Syrischen', ZDMG 57 [1903], 524), which may simply have been the form most familiar to the Chronicler himself. Even if

7. Sources and Redaction in the Chronicler's Genealogy of Judah

found again only where the Chronicler is himself constructing a genealogical introduction on the basis of his sources (3:1, and cf. 2:3; 3:4, 5, etc.).[24]

It follows from all these considerations that an important part of the Chronicler's contribution to the structure of these chapters was the introduction and positioning of 2:10-17 and of chap. 3. Both deal with David, the one tracing his ancestors, the other his descendants. The significance of this observation may be emphasized by the structure of the section as a whole:[25]

Descendants of Ram (as far as David)	– 2:10-17
Descendants of Caleb	– 2:18-24
Descendants of Jerahmeel	– 2:25-33
Supplementary material on Jerahmeel	– 2:34-41
Supplementary material on Caleb	– 2:42-55
Supplementary material on Ram (David's descendants)	– chap. 3

It should be clear on the basis of our foregoing discussion that this chiastic pattern is the Chronicler's own work. That this is so for the use of the Davidic material as an *inclusio* has already been established. In addition, we have seen that the basis of 2:18-24 has been separated rather unnaturally from its continuation at 2:50b, with two other fragments added to it by the Chronicler. Finally, 2:34-41, which is of particular importance as first introducing supplementary material, has been seen to come from a different source from 2:25-33. Its insertion here interrupts the second source we isolated, introduces a tension between vv 31 and 34 concerning whether Sheshan had sons or not, and comprises a linear, as opposed to segmented, genealogy.

We thus conclude that the central part of the genealogy of Judah has been deliberately structured by the Chronicler. We have discovered only one verse (2:9) which is likely to have been his own original composition, and even for that the materials already lay to hand. Any interpretation of his purpose in these chapters must thus be derived from the ordering of the material alone. Clearly,

---

the *yōd* were the result of textual confusion (see next note), the medial *wāw* would still distinguish the spelling here from v 42.

[24] The order of the three sons of Hezron in this verse has not been satisfactorily explained. We might have expected either Ram, Chelubai, Jerahmeel, the order in which they are treated in more detail, or the reverse, since the Chronicler often follows an inverted order in these genealogies. In fact, however, we have Jerahmeel, Ram, Chelubai, which does not seem to fit at all. CURTIS AND MADSEN (82) suggest that the present order is due to textual corruption. Postulating that Ram was originally at the end of the verse, they conjecture that it fell out by haplography before the *wěrām* at the start of v 10, and was later reinserted incorrectly. In that case the final *yōd* of Chelubai (see previous note) might represent the initial *wāw* of *wě'et-rām*. (The LXX, curiously, includes Ram both before and after Chelubai.) On the other hand, if the MT is correct, we might explain its order as an attempt initially to list Ram as central in his family, intelligible on the basis of the structure of the genealogy as a whole, discussed below.

[25] Cf. the commentaries of CURTIS AND MADSEN and of MICHAELI together with A.-M. BRUNET, 'Le chroniste et ses sources', RB 60 (1953), 481-508, esp. 491-92 n. 4, and M.D. JOHNSON, The Purpose of the Biblical Genealogies (SNTSMS, 8; Cambridge, 1969), 70.

the primary aim will have been to emphasize the position of David and his descendants within the tribe of Judah, and this is fully in line with his interests later on in the work.

It only remains to deal with the opening and close of the genealogy, 2:3–8 and 4:1–23. 4:21–23 treats the sons of Shelah. The whole genealogy thus ends with the oldest surviving son of Judah mentioned at the start, 2:3[26] – a further *inclusio*. 4:1–20 gives supplementary material on the sons of Perez (cf. 4:1), and thus may be said to balance 2:4–8. The whole genealogy, therefore, is arranged in a chiastic manner, the sons of Hezron (2:9–3:24) forming the middle element. This draws attention to the centrality of David's family in the tribe, just as the section we have been mainly concerned with here emphasizes its prominence.

This article has attempted to establish the nature of the Chronicler's own contribution to 1 Chron. 2:3–4:23. A more precise source analysis than has been heretofore achieved has brought to light the work of a writer who successfully arranged the materials at his disposal in order to express his own particular viewpoint. Though such an analysis should be the prerequisite of historical reconstruction, which our remarks may thus help to further,[27] that has not been our primary aim. We have sought rather to allow an author of antiquity to speak in his own way. His method is certainly quite foreign to us, but, once recognized, it may be appreciated as strikingly effective. It is, furthermore, my conviction that this passage is not an isolated example of such a method, but that it can be successfully traced both within other sections of 1 Chron. 1–9 and, indeed, in the ordering of the nine chapters themselves as a whole.

---

[26] Of the first three sons of Judah, Er and Onan both died without family; cf. Gen 38:7 and 10. Er's death is referred to in 1 Chron. 2:3, but surprisingly not that of Onan. Knowledge of Gen 38:10 may be presupposed, for the Chronicler quite often leaves his readers to fill in detail from their knowledge of his *Vorlage*, but RUDOLPH (Chronikbücher, 10, 15) conjectures that a reference to the incident has been lost by homoioteleuton.

[27] It should be noted that I have not attempted to establish the historical value of the sources on which the Chronicler has drawn. However, against the suggestion which has been made that everything not found elsewhere in the OT has been invented by the Chronicler to suit his purposes, it may be pointed out that a number of strong indications have been observed which point to his use of earlier material in these chapters, and if the argument that some of the material may have already passed through one stage of redaction before it reached the Chronicler be correct, then the suggestion of pure invention even at an earlier stage seems less probable, though it must be admitted, not impossible.

8. 'We are Yours, O David': The Setting and Purpose of 1 Chronicles 12:1-23

1 Chronicles 12:1-23[1] is made up of four short paragraphs, each one of which illustrates the accumulating support for David during the period before his elevation to the throne. The opening sentence of each paragraph makes this theme clear: 'Now these are they that came to David' (verse 1); 'And of the Gadites there separated themselves unto David ...' (verse 9); 'And there came ... unto David' (verse 17); 'there fell away some to David' (verse 20), while the concluding verse 23 emphasizes the theme even more strongly:

For from day to day there came to David to help him, until it was a great host, like the host of God.[2]

The section would thus seem to be closely related to the aim of 1 Chron. 11-12 as a whole.

Despite this, however, there are those – principally Noth and Rudolph[3] – who argue that these verses are a later addition to the Chronicler's work. They give two main reasons. First, it is thought that they interrupt the connection between 11:10-47 and 12:24ff.[4] Both these passages deal with those who came to David's coronation at Hebron. It is recognized, of course, that 11:11 ff., being based on 2 Sam. 23:8-39, was not originally concerned with this, but 11:10 shows clearly that this is indeed the new setting in which the Chronicler has

---

[1] In this article the verse numbers throughout refer to the Hebrew Bible. It should be noted that the English versions combine 1 Chron. 12:4 and 5 into one, so that thereafter until the end of the chapter the English verse numbers are one lower than the Hebrew.

[2] While we may recognize in the divine name here an expression for the superlative (e.g. KIMḤI; J.M.P. SMITH, AJSL 45 (1928-29), 212f., and C. HOUTMAN, VT 28 (1978), 38, n. 2), the context suggests that it may not refer so much to numerical strength (cf. NEB: 'an immense army') as to the quality of the troops who came to support David. P.D. MILLER, however, argues against attributing any superlative force to the divine name in this passage: 'In light of the prior use of gādôl, the sentences make better sense when it is seen as a comparison between the greatness or size of David's army and the greatness or size of God's army'; The Divine Warrior in Early Israel (Cambridge, Mass.,1973), 242.

[3] M. NOTH, Überlieferungsgeschichtliche Studien I (Halle, 1943), 115-16; W. RUDOLPH, Chronikbücher (HAT; Tübingen, 1955), 103-107. They have been followed more recently by J.M. MYERS, I Chronicles (AB; Garden City, 1965), 95, and R. MOSIS, Untersuchungen zur Theologie des chronistischen Geschichtswerkes (Freiburg, 1973), 49.

[4] Noth, in fact, argues that 12:24ff. is itself a secondary expansion of 11:10-47, and that 12:1-23 must therefore be an even later addition.

placed it. 12:1–23, however, equally clearly does not relate to this setting. Secondly, these verses are chronologically out of order. They refer back to the time before David became king (see especially verses 1 and 20), a period in which the Chronicler does not otherwise show much interest.

A response to these arguments may be made along three separate lines. First, several elements of the style of the passage are particularly characteristic of the Chronicler. This argument is not decisive in itself, for a later editor may always imitate the style of the text on which he is working. Nevertheless, it may be claimed that in the present case the evidence is at least sufficiently strong to make the negative point that authorship by the Chronicler cannot be ruled out on this basis, and, when combined with other evidence to be noted below, may also contribute to a positive claim that his hand is to be seen at work here. Thus we may note the combination ṣinnāh wārōmaḥ, 'shield and spear', verse 9, which only occurs otherwise at 1 Chron. 12:25; 2 Chron. 11:12 (plural); 14:7; 25:5 (where the words are inverted), and compare the similar ṣinnāh waḥ^{a}nît, 'shield and spear', at 1 Chron. 12:35.[5] Again, m^{e}ṣād, 'stronghold', verses 9 and 17, occurs like this in the singular only at 1 Chron. 11:7, against its *Vorlage* in 2 Sam. 5:9, which has m^{e}ṣudāh; the combination of two plural nouns in rā'šê hā'^{a}lāpîm, 'heads of thousands' (verse 21), is particularly characteristic of the Chronicler, being something which he several times introduces elsewhere against his *Vorlage*;[6] the expression 'the God of our fathers' (verse 18) is another special favourite of the Chronicler's,[7] while the combination of prepositions in ʿaḏ l^e, verse 17, though not quite unique to him, again occurs predominantly in his work.[8] In verse 19 we find that 'the Spirit clothed itself with Amasai', the result being that he prophesied. This may be compared with the almost identical 2 Chron. 24:20, whereas in the only other passage where this idiom is used (Jud. 6:34) the result is quite different. Finally, as most commentators have recognized,[9] verse 23 is completely steeped in the Chronicler's style, and yet this verse summarizes the whole section, and it cannot have stood alone without it.

Second, we may note that the leading themes of the passage relate closely both to the immediate context and to the wider theology of the books of Chronicles as a whole. The general point about support for David has already been

---

[5] Cf. P. WELTEN, Geschichte und Geschichtsdarstellung in den Chronikbüchern (WMANT, 42; Neukirchen, 1973), 100–102.

[6] Cf. A. KROPAT, Die Syntax des Autors der Chronik verglichen mit der seiner Quellen (BZAW, 16; Giessen, 1909), 8–9; R. POLZIN, Late Biblical Hebrew: Toward an Historical Typology of Biblical Hebrew Prose (HSM, 12; Missoula, 1976), 42–43, together with my Israel in the Books of Chronicles (Cambridge, 1977), 57–58.

[7] Cf. S. JAPHET, The Ideology of the Book of Chronicles and its Place in Biblical Thought (Jerusalem, 1977), 19–23.

[8] Cf. Israel in the Books of Chronicles, 59, and the literature cited there.

[9] See especially E. L. CURTIS and A. A. MADSEN, A Critical and Exegetical Commentary on the Books of Chronicles (ICC; Edinburgh, 1910), 195 and 200.

mentioned. An associated, and more specific, emphasis is that of 'help' for David, encapsulated in the poetic fragment in verse 19:

Peace to your helpers!
For your God helps you.

Basing our analysis on the occurrence of the root ʿzr in connection with the king, we may note three related uses in Chronicles. (a) God's 'help' for the king has long been noted as a distinctive feature of the Chronicler's writing.[10] Outside the present passage, it is found at 1 Chron. 5:20; 2 Chron. 14:10 (twice. Evv. verse 11); 18:31; 25:8; 26:7, 15; and 32:8. The striking point to notice about these occurrences is that they are all peculiar to Chronicles, even though they have sometimes been added within otherwise parallel passages, presumably by the Chronicler himself. Moreover, they all relate to help in a military sense, which contrasts with the usage at 1 Chron. 15:26, where ʿzr is used for divine assistance for the Levites, rather than the king. (b) The converse of this first point is that either to seek the help of others, or oneself to help the ungodly, will lead to disaster; cf. 2 Chron. 19:2; 28:16 and 23 (twice). Again, each occurrence is peculiar to Chronicles and comes in a military context. (c) The corollary of the first two points is that of several kings it is noted that the leaders – presumably military – of Israel also helped them: for David, cf. 1 Chron. 12:34 and 39;[11] for Solomon, cf. 1 Chron. 22:17; for Uzziah, cf. 2 Chron. 26:13; and for Hezekiah, cf. 2 Chron. 32:3, all found only in Chronicles.

If these remarks summarize the position in Chronicles as a whole, it may now be observed that all three uses of ʿzr are also attested in 1 Chron. 12:1–23.[12]

---

[10] S. R. DRIVER, An Introduction to the Literature of the Old Testament (9th edn. Edinburgh, 1913), 536; CURTIS-MADSEN, 32.

[11] In both these verses the Aramaic word ʿdr is used, though with no apparent difference in meaning, as comparison of verse 39 with verse 1 makes clear. There is in addition a slight textual problem in verse 34. I follow the most widely held solution as presented in BHS.

[12] A number of scholars have argued that some of the occurrences in this chapter should be attributed rather to a second root ʿzr, meaning 'to be strong, valiant; to strengthen, to fight'. The whole issue is discussed, with full references to earlier studies, in P. D. MILLER, 'Ugaritic gẓr and Hebrew ʿzr', UF 2 (1970), 159–175. This has now been strongly challenged, however, by A. F. RAINEY, 'Ilānu rēṣūtni lillikū!', in H. A. HOFFNER (ed.), Orient and Occident (AOAT, 22; Neukirchen, 1973), 139–142, and cf. his comments in L. R. FISHER (ed.), Ras Shamra Parallels, Vol. II (Rome, 1975), 74f. and 105f.; see also P. WELTEN, 90, n. 67. In my opinion, and as far as Chronicles alone is concerned, there is no compelling reason to understand any of the verbal occurrences of ʿzr as coming from the postulated second root. A stronger case can be made out for some of the nominal forms (as in 1 Chron. 12:1), but even there it cannot be regarded as in any way conclusive. Moreover, the discussion to date has not taken sufficient note of the fact that the Chronicler has some distinctive usages of his own of htḥzq which tend to overlap with those claimed for ʿzr II, a fact which weakens the claims of the latter. Finally it may be observed that since Miller suggests that nearly all the passages referred to above may include ʿzr II, my main point would still hold good, namely that in terms of its major theme 1 Chron. 12:1–23 is indistinguishable from the outlook of the remainder of Chronicles. It is unnecessary, too, to follow K. BALTZER in relating ʿzr to obedience in some, but not all, of these passages. As the poetic fragment in

God's help for the king receives emphasis in the last line of the poem in verse 19; association with the ungodly comes in by way of a negative in verse 20, while the theme of military leaders helping the king comes no less than five times, at verses 1, 18, 19, 22, and 23. Its occurrence in both the heading and the summary of the section marks it out as a dominant theme.

So far, it has been suggested that on the basis of style and of general outlook it seems very much as though 1 Chron. 12:1–23 comes from the same hand as the remainder of these books. We may now move on thirdly, therefore, to deal with the question raised by Noth and Rudolph of the passage's chronological setting. In some ways this is never a very strong point on which to argue when dealing with the Chronicler, because he can be seen on occasions to change the order of his *Vorlage* and thus to rearrange his material on grounds quite other than strict chronology. There is abundant evidence to suggest that he assumes knowledge on the part of his readers of the earlier account of Israel's history;[13] he will therefore have expected them to realize what he was doing, and to interpret accordingly. A few examples from his account of the first part of David's reign will be sufficient to substantiate this point.

Since both the start of 1 Chron. 11 and the close of 1 Chron. 12 are dealing with David's coronation at Hebron, it is clear that the Chronicler's account of the capture of Jerusalem in 11:4–9 must be out of order.[14] His purpose in this case may well have been to develop his ideal portrayal, already begun in 11:1–3, of a united Israel centred by David on Jerusalem. Next, reference has already been made to the fact that 11:11–47 has been given a completely new context by the Chronicler, for he has brought it forward from its position at the end of David's reign in 2 Sam. 23 in order to make it part of a larger and impressive series of lists of those 'who gave him (David) strong support in his kingdom, together with all Israel, to make him king' (11:10). Finally, we may note here 1 Chron. 14, which has been inserted for theological reasons[15] from 2 Sam. 5:11–25 into the middle of the account of the transfer of the ark to Jerusalem.

In the light of this general point, it becomes now of greater interest to observe that 1 Chron. 12:1–23 is itself not arranged on a chronological basis. Rothstein,

---

12:19 makes clear, the various uses of the root are to be closely compared, but there can be no allusion to obedience in 'your God helps you'; cf. Das Bundesformular (WMANT, 4; Neukirchen, 1960), 80, n. 6.

[13] Cf. T. WILLI, Die Chronik als Auslegung: Untersuchungen zur literarischen Gestaltungen der historischen Überlieferung Israels (FRLANT, 106; Göttingen, 1972), 56–59.

[14] It is unlikely that the order here is determined solely by that of the Chronicler's *Vorlage* (so Rudolph), since elsewhere he shows himself quite free of such restrictions. Moreover, the fact that he himself probably composed the verse immediately following (11:10) shows that he must have been aware that his account was detached from its chronological context. For some discussion of the actual course of events, cf. C. E. HAUER, 'Jerusalem, the Stronghold and Rephaim', CBQ 32 (1970), 571–578.

[15] Though overpressed in some of its details, the explanation of the passage by MOSIS, 55–79, is the most illuminating.

8. 'We are Yours, O David': The Setting and Purpose of 1 Chronicles 12:1-23   119

for instance, taking the material as historically reliable, argued that a likely order would be (a) verses 17-19; (b) verses 9-16; (c) verses 1-8; and (d) verses 20-22.[16] Rather, it may be suggested that a clue to the principle of arrangement here may be found in the geographical information supplied. For each paragraph of this particular section they are Ziklag (verse 1), the stronghold (verse 9), the stronghold (verse 17) and Ziklag (verse 21), a simple chiastic arrangement. However, the arrangement does not stop there, for the lists immediately preceding and following this passage are both set in Hebron, and if the verses which introduce them, and which are almost certainly to be ascribed to the Chronicler's own hand, are compared, it will be seen at once that he has brought them into close relationship with one another:

Now these are the chiefs of the mighty men whom David had, who shewed themselves strong with him in his kingdom, together with all Israel, to make him king, according to the word of the Lord concerning Israel (11:10),

and

These are the numbers of the heads of them that were armed for war, which came to David to Hebron, to turn the kingdom of Saul to him, according to the word of the Lord (12:24).

Finally, the outer limits of chapters 11 and 12, namely 11:1-9 and 12:39-41, may be similarly compared, as they describe the actual coronation of David by all Israel at Hebron.[17] For the sake of clarity, it may be helpful to set out the whole of the pattern which thus emerges:

David's coronation at Hebron	11:1-9	a
Support for David at Hebron[18]	11:10-47	b
Support for David at Ziklag	12:1-8	c
Support for David at the stronghold	12:9-16	d
Support for David at the stronghold	12:17-19	d'
Support for David at Ziklag	12:20-23	c'
Support for David at Hebron	12:24-38	b'
David's coronation at Hebron	12:39-41	a'

While I am aware that such an analysis as this is on the one hand becoming fashionable these days and that there is, on the other hand, a right and healthy scepticism on the part of many concerning its validity, I would urge its legitimacy in the present case on three grounds. First, it is based on the major topic of

---

[16] J.W. ROTHSTEIN and J. HÄNEL, Das erste Buch der Chronik (KAT; Leipzig, 1927), 242-243. Rothstein finds himself unable to explain the present order.

[17] Although 11:4-9 describes David's capture of Jerusalem, it is probable, for the reasons given above, that the Chronicler regarded these verses as an integral part of the opening paragraph; so too MOSIS, 49.

[18] Hebron is not actually mentioned in the introductory verse 11:10, but the context and the content of the verse make it clear that this is the intention. I know of no commentator who has disputed this conclusion.

each paragraph, highlighted several times, as has been noted, by the editorial insertions of the Chronicler himself. It does not depend merely on remote verbal reminiscences that have little to do with the substance of the material. Second, there are some other passages where the Chronicler uses a similar type of method in the arrangement of lists, particularly in certain parts of 1 Chron. 1–9.[19] Third, there, as here, the purpose of such an arrangement is quite clear to the reader. It is not simply an arbitrary patterning, but a specific literary device which the Chronicler uses to convey part of his message. Thus in the present instance the pattern has at its centre the earliest period at which David began to attract support (e.g. 1 Sam. 22:1–5; 23:14; 24:1) and then moves through the Ziklag period (1 Sam. 27:6 and chapters 29–30) and the assembling of the military personnel at Hebron finally to encompass the full extent of Israel at David's coronation. In this way a portrayal is artistically presented of the increasing recognition of and support for David by the people. It hardly needs saying that this fits in exactly with what has long been recognized as one of the major emphases in the Chronicler's treatment of the united monarchy. We may conclude, therefore, that to examine 1 Chron. 12:1–23 from a chronological point of view only, and then to dismiss it, is to overlook both the Chronicler's method in general, and his purpose and arrangement of material in this passage in particular.[20]

As 1 Chron. 12:1–23 is without any Biblical parallel, we have no certain way of determining to what extent the Chronicler has either invented or shaped its contents in order to arrive at the pattern just analysed. However, a discussion of the probable origins of one element of this material will enable us at least to formulate a hypothesis about this which may in turn lead to a fuller appreciation of the Chronicler's purpose and presentation.

It has already emerged from our discussion of the style and of the structure of the passage that the verses which introduce each paragraph and which conclude the whole should be attributed in their present form to the Chronicler himself. It is surprisingly widely agreed, however, that the lists and anecdotes themselves rest on good tradition and that they may doubtless be attributed to the Davidic period in general, if not to the exact time specified in the present text, rather as in the case already noted of 11:11ff.[21]

---

[19] See my 'Sources and Redaction in the Chronicler's Genealogy of Judah' in this volume, and my commentary, 1 and 2 Chronicles (NCB; London and Grand Rapids, 1982), especially on 1 Chron. 6.

[20] It should be noted that elsewhere the Chronicler does not entirely pass over the period before David's coronation in silence (contra NOTH); 11:13f. and 15ff. refer to that time, and yet all agree that the Chronicler was himself responsible for their inclusion; cf. J. GOETTSBERGER, Die Bücher der Chronik oder Paralipomenon (HSAT; Bonn, 1939), 107. One may also note 1 Chron. 17:7 and 29:27.

[21] See, for instance, A.C. WELCH, The Work of the Chronicler: Its Purpose and its Date (Schweich Lectures, 1938; London, 1939), 14; G. VON RAD, Das Geschichtsbild des chronistischen Werkes (BWANT, 54; Stuttgart, 1930), 34; also RUDOLPH; MYERS; JAPHET, 247,

Generally speaking, scholars have not been prepared to speculate further. An exception to this, however, is A. Zeron,[22] whose more detailed hypothesis must therefore be briefly examined. He argues that a number of features of the passage can best be explained if the section reflects capitulation to David by various groups at and after the time of Absalom's rebellion (2 Sam. 15-20). Thus, for instance, (a) Amasai (verse 19) is to be identified with Amasa, Absalom's general, who was later won over to David (cf. 2 Sam. 17:25; 19:13; 20:4ff.). David's initial hesitation in receiving him (verse 18) would be understandable in the circumstances; (b) the reference to crossing the Jordan (verse 16) does not fit well with the stories of David's flight from Saul, but is very appropriate in the setting proposed; (c) since David fled from Absalom to Mahanaim in Transjordan (2 Sam. 17:22, 24, 27), an explanation is provided on this view for the reference to Gad (verse 9) and part of Manasseh (verse 20), since both were Transjordanian tribes. Similarly, the men of Judah and Benjamin, mentioned in the other two paragraphs, would fit the account of 2 Sam. 19:16ff.; (d) verse 15 is closely comparable to 2 Sam. 18:1-4. Zeron conjectures that these traditions were not considered suitable for inclusion in the Succession Narrative of 2 Sam./1 Kgs, but were known to the Chronicler who, because he omitted the whole Absalom account, used the material here instead.

Zeron's theory is superficially attractive, and in view of the way the Chronicler has been seen to provide the material of his sources with quite new settings, no *a priori* objection can be raised against it. Unfortunately, however, it does not stand up to detailed scrutiny. For instance, if, as Zeron argues, David was already in Transjordan, why did the Gadites need to cross the river in order to get to him (verse 16)? Again, verses 20-22 are linked in every particular with 1 Sam. 29-30, referring not only to David's relationships with Saul, the Philistines and the people of Manasseh,[23] but also the Amalekites of 1 Sam. 30, with whom we must clearly identify 'the band of raiders' (verse 22). This paragraph, at least, is more securely linked to its overt historical setting than Zeron allows. Thirdly, Zeron's understanding of verse 15 is improbable. The final clause of the verse is admittedly cryptic. Zeron favours the interpretation represented, for instance, in the translation of RSV: 'the lesser over a hundred and the greater over a thousand'. This has the support of the Vulgate. However, as Keil observed long

---

etc. CURTIS and MADSEN (194-195), by contrast, argue strongly to the contrary, concluding that the chapter 'has no historical worth'. They fail to distinguish, however, between inherited material and the setting which the Chronicler has given it.

[22] A. ZERON, 'Tag für Tag kam man zu David, um ihm zu helfen, 1. Chr. 12, 1-22', ThZ 30 (1974), 257-261. A modified version of this article has appeared in Hebrew in Tarbiz 46 (1977), 8-16.

[23] David must have accompanied the Philistines at least as far as Aphek (1 Sam. 29:1), which lies near the territory of Manasseh, and if he had gone any further with them towards Jezreel (1 Sam. 29:11) he may even have passed through Manasseh. Either way, desertion to him at this point of 'some of the men of Manasseh' is credible.

ago,[24] we should then have expected the preposition '*al* rather than *l*ᵉ. The alternative understanding, supported by the Targum and followed by the medieval Jewish commentators and by most modern commentators and translators (e.g. RV, NEB), is thus more probably correct, namely 'the least of them a match for a hundred, the greatest a match for a thousand'. For this thought, compare Lev. 26:8; Deut. 32:30; Isa. 30:17. This verse cannot then be compared with 2 Sam. 18:1–4 to support Zeron's theory. Finally, the identity of Amasai with Amasa (the only name, apart from David, that would occur in both passages) remains conjectural. Since none of Zeron's other arguments fits the setting he proposes better than the one provided by the Chronicler, his theory must be rejected.

A quite different approach to the problem may be made by noting first that at the very heart of the chapter's structure analysed above lies a poetic fragment which most commentators have assumed to pre-date the Chronicler:

We are yours, O David;
    and with you, O son of Jesse!
Peace, peace to you,
    and peace to your helpers!
For your God helps you (verse 19).

In discussions of this verse known to me, only Ackroyd[25] has got as far as even suggesting a contrast with 2 Chron. 10:16, but the suggestion is worth exploring and developing. The verse referred to is the answer of the northern tribes to Rehoboam:

What portion have we in David?
    We have no inheritance in the son of Jesse.
Each of you to your tents, O Israel!
    Look now to your own house, David.

The contrast between the two passages is virtually complete, the one being a strong affirmation of loyalty to David, the other an equally strong rejection. The parallelism of 'David' and 'the son of Jesse' is common to both. The sentence 'each of you to your tents', indicating at best the northern tribes' withdrawal of support for the Davidic house, and at worst open hostility towards it,[26] may in either event be contrasted with 'peace to your helpers'. Finally, 'your God helps you' is the direct opposite of 'Look now to your own house'.

These are not, however, the only passages where such words are found. A shorter version of the rejection of David occurs in 2 Sam. 20:1 as the rallying call for Sheba's rebellion, and indeed there is a hint that the Chronicler was

---

[24] Cf. C.F. KEIL, Biblischer Commentar über die nachexilischen Geschichtsbücher: Chronik, Esra, Nehemia und Esther (Leipzig, 1870), 135.
[25] P.R. ACKROYD, I & II Chronicles, Ezra, Nehemiah (TBC; London, 1973), 55.
[26] Cf. P.A.H. DE BOER, Fatherhood and Motherhood in Israelite and Judean Piety (Leiden, 1974), 10.

aware of this, since in the third line his text is closer to this form of the saying than to the strictly parallel 1 Kgs 12:16.²⁷ There is one further possible example, if not of the same saying, yet at least of one that is comparable. In 1 Sam. 25, David sends ten young men to Nabal to ask for some sustenance. Their friendly greeting, 'Peace be to you, and peace be to your house, and peace be to all that you have' (verse 6), is rejected by Nabal's answer, 'Who is David? Who is the son of Jesse?' (verse 10). Since David's men had not referred to their leader as 'the son of Jesse', it is evident that Nabal is portrayed as already knowing a certain amount about him,²⁸ so that his questions are purely rhetorical, and are an expression of rejection. There are no other passages in the Old Testament where this particular parallelism occurs. (In 2 Sam. 23:1 the opening clause stands on its own as a heading and thus cannot be compared at this point.)

In attempting to evaluate this material, we may observe first that precisely in the days of the early monarchy such short sayings expressing approval or disapproval appear not to have been unusual. Two other well-known examples have survived. One is the song of the women:

Saul has slain his thousands
And David his ten thousands.

It occurs first at 1 Sam. 18:7, and is said to have been sung 'when David returned from slaying the Philistine' (verse 6). Its content, however, clearly suggests a much wider currency than just this, and this is confirmed by two later occurrences, 1 Sam. 21:12 and 29:5. The other example is the saying 'Is Saul also among the prophets?', which is said to have become proverbial. The significance of the question is by no means agreed; some suggest that it is positive towards Saul, others that it is negative, and some even think that it may be used both ways.²⁹ Fortunately, a decision on this is not necessary for our present purposes. It is enough to observe that it occurs twice (1 Sam. 10:11-12; 19:24), which suggests its widespread currency at the time.

We are now in a position to offer some conjectures about the development of the sayings concerning David. The hypothetical nature of this reconstruction is fully acknowledged, the more so as I am well aware that even what once could have been regarded as an agreed starting point, such as the historical nature of

---

²⁷ Note the inclusion of *'îš*, omitted by 1 Kgs. However, in the first words of the saying, Chronicles follows Kings rather than Samuel with *mah-lānû* rather than *'ên-lānû*. It is noteworthy that M. NOTH, Könige (BK; Neukirchen, 1968), 276f., regards the version favoured by the Chronicler as in each case more original.

²⁸ Cf. H.J. STOEBE, Das erste Buch Samuelis (KAT; Gütersloh, 1973), 447.

²⁹ In addition to the commentaries, cf. V. EPPSTEIN, 'Was Saul also among the Prophets?', ZAW 81 (1969), 287-304; L. SCHMIDT, Menschlicher Erfolg und Jahwes Initiative (WMANT, 38; Neukirchen, 1970), 103-119; J. STURDY, 'The original Meaning of "Is Saul also among the Prophets?"', VT 20 (1970), 206-213; J.H. GRØNBAEK, Die Geschichte vom Aufstieg Davids (Copenhagen, 1971), 118f.; J. LINDBLOM, 'Saul inter Prophetas', ASTI 9 (1974), 30-41; S.B. PARKER, VT 28 (1978), 278f.

the Succession Narrative, has now been forcefully questioned.[30] However, it seems reasonable to suggest on the basis of the comparable examples just mentioned that early in the days of David's rise a saying in his favour, almost in the nature of a slogan, was coined by his followers, namely, 'We are yours, O David; and with you, O son of Jesse', and that this was countered by adherents of Saul with such replies as that of Nabal. With David's establishment on the throne, however, the antagonism developed beyond a merely personal level, giving rise to Sheba's classic formulation:

We have no portion in David,
And we have no inheritance in the son of Jesse;
Every man to his tents, O Israel! (2 Sam. 20:1).

Such sayings, which circulated widely in oral form,[31] were long remembered because they expressed deeply held feelings even during the period of the united monarchy. It is no wonder, then, that it surfaced again at the division of the kingdom, but reapplied now in dynastic terms with the addition of the line, 'Look now to your own house, David'. Finally, the Chronicler, knowing the old pro-Davidic saying, developed it in the present context with vocabulary and theology of his own in order to counter the denial of God's choice of the Davidic house which this last addition implies. Hence the words '... and peace to your helpers! For your God helps you'.

Two factors point to this being both the process and the method of the Chronicler. First, these words express support for David from a group who come from Benjamin and Judah (verse 17).[32] A comparison with the position at the division of the kingdom is thereby reinforced. Secondly, it must be observed that in its present context the poem is clearly regarded as prophetic. This is apparent from the introduction, 'Then the Spirit clothed itself with Amasai', and from comparison with the other use of this expression in Chronicles at 2 Chron. 24:20. Von Rad long ago observed that in a form of speech which he labelled the levitical sermon[33] prophetic sayings are quite regularly detached from their original contexts and used almost as 'texts' by inspired speakers whose preach-

---

[30] Cf. D.M. GUNN, The Story of King David: Genre and Interpretation (JSOTSup, 6; Sheffield, 1978).

[31] Cf. M. NOTH, Könige, 276f.

[32] In view of the Chronicler's practice elsewhere, it is possible that he himself added the words 'Benjamin and', thereby underlining the contrast with the situation at the division of the kingdom; cf. WELTEN, 81, n. 18. A quite different view, however, is taken by B.Z. LURIA, 'David's Heroes from the Tribe of Benjamin' (Hebrew), Beth Mikra 60 (1974), 63–71.

[33] G. VON RAD, 'Die levitische Predigt in den Büchern der Chronik', in Festschrift Otto Procksch (Leipzig, 1934), 113–124 = Gesammelte Studien zum alten Testament (Munich, 1958), 248–261. For some recent discussion, see J.D. NEWSOME, 'Toward a New Understanding of the Chronicler and his Purposes', JBL 94 (1975), 201–217, and, more generally, D.L. PETERSEN, Late Israelite Prophecy: Studies in Deutero-Prophetic Literature and in Chronicles (SBLMS, 23; Missoula, 1977), ch. 3.

ing punctuates the Chronicler's narrative with theological interpretations of the events being recorded. The present verse is not, of course, an example of such a form, but it serves much the same purpose and has been handled in a comparable way. Bearing in mind that there has often been observed a close association between prophecy and monarchy in Chronicles,[34] we may therefore suggest that the Chronicler, knowing of this old poetic saying, was attracted to it because it provided an early indication of God's choice of David as king. He therefore emphasized its importance by presenting it as a prophetic saying, and he then added to it in order to reapply it dynastically by way of contrast with the account of the division of the kingdom. Finally, he drew attention to it by arranging it at the centre of a literary pattern which doubtless made use of other material known to him, and whose purpose is to demonstrate the steady growth of support for David up to the point of his coronation. Understood in this way, 1 Chron. 11–12 provides us with a further example of the interplay between inherited text and interpretative activity which has been at the centre of so much recent work on the books of Chronicles as a whole.

Postscript. In the discussion which followed the oral presentation of this paper the question was raised by several contributors about the translation of the poetic fragment in 1 Chron. 12:19, and of its first line in particular. The version used throughout this article (including its title) for the translation of that verse is the RSV. This represents a well established tradition of translation, and is certainly a possibility. Comparison of the ancient versions and modern commentaries on the Hebrew text, however, makes clear that there are several other reasonable possibilities, while recent research into the stylistic devices used in (especially early) Hebrew poetry suggests the further possibility of alternative line division. Clearly a full discussion would require, and deserves, an article of its own. Since no solution can claim certainty, and since my argument is not seriously affected by the issue, I have decided to retain the text as originally drafted while at the same time drawing attention by means of this note to the need for further work on this particular detail.

I should like to take this opportunity of thanking three friends who kindly read and helpfully commented on the first draft of this article: Professor J. A. Emerton, Dr. G. I. Davies and Mr. E. Ball.

---

[34] This should not be overpressed, however. See the recent balanced presentation in I. L. SEELIGMANN, 'Die Auffassung von der Prophetie in der deuteronomistischen und chronistischen Geschichtsschreibung', Congress Volume, Göttingen 1977 (VTSup, 29; Leiden, 1978), 254–284.

9. The Origins of the Twenty-Four Priestly Courses: A Study of 1 Chronicles 23–27

There is only one explicit reference in the Old Testament to the division of the Jewish priesthood into twenty-four courses, namely 1 Chron. 24:7–18. It is, nevertheless, clear from a growing wealth of evidence that the arrangement outlined there remained largely unchanged throughout the following centuries until the fall of the second temple. Since this fact is now widely recognized, there is no need to deal with it again here.[1]

At present, however, there is much less evidence on which to come to a decision about the time of origin of this system, even though such a decision is a prerequisite for establishing why it developed in the first place. The later sources do not provide much help here. E. Schürer[2] was able to show that they are not incompatible with a post-exilic date, but hesitated to be more specific. Similarly, studies of the history of Old Testament priesthood[3] tend either to avoid or to stop short of the issue, while those who approach the matter from the angle of the first century AD[4] can legitimately afford to leave the matter unresolved for their particular purposes.

---

[1] In addition to the works discussed more fully below, reference may be made in support of this statement to the following publications of texts and discussions based upon them: Y. AVI YONAH, 'A List of Priestly Courses from Caesarea', IEJ 12 (1962), 137–9; idem, 'The Caesarea Inscription of the Twenty-Four Priestly Courses', in E.J. VARDAMAN and J.L. GARRETT (ed.), The Teacher's Yoke: Studies in Memory of Henry Trantham (Waco, 1964), 46–57; J.T. MILIK, VTSup 4 (1957), 24–5; G.M. STEINDLER, 'Le mišmarōt in una iscrizione di Beit Ḥaḍir (Yemen)', AION 34 (1974), 277–82; S. TALMON in C. RABIN and Y. YADIN (ed.), Scripta Hierosolymitana 4 (1958), 168–76; P. WINTER, 'Twenty-six Priestly Courses', VT 6 (1956), 215–17; Y. YADIN, The Scroll of the War of the Sons of Light against the Sons of Darkness (Oxford, 1962), 204–6. References that have long been known were recognized to have supported this conclusion, though they could not establish it with quite the precision of the more recent discoveries; cf. 1 Macc. 2:1; Lk. 1:5–9; Josephus, Ant. vii, §§ 365f., and Life, § 2; on Against Apion ii, § 108, cf. J. JEREMIAS, Jerusalem zur Zeit Jesu (Göttingen, 1962³), 231 (ET, London, 1969, 204–5); and a number of later Jewish sources, such as M. Sukkah 5:6–8 and M. Ta'anit 4:2.

[2] Geschichte des jüdischen Volkes im Zeitalter Jesu Christi II (Leipzig, 1907⁴), 286–9 (ET II/1, 216–20).

[3] Reference need be made only to A.H.J. GUNNEWEG, Leviten und Priester (Göttingen, 1965), and A. CODY, A History of Old Testament Priesthood (Rome, 1969). R. DE VAUX, Les institutions de l'Ancien Testament II (Paris, 1960), 233, 242 and 246 (ET, London, 1965², 372, 379 and 382) refers these chapters to the post-exilic period, but gives little further detail.

[4] For instance J. JEREMIAS, Jerusalem zur Zeit Jesu, 224–34; F.F. BRUCE, New Testament History (London, 1969), 139.

Of the few who hazard a more specific discussion, the majority seem to favour the reforms of Nehemiah as the most likely setting for this development. Thus, for instance, although J. Liver[5] is right to reject the view of Y. Kaufmann[6] that there is an explicit reference to the institution in Neh. 13:30, yet he feels compelled to agree that there is no good reason why such a date should not be regarded as the most probable.

The present article, by contrast, will argue for a somewhat different conclusion, based on a more exact analysis of the setting of 1 Chron. 24:7–18 within its wider context of 1 Chron. 23–27. Two main problems will need to be dealt with. First, various literary levels have often been detected within these chapters even though no particular analysis of them can be said to enjoy a consensus. An attempt will here be made to improve on this situation. It will be suggested that there are in fact only two such levels, that 1 Chron. 24:7–18 belongs to the secondary level, and that the various passages which make up this secondary level are all ideologically inter-related. This is an important point because it gives the analysis a greater measure of self-authentication and at the same time provides a reasonable explanation, associated with the origins of the twenty-four courses, for the later process of expansion itself. Secondly, a number of commentators have observed that there is a close link between 1 Chron. 23:2 and 28:1, so that from a narrative point of view 23:3–27:34 seems to be intrusive. It will be necessary to examine this view also in order to be able to arrive at a closer dating of the material in relation to the date of the Chronicler's composition as a whole.

To start with the 'internal' analysis of these chapters, it should be observed at the outset that in their present position the context of these various lists is provided by 23:3–6a.[7] This makes clear (a) that David was personally responsible for the organization of the Levites into divisions;[8] (b) that only Levites were involved at this stage; and (c) that the Levites were sub-divided into four classes, namely those who had charge of the work in the house of the Lord, officers and judges, gatekeepers, and musicians.[9] In what follows, however,

---

[5] Chapters in the History of the Priests and Levites: Studies in the Lists of Chronicles and Ezra and Nehemiah (Hebrew. Jerusalem, 1968), 31–49.

[6] The History of Israelite Religion IV (Hebrew. Tel Aviv, 1972), 358–9 (ET, New York, 1977, 411–12).

[7] Despite most English translations, verse 6a (to $mahl^eqôt$) should be taken with what precedes, while the remainder of the verse is the heading for the following list; cf. A.C. WELCH, The Work of the Chronicler: Its Purpose and its Date (The Schweich Lectures, 1938; London, 1939), 84.

[8] It is universally agreed that the lists in their present form do not in fact go back to David's time, but reflect the arrangement of the post-exilic cult. Most telling in this regard is comparison with the related lists in Ezra-Nehemiah.

[9] The four groups of Levites are listed here in descending numerical order, whereas in the following more detailed lists which comprise the primary layer they are dealt with rather on the basis of their relationship to the centre of worship in the temple.

there is included a number of passages which are either not governed by this context or which may be held to contradict it. There is thus a *prima facie* case for assuming that some of the subsequent material has been added later, an assumption which other considerations also support.

The list of gatekeepers in 26:1–19 provides a convenient starting point for our analysis.[10] It is widely agreed first that verses 4–8 are intrusive, both because they interrupt the treatment of the family of Meshelemiah in verses 1–3 and 9, and because the house of Obed-edom, with which they deal, is not linked genealogically with the Levites, whereas the other two main families in the list are (Meshelemiah is linked with Korah in verse 1 and Hosah with Merari in verse 10). Furthermore, the numbers attributed to Obed-edom (sixty-two, verse 8) are out of all proportion with those attributed to Meshelemiah (eighteen, verse 9) and Hosah (thirteen, verse 11).[11]

If this is correct, then verses 12–18 must also have been included by the reviser, since the reference to Obed-edom (verse 15) is quite secure in its present context, and cannot be detached in the way that it could in verses 4–8. Two other considerations independently support the conclusion that verses 12–18 are secondary:

(a) Meshelemiah is here called Shelemiah. In itself, this causes no difficulty (the same man is referred to as Shallum in 1 Chron. 9:19), but we should certainly have expected that the same spelling would have been used within the same passage were it all to derive from the same author.

(b) The whole process of lot-casting for duties described in these verses seems to contradict the context as established by 23:3–6a. There, the organization of the Levites is ascribed to David, but here he is not mentioned and the implication of verse 13 is that the gatekeepers were themselves responsible for the arrangement of their duties.

Verse 19, finally, with its reference to the Korahites and the sons of Merari, seems best to be understood as the original conclusion to verses 1–3, 9–11 (cf. verses 1, 10). We may thus conclude that 1 Chron. 26:1–19 is composite. Verses 1–3, 9–11 and 19 have been later supplemented by the addition of 4–8 and 12–

---

[10] Cf. J. W. ROTHSTEIN AND J. HÄNEL, Kommentar zum ersten Buch der Chronik (Leipzig, 1927), *ad loc.,* followed by G. VON RAD, Das Geschichtsbild des chronistischen Werkes (Stuttgart, 1930), 116. WELCH, 91–3, also accepts the outline of ROTHSTEIN's literary analysis, though he reverses the historical development by which ROTHSTEIN explained his findings. W. RUDOLPH, Chronikbücher (Tübingen, 1955), 171–3, by contrast, argues that the passage is a unity. His view depends, however, on a rather different approach to these chapters as a whole which does not, in my opinion, do justice to the various lines of argument developed in this article which all point in the same direction. His discussion of the present paragraph is unsatisfactory because it does not get to grips with the substance of the arguments in favour of a literary division.

[11] It may be noted in passing that a progression can be outlined in the development of the lists of the gatekeepers in the post-exilic literature in terms of names, numbers and levitical status, namely Ezra 2:42 (Neh. 7:45); Neh. 11:19; 12:25; 1 Chron. 9:17ff. and 26:1–19. It is thus of interest to note that Obed-edom is also missing from 1 Chron. 9:17ff., which otherwise has very close links with 26:1–3 and 9.

18. The first block of material is a simple list of gatekeepers, arranged on a genealogical principle. The revision, however, has two effects. First, it introduces into a Levitical context the family of Obed-edom. Uncertainty about his status is reflected also in 1 Chron. 15–16, where it can be shown that the Chronicler himself included him amongst the singers, while a later reviser insisted that he was a gatekeeper.[12] His inclusion amongst the gatekeepers only at the stage of revision in chapter 26 thus agrees with a development attested elsewhere. Secondly, the revision supplies considerable detail about the nature of the gatekeepers' duties, arranged by the casting of lots. The numbers in verses 17–18 amount to a total of twenty-four. This cannot be directly equated with the twenty-four priestly courses, since, unlike the latter, they all functioned together, not by rotation. Nevertheless, the possibility cannot be ruled out that the number is not coincidental, and that it points to the same type of approach to cultic organization.

Moving back now to the lists of musicians in chapter 25, we find that the passage falls into two distinct parts. Verses 1–6 give a list of the musicians and their duties divided into three under the leadership of Asaph, Jeduthun and Heman. Verse 7 introduces the remainder of the chapter, since its figure of 288 is exactly the 24 x 12 of verses 9–31. This part gives an orderly presentation of the division of the singers into twenty-four courses.

Examination of these two parts of the chapter reveals that, although there are many points in common between them, there is also a number of unevennesses, indicating that here again the chapter was not originally a unity.[13] Not all the points noted here are of equal weight by any means, but it is suggested that when taken together they present a strong case for such a division of the chapter.

(a) In verses 1–6 there is a considerable emphasis on David's personal ordering of the musicians (verses 1, 2, 5, and 6), whereas in 7ff. not only is David not mentioned but also the musicians decide their duties by lot-casting (verse 8).

(b) Verses 2, 3 and 6 state that the musicians performed under the direction of their father. It is difficult to see how this could have worked out in the system of verses 9ff., where they are divided up into twenty-four separate courses.

(c) A similar point may perhaps be made about the use of instruments. In verses 1–6, these are to some extent distributed amongst the three groups (see especially verse 3), implying that they all needed to play together. In the system of twenty-four courses in 7–31, however, it must be assumed that each separate course would have contained those who could play on each type of instrument (though cf. point (f) below).

---

[12] For details, see my forthcoming commentary on 1 and 2 Chronicles in the New Century Bible series [subsequently published in 1982; cf. pp. 119–32].

[13] For some of the following observations see, in addition to the commentaries, D.L. PETERSEN, Late Israelite Prophecy: Studies in Deutero-Prophetic Literature and in Chronicles (Missoula, 1977), 64–8, although in other respects both the analysis and the conclusion presented here differ considerably from those of PETERSEN.

(d) Despite the practice of casting lots, verses 7–31 show a considerable degree of orderliness, and in many ways this corresponds to the order in verses 1–6.[14] Nevertheless, this correspondence is not complete: Joseph occurs first in verse 9, against the order of verse 2, and a few of the names occur in the two passages in slightly different forms.[15] This slight divergence within substantial overall agreement points away from the literary dependence of one passage upon the other, and indicates rather that the lists are based on the actuality of the situation at the time of composition, but that this had changed slightly between the two halves.

(e) The word *mispār* is used in different ways in verses 1 and 7. Despite the objections of most commentators,[16] its use in verse 1 with the meaning 'list' is quite acceptable as is shown by the fact that at 1 Chron. 11:11 it is introduced by the Chronicler with exactly this meaning against his *Vorlage* (2 Sam. 23:8). In verse 7, however, it is used with its more normal meaning of 'number', 'total'. An important subsidiary conclusion resulting from this observation is that it is no longer necessary to regard verses 2 ff. as intrusive in their present context, as the commentators referred to in note 16 above were obliged to do. Our much simpler analysis of the chapter into two straightforward parts is thus strengthened.

(f) Finally, I consider it possible that different types of music are intended by the two lists. In verse 7, the music is described as *šîr*, which, when used absolutely as here, means 'singing'. In verses 1–6, however, attention is focussed exclusively on the playing of instruments, and it is significant that when *šîr* is used (once only, in verse 6), it is immediately qualified by the words 'with cymbals, harps, and lyres'. Thus RSV correctly renders *šîr* in this verse by 'music'.

If, for these reasons, it is legitimate to detect two hands at work in this chapter, the question must be asked, which is secondary? Two main factors point quite

---

[14] See the diagrammatic presentation in ROTHSTEIN-HÄNEL, 453, repeated by PETERSEN, 67. Particularly striking is the fact that the order in verses 9–31 keeps together at the end the curious names of verse 4b which have been recognized as comprising either a hymnic fragment or a catalogue of five 'incipits'; for the former view, see originally H. EWALD, Ausführliches Lehrbuch der hebräischen Sprache des alten Bundes (Göttingen, 1870[8]), 680, and its development in various ways by (in addition to the commentators) E. KAUTZSCH, ZAW 6 (1886), 260; P. HAUPT, ZAW 34 (1914), 142–5; H. TORCZYNER, JBL 68 (1949), 247–9. For the latter view, cf. J. M. MYERS, I Chronicles (Garden City, 1965), 173. Whatever be the origins of this curious phenomenon, it is sufficient for our present purposes to observe with RUDOLPH (166–7) against WELCH (88–90) that the words are certainly used as proper names in the present context of both halves of the chapter.

[15] Apart from cases where the differences are merely orthographical, note *yiṣrî* (verse 11) for *ṣ^{e}rî* (verse 3), *^{a}zar'ēl* (verse 18) for *'uzzî'ēl* (verse 4) and *šûbā'ēl* (verse 20) for *š^{e}bû'ēl* (verse 4).

[16] E.g. I. BENZINGER, Die Bücher der Chronik (Tübingen and Leipzig, 1901), 75, and R. KITTEL, Die Bücher der Chronik (Göttingen, 1902), 94, followed by ROTHSTEIN-HÄNEL, WELCH, 88, et al. Their views were opposed by E. L. CURTIS and A. A. MADSEN, A Critical and Exegetical Commentary on the Books of Chronicles (Edinburgh, 1910), 276, but for unsatisfactory reasons.

clearly to verses 7–31 as the later addition. First, verses 1–6 relate closely to the context established by 23:3–6a. David is responsible for organizing the musicians, while the emphasis on the use of instruments corresponds exactly to what we would expect on the basis of 23:5. This is not true, however, of verses 7–31. Secondly, verses 7–31 have instead two links with 26:12ff., which we have already argued are secondary. Most impressive here is the close similarity between 25:8:

And they cast lots for their duties, small and great, teacher and pupil alike

and 26:13:

And they cast lots by fathers' houses, small and great alike, for their gates.

Linked with this is the orderliness of the duties in the two secondary passages, which is based upon the system of courses, and yet which is lacking in the earlier lists.

We may thus conclude our analysis of chapter 25 by noting the similarities to the results already achieved in chapter 26. The earlier strand (verses 1–6) contains genealogically based lists which correspond exactly with 23:3–6a and which, it will be argued later, are fully compatible with other parts of the Chronicler's work. The secondary material, on the other hand, seems to reflect the same outlook as that already detected in chapter 26.

We are now in a position to move back to the lists of Levites and priests in 23:6b–24:31. First of all, there is a fair measure of agreement that 23:25–32 cannot come from the same hand as the earlier part of the chapter.[17] This is principally because on the one hand verses 6b–24 (with the exception of the intrusive verses 13b–14)[18] give a genealogically related list of Levites who were to do the work for the service of the house of the Lord (verse 24), thus corresponding exactly with the context governed by 23:4, whereas, on the other hand, verses 25–32 link together both this type of Levite and the Levitical singers (verses 30–31), thereby ignoring the distinctions made in verses 4–5, distinctions which, moreover, the lists of 6b–24 and 25:1–6 evidently maintain.[19] In

---

[17] Cf. RUDOLPH, 156, etc.

[18] The explanatory expansion included in these verses is out of place in a list of heads of fathers' houses. Its outlook, however, fits in closely with the concerns of the priestly reviser who, it will be argued, was responsible for the rest of the secondary material in these chapters, together with a few short interpolations elsewhere in Chronicles.

[19] It may be mentioned here that some scholars argue towards the same conclusion on the basis of the discrepancies in verses 3, 24 and 27 over the age at which the Levites entered on their service. WELCH, 81, for instance, makes it the start of his whole analysis of these chapters. In fact, however, 24b and 27 are much later additions altogether, so that they cannot be drawn into our main discussion at all. 24b interrupts the connection between 24a and 25 (so ROTHSTEIN-HÄNEL, 419). Since verse 25 stands at the head of the passage from the reviser, 24b must be later still. For Levitical service to start at twenty years old is not envisaged in the Pentateuch, though cf. 2 Chron. 31:17; Ezra 3:8. Probably the age was changed from time to time under the pressure of circumstances. We may then surmise either

addition, it is clear from verses 28, 29 and 32 that the main purpose of these verses is to spell out the distinction between priests and Levites, in which the duty of the Levites was merely 'to assist' or 'to attend'. Here again, there is nothing in the context which would have led us to expect concentration on such a topic. In contrast with all this, however, the genealogical list which remains fits admirably after the heading in 3–6a, and provides, we may now observe, just the same sort of amplification of the first category of Levite mentioned in verse 4 as 25:1–6 and 26:1–3, 9–11 and 19 do for those in verse 5.[20]

Moving on now to 'the divisions of the sons of Aaron' in 24:1–19, we see at once that several factors already familiar from the preceding discussion mark the section in its entirety as secondary:

(a) It is intrusive in a context that is dealing exclusively with Levitical lists. It is true that priests are mentioned in 23:2, but the heading to the lists in question comes only in verses 3ff., and there the priests are not referred to. (In 23:2, the reference to priests is introduced only as a part of the stereotyped threefold division of the population current in his time; cf., for instance, 1 Chron. 13:2; 2 Chron. 30:25; 35:8; Ezra 2:70, etc. 1 Chron. 23:1–2 serves as an introduction to the whole of 23–29, and does not, therefore, oblige us to find specific references to each of the categories which it mentions in 23–27 alone, *contra* Curtis-Madsen, 260f.)

(b) That this is so is confirmed by the fact that 24:1 links closely with the end of 23, already seen as secondary.

(c) Contrary to what the context would lead us to expect, David does not act alone, but 'with the help of Zadok ... and Ahimelech' (verse 3, and cf. verse 6). This provides the first link with material already noted as secondary in 25 and 26.

(d) A further such link is that the courses of priests are organized by lot, rather than by royal appointment. In particular, we should note verse 5: 'They organized them by lot, all alike (*ʾēlleh ʿim ʾēlleh*)', which is similar to the distinctive expressions in 25:8 and 26:13 noted earlier.

---

that the glossator wished to invoke Davidic authority for the practice current in his own time, or that he simply aimed at explaining away the difference between 1 Chron. 23:3 and 2 Chron. 31:17. Verse 27 also interrupts the evident continuity between verses 26 and 28. It is a misplaced gloss on 24b, seeking to explain the discrepancy with verse 3. It is not very apt, however, because the whole extended section, introduced at 23:1, is properly to be regarded as 'the last words of David'.

[20] Many scholars have argued that there were originally twenty-four heads of fathers' houses in this passage, even though the present text gives only twenty-two (or twenty-three, according to CURTIS-MADSEN, 263–6); in addition to the commentaries, particularly the older ones, cf. M. BERLIN, 'Notes on Genealogies of the Tribe of Levi in 1 Chron. xxiii–xxvi', JQR 12 (1900), 291–8. There is no primary textual evidence for such speculations, however; they are based merely on the prior assumption, contested in this article, that the twenty-four courses should be reflected here. In the absence of other evidence, it is better method to accept the text as it stands.

(e) A final link with the other secondary material is provided by the fact that the courses number exactly twenty-four, a situation nowhere reflected in the primary material.

The passage as a whole is favourable to the priesthood. This is clear not only from its connection with the end of 23, but also from the way in which a past failing of the priestly house is covered over (verse 2; cf. Lev. 10:1-2; Num. 3:4). The pro-priestly inclinations of the reviser, apparent now from this chapter, as well as from 23:13b-14 and 28 ff., will enable us later to link the whole of his work in 23-27 with some other comparable revisions elsewhere in 1 Chronicles.

At the end of chapter 24 there is appended a fragmentary list of 'the rest of the sons of Levi' (verses 20-31). On the whole, it continues the genealogy of 23:6b ff. one generation further by recapitulating parts of it in the same order and then extending it. All reference to the family of Gershon, however, is omitted. This provides us with the first piece of evidence that the passage cannot have been included by the original author of 23, for, as Welch (84) observes, when David was organizing the Levites into divisions (23:6), 'he could not have both included and excluded the Gershonites: nor could he have set over his courses at the same time a body of men and their sons'. In support of this conclusion we may observe first that the paragraph is integrally tied to 24:1-19, itself secondary (compare verse 31 with verse 3, and note too the comparison with 'the sons of Aaron'; the expression $l^{e\zeta}ummat\ {}^{\gimel a}\hbar\hat{e}hem$ also occurs at 26:12), and, second, that the Levites cast lots for their duties rather than being organized by David.

Why did the reviser add this curious section? Clearly, he was bringing the situation up to date, which seems to have involved the addition of one generation.[21] In addition to this, however, verse 31 suggests that he intended to reach a total of twenty four courses for the Levites as in the previous case of the priests, thus marking an advance over the list in 23. Quite how he did so is not clear to us, especially as the sons of Gershon (23:7-11) are not taken into account here, but appreciation of his intention is sufficient for our present purposes.

At the end of chapters 23-27, there are two passages which have not yet been dealt with. Both raise many questions which cannot be discussed here. We shall confine our remarks exclusively to the prior issue of their literary status.

First, in 26:20-32 details are supplied of the duties of various Levites. Although many commentators divide it into several unconnected sections, it does in fact constitute a single unit because of the overarching genealogical framework supplied by the four Kohathites listed in verse 23 (cf. 23:12).[22] It seems probable that the paragraph has been extracted from some other more extensive source because (a) despite their introduction in verse 23, and unlike the other

---

[21] The text certainly seems to have suffered corruption in some places, but the emendations suggested by the majority of commentators do not alter the position set out above.

[22] So correctly in this respect RUDOLPH, 176-7.

three families mentioned there, the Uzzielites are not referred to in the sequel, and (b) some of the people mentioned here have already been listed in 23:6b ff.; as it is unlikely that they served simultaneously in two of the four categories of 23:4f., this discrepancy points to the separate origin of the material.

Such a slight inconsistency is insufficient in itself, however, to relegate the paragraph to the secondary level, for even if he was aware of it the compiler of the primary layer had strong motive to include this extract, namely that its reference to some Levites who acted as 'officers and judges' (verse 29) corresponds to the fourth category listed in the heading at 23:4f. Moreover, such other considerations as there are support the view that this passage is primary: all those listed are Levites, and they are grouped genealogically, as elsewhere in the primary material. Similarly, David's authority over them is exercised directly (vese 32). At the same time, however, none of the features of the secondary material is to be found here.

Finally, the whole of chapter 27 is to be regarded as secondary, since it is neither related to the Levites, nor deals with David's final arrangements, but describes rather his reign in general. It is thus quite unrelated to the context governed by 23:3–6a. The numbers in verses 1–15 (twelve divisions of 24,000 each), though not found elsewhere, reflect the orderly outlook of material already established as secondary; cf. especially 25:9–31.[23] Thus, while I believe it can be shown that for each of the four paragraphs which make up this chapter the reviser was drawing on earlier material and that he has reshaped this to make it serve his own particular purposes, yet nevertheless what matters for us in the present context is that none of this is to be attributed to the primary layer of 1 Chron. 23–27.

We may now summarize the discussion so far by observing that there are two main strands of material in 1 Chron. 23–27. The primary strand is made up of 23:6b–13a, 15–24, 25:1–6, 26:1–3, 9–11, 19, and 26:20–32. It may be stressed that each of these four short sections is governed by one of the categories of Levite listed in 23:3–6a. In each case David is himself responsible for their

---

[23] The artificial nature of 27:1–15 is clear from the fact that (a) the names of the commanders are drawn from the list of David's heroes in 11:11 ff., even though historically they could not also have been commanders of large divisions; Asahel (verse 7), for instance, was killed before David became king over the whole of Israel (2 Sam. 2:18–23), and though the inclusion of 'his son Zebadiah after him' shows awareness of this difficulty, it does not in fact remove the anachronism. It may be noted, however, that there are enough small differences between the two forms of the list to suggest that the dependence was not direct; and (b) a national, conscripted army, unlike a professional standing army, was called to arms only in time of war; cf. DE VAUX, II, 29 (ET, 227). There is no evidence whatever for the very improbable suggestion of this paragraph that civilians were conscripted for a month's service each year, despite the characteristically spirited discussion by Y. YADIN, The Art of Warfare in Biblical Lands (London, 1963), 279–84. In view of all this, the probability that the reviser was here working under the influence of the recently introduced system of twenty-four courses, which he has extended in a utopian manner to other areas of David's secular administration, is enhanced.

organization, and they each present little more than a genealogically based list (though there is rather more elaboration in the final paragraph).

Most of the secondary material likewise has a number of factors in common, a fact which lends support to the literary analysis for which I have argued. These have been noted during the discussion. Historically, the most significant of these is that only in this secondary layer, and then consistently, do we find reference to the twenty-four courses. Since this revision must at the earliest be later than the date of the Chronicler himself, it enables us to establish a *terminus post quem* for this development on more reliable grounds than those of general probability, and rather later than what was noted at the start of this article as the general view.

Is it possible, however, to be yet more specific? I believe it is, provided (a) the relationship of the primary layer to the work of the Chronicler himself can be established, and (b) there is some indication of the length of time between this layer and the work of the reviser.

Several factors favour the inclusion of the primary layer into his work by the Chronicler himself, despite the contrary view of many commentators, to be examined shortly. First, some such material is to be expected on the basis of the general context. From 1 Chron. 17 onwards, the Chronicler's overriding concern is David's preparations for the building of the temple. Just as in chapters 15–16 he is concerned to explain the new role of the Levites after the ark has been brought to Jerusalem, so it is not at all surprising to find that he goes on at this point to make some reference to the preparation by David for their ordering in the future temple. This point is further supported by such passages as 2 Chron. 8:14, 23:18 and 35:4, where explicit reference is made to David's ordering of the Levites. If we regard the whole of 23–27 as secondary, these passages are left without adequate antecedent. The same point may be urged even more specifically on the basis of 1 Chron. 29:8, which clearly presupposes 26:21, but which (despite Rudolph, 185 and 191) there is no reason to regard as a later addition.[24]

Secondly, the reconstructed lists of the primary layer fit in well with the stage of development in the Levitical orders during the postexilic period reflected in other parts of Chronicles, while the revision isolated here is similarly of a piece with that found elsewhere. A full discussion of this would take us far beyond our subject,[25] but one or two of the most obvious examples may be briefly referred to.

---

[24] Since RUDOLPH regards the whole of 1 Chron. 23–27 as additional, he is obliged also to regard various other allusions in 1 Chron. 28–29 as introduced later under its influence. Some of these become unnecessary in the context of the present analysis. The only convincing example is 28:1, where the titles seem to be based on those of 27. I should agree that here the reviser has continued his work for a few lines beyond the end of 27 by including these titles after 28:1a in order to integrate his additions with the continuing narrative of the Chronicler.

[25] The most detailed single collection of material for such comparative purposes is J. LIVER, Chapters in the History of the Priests and Levites, though my conclusions differ quite markedly from his.

The post-exilic development in the guilds of singers has been analysed in some detail by H. Gese.²⁶ He isolates the following four stages:

I. At the return from the exile, the singers are simply called 'sons of Asaph', and are not yet reckoned as Levites (Ezra 2:41; Neh. 7:44);

II. Neh. 11:3–19 and 1 Chron. 9:1–18, from Nehemiah's time. The singers are now reckoned as Levites, and are in two groups, the sons of Asaph and the sons of Jeduthun;

III. A 1 Chron. 16:4ff.; 2 Chron. 5:12, 29:13f., 35:15. The levitical singers are now in three groups, Asaph, Heman and Jeduthun;

III. B 1 Chron. 6:31ff. and 15:16ff. Jeduthun is replaced by Ethan, and Heman is now more prominent than Asaph.

In the passage under discussion, the singers in 25:1 are listed in the order Asaph, Heman and Jeduthun, which is the same as Gese's III A. However, the numbers attributed to each family indicate the increasing prominence of Heman (verse 5), thus bringing it a little closer towards III B. Against Gese, I take stage III B to reflect the period of the Chronicler himself.²⁷ He could thus well have included 25:1–6 in his account, whereas any attempt to make these verses later than him is virtually ruled out by the fact that Jeduthun has still not been replaced by Ethan.

Similarly, in the case of the gatekeepers it was shown above that Obed-edom was only included amongst them by the reviser, not by the primary layer. Although this is admittedly only negative evidence, this latter reflects the same outlook as the Chronicler himself, whereas it is the reviser of 1 Chron. 15–16 who insists on his status as a gatekeeper (cf. 15:21 and 16:5, but contrast 15:18, 24 and 16:38). Conversely, if 26:1–3, 9–11 and 19 be set within the development of the lists of gatekeepers in Ezra, Nehemiah and Chronicles, it will be found that it fits the period of the Chronicler admirably.²⁸

The clearest, though by no means the only, evidence that the work of the Chronicler has been revised by some one with priestly sympathies comes from 1 Chron. 15–16.²⁹ Thus, for instance, though 'the sons of Aaron' occur in 15:4,

---

²⁶ H. GESE, 'Zur Geschichte der Kultsänger am zweiten Tempel', in O. BETZ, M. HENGEL and P. SCHMIDT (ed.), Abraham unser Vater: Juden und Christen im Gespräch über die Bibel. Festschrift für Otto Michel zum 60. Geburtstag (Leiden, 1963), 222–34, = Vom Sinai zum Zion: Alttestamentliche Beiträge zur biblischen Theologie (Munich, 1974), 147–58.

²⁷ Here I can only refer to my commentary (above, n. 12), especially on 1 Chron. 15–16, for details. In fact, my main point holds even on GESE's view.

²⁸ Cf. note 11 above for the material.

²⁹ I should nevertheless dissociate myself quite emphatically from the radical divisions of the Chronicler's text proposed in different forms by ROTHSTEIN-HÄNEL, WELCH, and K. GALLING, Die Bücher der Chronik, Esra, Nehemia (Göttingen, 1954). Nor do I find nearly so much scattered secondary material as RUDOLPH; for one example, cf. my Israel in the Books of Chronicles (Cambridge, 1977), 71–82. The pro-priestly reviser's work generally consists of little more than the addition of a verse or two here and there to make clear the distinction

they are not mentioned in the more detailed list which follows (verses 5–10). Again, though 'the priests Zadok and Abiathar' are referred to in verse 11, David goes on to address only 'the heads of the fathers' house of the Levites' in verse 12. Further, although 'the priests and the Levites sanctified themselves to bring up the ark' in verse 14, verses 15 and 25 ff. refer only to the activity of the Levites. It is likely, therefore, that these references were added by someone who took his cue from the mention of sacrifices later on, just as the inclusion of 'trumpets' in 15:28 (contrast their absence from the list of 19–21) probably led to the addition of 24b*a* on the basis of the fact that in the Pentateuch and elsewhere it was the priests alone who blew them (Num. 10:8; 31:6; cf. Neh. 12:35, 41).

It may thus be concluded both that the primary layer of 1 Chron. 23–27 can be attributed to the Chronicler,[30] and that it has been subjected to the same type of revision, even if more extensive, as his work in other passages.

Why, then, have so many commentators adopted a contrary view? The answer is simply that the passage as a whole appears to interrupt the connection between 23:2 and 28:1.[31] Such an argument is not sufficient to overthrow our earlier conclusion. First, once it is realized how relatively small is the amount of material to be attributed to the primary layer, full weight may be given to R.J. Coggins's comment that 'this would not have been regarded as an interruption by the original readers in the way that we should so consider it'.[32] We have always to beware of imposing modern standards of literary appreciation on an ancient author.

Secondly, closer examination of 23:2 and 28:1 leads us to question whether they really support the process of interruption which has been claimed. If the material was inserted quite so clumsily as is suggested, we should not have expected any overlap between 23:2 and 28:1, whereas if a later scribe were trying to point out the interruption we should have expected him to repeat the sentence exactly. In fact from the point of view of vocabulary they have very little in common (for instance, the word for 'assembled' is different in each case, 23:2 using *'sp*, 28:1 using *qhl*).

---

between priests and Levites. Thus his treatment of 1 Chron. 23–27 is quite unparalleled in its extent.

[30] Where there are some slight inconsistencies (actually barely noticeable in the primary layer), on which RUDOLPH particularly lays heavy emphasis, they may be explained as due to the Chronicler incorporating originally independent material without feeling the need to make them conform in every particular. This too is attested elsewhere in his work; for an example, cf. my 'Sources and Redaction in the Chronicler's Genealogy of Judah', JBL 98 (1979), 351–9 (above, 106–14).

[31] So, for instance, M. NOTH, Überlieferungsgeschichtliche Studien 1 (Halle, 1943; Tübingen, 1967²), 112–15; RUDOLPH, 152; T. WILLI, Die Chronik als Auslegung: Untersuchungen zur literarischen Gestaltung der historischen Überlieferung Israels (Göttingen, 1972), 196f.

[32] The First and Second Books of the Chronicles (Cambridge, 1976), 118.

Thirdly, what we do have here is a literary device that seems to have been quite popular at this time and which is found elsewhere in the Chronicler's work, namely 'repetitive resumption'.[33] Other examples of this device show both that it need not involve verbally exact repetition, so long as the resumption is clear, and that it is used precisely to allow the inclusion of material germane to the author's main purpose which does not, however, exactly fit his narrative sequence. This, it may be suggested, was just the Chronicler's position. He wanted to include details of David's final ordering of the Levites because of their great importance to his overall interests, but could not find a point at which to fit them smoothly into his narrative. His use of this device, therefore, far from supporting the view of those who regard the whole of 23–27 as secondary, encourages us rather to trace the inclusion of the Levitical lists in their original short form back to the Chronicler himself.

The date of Chronicles remains a controversial issue, but one in the later part of the Persian period, around 350 BC, still seems to satisfy the evidence best.[34] Most recently the attempt has been made by several scholars to revive the theory of a sixth century date,[35] but I have set out elsewhere my reasons for disagreeing with this position.[36] The important question that remains, however, is the length of time between the work of the Chronicler and that of the reviser. Our preceding discussion has revealed one or two factors that suggest it was not more than a single generation.

First, in the case of the supplement to 23:6b–24 in 24:20–31, it was necessary to add only one generation to the earlier material, presumably amongst other things to bring it up to date. Secondly, it was found that the differences in order and names of the singers between the two halves of chapter 25 could best be explained on the basis of a development of the actual situation at the time of composition. Since these differences are only slight, and since overall there is substantial agreement, the time gap is likely to have been quite short. I thus conclude that the priestly reviser worked only a single generation after the Chronicler himself, and that he already presupposed the completed develop-

---

[33] The term seems to have been coined by S. TALMON, The Interpreter's Dictionary of the Bible, Supplementary Volume (Nashville, 1976), 322, who gives examples from Ezra-Nehemiah. See also the remarks of P. WELTEN, Geschichte und Geschichtsdarstellung in den Chronikbüchern (Neukirchen-Vluyn, 1973), 190f., and T.C. BUTLER, VT 28 (1978), 146. The device is found, *inter alia*, at 1 Chron. 4:1 (see the article referred to in note 30 above), 5:3 (resumption of 5:1a), 15:11 (resumption of the substance of verses 4–10), 16:37 (resumption of 16:4–7), and so on.

[34] See Israel in the Books of Chronicles, 83–6, for a survey of the main points at issue.

[35] F.M. CROSS, 'A Reconstruction of the Judean Restoration', JBL 94 (1975), 4–18; J.D. NEWSOME, 'Toward a New Understanding of the Chronicler and his Purposes', JBL 94 (1975), 201–17; D.L. PETERSEN, Late Israelite Prophecy, 57–60. These writers acknowledge the stimulus of an earlier, brief article by D.N. FREEDMAN, 'The Chronicler's Purpose', CBQ 23 (1961), 436–42.

[36] In the course of an article entitled 'Eschatology in Chronicles', Tyndale Bulletin 28 (1977, but published in 1979), 115–54 (below, 162–95).

ment of the system of twenty-four courses. A date for this development at the close of the Persian period thus seems most probable.[37]

The only evidence which might tell against this conclusion is the reference to Jehoiarib in 24:7. It has been argued by a number of scholars that since in other lists he occurs further down, if at all, the present order can date only from the Maccabean period, since the family of the Maccabees belonged to this family (1 Macc. 2:1).[38] This point is not sufficient, however, to overthrow our previous conclusion. First, the most that this evidence could prove would be that the position of Jehoiarib within the list had been altered through later influence.[39] Liver, for instance, has argued (pp. 36–7) that, since the sectarians at Qumran presupposed the existence of the twenty-four courses in their alteration of it to twenty-six, the system itself must pre-date the Hasmonaean period. Secondly, however, it is not necessarily so certain that the family of Jehoiarib was not prominent before the rise of the Maccabees. Rothstein-Hänel, 433 ff., argued that he was on the basis of his ascendancy through some of the lists in Ezra, Nehemiah and Chronicles, though it must be admitted that not all would accept the integrity of the text in the passages they cite. Others have argued towards a similar conclusion on the basis of the phraseology of 1 Macc. 2:1 itself.[40] Finally, Myers (pp. lxxxvii and 165), on the basis of the attestation of Chronicles from Qumran, finds it hard to accept that any part of it could derive from so late a date, though this argument is questionable. We may nevertheless conclude that various explanations for the position of Jehoiarib in 1 Chron. 24:7 are possible, and that therefore the date for the origins of the twenty-four courses argued for above on the basis of wider and more reliable considerations is not affected by it.

The sources available do not suggest any particular reason for the development of the system of twenty-four courses, nor are we sufficiently well informed about the situation in Jerusalem at the end of the Persian period to do more than indulge in speculation on this issue. It is possible that it represents no more than another, though in this case ultimately definitive, step in that development

---

[37] This date, of course, depends on accepting my date for the composition of Chronicles as a whole. Nevertheless, the literary analysis of 1 Chron. 23–27 and the consequent *relative* dating of the two strands presented above is not affected by this, and may be judged separately on its own merits.

[38] This argument goes back at least as far as SCHÜRER. In addition to a number of the commentaries and other works already referred to, see the cautious remarks of P.R. ACKROYD, 'Criteria for the Maccabean Dating of Old Testament Literature', VT 3 (1953), 113–32 (126–7).

[39] This is the view, for instance, of CURTIS-MADSEN, 269, and DE VAUX, 266 (ET, 397), and it is allowed, at least, by RUDOLPH, 161–2.

[40] P.R. ACKROYD, 127, n. 2, develops this suggestion with appeal to the comments of F.-M. ABEL, Les livres des Maccabées (Paris, 1949²), 30. It is also assumed in the recent major commentary of J.A. GOLDSTEIN, I Maccabees (Garden City, 1976), 17, and see the discussion of the issue by M. STERN, in S. SAFRAI and M. STERN (ed.), The Jewish People in the First Century II (Assen, 1976), 589.

which has often been traced through the historical books of the post-exilic period. On the other hand, it seems more probable that some specific cause underlies what must have been a quite widespread reform of the temple personnel. Two possibilities may be suggested. First, a strong case has been made out for the view that at about this time a substantial number of priests left Jerusalem for Shechem, where they became an important element in the development of the Samaritan community as known from later times.[41] This secession would certainly have necessitated a measure of reorganization in Jerusalem, and it is noteworthy in this respect that the list of priests in 24:7-18 has far less contact with earlier lists of priests than do the lists of other cultic officials in the revision of 1 Chron. 23-27 with their antecedents.

A second possibility relates to the rather obscure incident related by Josephus (Ant. 11 §§ 297-301), which tells how the high priest Joannes murdered his brother in the temple, as a result of which the Persian Bagoses (Bagoas)

> defiled the sanctuary and imposed tribute on the Jews, so that before offering the daily sacrifices they had to pay from the public treasury fifty drachmae for every lamb,

a measure which we are told lasted for seven years. Since this incident is to be dated to our period,[42] and indeed may not be unconnected with the first possibility outlined above, the disruption it undoubtedly caused to the regular temple services may have contributed to the development of the courses.

The main conclusions of this discussion may now be briefly summarized. There are two main literary layers in 1 Chron. 23-27. The earlier, very much shorter, layer was part of the Chronicler's original composition. The second was added about a generation later by a pro-priestly reviser under the impact of the institution of the system of twenty-four courses. This establishes a date for the introduction of this institution in the closing years of the Persian period, a time when at least two events for which we have independent evidence connected with the Jerusalem priesthood might well have demanded such a reorganization.

---

[41] Cf. H.G. KIPPENBERG, Garizim und Synagoge: Traditionsgeschichtliche Untersuchungen zur samaritanischen Religion der aramäischen Periode (Berlin, 1971), 50-9, and my development of his arguments in Israel in the Books of Chronicles, 137-8.

[42] See my discussion in 'The Historical Value of Josephus' *Jewish Antiquities* xi. 297-301', JTS, ns 28 (1977), 49-66 (above, 74-89). M. STERN, 589-90, also draws attention to the relevance of this incident to our present concern, but he dates it considerably earlier than I do.

10. The Accession of Solomon in the Books of Chronicles

Scholarly interest in the nature and purpose of the books of Chronicles has increased rapidly in recent years. Whilst this in itself is to be greatly welcomed, there remains the danger that general surveys and studies may outstrip the detailed analyses upon which such generalizations should be based. In this article, it will first be argued that the Chronicler modelled the transition of rule from David to Solomon on that from Moses to Joshua at the end of Deuteronomy and the beginning of Joshua; secondly, reasons will be suggested as to why the Chronicler may have drawn this parallel; and finally, attention will be directed to a few implications of this observation for study of the books as a whole.

A.

There are five main elements in the Chronicler's account of Solomon's accession which suggest that he was influenced by the narrative of the succession of Joshua. It is in this accumulation of parallels that the force of the Chronicler's intention is felt.

Firstly, David's disqualification from building the temple is directly linked in Chronicles with the succession of Solomon in a way that is not the case in Samuel/Kings. This is brought out both in David's private charge to his son (1 Chron. 22:6ff.) and in his public declaration (28:2–8). Similarly in Deuteronomy, the fact that Moses is not allowed to lead the people across Jordan into Canaan is directly associated with the appointment of Joshua as his successor in order to fulfil this function (Deut. 1:37f.; 31:2f.). It may perhaps have been this that influenced the Chronicler in his reasoning as to the cause of Solomon's suitability to build the temple, namely that he was a man to whom the Lord gave peace and rest (1 Chron. 22:9, 18),[1] for this was also the mark of the successful completion of Joshua's task (Josh. 11:23; 21:44 etc.).

Secondly, both in form and expression, the 'installation' of Solomon itself parallels that of Joshua. From the form-critical point of view, the installation of

---

[1] Cf. R. Mosis, Untersuchungen zur Theologie des chronistischen Geschichtswerkes (Freiburger theologische Studien, 92; Freiburg, 1973), 94–101.

Joshua has been made the subject of a special study by Lohfink,[2] and although he had already suggested parallels from other parts of the Bible (including 1 Chron. 22 and 28), it was left to McCarthy to work these out more fully.[3] McCarthy accepted Lohfink's general position, but suggested that he had sought to define the elements of the *genre* too rigidly. After a study of all the relevant texts, McCarthy proposed the following definition: (I) Encouragement; (II) Description of task; (III) Assurance of divine aid. The phrases used, and indeed the order in which they occur, are governed by the demands of the task in hand. The *genre* is found in its simplest form at Deut. 31:23: 'And he gave Joshua the son of Nun a charge and said, (I) Be strong and of a good courage: (II) for thou shalt bring the children of Israel into the land which I sware unto them: (III) and I will be with thee'. If this refers to the first of Joshua's tasks, whose fulfilment is described in Josh. 1-12, installation to the second of his tasks (fulfilled in Josh. 13-21) is found in Josh. 1:6, 9b: '(I) Be strong and of a good courage: (II) for thou shalt cause this people to inherit the land which I sware unto their fathers to give them .... (III) The Lord thy God is with thee whithersoever thou goest'.[4]

Now whilst it may not be compelling to speak here of a fixed and widespread form, these studies do at least help point out similarities to the charge of David to Solomon. The elements as analysed by McCarthy, and indeed often the very same words, are found three times in 1 Chronicles. In chapter 22, after the introductory statement of vv. 1-10, David turns to the essence of his charge: 'Now, my son, (III) the Lord be with thee; (I) and prosper thou, (II) and build the house of the Lord thy God'. In I Chron. 28:10, the same elements occur, as observed by McCarthy, who analyses the verse thus: 'Yahweh's assistance is assured (he has chosen Solomon), the task is stated (build the temple), and the encouragement given, "be brave and active" ($h^azaq\ wa^{\prime a}\acute{s}\bar{e}h$). Once more, all the elements are there and in language fitted to the occasion'.[5] Finally, we may point to 1 Chron. 28:20: 'And David said to Solomon his son (I) be strong and of good courage, (II) and do it: (III) fear not, nor be dismayed: for the Lord God, even my God, is with thee; he will not fail thee, nor forsake thee'.

Not only in form, but also in phraseology, there is much that directly parallels Deut. 31 and Josh. 1, both in the verses already cited, and in others from the

---

[2] N. LOHFINK, 'Die deuteronomistische Darstellung des Übergangs der Führung Israels von Moses auf Josue. Ein Beitrag zur alttestamentliche Theologie des Amtes', Scholastik 37 (1962), 32-44.

[3] D.J. MCCARTHY, 'An Installation Genre?', JBL 90 (1971), 31-41, amplifying his remarks in Treaty and Covenant: A Study in Form in the Ancient Oriental Documents and in the Old Testament (Analecta Biblica, 21; Rome, 1963), 143f.

[4] According to LOHFINK (p. 37), Josh. 1:7-9a is secondary to the main thought of the passage (if not to the composition itself), and hence should not be included in the form-critical analysis.

[5] MCCARTHY, 'An Installation Genre?', 33. On page 37, he conjectures that the whole of chapter 22 'has grown out of 1 Chron 28:10'.

10. The Accession of Solomon in the Books of Chronicles 143

same context. The following is a list of the commonest of these recurring phrases and ideas:

$h^a zaq\ we^{,e} mas$ – Deut. 31:7, 23; Josh. 1:6, 7, 9; 1 Chron. 22:13; 28:20 (cf. Deut. 31:6 and 1 Chron. 28:10).

$^{,}al$-$tîrā^{,}\ w^{e,}al$-$tēḥāṯ$ and equivalents – Deut. 31:8; Josh. 1:9; 1 Chron. 22:13; 28:20 (cf. Deut. 31:6).

$^{c}imm^{e}kā\ yhwh\ ^{,e}lohêkā$ and equivalents – Deut. 31:6, 8, 23; Josh. 1:5, 9; 1 Chron. 22:11, 16; 28:20; 2 Chron. 1:1.

$lo^{,}\ yarp^{e}kā\ w^{e}lo^{,}\ ya^{c}az^{e}ḇekā$ and equivalents – Deut. 31:6, 8; Josh. 1:5; 1 Chron. 28:20.

The stress on prospering through observance of the law – Deut. 31:5; Josh. 1:7f.[6]; 1 Chron. 22:12f.; 28:7f., 9.

Attention has been drawn to another related term by J.R. Porter in his discussion of 'The Succession of Joshua'.[7] Porter's main concern is to demonstrate that the Deuteronomic account of the succession of Joshua was based upon 'the practice that marked the transmission of the royal office from one king to another'.[8] He thus approaches these passages from the opposite angle to that of the present paper. Of the points that he adds to the analyses of Lohfink and McCarthy, one is relevant here, namely that 'the words of installation are described as a solemn charge, expressed by the *Pi'ēl* of the root צוה' (p. 107). He refers to Num. 27: 19, 23; Deut. 31:14, 23; Josh. 1:9; 1 Kgs 2:1; 1 Chron. 22:6; 2 Chron. 19:9.

Closer examination, however, reveals that Porter has overlooked a small but significant distinction between some of these passages which would tend to draw closer together the passages which we are considering here against the others which he lists. In each case apart from the verses in Deuteronomy and Joshua, the subject of the verb is the man concerned: Moses, David, Jehoshaphat. In Deut. 31:14, 23 and Josh. 1:9, by contrast, the subject of the verb is God Himself. Similarly, in 1 Chron. 22:12, not mentioned by Porter, we find the same situation prevailing: David says to Solomon, 'Only the Lord give thee discretion and understanding, and give thee charge concerning Israel ($wîṣaww^{e}kā\ ^{c}al$-$yiśrā^{,}ēl$); that so thou mayest keep the law of the Lord thy God'. This may then be compared with Deut. 31:14, but contrasted with 1 Kgs 2:1.[9]

---

[6] Naturally, the influence of such a verse as this upon the Chronicler would not have been diminished out of consideration for Lohfink's form-critical analysis!

[7] In J.I. DURHAM and J.R. PORTER (eds.), Proclamation and Presence. Old Testament Essays in Honour of Gwynne Henton Davies (London, 1970), 102–132.

[8] If the argument of the present paper is sound, namely that there is direct literary influence of Deuteronomy/Joshua on Chronicles on in this matter, then PORTER's thesis will be weakened in that a good deal of the evidence he presents is based on Chronicles.

[9] In 1 Chron. 22:6, where David 'charges' Solomon, it is only, and explicitly, to build the temple, a use comparable, therefore, with v. 17 of the same chapter. As Porter observes, this may imply his succession to the throne, but it does not directly say so, as v. 12 does.

The concentration of these phrases and ideas within a few short passages that are all dealing with the installation of a successor is most striking. It is true that in David's charge to Solomon in 1 Kgs 2:1 ff. there is also an echo of these thoughts, but it is not nearly so strongly marked as in Chronicles, nor is it part of a consistent portrayal such as we are suggesting may be found in Chronicles. That the Chronicler was not influenced by this passage in his interpretation may be seen from the fact that he did not even bother to include it in his account!

The third element common to both accounts of the transition of leadership is the manner in which it is announced. In each case, the charge is given in private (Deut. 31:23; 1 Chron. 22:6ff.), only then to be repeated 'in the sight of all Israel ($l^{e^c}\hat{e}n\hat{e}$ $kol\text{-}yi\acute{s}r\bar{a}\,{}^{\circ}\bar{e}l$)' (Deut. 31:7; 1 Chron. 28:8).[10] Moreover, in each case, the formal, private charge is followed by a later imperative command to put it into practice (Josh. 1:2ff.; 1 Chron. 28:8ff.). To McCarthy, indeed, this element is so striking that he thinks it 'almost gives the impression that the Chronicler has studied Deut-Josh with great care .... The sequence between 1 Chronicles 22 and 1 Chronicles 28 is like that between Deuteronomy 31 and Joshua 1 and 13' (p. 36).

Fourthly, we find that in both cases, the people fully accept this situation, such that in the narrators' notices of the rise of the new leader, the obedience of the people is singled out. Thus Deut. 34:9 reads, 'And Joshua the son of Nun was full of the spirit of wisdom; for Moses had laid his hands upon him: and the children of Israel hearkened unto him ($wayyi\check{s}m^{e^c}\hat{u}\,{}^{\circ}\bar{e}l\hat{a}w\,b^e n\hat{e}\text{-}yi\acute{s}r\bar{a}\,{}^{\circ}\bar{e}l$), and did as the Lord commanded Moses' (and cf. Josh. 1:16–20). The case is similar in the account of the succession of Solomon, 1 Chron. 29:23: 'Then Solomon sat on the throne of the Lord as king instead of David his father, and prospered; and all Israel obeyed him ($wayyi\check{s}m^{e^c}\hat{u}\,{}^{\circ}\bar{e}l\hat{a}w\,kol\text{-}yi\acute{s}r\bar{a}\,{}^{\circ}\bar{e}l$)' (and cf. 1 Chron. 29:24).

Finally, in the book of Joshua the continuity of office from Moses to Joshua is underlined by means of the fact that God 'magnified' Joshua: 'And the Lord said unto Joshua, This day will I begin to magnify thee in the sight of all Israel (${}^{\circ}\bar{a}h\bar{e}l$ $gaddel^e k\bar{a}\,b^{e^c}\hat{e}n\hat{e}\,kol\text{-}yi\acute{s}r\bar{a}\,{}^{\circ}\bar{e}l$), that they may know that, as I was with Moses, so I will be with thee' (Josh. 3:7); 'On that day the Lord magnified Joshua in the sight of all Israel ($giddal\,yhwh\,{}^{\circ}e\underline{t}\text{-}y^e h\hat{o}\check{s}ua^c\,b^{e^c}\hat{e}n\hat{e}\,kol\text{-}yi\acute{s}r\bar{a}\,{}^{\circ}\bar{e}l$); and they feared him, as they feared Moses, all the days of his life' (Josh. 4:14). Similarly, the Chronicler twice picks up this same idiom with reference to Solomon, and although he does not explicitly draw the parallel with David (indeed, in the first

---

[10] It is curious indeed that in Deuteronomy, the public announcement should precede the formal charge! The Chronicler has the logical order, and the problem remains one for the internal structure of Deuteronomy only. LOHFINK fails to deal with this in his overall harmonization (41–43). The command to the princes of Israel to help Solomon (1 Chron. 22:17–19) is not to be put on the same level as the public announcement. 'This little pericope is directed to the officials alone', J.M. MYERS, I Chronicles. Introduction, Translation and Notes (AB; Garden City, 1965), 155. Many commentators, indeed, regard it as altogether secondary; cf. W. RUDOLPH, Chronikbücher (HAT; Tübingen, 1955), 153f., and others cited there.

10. The Accession of Solomon in the Books of Chronicles

case he even says that it superseded David), yet it is safe to say, in view of the position of David in Chronicles as a whole, that the intention here is much the same as in the book of Joshua: 'And the Lord magnified Solomon exceedingly in the sight of all Israel (*way^{e}gaddēl yhwh 'et-š^{e}lomoh l^{e}ma'lāh l$^{e\,c}$ênê kol-yiśrā'ēl*)' (1 Chron. 29:25, and cf. 2 Chron. 1:1).

The cumulative effect of these five points, which start with the situation prior to the designation of the successor, go through his appointment and finish with its result, enables us to say that the transition of leadership from Moses to Joshua clearly served as a model for the Chronicler in his understanding of the transition from David to Solomon.

B.

Two related purposes in the Chronicler's narrative are served by this device. Firstly, it is part of the method by which he welded together the reigns of David and Solomon in order to present them as a single, unified 'event' in the history of his people.[11] The close relationship between Deuteronomy and Joshua is well known.[12] As Lohfink has clearly shown, the installation of Joshua himself is a

---

[11] This aspect of the Chronicler's presentation of his people's history has not received sufficient attention from the commentators. The other main technical device (leaving aside for the moment considerations of actual content) by which he achieves this effect is by a structural contrast with his *Vorlage*. The whole suspense of the Succession Narrative in 2 Samuel gives way in Chronicles to an early announcement by David that Solomon is to reign after him (1 Chron. 22:6ff.). This large-scale interlocking structure between the two reigns is reflected on a smaller scale in the formal notices of the end of David's reign and the start of Solomon's. Normally, in both Kings and Chronicles, the death of the monarch is announced first, and the succession of his son comes next (e.g. 1 Kgs 2:10–12; 2 Chron. 9:29–31). Uniquely, this order is reversed at the end of 1 Chronicles: the accession of Solomon is announced first (29:23–25), followed by the notice of David's death (vv. 26–30). It is true that at v. 28b it is repeated that 'Solomon his son reigned in his stead', replacing a notice to the same effect from 1 Kgs 2:12, but then the Chronicler again breaks away from his *Vorlage* to give his sources for, and final summary of, David's reign (vv. 29–30) – a further reversal of his usual procedure. Thus, in these few verses, as in the structure of the surrounding chapters as a whole, the reigns of David and Solomon are linked together as far as is possible into a single unit.

[12] For a concise presentation of the evidence, cf. G.J. WENHAM, 'The Deuteronomic Theology of the Book of Joshua', JBL 90 (1971), 140–148. WENHAM argues that the role of Joshua is 'one of the strongest links between the two books' (145). Similarly, K. MÖHLENBRINK can speak of the succession of Joshua as 'die wichtigste Klammer zwischen den Mosesagen und den Traditionen der Landnahmezeit', on page 49 of 'Josua im Pentateuch. (Die Josuaüberlieferungen ausserhalb des Josuabuchs)', ZAW 58 (1942/43), 14–58. See also M.G. KLINE, The Treaty of the Great King. The Covenant Structure of Deuteronomy: Studies and Commenatry (Grand Rapids, 1963), 35, reprinted in The Structure of Biblical Authority (Grand Rapids, 1972), 141f.

vital hinge between the two books, with Josh. 1 in particular as the passage that has links back into Deuteronomy and forward into Joshua.[13] If this association influenced the Chronicler as suggested here, then it is only reasonable to assume that his intention was to underline the unity of the reigns of David and Solomon.

Secondly, in further emphasis upon this unity, the parallel drawn with Moses and Joshua contributes to the Chronicler's demonstration that Solomon's function was to bring to fulfilment the work begun by David. It is not so much that he seeks to equate their roles as to show that the work of David on the one hand was incomplete, and on the other that that of Solomon would have been impossible without the preparations which David made.

It is this that Braun has overlooked in his recent article,[14] which otherwise has useful material for our purpose, for he there maintains (correctly) against many expositors that the Chronicler's estimation of Solomon was not inferior to that of David, but that he has introduced various elements in order to equate them. We would wish to point further, however, to a number of passages that demonstrate the *complementary* nature of the two kings' functions.

Twice, in passages peculiar to Chronicles, David is represented as saying that, unaided, Solomon would be unable to meet the demands posed by the task of temple building; in each case, it is then stressed that as a result of this, David made full preparation for the building (1 Chron. 22:5; 29:1 f.). It is thus made quite clear that the extensive preparations which are such a well-known feature of the later chapters of 1 Chronicles derive from Solomon's inability to complete the task unaided, an inability only heightened by the comprehensive nature of those preparations: they include the site for the temple (1 Chron. 22:1 with 2 Chron. 3:1),[15] initial organization of the workforce (1 Chron. 22:2, 15 with 2 Chron. 2:6, 14, 16),[16] materials both for the buildings and furnishing (1 Chron. 18:8[17]; 22:3 f., 14, 16; 29:2–9 with 2 Chron. 5:1), the 'pattern' of the buildings,

---

[13] This is taken further by Wenham, who finds all five of the theological *Leitmotifs* that bind Joshua to Deuteronomy already present in this chapter, *viz*: the holy war (vv. 2, 5, 9, 11, 14), the land (vv. 3, 4, 15), the unity of Israel (vv. 12–26), the role of Joshua (vv. 1–2, 5, 17) and the covenant (vv. 3, 7–8, 13, 17–18).

[14] R. L. BRAUN, 'Solomonic Apologetic in Chronicles', JBL 92 (1973), 503–516. Whilst doing justice to the statements that Solomon surpassed David (e. g. 1 Chron. 29:25), BRAUN'S overall estimation of the balance between the two reigns is preferable to the exaggerated claims that MOSIS makes for Solomon (125–163 *et passim*).

[15] The story of David's census, the plague and consequent purchase of the threshing floor is, of course, found also in the Chronicler's *Vorlage* (2 Sam. 24), but nowhere in the Deuteronomic History is the link explicitly made with the temple site, as it is twice in Chronicles.

[16] Again, all peculiar to Chronicles; Kings knows only of the corvée raised by Solomon himself, 1 Kgs 5:27 ff.; 9:15, though 2 Sam. 20:24 suggests that the Chronicler's view may have a sound historical basis.

[17] In the present form of the MT, the Chronicler has here added to his *Vorlage* the observation that the brass which David took as spoil was that 'wherewith Solomon made the brasen sea, and the pillars, and the vessels of brass'. There is doubt, however, whether this

priesthood and vessels (1 Chron. 28:11-12, 13a, 13b-18) and not least the peaceful conditions which were the necessary prerequisite for building. This seems to be the main reason for the Chronicler's retention of the accounts of David's wars in 1 Chron. 18-20, as David's charge to the princes in 1 Chron. 22:18f. makes clear.

The complementary side of this situation is that the Chronicler has heightened the stress on David's inability to complete the task of temple building (and hence of establishing the full round of cultic services), whilst underlining that Solomon was the one who brought the task to its fulfilment. In common with the Deuteronomic History, this note is first struck with the prophecy of Nathan to David (1 Chron. 17), but thereafter the Chronicler develops it in his own way. Twice David expresses his desire to build a temple, and his disqualification because he was a man of war, who had shed blood: 1 Chron. 22:7f.; 28:2f. (cf. 2 Chron. 6:7-9). In each case, however, the Chronicler takes up the promise through Nathan in order to apply it in this context specifically to Solomon, who is named as the one who shall realize David's desire (1 Chron. 22:9f.; 28:4-10). This interpretative application of the dynastic oracle thus forges a powerful link between the functions of the two kings.

Within this overall setting, the movement of the Ark also receives particular attention from the Chronicler. Here again, though the starting point may be the same as in Samuel/Kings (David's desire to build the temple having been initially fired by a wish to house the Ark, 2 Sam. 7:2; 1 Chron. 17:1), the Chronicler returns to it as part of David's unfinished legacy (1 Chron. 22:19; 2 Chron. 1:4). Correspondingly, he emphasizes in his account of the dedication of the temple that this aspect too was fulfilled by Solomon. In addition to the

---

half verse may not have dropped out accidentally from 2 Sam. 8:8. It is found in the LXX of Samuel and without it the *gam* of v. 11 is apparently left without an antecedent (so RUDOLPH, 135). It is thus not surprising that Lemke has used this case as an example of a passage where only text-critical, not theological, considerations are in play (W. E. LEMKE, 'The Synoptic Problem in the Chronicler's History', HTR 58 [1965], 349-363). The situation does not seem so clear-cut, however: there is quite a large number of major additions in the LXX of Samuel/Kings, and Rehm has shown that six of these (including our verse) 'gehören zusammen, da sie sich mit Gerätschaften und Einrichtungen am Tempel und königlichen Palast befassen' (M. REHM, Textkritische Untersuchungen zu den Parallelstellen der Samuel – Königsbücher und der Chronik [Alttestamentliche Abhandlungen, 13,3; Münster, 1937], 25). If, therefore, this half verse becomes part of a clear *Tendenz* on the part of the LXX translators in these books, then its witness to an original form of the MT is weakened, and the view of older commentators such as E. L. CURTIS and A. A. MADSEN, A Critical and Exegetical Commentary on the Books of Chronicles (ICC; Edinburgh, 1910), 234, that the half verse was added to the LXX of Samuel from Chronicles gains in strength. Lemke's counterargument that then we should expect a form of text identical with Paralipomena would be valid only if we were certain that the translators were influenced directly by Paralipomena and not by the MT of Chronicles; but this we do not know. Rudolph's argument on the basis of the *gam* in v. 11 is strong, but not conclusive, since it could be anticipatory of the following '*im hakkesep wᵉhazzāhāḇ ᵃšer hiqdîš mikkol-haggôyīm ᵃšer kibbēš*. Neither side

passages to this effect adopted from his *Vorlage* (2 Chron. 5:2-14;[18] 6:11), he supplies a divergent ending to Solomon's prayer of dedication that has this very point as its main theme (2 Chron. 6:41 f.), and then draws further attention to it by the account of a second (and additional) theophany (2 Chron. 7:1-3).

A final aspect of this same line of interpretation concerns the ordering of the cultic officials and their duties, since again they are installed by Solomon, following the ordering of David (2 Chron. 7:6; 8:12-15).

In the light of all these details of preparation and fulfilment, we may conclude not only that they support the case maintained in the first part of this paper, but further that reflection upon the relationship between Moses and Joshua and their complementary roles may have influenced the Chronicler in this aspect of the presentation of his account of the succession of Solomon.

C.

We may finally draw attention to a few implications of this study for the books of Chronicles as a whole. A first and clear conclusion will be to underline the consciously creative literary nature of the Chronicler's work. Various scholars have previously sought to emphasize this, though admittedly from widely differing standpoints.[19] It is doubtful, however, whether the evidence can be used to support Willi's more specific definition of *Die Chronik als Auslegung*.[20] It is true that Willi's explanation of 'exegesis' allows him to include a good deal of recensional, interpretative and even typological material (cf. pp. 132–169), and further that the virtual citation of the Deuteronomy/Joshua passages would fit his designation of the Chronicler's own compositions as *Musivstil*;[21] but in each case, Willi's examples are drawn from little more than scattered phrases and

---

of the argument seems to be compelling, therefore; all we can say is that, whether or not it is an addition from the Chronicler's hand, the half verse fully agrees with his point of view as set out above.

[18] Verses 11-13a are in fact added by the Chronicler, but they do not add anything relevant to our present concern.

[19] For instance, C.C. TORREY, 'The Chronicler as Editor and as Independent Narrator', AJSL 25 (1908–1909), 157–173 and 188–217 = Ezra Studies (Chicago, 1910), 208–251; M. NOTH, Überlieferungsgeschichtliche Studien 1 (Halle, 1943), 155–161, and more recently, P. WELTEN, Geschichte und Geschichtsdarstellung in den Chronikbüchern (WMANT, 42; Neukirchen, 1973), 5 and 205, and P.R. ACKROYD, 'The Theology of the Chronicler', Lexington Theological Quarterly 8 (1973), 101–116.

[20] T. WILLI, Die Chronik als Auslegung. Untersuchungen zur literarischen Gestaltung der historischen Überlieferung Israels (FRLANT, 106; Göttingen, 1972).

[21] *Ibid.*, p. 177, and cf. G. VON RAD, 'Die levitische Predigt in den Büchern der Chronik', Festschrift Otto Procksch (Leipzig, 1934), 113–124, reprinted in Gesammelte Studien zum Alten Testament (München, 1958), 248–261.

sentences. To seek to expand his categories to cover such an extended composition as has been argued for here (even if it were claimed that it was exegesis of 1 Kgs 2:1 ff., which we discounted above) would be to empty them of any distinctive significance. There is no need, therefore, to deny that the Chronicler had a positive purpose of his own in writing, which will then have governed both his choice of literary *genre* and his selection and use of source materials.

Secondly, the abundance of parallels drawn between this narrative and Deut. 31-Josh. 1 renders less probable the view of Goulder[22] that these chapters of Chronicles were intended as a liturgical correspondence to Exod. 19 ff., within the framework of his theory that 'the Chronicler saw himself as writing a continuous series of *haphtarah* readings to run parallel with the Law' (p. 219). Moreover, the parallels which he cites for Deut. 31-Josh. 1 in 2 Chron. 36:22-Ezra 1 are more remote than those that have been traced here (quite apart from the now questionable assumption that Chronicles and Ezra/Nehemiah are parts of a single work).

Finally, our findings provide fresh evidence against any attempt to divide up the work of the Chronicler on the basis of his adherence to one or other of the Pentateuchal sources,[23] and even suggest that the effort so frequently made to establish which of the sources had the greatest influence upon him is misguided. The main influence in the chapters studied was Deuteronomic, but his use of Deut. 34:9 in this connection shows that it was already in its present position. This verse is usually regarded as either a direct continuation or a recapitulation of the account of Joshua's appointment in Num. 27:12-23.[24] The implications of this observation will depend upon one's views both of the date of Chronicles and of the formation of the Pentateuch, but at least we may confidently assert that the Chronicler had the Pentateuch before him in its final and completed form.

---

[22] M. D. GOULDER, Midrash and Lection in Matthew (London, 1974), 202-224. P. R. ACKROYD has reacted favourably to the theory in principle, though he too feels that it 'tends to suffer from attempts at over-precision'; cf. The Age of the Chronicler (The Selwyn Lectures, 1970. Supplement to Colloquium – The Australian and New Zealand Theological Review; Auckland, 1970), 45.

[23] Thus, for instance, the commentary of J. W. ROTHSTEIN and J. HÄNEL, Kommentar zum ersten Buch der Chronik (KAT; Leipzig, 1927), argued that the original work of the Chronicler still knew of P as a separate document, but was later revised on the basis of the Hexateuch as a whole (*passim*, but cf. especially page LX), whilst A. C. WELCH, The Work of the Chronicler: its Purpose and its Date (The Schweich Lectures for 1938; London, 1939), argued that the basic narrative was in line with D, being later revised in the light of P. The most comprehensive study of the Chronicler's use of the Pentateuch is G. VON RAD, Das Geschichtsbild des chronistischen Werkes (BWANT, 4/3; Stuttgart, 1930).

[24] Cf. K. MÖHLENBRINK, 51 f.; J. R. PORTER, 103, and the standard Introductions to the Old Testament.

11. The Temple in the Books of Chronicles

Several years ago, Ernst Bammel kindly but firmly persuaded me to present a paper on the topic of the temple in the books of Chronicles to his graduate seminar. Since at the time he urged me to publish it, and in view of the subject chosen for this volume in his honour, he will, I hope, be prepared to accept this revised version of what was said on that occasion as a token of admiration and respect.

One of the few points about which all commentators on Chronicles are agreed is that the temple was of central significance to its author. While some aspects of its importance to him will be our primary concern in the bulk of what follows, it may serve as a useful introduction to the subject to remind ourselves of one or two of the devices by which the Chronicler draws attention to the centrality of the temple in his thinking.

To start with a simple example, we may note his introduction to Solomon's reign. Solomon was popularly remembered as a man of wealth and wisdom, and as the one who built the first temple. These three points are grouped together in 2 Chronicles 1.[1]

(a) Verses 2–6 are based on 1 Kgs 3:4, which serves in its context merely as an introduction to the dream which follows. Here, however, the Chronicler has developed the material into a narrative in its own right, in which the king leads the people in a major act of sacrificial worship. Moreover, he has made it the first recorded incident of Solomon's reign. It thus serves as a pointer to the aspect of the reign which the Chronicler deemed to be of greatest significance and invites us to read the following chapters in its light.

(b) Verses 7–13 represent a radical abbreviation of 1 Kgs 3.5–15 for reasons that need not concern us here.[2] The gift of wisdom to Solomon was, of course, one of the topics most widely remembered about this king. Against his *Vorlage*, however, the Chronicler no longer has the account of the dream at Gibeon followed by the illustrative example of the exercise of Solomon's wisdom in the story of the judgment between the two prostitutes (1 Kgs 3:16–28) In his view, the primary purpose of Solomon's wisdom was not to equip him for civil rule but

---

[1] For other aspects of the significance of 2 Chron. 1 for the Chronicler's portrayal of Solomon, cf. R.B. DILLARD, 'The Chronicler's Solomon', WTJ 43 (1980), 289–300; 'The Literary Structure of the Chronicler's Solomon Narrative', JSOT 30 (1984), 85–93; and 2 Chronicles (WBC, 15; Waco, 1987), 1–15.

[2] Cf. my 1 and 2 Chronicles (NCB; Grand Rapids and London, 1982), 195–96.

to enable him to undertake the task of temple-building retold in the following chapters.

(c) A further well-known feature of Solomon's reign was his wealth. In Kings, the details of this come at the end of the faithful part of his reign (1 Kgs 10:26-29), before his fall from grace. The Chronicler, however, has given this paragraph a completely new position in 2 Chron. 1:14-17; clearly, his purpose is again to show how this aspect too of Solomon's glory was channelled into the building of the temple, the account of which follows directly.

What is seen here in miniature in 2 Chronicles 1 is, in fact, largely true of the whole of his preceding narrative. Since clearly we cannot deal with so much material here even in brief, let us again take three representative examples.[3] First, in the period before the temple was built, its role in the religious life of the people was largely fulfilled by the ark. This may be seen by the facts that the temple was built explicitly to house the ark, that the Chronicler heightens the centrality of the bringing of the ark into the sanctuary at the dedication of the temple (2 Chron. 5:2–6:11), and that he uses the same loaded theological vocabulary of it as he does later of the temple. Now, when 1 Chron. 10:13-14 (the Chronicler's own comment on the reasons for Saul's death) is read in the light of 1 Chron. 13:1-5, the use of the same stereotyped vocabulary strongly suggests that a major contribution to Saul's failure was his neglect of the ark, and that David made the rectification of this abuse one of his first priorities. But then in turn, while David's care for the ark is drawn out to dominate the whole of 1 Chronicles 13–16 (contrast 2 Sam. 6), the Chronicler deliberately introduces a drastic change in the sequence of his *Vorlage* in order to work into the middle of this narrative the events of 1 Chronicles 14. Naturally, this was not meant to be a chronological improvement: in the space of three months (1 Chron. 13:14), even David could hardly have fathered more than thirteen children and still have had the strength to wage two successful campaigns against the Philistines! Rather, these are stereotyped markers of divine blessing for faithful kings. Welten[4] has isolated in particular building, military victory and large families as such tokens in Chronicles, and it is precisely these three that are assembled in 1 Chronicles 14. It is obvious, therefore, that even under the guise of the ark, the temple dominates much of David's reign. Proper attention to it is the source of blessing for the life of the nation.

Second, this same concern is the trigger for the dynastic promise which follows in 1 Chronicles 17. To cut a long story short,[5] the net result of the slight

---

[3] For fuller discussions, cf. especially R. Mosis, *Untersuchungen zur Theologie des chronistischen Geschichtswerkes* (Freiburger theologische Studien, 92; Freiburg, 1973), 44-124; T.-S. Im, *Das Davidbild in den Chronikbüchern* (Europäische Hochschulschriften, XXIII/263; Frankfurt am Main, 1985).

[4] P. Welten, *Geschichte und Geschichtsdarstellung in den Chronikbüchern* (WMANT, 42; Neukirchen-Vluyn, 1973).

[5] Cf. my 'The Dynastic Oracle in the Books of Chronicles', in A. Rofé and Y. Zakovitch

changes which the Chronicler introduces by comparison with 2 Samuel 7 is first to focus the oracle more exclusively on Solomon himself as the temple builder, and secondly to relate the more general conditional elements in the Deuteronomic forms of the oracle to the one specific condition of Solomon's faithfulness in regard to temple building. It thus emerges that the future of the dynasty is made dependent upon Solomon bringing to completion the work of his father David – David himself being ritually debarred[6] from undertaking the work 'because you have shed much blood upon the earth in my sight' (1 Chron. 22:8).

Third, it now becomes understandable why the rest of the account of David's reign is completely dominated by preparations for the building: site, materials, plans, personnel, political conditions, nothing that can be anticipated is left undone. Even David's extensive military campaigns are reinterpreted as the source for the precious metals that Solomon would need later on (1 Chron. 18:8,[7] 11; 2 Chron. 5:1).

In view of this and much more that could be said, it is obvious that the Chronicler set enormous store by the temple. But why? Wherein did its importance lie? And what kerygmatic purpose did he think would be served by his emphasis?

For many years it has been customary to respond to such questions in terms of the Chronicler's negative polemic. It is contended that his stress on the Jerusalem temple was intended to uphold its legitimacy in face of the claims of other comparable centres, most notably the Samaritan temple on Mount Gerizim. This in turn is linked with an interpretation of his work as a whole as being fundamentally anti-Samaritan in tone and purpose.[8]

While such sentiments may still be found in some standard text-books and reference works on the subject, this position has in fact been abandoned by almost all major scholars working in this field during the past fifteen or twenty years. This dramatic turn-around in interpretation has largely focused, however, upon the Chronicler's attitude to the northern kingdom.[9] Less attention has been

---

(eds.), *Essays on the Bible and the Ancient World: Isac Leo Seeligmann Volume* (Jerusalem, 1983), vol. 3, 305–18.

[6] As correctly observed by J. GOETTSBERGER, *Die Bücher der Chronik oder Paralipomenon* (HSAT, IV/1; Bonn, 1939), 163.

[7] For the difficult question of the Chronicler's *Vorlage* here, where the LXX of 2 Sam. 8:8 is closer to Chronicles than to the MT of Samuel, cf. M. REHM, *Textkritische Untersuchungen zu den Parallelstellen der Samuel-Königsbücher und der Chronik* (Alttestamentliche Abhandlungen, 13, 3; Münster, 1937), 25; H. G. M. WILLIAMSON, 'The Accession of Solomon in the Books of Chronicles', VT 26 (1976), 351–61 (357f.) (above, 141–49); R. BRAUN, 1 Chronicles (WBC, 14; Waco, 1986), 204–205, *contra* W. RUDOLPH, Chronikbücher (HAT, 21; Tübingen, 1955), 135, and W. E. LEMKE, 'The Synoptic Problem in the Chronicler's History', HTR 58 (1965), 349–63 (354–55).

[8] See the fundamental studies of C. C. TORREY, *Ezra Studies* (Chicago, 1910), 208–51, and M. NOTH, *Überlieferungsgeschichtliche Studien* (Halle, 1943), 171–80 (= *The Chronicler's History* [JSOTSup, 50; Sheffield, 1987], 97–106).

[9] In addition to most of the recent works on Chronicles cited elsewhere in this article, cf.

directed to the consequences which this shift might have for an appreciation of his temple theology. It is appropriate, therefore, to attempt such a reappraisal within the new context which Chronicles studies have established. I shall seek specifically to defend the view that the temple in Chronicles is not a litmus test of an orthodoxy that would exclude the non-conformist but rather a focus of unity for the people of Israel as a whole. We shall then in conclusion test this hypothesis by contrasting it with a different presentation from a slightly later date which in fact comes much closer to the exclusive model so frequently postulated of the Chronicler.

It is often thought to be a good approach in ecumenical discussions to start by going back in time to the common fount in history which unites various groups that may have diverged over lesser issues in subsequent time.[10] In the light of that unity one may then have a better perspective from which to approach those divisions. This, at any rate, is what the Chronicler patently does in his presentation of the temple. His concern is always to link it back by physical ties of unbroken continuity with institutions or settings of far earlier days, before the divisions of the monarchical period, let alone his own much later time, had surfaced. Let us examine two main examples of this: the temple site and its design.

(a) *The temple site.* The choice of temple site is explained in 1 Chronicles 21, the account of David's census, the consequent plague and David's purchase of the threshing floor of Ornan the Jebusite, the point where the plague stopped. In the Chronicler's *Vorlage*, 2 Samuel 24, the narrative is closely linked with 2 Samuel 21 for purposes of its own, and it is not explicitly stated that the threshing floor which David purchased became the future temple site. The text of this chapter had, we now know, already passed through some intermediate stage of development before it reached the Chronicler. Nevertheless, it is equally certain that he has himself taken this development further in ways that are important for our theme.[11]

H. G. M. WILLIAMSON, Israel in the Books of Chronicles (Cambridge, 1977); R L. BRAUN, 'A Reconsideration of the Chronicler's Attitude toward the North', *JBL* 96 (1977), 59–62; S. JAPHET, The Ideology of the Book of Chronicles and its Place in Biblical Thought (Jerusalem, 1977), 228–333 [Hebrew].

[10] See, for instance, S.C. NEILL in R. ROUSE and S.C. NEILL (eds.), A History of the Ecumenical Movement 1517–1948 (2nd edn; London, 1967), 726.

[11] For discussion of the textual and literary arguments that lead to this conclusion, see (in addition to the commentaries) LEMKE (above. n. 7), 355–57; E.C. ULRICH, The Qumran Text of Samuel and Josephus (HSM, 19; Missoula, 1978), 156–59; R. MICHEEL, Die Seher- und Prophetenüberlieferungen in der Chronik (BET, 18; Frankfurt am Main, 1983), 20–23; P.E. DION, 'The Angel with the Drawn Sword (II [sic!] Chr. 21,16): An Exercise in Restoring the Balance of Text Criticism *and* Attention to Context', ZAW 97 (1985), 114–17; S.L. MCKENZIE, The Chronicler's Use of the Deuteronomistic History (HSM, 33; Atlanta, 1985), 55–58, 67–71; E. NICOLE, 'Un cas de relecture: 2 Samuel 24 et 1 Chroniques 21', Hokhma 26 (1983), 47–55; and S. ROMEROWSKI, 'A propos de la relecture de 2 Samuel 24 par 1 Chroniques 21', Hokhma 28 (1985), 54–60.

First, the closing verses of the passage (21:26–22:1) are his own addition and, as is his customary method, they provide us with his interpretation of the foregoing narrative. Here we find that he aims to establish the divinely willed continuity between the Mosaic sanctuary and the future Jerusalem temple. The acceptance of the burnt offering by fire from heaven not only confirms the choice of the present site, but establishes a link with the altar of the tabernacle (cf. Lev. 9:24) and points forward to the similar occurrence at the dedication of the temple (2 Chron. 7:1). At the same time, although vv. 29–30 are circumstantial, and hence almost parenthetical, there is a conscious contrast between 'the tabernacle of the Lord' with its 'altar of burnt offering' (v. 29) on the one hand, and 'the house of the Lord God' and 'the altar of burnt offering' (22:1) on the other. Sandwiched in between, v. 30, which is rich in allusion to the preceding narrative, reminds us of the divine will which had deflected David away from the tabernacle at Gibeon to this new and unexpected setting.[12] The other relevant aspect of the Chronicler's treatment of this chapter is his characteristic use of typology. Typology in this context, it should be said, does not quite have the force that it does when used between the New Testament and the Old. It is not used to point to one incident or institution as the fulfilment of its shadowlike predecessor; rather, it serves as a cross-reference from one incident to another, inviting the reader to draw parallels and conclusions that go beyond the immediate statement of the text. There are two examples of this procedure in this passage.[13]

Verse 20 has little connection with its *Vorlage* in 2 Sam. 24:20; a number of features, however, suggest that a deliberate comparison with the story of Gideon in Judges 6 has been introduced. The basic theme is the same: the encounter of an angel with one who was threshing wheat and the offering received by supernatural fire, while some points of detail further support the analogy, such as the expressions 'hid themselves', 'he turned', and 'saw' in the sense of 'perceived'. Even if some of this evidence is overplayed, the basic analogy is attractive, for the appearance of the angel to Gideon also led to the establishment of a permanent holy place to the Lord. Moreover, Gideon went on from there to

---

[12] It is worth noting in passing that this passage has previously been understood in terms of anti-Samaritan polemic: David's statement in 22:1, which starts זה הוא בית יהוה האלהים, 'this is the house of the LORD God', is said by J. W. ROTHSTEIN and J. HÄNEL, Kommentar zum ersten Buch der Chronik (KAT, XVIII/2; Leipzig, 1927), 376–77, 385, and by RUDOLPH (above, n. 7), 148, to echo Jacob's statement in Gen. 28:17 – מה־נורא המקום הזה אין זה כי אם בית אלהים, 'How dreadful is this place! This is none other but the house of God.' This echo, however, is weak at best (it is not exact, for in Chronicles it refers to the future rather than to present realization) and in any case is not necessarily anti-Samaritan as such: the Samaritans revered Gerizim rather than Bethel. At the most it should be regarded as critical of the pre-exilic northern royal cult, which is not at all the same thing. But, as I have tried to indicate, it is better taken as a positive statement about the future temple site than as a purely polemical outburst.

[13] Cf. T. WILLI, Die Chronik als Auslegung (FRLANT, 106; Gottingen, 1972), 157–58.

contend for the Lord against Baal; did the Chronicler see in his account a similar development from a Jebusite sanctuary to one consecrated to the Lord? It is, at least, noteworthy that he introduces the term מקום in vv. 22 and 25, for this, as is well known, can have the extended meaning of 'holy site'.[14]

In vv. 22–25, the Chronicler introduces a more significant comparison by patterning David's purchase on Abraham's purchase of the cave of Machpelah from Ephron in Genesis 23. To the underlying similarity of the leading representative of the people of God buying a site for sacred purposes from a member of the indigenous population is added a number of details to make the analogy clear. Most noteworthy is his addition twice of the phrase בכסף מלא, 'at its full price', exactly as at Gen. 23:9 and occurring nowhere else in the OT. Further, against his *Vorlage* he twice uses the verb נתן 'give' for 'buy' in v. 22 as at Gen. 23:4 and 9, has David initiate the conversation (v. 22) as Abraham did at Gen. 23:3f., and in v. 23 he gives added emphasis to Ornan's initial response of wishing to 'give' (twice) the site to David, just as Ephron did with Abraham (Gen. 23:11). Perhaps also the Chronicler's extension of the area to be purchased from the threshing floor to the whole site (vv. 22, 25) was influenced by the similar dispute in Genesis 23 about the cave and the field in which it was found.

Preachers are fond of drawing out lessons from the fact that the cave of Machpelah was the only piece of real estate which the patriarchs secured in the promised land. There is no reason why the Chronicler should not also have been aware of this and made conscious use of the fact in his valuation of the temple site. It became in his view a firstfruit, so to speak, of the land of promise, so that all who revered Abraham as patriarch might feel a bond with this place.

A similar point is made even more obviously in the other passage which centres on the temple site, 2 Chron. 3:1:

Then Solomon began to build the house of the LORD at Jerusalem in Mount Moriah, where the LORD appeared to David his father, which he made ready in the place that David had appointed, in the threshing floor of Ornan the Jebusite.

Mount Moriah is referred to elsewhere only at Genesis 22 as the site where Abraham was commanded to offer up Isaac.[15] The important verses for our present concern are 2 and 14, though they contain several difficulties of their own. It is probable that in their present form they already interpret the narrative

---

[14] Cf. A. COWLEY, 'The Meaning of מקום in Hebrew', JTS 17 (1916), 174–76, and J. GAMBERONI, TWAT, IV, cols. 1113–24.

[15] It does not, as was once thought, occur in one of the Khirbet Beit Lei inscriptions; cf. F.M. CROSS, 'The Cave Inscriptions from Khirbet Beit Lei', in J.A. SANDERS (ed.), *Near Eastern Archaeology in the Twentieth Century* (Garden City, 1970), 299–306; A. LEMAIRE, 'Prières en temps de crise: les inscriptions de Khirbet Beit Lei', RB 83 (1976), 558–68; and P.D. MILLER, 'Psalms and Inscriptions', in J.A. EMERTON (ed.), Congress Volume: Vienna 1980 (VTSup, 32; Leiden, 1981), 311–32, *contra* J. NAVEH, 'Old Hebrew Inscriptions in a Burial Cave', IEJ 13 (1963), 74–92, and J.C.L. GIBSON, *Textbook of Syrian Semitic Inscriptions. Volume 1: Hebrew and Moabite Inscriptions* (Oxford, 1971), 57–58.

as a pointer towards the future temple. Particularly noteworthy is the use in v. 14 of the phrase 'the mount of the LORD', which elsewhere refers to the temple hill (Ps. 24:3; Isa. 2:3; 30:29). Further, the phrase 'as it is said this day' suggests association with a well-known location, and the word-play between 'it shall be provided' (which links back to v. 8 of the narrative) and 'he will be seen' could well be understood in cultic terms. Possible, but less certain, is the argument that if the popular view is right which sees in Genesis 22 an aetiology for the abolition of human sacrifice, then a reference to Jerusalem (apparently the centre of the 'Molek cult', which practised this form of sacrifice) is to be expected.[16] Now, while it is clear that v. 14 is important for determining one aspect of the narrator's purpose, it cannot be divorced from v. 2 in which the mention of Moriah is found. These are the only two verses which suggest that the altar was built on a mountain; the phrase 'one of the mountains of which I shall tell you', by its resemblance to the expression of God's choice of the sanctuary in, for instance, Deuteronomy 12, seems to be making a similar allusion to that in v. 14; and finally, the name Moriah itself may well, by a popular form of etymology, have been understood as 'the vision of the Lord', or the like, and so again be a pointer to one element in v. 14.

In 2 Chron. 3:1 the Chronicler has picked up and made explicit these major interpretative themes from Genesis 22. First, the identity of Moriah with the temple site is, of course, plainly stated. Second, the use of the word 'mount' relates to that feature already noted which seems to have entered Genesis 22 only as an element of interpretation, and third, the description 'where the Lord appeared to David his father' is subtly introduced to link an important feature of Gen. 22:14 ('he will be seen') with the more immediate designation of the temple site in 1 Chronicles 21, analysed above.

It may thus be concluded that the Chronicler's association of the temple site with Moriah is not arbitrary; rather, he has drawn on a tradition which was sufficiently deeply rooted and well established as to have influenced the Genesis text itself.[17] His own contribution is first to spell out what is alluded to in the earlier texts (exactly as was shown above to be the case with his handling of 2 Sam. 24 in 1 Chron. 21), and, second, to link these three episodes together in such a way as to emphasize the continuity of worship at this site and so indirectly to link the temple of his own day with some of the major religious leaders of Israel's past.

---

[16] See the discussion in G.C. HEIDER, The Cult of Molek: A Reassessment (JSOTSup, 43; Sheffield, 1985), 273-77. Heider himself rejects any association of Gen. 22 with the Molek cult.

[17] For the reasons given above, this conclusion seems more probable than the suggestion that 'Moriah' entered the text of Gen. 22 under the influence of Chronicles itself; cf. R. KILIAN, Isaaks Opferung: Zur Überlieferungsgeschichte von Gen 22 (SBS, 44; Stuttgart, 1970), 31-46.

For all of these reasons, then, the Chronicler saw in the site of the Jerusalem temple a focus of continuity with the nation's earliest history and one that should therefore override more recent differences. It is, of course, impossible to be sure what was happening in the north at the time that he was writing (mid-fourth century BC), but it appears that it was not much: Shechem was still deserted, as it had been for a century previously, so that clearly it was not yet a revered cult centre; that came only later, in my opinion under the impetus of a division in the Jerusalem priesthood, a breakaway group from which united with lay northern Israelites to form what we know as the Samaritan community.[18] If this is even approximately correct, it will mean that the later Samaritan characteristic of linking all previous events in Israelite history with Gerizim[19] will be a response to the type of approach attested in Chronicles. The latter may then be seen not as negative polemic, since it had no opposite view to counteract in this sphere, but rather as the positive presentation of a point of unity.

(b) *The temple design.* We have already seen that a connection is made in 1 Chronicles 21 between the Mosaic tabernacle and the Jerusalem temple. This, however, is only one small element in a rich vein concerning the Chronicler's understanding of the temple.

In 2 Chron. 5:5, the Chronicler follows his *Vorlage* in saying that, at the dedication of the temple, 'they brought up the ark, and the tent of meeting, and all the holy vessels that were in the tent'. However the Kings text should be understood,[20] the Chronicler has given it a clear significance of his own by his references to the presence of the Mosaic tabernacle at Gibeon: 1 Chron. 16:39; 21:29; 2 Chron. 1:3–6. The temple has thus become the final resting place not only of the ark, but also of the tabernacle and all its sacred vessels.

Now, in the Chronicler's presentation this is wholly appropriate, for he emphasizes the parallels between the two structures far more than does Kings. We need here only pick out a few of the most obvious elements that contribute to this typological patterning.

First, in 1 Chron. 28:11–19, a passage which has no parallel elsewhere,[21] David gives to Solomon the plans for the temple which he is being commissioned to build. The word תבנית, used four times in these nine verses with reference to

---

[18] Cf. H.G. KIPPENBERG, Garizim und Synagoge (RVV, 30; Berlin, 1971), and my 'Early Post-Exilic Judaean History', above, 3–24.

[19] As attested, for instance, throughout the *Memar Marqah*; cf. J. MACDONALD, Memar Marqah: The Teaching of Marqah (BZAW, 84; 2 vols; Berlin, 1963).

[20] It is believed by many to betray the hand of a late priestly editor, working in the light of Chronicles. By contrast, R.E. FRIEDMAN (The Exile and Biblical Narrative: The Formation of the Deuteronomistic and Priestly Works [HSM, 22; Chico, 1981], 48ff.,) has argued that it rests on sound historical memory; even if he is right, that does not invalidate discussion of what the significance of this might have been for the Chronicler.

[21] Against attempts to deny this paragraph to the Chronicler, see my 1 and 2 Chronicles, 181–82.

most aspects of the building, is clearly intended as an echo of the 'pattern' of the tabernacle and its furnishings, shown to Moses on Mount Sinai in Exod. 25:9, 40. There is a difference, however. Unlike the position in Exodus, there is no suggestion in Chronicles that David drew up a plan as a copy of something he had seen. Rather, David says in his summary, 'All this have I been made to understand in writing by the hand of the Lord upon me, all the works of the pattern'. The verse is difficult to construe in detail, but probably implies that David wrote the plans under conscious divine inspiration. It may be suggested, therefore, that since there was so much in common between the basic plan of the tabernacle and the temple, and since they stood in continuous tradition with each other, David did not need to see the heavenly pattern afresh: he could visit it at Gibeon. All he needed to do was to adapt the pattern under inspiration to the new conditions.

Second, it is necessary to do no more than mention that the parallel with the account of the building of the tabernacle is continued in both substance and vocabulary in the next chapter, 1 Chronicles 29, as David first appeals for offerings and the people then respond generously; cf. Exodus 25 and 35.

Third, we should consider the temple builder – Hiram in Kings, but Huramabi in 2 Chron. 2:13–14. Granted the context of a tabernacle-temple typology, it is striking that the list of his skills is amplified in Chronicles to include craftsmanship in materials that Bezalel had to be able to work in for the tabernacle (2 Chron. 2:7, 14; cf. Exod. 35:35). In the light of this, it is likely that the ascription of his mother to Dan in Chronicles rather than Naphtali in Kings is based on the help Bezalel received from Oholiab, who belonged to the tribe of Dan. Furthermore, it has been suggested that the additional *ab* element which the Chronicler has given to his name is also a reflection of the final syllable of Oholiab. Both builders of the tabernacle are thus typologically brought together in the one figure of Huramabi.[22]

Finally, a number of elements in the construction of the temple differ in Chronicles from Kings in ways that agree with the description of the tabernacle. I limit myself here to the most obvious example, the veil of 2 Chron. 3:14. Nowhere else does the OT refer to such a veil in the temple. The suggestion that a sentence to this effect has dropped out of 1 Kgs 6:21 is textually improbable and would contradict 6:31–32 which speaks of doors at this point. Rather, the Chronicler has introduced here a verbal citation from Exod. 26:31 and 36:35.

We are now in a position to suggest, therefore, that as the temple was associated with the patriarchs by its site, so it was associated by its design with Moses. Added to this, a fuller treatment of the subject than is possible here could also catalogue the many passages in which the Chronicler draws attention to the continuity of cultic observance and personnel with those of the Mosaic period.[23]

---

[22] See further, in addition to the commentaries, Mosis (above, n. 3), 136–47.

[23] Cf. S. J. DE VRIES, 'Moses and David as Cult Founders in Chronicles', JBL 107 (1988), 619–39.

In all this too, he was presenting his contemporaries with a focus for unity. Ark, tent, vessels; associations with Gibeon, and perhaps Shiloh and Shechem too – all these diverse strands, which were potential sources of fragmentation, were now drawn into the one sanctuary.[24] Once again, therefore, it is possible that the later Samaritan tradition of hiding the tabernacle vessels during the present age should be seen in part as a reaction to this viewpoint, the Chronicler's own presentation being intended positively rather than as negative polemic.[25]

Of the many points that ought to be noted from the post-Solomonic chapters in 2 Chronicles, I will mention just two that cannot be left unsaid. First, Abijah's 'sermon on the mount' in 2 Chron. 13:4–12 is not to be regarded as anti-Samaritan temple polemic, as has frequently been maintained. One of its twin foci is the legitimacy of the Davidic dynasty, which would have been an irrelevance in the postexilic debate; then, as Kippenberg (pp. 49f.) has shown, to single out 'the sons of Aaron' for mention would have been to play into the hands of the Samaritans at one of their strongest points. Finally, the point of deepest division between the two later communities – namely, the relative virtues of the locality of their respective sanctuaries – receives no mention here at all. Rather, the speech is to be entirely explained on the basis of its present narrative context where it plays an important role in a somewhat different aspect of the Chronicler's ideology.[26]

The other point is the use and role of the temple as a focus for unity in the reform of Hezekiah. This reform is of the greatest importance to the Chronicler, for in it he presents his solution to the problem of the divided kingdom. With the northern royal house now finally removed, he portrays Hezekiah as a second Solomon[27] over all Israel in a wide variety of spheres. Prominent amongst these are the arrangements which the two kings made for the temple. For instance, in his account of Solomon's building of the temple, the Chronicler singles out eight items and practices as being specifically 'an ordinance in Israel'. In each case, this reference is in addition to Kings. Without going into detail,[28] it may here be stated in summary fashion that in his account of Hezekiah's reformation, the Chronicler (again without parallel in Kings) exactly picks up each one of these eight items. His summarizing conclusion in both cases may serve as our summary of this point too:

---

[24] Cf. J. W. FLANAGAN, David's Social Drama: A Hologram of Israel's Early Iron Age (JSOTSup, 73; Sheffield, 1988), 212, who writes, 'The terminology and action betray the strength of lingering loyalties for religious centers other than Jerusalem'.

[25] Cf. KIPPENBERG (above, n. 18), 234–54; M. F. COLLINS, 'The Hidden Vessels in Samaritan Traditions', JSJ 3 (1972), 97–116. For the temple vessels as a focus for continuity, cf. P. R. ACKROYD, 'The Temple Vessels – A Continuity Theme', in Studies in the Religion of Ancient Israel (VTSup, 23; Leiden, 1972), 166–81.

[26] Cf. Israel in the Books of Chronicles (above, n. 9), 110–14.

[27] Or David and Solomon combined; cf. M. A. THRONTVEIT, When Kings Speak: Royal Speech and Royal Prayer in Chronicles (SBLDS, 93; Atlanta, 1987), 121–24.

[28] For which see Israel in the Books of Chronicles, 119–25.

2 Chron. 8:16 ותכן כל־מלאכת שלמה עד־היום מוסד בית יהוה
2 Chron. 29:35 ותכון עבודת בית־יהוה

Another aspect of this presentation of Hezekiah is his attempt, partially successful, to reunite the hitherto divided tribes of Israel. Careful study reveals, however, that his appeal to the northerners is integrally linked with the temple, both because the invitation is to a centralized celebration of Passover and also because the appeal is couched in terms that suggest that it is to be understood as a paradigm of how to act in conformity with Solomon's prayer of dedication; cf. 2 Chron. 30:6–9. Especially noteworthy here is v. 9, which is drawn from the Kings account of Solomon's prayer (1 Kgs 8:50), but which the Chronicler had earlier omitted from his account of the same event.

While this summary has been both sketchy and compressed, enough has been said to conclude that the Chronicler did not regard Solomon's reign merely as a story from ancient history. By his reworking of some of its central themes in the account of Hezekiah's reign, he showed that many of its characteristics were paradigmatic of national salvation; and central to this paradigm stands the temple as a focus for the reunification of the divided and scattered people of Israel.

As a concluding point, it may be worth noting how distinctive is this viewpoint of the Chronicler's by comparing it with that of another who, in my opinion, worked two or three generations later in the early Hellenistic period and was himself a member of a circle which valued Chronicles sufficiently to have been influenced by it in a number of respects. I refer to the editor of Ezra 1–6, the latest part of Ezra-Nehemiah to have been composed.[29] This editor had some primary sources at his disposal and he worked directly from these; his usual method was to cite the source verbatim and then to construct a narrative join with the next source directly out of its wording. In this, however, it can be shown that he too worked with a strong ideology of continuity: the second temple is continuous with the first; its sacred vessels are the same; priesthood and people are pure descendants of the first temple generation, and so on. But to what purpose was this continuity put? Not to the kind of inclusive policy which we have seen characterizes Chronicles, but rather the reverse. The whole drift of the work is to use continuity as a means of excluding some who might at first have been thought to have a rightful claim to participation, whether they are members of the Judaean community (cf. Ezra 2:59–63) or those who come from the northern part of the land (4:1–3). The contrast could scarcely be more marked.

If our view, hinted at earlier, of the rise of the Samaritans proper is approximately correct, and if the first temple was built on Gerizim in the early years of

---

[29] See my 'The Composition of Ezra i–vi', JTS ns 34 (1983), 1–30 (see below, 244–70). This suggestion has recently been challenged by J. BLENKINSOPP, Ezra-Nehemiah (London, 1989), 43–44, though I do not find his arguments persuasive.

the Hellenistic period, then this all makes admirable sense. During the earlier reforms of Ezra and Nehemiah, it is clear that there were at least two groups in Jerusalem. Particularly amongst the priests and aristocracy, there were those who favoured a fully open attitude to other inhabitants of the land, whether truly Israelites or not. On the other hand, the reform party took a rigorously exclusive view for ideological reasons. During the decades which followed, attitudes vacillated, but tended on the whole to polarize. The Chronicler's programme for reconciliation in the mid-fourth century BC failed, and not long after a group of the assimilationists found themselves forced out. What was more natural than that they should remove to the ancient and sacred site of Shechem to establish a new community more truly representative of Israel as they saw it (cf. n. 18 above)? When eventually they found themselves able to build a temple, the author of Ezra 1–6 compiled his polemical response, asserting emphatically the legitimacy of the Jerusalem sanctuary alone.

Thus we may conclude that at each step of this chequered history, much of which was determined by sociological and political as much as by theological factors, each faction presented an ideology of the temple to bolster its broader programme. Once the Chronicler's attempt at mediation had failed, the map was irrevocably drawn: the temple would not only be claimed as a touchstone of orthodoxy by Jerusalem and Shechem, but also in later years and in different ways by such other breakaway groups as Qumran and even – though here I stray beyond my competence and very much into Ernst Bammel's – by the early Christians.[30]

---

[30] Cf. B. GÄRTNER, The Temple and the Community in Qumran and the New Testament (SNTSMS, 1; Cambridge, 1965).

12. Eschatology in Chronicles

The title of this lecture requires a rather careful explanation of both its main elements. The word 'eschatology' has been deliberately chosen because of its appearance in the title of an influential book by O. Plöger, translated into English as *Theocracy and Eschatology*.[1] Stated very briefly, Plöger's thesis is that in the post-exilic community centred on Jerusalem there arose during the Persian and Hellenistic periods a sharp tension in which 'the various attitudes to the eschatological question may be regarded as the decisive point of difference' (p. 46). On the one hand, Plöger finds evidence in a number of texts, principally Isaiah 24–7, Zechariah 12–14 and Joel, for a strongly eschatological faith which over the years developed the hopes of the earlier restoration prophecies into the apocalyptic expectations of the *Hasidim* of Maccabean times, expressed particularly in the book of Daniel. Quite opposed to these groups stood a theocratic party whose adherents believed that the purposes of God were realized in the present community to such an extent that there was little if any place for eschatological expectation. In seeking to establish his case, Plöger argues that 'the non-eschatological view of the Chronicler... represents the official line within the theocracy' (p. 111).

In Old Testament scholarship, 'eschatology' is used in a wide variety of ways,[2] so much so that some even try to avoid it altogether. As it is by no means my intention to add to this confusion, let it here be stressed that our title means to imply no more than to ask how far Plöger's categorization is justified.

By 'Chronicles', I mean just that. For most scholars (Plöger included; cf. p. 37), the work of the Chronicler is thought to include either the whole or a substantial part of Ezra and Nehemiah.[3] I do not share this view, for reasons which I have set out elsewhere.[4] If I am mistaken in this view, then that ought not

---

[1] Oxford, 1968; translated by S. RUDMAN from the second edition of Theokratie und Eschatologie (WMANT, 2; Neukirchener Verlag, 1962).

[2] For a recent, clear statement of this variety, see J. BRIGHT, Covenant and Promise (London, 1977), 18–19.

[3] In recent years, a number have adopted the position maintained by K.-F. POHLMANN, Studien zum dritten Esra: Ein Beitrag zur Frage nach dem ursprünglichen Schluss des chronistischen Geschichtswerkes (FRLANT, 104; Göttingen, 1970), who argues, mainly on the basis of 1 Esdras, that the Chronicler's work originally concluded with Ezra 1–10 and Neh. 8.

[4] Israel in the Books of Chronicles (Cambridge, 1977), 5–70. On page 3, I observed in passing that the question of the extent of the Chronicler's work might have implications for

to affect the present study, for we would expect the conclusions which emerge from the major part of a writer's work at least not to contradict his viewpoint as a whole. At the same time, however, it seems worthwhile to take as a working hypothesis the view that 1 and 2 Chronicles constitute a separate work, for only then are we likely to make a serious attempt to establish their approach to any given topic and hence to have a firmer basis on which finally to assess the strengths and weaknesses of the hypothesis itself.

It is, then, our intention to examine the quite widespread contemporary understanding of one aspect of the Chronicler's theology that is typified by Plöger's work. What appears at first sight to be the study of a rather detailed point concerning a somewhat neglected book of the Old Testament may be justified on at least three grounds. First, it is agreed that this view of Chronicles differentiates it from the mainstream of Old Testament thought, setting it at the very edge of the Canon,[5] which so far as the Old Testament is concerned is usually thought to be characterized by an openness to the future of whatever sort.[6] Such a concession should not be made without first subjecting it to the most rigorous scrutiny. Secondly, in Plöger's view, Chronicles plays an important role in reconstructing one side of the divisions which are to be seen in the post-exilic period. Though this period is often shrouded in obscurity, it was a vital one both for the development of the Jewish people, and, hence, of their Bible in the form in which we have it today. Thirdly, the groups and parties with which we are more familiar from the background of the New Testament will have started to take shape at this time.[7] To the elucidation of this important topic too, our study may be seen as a small contribution.

A. The Present Position

We must start, then, by setting out in rather more detail Plöger's understanding of the Chronicler's view of theocracy. First, he draws on von Rad's conclusion that just as in Ezra and Nehemiah the term Israel is used for the tribes of Judah and Benjamin which made up the bulk of the post-exilic community, so too in

---

the usual assessment of his understanding of eschatology, messianism and theocracy. The present lecture may be seen as an attempt to justify this suggestion.

[5] W. RUDOLPH, Chronikbücher (HAT, 21; Tübingen, 1955), xxiii.

[6] See D.L. BAKER, Two Testaments, One Bible (Leicester, 1976), for a full survey with abundant bibliography.

[7] Note how many books on the background to the New Testament start their survey with the Persian period; e.g. F.F. BRUCE, New Testament History (London, 1969); E. LOHSE, Umwelt des neuen Testaments (Göttingen, 1971) ET, The New Testament Environment (London, 1976); R. H. PFEIFFER, History of New Testament Times (London, 1949); B. REICKE, Neutestamentliche Zeitgeschichte (Berlin, 1964) ET, The New Testament Era (London, 1968).

the history of the divided monarchy the name could only properly be used for those who still adhered to the house of David (p. 37).[8] This emphasis on David, which leads to the centrality of Jerusalem and the temple in the theocracy, was in part derived from the Deuteronomic history, but Plöger follows Noth[9] and Galling[10] in arguing that it received added significance in the Chronicler's day because of the controversy with the Samaritans. They, of course, shared the same views on the earlier period of Israelite history, but the Chronicler drew a sharp distinction between the respective communities by tracing the history of the people of God down through the period of the monarchy centred on Jerusalem and showing its continuity with the theocracy re-established under Ezra and Nehemiah (p. 39). This brings us to the heart of Plöger's exposition, for which he is explicitly indebted to W. Rudolph,[11] for he sees this realization of the theocracy as 'influenced not only by an outward looking anti-Samaritan aim, but also by an inward looking anti-eschatological point of view' (p. 40). According to Rudolph, the Chronicler's purpose was 'to present the realisation of theocracy in Israel' (p. 404). The twin pillars of this theocracy were the Davidic dynasty and the Jerusalem temple. However, hardly any messianic expectation is to be found, so it is unlikely that the Davidic dynasty had abiding significance for the Chronicler. On the other hand, he says:

we must not overlook the fact that in the second part of his presentation, the Books of Ezra and Nehemiah, he is pursuing the aim of describing the founding of the new people of God as it should be in accordance with the will of God – a community gathered around its Temple in zealous worship, protected by secure walls, in obedience to the divine Law, and inwardly separated from everything alien. This means that the actual Jewish community, especially as it is presented in Neh. xii 44-xiii 3, so fully realised the idea of theocracy for the Chronicler that there was no need of any further eschatological hope. The failure of the Davidic dynasty could be borne, so long as the second pillar of the theocracy, the Jerusalem Temple, stood firm. God had made this possible by moving the hearts of the Persian kings. The significance of the house of David for salvation was then limited to the fact that David and Solomon had created for the Temple those ordinances upon which the acceptable worship of the present community depended (p. 408f.).

In taking up this exposition, Plöger links it with his understanding of the Priestly Writing's view of history, namely that after the establishment of the cultic community on Mount Sinai, 'there was no prospect of fundamental change' (p. 40).

---

[8] See G. VON RAD, Das Geschichtsbild des chronistischen Werkes (BWANT, IV/3; Stuttgart, 1930), 18–37.

[9] M. NOTH, Überlieferungsgeschichtliche Studien 1 (Halle, 1943), 171–80.

[10] K. GALLING, Die Bücher der Chronik, Esra, Nehemia (ATD, 12; Göttingen, 1954), 14f.

[11] W. RUDOLPH, Chronikbücher. Parts of the introduction to this commentary, including the sections on which PLÖGER drew, were translated into English by P. R. ACKROYD, and read by RUDOLPH at a meeting of the Society for Old Testament Study in Edinburgh, July, 1954. They were subsequently published under the title 'Problems of the Books of Chronicles' in VT 4 (1954), 401–9. English citations here are from this article.

12. Eschatology in Chronicles

As already mentioned, Plöger's whole thesis has had a very considerable influence on current understanding of the development of the theology of the post-exilic community, and although the recent major work of P.D. Hanson[12] expresses reservations about some of Plöger's analysis, particularly his association of the opposing viewpoints with parties and sects, yet its own presentation of a struggle between a 'visionary' element on the one hand and a 'realistic' or 'pragmatic' element on the other, based upon their respective sociological status, is in a number of respects close to Plöger's view as far as the early post-exilic period is concerned,[13] for this latter element is defined as 'the hierocratic party dominated by the Zadokite priests which controlled the high priesthood' (p. 210). Hanson's analysis of the development of this struggle is far more detailed and subtle than Plöger's, so that he finds in the work of the Chronicler a more conciliatory position of the (at that time) victorious hierocratic party after the very exclusive claims of what he sees as a Zadokite revision of the book of Ezekiel. Nevertheless, the Chronicler's history remains a product of the hierocratic party, one of whose main emphases,[14] which would have alienated it from the visionary group, was its 'absence of an eschatological dimension' (p. 276). Hanson concludes that there is a marked interest in David and his establishment of the temple cult, but

the eschatological element implicit in the Davidic covenant is neglected... The fulfillment of history is not envisioned in an event of the future which would supersede and even negate past history, but is recognized in the present order (pp. 276f.).

Again

The Chronicler, living at a time when the temple was erected and standing at the very center of the life of the community, sees in the present order the fulfillment of history; past history is used not to point beyond the present to a future fulfillment, but to prove that the present represents the culmination toward which past history has been moving (p. 277).

---

[12] The Dawn of Apocalyptic (Philadelphia, 1975).

[13] It is only fair to point out that HANSON sees a change in the later period when he argues: 'The untenability of the "party" theory for the origins of apocalyptic becomes clear when one then moves on to consider developments in the second century, and finds Zadokites, themselves supplanted as temple priests, belonging to the apocalyptically orientated community of Qumran' (p. 20). Nevertheless, one would have welcomed more interaction with PLÖGER in HANSON's book.

[14] The other is the Chronicler's pro-Persian proclivity. However, as all the evidence for this is drawn from Ezra-Nehemiah (274-5), it need not be treated here. It should be noted in this connection that in our view, the last two verses of the present books of Chronicles were not part of the original composition, but were added subsequently from Ezra 1; see Israel in the Books of Chronicles, 7-10.

B. Alternative Viewpoints: Survey and Critique

In modern studies of Chronicles, two approaches have been adopted which present an alternative viewpoint to that just outlined. The first, adumbrated in a brief, but suggestive, study of D.N. Freedman[15] some while ago, has recently been developed independently by F.M. Cross[16] and J.D. Newsome.[17] Although in certain important points of detail there are differences between these scholars' positions, they do all agree that the most plausible setting for Chronicles is the post-exilic restoration of the temple under the leadership of Zerubbabel and Joshua the high priest. Its ideology is close to that of Haggai and Zechariah 1–8, and may have been the historical expression of the movement with which they were associated.

This understanding of the Chronicler is in marked contrast to that of Plöger. It makes of him one who shared in the hopes for the restoration of the Davidic dynasty in the person of Zerubbabel and for whom the future was wide open. There is certainly no question of an acquiescence in the present order of things, but rather an encouragement to faith in a new work which God is about to initiate. Furthermore, there is a certain attractiveness to this view in that it suggests a specific reason for the composition of Chronicles, and because it clearly was a period in which what Newsome calls the 'cluster of concerns' (p. 215) for kingdom, prophecy and cult, all prominent in Chronicles, are known to have converged.

However, our knowledge of the history of Judah in the Persian period is so episodic that we have to be aware of the temptation to bunch together around such fixed points as we do have all those unknown quantities which might in reality have filled one or another of the many gaps. In the present case, it may be argued first that evidence for a date for Chronicles substantially later than the last quarter of the sixth century BC[18] is dismissed too casually by these scholars, and secondly that the superficial attractiveness of their solution conceals difficulties to which they have not done justice.

The dating of Chronicles is a matter of the greatest delicacy; the more one investigates the evidence and usual arguments advanced, the more uncertain it

---

[15] 'The Chronicler's Purpose', CBQ 23 (1961), 436–42.

[16] 'A Reconstruction of the Judean Restoration', JBL 94 (1975), 4–18.

[17] 'Toward a New Understanding of the Chronicler and his Purposes', JBL 94 (1975), 201–17, reproducing, for the most part, the conclusions of his unpublished doctoral thesis, The Chronicler's View of Prophecy (Vanderbilt University, 1973).

[18] It should be observed that this revival of an early date for Chronicles is based on grounds quite separate from those previously advocated by A.C. WELCH in Post-Exilic Judaism (Edinburgh and London, 1935), 241f., and The Work of the Chronicler: its Purpose and Date (The Schweich Lectures, 1938) (Oxford, 1939), and that the one approach cannot appeal to the other for support. In fact, Welch's conclusions in this particular were based on a literary division of the text of Chronicles which would find few, if any, adherents today, despite the perspicacity of many other aspects of his presentation.

all becomes. What is clear, however, is that if 1 Chron. 3:19–21 is part of the original composition, then it cannot date from earlier than the second generation after Zerubbabel.[19] It is thus not surprising to find that Freedman, Cross and Newsome all deny that the genealogies of 1 Chron. 1–9 were an original part of the Chronicler's work. It must be observed, however, that their only argument for this position is that the genealogies contradict their dating.[20] This at once raises suspicion, and it is increased by the fact that neither Cross nor Newsome (whose articles are quite recent) makes any attempt to deal with such studies as have tried to show that in fact 1 Chron. 1–9 is both consistent with the thought and style of the remainder of the book, and that it contributes to its overall presentation.[21] It could never be proved, of course, that a later editor has not added a few generations to the Davidic genealogy in order to bring it down to his own day, but many theories of far reaching addition to an original genealogical core[22] have been shown to be less than securely based,[23] and in the case of the Davidic genealogy in particular, Johnson has demonstrated (pp. 69–71) that its structure conforms to that which the Chronicler uses elsewhere. Finally, from a literary point of view, there is no break at all in the genealogy as far as Zerubbabel's grandchildren (verse 21a), but thereafter in the text as we now have it (and it must be admitted that it is not above suspicion) there is a break,[24] 'the sons of Rephaiah' etc. being loosely attached without the copula. Thus, if we are going to look for editorial additions, this is the most likely place; but, as indicated above, it is already substantially after the period of Zerubbabel.

A related point concerning Cross's more elaborate theory of three successive editions of Chronicles should be mentioned here. Chr_3 is his name for the final edition, dated c. 400 BC and comprising the whole of our Chronicles-Ezra-Nehemiah. Cross then uses the evidence of 1 Esdras and Josephus to argue for a Chr_2 c. 450 BC. Its ending will accordingly have consisted of (approximately) Ezra with Neh. 8. Cross also argues, however, that 'the two editions differ at the beginning, Chr_3 introducing the genealogies of 1 Chronicles 1–9' (p. 11). For

---

[19] There is little agreement over how to construe vv.21b–24, as the commentaries show. It may take the genealogy further, but as this is not agreed by all (see R.K. HARRISON, Introduction to the Old Testament [London, 1970], 1155), it has seemed safest to stop here at the point on which all do agree, and which is sufficient for our present purposes.

[20] WELCH, Post-Exilic Judaism, 185 f., did at least suggest reasons for his relegation of these chapters to a secondary status. However, his main arguments, namely that they lack unity and do not fit with the themes of the rest of Chronicles, have been refuted by more recent studies; see the next note.

[21] M.D. JOHNSON, The Purpose of the Biblical Genealogies (SNTSMS, 8; Cambridge, 1969), 44–76; S. JAPHET, The Ideology of the Book of Chronicles and its Place in Biblical Thought (Hebrew: Doctoral Thesis, The Hebrew University, Jerusalem, 1973), 283–90.

[22] See principally M. NOTH, Überlieferungsgeschichtliche Studien I, 117–22, and W. RUDOLPH, Chronikbücher, ad loc.

[23] Israel in the Books of Chronicles, 72–82.

[24] See C.F. KEIL, Biblischer Commentar über die nachexilischen Geschichtsbücher: Chronik, Esra, Nehemia und Esther (Leipzig, 1870), 58.

this assertion there is no evidence. 1 Esdras[25] and Josephus, of course, cannot help us here, and, as Cross concedes, the Davidic line is traced in Ezra 8:3 as far as Hattush, who is already in what we have suggested might be the additional material at 1 Chronicles 3:22. Thus, even if we were to concede for the sake of this particular discussion that 1 Esdras could be used to reconstruct an earlier stage of the growth of Chronicles, that still would not necessarily involve the exclusion of 1 Chronicles 1–9. We may then observe finally that for Cross's postulated Chr_1 (1 Chron. 10-Ezra 3:13) there is no additional evidence beyond that already suggested by Freedman. The Greek versions and Josephus can certainly be adduced to open discussion of the postulated Chr_2 and $_3$, but we should not be misled into thinking that any new evidence has thereby been advanced to support an even earlier Chr_1.

A further difficulty for Cross and Freedman (though not for Newsome, since he separates the whole of Ezra from Chronicles) is raised by Ezra 4, which includes references, out of their strict chronological place, as late as Artaxerxes, who ascended the throne only in 465 BC. Thus Freedman guesses that an original narrative about Zerubbabel and the temple has been supplanted by the Aramaic record now found in Ezra 4:6–6:18, while Cross simply has his Chr_1 end at Ezra 3:13. This is not the place for an examination of the intricate problems surrounding the composition of Ezra 1–6, but no view that has to speculate to this extent without any external evidence against the present form of the text can be wholly self-authenticating.

Finally, on the issue of dating, we must not overlook the probable reference to Darics in 1 Chronicles 29:7. Two points are at issue here that need to be settled before the reference can be used with any confidence for dating purposes. The first seems now to command widespread agreement, namely that Darius I was the first to mint Darics, and that only some years after his accession. It used to be objected to this view that this would leave an awkward gap between the conquest by Cyrus of Croesus of Lydia, whence the Persians derived their own coinage.[26] It is now apparent, however, that in fact the Persians at first simply continued to mint Croeseids,[27] and indeed Greek coins in both silver and gold

---

[25] 1 Esdras in its present form starts at 2 Chron. 35. However, the work is almost certainly only the fragment of an originally more extensive compilation; see POHLMANN, Studien zum dritten Esra. We have no proof of its original opening, however, although I have argued against POHLMANN that it is unlikely to have been co-extensive with the whole of Chronicles; see Israel in the Books of Chronicles, 14–21.

[26] So, popularly, P. GARDNER, A History of Ancient Coinage, 700–300 BC (Oxford, 1918), 87–8.

[27] Cf. J.H. JONGKEES, 'Kroiseios en Dareikos', Jaarbericht No. 9 van het Vooraziatisch-Egyptisch Gezelschap: Ex Oriente Lux (1944), 163–8, drawing on evidence from the hoard of coins discovered in the American excavations at Sardis, one group of which were certainly minted under the Persians; see T.L. SHEAR, 'Sixth Preliminary Report on the American Excavations at Sardes in Asia Minor' AJA, second series, 26 (1922), 389–409 (397–9), and S.P. NOE, A Bibliography of Greek Coin Hoards (second edition; Numismatic Notes and

12. Eschatology in Chronicles

were found in the foundation deposit of Darius' own throne room at Persepolis.[28] The evidence thus points strongly to a later date for the introduction of Darics, 515 BC at the earliest. Secondly, however, can we be sure that it is to Darics that 1 Chronicles 29:7 refers? (a) No word for Daric is known in Old Persian. *darika- has been suggested[29] and is etymologically possible,[30] but remains unattested. What does now seem likely, however, is that this is not an abbreviation of the superficially similar word for gold, *daraniya-*,[31] which some have then suggested was used for coins throughout the period of the Persian empire. Furthermore, such an abbreviation would in any case leave the silver Darics unexplained,[32] and would not of itself prove that the Daric necessarily went back to an earlier date.[33] (b) On the Greek side, it is well known that classical authors understood *dareikos* to be derived from the name Darius,[34] attesting their belief that he was the first to mint these coins. Since this fits in exactly with the numismatic evidence referred to above, and is acceptable on linguistic grounds,[35] there is no need to doubt the value of this evidence. What remains uncertain, however, is whether this is a loanword from the Old Persian for Daric, its explanation being merely a Greek *Volksetymologie*, or whether the name was in fact Greek from the start. (c) In the Old Testament, there are two similar words that appear to refer to coins in texts of the Persian period: *ʾadarkōnîm* in our 1 Chronicles 29:7 and Ezra 8:27, and *darkᵉmōnîm* in Ezra 2:69=Nehemiah 7:70

Monographs, 78; 1937), no. 927. Again, E. S. G. ROBINSON, 'The Beginnings of Achaemenid Coinage', The Numismatic Chronicle, 6th series, 18 (1958), 187–93, comes to similar conclusions on the basis of two hoards from Tchai (45 miles east of Smyrna), published by S. P. NOE, Two Hoards of Persian Sigloi (Numismatic Notes and Monographs, 136; 1956).

[28] E. HERZFELD, 'Notes on the Achaemenid Coinage and some Sassanian Mint-Names', Transactions of the International Numismatic Congress 1936, edited by J. ALLAN, H. MATTINGLY and E.S.G. ROBINSON, 413–26 (413–16); E.F. SCHMIDT, The Treasury of Persepolis and Other Discoveries in the Homeland of the Achaemenians (Communications of the Oriental Institute of the University of Chicago, 21; Chicago, 1939), 76; full publication by S. P. NOE et al., in E.F. SCHMIDT, Persepolis II, Contents of the Treasury (Oriental Institute Publications, 69; Chicago, 1957), 110–4, pl. 84.

[29] A. MEILLET, Grammaire du vieux-perse (1915), 67 (not available to me).

[30] E. SCHWYZER, in an article in Indogermanische Forschungen 49 (1931), 1–45, discusses the main philological problems of Old Persian, Greek and Hebrew references to Darics (8–21). I am grateful to Dr I. GERSHEVITCH for initially drawing my attention to this article, which has generally been overlooked by the commentators, though it is now included in the new German lexicon: W. BAUMGARTNER et al., Hebräisches und aramäisches Lexikon zum alten Testament (Lieferung 1; Leiden, 1967), 16.

[31] Cf. SCHWYZER, 13, and R.G. KENT, Old Persian: Grammar, Texts, Lexicon (New Haven, 1950), 189.

[32] G.F. HILL, Catalogue of the Greek Coins of Arabia, Mesopotamia and Persia (Oxford, 1922), cxx f., observes that *dareikos* was also sometimes used by the Greeks for silver Persian coins.

[33] JONGKEES, 'Kroiseios en Dareikos', 166.

[34] Herodotus IV, 166; Pollux III, 87.

[35] SCHWYZER, 8–12.

and Nehemiah 7:69, 71. Although the LXX is not of great help at this point, unfortunately, yet as far as it goes[36] it would tend to support what is certainly on the surface the most attractive suggestion[37] of seeing Drachmas in *dark^{e}mōnîm* and Darics in *'^{a}darkōnîm*, the *mem* of *dark^{e}mōnîm* being the distinguishing factor. In both cases, the *-ōn* ending would reflect the Greek genitive plural.[38] Both types of coin were, of course, current in the Persian period.[39]

I thus conclude that the author of 1 Chronicles 29:7 was most probably representing part of the offering for the preparation for temple building at the end of David's reign in terms of the Darics that were current in his own day,[40] an innocent enough anachronism which is by no means unparalleled in modern translations and paraphrases of the Bible today. However, since no one has suggested relegating this passage to a secondary level of composition it appears that he could not then have written as early as Freedman, Cross and Newsome have suggested.[41] With that conclusion, however, their understanding of the Chronicler's purpose as somehow intending to support the hopes vested in Zerubbabel in the early years of Darius' reign and as attested in Haggai and Zech. 1-8 must be rejected.

It is perhaps worth taking this discussion yet one step further, for even if it were possible to date Chronicles as early as these scholars suggest, we would not necessarily then have to conclude that such a date was the most plausible on

---

[36] Darics are nowhere mentioned in the Greek Bible. Drachmas are mentioned in several passages, of which two are relevant to the present discussion. In the A text of Ezra 2:69 it is used to translate *dark^{e}mōnîm*, and this supports the position defended above. At Ezra 8:27, the A text also translates *'^{a}darkōnîm* by 'Drachmas'. This may suggest that the two words in Hebrew were not distinguished, but it is equally possible to suppose that the *Vorlage* of LXX A also read *dark^{e}mōnîm* here; cf. SCHWYZER, 16.

[37] See E. MEYER, Die Entstehung des Judenthums (Halle, 1896), 196-7, who also adduces further supporting evidence from a bilingual Greek and Phoenician inscription from Piraeus in which both forms again occur. MEYER has been followed by, for instance, SCHWYZER, 17-19, and W. RUDOLPH, Esra und Nehemia samt 3. Esra (HAT, 20; Tübingen, 1949), 24.

[38] For the use of prosthetic *'aleph* in a number of Iranian loan words, see E. MEYER, Die Entstehung des Judenthums, 38.

[39] There is thus no need to follow W.F. ALBRIGHT who revised his earlier opinion to suggest that all these passages refer to Drachmas; contrast JBL 40 (1921), 113, with BiOr 17 (1960), 242.

[40] The suggestion that the word reflects the Assyrian *darag mana* (so conveniently H. HAMBURGER, IDB I, 769) is rejected by SCHWYZER, 14, and rightly, for the Assyrian phrase is not found in the modern dictionaries.

[41] They are, of course, at liberty to suggest alternative explanations, for instance that Darics were, despite the evidence we have referred to, minted before the time of Darius I, or that a later editor altered the original text of 1 Chron. 29:7 to suit it to the currency of his own day. The disadvantage of any such suggestion is its appearance of special pleading, seeking to avoid the implications of what is potentially one of the very few pieces of solid evidence for dating in the interests of a wider theory which must inevitably remain hypothetical. It would appear to be sounder method to move from what is more certain to what is less, rather than *vice versa*.

the evidence they themselves have advanced; indeed, there are certain difficulties in the way of this conclusion that have not so far been faced. These difficulties centre chiefly on the fact that despite the many similarities between Haggai and Zechariah, there are also differences of emphasis between them that should not be underestimated. It would take us far beyond our subject to discuss these points in detail, for there are several difficult matters concerning text (especially in Zech. 6:11-14), redaction and interpretation which would all require close examination first. Suffice it to say for the present, however, that virtually all major recent comparative studies of Haggai and Zechariah 1-8 agree that there are such differences of emphasis, and that they concern particularly the understanding of the role of Zerubbabel.[42] Most noteworthy in this regard is that in Zechariah Joshua the high priest is far more prominent than in Haggai to the point where it is necessary to speak of the vision of a dyarchic form of leadership for the community. We may also observe a slight modification in Zechariah of Haggai's more overtly religio-political involvement.[43]

Although we must here enter the realm of speculation, it would seem most likely that this change was caused principally by two factors. On the one hand, although Ackroyd has demonstrated the difficulties of establishing any precise correlation between the dates supplied in these books and the turbulent course of events that marked the start of Darius' reign,[44] yet even he finds significance in the date in Zechariah 1:7. He writes of the immediately following passage (1:8-17):

> here the message given to the prophet is 'behold, all the earth remains at rest.' This message – indicating that rebellions in the empire are at an end – is so appropriate to the date given immediately before (1:7, February 520)... that it would appear to be a strong argument in favor of the general correctness of that date, at least for this particular utterance (p. 18).

On the other hand, despite the persistent efforts of a number of scholars[45] to implicate Zerubbabel in some conspiracy or rebellion, for which he was subse-

---

[42] E. g. P. R. ACKROYD, Exile and Restoration: A Study of Hebrew Thought of the Sixth Century BC (OTL; London, 1968), 153-217; W. A. M. BEUKEN, Haggai-Sacharja 1-8: Studien zur Überlieferungsgeschichte der frühnachexilischen Prophetie (Studia Semitica Neerlandica, 10; Assen, 1967); K.-M. BEYSE, Serubbabel und die Königserwartungen der Propheten Haggai und Sacharja: Eine historische und traditionsgeschichtliche Untersuchung (Arbeiten zur Theologie, I/48; Stuttgart, 1972); K. GALLING, 'Serubbabel und der Wiederaufbau des Tempels in Jerusalem', in A. KUSCHKE (ed.), Verbannung und Heimkehr: Beiträge zur Geschichte und Theologie Israels im 6. und 5. Jahrhundert v. Chr. (Tübingen, 1961), 67-96; idem., Studien zur Geschichte Israels im persischen Zeitalter (Tübingen, 1964), 109-26 and 127-48; W. RUDOLPH, Haggai-Sacharja 1-8-Sacharja 9-14-Maleachi (Gütersloh, 1976), especially 153-6; G. SAUER, 'Serubbabel in der Sicht Haggais und Sacharjas', in F. MAASS (ed.), Das ferne und nahe Wort (BZAW, 105; Berlin, 1967), 199-207; K. SEYBOLD, 'Die Königserwartungen bei den Propheten Haggai und Sacharja', Judaica 28 (1972) 69-78.

[43] BEYSE, 37, who is more restrained in this regard than SAUER.

[44] P. R. ACKROYD, 'Two Old Testament Historical Problems of the Early Persian Period', JNES 17 (1958), 13-27.

[45] The most extreme statement of this position is L. WATERMAN, 'The Camouflaged

quently executed or removed from office, there is reasonable evidence to suggest that in fact the very opposite was the case. First, Darius explicitly confirmed Zerubbabel in his role as governor and temple builder after Tattenai and his colleagues had inquired (Ezra 5:3–17) whether the rebuilding of the temple, which had already started, was permissible:

> Now therefore, Tattenai, governor of the province Beyond the River, Shethar-bozenai, and your associates the governors who are in the province Beyond the River, keep away; let the work on this house of God alone; let the governor of the Jews and the elders of the Jews rebuild this house of God on its site (Ezra 6:6–7).

This permission would not have been given if there was any suspicion of involvement in seditious activity.[46] Second, it appears from the problematic Ezra 4 that 'the adversaries of Judah and Benjamin' waited until the walls of Jerusalem were being rebuilt in the reign of Artaxerxes before accusing the city and its inhabitants of being 'rebellious and wicked'. Again, this delay would be hard to explain if there had been occasion for such an accusation in the earlier period.[47] We may thus conclude that Zerubbabel himself preferred not to make any capital whatever out of his Davidic ancestry.

Now Newsome speaks (p. 214) of the author of Chronicles and the prophets Haggai and Zechariah cherishing a political hope focussed upon the house of David in the person of Zerubbabel. If he wishes to be as particular as that, however, then we must observe that the evidence just adduced would strongly suggest that both external and internal developments caused these political hopes to be modified within months at most of their formulation. Since part of that modification is to introduce the high priest in a role and status which, as Beuken has shown,[48] could not have claimed support from Chronicles, we are left, on Newsome's understanding, with far too short a time to allow for the composition of so long and well structured a work as 1 and 2 Chronicles, quite apart from the time that would have been needed to collect the material for that composition. If, on the other hand, Newsome does not wish to tie his interpretation so closely to political developments, then at once we must ask why Chronicles should be tied to the late sixth century BC at all. He argues that by 400 BC 'the prophetic decline was far advanced, and the Davidic kingdom was merely a memory' (p. 216). But how do we know? Newsome gives no evidence to support this assertion, whereas against it many would claim that there were still prophets active in Jerusalem considerably later than Haggai and Zechariah:

Purge of Three Messianic Conspirators', JNES 13 (1954), 73–8, but it has also been held by others in more moderate forms; e.g. A. T. OLMSTEAD, History of the Persian Empire (Chicago, 1970), 142. Earlier suggestions along this line were criticized in particular by A. BENTZEN, 'Quelques remarques sur le mouvement messianique parmi les Juifs aux environs de l'an 520 avant Jésus-Christ', RHPhR 10 (1930), 493–503.

[46] Cf. K.-M. BEYSE, 45.
[47] Cf. K. GALLING, 'Serubbabel', 94–6, and Studien, 147–8.
[48] W. A. M. BEUKEN, Haggai-Sacharja 1–8, 309–16.

Malachi certainly, Joel and Obadiah probably,[49] and perhaps parts of other prophetic books according to one's views of their composition. As to the Davidic kingdom, the genealogy in 1 Chronicles 3 certainly comes down to a later date, as we have seen, and, whatever its relationship to the remainder of the book, it stands in its own right as a witness to a continuing interest in the Davidic line. Moreover, the fact that Nehemiah's opponents even considered it worth bringing a charge against him which said 'you have also set up prophets to proclaim concerning you in Jerusalem, "there is a king in Judah"' (Neh. 6:7) would suggest that they considered it possible that they would be believed.[50] The attribution of Chronicles to the period of Haggai and Zechariah may thus be said to have difficulties which its proponents have not yet faced, and moreover to rest in the last resort on an argument from a silence which is in imminent danger of being broken.

Finally, Freedman, Cross and Newsome imply that the prophets and the Chronicler come from the same circle. It need hardly be said, however, that a general similarity on certain prominent issues is not sufficient to maintain this more specific hypothesis. The issue has been one of quite separate debate in recent years following the publication of Beuken's work already referred to. He argues with commendable thoroughness that Haggai and Zechariah 1–8 received their final editing in what is called a 'Chronistically orientated milieu'. We should observe at once that, of course, this in itself implies a certain distinction between the original oracles of the prophets and their editors who intended to interpret and reapply their message to a later generation, a distinction which forms the main basis for Beuken's detailed exposition. Beuken's view (which in any case presupposes the common authorship of Chronicles, Ezra and Nehemiah) has recently come in for a measure of what, in my opinion, is justified criticism,[51] to which further points could be added without great difficulty.[52] It follows, therefore, that here again we should be careful of associating these various works too closely.

---

[49] Cf. R. K. HARRISON, Introduction, 879 and 902.

[50] This would be even more significant if the suggestion that Nehemiah himself was of Davidic descent could be substantiated; but it remains very speculative: U. KELLERMANN, Nehemia: Quellen, Überlieferung und Geschichte (BZAW, 102; Berlin, 1967), 154–9, and W.TH. IN DER SMITTEN, 'Erwägungen zu Nehemias Davidizität', JSJ 5 (1974), 41–8, but cf. the critical comments of J. A. EMERTON, JTS ns 23 (1972), 177–81.

[51] W. RUDOLPH, Haggai-Sacharja 1–8, 23, 38f., etc., and especially R. A. MASON, 'The Purpose of the "Editorial Framework" of the Book of Haggai', VT 27 (1977), 413–21.

[52] For instance, we might expect that in a 'neutral' matter such as the use of titles there would be a similarity between the various works of a single school. However, in this case, we find just the opposite. A frequent and characteristic title for God in Haggai and Zech. 1–8 is 'the Lord of Hosts', and some of its occurrences are generally attributed to the editor(s) of the books. Chronicles, however, shows a dislike for it: it is never found in material peculiar to Chronicles, and in three out of six cases where it is found in his *Vorlage*, it has been suppressed; cf. S. JAPHET, Ideology, 25–6. Similarly, for the title 'high priest', Haggai and Zech. 1–8 regularly use the expression *hkhn hgdwl*, and again, this is frequent in passages

On the basis of these various considerations, it may thus be concluded that the recent attempts to find an eschatology of a rather particular kind in Chronicles by way of an early dating must be rejected. We learn from this discussion, however, that our examination will need to be rather more closely involved with the texts themselves. The dangers of seeking to relate a historical book to a particular event in a later period are clear, and without much more evidence such attempts are likely to fail.

An alternative approach to our problem may be said to link some aspects of the works of a number of scholars which otherwise differ quite markedly.[53] On this view, the Chronicler is thought so to have heightened his portrayal of the glories of a past age as to stimulate within his readers the hopes for a return to these conditions in an eschatological, or quasi-eschatological, dimension. This is usually discussed with particular reference to the person and reign of David, though in a more recent study Mosis has attempted to refine this approach much further.[54] In his view, the reigns of Saul, David and Solomon are paradigms of three possible situations in which later Israel may find herself; Saul is representative of apostasy and failure, in brief, of exile, whereas David is more the pattern for restoration, a transition from loss to salvation, and yet (and this is Mosis' distinctive contribution) his reign is not in itself a period of final attainment. It is, rather, preparatory to ultimate fulfilment, typified by the Chronicler's presentation of the reign of Solomon.[55] Subsequent kings, and indeed the post-exilic restoration, are found to have parallels with either the reign of Saul or of David; the Solomonic epoch remains as a pattern for future, even eschatological, hope and aspiration.[56]

---

that are most naturally understood as editorial, such as the narrative introductions to the oracles. In Chronicles, however, this title is only found once, at 2 Chron. 34:9, where it is drawn unchanged from 2 Kgs 22:4. Elsewhere, both in passages peculiar to Chronicles, and in passages where the Chronicler has altered or suppressed his *Vorlage*, he uses instead *khn hr'š*; see S. JAPHET, VT 18 (1968), 343–4.

[53] E.g. G. VON RAD, Geschichtsbild, 119–32, and Theologie des alten Testaments I (Munich, 1958), 347–8 (ET, Old Testament Theology I [Edinburgh and London, 1962], 350–1); A. NOORDTZIJ, 'Les intentions du Chroniste', RB 49 (1940), 161–8; A.-M. BRUNET, 'Le Chroniste et ses sources', RB 60 (1953), 481–508 and 61 (1954), 349–86, and 'La théologie du Chroniste: théocratie et messianisme', in J. COPPENS et al. (eds.), Sacra Pagina I (ETL 12–13; 1959), 384–97; G.J. BOTTERWECK, 'Zur Eigenart der chronistischen Davidgeschichte', ThQ 136 (1956), 402–35; W.F. STINESPRING, 'Eschatology in Chronicles', JBL 80 (1961), 209–19; R. NORTH, 'Theology of the Chronicler', JBL 82 (1963), 369–81; F. MICHAELI, Les Livres des Chroniques, d'Esdras et de Néhémie (CAT, 16; Neuchâtel, 1967), 31–2.

[54] R. MOSIS, Untersuchungen zur Theologie des chronistischen Geschichtswerkes (Freiburg, 1973). MOSIS's approach to the Chronicler has received a measure of approval, at any rate by comparison with that of T. WILLI, Die Chronik als Auslegung (FRLANT, 106; Göttingen, 1972), from P.R. ACKROYD, 'The Chronicler as Exegete', JSOT 2 (1977), 2–32.

[55] See in particular 164–9.

[56] 'Der Chr gestaltet also seine Salomogeschichte nach der in 2 Makk 2, 1 ff bezeugten, endzeitlichen Heilserwartung und entwirft damit ein Bild des Heils, das zu seiner Zeit, der Zeit des zweiten Tempels, noch aussteht und dessen Kommen er für eine noch zukünftige Zeit erwartet' (163).

12. Eschatology in Chronicles

Concerning the first group of studies just mentioned, it must be said that although it may superficially seem difficult to find any major objection, yet often they are expressed in such general terms that the conclusions drawn are inevitably somewhat subjective. This is shown particularly by the fact that the same evidence has clearly failed to impress Rudolph, Plöger and others. In fact, however, although it is certainly true that the portrayal of David is more favourable in Chronicles than in Samuel and Kings, yet, as Japhet has shown,[57] enough unfavourable elements remain to suggest that it cannot be termed 'idealized'. How, then, can we be sure that the Chronicler's purpose was that which these scholars claim? Their approach could only win approval if first they could point to some specific texts which indicated that this was in fact in the mind of the Chronicler.

Mosis, on the other hand, might claim that his detailed study avoids these dangers. In consequence, however, it lays itself open to more rigid scrutiny which suggests that he may have erred in three important respects.[58] First, whereas it is true that Solomon's character is portrayed in Chronicles as blameless, yet that again does not make of him the idealized figure that Mosis suggests. His dependence upon his father's preparations for the successful building of the temple is only the most striking example of this fact.[59] Secondly, as will become apparent later, I agree with Japhet and Braun[60] that the Chronicler has endeavoured to present the reigns of David and Solomon as a unity. Though neither on his own is an idealized figure, yet the period of their rule as a whole is presented in a most positive fashion. It is thus questionable whether the division which Mosis draws between them, so crucial for his interpretation, can be maintained in the form that he sets out. Thirdly, it has been suggested that the Chronicler modelled his presentation of the reign of Hezekiah on that of Solomon, not David, and that Mosis' attempts to find 'Davidic' elements in Hezekiah are unsuccessful.[61] If this suggestion is correct, Solomon's reign can no longer serve as a unique pattern of eschatological bliss.

We conclude from these observations, therefore, that although this second main approach to our topic has much to commend it over the first, it by no means

---

[57] JAPHET, Ideology, 468–72, drawing attention in particular to 1 Chron. 21, 1 Chron. 13 with 15:11–15 and 1 Chron. 22:7–8, 28:3.

[58] ACKROYD, 'Chronicler as Exegete', makes a number of criticisms of details in MOSIS's arguments, though he does not necessarily think that these invalidate MOSIS's position as a whole. They are thus in a rather different category from those listed above, and so need not be pursued further here.

[59] I have developed this theme more fully in 'The Accession of Solomon in the Books of Chronicles', VT 26 (1976), 351–61 (see above, 141–49); see further JAPHET, Ideology, 476–81.

[60] See the references in the previous note, together with R.L. BRAUN, 'Solomonic Apologetic in Chronicles', JBL 92 (1973), 503–16; 'Solomon, the Chosen Temple Builder: the Significance of 1 Chronicles 22, 28, and 29 for the Theology of Chronicles', JBL 95 (1976), 581–90, and 'The Message of Chronicles: Rally 'Round the Temple', CTM 22 (1971), 502–14.

[61] Israel in the Books of Chronicles, 119–25.

exhausts the subject. In particular, there is a clear need to deal with the texts themselves, rather than resting content with vague generalizations about the Chronicler's portrayals of character.

C. The Dynastic Oracle

The most promising approach is likely to be by way of a study of the position of the king in Chronicles since, as is well known, the whole work is very much built around the Davidic dynasty. Clearly, our particular concern must be to examine whether the Chronicler thought that the promises to David, which of course were of eternal significance, were of such a kind as to lead him to expect the emergence of a king some time in the future in Jerusalem, or whether, as so many have argued, he presented his history in such a way as to suggest that the significance of these promises had been transferred to the temple and its cultus, so that no particular further change in the theocracy was to be expected. Inevitably, we must start with an examination of the Chronicler's presentation and interpretation of the dynastic oracle.

Two main types of evidence have been advanced in the past in the attempt to resolve this point, and it is noteworthy that both have been claimed in support of each position. A brief review of the salient points of this discussion will provide the context in which a new suggestion for the resolution of this difficulty may be understood.

Comparison of 1 Chronicles 17 with 2 Samuel 7 (the Nathan oracle) shows that there is a clear literary relationship between the two. The differences between them, however, have been variously explained. We may most easily begin with a comparison of the parallel forms of the verse that lies, in our present texts, at the very heart of the oracle, and move out thence to the wider context.

2 Sam. 7:12　כי ימלאו ימיך ושכבת את אבתיך והקימתי את זרעך אחריך
אשר יצא ממעיך והכינתי את ממלכתו

1 Chron. 17:11　והיה כי מלאו ימיך ללכת עם אבתיך והקימתי את זרעך
אחריך אשר יהיה מבניך והכינותי את מלכותו

The only difference of any real substance between these two verses lies in the underlined clauses. Most scholars (excepting, of course, those who find in the Chronicler's מבניך no more than a textual corruption of ממעיך[62]) argue that 'The change in Ch. has been made to point more definitely to Solomon',[63] so

---

[62] E. g. I. BENZINGER, Die Bücher der Chronik (KHAT, 20; Tübingen and Leipzig, 1901), 56.

[63] E. L. CURTIS and A. A. MADSEN, A Critical and Exegetical Commentary on the Books of Chronicles (ICC; Edinburgh, 1910), 229.

12. Eschatology in Chronicles

that translations such as 'one of your own sons' (RSV), 'der einer von deinen Söhnen sein wird'[64] or 'qui sera un de tes fils'[65] are commonplace. Few writers seem to regard it as necessary to justify this understanding, though Rudolph (p. 133) advances three supporting arguments. First, the continuation (2 Sam 7:13; 1 Chron. 17:12) points clearly to Solomon; secondly, the whole of 1 Chron. 17:11-14 is said to refer to Solomon, whilst, thirdly, the later application of the oracle to Solomon in 1 Chron. 22:9-10; 28:5-6 and 2 Chron. 6:9 should be decisive in determining our interpretation of it.

This last point is not compelling, however, for, as Rudolph later concedes (pp. 135-137), the Chronicler himself applies the promise to kings later than Solomon (cf. 2 Chron. 13:5; 21:7 and 23:3). Moreover, in a footnote to his translation (p. 131), he admits that an alternative interpretation is grammatically possible, namely '(d. Samen,) der aus deinen Söhnen hervorgehen wird'. This would be, of course, the translation defended by proponents of the 'messianic' position, and is generally attributed by modern writers to von Rad.[66] He in turn, however, derived his understanding from Keil, and it is only in his commentary,[67] which seems to have been completely ignored in the modern debate, that we find a real attempt to defend this alternative translation. He maintains, first, that if the Chronicler had wished to limit the reference to Solomon, he would have omitted the relative clause altogether, since 'thy seed', without further qualification, would include the sons of David. Secondly, if more precise specification were needed, אשר מבניך would have been the form expected. Thirdly, היה מן is stated not to denote *to be of* one, i.e., *to belong to* him, but rather *to arise, be born* or *go forth from* one; Gen. 17:16 and Eccl. 3:20 are compared. Finally, this messianic interpretation is said best to account for the other divergences of the Chronicler's text from Samuel, such as the omission of 2 Sam 7:14b.

Since this last point is disputed on other grounds, and since the first two can be explained away on the supposition that the Chronicler was attempting to follow the verbal outline of his *Vorlage* in as close a manner as his own distinctive viewpoint would allow, it would appear that the substance of Keil's case rests upon his third point.

The two passages he cites for comparison certainly lend strong support to his position. Eccl 3:20b and c reads: הכל היה מן העפר והכל שב אל העפר. There is a clear allusion here to Gen 3:19: כי עפר אתה ואל עפר תשוב, but whereas

---

[64] RUDOLPH, Chronikbücher, 130.
[65] A. CAQUOT, 'Peut-on parler de messianisme dans l'oeuvre du Chroniste?, *RTP* 3/16 (1966), 116.
[66] VON RAD, Geschichtsbild, 123-124, and Theologie des alten Testaments I, 348, n. 9. It is adopted without further discussion by *(inter alia)* NOORDTZIJ, 'Les intentions du Chroniste', 163; GALLING, Chronik, Esra, Nehemia, 54; BOTTERWECK, 'Zur Eigenart der chronistischen Davidgeschichte', 402-435, esp. 422.
[67] KEIL, Chronik, 163-164.

Adam himself can be called 'dust' directly and without qualification (cf. Gen 2:7), his descendants, to whom Koheleth refers, can be described thus only in an indirect manner; hence the qualifying use of היה מן.

The situation is comparable at Gen 17:16b*b*: מלכי עמים ממנה יהיו,[68] for it is clear that it is not Sarah's own son, but rather her more distant descendants who are to be kings. On the basis of these two verses, therefore, Keil's interpretation of 1 Chron. 17:11 cannot be so lightly rejected as some have implied.

While it is thus clearly possible to understand the phrase in isolation in the way Keil proposes, he has nevertheless failed to prove that this is the only possible interpretation. If it can be established that the phrase is in fact ambiguous, then it must be left to a consideration of the wider context to settle the issue. The examples Keil cites are selected to support his case.

Others, however, can equally well be adduced which point in a contrary direction. Without in any way needing here to undertake a full analysis of the use of היה מן, we may in the first place point to 1 Kgs 12:31b – ויעש כהנים מקצות העם אשר לא היו מבני לוי – to show that in some cases מן has no further significance than 'from amongst'. Deut 23:18 is similar. Also expressing immediacy rather than the indirectness that Keil seeks to defend (although not quite so close because of the absence of ב from the context) is the use of מן after היה in 2 Sam. 3:37b; 1 Kgs 2:15b; Isa. 50:11c; Jer. 30:21a; Mal. 1:9b and 2 Chron. 22:7 (*inter alia*). Finally, we may note the use of היה מן to express the idea of 'to be of one piece with', in, for instance, Exod. 25:31, 36; 27:2; 28:8; 37:17, 22, 25 and 38:2.

We conclude, therefore, that the contentious phrase אשר יהיה מבניך is in itself ambiguous, and that Keil was wrong to deny that it could possibly mean 'to be of' one. In consequence, we are now at liberty to suggest that other factors point to its reference in the mind of the Chronicler to Solomon alone. In particular, the continuation in the next verse – הוא יבנה לי בית – must, in the context of the chapter as a whole, refer to Solomon as the temple-builder. It is thus hard to refrain from endorsing the first of Rudolph's arguments in support of his rendering of 1 Chron. 17: 11 noted above.

---

[68] The text of the second half of this verse is not at all certain, the witnesses to it falling into three main groups: (a) the MT applies the whole to Sarah, וברכתיה והיתה לגוים מלכי עמים ממנה יהיו. This is broadly supported by the Targumim (except Tg. Ps.-J.), though Tgs. Onkelos and Neofiti mg have second person singular suffixes for the first word (ואברך יתך/ואברכינך); (b) The Sam. Pent. reads וברכתיו referring to the son who has been promised. This is presupposed also by the LXX, Vg, Pesh, Jub and Tg. Ps.-J., and is adopted, for instance, by E. A. SPEISER, Genesis (AB; Garden City, 1964), 125; (c) These latter versions (except T. Ps.-J.) go further than the Sam. Pent., however, in also referring the final clause, in which we are here primarily interested, to Isaac, not Sarah, but they have generally not been followed in this by the commentators. Even if this were correct, it would not affect the point of syntax which KEIL upholds, for neither Jacob nor Esau are said to have been kings, but only their more distant descendants.

12. Eschatology in Chronicles

Secondly, however, there is little justification for the view which sees in the Chronicler's text an attempt specifically to intensify the individual reference to Solomon.[69] It is probable, rather, that in this instance he has merely furnished us with no more than a straight alternative to his *Vorlage*. Seeligmann has pointed to the precise parallelism of היה מן in Gen. 17:16 with יצא מן in v. 6 of the same chapter,[70] to which we might add the parallel couplet at the start of Jer. 30:21 as comparing very closely with the texts under discussion:

והיה אדירו ממנו

ומשלו מקרבו יצא

In addition, it has been observed by Japhet[71] that בניך and מעיך יצאי are also synonymous expressions, as comparison of the parallel texts 2 Kgs 19:37 *(Qere)*, Isa. 37:38 and 2 Chron. 32:21 shows. It would thus appear that both parties to the discussion have sought to read too much into 1 Chron. 17:11. Our contention is rather that the Chronicler understood his *Vorlage* at this point to refer to Solomon, and that he reproduced it accordingly. General probabilities suggest that he introduced a slight change for stylistic purposes,[72] though recent studies have tended to underline the difficulties of pinpointing the origin of such changes,[73] so that in the end we cannot be sure that the Chronicler was not just reproducing his *Vorlage* faithfully, or even that the Samuel text is not secondary at this point.[74]

If it be allowed that the differences between 1 Chron. 17:11 and 2 Sam 7:12 are in fact of little substantial significance, we can then move on to observe that

---

[69] *Contra* WILLI, Die Chronik als Auslegung, 105–106.
[70] I.L. SEELIGMANN, Tarbiz 25 (1955–6), 129.
[71] JAPHET, Ideology, 417.
[72] H. VAN DEN BUSSCHE, ETL 24 (1948), 386 has even suggested that a later scribe may have changed the text of Chronicles, which will have originally been identical with Samuel, because he found the expression יצא ממעיך too crude for a divine speech.
[73] Cf. S. TALMON, 'Synonymous readings in the textual traditions of the Old Testament', Scripta Hierosolymitana 8 (1961), 335–383, who intends to point out on p. 358 that the LXX of both verses underlines our difficulties in this regard, since it takes its verb form from Chronicles and its noun from Samuel (not *vice versa*, as TALMON actually says); W.E. LEMKE, 'The Synoptic Problem in the Chronicler's History', HTR 58 (1965), 349–363.
[74] There are, of course, some standard examples in these chapters where, from a purely textual point of view, Chronicles is to be preferred to Samuel; e.g. שפטי in 1 Chron. 17:6 against שבטי in 2 Sam. 7:7 (I am not persuaded by the contrary opinion of PH. DE ROBERT, 'Juges ou tribus en 2 Samuel VII?', VT 21 [1971], 116–118, or of P.V. REID, '*šbty* in 2 Samuel 7:7', CBQ 37 [1975], 17–20); והיה at the start of 1 Chron. 17:11, which is omitted in 2 Sam 7:12, probably by dittography with the end of the preceding verse. H. VAN DER BUSSCHE, 'Le texte de la prophétie de Nathan sur la dynastie davidique (II Sam., VII – I Chron., XVII)', ETL 24 (1948), 354–394, has gone much further than this in suggesting that in virtually every case, stylistic, linguistic or theological considerations point to the secondary nature of the text in Samuel. Whilst no other scholar seems to have adopted this extreme position, it should at least serve to remind us that all too often we tend to jump to conclusions on the presupposition that every divergence in a parallel text is due to the Chronicler himself, without first weighing other possibilities in each particular and individual case.

the emphasis of the remainder of the oracle is slightly directed towards Solomon.[75] This is made most clear in 1 Chron. 17:14: 'But I will confirm him in my house and in my kingdom for ever and his throne shall be established for ever', where the third person singular pronouns, which in the context (see verse 12) can refer only to Solomon, should be compared with the second person singular pronouns (referring to David) of the *Vorlage* in 2 Sam. 7:16:[76] 'And your house and your kingdom shall be made sure for ever before me; your throne shall be established for ever'.

It follows from this conclusion, first, that the significance of the omission from 1 Chron. 17 of the sentence in 2 Sam. 7:14 about the possible need to discipline David's successor should be interpreted exclusively in terms of the Chronicler's understanding of the role of Solomon, to which we must return below; and secondly, that at this stage in the Chronicler's narrative we may even have to concede that the expression 'the Lord will build you a house' (1 Chron. 17:10) has been applied by the context to Solomon alone, with the promise of an established dynasty thrown forward on to Solomon for purposes and with consequences which remain to be determined.

Up to this point, therefore, we agree with those whose understanding of 1 Chron. 17 leads them to oppose a messianic, and on the whole even a royalist, interpretation. This conclusion, however, by no means exhausts the subject, for the Chronicler often conveys his message by way of his larger narrative structure. His handling of the dynastic oracle in 1 Chron. 17 is but one element of this larger whole, and rash conclusions concerning his *Tendenz* should thus not be drawn hastily from a single text without further ado.

The second approach to an understanding of the Chronicler's interpretation of the dynastic oracle is through the references to it in his subsequent narrative.

---

[75] It should be noted that David's prayer in response to the oracle (1 Chron. 17:16–27) is apparently adopted by the Chronicler without any significant or tendentious alteration. Its stress on the eternal validity of the promise may be thought to create a certain tension with the focussing of the oracle itself on Solomon, as maintained above, and this must be discussed later. The heart of the prayer (1 Chron. 17:25), however, could well be interpreted as applying primarily to Solomon, and was probably so understood by the Chronicler.

[76] It has recently been pointed out by T. N. D. METTINGER, King and Messiah (ConB. Old Testament Series, 8; Lund, 1976), 57–8, that the LXX of 2 Sam. 7:16 here agrees with 1 Chron. 17:14 (MT and LXX) against its MT *Vorlage*. His suggestion that 'the LXX reading has preserved a tradition that goes back to the original Solomonic document of Solomon's legitimation', of which the MT is a later, dynastic redaction, must be judged implausible. Unless we are to take the view that the text in Samuel is the outcome of very much later editorial manipulation, two possibilities remain open: either the Chronicler had a *Vorlage* which already differed from the MT of Samuel, and whose reading is attested in the LXX, as suggested for comparable situations at a number of other texts by LEMKE, or the LXX of 2 Sam. 7:16 reflects an assimilation to the Chronicler's text at either the Hebrew or Greek stage of its development. Whilst certainty is completely unattainable here, it remains true that the MT of Samuel and Chronicles at this point seems so to coincide with the overall thrust of its context in the respective passages that the second alternative is the more probable (cf. M. SIMON, RHPhR 32 [1952], 46–7).

12. Eschatology in Chronicles

Here again, the significance of this material has been assessed in widely differing ways.

On the one hand, Newsome has most recently argued,[77] on the basis of 1 Chron. 22:9-10 and 28:6-7, that 'Chronicles' interest in the Davidic kingdom is actually an interest in eschatology' (p. 213), for these texts are said not only to amplify the oracle of Nathan, but particularly to heighten the stress on the perpetuity of the Davidic dynasty (pp. 208-10). (Whilst we have already noted some difficulties for Newsome's conclusions about the dating of Chronicles, his interpretation of the texts is a separate issue which still requires examination.)

On the other hand, as far as our present interest is concerned, it is a serious weakness in Newsome's case that he completely fails to deal with two important emphases of these texts to which other scholars have drawn attention, and from which they have arrived at quite contrary conclusions. First, it is impossible to deny that in the speeches of David in 1 Chron. 22, 28 and 29 the dynastic oracle is linked very closely indeed with the election of Solomon as David's successor. Thus, in 1 Chron. 22:6-10, David relates to Solomon what must be intended as a *verbatim* account of the oracle as he received it, and indeed there are some clear and substantial points of literary contact (compare 1 Chron. 17:12-13a with 22:10). Included in the oracle, however, is a reference to Solomon by name, 1 Chron. 22:9:

> Behold, a son shall be born to you; he shall be a man of peace. I will give him peace from all his enemies round about; for his name shall be Solomon, and I will give peace and quiet to Israel in his days.

It is curious that Newsome, who cites part of this and the following verse, chooses to omit from his citation those very phrases in which the application of the promise to Solomon is made explicit.

Similarly, in 1 Chron. 28, where David addresses the people, he again refers to the dynastic oracle in such a way as to link it inseparably with Solomon:

> He said to me, 'It is Solomon your son who shall build my house and my courts, for I have chosen him to be my son, and I will be his father. I will establish his kingdom for ever if he continues resolute in keeping my commandments and my ordinances, as he is today' (verses 6-7).

Whilst Newsome cites this passage in full, he again completely fails to take account of the emphasis on Solomon as the recipient of the promise.

A related theme to which this passage also refers is that of the divine election of Solomon as king. Several scholars have noted that Chronicles is unique in making Solomon the object of God's choice *(bḥr)*,[78] and although at 1 Chron.

---

[77] NEWSOME, 'Toward a New Understanding'. NEWSOME'S presentation is the most extreme of a line of interpretation found also *(inter alia)* in J. W. ROTHSTEIN and J. HÄNEL, Kommentar zum ersten Buch der Chronik (KAT, 18; Leipzig, 1927), xliv; BOTTERWECK, 'Eigenart', 422, 430-31; BRUNET, 'La théologie du Chroniste'.

[78] E.g. G.E. MENDENHALL, IDB II, 78; I.L. SEELIGMANN, 'mmṣy'wt hyṣṭwryt ltpysh

28:10 and 29:1 it is related only to the building of the temple,[79] yet at its other two occurrences (1 Chron. 28:5 and 6) it is brought into the closest possible association with the dynastic oracle. In consequence, the first point to be made from the Chronicler's own interpretation of this oracle in his subsequent narrative is that there is a heavy emphasis upon its particular application to Solomon. That this does not fully exhaust its significance is clear from several passages that relate to kings later than Solomon, as will shortly be seen more fully, but there is nevertheless a stress here in the Chronicler's narrative which is lacking in his *Vorlage,* and to which Newsome has failed to do justice. It need hardly be added that this conclusion confirms the approach to the Chronicler's *Tendenz* in 1 Chron. 17 itself which we favoured above.

The second feature of these speeches of David that deserves fuller attention is the conditional element which they import into the promise of a dynasty,[80] apparent particularly at 1 Chron. 28:7 and 9; 2 Chron. 6:16; 7:17-18. 1 Chron. 22:12-13, which is usually compared at this point, is in reality to be distinguished from these other passages, for though it is certainly conditional, it is not directly linked to the establishment of the dynasty, but rather with Solomon's prosperity.[81] It is true that just previously (verse 10) the promise of an eternal dynasty has been referred to, but the immediate context (verses 11 and 14) shows that this 'prosperity' is to be understood primarily in terms of temple building. This leaves 1 Chron. 22:10 as an isolated example of an unconditional repetition of the promise of a dynasty.

A way quite different from Newsome's silence of avoiding the implications of this material is that advanced by Mosis (whose position is otherwise at the opposite extreme), who attempts to relegate 1 Chron. 22: 12-13 and 28:7b-10 to

---

hystwrywswpyt bmqr', prqym 2 (1969-74), 273-313 (300); JAPHET, Ideology, 448-51; BRAUN, 'Solomon, the Chosen Temple Builder'.

[79] It should nevertheless be noted that this is itself a major theme of 1 Chron. 17, and that the designation during David's lifetime of Solomon as the temple builder is already a step towards the application of the oracle to Solomon, whereas in Kings this connection is not made until after the temple has been built (1 Kgs 8:19-20), as observed by JAPHET, Ideology, 449.

[80] NEWSOME is aware of this element, but merely refers in a footnote to the treatment of FREEDMAN, 'The Chronicler's Purpose'. However, this is not sufficient for the present purpose, for Freedman does not explain the intention of these verses in both Chronicles and Kings where the whole future of the dynasty itself is made conditional on the king's obedience. In fairness, it should be said that in his unpublished doctoral dissertation (The Chronicler's View of Prophecy, 136), NEWSOME does agree that '1 Chronicles 28:7 depicts David (in a prophetic utterance) affirming that the eternity of the Davidic house is conditional upon the king's faithfulness to Yahweh', but even there he fails to integrate this observation into his overall conclusions.

[81] *Contra* JAPHET, Ideology, 461. A similar objection may be levelled against CAQUOT, 'Peut-on parler de messianisme ...?', 116, who refers only to 1 Chron. 28:20 to support his claim that the Chronicler has no interest in Solomon's future apart from temple building. However, since he makes no reference whatsoever to such passages as 1 Chron. 22:10, 28:7 etc., his interpretation must be discounted as one-sided.

the realm of secondary expansion, to be ignored, in consequence, in any estimate of the Chronicler's ideology.[82] Mosis' main argument in favour of this suggestion is that these verses are impossible to reconcile with other passages where the Chronicler has deleted a concession in his *Vorlage* to the very possibility that Solomon might sin: 1 Chron. 17:13 and 2 Chron. 1:12 (contrast 1 Kgs 3:14). This, however, is quite unacceptable, for such a possibility *is* conceded by the Chronicler at 2 Chron. 6:16 and especially 7:17. It is not true to say that 6:16 refers only to the later Davidides,[83] for the antecedent of the pronoun in 'your sons' is David himself, so that Solomon must at least be included; in fact, however, it would even seem that the reference is primarily to him, for verse 15 speaks of the fact that the first part of the promise to David (that his son would build the temple) has been fulfilled 'this day'. In 7:17, the case is even stronger, the text making it quite clear that Solomon alone is referred to: 'And as for you, if you walk before me, as David your father walked ...'.[84] Finally, not only do these passages not contradict the position of the Chronicler as expressed elsewhere, but we shall in fact seek to show that they contribute substantially to his overall presentation.

In contrast to these rather extreme positions, a more moderate line is advanced in this regard by Japhet.[85] She reminds us first of the tension in the books of Samuel and Kings between the two presentations of the oracle of Nathan, for in 2 Sam. 7 the promise of an eternal dynasty to the Davidic family is absolute and unconditional, whereas in 1 Kgs 8:25 (and cf. 2:4 and 9:5) there is a change of emphasis by which the establishment of the promise is made dependent on (Deuteronomistically expressed) obedience to God's law. In Chronicles, however, Japhet argues first that the omission of 2 Sam. 7:14b in fact softens the unconditional nature of the promise, for its purpose in 2 Samuel was to emphasize that even if an individual king sinned and was punished, this would not affect the continuity of the dynasty itself. She is then able to go on to show that the passages in 1 Chron. 22 and 28 confirm this impression, for though for the most part they virtually cite the oracle of 1 Chron. 17 *verbatim,* yet they harmonize it with the Deuteronomic presentation by introducing a conditional clause at the very point where 2 Sam. 7:14b was omitted (cf. 1 Chron. 28:7).

Japhet has more difficulty, however, in fitting into her scheme the allusions to the dynastic oracle in 2 Chron. 13:5, 21:7 and 23:3. She explains away the first

---

[82] Mosis, Untersuchungen, 90–2.

[83] *Contra* Mosis, Untersuchungen, 90.

[84] Mosis's other arguments for deleting these verses are even less convincing. For instance, he notes that a number of scholars (e. g. RUDOLPH, Chronikbücher, 151–2) regard the end of 1 Chron. 22 as secondary, but this concerns verses 14–19 only, so that there is really no good reason to extend the expansion back to include verses 12–13, as Mosis suggests. Moreover, the verses in 1 Chron. 22 and 28 are integral parts of larger forms which, it has been argued, play a significant role in the structure of the Chronicler's work as a whole; cf. my 'The Accession of Solomon', and BRAUN, 'Solomon, the Chosen Temple Builder'.

[85] JAPHET, *Ideology,* 457–63; and cf. in part SEELIGMANN, '*mmṣy'wt hystwryt*', 301 ff.

by observing that though no condition is expressed, there is at least a heavy emphasis on the assertion of cultic obedience by Abijah and the Jerusalem community. The other two occurrences come from a period of grave threat to the dynasty, so that the Chronicler was justified in returning to the aspect of unconditional promise to David.

From this discussion of studies of 1 Chron. 17 and its echoes in the later chapters of the Chronicler's work, apparently conflicting viewpoints have emerged. This concerns chiefly the fact that on the one hand we have noted a marked tendency to concentrate the attention of the oracle exclusively on Solomon, whilst on the other there is an emphasis on those conditional elements which in the Deuteronomic presentation were intended primarily to refer to the failings of the later kings as an explanation for the fall of the dynasty in the Babylonian exile.[86] Furthermore, the Chronicler has retained the references of his *Vorlage* to 'eternity' in connection with the dynastic promise, and carried them over into his own later applications of the oracle (cf. 1 Chron. 17:12, 14, 17, 23, 24, 27; 22:10; 28:7, 8), which again might be considered inappropriate if the promise relates to Solomon alone.[87]

It may, however, be suggested that all these factors can be explained on the basis of a feature of the Chronicler's narrative to which attention has already been drawn,[88] namely his concern to present the reigns of David and Solomon as a single, unified event within the divine economy for the life of the nation, in which the complementary nature of the two kings' functions plays an important role, a feature most marked in the Chronicler's handling of the theme of temple building.

In the books of Samuel and Kings, Solomon makes no particular contribution to the establishment of the dynasty. The unconditional promise is addressed directly to David (2 Sam. 7) in such a way that, although it arises from a concern for, and remains closely associated with, the emergence of Solomon as the temple builder, the two themes can nevertheless be kept apart and treated in isolation. Equally, the interpretation of the promise on a conditional basis which comes later does not distinguish Solomon from his successors, and indeed, it is in particular the sin of Manasseh which is said to lead to the final catastrophe.

The Chronicler, in contrast, by way of his distinctive presentation of the united monarchy, would seem to have attempted to harmonize the tensions of his *Vorlage:* just as the dynastic oracle, as delivered originally to David, is concentrated upon the person of his son Solomon, so too the conditions of obedience, whose fulfilment will lead to the establishment of an eternal dynasty,

---

[86] See SEELIGMANN, '*mmṣy'wt hyṣṭwryt*', 308–10.

[87] This point is conceded by RUDOLPH, Chronikbücher, 137, and is emphasized by J. M. MYERS, 1 *Chronicles* (AB, 12; Garden City, 1965), 129. The 'elasticity' of the oracle itself is stressed particularly by N. POULSSEN, König und Tempel im Glaubenszeugnis des Alten Testaments (SBM, 3; Stuttgart, 1967), 171–4.

[88] See the works referred to in notes 59 and 60 above.

are focussed upon him (1 Chron. 28:7).[89] This at once, of course, has the effect of making Solomon's role a foundation for the future of the dynasty equal with David's for upon Solomon's obedience the whole of that future will depend. The establishment of an eternal dynasty thus rests on two indispensable elements: the promise of God to David, and the carrying out of God's conditions by Solomon. Neither element would suffice in itself, and equally neither David's nor Solomon's part in this scheme could have been fulfilled without the other, for the promise to David would clearly have been void without Solomon, whilst of Solomon it is said that he could not have managed to complete the temple (and thus fulfil the major demand upon him) without the help of David's preparation (1 Chron. 22:5; 29:1-2).

In the passages where this theme is explicit, two aspects of obedience receive attention; the one is specific, the building of the temple, and the other quite general, the keeping of God's commandments and ordinances. What is more, it is well known that the Chronicler's account of Solomon's reign presents him as one who did in fact keep both these conditions,[90] and that in as positive a way as it is possible to conceive.[91] Finally, the Chronicler's omission of 2 Sam. 7:14b may be explained at this point, for it becomes clear that this was certainly not a matter of his hesitation in even granting the possibility that Solomon might be disobedient *(contra* Mosis); nor was it only – though we readily agree that it may have included – an attempt to eliminate from the oracle a sentence whose effect was to make the promise of the dynasty as a whole so definitely unconditional *(contra* Japhet). It was rather, we suggest, that the Chronicler's focussing of the oracle upon Solomon made the inclusion of this clause quite irrelevant. In the Samuel text, it refers to the whole future line of Davidic kings, to many of whom the saying could have applied, whereas for Solomon in the Chronicler's scheme it could have no application whatever. Either he was going to obey, in which case the dynasty would be established, or he would fail, and his house with him; the possibility was not foreseen that he would fail personally, but the dynasty nevertheless endure.

---

[89] This will explain the Chronicler's omission of 'or your children' from 1 Kgs 9:6 at 2 Chron. 7:19, which has not been adequately treated by the commentators. In Kings, the condition of obedience is laid by God on Solomon and his descendants without distinction. This is changed in the present form of the Chronicler's text *(contra* J. GOETTSBERGER, Die Bücher der Chronik oder Paralipomenon [Die heilige Schrift des alten Testaments, 4/1; Bonn, 1939], 236) to a reference to Solomon and his people. The effect of this is to limit the conditional aspect of the promise of a dynasty in verses 17-18 to Solomon alone; see further below.

[90] Cf. MOSIS, Untersuchungen, 125-63, and especially BRAUN, 'Solomonic Apologetic'. 1 Chron. 28:7 states explicitly that at that time Solomon was keeping the necessary conditions; the subsequent narrative would give the reader of Chronicles no cause to suppose that this changed in any particular.

[91] See 1 Chron. 28:23; 2 Chron. 1:1, 9-10 with God's positive answer; 2:11; 6:8-10, 15-16; 9:22, in addition to the well-known passing over of the apostasy of Solomon in 1 Kgs 10.

D. Later development

Our contention, then, is that, with the completion of the period of Davidic-Solomonic rule, the Chronicler intends his readers to understand that the dynasty has been eternally established. We have not found evidence to justify the view that with Solomon's building of the temple the content of the promise was exhausted, but rather that the completion of the temple was a contributory factor to the establishment of the promise. We must now move on, therefore, to see whether there are any other indications to support this understanding.

(l) 2 Chron. 6:41–2. 2 Chron. 6 is mainly taken up with Solomon's prayer at the dedication of the temple. On the whole, it follows 1 Kgs 8 very closely. A change of emphasis that does seem to be deliberate, however, is seen in the fact that the three references to the Exodus and Sinai at 1 Kgs 8:21, 51 and 53 have been either reduced or altered.[92] The third instance is in fact the close of the prayer, the reference to the Exodus forming the basis for Solomon's appeal to God to answer him. The full explanation of this phenomenon cannot concern us here,[93] but it is relevant to observe that the Chronicler has substituted new material to form a quite different conclusion to the prayer (2 Chron. 6:41–2):

And now arise, O Lord God,
   and go to thy resting place,
thou and the ark of thy might.
   Let thy priests, O Lord God, be clothed with salvation
and let thy saints rejoice in thy goodness.
O Lord God, do not turn away the face of thy anointed one!
Remember thy steadfast love for David thy servant.

These lines comprise mainly a citation of Ps. 132:8–10. Although there are several minor differences between the texts, the only one of immediate significance comes in the last two lines, for Ps. 132:10 reads:

For thy servant David's sake
   do not turn away the face of thy anointed one.

It is to be noted first that the order of the two lines has been inverted by the Chronicler, and secondly that he has altered it to 'Remember thy steadfast love for David' by introducing what we can only understand as an allusion to Isaiah 55:3b ('And I will make with you an everlasting covenant, my steadfast sure love for David'). We would suggest that this was both to give added emphasis to this line and to remove a possible ambiguity inherent in the words 'for David's sake'.

The first of these two points is clear enough. Concerning the second, we need to remember that Ps. 132 deals with two related themes, the transfer of the Ark to Jerusalem and God's promise to David. Verse 10 marks the transition between

---

[92] See BRUNET, 'La théologie du Chroniste', and JAPHET, Ideology, 382–8.
[93] See Israel in the Books of Chronicles, 64–6, for an introductory account.

the two halves, so that it is not clear whether 'for David's sake' means because of his faithfulness and loyalty[94] or because of God's promise to him. The former could find support in the first verse of the Psalm: 'Remember, O Lord, in David's favour, all the hardships he endured', whereas the latter can appeal to the verses that follow (11–12, 17).[95]

Whatever be the true interpretation of the Psalm, three considerations lead me to conclude that the Chronicler means us to understand his rephrased line as a reference to God's promise to David. First, this is the meaning of the phrase in Isa. 55:3. It is true that there have recently been some attempts to suggest that it is a subjective genitive there too ('David's loyal acts'),[96] but I have endeavoured to show in considerable detail elsewhere[97] both that the arguments in favour of this position are not compelling, and that others point very forcibly indeed to the rendering 'steadfast love for David'.[98] Secondly, the context in the prayer of Solomon points the same way, for it will then balance the opening of the prayer in 2 Chron. 6:15–17, with its strong emphasis upon God's keeping his promise to David up until the time of temple building and its request that God will now go on to confirm that word of promise.[99] Thirdly, as we have seen, in the

---

[94] So, for instance, A. A. ANDERSON, The Book of Psalms, Vol. 2 (NCB; London, 1972), 883.

[95] For an analysis of the Psalm along these lines, see T. E. FRETHEIM, 'Psalm 132: a Form-Critical Study', JBL 86 (1967), 289–300. W. A. M. BEUKEN understands the implications of FRETHEIM's study in this regard differently; see 'Isa. 55, 3–5: the Reinterpretation of David', Bijdragen 35 (1974), 49–64 (52, n. 19). It is true that FRETHEIM points to some parallels between verses 1 and 10, but he then goes on (p. 292) to stress that there are also 'some notable differences between the two strophes' 1–5 and 10–12, the main one being precisely the difference between a supplication to remember the Davidic hardships in fulfilling his vow to God in the past (v.1) and (v.10) God's fulfilling his vow to David in the present.

[96] Principally A. CAQUOT, 'Les "grâces de David". A propos d'Isaïe 55/3b', Semitica 15 (1965), 45–59, and BEUKEN, 'Isa. 55, 3–5'.

[97] '"The Sure Mercies of David": Subjective or Objective Genitive?', JSS 23 (1978), 31–49.

[98] Proponents of the alternative view point in particular to the use of this same word (ḥsdym) with the meaning of 'pious deeds' at 2 Chron. 32:32 and 35:26 and compare also the use at Neh. 13:14; in addition to the works cited above, see in particular M. ADINOLFI, 'Le "opere di pietà liturgica" di David in 2 Cron. 6,42', Bibbia e Oriente 7 (1966), 31–6. It should be said in reply, however, that whereas these passages show that the word *may* be used of 'pious deeds', in my view the even closer parallel of Is. 55:3 and the context in 2 Chron. 6 should, from the point of view of method, be given greater weight, and both strongly favour the translation adopted above. As for the use of the word 'remember', it is true that at Ps. 132:1 and Neh. 13:14 *(inter alia)* it is used in connection with an appeal to God to take note of someone's faithfulness, but that does not, of course, exclude its use of God making his promises effective; see W. SCHOTTROFF, 'Gedenken' im alten Orient und im alten Testament (WMANT, 15; 2nd edn; Neukirchen, 1967), 199–217. SCHOTTROFF seems himself inclined to support the alternative understanding of 2 Chron. 6:42 (see pp. 222–6), but is very hesitant about it, and certainly allows the possibility of the interpretation offered above.

[99] BEUKEN, 'Isa. 55, 3–5', argues against this parallel that 'the connection with vss. 7f., where God praises David because of his "good" intentions to build a house for Yhwh, has as much weight' (p. 52). This seems less likely, however, because (i) verses 7f. are not part of

Chronicler's understanding of the united monarchy, the emphasis falls on the promise to David and obedience to the conditions by Solomon. Thus an appeal to David's pious deeds at this point would be less appropriate to his overall presentation.

We are now in a position to see the significance of these verses for the Chronicler's theology. On the one hand, his allusion to Isa. 55:3 must be seen as an attempt to re-emphasize the royalist interpretation of the promise to David over against Isa. 55:3 which, as is now generally recognized, appears to transfer the promise to the people as a whole.[100] The application of this very phrase back again to the context of the Davidic dynasty must thus be seen as telling evidence against Rudolph's and Plöger's view that the Chronicler intended to move away from any kind of royalist hope.

On the other hand, the use of this verse at the conclusion of Solomon's prayer of dedication is also noteworthy. We have seen that one of the main conditions that he had to fulfil if the dynasty was to be established was the building of the temple. With that now accomplished, it becomes fully intelligible that he should request God to 'remember (his) steadfast, sure love for David'. The positioning of this verse thus helps to confirm our interpretation of the dynastic oracle offered above, and again tells heavily against the view that the promise is exhausted with the completion of the temple building. Rather, on this basis, the exact opposite seems to be the case.

Immediately after Solomon's prayer, the Chronicler departs from his *Vorlage* in 1 Kings by recording that

When Solomon had ended his prayer, fire came down from heaven and consumed the burnt offering and the sacrifices, and the glory of the Lord filled the temple.

This dramatically underlines God's willingness to answer Solomon's request (expressed more conventionally at 2 Chron. 7:12ff.) and suggests to the reader that he may henceforth expect the unconditional guarantee that a king will rule in Jerusalem. Three passages in his subsequent narrative demonstrate that this is, in fact, the case.

(2) 2 Chron. 13:5–8. It is widely agreed that, without prejudice to the question of a source for the material in this chapter, the speech of Abijah in verses 5–12 coincides with, and hence reflects, the Chronicler's own viewpoint. The themes

---

Solomon's prayer, which starts rather at verse 14; (ii) there is no evidence that good intentions could be described as *ḥsdym*. Ps. 132 would allow the possibility that David's care for the Ark might be involved, but that is not mentioned in verses 7f.; (iii) the same passage goes on immediately to relate that David was unable to realise his good intention, but that God kept his promise to David in allowing his son Solomon to complete the task (verse 10). The emphasis of these verses, therefore, is similar to those at the start of Solomon's prayer, and so cannot support BEUKEN's case.

[100] P. VOLZ, *Jesaia II* (KAT; Leipzig, 1932), 139–43, and especially O. EISSFELDT, 'The Promises of Grace to David in Isaiah 55:1–5', in B. W. ANDERSON and W. HARRELSON (eds.) *Israel's Prophetic Heritage* (London, 1962), 196–207.

12. Eschatology in Chronicles

with which it deals are prominent concerns of his elsewhere, and it appears furthermore to be crucial to a correct understanding of his narrative structure.[101] As far as I am aware, only Caquot has challenged this consensus,[102] but since he gives no reasons to support his assertion, whereas at the same time the implications of these verses conflict with the rather extreme view he wishes to present, we need not delay to consider his opinion in detail.

Two aspects of kingship as presented here call for comment. First, we find reference to a theme emphasized elsewhere in Chronicles, namely the description of 'the kingdom of the Lord in the hand of the sons of David' (verse 8). This concept is also introduced (sometimes by way of a slight change from the *Vorlage*) at 1 Chron. 17:14; 28:5; 29:11 and 23; and 2 Chron. 9:8. Equally, it provides the conceptual background necessary to understand 1 Chron. 10:14b. In his speech, Abijah employs the expression to prove the senselessness of the rebellious Northerners trying to withstand Davidic rule. This implies that included in the Chronicler's understanding was the idea both that the kingdom of the Lord coincided with its expression in Israel on earth and that, naturally enough, being God's kingdom, it was permanent and indestructible. This leads directly to our second consideration, for it must inevitably be asked whether there is any guarantee that the Lord will continue to express his kingship through the Davidic house. Verse 5 supplies a clear answer:

Ought you not to know that the Lord God of Israel gave the kingship over Israel for ever to David and his sons as[103] a covenant of salt?

That God could pass the kingship from one dynasty to another is made clear from the explicit reference to its transfer from Saul to David (1 Chron. 10:14), but already in 1 Chron. 17:13 it was promised that this would not happen again, and the analogy of this promise with 'a covenant of salt' in our passage is intended to confirm this stability, for whatever be the origins of the expression in ancient custom, its use elsewhere in the Bible (Num. 18:19 and cf. Lev. 2:13) points clearly to its eternal significance.[104] Thus, the collocation of these two aspects of the speech of Abijah shows that by his time the members of the Davidic family were unchangeably established as those through whom God had chosen to exercise his kingship.

---

[101] See Israel in the Books of Chronicles, 111–15, 122.

[102] CAQUOT, 'Peut-on parler de messianisme ...?', 119.

[103] RSV: 'with'. As there is, in fact, no preposition, the translation above, representing an accusative of nearer definition, seems slightly to be preferred; see KEIL, *ad loc.;* RUDOLPH, Chronikbücher, 236–7; JAPHET, Ideology, 452–4. Strictly speaking, the relationship between God and David is not here described as covenantal (though cf. 2 Chron. 21:7); the covenant of salt is used, rather, as an analogy.

[104] In addition to the standard Bible Dictionaries and Encyclopaedias, see H.C. TRUMBULL, Studies in Oriental Social Life (London, 1895), 111–12; RUDOLPH, Chronikbücher, 237; JAPHET, Ideology, 452–4.

(3) 2 Chron. 21:7:

Yet the Lord would not destroy the house of David, because of the covenant which he had made with David, and since he had promised to give a lamp to him and to his sons for ever.

Two apparently[105] significant changes distinguish this verse from its *Vorlage* in 2 Kgs 8:19. First, the Chronicler has altered a reference to 'Judah' to 'the house of David' as that which the Lord did not want to destroy; secondly, while Kings says simply 'for the sake of David his servant', Chronicles introduces 'the covenant which he had made with David'.

In this editorial passage, the Chronicler adopts the negative assessment of Kings on Jehoram, the king in question. Nevertheless, even in such a case, the Chronicler strengthens the allusion to the unconditional promise to the Davidic dynasty,[106] thus supporting once more our overall understanding of his position. Japhet argues that the importance of this verse within the book as a whole is quite secondary.[107] It is true that it is based upon the account in Kings, but the fact that the Chronicler altered the text precisely, as we understand it, to heighten its force would suggest that he did not take it over mechanically, but because it suited his purpose to include it at this point.

(4) 2 Chron. 23:3. For the story of the initiative of Jehoiada the high priest in overthrowing Queen Athaliah and restoring Joash, the sole survivor of the Davidic house, to the throne in Jerusalem, the Chronicler clearly bases himself squarely on the account in 2 Kgs 11. There are, however, more than the usual number of additions and omissions, suggesting that it is likely to be his own hand that lies behind the changes rather than more mechanical textual considerations. In 23:3, therefore, it is of interest to note an addition in line with the evidence we have already accumulated. When Jehoiada presents Joash as the king's son, the Chronicler adds, 'Let him reign, as the Lord spoke concerning the sons of David'. The reference to God's promise to David, established by Solomon as unconditional, is unmistakable.

---

[105] In cases of small variations between Kings and Chronicles, it is acknowledged that the variation may not in every case be due to the Chronicler himself, but that his text of Kings may have already existed in a form different from that of the MT; see LEMKE, 'The Synoptic Problem in the Chronicler's History'. In the present instance, however, the only alternative published witness which might indicate such a situation in fact supports the MT of Kings and Chronicles respectively in the matters with which we are concerned, while at the same time the alterations are in such accord with the Chronicler's outlook generally that attribution of the change to him remains the most probable explanation.

[106] Nor should it be forgotten that he also adopts the second half of the verse unchanged, and that it has the same point as its emphasis. Unfortunately, it is not fully clear what is meant by 'a lamp', nor that the Chronicler necessarily understood it in the same way as Kings. For a number of suggestions, see the references in P.D. HANSON, HTR 61 (1968), 297–320.

[107] JAPHET, Ideology, 454–6. It is possible, however, that she is correct in detecting the influence of the Chronicler's doctrine of individual retribution on the change of 'Judah' to 'the house of David'.

12. Eschatology in Chronicles

In concluding this section, it is of interest to note the variety of situations that lies behind the last three passages we have discussed. The first was related to Abijah, of whom the Chronicler evidently approves, the second to Jehoram, of whom he has not a good word to say, and the third to a period when the dynasty as a whole came as close as imaginable to total destruction. It is admitted that by and large the allusions are brief, and that apparently not a great deal is made of them. Nevertheless, it may be asked whether it is not significant that, having established his position through his account of the united monarchy, the occasions on which he chooses to remind his readers of this theme are illustrative of the three major situations through which the dynasty could pass whilst remaining intact.

E. The Significance of 2 Chronicles 7:12–22

Our examination of the Chronicler's attitude towards the Davidic dynasty has attempted to show that in his opinion the promise to David, confirmed by Solomon's obedience, was of eternal validity. One objection to this understanding remains to be considered, and that is: is it at all probable that anyone living in Jerusalem during, as we understand it, the relatively stable period of Persian rule, a long period during which there was no Davidic king, nor any likelihood of one being enthroned, could have conceivably even dared hope that a descendant of David would ever again emerge as ruler? The analysis of one final passage, 2 Chron. 7:12–22, may help to resolve this dilemma.

We have already had occasion to stress the importance for the Chronicler of Solomon's completion of the temple and his prayer at its dedication. We would thus expect 2 Chron. 7:12–22, which contains God's answer to that prayer, to be equally significant in the presentation of his theological position. Its main aim is to show that God has answered Solomon's prayer by 'choosing' the new sanctuary, this being also the aim of 1 Kgs 9:3–9, on which the Chronicler has based his account. He has also, however, adapted his *Vorlage* along characteristic lines.

The first major section, verses 13–15, is completely additional to Kings. It relates to the people as a whole, and although it has generally been passed over very briefly by the commentators, yet it is in fact crucial for his well known doctrine of immediate retribution. This is a dogma of his that is always referred to, but has not, in my opinion, been analysed in anything like the detail it deserves.[108] Such an analysis would take us beyond our present subject, but 7:14

---

[108] The basic examples have often been set out, e.g. by J. WELLHAUSEN, Prolegomena zur Geschichte Israels (6th edition; Berlin, 1905), 198–205 (ET, Prolegomena to the History of Israel [Edinburgh, 1885], 203–10); G. VON RAD, Theologie I, 345–7. VON RAD here also makes a better attempt than most to appreciate the theological significance of this doctrine,

would be central to it. In this verse, the Chronicler gives four possible responses of the people to imminent or actual disaster on the basis of which God will intervene with forgiveness and restoration. These four words are then each used in the subsequent narrative as markers at one point or another to introduce one of the miraculous interventions that are such a characteristic feature of the Chronicler's work. For instance, the verse starts, 'If my people... humble themselves...'. The first king after Solomon, Rehoboam, faced an invasion by Shishak, king of Egypt, in the fifth year of his reign (2 Chron. 12:1-12). Urged by the prophet Shemaiah, however,

the princes of Israel and the king *humbled themselves* and said 'The Lord is righteous'. When the Lord saw that they *humbled themselves,* the word of the Lord came to Shemaiah: 'They have *humbled themselves;* I will not destroy them, but I will grant them some deliverance, and my wrath shall not be poured out upon Jerusalem...' (verses 6-7).

Similarly, of Rehoboam, it is said,

When he *humbled himself* the wrath of the Lord turned from him, so as not to make a complete destruction (verse 12).

This word is used in a comparable way at 2 Chron. 30:11; 32:26; 33:12, 19, 23; 34:7 and 36:12. Remarkably, however, though it is used on three occasions in the earlier narrative (1 Chron. 17:10; 18:1 and 20:4), these are all quite neutral theologically, and do not mark similar miraculous turning points. When it is now added that precisely the same situation holds for the other three programmatic words of 2 Chron. 7:14 without a single exception,[109] it will be apparent that the Chronicler intends us to understand God's answer to Solomon's prayer as both literal and as in some way initiating a new phase in God's relationship with his people.[110] It is equally apparent that, as far as this promise goes, since we can check his attitude from his subsequent narrative, he was of the opinion that no external circumstances were too formidable to prevent God's immediate, direct and, if need be, miraculous move to fulfil it.

---

as also does JAPHET, Ideology, 159-208, but neither deals with the particular passage under analysis above.

[109] (a) For 'to pray', cf. 2 Chron. 32:20, 24 and 33:13, but contrast the 'neutral' use at 1 Chron. 17:25 and 2 Chron. 7:1. (b) For 'to seek (my face)', cf. 2 Chron. 11:16; 15:4, 15; 20:4, and contrast 1 Chron. 4:39; 14:8; 16:10, 11; 21:3. (c) 'To return' is used frequently, but with theological significance of the sort referred to here only at 2 Chron. 15:4; 30:6, 9 and 36:13. It is true that the words 'to pray' and 'to return' occur a number of times in Solomon's prayer, 2 Chron. 6. However, since 2 Chron. 7:14 is the direct answer to that prayer, this fact would seem to strengthen, not undermine, our present contention.

[110] It is not suggested that 2 Chron. 7:14 contains the only words that have this kind of significance in Chronicles. There are several others, some of which seem to be based in a comparable way on 1 Chron. 10:13-14. Nevertheless, the facts set out above and in the previous note are too striking to be coincidental.

With this in mind, we turn to the second part of God's answer to Solomon, 2 Chron. 7:17–18. Just as the first part dealt with Solomon's request for his people, so this one deals with his request concerning the status of the king, which we have already noted is intensified over against 1 Kgs 6. We have also seen the general importance that these verses have in the Chronicler's interpretation of the dynastic oracle. In the light of these factors, two slight changes that the Chronicler introduces here are to be regarded as significant. If they were quite isolated, we would probably agree with those who regard them as trivial at best,[111] but since they come in this passage whose careful construction is becoming apparent, I am now of the opinion that we should not pass over them so lightly.

First, in verse 18, the Chronicler appears to have strengthened the reference to a covenant with David, substituting $k\bar{a}ratt\hat{\imath}\ l^e$ for $dibbart\hat{\imath}\ {}^{\varsigma}al$ (1 Kgs 9:5). It is true that some have suggested mere textual confusion here,[112] and it must be agreed that this remains a possibility. However, there is no versional or other evidence that I am aware of to support this conjecture, so that we ought first to reckon with the evidence as it stands.

Secondly, at the end of the same verse, 'a man upon the throne of Israel' has become 'a man to rule Israel', which, of course, is an exact echo of Mic. 5: 1 (ET 5:2). Though there is no evidence that this is to be understood in a technical messianic sense here,[113] yet it points once more, as do the other considerations already adduced, to an emphasis upon the promise of an eternal dynasty, once Solomon has fulfilled the necessary conditions.

The last section of this passage, verses 19–22, has just one significant difference from its *Vorlage* for our purposes, for it omits from verse 19 the reference in 1 Kgs 9:6 to the sons of Solomon.[114] By retaining the second person plural form of address, however, it must be taken, on the basis of the foregoing context, to refer to Solomon and the people rather than Solomon and his descendants. Just as in the previous two sections, the conditions for the blessing of people and king have been treated separately, as in the prayer, so here they are brought together at the point where there is a warning of the dangers of judgement that would follow disobedience. However, we cannot help noticing that, although Solomon is included in the warning, and although the judgement explicitly covers matters already dealt with in God's answer to him (exile, loss of land and destruction of the temple), yet there is no hint of any sort that the dynastic promise would lose its validity. Since the apostasy alluded to in verse 19 is as

---

[111] E.g. RUDOLPH, Chronikbücher, 218; JAPHET, Ideology, 490. VON RAD, Geschichtsbild, 124, draws attention to the changes in his treatment of the Davidic covenant in Chronicles, but without regard to the immediate context of the verse.

[112] E.g. CURTIS and MADSEN, Chronicles, 351.

[113] Contra MYERS, II Chronicles, 44.

[114] See above, n. 89. Again, I know of no textual evidence to prevent us exploring the possibility that this is a deliberate omission by the Chronicler.

drastic as can be imagined, this fact would seem once again to underline the unconditional nature of the promise.

Certain conclusions may be drawn, therefore, from this analysis of 2 Chron. 7:12–22. On the one hand, it is clear that the Chronicler's presentation is in part an encouragement to his readers so to return to God in self-humbling and prayer that he will again intervene in their own generation as he had so manifestly done in the past in similar circumstances. There is no suggestion here of satisfaction with the present, but rather every encouragement to look towards a dramatic transformation in the future.

Alongside this hope, towards the realization of which the people can contribute, stands the promise of a restoration of the Davidic dynasty. For this, however, there is no indication that anything can be done to speed its realization, for throughout the Chronicler's history the rigid application of the concept of retribution leads also towards what might loosely be termed a democratic[115] outlook, in which the individual's personal responsibility is more marked over against the earlier literature. Although there are still occasions where the king's activity inevitably affects the wellbeing of his people (most notably in 2 Chron. 28), yet more normally the people's own share in responsibility is clearly set out (e.g. 2 Chron. 12:1, 6; 13:13–18; 15:2, but contrast with 16:7–10, 12; 20:2–4, 13–23; 36:12–16, etc.). Nowhere, however, is the possibility envisaged that the people's faithfulness will affect the king for blessing.

F. Conclusions

The main conclusions of this lecture may now be presented in summary form:

(1) Despite the widespread influence of the approach to the Chronicler's work typified by Plöger's book, some scholars have nevertheless attempted to find in it a more positive attitude towards the future. However, the main arguments on which these studies were based have not been found entirely satisfactory.

(2) By his interpretation of the united monarchy of David and Solomon, and his handling of the dynastic oracle in the light of this, the Chronicler showed that in his view with the death of Solomon that promise was established as unconditional.

(3) A number of other texts, though not numerous, were sufficient to confirm that this remains his position throughout the work.

(4) His doctrine of immediate and individual retribution, including as it does a firm belief in God's direct involvement in history, suggests both that the people themselves should be encouraged to look to the future for improvement

---

[115] See WILLI, Die Chronik als Auslegung, 161.

in their present sorry condition, and that it is by no means absurd to maintain that the Chronicler could have inherited and passed on a continuing tradition of hope centred on the Davidic family. We have found no evidence that this is 'messianic' in the strict sense (we prefer in consequence the expression 'royalist'), nor do we wish to deny that with regard to some other prophetic hopes he may have presented a realized or inaugurated eschatology.[116] This is not the same, however, as asserting that he was closed to the future; on the contrary, it would appear that he too was one who would have heartily endorsed the words of Jehoshaphat which he cites:

Hear me, Judah and inhabitants of Jerusalem! Believe in the Lord your God, and you will be established; believe his prophets, and you will succeed (2 Chron. 20:20).

---

[116] For an attempt to support this position in connection with the prophecies of the reunification of Israel and Judah, see Israel in the Books of Chronicles, 125–6.

Ezra-Nehemiah

13. Post-Exilic Historiography

'Post-exilic historiography' ought to reflect on the methods and motives of those who wrote history in the post-exilic period, principally the authors of the books of Chronicles and of Ezra-Nehemiah.[1] There are, of course, a number of other Biblical books which relate to this period amongst both the Prophets and the Writings. However, whilst they undoubtedly contribute to our meagre knowledge of the history of the period, they are not historiographical as such, and so cannot be considered directly in the present paper. The same is true of the various extra-biblical sources of information[2] whose value for historical reconstruction can scarcely be overestimated but which again cannot be called historiographical in the strict sense of the word.

In order to allow myself space to say anything worthwhile, however, it has proved necessary to narrow even this restricted area still further. Because my views on Chronicles are already available in published form,[3] it may be of more interest here to reflect chiefly on the books of Ezra and Nehemiah. I shall therefore take my title to refer to historical works written both during *and concerning* the post-exilic period.

To those who do not specialize in this period, mention of Ezra and Nehemiah probably raises at once a number of celebrated, but very specific, historical questions, chronology not least amongst them. In terms of many studies which make use of these books, however, this fact has had the most doleful effect: a few specific texts are repeatedly examined without what should surely be the necessary pre-requisite of a thorough analysis and comprehension of the books as a whole and the inter-relationships of their constituent sources. (This is, I suspect, a criticism which many would wish to make within their own areas of specialization, and the general principle is illustrated by the comments of other contributors to this volume.) But such a study is a lengthy business, involving

---

[1] Some would want also to include works such as Esther and Daniel 1–6. However, in addition to the problem of literary *genre* which they raise, they stand apart by reason of the fact that they do not relate to the life of the community in Palestine.

[2] Recent surveys of the relevant material include G. WIDENGREN, 'The Persian Period', in J. H. HAYES and J. M. MILLER (eds.), Israelite and Judaean History (London, 1977), and W. D. DAVIES and L. FINKELSTEIN (eds.), The Cambridge History of Judaism. Volume One: Introduction; The Persian Period (Cambridge, 1984). On the latter, however, see my comments in VT 35 (1985), 231–38.

[3] See my 1 and 2 Chronicles (Grand Rapids and London, 1982), with bibliography of other relevant works on xviii-xix.

the close analysis of every part and facet of the work in order to evolve a hypothesis for their development which takes full account of all the evidence. Generalizations[4] which ignore significant items of relevant but contrary evidence are of little help. More useful are those who sketch out the options and so clear the ground, but are themselves hesitant to push the frontiers back with fresh suggestions.[5] Better still are detailed studies of particular parts or aspects of these books which attempt to take into account the whole range of evidence on their selected topic. As examples of this category, mention should be made of the monographs of Schaeder[6] and of In der Smitten[7] on the Ezra Narrative, Kellermann[8] on the Nehemiah material, Pohlmann[9] on the problems of 1 Esdras, Polzin[10] on the language of the books, and the recent articles of Japhet[11] on the composition of Ezra 1–6. Best of all, however, are those who have attempted a fully integrated analysis of the books, though naturally in saying this I do not imply that I agree with them in all their conclusions. Amongst commentaries, where we should expect to look first, I know of none since the magisterial work of Rudolph,[12] whilst significant monographs have been contributed by Torrey,[13] Noth[14] and Mowinckel.[15] It should be clear, therefore, from even this brief survey that there remains plenty of scope for the present generation of scholars.

---

[4] F.M. CROSS, 'A Reconstruction of the Judean Restoration', JBL 94 (1975).

[5] Mention might be made here, for instance, of H. SCHNEIDER, Die Bücher Esra und Nehemia (Bonn, 1959); J.M. MYERS, Ezra. Nehemiah (AB, 14; Garden City, 1965); and a number of publications by P.R. ACKROYD, most recently 'The Jewish Community in Palestine in the Persian Period, in DAVIES and FINKELSTEIN, Cambridge History of Judaism, I, 130–61.

[6] H.H. SCHAEDER, Esra der Schreiber (Tübingen, 1930).

[7] W. TH. IN DER SMITTEN, Esra: Quellen, Überlieferung und Geschichte (Studia Semitica Neerlandica, 15; Assen, 1973); see also F. AHLEMANN, 'Zur Esra-Quelle', ZAW 59 (1942–43), 77-98; and K. KOCH, 'Ezra and the Origins of Judaism', JSS 19 (1974).

[8] U. KELLERMANN, Nehemia: Quellen, Überlieferung und Geschichte (BZAW, 102; Berlin, 1967).

[9] K.-F. POHLMANN, Studien zum dritten Esra: Ein Beitrag zur Frage nach dem ursprünglichen Schluss des chronistischen Geschichtswerkes (FRLANT, 104; Göttingen, 1970).

[10] R. POLZIN, Late Biblical Hebrew: Toward an Historical Typology of Biblical Hebrew Prose (HSM, 12; Missoula, 1976).

[11] S. JAPHET, 'Sheshbazzar and Zerubbabel, Against the Background of the Historical and Religious Tendencies of Ezra-Nehemiah', ZAW 94–95 (1982–83).

[12] W. RUDOLPH, Esra und Nehemia (HAT, 20; Tübingen, 1949); limiting ourselves to the present century, mention should also be made of A. BERTHOLET, Die Bücher Esra und Nehemia (KHAT, 19; Tübingen, 1902) and G. HÖLSCHER, 'Die Bücher Esra und Nehemia', in E. KAUTZSCH and A. BERTHOLET (eds.), Die heilige Schrift des Alten Testaments (4th ed. Tübingen, 1923).

[13] C.C. TORREY, The Composition and Historical Value of Ezra-Nehemiah (BZAW, 2; Giessen, 1896); Ezra Studies (Chicago, 1910; reprinted, New York, 1970).

[14] M. NOTH, Überlieferungsgeschichtliche Studien (Halle, 1943; reprinted, Tübingen, 1967). [Translation of first half in The Deuteronomistic History (JSOTSup, 15; Sheffield, 1981); translation of second half in The Chronicler's History (JSOTSup, 50; Sheffield, 1987)]

[15] S. MOWINCKEL, Studien zu dem Buche Ezra-Nehemia I–III (Oslo, 1964–65); see also S. TALMON, 'Ezra and Nehemiah', IDBS (1976), 317–28.

Appropriate methods for the study of these books will naturally vary according to the kind of information which we are asking of them. Nevertheless, a fundamental key for most approaches lies in a comprehensive literary history. Source and redaction criticism are in my judgement a *sine qua non* for all further work.[16] This clearly applies to linguistic studies, since all are agreed that allowance must be made for the idiosyncracies of the different writers of the component parts of the books. It should be true too of sociological research,[17] because it is necessary to understand the social position and hence viewpoint of the writers if adequate allowance is to be made for their presuppositions in this sphere. No one, I imagine, will quarrel with its importance for historical reconstruction, nor should they, by extension, for theological and, finally, historiographical concerns as well.

Since none of this is in any sense new or even controversial, it is surprising to find that research in this area has remained virtually static for many years. With a few notable exceptions, most writers simply choose between, or slightly rearrange, the options which were already on offer in the early decades of this century. Claims of fresh light or a breaking of the impasse (whether justified or not) have generally been restricted to individual topics rather than the works as a whole.

Now, it may be, of course, that the reason for this state of affairs is that one of the established options is correct. This is a possibility which Biblical scholars are loathe to admit, however, and in the present instance they have good reason. There are several disquieting factors which suggest that the search for solutions at a quite fundamental level remains necessary. I here mention just four:

(i) No one has satisfactorily resolved the problem of the *genre* of the Nehemiah Memoir. Five theories about this are currently canvassed,[18] but none does justice to all the material. Yet the Nehemiah Memoir is usually paraded as one of the most established results of source criticism in these books, if not in the whole OT.

(ii) There is a substantial body of material in the later chapters of Nehemiah whose provenance and literary associations have received little attention. It is widely agreed that not all can be attributed to either the Ezra or the Nehemiah sources, but few have penetrated beyond this negative position.

(iii) The extent, original order, *genre* and authenticity of the Ezra material continue to elicit such a plethora of contradictory views that there can be little

---

[16] The continuing importance of these now traditional disciplines is shown with reference to other texts in the essays of FRIEDMAN and ISHIDA elsewhere in this volume. [R.E. FRIEDMAN and H.G.M. WILLIAMSON (eds.) The Future of Biblical Studies: The Hebrew Scriptures (Semeia Studies; Atlanta, 1987), 81–101 and 165–87.]

[17] Note the importance attributed to these works by H.G. KIPPENBERG, Religion und Klassenbildung im antiken Judäa (SUNT, 14; Göttingen, 1978).

[18] Four are summarized by KELLERMANN, Nehemia, 76–84. He then adds his own fresh suggestion (84–88 *et passim*), in which he compares the NM with the 'Prayer of the Accused'.

confidence in the methods that have produced them. Whilst much of the older evidence based on literary style[19] is now seen to have been based on faulty method, nothing of potentially equal objectivity has emerged to replace it.

(iv) There has recently been a heartening response, from my point of view, to the arguments for the separation of Chronicles from Ezra-Nehemiah as regards authorship. Under the old consensus, certain parameters were established for the composition of Ezra-Nehemiah. With these removed, it is possible to look with fresh eyes at the process of our books' composition and to find quite novel results imposing themselves. I have already tried to illustrate this in a lengthy article on Ezra 1–6,[20] in which amongst other things I conclude that these chapters presuppose a knowledge of the combination of the material about Ezra and Nehemiah and so represent the latest phase in the books' composition. Furthermore, opinions and prejudices about the Chronicler's historiographic method have often in the past been assumed to hold true for Ezra and Nehemiah too.[21] In the present climate, it becomes possible to study our books afresh without such preconceived ideas.

If, then, there is reason enough to believe that fresh research is desirable, in what directions may we expect it to go? To answer this question, I shall first sketch some of the results of my own investigation. I do this in order to illustrate why I consider that a major *desideratum* is for those who will allow themselves enough time and effort to immerse themselves in these books. The kind of analysis which is necessary and which I shall just begin to illustrate will never emerge from those who are merely seeking solutions to predetermined historical or other questions. I shall then move on to outline one or two wider issues where further work seems desirable.

To start with, I find it quite extraordinary that no one has ever pointed out the extent to which all of Nehemiah's major achievements are paralleled in other passages not derived from his first person account. The list of participants in the wall building in Neh. 3 was certainly not composed at first by Nehemiah, though I consider it probable that he incorporated it later into his own account.[22] Its

---

[19] See especially the works of TORREY, Composition and Historical Value of Ezra-Nehemiah; Ezra Studies; and A. S. KAPELRUD, The Question of Authorship in the Ezra-Narrative: a Lexical Investigation (Oslo, 1944). For a preliminary response, cf. RUDOLPH, Esra und Nehemia, 163–65; more recent discussions from differing points of view but all with a conscious concern for method include H. G. M. WILLIAMSON, Israel in the Books of Chronicles (Cambridge, 1977), 37–59; POLZIN, Late Biblical Hebrew, and M. A. THRONTVEIT, 'Linguistic Analysis and the Question of Authorship in Chronicles, Ezra and Nehemiah', VT 32 (1982), 201–216.

[20] H. G. M. WILLIAMSON, 'The Composition of Ezra i–vi', JTS n.s. 34 (1983), 1–30 (see below, 244–70).

[21] TORREY, Ezra Studies, 223; H. CAZELLES, 'La Mission d'Esdras', VT 4 (1954), 113–140 (119); H. H. ROWLEY, 'The Chronological Order of Ezra and Nehemiah', in The Servant of the Lord (2nd edn; Oxford, 1965), 137–68 (147).

[22] I defend this conclusion and others of a similar sort throughout this paper at greater

standpoint is that of the work completed, with the 'doors, bolts and bars' of the gates all in place. In Nehemiah's first person account, however, the work is not completed until chap. 6, and even then it is explicitly stated that 'at that time I had not yet hung the doors in the gates' (v 1). Second, the account is in the third person, whereas Nehemiah's account is always in the first person, and third, the use of *'addîrîm*, 'nobles', contrasts with Nehemiah's own ways of referring to the local leaders. The prominence given to Eliashib the high priest (v 1) suggests that the list was originally drawn up under priestly influence, and so is likely to have been preserved in the temple archives. It is of further interest to note the use of *'ᵃdōnêhem*, 'their lord', in probable reference to Nehemiah (v 5). The same title is used for Ezra in Ezra 10:3 on the lips of one whose family had participated in the first return many years previously (cf. Ezra 2). An origin for our present list in the same circles is not unlikely. It may be suggested as a speculation that, in view of the prominence of Eliashib, and the reference to the Meshullam who was related by marriage to Tobiah (cf. v 30 and 6:18), the list may have been drawn up originally at the instigation of those who later became antagonistic to Nehemiah in an attempt to claim from him some of the credit for the successful completion of the task.

It is generally assumed that from a chronological point of view Nehemiah's next concern was the dedication of the walls, though for separate reasons his account has been moved to 12:27–43. Commentators are agreed, however, that this paragraph cannot have been extracted as a whole from his Memoir. The first four verses include no reference to Nehemiah, the lists of the names of the priests and musicians interrupt the narrative flow and are not elsewhere the object of Nehemiah's concern, and the narrative itself is fragmentary: we are not told, for instance, where the processions started from, what happened to most of the members of the processions as they approached the temple, how the first choir reached the temple, and so on. It is therefore generally agreed that an extract from the Nehemiah Memoir has here been heavily reworked. For technical reasons that need not detain us now, we may ascribe vv 31–32, 37–40 and 43 to Nehemiah's account.

Unlike earlier commentators, however, I do not find it possible simply to ascribe all the remaining material to editorial expansion. There are elements of overlap between the descriptions of the processions and of the ceremony itself; there is some apparently valuable archival material in vv 28–29; and there are some slight tensions between this additional material and the surrounding narrative context, all of which makes it probable that two separate descriptions have been spliced together rather than that the final account has evolved directly out of an earlier, shorter one. The clerical and religious interests of the alternative account stand out clearly on even a superficial survey.

---

length in a forthcoming commentary on Ezra-Nehemiah for the Word Biblical Commentary series [subsequently published in 1985].

A third early action by Nehemiah was to arrange for the repopulation of the city of Jerusalem. He tells of his preparations for this in the opening verses of chap. 7. At this point, as is well known, his account breaks off. From a narrative point of view, the subject is resumed at the beginning of chap. 11. Most commentators assume that vv 1-2 represent an editorially reworked version of the continuation of Nehemiah's account. Closer examination shows that this cannot be the case: (i) the verses are not couched in Nehemiah's first person narrative style; indeed, he is not mentioned here at all. As they stand, therefore, these verses could contribute nothing to the purpose of his account; (ii) the style of writing differs from that of Nehemiah.[23] We here find *šeʾār*, 'rest, remainder', where Nehemiah uses *yeter* (2:16; 4:8, 13; 6:1, 14), *śārîm*, 'leaders', where Nehemiah consistently uses words like *seḡānîm* and *ḥōrîm*,[24] and the use of *ʿîr haqqōdeš* for Jerusalem; (iii) despite the fact of continuity with chap. 7, these verses do not supply what we have been led to expect from Nehemiah's own account. He tells how he gathered the leaders of the people in order to make a genealogical record of them, and that he then found an older record to help him (7:4-5). We thus expect him to organize the repopulation of Jerusalem with reference to family connections. What we find here instead, however, is that the people (not Nehemiah) make the arrangements on the haphazard basis of lot-casting.

It therefore appears that here too we have a fragment of an alternative account of one of Nehemiah's actions. Lot-casting at this period was a cultic, even priestly, affair.[25] If the passage describes an activity undertaken with priestly supervision, then its preservation in the temple archives is a plausible speculation. Its attachment to the following list, which we cannot deal with now, enhances this probability.

Finally, we must consider Nehemiah's various social and religious reforms recorded in chaps. 5 and 13. Some connection with Neh. 10 has long been recognized.[26] Neh. 10 is a first-person account by the community of a one-sided agreement into which the people entered to observe the Law of God. Quite rightly, no one has ever suggested that it was part of the Nehemiah Memoir. There have been occasional attempts to relate it to the Ezra source, but in my

---

[23] MOWINCKEL, Studien zu dem Buche Ezra-Nehemia, I, 48-49; KELLERMANN, Nehemia, 43.

[24] 2:16; 4:8, 13; 5:7, 17; 6:17; 7:5 (a reference of particular significance since it is in the same narrative context as our present verses); 12:40; 13:11, 17. *śārîm* occurs only at 12:31-32 with a comparable meaning in material possibly to be attributed to Nehemiah, but even there other considerations make it equally likely that it is due to editorial adaptation. Elsewhere in Nehemiah's writing, *śārîm* carries a more specific nuance.

[25] Cf. 1 Chron. 24:5, 7, 31; 25:8, 9; 26:13, 14, all passages which should, in my view, be attributed to a priestly reviser of the Chronicler's original work; cf. WILLIAMSON, 'The Origins of the Twenty-Four Priestly Courses: a Study of 1 Chronicles xxiii-xxvii', VTSup 30 (1979), 251-68 (see above, 126-40).

[26] See BERTHOLET, Die Bücher Esra und Nehemia.

opinion it should be regarded as a document of independent origin.[27] Its affinities with the temple archives are suggested by (i) the conclusion of the chapter, with its summarizing note of strong support for the temple; (ii) the use of *'addîrêhem* (v 30), which is to be compared with 3:5 and our remarks earlier about the likely origin of that chapter; and (iii) the temple as the most likely place in which, to judge from its content, some secondary material in v 40a would have been added.[28]

Now, it is remarkable to observe to what extent the individual clauses of this pledge overlap with reforms for which Nehemiah also takes credit. It is necessary only to list them to realize that the coincidence goes beyond the possibilities of chance:

mixed marriages (10:31; 13:23-30)
Sabbath observance (10:32; 13:15-22)
abandonment of the practice of taking loans on pledge (10:32; Neh. 5)
the wood offering (10:35; 13:31)
firstfruits (10:36-37; 13:31)
Levitical tithes (10:38-39; 13:10-14)
neglect of the temple (10:40; 13:11).

Before reflecting on these observations, we must now draw in some further relevant evidence concerning the Nehemiah Memoir itself. As I have already indicated, scholars ought to have been alerted to the existence of a problem by the complete lack of agreement over the work's literary *genre,* and by the fact that most of the proposed solutions are based upon only a narrow selection of relevant evidence. Three further points also cry out for explanation:

(i) There is a long and unexplained gap between the account of the wall-building with related events and the incidents recounted in chap. 13. Taking the chronological notices of the book as they stand, we are presented with the description of less than one year's activity in considerable detail followed by several isolated topics from perhaps as much as fifteen years later. It is hardly adequate merely to reply that nothing of significance happened in the meanwhile.

(ii) Few will disagree that a solution to the problem of the Nehemiah Memoir must account adequately for the distinctive 'remember' formula. Perusal of the

---

[27] See especially MOWINCKEL, Studien zu dem Buche Ezra-Nehemia, III, 142-156. In this discussion, I deal only with the account of the pledge in vv 1, 29-40. The list of those who signed the document (vv 2-28) has been added secondarily, as nearly all commentators recognize.

[28] The extent of these additions throughout the closing verses of the chapter is disputed, but clearly v 40a must be included amongst them: its switch to third person narration is out of place, and it seems to offer a summary of what is to be brought into the storerooms, which is inappropriate in the context of the pledge.

six passages where it occurs reveals something that I have never seen even noted, namely that not one of them relates to the building of the wall. With only one possible exception (and that a negative use of the formula),[29] none even relates to the early period of Nehemiah's work at all, but can only have been written twelve years later at the earliest. It would be strange, to say the least, that if Nehemiah composed the whole Memoir as some kind of votive inscription, however defined, he should not have specifically offered his most outstanding achievement as a major reason for God to remember him.

(iii) If we concentrate for the moment on the deeds which Nehemiah asks God to have in remembrance, we find that they are as follows:

- 5:19 Nehemiah has desisted from eating 'the bread of the governor' throughout his first term of office because of the people's economic burdens. The earlier part of the chapter shows that much of this was due to debt slavery.
- 13:14 Two points are included here, care for the house of God, which may refer to the expulsion of Tobiah, and 'its services', referring to the restoration of the Levitical tithes.
- 13:22 Sanctification of the Sabbath Day.
- 13:31 The foregoing paragraph treats mixed marriages, the duties of the priests and Levites, the wood offering and the first-fruits.

Perusal of this list at once reveals that every item mentioned can be directly associated with one or other of the clauses of the pledge in chap. 10, as analysed above.

This whole catalogue of observations about the Nehemiah Memoir seems to me to go beyond the possible bounds of coincidence and to demand some sort of explanation. Though such a solution may appear old-fashioned, a literary division of the material provides far and away the easiest way out. No difficulty confronts the relegation of 5:14–19; 13:4–14, 15–22 and 23–31 to a subsequent phase of composition. These few paragraphs have much in common: each concludes with a positive 'remember' formula; each is a brief description without particular chronological setting; each comes long after the building of the wall, and each can be linked in some way with chap. 10. On the other hand, the rest of the Nehemiah Memoir now also takes on a degree of coherence: all is related to the task of building the wall together with its immediate sequel;

---

[29] Neh 6:14. This verse introduces a 'remember' formula into an account of the first phase of Nehemiah's work. Two possible explanations suggest themselves: (i) This is the only occurrence of the formula which refers to something unmentioned in the preceding narrative, namely 'Noadiah the prophetess and the rest of the prophets ...' . This may indicate that the verse was worked in at a later stage. (ii) Since this verse is a prayer against the enemy rather than a positive use of the 'remember' formula, it may be intended as a prayer uttered within the historical context itself, as 3:36–37 clearly is. Either of these possibilities would remove the difficulty of 6:14 for the general view advanced above. Either seems to me easier to accept than that all the other factors referred to here are purely coincidental.

nothing need come later than a year after Nehemiah's arrival in Jerusalem, if that. Furthermore, the removal of the 'remember' formula leaves the narrative much more as a report on a limited project – to be expected after 2:6 – than a votive or dedication text. Years later, as our earlier discussion of the alternative, priestly material has suggested, Nehemiah felt that justice was not being done to him within his own community. I suggest that he was thus moved to rework his old report, adding to it a number of short paragraphs dealing specifically with those points for which he felt he was not being given due credit. As an aside, therefore, we may conclude that the Nehemiah Memoir represents a mixture of literary *genres* and that previous discussions have been vitiated by their failure to commence with a proper source analysis.

At this point, I should like to reemphasize that all this material is presented by way of illustration alone. Wearisome as this survey may have become, it is still only a beginning. What I have sketched in itself needs refinement and extension, and even then nothing has been said of the Ezra material, of Ezra 1–6 and more besides. Even so, it may be hoped that sufficient indication has been given both of the primacy of literary analysis for a correct approach to these books, and of the sort of methods by which it should be conducted. If that be allowed, then we may turn our attention to some consequences of what we have noted that may also point the way forward for further work.

First, and rather obvious, it is impressed upon us yet again to what an extent we are dependent upon the somewhat spasmodic light which our sources shed upon this period. Well illuminated are the building of the second temple, the twelve months of Ezra's work, the building of the wall under Nehemiah and its immediate sequel (say twelve months), and an unchronological account of various reforms some twelve or fifteen years later. Limiting ourselves to the Persian period, I have endeavoured in various articles[30] to accumulate evidence which enables us to say something about the end of that period when, I believe, there was a major split in the Jerusalem priesthood and many of its members left to join with other elements at a resettled Shechem to found what we know as the Samaritan community. To these five moments some further information can, of course, be added from other sources of various kinds. However, when we remember that we are dealing with a time span of over 200 years, it is quite clear that we cannot expect to write anything like the kind of connected history with which we are familiar. As related, each episode is virtually self-contained, and there can be no question of a cause-and-effect continuum between them. Our approach to these materials must respect and take account of this fundamental limitation.

Second, from even the small sample of an analysis offered above, it emerges that the divisions of opinion within the Jerusalem community were more com-

---

[30] H. G. M. WILLIAMSON, 'The Historical Value of Josephus' *Jewish Antiquities* xi. 297–301', JTS n. s. 28 (1977), 49–66 (see above, 74–89); 'Origins of the Twenty-Four Priestly Courses'; 'Composition of Ezra i–vi'.

plicated than has been assumed hitherto. This is not the place for me to repeat my reservations[31] about the approach to this issue by Plöger[32] and its separate, but in many respects comparable, treatment by Hanson.[33] Rather, we should observe on the basis of the juxtaposition of material in Nehemiah that there were clearly quite sharp differences of opinion even within what are generally regarded as theocratic or hierocratic circles. It is true that the literary evidence I have adduced would not yet allow us to say that these were more than matters of style or approach, but should these be dismissed as of no consequence? Sociological examination of these texts has only just begun, but it already tempts me to feel that it has as much to teach us about the growth of sects within Judaism as do genuinely theological or religious differences. Perhaps I may amplify this with reference to Neh 9.

It is a fundamental conviction of scholars like Plöger that the books of Chronicles, Ezra and Nehemiah contain no hope of radical change in Israel's future. He summarizes and quotes with approval the following passage from Rudolph:

We must not overlook the fact that in the second part of his presentation, the Books of Ezra and Nehemiah, he is pursuing the aim of describing the founding of the new people of God as it should be in accordance with the will of God – a community gathered around its Temple in zealous worship, protected by secure walls, in obedience to the divine Law, and inwardly separated from everything alien. This means that the actual Jewish community, especially as it is presented in Neh. xii 43--xiii 3, so fully realised the idea of theocracy for the Chronicler that there was no need of any further eschatological hope. [34]

Comparable opinions find expression in a number of studies of these works written during the last thirty years or so, especially those which regard Ezra and Nehemiah as the culmination of the Chronicler's writing.

A different viewpoint emerges, however, if we take more seriously the work of the editor who combined the accounts of the activity of Ezra and Nehemiah as an independent narrative. Neh 8–10 takes on central significance. For Rudolph, the present ordering was no more than the result of an accidental textual transmission. Others, like Mowinckel and Pohlmann, see the growth of these chapters as a secondary development, for they uphold the priority of 1 Esdras, where Neh 8 immediately follows Ezra 10, and they see the inclusion of the Nehemiah Memoir as coming only at a very late stage. For a number of reasons which need not detain us now, however, these chapters are better regarded as the thoughtful

---

[31] See WILLIAMSON, Israel in the Books of Chronicles, 132–140; 'Eschatology in Chronicles', TynB 28 (1977), 115–154 (see above, 162–95).

[32] O. PLÖGER, Theokratie und Eschatologie (WMANT, 2; Neukirchen, 1959) = Theocracy and Eschatology (Oxford, 1968).

[33] P.D. HANSON, The Dawn of Apocalyptic (Philadelphia, 1975).

[34] Cited from W. RUDOLPH, 'Problems of the Books of Chronicles', VT 4 (1954), a translation by P.R. ACKROYD of parts of the introduction to RUDOLPH's Chronikbücher (HAT, 21; Tübingen, 1955), which is itself, of course, the source on which PLÖGER drew.

combination of three originally discrete literary elements into a single, focal description of a climax in the reformers' work. Presentation of the Law (Neh 8), confession (Neh 9) and a pledge by the community to keep God's Law (Neh 10) may be loosely termed a process of covenant renewal which gives coherence and direction to the other reforms which have been described.[35]

In this, the great prayer of confession in Neh 9 is central. Here, moreover, is a text which cries out for rhetorical analysis, but which has not hitherto received such attention. Of the many insights which such an analysis affords, I single out just one for mention here.

The final stanza of the long historical retrospect is to be found in vv 22–31. It deals with entry into and life in the land, the promise of which has been prominent in the earlier sections. After treating the entry into the land in vv 22–25, the description moves on into three cycles on the pattern of rebellion, handing over to a foreign power, cry for help, and response by God in mercy and deliverance (vv 26-27; 28; 29–31). A number of phraseological parallels between these units makes the cyclical pattern stand out clearly. Naturally, we may see in this the influence of the Deuteronomic presentation of the people's history.

Within this recurring pattern, the author probably intends us to see an intensification of the severity of God's judgement. Certainly v 28b is markedly more forceful than 27a, but what of v 30c? While at first glance it seems milder, it is in fact probably to be seen as a statement about the Babylonian conquest and exile. It is difficult to see otherwise the force of $l\bar{o}^{\jmath}$ $^{ca}\dot{s}\hat{\imath}t\bar{a}m$ $k\bar{a}l\hat{a}$, 'you did not eliminate them', in v 31, and the fact that this stands at the very end of the historical retrospect adds some support to this conclusion.

Now, it should not escape notice that this third cycle breaks off abruptly without the expected elements of a cry to God for help and his consequent deliverance. Evidently, the author considered that the restoration from that severe judgement was not yet complete; rather, he includes himself and his contemporaries as living still within a theologically exilic situation. Then, with a most powerful shift of perspective, he immediately actualizes the cry for help as in vv 32–37 he presents words of confession, petition and lament which arise from his current situation. And this is made the more poignant in the wider context of these chapters by the fact that he has already equated rebellion against God with rejection of his Law (e.g., v 29),[36] whereas it is precisely a return to this law that characterizes Neh. 8–10 as a whole. With the prayer breaking off at this point of bringing the congregation inside the recurrent pattern of confession

---

[35] See K. BALTZER, Das Bundesformular (WMANT, 4; Neukirchen, 1960), 51–55 = The Covenant Formulary (Oxford, 1971), 43–47; IN DER SMITTEN, Esra, 35–53; KELLERMANN, Nehemia, 90–92; D.J. MCCARTHY, 'Covenant and Law in Chronicles-Nehemiah', CBQ 44 (1982), 25–44.

[36] Cf. M. GILBERT, 'La place de la loi dans la prière de Néhémie 9', in J. DORÉ, P. GRELOT and M. CARREZ (eds.), De la Tôrah au Messie: Mélanges Henri Cazelles (Paris, 1981), 307–316.

and deliverance, we cannot but be left on the tiptoe of expectation as regards the future. Moreover, the substance of the lament concerning the oppressive nature of foreign domination does not allow us to interpret this expectation in any other than political terms.

Now, it may well be that Neh. 9 stands somewhat isolated in this regard within Ezra-Nehemiah. Nevertheless, its centrality within the structure of the books as a whole obliges us to look again at the types of division which existed within the post-exilic community, and so reinforces the questions we have posed from other points of view as well.[37]

A third and final conclusion of our discussion, again with acknowledgement of the need for further study, is a heightened appreciation of the historiographical concern of the writers in its fullest sense. As we have seen, there was available to the editor(s) an assortment of primary sources, each giving considerable detail about some particular event or activity, but unrelated in any way to the other sources, and often at a long chronological remove from them.

As they have reached us, however, there can be no doubt that these books confront us with a single and united account of the postexilic restoration of the people, their city and their cult. Not only is all sense of the passage of time eliminated, but isolated events have now been lifted from their strictly historical moorings to be judged instead by their theological significance. It is at this level, the level of divine causality, that continuity is to be perceived; the normal laws of cause and effect are totally subordinated to this perspective. We thus have in these books a most instructive example, whose steps we can clearly trace, of the development of what in other books would be called a history of salvation.

This process is characteristic of all the major redactional layers in these books,[38] and may be summarized under three general headings.

First, a number of chronological summaries group widely diverse periods as though they were to be regarded as parts of a single whole. For instance, at Ezra 6:14 the restoration of the temple is linked with Cyrus, Darius and Artaxerxes and so covers the whole span of the books rather than the point which has been reached in the narrative. Again, at Neh. 12:47 Zerubbabel and Nehemiah are

---

[37] Of course, PLÖGER and HANSON are not without their critics from many other points of view as well. For a recent example, cf. R. MASON, 'The Prophets of the Restoration', in R. COGGINS, A. PHILLIPS and M. KNIBB (eds.), Israel's Prophetic Tradition: Essays in Honour of Peter R. Ackroyd (Cambridge, 1982), 137–154. See also a number of passages in the wide-ranging study of C. C. ROWLAND, The Open Heaven: A Study of Apocalyptic in Judaism and Early Christianity (London, 1982). A noteworthy dissenting voice from a critical standpoint which in other respects is closer to that of RUDOLPH and PLÖGER is R. MOSIS, Untersuchungen zur Theologie des chronistischen Geschichtswerkes (Freiburg/Basel/Wien, 1973).

[38] In my opinion, there are three such layers, (i) the combining of the narratives concerning Ezra and Nehemiah together with some of the other material from the period of Nehemiah noted earlier in this paper, (ii) the later addition of the lists in 11:21–36 and 12:1–26, and (iii) the prefixing of Ezra 1–6. It may be observed that the examples noted above draw on all three of these layers.

noted in parallel in connection with the support of the cultic personnel, while at 12:26 the lists of priests and Levites are summarized as spanning the whole period of Joiakim, the high priest next after the initial return, Nehemiah the governor and Ezra the priest and scribe. Here the emphasis is clearly on the complementarity of function rather than on chronological separation.

Second, the even flow of dates through the books serves to give a sense of continuity to what we know otherwise was a series of disjointed acts. Thus not only are the two parts of the book of Ezra, which are historically separated by several decades, joined theologically by the astonishing phrase 'After these things' at Ezra 7:1, but also, perhaps, by the dating of the events of chap. 6 to the sixth year (of Darius) and those of chaps. 7ff. to the seventh year (of Artaxerxes). Similarly, whereas historically, I believe, Ezra's reading of the Law in Neh. 8 preceded Nehemiah's mission by thirteen years, it is integrated into its new setting by being dated without further qualification in the seventh month, which appears to follow smoothly after the sixth month, Elul, on which the wall was completed in Neh. 6:15. Then the originally independent Neh. 9 follows on 'the twenty-fourth day of this month' (9:1), while Neh. 10 is joined on by its introductory phrase 'And yet for all this'. Finally, the various reforms which close the book are also joined by their redactional chronological notations: 'on that day' (the day of the dedication of the wall!) in Neh. 12:44 and 13:1, 'Now before this' in 13:4 and 'in those days' in 13:15 and 23.

Third and last, the major divisions of the work are linked by having been given a parallel structure in each case which is clearly the result of editorial arrangement of source materials. Space forbids an exposition of this panel effect that runs through the books, but suffice it to say that it helpfully accounts for the two most celebrated chronological discontinuities which the books contain, namely the account of opposition that the community faced in Ezra 4 and the suspension of Ezra's reading of the Law until Neh. 8. Some helpful remarks towards the elucidation of this patterning have already been offered by Gunneweg[39] and Childs.[40] I have endeavoured to carry their insights forward a little in a forthcoming commentary, but it is clear that here too much remains to be done. This is an approach to Old Testament study which has attracted much attention in recent years in connection with a number of other books, and I do not doubt that the time is ripe for similar attention to Ezra and Nehemiah. Let me conclude, however, by reemphasizing that so far as my own tentative probes in this direction are concerned, our appreciation of such patterning is likely to be heightened and so best served by an initial thorough examination of the more traditional disciplines of source and redaction analysis.

---

[39] A.H.J. GUNNEWEG, 'Zur Interpretation der Bücher Esra-Nehemia', VTSup 32 (1981), 146–161.

[40] B.S. CHILDS, Introduction to the Old Testament as Scripture (London, 1979), 631–637.

14. Ezra and Nehemiah in the Light of the Texts from Persepolis

Between the years of 1931 and 1939 a major excavation of Persepolis, one of the capitals of the Achaemenid empire, was undertaken by the Oriental Institute of the University of Chicago.[1] During the course of these excavations, many discoveries of texts were made, of which three are of particular concern to us here. The first and largest group to be unearthed was found initially by accident during the third season (1933), when E.E. Herzfeld was still leader of the excavation. 'When leveling debris for the construction of a road, Herzfeld discovered great numbers of cuneiform tablets in the northeastern remnants of the Terrace fortification.'[2] These 'remnants' proved to have been a bastion on the northern edge of the terrace, the tablets being located in its southeastern portion.[3]

In 1935, when E.F. Schmidt had succeeded Herzfeld as director, work was begun on the Treasury, and here in 1936 a further, though much smaller, group of tablets was found in Room 33.[4] Finally, principally in Hall 38 of the Treasury, a number of (probably) ritual objects, such as pestles, mortars and plates, were

---

[1] The following special abbreviations should be noted: AD = G.R. DRIVER, Aramaic Documents of the Fifth Century B.C. (Oxford, 1957); AP = A. COWLEY, Aramaic Papyri of the Fifth Century B.C. (Oxford, 1923); BMAP = E.G. KRAELING, The Brooklyn Museum Aramaic Papyri (New Haven, 1953); CHI = I. GERSHEVITCH (ed.), The Cambridge History of Iran. Volume 2: The Median and Achaemenid Periods (Cambridge, 1985); PFa = R.T. HALLOCK, 'Selected Fortification Texts', Cahiers de la Délégation Archéologique Française en Iran 8 (1978), 109-36; PFT = R.T. HALLOCK, Persepolis Fortification Tablets (University of Chicago Oriental Institute Publications, 92; Chicago, 1969); PTT = G.G. CAMERON, Persepolis Treasury Tablets (University of Chicago Oriental Institute Publications, 65; Chicago, 1948). In all cases where these abbreviations refer to collections of texts, the references in what follows are to the number of the text cited unless otherwise stated.

[2] E.F. SCHMIDT, Persepolis I. Structures, Reliefs, Inscriptions (The University of Chicago Oriental Institute Publications, 68; Chicago, 1953), 3; cf. E.E. HERZFELD, Iran in the Ancient East (London, 1941), 226. See more popularly E.F. SCHMIDT, The Treasury of Persepolis and Other Discoveries in the Homeland of the Achaemenians (Chicago, 1939).

[3] SCHMIDT, Persepolis I, 40.

[4] Ibid. 4 and 173-74; see also N. CAHILL, 'The Treasury at Persepolis: Gift-Giving at the City of the Persians', AJA 89 (1985), 373-89. Aspects of CAHILL's interpretation of the treasury's function have been challenged by C. TUPLIN ('The Administration of the Achaemenid Empire', in I. CARRADICE [ed.], Coinage and Administration in the Athenian and Persian Empires [BAR International Series, 343; Oxford, 1987], 109-66, esp. 139).

discovered. Made of a hard green stone known as (impure) chert, and usually highly polished, many of these objects were found to have Aramaic inscriptions written on them.[5]

Although the three groups of texts, and especially the fortification and treasury tablets, share a number of points in common, it is important to distinguish carefully their individual characteristics.

Most obviously distinctive is the small group of about 200 texts in Aramaic (not all legible). Cameron was the first to study these texts, and he came to the conclusion that they referred to the delivery of the objects on which they were written at Persepolis.[6] Bowman, however, to whom was entrusted the publication of the material,[7] rejected this conclusion in favour of the view that they described the objects' use in the religious *haoma* ceremony. Subsequent study has vindicated Cameron's basic approach,[8] so that although several differences of opinion, to say nothing of a number of obscurities, remain in the realm of detail, the general approach that should be taken to these texts is now agreed. For instance, instead of Bowman's translation of text no. 18:

בסרך בירתא ליד מתרך סגנא	1)	In the ritual of the fortress, beside Mithraka the *segan*,
בגפשת / עבד סחר זנה רב /	2)	I Bago-paušta used this plate, a large one,
[ליד ב]גפת גנזברא קדם מזדדת	3)	[beside Ba]ga-pāta the treasurer (and) before Mazda-dāta
אפגנזברא אשכר שנתי ר— /// /// ///	4)	the sub-treasurer. '*škr* of year 19

---

[5] SCHMIDT, Persepolis I, 181 ff.; E. F. SCHMIDT, Persepolis II. Contents of the Treasury and Other Discoveries (The University of Chicago Oriental Institute Publications, 69; Chicago, 1957), 53–56.

[6] Cf. G. G. CAMERON in SCHMIDT, Persepolis II, 55.

[7] R. A. BOWMAN, Aramaic Ritual Texts from Persepolis (University of Chicago Oriental Publications, 91; Chicago, 1970).

[8] For reviews that support this, see especially J. B. SEGAL, BSOAS 35 (1972), 354–55; PH. GIGNOUX, RHR 181 (1972), 86–87; J. R. HINNELLS, 'Religion at Persepolis', Religion 3 (1973), 157–60; R. DEGEN, BibOr 31 (1974), 124–27; for studies, see P. BERNARD, 'Les mortiers et pilons inscrits de Persépolis', Studia Iranica 1 (1972), 165–76; B. A. LEVINE, 'Aramaic Texts from Persepolis', JAOS 92 (1972), 70–79; W. HINZ, Neue Wege im Altpersischen (Göttinger Orientforschungen, III/1; Wiesbaden, 1973), 43–52; J. NAVEH and SH. SHAKED, 'Ritual Texts or Treasury Documents?' Orientalia ns 42 (1973), 445–57; J. A. DELAUNAY, 'À propos des "Aramaic Ritual Texts from Persepolis" de R. A. Bowman', Acta Iranica 2 (1974), 193–217; I. GERSHEVITCH, 'An Iranianist's View of the Soma Controversy', in PH. GIGNOUX and A. TAFAZZOLI (eds.), Mémorial Jean de Menasce (Louvain, 1974), 45–75, especially 52–54 and 69–71; W. HINZ, 'Zu den Mörsern und Stösseln aus Persepolis', Acta Iranica 4 (1974), 371–85; K. KAMIOKA, 'Philological Observations on the Aramaic Texts from Persepolis', Orient 11 (1975), 45–66; W. VOGELSANG, 'Early Historical Arachosia in South-East Afghanistan', Iranica Antiqua 20 (1985), 55–99, esp. 82–86. I regret that M. N. BOGOLJUBOV, 'Aramejskie nadpisi ne ritual 'nyh predmetah iz Persepolja', Izvestija Akademii Nauk SSSR, Serija Literatury i Jazyka 32 (1973), 172–77, is not accessible to me.

we should probably translate along the lines:

1) In the fortress of Sāruka,[9] (which is) under the authority of[10] Mithraka the prefect,[11]
2) I Bago-paušta handed over[12] this plate, a large one,
3) under the authority of /to (*or* 'made for') Baga-pāta the treasurer in the presence of Mazda-dāta
4) the sub-treasurer (as) tribute/a gift[13] of year 19.

The texts are dated to the years 479/78–436/35 BC or perhaps a little later, during the reigns of Xerxes and Artaxerxes I, so that they overlap with the work of Ezra and Nehemiah on a traditional dating.

By far the largest group of texts, of which over two thousand have been published to date,[14] are the so-called fortification tablets, which date from the earlier period of 509–494 BC. Being written in Elamite,[15] they are by no means

---

[9] Three words with the preposition *b* stand in this initial position: *prkn, srk,* and *hst.* BOWMAN related them to his ritual interpretation (e.g., *prkn* = '(haoma)-crushing ceremony'), but others all find an indication of place, as suggested by comparable formulae with *b ... byrt*' in other texts (so frequently, *inter alia,* in AP and BMAP; the most recent example is reported to be in the as yet unpublished Samaria Papyri 4:1, where *bšmryn byrt*' stands in an equivalent position to *bšmryn qryt*' at 14:1; this shows that 'fortress' is not a fully satisfactory translation of *byrt*'; cf. F. M. CROSS, 'Samaria Papyrus 1: An Aramaic Slave Conveyance of 335 B.C.E. found in the Wâdi ed-Dâliyeh', ErIsr [1985], 7*–17* [11* with nn 9 and 10]); A LEMAIRE and H. LOZACHMEUR, 'Birāh/birtā' en araméen', Syria 64 (1987), 261–66. Whereas LEVINE, GERSHEVITCH and DELAUNAY argue that reference is to rooms within the palace or treasury, BERNARD and especially HINZ ('Zu den Mörsern') have advanced strong arguments for finding here three place names in the eastern part of the empire known as Arachosia, itself mentioned several times in these texts (e.g., 9:4; 13:4; 19:4; 43:6). It will have been in this region that the objects were made before being sent to Persepolis. KAMIOKA's compromise suggestion, that these are place names in the vicinity of Persepolis ('Philological Observations', 60–61) has nothing to commend it.

[10] For this meaning of *lyd,* cf. AD iv 1.

[11] The plural is familiar from Dan 2:48; 3:2, 3, 27; 6:8. In BOWMAN 2:2, *rb*' has apparently been added secondarily after *sgn*', making an interesting parallel with Dan 2:48.

[12] Or 'made', Aram. *ʿbd.* Uncertainty over the precise significance of these texts remains because of the double use of *lyd.* Both occurrences could mean 'under the authority of', or the second might mean more simply 'to' or 'for'.

[13] BOWMAN thought that *ʾškr* meant 'intoxicant', though he regularly left it untranslated. For the now generally accepted association with Akkadian *iškaru,* either as 'finished products, staples, or material to be delivered' or as some kind of tax (CAD 7, 244–49), cf. LEVINE, 78, and for criticism of BOWMAN in this regard, cf. KAMIOKA, 52–54.

[14] Cf. PFT and PFa; it appears from PFT (1) that there are over three and a half thousand tablets in all. It should also be noted that an unspecified number of texts in Aramaic from the same source remain unpublished. For introductory studies, cf. R. T. HALLOCK ('The Evidence of the Persepolis Tablets', CHI 588–609); J. M. COOK (The Persian Empire [London, 1983], 85–90); D. M. LEWIS ('Postscript', in A. R. BURN, Persia and the Greeks: the Defence of the West, c. 546–478 BC [London, 1984²], 587–609). For a major effort to integrate the evidence from these texts with that of other sources relating to the geographical divisions and tribute of the empire, cf. TUPLIN ('The Administration of the Achaemenid Empire'), and for historical geography cf. W. M. SUMNER ('Achaemenid Settlement in the Persepolis Plain', AJA 90 [1986], 3–31).

[15] I freely admit to knowing no Elamite; this aspect of the present study is based on the

perfectly understood, but the number of them, together with the degree of overlap between one text and another, means that there is no doubt about the general situation. For the most part they record receipts or payments in kind for a variety of purposes. Their discovery in the 'fortifications' of Persepolis is an explicable accident of history[16] which has no bearing on the fact that they give us a direct insight into various aspects of administration at one of the Achaemenid capital cities.

The situation with regard to the treasury tablets is not dissimilar. Published in a variety of works by G.G. Cameron,[17] they date from 492–458 BC. The chief difference from the fortification tablets is that payments are now made in cash rather than in kind.

So far as I can tell, this wealth of material has largely been ignored by biblical scholars, and even occasional references that may be found in commentaries[18] hardly do justice to their potential. In what follows I cannot, of course, attempt fully to remedy this situation. The most I can set out to achieve is to draw attention to the relevance and scope of this material, in the hope that others with the necessary linguistic skills may be able later to refine what will, I fear, be seen in retrospect as a very crude comparison.[19]

---

translations of HALLOCK and CAMERON, together with the published comments of the few other specialists in that field. The linguistic position is probably in any case complicated by the peculiar circumstances of having Elamite scribes to record business which was basically conducted in Old Persian; cf. I. GERSHEVITCH, 'The Alloglottography of Old Persian', TPS (1979), 114–90.

[16] SCHMIDT linked the dates of the tablets with the phases in the development of the building of the treasury (Persepolis I, 41–42). He believed that the original treasury was completed at about the time when the series of fortification tablets begins, so that it cannot be deduced that there were no administrative texts, since lost, at an earlier time. Later, the treasury was twice expanded, the date of the first of these expansions coinciding with the break between the fortification and the treasury tablets. 'We believe that the fortification tablets had been removed – sometime after 494/93 B.C. – from their original archives to be stored (or discarded) in rooms of the fortification' (41). He further argued that the cessation of the treasury tablets indicated another change in the location of the administration, though others have argued that at that time the scribes went over to making their records (presumably in Aramaic) on perishable material; cf. W. HINZ, 'Zu den Persepolis-Täfelchen', ZDMG N.F. 35 (1961), 236–51. R.T. HALLOCK further believes that the use of Aramaic on perishable material accounts for the many gaps in even what we do have of the archive ('The Persepolis Fortification Archive', Orientalia ns 42 [1973], 320–23).

[17] PTT; see also G.G. CAMERON, 'Persepolis Treasury Tablets Old and New', JNES 17 (1958), 161–76; 'New Tablets from the Persepolis Treasury', JNES 24 (1965), 167–92.

[18] E.g., R.A. BOWMAN, IB 3, 613; J.M. MYERS, Ezra, Nehemiah (AB, 14; Garden City, 1965), 43, 51, referring quite reasonably to the association attested between archives and treasury (Ezra 5:17; 6:1). On this, see now J.C. GREENFIELD, 'Aspects of Archives in the Achaemenid Period', in K.R. VEENHOF (ed.), Cuneiform Archives and Libraries (Leiden, 1986), 289–95.

[19] The comments of D.M. LEWIS in his pioneering work on bringing this material to the attention of classicists are appropriate in our context too; he writes of the new evidence that 'although it seldom bears directly on the points which principally concern us, (it) neverthe-

Towards the conclusion of my 1987 Tyndale Biblical Archaeology Lecture,[20] I made a start on this comparison by suggesting six ways in which the Persepolis material could help forward our understanding of Neh. 5:14–19. I shall not repeat that discussion here, but will provide rather an introduction to three more general topics – language, religion, and travel – while emphasizing once more that this is far from an exhaustive survey.

A. Language

We may begin by noting, then, that despite the geographical distance which separates Arachosia from Judah, there are several points of contact between the language of the Aramaic texts from Persepolis and that of Ezra and Nehemiah. This is due, of course, to the fact that both reflect the current language of Persian administration, and to that extent little is added to what was already known or strongly surmised from other sources. Thus, for instance, we have the regular opening of the texts with b + place name + $byrt^{\,\prime}$, 'in the fortress of X', to set alongside $b^{e\,\prime}ahm^et\bar{a}^{\,\prime}$ $b\hat{\imath}rt\bar{a}^{\,\prime}$ of Ezra 6:2[21] and the Hebrew $b^e\check{s}\hat{u}\check{s}an$ $habb\hat{\imath}r\hat{a}$ of Neh 1:1; the official title $gnzbr^{\,\prime}$,[22] 'the treasurer', to compare with Hebrew $haggizb\bar{a}r$ at Ezra 1:8 and the Aramaic plural $gizzabrayy\bar{a}^{\,\prime}$ at Ezra 7:21; the use of the anarthrous kl in the summary of a list,[23] which may help explain the unusual Hebrew $kol\text{-}k\bar{e}l\hat{\imath}m$ at Ezra 1:11;[24] and the use of PN + $\check{s}mh$ (literally, 'his name') to mean 'a man named PN', exactly like $\check{s}\bar{e}\check{s}bassar$ $\check{s}^em\bar{e}h$ at Ezra 5:14.[25]

---

less sometimes suggests new approaches', Sparta and Persia (Cincinnati Classical Studies, ns 1; Leiden, 1977), 3.

[20] 'The Governors of Judah under the Persians', TynB 39 (1988), 59–82 (see above, 46–63). To the literature cited there, there should now be added TUPLIN, 'The Administration of the Achaemenid Empire', and D. M. LEWIS, 'The King's Dinner (Polyaenus IV 3,32)', in H. SANCISI-WEERDENBURG and A. KUHRT (eds.), Achaemenid History II. The Greek Sources: Proceedings of the Groningen 1984 Achaemenid History Workshop (Leiden, 1987), 79–87.

[21] For the omission of b before $byrt^{\,\prime}$ as a dittograph, cf. W. RUDOLPH, Esra und Nehemia (HAT; Tübingen, 1949), 54.

[22] A loan-word from Old Persian ganzabara, not previously attested in Aramaic with retention of the nun, but cf. Late Babylonian ganzabaru; CAD 5, 43.

[23] Misunderstood as a proper name by BOWMAN, 94:3 and 95:3; see rather SEGAL, 354; NAVEH and SHAKED, 453; and HINZ, 'Zu den Mörsern', 378. One should compare the regular use of PAP, 'total', to similar effect in many of the Elamite texts.

[24] For the suggestion that the inventory and its heading in Ezra 1:7–11 are based on an Aramaic original, see my Ezra, Nehemiah (WBC, 16; Waco, 1985), 7.

[25] Both Persian and Akkadian origins can be proposed for this idiom; cf. BOWMAN, p. 66, and DELAUNAY, 206f. It was already misunderstood by the Greek versions as well as by some more modern commentators; cf. L.W. BATTEN, The Books of Ezra and Nehemiah (ICC; Edinburgh, 1913), 140: 'its omission seems necessary', an opinion still tentatively favoured by A.H.J. GUNNEWEG, Esra (KAT; Gütersloh, 1985), 100. Dr. W. HORBURY has suggested to me that $\check{s}em\hat{o}$ in Zech 6:12 may be an example of the use of the same idiom in Hebrew.

Although we should not, therefore, expect any major new advance of understanding in this area, there are nevertheless a few matters, of which we will here consider three examples, concerning which our texts can add clarification.[26] To take first the idiom just referred to, Clines has observed that it 'is found regularly in contemporary papyri in reference to slaves', from which he concludes that 'the possibility must be considered that he (Sheshbazzar) was a high-ranking Babylonian official of slave status.'[27] Hinz, however, has made out a strong case for the suggestion that those so designated in the Persepolis texts were wealthy nobles in the area of the three named fortresses who regarded it as a privilege to supply the vessels needed for the periodic festival at Persepolis.[28] If he is right, then, of course, no deductions can be drawn from the use of this idiom about the social status of the individuals concerned.[29] We might surmise that it was used rather in cases where the individual was unknown personally to the recipient of the document,[30] for in our texts it is striking that it is only used in connection with the donors of the vessels, whose names are hardly ever repeated, but never in connection with the various officials, whose names recur frequently and who would have been known to others in the state bureaucracy. This would also, of course, readily explain its use with slaves – and with Sheshbazzar in the context presupposed by Ezra 5:14.

Second, light can be shed from these texts on the troublesome $’eben\ g^elāl$ referred to in connection with the building of the temple at Ezra 5:8 and 6:4, and which has generally been translated into English by 'large stones' or the like.[31] A number of other translations have been proposed, however, among which we

---

[26] For some examples of refinements to, or support for, views already held about, for instance, $’uššarnā’$ (Ezra 5:3, 9), $š^etar\ bôz^enay$ (Ezra 5:3; 6:6), $ništ^ewān$ (Ezra 4:7; 7:11), and especially $tiršātā’$ (Ezra 2:63; Neh. 7:65, 69; 8:9; 10:2), cf. HINZ, Neue Wege im Altpersischen, 39–45.

[27] D.J.A. CLINES, Ezra, Nehemiah, Esther (NCB; Grand Rapids and London, 1984), 87, citing AP 28:4; BMAP 5:2, 4; 8:3; AD 5:2–3; 8:1; 9:1. Without reference to the case of Sheshbazzar, this explanation of the idiom's significance had already been advanced by KRAELING, BMAP (145, 208). The idiom is attested most recently in J.B. SEGAL, Aramaic Texts from North Saqqâra (London, 1983), 5:1; 9:3; 17:1; 29:3, 6; 55a:4; 60:4; 63:2, 3; and in the Samaria Papyrus 1:2 (cf. CROSS, 'Samaria Papyrus I') and in a reconstructed part of papyrus 2; cf. F.M. CROSS, 'A Report on the Samaria Papyri', VTSup 40 (1988), 17–26.

[28] Cf. HINZ, 'Zu den Mörsern', 380: 'adlige Herren und Grundbesitzer im Bezirk der drei Festungen Parikāna, Sāruka und Hasta ... Vermutlich gehörte diese besondere Abgabe zu den Ehrenpflichten jener iranischen Gutsbesitzer, die zugleich dem Reichsheer als Offiziere zu dienen hatten.'

[29] In fact, CLINES's theory might already have been found questionable in light of, for instance, AP 33.

[30] I have subsequently discovered that this suggestion has already been advanced by E.Y. KUTSCHER ('New Aramaic Texts', Hebrew and Aramaic Studies [Jerusalem, 1977], 37–52, esp. 40, 45).

[31] AV, RV: 'great stones'; RSV: 'huge stones/ great stones'; ASB: 'huge stones'; NEB: 'massive stones'; JB: 'blocks of stone/stone blocks'; GNB: 'large stone blocks'; but note now the JPS version, 'hewn stone'.

may notice most recently the suggestion that the reference is to cobble or rubble fill in connection with what is known as pier-and-rubble construction.[32]

In something like a quarter of the Aramaic texts from Persepolis, the objects described are said to be *zy gll*, which Bowman translates 'of stone'. In some cases, a further modifier is added, varying from one text to another. Sometimes an adjective is used, and on other occasions another noun joined by *zy*. The meaning of these words is uncertain, but the suggestion that the first group refers to something like colouring or patterning and the second to the type of stone seems reasonable.

On the basis of this material, together with the evidence collected concerning Akkadian *galālu* for the Chicago Assyrian Dictionary,[33] Bowman wrote an article in 1965 arguing, *inter alia*, that (i) a distinction should be drawn between *galālu* (and some later Aramaic uses of *gll*) meaning 'pebble', 'cobble', and the many passages in Akkadian of the Persian period where such a meaning is inappropriate; he reckoned Ezra 5:8 and 6:4 among the latter; (ii) because of the variety of objects described by *gll* (including stelae, pillars, window frames and dishes), *gll* cannot refer to either the shape or type of stone: it 'should be translated simply as "stone", without further specification' (67); (iii) the use of *'bn* should be regarded as a determinative; whether or not *gll* once had a more specific meaning, by the time of Ezra, with or without the determinative *'bn*, it simply meant 'stone'.[34]

Although Bowman's article is a helpful collection of material and is certainly moving in the right direction, its conclusion nevertheless raises two particular difficulties. First, Aramaic is not Akkadian, and to speak of *'eben* as 'a determinative' is inappropriate. It is simply not a usage that would have been recognized by Aramaic speaking Jews in Judah. Whatever its history, the phrase must have meant something more to them than just 'stone', for which *'eben* alone would have sufficed. Secondly, Delaunay[35] has argued that 'stone' is also inappropriate for *gll* in the Persepolis texts on the ground that it would be superfluous, and even absurd, so to qualify certain vessels when in fact they are all made of stone in any case. (It should be remembered, however, that the Persians were obsessed with bureaucratic pedantry, so that Delaunay's objection may not be so strong as

---

[32] Cf. L. E. STAGER, 'The Archaeology of the Family in Ancient Israel', BASOR 260 (1985), 1–35, esp. 13; for the method of construction, cf. E. STERN, 'The Excavations at Tel Mevorach and the Late Phoenician Elements in the Architecture of Palestine', BASOR 225 (1977), 17–27, and Excavations at Tel Mevorakh (1973–1976) (Qedem 9; Jerusalem, 1978), 71–75.

[33] CAD 5, 11.

[34] R. A. BOWMAN, 'אֶבֶן גְּלָל – *aban galâlu* (Ezra 5:8; 6:4)', in I. T. NAAMANI and O. RUDAVSKY (eds.), Dōrōn. Hebraic Studies. Essays in Honor of Professor Abraham I. Katsh (New York, 1965), 64–74; see also Aramaic Ritual Texts, 44–45; IB 3, 610.

[35] DELAUNAY, 'A propos', 204f.

at first appears.) Delaunay thus returns to a proposal of Herzfeld[36] that, in accordance with the root meaning of *gll*, the reference is to turning or polishing, and so work that might attract extra remuneration.

This suggestion seems to fit the varied uses of both *gll* and *galālu*, and one may well imagine how it could come to be used without the pedantically correct use of *'eben*, 'stone', with it; compare, for instance, how we regularly speak of 'hardback' and 'paperback' without thereby implying that either is the exact equivalent of 'book'. Bowman seems to have fallen into the trap of asserting that 'all *gll* is *'bn*, therefore all *'bn* is *gll*'. Thus 'dressed/hewn/polished stone' seems appropriate for the Biblical occurrences.

A final line of support for this understanding may come from an Aramaic gloss on one of the fortification tablets. PFT 1587 is translated by Hallock, '185 (BAR of) grain, supplied by Hatarbanus, Ramakka received. It was taken (to) Persepolis (for) rations of makers of stone (sculptures). Second month, ... th year'. The Aramaic gloss reads *rmk ybl prs ptp lnqry gll*, and is translated (apparently by Bowman; cf. PFT, p. 82) 'Ramakka brought (it to) Persepolis, (for) rations of diggers of stone'. The Elamite text, however, as Hallock's bracketed explanation suggests, implies something more than just quarrymen, for which other terms are used (cf. PTT 9); the word in question translated 'makers' is elsewhere used with such other finished products as wine and oil. The Aramaic translation *nqr* can reasonably fit with this, for although in all the cognate languages the root can have the meaning 'to quarry, bore',[37] it is also used, both in Aramaic and Akkadian, for carving stone or the like. Indeed, when it is thought by Bowman to occur in a very damaged text on one of his mortars (no. 160), he translates 'chiseled(?)', and comments, 'The word *nqwr* may be from the root *nqr* meaning "to chisel", "to shape stones by chiselling", "to whet a millstone"'.[38] It may be suggested that here again the evidence is best explained if *gll* means not just 'stone', but stone that has been worked in some particular manner.

A final area where our texts may help towards a better understanding of the vocabulary of Ezra and Nehemiah derives, strangely enough, not from the Aramaic texts at all, but the Elamite.[39] Not infrequently in the records of payments in kind to some individual, there is reference also to what Hallock

---

[36] DELAUNAY refers only to the citation of HERZFELD's views *apud* SCHMIDT, Persepolis II, 55, n. 68; cf. E. HERZFELD, Altpersische Inschriften (Berlin, 1938), 100.

[37] Cf. CAD 11, 329–32; BDB, 669; PAYNE SMITH, 352.

[38] Aramaic Ritual Texts, 185, with reference to M. JASTROW, A Dictionary of the Targumim, the Talmud Babli and Yerushalmi, and the Midrashic Literature (New York and Berlin, 1926), 935a.

[39] A further potential example from this source is unfortunately inconclusive in the present state of knowledge. Elamite *baribara* (PFT 107:7; 161:7–8; 586:3–4 and 995:3-4) probably represents Old Persian *paribāra, whence the enigmatic Hebrew loan-word *parbār/parwār* (2 Kgs 23:11; 1 Chron. 26:18). However, the meaning of *baribāra* is disputed; cf. I. GERSHEVITCH in HALLOCK, PFT, p. 675, and W. HINZ, Orientalia ns 39 (1970), 436.

translates as his 'boys' *(puhu)*; for instance, we are told concerning Parnaka, a well-known senior official, that 'Daily (by) Parnaka together with his boys 48 BAR is received. (By) Parnaka himself 18 BAR is received. (By) his 300 boys 1 QA each is received'.[40] There is a good deal of evidence, however, that 'boy' is a reference to status rather than age. For instance, though rations vary, theirs are often as much as an adult male,[41] they receive rations of wine, they do 'men's' work, and occasionally are even referred to in the same text as 'men' *(ruh)*.[42] It thus looks as though *puhu* has a similar semantic range as Hebrew *naʿar* in Nehemiah 4 and 5 (and 13:19; perhaps also at 6:5), where the $n^{eʿ}ārîm$ are clearly a group who owe particular and personal loyalty to Nehemiah (or whoever).[43] And since it is clear from the Persepolis texts that their rations or salary were a designated fraction of their master's, we may perhaps understand better why, after complaining about the heavy burdens that his predecessors as governor had laid upon the people in terms of both cash and kind, Nehemiah adds, 'Even their $n^{eʿ}ārîm$ lorded it over the people' (Neh. 5:15).

B. Support of Local Cults

At Ezra 6:9-10 and 7:17-20 we are told that Darius I, and later Artaxerxes I, gave instructions that material support should be given by the empire for the regular sacrifices in the Jerusalem temple. Earlier skepticism about the likelihood of such support was countered most effectively by de Vaux,[44] who was able to adduce several examples of Achaemenid concern for the continuation of local cults, no doubt partly in order that they might be able effectively to pray for 'the life of the king and his sons' (Ezra 6:10; cf. Jer. 29:7; AP 30:25-26; and the

---

[40] PFa 4, lines 8-16. 10 QA = 1 BAR, 1 QA being roughly equivalent to a quart (cf. PFT, p. 72).

[41] Cf. PFT, pp. 29-30, and R.T. HALLOCK, 'A New Look at the Persepolis Treasury Tablets', JNES 19 (1960), 90-100, esp. 93-94; for references, compare especially the figures throughout PFT, 847-994. In 1239-69, boys generally receive 1 QA, as do a horseman (1244, 1266-68), servants (1258, 1262, 1264 and 1265) and some others (1260).

[42] These last three points are all illustrated by PFT 1137; see also variously (as examples only) PTT 47, 58, 72 and 77; HINZ, Neue Wege im Altpersischen, 72-74; H. KOCH, 'Zu den Lohnverhältnissen der Dareioszeit in Persien', in H. KOCH and D.N. MACKENZIE (eds.), Kunst, Kultur und Geschichte der Achämenidenzeit und ihr Fortleben (Berlin, 1983), 19-50, esp. 21.

[43] For discussion of *naʿar* with further bibliography, cf. my Ezra, Nehemiah, 227-28, and add L.E. STAGER, BASOR 260 (1985), 25 f.

[44] R. DE VAUX, 'Les décrets de Cyrus et de Darius sur la reconstruction du temple', RB 46 (1937), 29-57 = 'The Decrees of Cyrus and Darius on the Rebuilding of the Temple', The Bible and the Ancient Near East (London, 1972), 63-96.

Cyrus Cylinder, ANET 316), and today most commentators accept that there is little difficulty in principle with the biblical statement.[45]

The Persepolis fortification tablets lend strong support to this conclusion and illuminate some of the practicalities involved. PFT 303, 336–77 and 2029–30 record delivery of various goods for use in the service of a number of different named and unnamed gods; for example, '7 (BAR of) grain, supplied by Bakamira, Anbaduš received, and utilized (it) for (the god) Humban. 22nd year' (PFT 340). Within the region covered by these texts, the following are some of the gods mentioned: Ahuramazda, Humban, Mišduši, Mithra, Ṣimut, Pirdakamiya, Turma, Marirāš, Narišanka and Adad.[46] Here we have Persian, Elamite and Babylonian gods all being honoured by their separate devotees within a circumscribed area, and all being supported equally by funds from the imperial treasury.[47] Viewed in this light, the addition of another god to whatever list may have been supported by the treasury of 'Beyond the River', specifying the quantities to be supplied, need have surprised nobody.

The commodities listed as being supplied for the gods are grain, wine, flour, beer and *tarmu* grain, which at first sight overlaps only very partially with the biblical lists. Quite apart from the fact that naturally the needs of the individual cults concerned will have had to be considered, there are other reasons why this dissimilarity need not worry us unduly; to appreciate this, however, each piece of evidence needs to be considered in its chronological and religious context.

First in time comes Darius' order that 'whatever is needed – young bulls, rams, or sheep for burnt offerings to the God of heaven, wheat, salt, wine or oil, as the priests at Jerusalem require – let that be given to them ...' (Ezra 6:9). As noted, there is no direct parallel for this, because it is so much earlier than our other sources, but in principle it is not unreasonable in the light of what we have already seen.

Second come the fortification tablets, and here it is of interest to observe that the grain rations could quite openly be used for the purchase of sheep for sacrifice. For instance:

80 (BAR of) grain, supplied by Mamannuwiš, Ururu the priest received and delivered, and in its stead he received 8 sheep, and utilized (them) for the gods.

---

[45] GUNNEWEG emphatically rejects the authenticity of the documents in Ezra 6 and 7, but nevertheless adds with regard to 6:10: 'Daß tatsächlich – in der historischen Faktizität – die persische Zentralregierung die Wiederherstellung von Tempel und Kult gestattete und anordnete, ist damit nicht bestritten, das ist vielmehr als sehr wahrscheinlich anzusehen' (110).

[46] For a fuller list with discussion, cf. H. KOCH, Die religiösen Verhältnisse der Dareioszeit: Untersuchungen an Hand der elamischen Persepolistäfelchen (Göttinger Orientforschungen, III/4; Wiesbaden, 1977), and 'Zur Religion der Achämeniden', ZAW 100 (1988), 393–405. KOCH also includes among the Babylonian gods the Sumerian KI, 'the earth', but this seems more likely to be an ideogram for the Elamite earth-god.

[47] Cf. M. DANDAMAEV, 'La politique religieuse des Achéménides', Acta Iranica 4 (1975), 193–200, and P. BRIANT, Rois, Tributs et Paysans (Paris, 1982), 225, n. 398a.

2 sheep for (the god) Adad, 2 sheep for the shrine (?), 2 sheep for (the place) Tikrakkaš, 2 sheep for (the place) Hapidanuš, total 8 yearling sheep, were issued (at) the granary (?) (PFT 352; cf. 362–64 and 2030).

A possible reason for this cumbersome procedure is suggested by Hinz,[48] who sees in it a somewhat artificial means whereby a Zoroastrian, who of course could not accept animal sacrifice in any shape,[49] was nevertheless able to support a cult in which such sacrifice was normal. The date at which, if at all, or to what extent, the Achaemenids embraced Zoroastrianism is a highly contentious issue,[50] but a move in that direction between the early years of Darius I and the period of the fortification tablets is not unreasonable, and could explain the difference between them and Ezra 6. Alternatively, grain may simply have been used as the basic unit of currency in the treasury, with the system of reckoning up for animals in terms of grain in place from the start, in which case there is no real development to be detected between the two periods.

Next in order come the treasury tablets which, while not dealing directly with support for local cults, are relevant here because of their testimony that for a number of years up until the time of Ezra payment in kind was being supplemented, if not replaced, by payment in silver in the imperial treasuries.[51] And this, then, leads straight back, fourthly, to the text of Ezra 7:15–20, where Ezra is given cash to enable him to buy both animals and other materials for the sacrificial cult. The different manner in which these grants were paid to the Jews by Darius and Artaxerxes is thus neatly explained by factors which we could only have learned about from the two collections of Elamite texts from Persepolis which come in between.

Four other smaller matters also deserve mention here. First, several of these texts specify a particular ceremony for which the supply is made; for instance, '3 *marriš* (of) wine, supplied by Parsauka, Mardonius the priest received, and (utilized it for) the divine *tamšiyam* (ceremony) of (the god) Humban. (At) Uratukaš. 23rd year' (PFT 348). The meaning of *tamšiyam* is uncertain, but Hallock himself favours the suggestion of I. Gershevitch, which he reports as follows: 'it is to be connected with Av. *zaoša-*, "pleasure". Thus it would represent OP **daušiyam*, a neuter adjective used as a substantive, meaning

---

[48] W. Hinz, 'Die elamischen Buchungstäfelchen der Darius-Zeit', Orientalia ns 39 (1970), 421–40, esp. 427–30.

[49] As is well known, this is often advanced as the explanation for the omission (if not indeed deletion; cf. B. Porten, 'Aramaic Papyri and Parchments: A New Look', BA 42 [1979], 74–104, esp. 99) of w‘lwh, 'and burnt offering', from AP 32:9 by comparison with 30:25 (and see also 33:10–11), but other explanations are possible.

[50] For a recent survey, cf. M. Schwartz, 'The Religion of Achaemenian Iran', CHI 664–97, with further bibliography on pp. 916–18; see also H. Koch, 'Zur Religion der Achämeniden'.

[51] Though apparently resort was made to this mode of payment particularly in times of shortage, such as in 467–466 BC, treasury payments of this kind are attested as late as 458 BC, the probable year of Ezra's commission; cf. R.T. Hallock, 'A New Look', 91.

"what serves for satisfaction, propitiatory offering"' (19). If this is so, then one may more readily understand how so very 'Jewish' a word as *nyḥwḥyn*, 'pleasing sacrifices, soothing offerings', could be included in Darius' decree at Ezra 6:10.[52] It is generally believed that Jewish scribes would have had a hand in drafting such a document.[53] It was a happy coincidence for them that they could pass off one of their most technical items of cultic vocabulary as though it were the Aramaic equivalent of a ceremony better known in Achaemenid circles.

Second, PFT 741–74 record rations paid to individuals who exercised religious functions, for instance: '12 (*marriš* of) wine, supplied by Miššabadda, Harima received (for) performing (?) the *lan* (ceremony at) Harbus. It was given to him as rations by the king, (for) a whole year. 23rd year' (PFT 753).[54] This may be set alongside Ezra 7:24, where Artaxerxes orders the treasurers in Beyond the River: 'Be it further known to you that you have no authority to impose tribute, tax, or dues upon any of the priests and Levites, the musicians, gatekeepers, temple servants, or (other) servants of this house of God'. The specific mention of support for officially recognized cultic officials is thus common to both contexts, and this further undermines Weinberg's attempt to argue that the community as a whole was exempt from tax.[55]

Third, most of these rations to individuals engaged in religious functions are given for a specified period, as in the text just cited, and as in this further typical example: '12 *marriš* (of) wine, supplied by Parnizza, Kurka the Magus, the lan performer (?) (at) Marsaškaš, received (for) the libation of the *lan* (ceremony). From the sixth month through the fifth month, total 12 months, (starting in?) the 17th year' (PFT 757). The time involved in the grants recorded in Ezra is not specified, but on the basis of the quantities involved the suggestion has been advanced that the allowance at Ezra 7:22 was intended to last for two years.[56] Some such limitation certainly seems plausible in the light of our texts.

Finally, alongside Ezra 6:9, in which it is stated that the necessary supplies are to be given them 'day by day', a phrase often attributed to the Chronicler, it is worth setting a text such as PFT 748, where concerning the allocation of a ration of beer for the lan ceremony we are told, '(For) a period of 12 months he received (for) 1 month 3 *marriš*. Daily he receives 1 QA' (lines 7–11). It was

---

[52] Contrast the doubts expressed by, for instance, C.C. TORREY (The Composition and Historical Value of Ezra-Nehemiah [BZAW, 2; Giessen, 1896], 10, and Ezra Studies [Chicago, 1910], 158, 194).

[53] Cf. P. FREI, 'Zentralgewalt und Lokalautonomie im Achämenidenreich', in P. FREI and K. KOCH, Reichsidee und Reichsorganisation im Perserreich (OBO, 55; Freiburg and Göttingen, 1984), 7–43.

[54] The significance of the *lan* ceremony is discussed by H. KOCH ('Zur Religion der Achämeniden').

[55] J.P. WEINBERG, '$N^e tînîm$ und "Söhne der Sklaven Salomos" im 6.–4. Jh. v.u.Z.', ZAW 87 (1975), 355–71, esp. 367–68.

[56] Cf. RUDOLPH, Esra und Nehemia, 75, citing A. BERTHOLET, Theologie des AT II (1911), 30 (not available to me).

clearly not unusual for an allowance to be made for an extended period but for it to be released on a day-by-day basis.

C. Travel and Transportation

There are several accounts in Ezra and Nehemiah of journeys between Babylon and Jerusalem, included in which there is reference to the transportation of specified items for the temple or city. Ezra 1:7–11 includes an inventory of the temple vessels, and concludes, 'all these did Sheshbazzar bring up, when they of the captivity were brought up from Babylon to Jerusalem'. Ezra 8 comprises a fuller account of Ezra's journey, again with a list of valuable items transported, but this time with the details of the accounting procedures at both the start and the conclusion of the journey. Finally, in Nehemiah 2 we are told how Nehemiah travelled with a smaller party from Susa to Jerusalem carrying letters to various officials requesting both a safe conduct on the journey and materials for rebuilding after his arrival. Although a number of other such journeys are mentioned or presupposed by the narrative,[57] these three provide the most detail for comparative purposes.

The texts from Persepolis contain a great deal of information which can be treated as background against which to read these various accounts. Because they are not narrative documents, it is necessary to combine information from different groups of texts in order to build up a composite whole. There is admittedly a danger of misrepresentation in this procedure, but this is partly offset by the number of texts at our disposal which helps to develop a reasonably rounded picture.

The first point to be made is the simple observation that without question the Achaemenid bureaucracy went to enormous lengths to record carefully all manner of payments and receipts at the central treasuries. Hallock's A texts (PFT 1–57), for instance, record details of the transport of commodities in the sense of how they were taken away from a given centre; they are thus comparable to a receipt by the bearer; for example, '22 (BAR of) barley loaves (?), supplied by Bakabada, was taken to Persepolis for the (royal) stores. 24th year' (PFT 3). The B texts (PFT 58–137), on the other hand, record how commodities were delivered to a given centre; they are thus comparable to a receipt by the recipient to the bearer. As a brief example, '22 (BAR of) *tarmu* (grain) Sunkišip took, and delivered (it at) Tandari. Hapikra received (it). 24th year' (PFT 114). Other

---

[57] For instance, it is generally supposed that there was more than a single journey of return during the period 538–520 BC; Ezra 4:6, 7 and 8–23 refer to three exchanges of letters between Beyond the River and the court, while Ezra 5–6 includes details of a further similar exchange. Nehemiah 13:6–7 refers to a further journey in each direction by Nehemiah.

collections of texts deal with tax receipts and other deposits, payments of salaries and making provision for special officials and for royal occasions, payments of allowances to mothers who have just had babies, travel rations and the like.

These texts were not just receipts, however, but were clearly used as part of a broader accounting procedure. One group of texts (PFT 233-58) is accounting balances, noting the total amount that was being 'carried forward as balance', and sometimes a note of the date on which the calculation was made; for instance, '9,502 (BAR of) grain has been carried forward (as) balance, entrusted to Bakasušta, (at) Liduma. In the 22nd year, twelfth month, the accounting was done' (PFT 240). Finally, in PFT 1961-2014 there are longer and more elaborate accounting texts itemizing payments and receipts and balances brought or carried forward. The treasury texts too, though somewhat different in nature, demonstrate not dissimilar concerns, while the Aramaic texts remind us that sometimes special items which had been supplied (under whatever circumstances and for whatever purpose) could be individually marked with all necessary detail.[58]

In this context, it should come as no surprise to find the detailed care attested in the biblical texts enumerated above regarding procedures of payments and receipt. To Sheshbazzar an itemized list was brought out and counted over by the treasurer (Ezra 1:8), while in Ezra's case the items were first weighed out by Ezra to specified individuals (8:25-27) who then in turn weighed them out to other officials on their arrival in Jerusalem:[59] 'everything was checked by number and by weight and the total weight was recorded in writing' (Ezra 8:34). Indeed, by now we should have learned from Persepolis to expect nothing less.

The formula used when noting such payments, attested at Ezra 1:8, has already been compared with AP 61, but a further point of comparison comes now from the Aramaic texts at Persepolis. As was seen above, there are at least two levels of authority involved with the manufacture or delivery of the items in question, one introduced by *lyd*,[60] the other by *qdm*. The latter is used only with the sub-treasurer (*'pgnzbr'*), and is probably to be understood as indicating that he was personally present when the vessel was made/made over. The other indicates only more generally under whose authority the work was done. In Ezra

---

[58] It is tempting here to compare the 'two vessels of brightly gleaming copper as precious as gold' of Ezra 8:27. We should note that in the Aramaic texts the size is often mentioned, and occasionally even the measurements, reading *lpty 'ṣb'n* X ('x fingerbreadths wide') at 43:4; 73:5; 114:3, with DEGEN, 126, NAVEH and SHAKED, 455, HINZ ('Zu den Mörsern', 385) *et al.*, against BOWMAN's original idea that these words indicate the value of the vessel (which would then have been comparable with Ezra 8:26).

[59] PFT 388 provides a good parallel to this record of accounting both before and after transportation: '130 (BAR of) ŠE.GIG.lg (grain), supplied by Bakubeša, Teispes received, and took (it to the place) Zila-Umpan. Tiriya received (it), and utilized (it) for the royal food supply (?). 19th year.'

[60] In fact this is used both with the prefect (*sgn*) and with the treasurer. It is not clear whether the vessels were made 'under the authority' of both these officials, or whether in one case *lyd* should be translated rather as '(made over) to'; see above, n. 12.

1:8, when we are told that Cyrus brought out the temple vessels by the hand of Mithredath the treasurer who then counted them out to Sheshbazzar, we should probably see a similar procedure, Cyrus himself, of course, not being personally responsible for bringing out the vessels.

Despite all the care that went into these recording and accounting procedures, mistakes were sometimes made. These usually involve a mistake in the numbers concerned, the causes being anything from a simple slip to more serious miscalculations in accountancy. For example, at PFT 661 we seem to have a simple error of 6 for 8; at 855 a slip in the list (23 for 32) has led to an error in the final total; at 864 the total (228) is out by one in the tens unit, but in 1023 the total (88) is out by one in the ones unit; in 1011 a figure in the body of the list is out by a factor of one, but in 1028 by a factor of ten. Sometimes, it is possible to trace how an error has arisen. At PFT 865 the scribe put only one month's ration total instead of the three months that the account was for; at 932 a line has been left out accidentally as the scribe's eye jumped from one figure of 15 to the next (parablepsis); at 860 Hallock tells us that an erasure left some signs undeleted even though the scribe wrote his new text over the top – it is not difficult to imagine that a later copyist, when drawing up a combined account, might have been led into error as a consequence; PFT 259–66 involve large quantities of wine together with some kind of fractional charge or deduction. In his discussion Hallock (15) sets out the somewhat complicated procedure by which this deduction is calculated, but even then, when applying his results to the related account text 2006 two errors of figures have additionally to be conjectured. Finally, an occasional glimpse allows us to see why such miscalculations might have occurred. PFT 77 reads:

12 'cowhides' of camels, 7 'cowhides' of yearling camels, 2 'cowhides' of camel calves (?), total 21 'cowhides', supplied by Takmašbada, Šandupirzana received. Included among these 'cowhides' (were) 2 *aššana*. They were received (in) the ninth month, on the first day, 24th year.

It is not difficult to see how the two 'included' items could be misunderstood as additional by a careless scribe.

It has long bothered commentators that we are faced with errors of similar kinds in some of the lists in Ezra and Nehemiah. For example, there are differences between some of the figures in what purports to be the same list in Ezra 2 and Nehemiah 7, and neither there nor in Ezra 1:11 do the totals equal the sum of the parts. Not a few of these discrepancies can be accounted for on the basis of the system of numeral notation probably used at some stage in the transmission of the text,[61] but that does not account for every case. It is thus reassur-

---

[61] H.L. ALLRIK, 'The Lists of Zerubbabel (Nehemiah 7 and Ezra 2) and the Hebrew Numeral Notation', BASOR 136 (1954), 21–27.

ing to find that the sources which may lie behind the biblical text are no worse off than the products of the royal scribes and accountants at Persepolis.

A substantial group of over 300 of our texts (PFT 1285–1579; 2049–57; cf. 1780–87; 1942: 19–22; 1953: 34–35) deal with the provision of rations for travellers, and contain several matters of interest for us. We learn of journeys by both small and large groups of workers and others over shorter and longer distances. Kandahar, India, Arachosia, Babylon, Sardis and Egypt, for instance, are all mentioned as starting points or destinations. The rations referred to, however, are generally only sufficient for a single day (1 or 1½ QA of flour per person), from which it has been not unreasonably deduced that there must have been supply stations at single day's journey intervals along the major routes of the empire.[62]

The authorizing and accounting system appears to have operated as follows: the leader of each group of travellers was given some kind of document (of which more below) by the king or other senior official, authorizing him to draw so much each day in the way of rations from the supply stations. Each time he did this, a document such as those that we have was drawn up by an official at the supply station and sent to Persepolis. There, the commodities issued will have been credited to the account of the supply station by debiting the account of the official who had issued the authorizing document.[63]

There are two words for this kind of authorizing document: *halmi* is usually translated 'sealed document', and Cameron suggested that it might be a loan-word from Aramaic *ḥtm*.[64] The other is *miyatukkam*, which is thought to derive from Old Persian with some such meaning as 'authorisation',[65] so that semantically the two words are not far removed from each other. They seem to be used more or less interchangeably.

Sadly, no example of such an authorizing document has survived at Persepolis, partly, no doubt, because they would often have been written in Aramaic on papyrus or parchment. It has been suggested by Benveniste,[66] however, that AD 6 is just such a document, for in it Arsames, the satrap of Egypt who is temporarily on leave back home in Babylon, writes to various of his subordinates along the way to Egypt, commanding them to provide daily rations for Neḥtiḥur, his officer. In Driver's translation, the first five lines read:

From Aršam to Marduk the officer who is at..., Nabû-dalâni the officer who is at Laʿir, Zātōhi the officer who is [at] ʾArzūḥin, ʾUpastabar the officer who is at Arbel, Ḥalšu

---

[62] Cf. PFT 6, 40.
[63] Ibid., and BRIANT, Rois, Tributs et Paysans, 208–9.
[64] CAMERON, PTT, p. 53, with justification for the phonetic shift involved; R.T. HALLOCK, 'New Light from Persepolis', JNES 9 (1950), 237–52, esp. 247–48.
[65] PFT, pp. 40, 733–34.
[66] E. BENVENISTE, 'Notes sur les tablettes élamites de Persépolis', JA 246 (1958), 49–65, esp. 63–65; see also LEWIS, Sparta and Persia, 6.

(?) and Māt-âl-Ubaš (?), Bagafarna the officer who is at Sa'lan, Frādafarna and Gavazāna (?) the officers who are at Damascus.

And now: – behold! one named Neḥtiḥur, [my] officer, is going to Egypt.

Do you give [him] (as) provisions from my estate in your provinces every day two measures of white meal, three measures of inferior (?)[67] meal, two measures of wine or beer, and one sheep, and for his servants, 10 men, one measure of meal daily for each, (and) hay according to (the number of) his horses; and give provisions for two Cilicians (and) one craftsman, all three my servants who are going with him to Egypt, for each and every man daily one measure of meal; give them these provisions, each officer of you in turn, in accordance with (the stages of) his journey from province to province until he reaches Egypt ...

Clearly, some distinction needs to be drawn between this text and the *halmi* of the Persepolis tablets on account of the fact that Arsames refers only to his personal estates, not the more official supply stations, but in general the comparison drawn by Benveniste seems apposite.

Turning with these introductory remarks on the travel ration texts to a comparison with the biblical data, several points stand out:

(1) Both Ezra (Ezra 8:36)[68] and Nehemiah (Neh. 2:8–9) took with them letters from the king authorizing the payment of certain grants for their work. While these cannot be equated with the documents carried by the travellers in the Persepolis tablets, since they do not refer to supplies for the journey, they would doubtless have functioned in exactly the same way. Indeed, it may be wondered whether the unusual use of an Old Persian loan-word at Ezra 8:36 (*dātê hammelek*; in Hebrew elsewhere only in Esther) may not be intended precisely as the equivalent of *miyatukkam*.[69]

(2) In addition, Nehemiah requested that he be given letters 'addressed to the governors of Beyond the River so that they may grant me a safe conduct until I reach Judah' (Neh. 2:7). These too are likely to have been recognizably in the same class as the *halmi*.

(3) Ezra's letters are addressed 'to all the treasurers of Beyond the River' (Ezra 7:21). In the light of the administrative structures probably to be deduced from the Aramaic texts considered above, we may say that these are likely, strictly speaking, to have been 'subtreasurers' (*'pgnzbr'*), who were actually responsible for making the payments, and who operated under the authority of

---

[67] HINZ (Neue Wege im Altpersischen, 40) proposes a Persian derivation for this word with the meaning 'fine'.

[68] I have suggested at Ezra, Nehemiah, 98 that the essential text of these 'letters' is included in Artaxerxes' edict at 7:21–24.

[69] Note the possible support for this semantic equivalent in the remarks of I. GERSHEVITCH, '*miyatukkam* "authorization": *vy-$\bar{a}$-$duga$-, a neuter noun belonging to the OP fem. *han-duga-* "proclamation, declaration (or sim.)"?' 'Iranian Nouns and Names in Elamite Garb', TPS (1969), 165–200, esp. 177. HINZ, however, suggests that it represents OP *$viy\bar{a}tika$, meaning 'a pass', comparing Old Indian *viyāti*, 'travel through', with the characteristic OP *-ka* ending (Neue Wege im Altpersischen, 39–40).

the treasurer of the satrapy.[70] The plural $^{ʾa}ḥašdarp^enê\ hammelek$, 'the royal satraps', at Ezra 8:36, remains a puzzle, however.[71]

(4) According to the figures supplied in the biblical text, Ezra's caravan will have numbered approximately 1,500 men, and we are not told how many women and children accompanied them. Nehemiah's group, of course, was much smaller, though he had an armed escort with him. It is unlikely, in my opinion, that the list in Ezra 2 is intended to describe a single caravan, but it is rather a summary of all in the land by 520 BC, including some who had not been in exile.[72] We cannot, therefore, say anything about the size of the first parties which returned.

Travelling parties of many sizes are attested in our texts, and since more than 72 percent of the dated texts come from only two years it must be assumed that such travelling companies were by no means an uncommon sight on the empire's highways. PFT 1532, for instance, speaks of 2,454 gentlemen, and no. 1527 of 1,150 workers,[73] though the majority of texts deal with smaller numbers.

(5) With regard to Nehemiah's armed guard (and Ezra's refusal of such an escort) we may observe that a number of titles of uncertain meaning crop up in these texts which Hallock tentatively associates with those who might have accompanied the caravans. We should note especially the 'elite guide' (literally, 'safe-keeper'), and his comment that 'Persons with this title... are involved particularly with groups of foreigners, for whom special guidance and protection would be required' (42). In addition, as is probably attested by these texts, and as is already known from other sources,[74] there were mounted couriers, who must have been armed, moving rapidly from one station to the next, as well as many other travellers. Whatever risks he took, Ezra is certainly not to be pictured as leading his party through totally deserted and trackless wastes.

(6) Part of Ezra's anxiety was doubtless caused by the fact that he was transporting gold, silver, and valuable vessels for the temple (Ezra 8:25–27). In this connection, it is hard to resist citing PFT 1342, even though it is not fully understood: '8 BAR (of) flour (was) supplied by Karma. Mannuya the treasurer took silver from Susa, and went to Matezziš. 2 gentlemen daily received each

---

[70] See also HALLOCK, CHI, 592–95. It has been calculated that there were at least 19 treasuries in the Persis/Elam region outside Persepolis itself; cf. TUPLIN, 'The Administration of the Achaemenid Empire', 130, with reference to H. KOCH, '"Hofschatzwarte" und "Schatzhäuser" in der Persis', ZA 71 (1981–82), 232–47; cf. also W. HINZ, 'Achämenidische Hofverwaltung', ZA 61 (1971), 260–311.

[71] See most recently T. PETIT, 'L'évolution sémantique des termes hébreux et araméens *pḥh* et *sgn* et accadiens *pāḫatu* et *šaknu*', JBL 107 (1988), 53–67.

[72] Cf. Ezra, Nehemiah, 28–32.

[73] Indeed, LEWIS, Sparta and Persia, 6–7, goes so far as to speak of 'people moving round in large ethnic groups' and of 'a whole population transplanted', though this needs to be read carefully in its historical context.

[74] Cf. HALLOCK, CHI, 606–7.

1½ QA. Ninth (Elamite) month, (for) a period of 16 days, 22nd year'. There are several unusual points about this text: we do not normally find references to someone of the rank of treasurer among the travellers; nor to the transportation of silver (but cf. PFT 1357 and PFa 14); nor are the rations ever for so long as 16 days.[75] It is clearly tempting to assume that these three factors are somehow related, but it remains strange that Mannuya did not make all haste to deposit his silver safely. Did he have to wait for an escort, or until the road had been made safe? Perhaps there is a hint that Ezra had good cause to pray earnestly for a safe journey and to give thanks after his arrival in Jerusalem.

(7) Finally, in view of both Ezra 2:66–67 and Neh. 2:9, it is worth pointing out that animals (especially horses) are sometimes included in these texts as receiving rations,[76] and indeed that PFT 1780–87 relate exclusively to rations for animals on journeys (e.g., PFT 1785: '17.4 BAR [i.e., 17 BAR, 4 QA] (of) grain, Miramana received for rations, and gave (it) to horses of Abbalema, (as) rations (for) 2 days. He carried a sealed document of the king. 19 horses, 1 received 3 QA. And 15 mules, 1 received 2 QA. In the second (Elamite) month, 23rd year').

D. Conclusion

In drawing these remarks to a close, it is worth reminding ourselves that the chronologically restricted testimony of the Persepolis tablets is probably an accident of history, and that the type of administration which they reflect will have lasted throughout the years of the Achaemenid empire.[77] There can thus be no objection to comparing them closely with Ezra and Nehemiah, with which we have seen they demonstrate some striking points of contact. Furthermore, as in the case of Neh. 5:14–19, dealt with on a previous occasion (see above, n. 20), the biblical passages referred to here have tended to be clustered in concentrated sections, despite the more thematic nature of the discussion. Not surprisingly, it will be found that these are passages which deal with points of closest contact between the Persian administration and the Jewish leaders. To

---

[75] Nearly all are for one day, a few for two days; above that, HALLOCK (43) lists one tablet each relating to three days (1344), four days (1311), six days (1408), seven days (2057), and ten days (1395).

[76] See, for instance, PFT 1397: '29 (BAR of) flour, supplied by Mirizza, Karabba the Indian, sent forth from the king (to) India, received for rations, (for) 1 day (in) the third month, 24th year. He himself received 2 QA. 180 'people' (passengers?) received each 1½ QA. 50 boys received each 1 QA. 3 horses consumed each 3 QA. 3 mules consumed each 2 QA. He carried a sealed document of the king'.

[77] Cf. especially BRIANT, Rois, Tributs et Paysans, 208 ff., and above, n 16.

that extent, our discussion has not only illuminated some obscurities in our texts, but has also shown how well they fit into their purported setting.

On the other hand, it is important to be careful not to try to prove too much from such comparisons. There is still a great deal of uncertainty surrounding the detailed understanding of these texts, some of the points raised above could well be coincidental, and it may be assumed that government practices were as well known to storytellers as to historians. Nevertheless, when due allowance has been made, it remains the case that the more we learn of the system of Persian rule, the more the objections of an earlier generation of scholars to the substantial authenticity of the accounts in Ezra and Nehemiah may be seen to have been unwarranted; and with that we must remain content.

15. Scripture Citing Scripture:
The Historical Books

There are two principal ways in which the historical books of the Old Testament make use of earlier scriptural material. One is the interpretation and application of the law of Moses, attested especially in the books of Ezra and Nehemiah, but not lacking from Chronicles or even the Deuteronomic History. The other is the Chronicler's use of Samuel and Kings. In these two areas is to be found a major stimulus towards both the halakhic and the haggadic readings of Scripture which became so pervasive in later centuries, and we shall therefore concentrate on these in the present chapter. Of the many other topics which clamour for attention, none is of greater theological interest than the use of prophetic sayings in late Old Testament historical writing, so that a third brief section has been devoted to them. Needless to say, for reasons of space it has been necessary severely to limit the number of examples adduced in each case.

A. The Law

The books of Ezra and Nehemiah refer to the book of the law under an astonishing variety of titles: the law of Moses (Ezra 3:2; 7:6; cf. 2 Chron. 23:18; 30:10); the book of Moses (Ezra 6:18; Neh. 13:1; cf. 2 Chron. 35:12); the law of the Lord (Ezra 7:10, and popular also in Chronicles; cf. 1 Chron. 16:40; 2 Chron. 31:3, 4; 35:26); the law of your God (Ezra 7:14, 26); the book of the law of Moses (Neh. 8:1); the book of the law (Neh. 8:3; cf. 2 Chron. 34:15); the book (Neh. 8:5, 8); the law (Ezra 10:3; Neh. 8:2, 7, 9, 13, 14; 10:35, 37; 13:3; cf. 2 Chron. 34:19); the book of the law of God (Neh. 8:18); the book of the law of the Lord (Neh. 9:3; cf. 2 Chron. 17:9; 34:14); and the law of God (Neh. 8:8; 10:29, 30. 2 Chron. 34:30 also speaks of the book of the covenant). It is clear from the interchange of titles in passages such as Nehemiah 8 that these all refer to one and the same law. This is further confirmed by Neh. 10:30 and 2 Chron. 34:14, where the law of God is said to have been given through Moses, and by 2 Chron. 25:4, where 'that which is written in the law, in the book of Moses' is substituted for 'that which is written in the book of the law of Moses' in 2 Kgs 14:6.

Discussions about the extent to which this work should be identified with the Pentateuch as we know it were intensified by the development of a consensus of critical opinion that Moses was not directly responsible for the first five books of the Bible. During the past two centuries, Ezra's law book has been associated with P, with D, with an unknown collection of laws which lies behind the Pentateuch as well as with the Pentateuch itself.[1] Because there appear to be references to most major strands of the Pentateuch both in passages concerned with the law (e.g. Nehemiah 10) and with the early history of Israel (e.g. Nehemiah 9), the majority of scholars have continued to associate the book of the law with the Pentateuch. It is true that in recent years Kellermann[2] has argued that Ezra's law book was a form of the deuteronomic law, but this is the result of his limiting what can be known of the historical Ezra to the edict of Artaxerxes in Ezra 7:12–26. On similar grounds, Rendtorff[3] has denied any connection between Ezra's law (Aramaic *dāt*) and the torah, the law of the Lord; again, however, this is an historical conclusion relating to Ezra's mission, and Rendtorff does not extend it to the books of Ezra and Nehemiah as a whole.

Quite different, however, is the radical proposal of Houtman.[4] After surveying the prescriptions in Ezra and Nehemiah which purport to come from the book of the law, he concludes that this cannot have been the Pentateuch but must rather have been some quite separate law book which has not been transmitted to us. He cites the recently published Temple Scroll as an analogy. Clearly, if Houtman is right we cannot learn anything from these books about the innerbiblical use of Old Testament law.

General considerations lead to the conclusion that Houtman's hypothesis is improbable. Being in the form of a first-person address by God (and so never called 'the law of Moses' or equivalents), the Temple Scroll cannot be cited as evidence for the view that 'there were circles of men who held themselves entitled to promulgate existing laws anew in the name of Moses' (p. 110). In any case, we are not dealing in Ezra and Nehemiah with a breakaway group, like the people of Qumran, nor is there any evidence that the latter had doubts about the supreme authority of the Pentateuch, despite the existence of the Temple Scroll. It is thus very difficult to believe that a document which was, *ex hypothesi*, a major formative influence in the development of post-exilic Judaism should have

---

[1] Cf. the surveys of research by S. MOWINCKEL, Studien zu dem Buche Ezra-Nehemia III: Die Ezrageschichte und das Gesetz Moses (Oslo, 1965); U. KELLERMANN, 'Erwägungen zum Esragesetz', ZAW 80 (1968), 373–85; R.W. KLEIN, 'Ezra and Nehemiah in Recent Studies', in F.M. CROSS, W.E. LEMKE and P.D. MILLER (eds.), The Mighty Acts of God: In Memoriam G. Ernest Wright (Garden City, 1976), 361–76; C. HOUTMAN, 'Ezra and the Law', OTS 21 (1981), 91–115.

[2] 'Erwägungen zum Esragesetz'; and cf. W. TH. IN DER SMITTEN, Esra: Quellen, Überlieferung und Geschichte (SSN, 15; Assen, 1973), 124–30.

[3] R. RENDTORFF, Das Alte Testament: eine Einführung (Neukirchen, 1983), 71 = The Old Testament: an Introduction (London, 1985), 68; 'Esra und das "Gesetz"', ZAW 96 (1984), 165–84.

[4] 'Ezra and the Law'.

been lost without trace whilst the Pentateuch, unmentioned in these books on Houtman's view, should have risen silently to its position of supreme authority.

That Houtman has been able to formulate such a theory at all, however, alerts us to the fact that the citation and application of pentateuchal laws were already displaying a sophisticated hermeneutic at that time. Awareness of this should help explain the difficulties which Houtman has exposed. Two recent studies in particular call for attention.

First, in a brief but illuminating article on Nehemiah 10, Clines[5] has argued that although all the particular stipulations listed in vv. 31–40 include novel material, they nevertheless are 'the result of exegetical work upon previously existing laws' as known to us from the Pentateuch. The basic exegetical principles at work are much as we should expect: being authoritative and considered to be comprehensive, the law can be harmonised to supply clear directives. This may require supplementary laws or reinterpretation along the lines of the law's intention rather than explicit requirement. Five types of legal development are then observed to follow from this basis, namely (i) creation of facilitating law, enabling earlier regulations to be carried out; (ii) revision of facilitating law; (iii) 'creation of a new prescription from a precedent in Pentateuchal law'; (iv) 're-definition of categories, always in the direction of greater comprehensiveness'; and (v) the integration of separate legal prescriptions. To give but one simple example of the first category, Lev. 6:5–6 prescribes that the fire on the altar of sacrifice must be kept burning continually. In the wording of Neh. 10:35, it is clearly to this that the phrase 'as it is written in the law' refers. In earlier times it had been the responsibility of the Gibeonites to provide the necessary wood (cf. Josh. 9:27), but that no longer obtained after the exile. Consequently, there was now a need to establish a 'wood offering' on a rota basis in order to facilitate obedience to the pentateuchal law. As with the other stipulations in this passage, it was a perfectly intelligible first step towards what later became known as *sĕyāg lattôrâ*, 'a hedge for the torah'.

If Clines's essay is brief and programmatic, the other recent study in this field – that of Fishbane[6] – is lengthy and detailed. Indeed, Fishbane makes so bold as to conclude his book with the claim that it is 'the first comprehensive proof and analysis' of inner-biblical (i.e. Old Testament) exegesis. Of particular relevance for our immediate concerns are his chapters on legal exegesis in historical sources (pp. 107–62) in which he divides his analysis into two parts. In the first, he examines examples of what he calls 'legal exegesis with verbatim, paraphrastic, or pseudo-citations' (principally 2 Chronicles 35; Ezra 9; Neh. 8; 10:30–31; Jer. 17:19–27 and Ezekiel 44) and in the second 'legal exegesis with covert citations' (principally Josh. 5:10–12; 1 Kgs 6:7; 2 Chron. 7:8–19; 30).

---

[5] D. J. A. CLINES, 'Nehemiah 10 as an Example of Early Jewish Biblical Exegesis', JSOT 21 (1981), 111–117; cf. Ezra, Nehemiah, Esther (London and Grand Rapids, 1984), ad loc.

[6] M. FISHBANE, Biblical Interpretation in Ancient Israel (Oxford, 1985).

Not surprisingly, Fishbane is able to demonstrate a wide variety of exegetical techniques not far from the surface of these texts. Most of his examples have been observed piecemeal by previous commentators, and many of the principles which he sees to have been at work are those which Clines has also catalogued. Thus, to give a simple and well-known example of Clines's fifth category – the integration of separate legal prescriptions – Fishbane rightly defends the widely-held view that 2 Chron. 35:13, 'they boiled the Passover in fire, according to the ordinance (*kammišpāṭ*)', can only be understood as an attempt to harmonise the apparently contradictory stipulations in Deut. 16:7 and Exod. 12:8–9. Thus much of the value of Fishbane's work lies in the collecting, ordering and re-evaluating of this wealth of material, even if a number of obvious examples, such as some other clauses of the pledge in Nehemiah 10, receive no mention.

Interaction with Fishbane's work will not, therefore, be at the level of major disagreement in principle, but rather of detail and the specific interpretation of particular passages. So here we may take just one area of relevance to our present concern which perhaps deserves further examination. In several of the passages with which Fishbane deals there is the comment that something was done *kakkātûb*, 'as prescribed' (or equivalents). Fishbane seems to take this as a rather broad qualification of the preceding context, and since there is often mention of practices for which there is no direct pentateuchal warrant, he finds here evidence for the process by which exegetical conclusions became an authoritative part of the law itself. Houtman too based his argument on some of the same passages, but drew the more radical conclusion which we have already noted. Thus, as well as modifying Fishbane's position, our discussion should also help to cast further doubt on Houtman's hypothesis.

Examination of all the passages where this word and its equivalents occurs points to a different explanation. It may be suggested that *kakkātûb* is used to qualify only the word or phrase which immediately precedes it,[7] and that such a word or phrase is thus *distinguished* from its prevailing context. By stating that some specific act was in accordance with *tôrâ*, the writers acknowledge that other matters may not have been.

We have already argued above that this is so at Neh. 10:35 – 'as it is written in the law' qualifies only the continually burning fire on the altar, not the (nonpentateuchal) wood offering. Similarly two verses later, 'as it is written in

---

[7] An apparent exception to this rule might be claimed for Bar. 2:2, especially if E. Tov's translation (The Book of Baruch [SBL Texts and Translations, 8; Pseudepigrapha Series, 6; Missoula, 1975], 19) is followed, for there *kakkātûb* refers forward to the following clause. Bar. 2:2, however, is clearly related to Dan. 9:12–13, where the relevant words (also referring forward) are *ka'ăšer kātûb bětôrat mōšeh*, and it would have been better if Tov had followed this lead. (The LXX renders *kakkātûb* in a variety of ways, so that there is no reason to prefer this form to that of Dan. 9:13.) Although there is no other OT parallel for the use of this construction in relation to the pentateuchal law, it does not seem impossible that the differences in phraseology and in usage are related.

the law' relates 'the firstborn of our sons and of our cattle' to the law of Num. 18:15 (note the unusual use of *bĕhēmâ* in both cases) in contrast to the (non-pentateuchal) 'first-fruits of every kind of fruit tree' in the previous clause.[8] In 2 Chron. 23:18 'as it is written in the law of Moses' obviously qualifies only 'to offer the burnt offerings of the Lord' immediately before, since the disposition of the Levites earlier in the verse is explicitly attributed to David. At 2 Chron. 35:26 no one can suppose that 'the rest of the acts of Josiah' were all 'according to that which is written in the law of the Lord'; rather, that phrase qualifies only the word *ḥăsādâw* which immediately precedes it, explaining in what sense Josiah's deeds were good or pious.

Space precludes a full survey of every relevant passage; we must therefore be content, now that some clear examples have established the principle, to look briefly at those passages which directly affect Fishbane's interpretation before concluding this section with a more detailed analysis of Nehemiah 8. At 2 Chron. 35:12, Fishbane appears to suppose that 'as it is written in the book of Moses' refers to the whole passage in which the paschal slaughter, originally a lay performance, is now the duty of the Levites. In our view, however, it qualifies only *lĕhaqrîb lyhwh*, which even in the present context can be regarded as conforming to pentateuchal law.[9] The situation is similar in v. 6 of the same chapter, where 'to do according to the word of the Lord by the hand of Moses' again does not relate to the Levites killing the passover lambs, but to their 'preparing for their brethren' with reference forward to v. 13.[10] Finally, in 2 Chron. 30:5, 'as it is written' should be taken closely with the observation that the Passover had not been celebrated before 'in great numbers'. When we ask why, we are directed to v. 3, where a similar concern is expressed in relation to the people's coming to Jerusalem. Here, then, there is a specific allusion to Deut. 16:1-8 as the written text to which reference is made.[11]

---

[8] Cf. H.G.M. WILLIAMSON, Ezra, Nehemiah (WBC, 16; Waco, 1985), 337, for fuller detail.

[9] Cf. W. RUDOLPH, Chronikbücher (HAT, 21; Tübingen, 1955), 327.

[10] Cf. H.G.M. WILLIAMSON, 1 and 2 Chronicles (London and Grand Rapids, 1982), 406.

[11] The strongest case for an exception to this consistent pattern is Ezra 6:18 (Aramaic), to which FISHBANE makes no reference. Here, it looks as though the system of priestly and Levitical courses and divisions is being ascribed to 'the book of Moses'. If so, we should note (i) that this is not a widely-held position, because elsewhere these arrangements are carefully ascribed to David (e.g. 1 Chron. 23-4); (ii) that the reference to 'Jerusalem' makes clear that this cannot be intended as a direct citation from the Pentateuch; (iii) that the author of this verse is likely to have worked long after Ezra, Nehemiah and the Chronicler (cf. WILLIAMSON, 'The Composition of Ezra i-vi', JTS n.s. 34 [1983], 1-30 [below, 244-70]). By this time HOUTMAN's suggested explanation by way of a book quite separate from the Pentateuch is even less plausible; and (iv) that his position is a further development of that already taken by a later reviser of the Chronicler's work in 1 Chron. 24:1-2. An alternative explanation should not be ruled out, however, namely that the phrase qualifies only 'the service of God'.

It should be emphasised that in these and comparable texts which could be cited we are not for one moment denying that in the passages as a whole there is much of the type of exegesis which Fishbane patiently unravels. Our concern rather is to emphasise that in this exercise the writers were perhaps more aware of the distinction between text and interpretation than Fishbane gives them credit for. In other words, so far as the law is concerned it is by no means inappropriate to talk in terms of 'the use of Scripture' for this later post-exilic period.

An instructive example to which we may now give a little more detailed attention is found in Nehemiah 8. The first half of the chapter, vv. 1–12, recounts the reading and explanation of the law in a general way to the people. Then we are told:

On the second day the heads of families of all the people, together with the priests and the Levites, gathered around Ezra the scribe in order to study the words of the law which the Lord had commanded through Moses, that the Israelites should live in booths during the feast of the seventh month, and that they should proclaim the following words and spread them throughout their cities and Jerusalem: 'Go out into the hill country and bring branches of olive and of oleaster, of myrtle, palm and leafy trees in order to make booths as it is written'. (Neh. 8:13–15, author's translation)

The difficulty which this passage poses is that it includes material which does not appear to have pentateuchal warrant. However, this is less than is generally supposed (e. g. by Houtman) and the remainder may be deduced from the law by the kind of techniques which Clines and Fishbane have described. Nevertheless, in the present case it is simpler than Fishbane perhaps realises, and thus we do not accept that this passage justifies some of the more elaborate conclusions which he draws from it.

The first point to notice is that the primary text under consideration is Lev. 23:39–43, because of all the passages in the Pentateuch which deal with the feast of Tabernacles this is the only one to stipulate that the Israelites should dwell in booths during its celebration (cf. v. 42). The significance of this for the occasion under discussion is apparent not only from the verses cited above ('They found written in the law... that [*'ăšer*] the Israelites should live in booths ...'), but also from the continuation in vv. 16–17 which relates how the people made their booths and lived in them during the festival, 'something', we are told, 'that the Israelites had not done from the time of Jeshua the son of Nun until that day' (v. 17). Indeed, so great is the concentration on this new aspect of the celebration that we learn very little about what else happened, warning against the dangers of an argument from silence in this regard. We may conclude from this first point that *kakkātûb* at the end of v. 15 probably qualifies only the clause which immediately precedes it, namely 'to make booths'.[12] This would fit well with our study of the use of this word earlier as well as with the emphasis of the

---

[12] Strictly speaking, Lev. 23:42 speaks only of 'dwelling' in booths, so that we must allow that there is a minimum of obvious interpretation involved in the use of *laʿăśōt*.

present passage in particular. It also alerts us to the possibility that the writer may be aware that some of the other material in the context is not directly cited from the law.

Second, however, our passage states that more than just the dwelling in booths was 'found written in the law'. An additional indirect clause, also introduced by *'ăšer*, speaks of a proclamation to be made. Commentators have usually passed this over in silence or used it as evidence for differences between Ezra's law book and the Pentateuch. The suggestion may rather be advanced, however, that it derives from the introduction to the whole calendar in Leviticus 23, which states, 'These are the set feasts of the Lord ... which you shall *proclaim* in their appointed season' (v. 4; see also v. 37). Admittedly, Lev. 23:4 uses a different verb (*qr'*) from Neh. 8:15 (hiph. of *šm'*), but that is not an insuperable difficulty. Naturally, the question will have been raised as to what precisely the proclamation should include, and it is at *this* point, we submit, that 'exegesis' played its part, and that in two ways: (i) concentrating on the discovery of the importance of living in booths during the festival, the leaders told the people to bring materials suitable for the purpose – another example of 'facilitating law' (Clines's first category). Some of the types of tree listed coincide, not unnaturally, with the types that were to be brought in any case for *other aspects* of the festivities (cf. Lev. 23:40), but the remainder are types more generally available. However, the legal prescription of Lev. 23:40 for one aspect of the festival is not to be confused with this facilitating law, as the lack of reference to the bringing of fruit further demonstrates. As a harvest celebration, Tabernacles had been observed regularly before (cf. Ezra 3:4, to go no further); the present description dwells exclusively on the new (or renewed) aspects of the celebration. There is thus no need to follow Fishbane in his less plausible suggestion that it was by way of etymological speculation on the root *skk* that they arrived at the idea of bringing branches. (ii) Though not explicitly stated in so many words, it is clearly implied that the proclamation summoned the people of Judah to Jerusalem for the festival. Though denied by Fishbane, this is the probable implication of v. 16: the residents of Jerusalem built their booths on their roofs or in the courts of their houses, whilst those who came in from the surrounding districts did so in the temple courts or other open spaces in the city. Furthermore, the implication of v. 18 is that the festival was celebrated by all the people together. In that case, we may see the influence of Deut. 16:13–15 on the framing of the proclamation – an example of Clines's fifth category, the integration of separate legal prescriptions.

We may conclude, therefore, from this and other examples that could be mentioned[13] that on close examination the post-exilic historians appear to have

---

[13] Perhaps the most involved passage from the point of view of legal exegesis is Ezra 9:1–2, treated independently by WILLIAMSON (Ezra, Nehemiah, *ad loc.*) and FISHBANE (Biblical Interpretation, 114–23). Together with some shared conclusions we also both include some material not considered by the other, pointing to the complexity of the exegetical process.

been remarkably self-conscious in their use of legal Scripture and that they drew a sharper distinction than has generally been recognised between text and exegesis. They were well aware of the difficulties of applying the written law in situations for which it had not been originally intended, and they quickly developed a wide range of exegetical tools to help them in their task. It seems clear, however, that they took pains to distinguish between the letter and the spirit of the law, and generally left clear lexical markers to prevent confusion in this regard. What we must now turn to investigate is the use they made of narrative rather than legal material.

B. Narrative

Although narrative material from earlier biblical sources is used by citation or allusion in a variety of later works (cf. Nehemiah 9, for example, and the typological use of the exodus in various parts of Ezra), it is inevitable that our attention in this section should be directed primarily towards the Chronicler's use of Samuel and Kings. After a period of relative neglect, the books of Chronicles have been the subject of renewed interest during the last fifteen or twenty years, and much of this activity focuses precisely on the topic in hand.

A preliminary point that has to be made concerns the form of the text of Samuel and Kings which the Chronicler used. Despite warning signs to the contrary from the LXX, it was assumed until comparatively recent times that the MT of the respective works could be compared without difficulty. The discovery of the Qumran scrolls – and especially the still unpublished 4QSam^a – has shown, however, that this is by no means always justified. In a string of publications, Cross and his pupils who have had access to this material have demonstrated that not infrequently the Chronicler followed a text of Samuel which was markedly closer to his own than the MT.[14] Great caution must therefore be exercised when undertaking detailed comparative study not to confuse theological or tendentious issues with purely textual matters.

Despite this warning, there are several mitigating factors which enable us to proceed, albeit with caution. First, in what is probably the most valuable part of his controversial thesis, McKenzie[15] has shown that the situation in Kings

---

[14] Cf. F.M. CROSS, 'The History of the Biblical Text in the Light of Discoveries in the Judean Desert', HTR 57 (1964), 281–9; W.E. LEMKE, 'The Synoptic Problem in the Chronicler's History', HTR 58 (1965), 349–63; E. ULRICH, The Qumran Text of Samuel and Josephus (HSM, 19; Missoula, 1978). P.K. MCCARTER (I Samuel [AB, 8; Garden City, 1980]; II Samuel [AB, 9; Garden City, 1984]) provides further valuable information.

[15] S.L. MCKENZIE, The Chronicler's Use of the Deuteronomistic History (HSM, 33; Atlanta, 1985), 119–58.

differs from that in Samuel in this regard. Where the Chronicler is following Kings, it appears that his text was after all closer to MT. Secondly, as work on the LXX of Samuel and of Chronicles develops, so comparative work may be put on a sounder footing even in the absence of corroborative Hebrew sources such as 4QSam^a. Finally, as we shall see, there is a great deal that can usefully be said which is based upon far broader considerations than intricate synoptic comparisons alone.

There is one recent work whose thesis, if correct, would render further discussions more or less otiose, and that is the study already referred to by McKenzie.[16] Briefly stated, McKenzie works on the basis of material found only in Chronicles to isolate a few well-known characteristics which represent the writer's *Tendenz*. Looking then at the passages where Chronicles runs parallel with Samuel and Kings, he allows differences which can be explained by this *Tendenz* to be due to the Chronicler himself. Otherwise, however, he argues that the Chronicler followed his *Vorlage* quite slavishly; the exegetical techniques which others have claimed to find do not come into the picture at all. On this basis, he then advances his view that the Chronicler used Cross's Dtr_1 as his source and that Chronicles is therefore of some value in disentangling Dtr_2 from Dtr_1.

McKenzie's work raises a host of questions which cannot be discussed here.[17] It must suffice to say for the moment that he has not, in my opinion, done justice to the many ways – some delicate and some quite radical – in which the Chronicler handled his *Vorlage*. In referring to some of these below we shall already be indicating areas where his initial analysis needs far greater refinement before his overall theory can be taken more seriously.

A number of studies, both old and new, which have broached the subject of the Chronicler's use of Scripture have tried to subsume all the evidence under a single rubric as though this contained the clue to the Chronicler's 'purpose' as a whole. Of these, by far the most impressive is that of Willi,[18] who seeks to explain all the material as 'exegesis'. With a prodigious compilation of detail, he marshalls the differences between Samuel-Kings and Chronicles into nine categories which move from such minor matters as textual, orthographic and grammatical differences through more important minor omissions and additions to significant interpretative devices including recension and the use of typology. Whilst inevitably scholars will differ on this or that detail, no one can work through Willi's comparative study without learning a very great deal about the methods which the Chronicler used in his composition.

Despite this positive evaluation, it remains questionable whether Willi's theory is adequate to account for the books of Chronicles as a whole. We must

---

[16] The Chronicler's Use of the Deuteronomistic History.

[17] Cf. my review of McKenzie, The Chronicler's Use of the Deuteronomistic History, in VT 37 (1987), 107–14.

[18] T. Willi, Der Chronik als Auslegung: Untersuchungen zur literarischen Gestaltung der historischen Überlieferung Israels (FRLANT, 106; Göttingen, 1972).

agree that no appraisal of Chronicles which does not take the synoptic passages fully into account can be considered adequate and further that the general shape and order of the Chronicler's work is largely dependent upon the earlier composition. Nevertheless, these passages alone are not sufficient to explain the whole: the Chronicler's selective use of Samuel-Kings shows that he regarded them as a source rather than as a text; there are occasions such as 1 Chronicles 14 and 2 Chronicles 1 where he alters the order of his *Vorlage* for purposes of his own; the considerable amount of additional material which he includes (even if it is reduced by following Noth's 1943[19] literary-critical surgery) cannot be explained on this basis either; and finally the Chronicler used techniques which go far beyond the exegetical, particularly the paradigmatic patterning of his material in terms of 'exilic' and 'restoration' situations.[20]

In my view, it is therefore preferable not to seize on any one aspect of the Chronicler's use of earlier scriptural material as the key to his method and purpose. Rather, his aim in writing should be sought elsewhere, leaving us free to observe the very considerable range of techniques which he presses into service as he makes use of antecedent material. As well as all those discussed by Willi, they also include adumbrations of much that was later to be developed in the midrashim and targumim.[21]

Sketchy as this survey has been, it should be clear by now that the Chronicler's treatment of his narrative *Vorlage* differs to a certain extent from what we saw earlier with regard to the law. There, the few examples which we drew from his work (2 Chronicles 30 and 35) show no appreciable difference in approach from that of Ezra and Nehemiah, where the distinction between text and interpretation seems already quite advanced. It is true that if style is a valid criterion, then the Chronicler exercised greater freedom with respect to his extra-biblical sources than he did with Samuel-Kings. This may indicate that the latter was in some way more 'authoritative' in his estimation, if only because it was undoubtedly the familiar version of his people's history. He was thus in no position to deal with it so freely. Equally it must be remembered, however, that this material had already been subjected to a deuteronomic redaction and was thus *ipso facto* more amenable to the Chronicler's own outlook. Even so, he frequently finds it necessary to draw out the compatibility of the narrative with the pentateuchal law[22] whilst his use of typology and paradigm seeks to draw from the historically bound narra-

---

[19] M. NOTH, Überlieferungsgeschichtliche Studien (Halle, 1943) = The Chronicler's History (JSOTSup, 50; Sheffield, 1987).

[20] Cf. R. MOSIS, Untersuchungen zur Theologie des chronistischen Geschichtswerkes (Freiburger theologische Studien, 92; Freiburg, 1973); P.R. ACKROYD, I & II Chronicles, Ezra, Nehemiah (London, 1973); 'The Chronicler as Exegete', JSOT 2 (1977), 2-32.

[21] Cf. I.L. SEELIGMANN, 'Voraussetzungen der Midrashexegese', VTSup 1 (1953), 150-81; R. BLOCH, 'Midrash', DBSup 5 (Paris, 1957), cols. 1263-81; FISHBANE, Biblical Interpretation, 380-440.

[22] Cf. G. VON RAD, Das Geschichtsbild des chronistischen Werkes (BWANT, 54; Stuttgart, 1930).

tives of the Deuteronomic History a number of timeless theological values and lessons which he has learned from elsewhere, namely the prophets. Thus in terms of religious authority, the law and the prophets ranked higher for the Chronicler than the narrative history. The latter illustrated and explained the former and could be retold to drive home the lessons which they taught. The lessons themselves, however, derived from these other sources. It is thus appropriate that we should turn in conclusion to the use of the prophetic books in his work.

C. The Prophets

The Chronicler's treatment of prophecy and the prophets has been the subject of several recent studies.[23] Our concern here, however, is with just one aspect of this subject, namely the citation of prophetic 'texts' in the so-called Levitical sermons.

It was von Rad[24] who first dealt with this material from a form-critical perspective. He noted that at a number of places in his narrative the Chronicler included a 'sermon' on the lips of a prophet, Levite or king, and that it generally included the following elements: 'the conditions on which God is prepared to give his help – i.e. the doctrine'; application of that principle to some aspect of Israel's history; and an exhortation to faith on the part of the hearer. This influential classification has been accepted by many, and in some cases further refined.[25] More recently, however, there have been signs of a growing dissatisfaction with aspects of von Rad's theory,[26] and Mathias[27] has now published a

---

[23] C. WESTERMANN, Basic Forms of Prophetic Speech (Philadelphia, 1967), 163–8 (= Grundformen prophetischer Rede [BEvTh, 31; Munich, 1960]); D.L. PETERSEN, Late Israelite Prophecy: Studies in Deutero-Prophetic Literature and in Chronicles (SBLMS, 23; Missoula, 1977); I.L. SEELIGMANN, 'Die Auffassung von der Prophetie in der deuteronomistischen und chronistischen Geschichtsschreibung', VTSup 29 (1978), 254–79; S. JAPHET, The Ideology of the Book of Chronicles and its Place in Biblical Thought (Jerusalem, 1977), 154 ff.; R. MICHEEL, Die Seher- und Prophetenüberlieferungen in der Chronik (BET, 18; Frankfurt am Main, 1983).

[24] G. VON RAD, 'The Levitical Sermon in I and II Chronicles', in The Problem of the Hexateuch and Other Essays (Edinburgh and London, 1966), 267–80 = 'Die levitische Predigt in den Büchern der Chronik', in Festschrift Otto Procksch (Leipzig, 1934), 113–24 = Gesammelte Studien zum alten Testament (Munich, 1958), 248–61.

[25] E.g. J.D. NEWSOME, 'Toward a New Understanding of the Chronicler and his Purposes', JBL 94 (1975), 201–217.

[26] E.g. R.L. BRAUN, 'Chronicles, Ezra and Nehemiah: Theology and Literary History', VTSup 30 (1979), 52–64 (54 n. 11); M.A. THRONTVEIT, The Significance of the Royal Speeches and Prayers for the Structure and Theology of the Chronicler (unpublished dissertation, Union Theological Seminary, Richmond, 1982), 163. [This was subsequently published as When Kings Speak (SBLDS, 93; Atlanta, 1987).]

[27] D. MATHIAS, '"Levitische Predigt" und Deuteronomismus', ZAW 94 (1984), 23–49.

full-scale attempt at a rebuttal. Whilst many of the points Mathias raises are apposite, they do not empty von Rad's work of all significance. Thus, we may agree that the title 'Levitical' is too specific, that no sure *Sitz im Leben* for this genre can be established, and that the material which we now have probably derives from the Chronicler himself rather than being, as von Rad thought, independent summaries clumsily worked into his narrative by the Chronicler. Despite all this, however, these passages have characteristics in common which are suggestive of sermonic style, even if in imitation. Though they should not be forced into a rigid form-critical mould, Mason[28] has described the features which they have in common (appeal to an agreed authority; proclamation of some theological teaching about God; and call for response) as well as the literary devices which they regularly use (rhetorical questions; play on words; and illustrations from past history).

Even on Mason's more flexible analysis, it is clear that the use of citations from the prophets remains a fundamental feature. This marks a significant divergence from the speeches in the Deuteronomic History. A probable explanation is that the deuteronomists, who were also responsible for much editorial work on the pre-exilic prophetic corpus, incorporated the insights of the prophets directly into their work. In his much later situation, however, the Chronicler was conscious of standing in a quite different relationship to the writings of the prophets: he derived his theology of history from them at second hand and he could appeal to them as an authority shared both by himself and by his readers. To some extent, therefore, the debate about whether he regarded them as already 'canonical' is beside the point. The use he makes of them in his work shows that within his community they had already been accepted as authoritative religious texts. The Chronicler understood the prophets to be teaching such central doctrines as God's righteousness (Zeph. 3:5 at 2 Chron. 19:7), his universality and omniscience (Zech. 4:10 at 2 Chron. 16:9), the importance of repentance (Jeremiah and Zech. 1:2–6 at 2 Chron. 29:5–11 and 30:6–9), the need for faith (Isa. 7:9 at 2 Chron. 20:20), and the fact of divine response to human initiative (Jer. 29:13–14 at 2 Chron. 15:2). Though this list by no means exhausts the Chronicler's use of the prophets, it shows the extent to which they gave shape to the characteristic parameters of his thought. Indeed, it may not be too much to say that they provided him with the theological context within which to read – and hence retell – his people's history. Since they are never marked out by the formula *kakkātûb*, the writings of the prophets were not to be put on a level with the law so far as religious practice was concerned; but as a resource for broader theological awareness, it appears that the prophets had already attained pre-eminence.

---

[28] R. MASON, 'Some Echoes of the Preaching in the Second Temple? Tradition Elements in Zechariah 1–8', ZAW 96 (1984), 221–35.

16. The Composition of Ezra 1–6

It is a widely recognized fact that a satisfactory historical reconstruction of the reforms of Ezra and Nehemiah is dependent upon a resolution of the many literary problems associated with Ezra 7–10 and Nehemiah.[1] This is no less true of the account earlier in Ezra of the return of a number of the Jews from the exile in Babylon and the subsequent building of the second temple. Generally speaking, however, less attention has been devoted to analysing the relationship of sources and redaction in these six chapters, and this is for one simple reason. Until recent years it has been almost universally believed that the Chronicler was responsible for the present shape of the material. Consequently, conclusions drawn from what can be more securely learnt of his method by comparing his account with the parallel accounts in Samuel and Kings could be applied to the present passage as well.[2] Ezra 1–6 was not seen as a particular or separate problem.

For the increasing number of scholars who have recently expressed their conviction that the books of Ezra and Nehemiah should not be associated so closely with the Chronicler, however, the position is very different. Although one recent study which shares this conviction has concluded that 'the contents of Ezra 1–3 and 6:14–18 lie closest to the thought world of the Chronicler'[3] (and a possible explanation of this will be suggested later), yet the aim of the present article is to indicate that a source- and redaction-critical approach to Ezra 1–6 which does not start out with the presupposition that the Chronicler was their editor can be fruitful in supplying a simple and readily intelligible account of their composition. It should be emphasized at the outset that our concern goes no further than this. The earlier history of the sources isolated, a necessary second step in historical reconstruction, cannot be treated here unless it bears directly on our primary purpose.

---

[1] I am indebted to Professor J.A. Emerton for his helpful comments on a draft of this article. His solution to some of the problems treated here differs from mine, and this has helped me to clarify my arguments at a number of points.

[2] See, for example, P.R. ACKROYD, Exile and Restoration: A Study of Hebrew Thought of the Sixth Century BC (London, 1968), 138–52; O. EISSFELDT, Einleitung in das Alte Testament (3rd edn; Tübingen, 1964), 736f. (ET The Old Testament: an Introduction [Oxford, 1965], 542), and most recently A.H.J. GUNNEWEG, 'Zur Interpretation der Bücher Esra-Nehemia', VTSup 32 (1981), 146–61.

A. Ezra 2

The list in Ezra 2 of the exiles who returned from Babylon provides a convenient way into the material. This is because it is the only passage in Ezra 1–6 which has a parallel elsewhere in the Old Testament, namely Neh. 7:6–72.[4] Most of the differences between the two passages are to be explained on the basis of later, textual corruption.[5] They are therefore of no importance to us here. Towards the end of the list, however, there are some more substantial differences. Examination of these should be more rewarding.

The first point to observe is that the two texts in fact run parallel beyond the conclusion of the list itself, as comparison of Ezra 3:1 with Neh. 7:72b–8:1 clearly shows. In both cases these verses introduce the following narrative rather than serving as a summary or conclusion to the preceding list. It is thus quite clear that one passage must be directly dependent upon the other. The facts cannot be explained on the hypothesis that both drew independently from some common original source, as J. Nikel, for instance, supposes.[6]

This being so, it should be possible to establish which passage borrowed from which. Since the rise of critical scholarship, the overwhelming majority of those who have studied the issue have concluded that Ezra 2 is dependent on Neh. 7.[7] Two main reasons have been advanced in support of this, and to these we would add two new ones.

First, in the continuation of the narratives, 'the seventh month' of Neh. 7:72 is shown to be an integral part of its context by the reference to the same month in 8:2, whereas in Ezra 3:1 it is left completely in the air.

Secondly, it is generally argued that Ezra 2:68–69 represents a summarizing of Neh. 7:69–71 rather than Nehemiah an expansion of Ezra, and the figures involved seem to bear this out. For instance, in the matter of priestly garments,

---

[3] R.L. BRAUN, 'Chronicles, Ezra and Nehemiah: Theology and Literary History', in J.A. EMERTON (ed.), Studies in the Historical Books of the Old Testament (VTSup, 30; Leiden, 1979), 52–64.

[4] Verse enumeration throughout this article is that of the Hebrew Bible.

[5] Cf. H.L. ALLRIK, 'The Lists of Zerubbabel (Nehemiah 7 and Ezra 2) and the Hebrew Numeral Notation', BASOR 136 (1954), 21–7; L.W. BATTEN, The Books of Ezra and Nehemiah (ICC; Edinburgh, 1913), 71–103; J.A. BEWER, Der Text des Buches Ezra (Göttingen, 1922), 17–36; W. RUDOLPH, Esra und Nehemia samt 3. Esra (HAT; Tübingen, 1949), 8–27.

[6] Cf. Die Wiederherstellung des jüdischen Gemeinwesens nach dem babylonischen Exil (Freiburg im Breisgau, 1900), 71f.

[7] No purpose would be served by a comprehensive listing of authorities. Representative discussions may be found in K. GALLING, 'Die Liste der aus dem Exil Heimgekehrten', Studien zur Geschichte Israels im persischen Zeitalter (Tübingen, 1964), 89–108; RUDOLPH, Esra und Nehemia, 11–15; R. SMEND, Die Listen der Bücher Esra und Nehemia (Basel, 1881), 15–23; J. THEIS, Geschichtliche und literarkritische Fragen in Esra 1–6 (Münster, 1910), 60–7.

Neh. 7:69–70 has 67 + 30 items,[8] which Ezra 2:69 has rounded up to 100. Again, for silver minas the sum in Nehemiah is 500 + 2,200 + 2,000, which Ezra 2 has rounded up to 5,000. The suggestion that the process was the other way round (see the works of Mowinckel and Pohlmann cited below) fails to explain why the totals were not divided accurately, whereas on the usual view one need only suppose that the totals were brought up to the nearest round number, an eminently more sensible suggestion.

To these arguments, we may add two more. First, the manner in which the date is given in Ezra 3:1 ('the seventh month') does not fit the practice adopted elsewhere in Ezra 1–6. Here the narrator usually relates events to a given year of the king (e.g. 1:1; 4:24; 6:15) or to some other fixed occasion (e.g. 3:8). If the year is not stated, as at 6:19, the context leaves no doubt as to what is meant. Nowhere else do we find an unattached reference to a named month as at 3:1. On the other hand, this system of dating is exactly what we find regularly in the Ezra material, to which Neh. 7:72b belongs; cf. Ezra 8:31; 10:9, 16–17; Neh. 8:2.

Secondly, within the usually shorter account of Ezra 2:68–69, v. 68 in fact constitutes a clear plus over against Neh. 7:70. This plus, however, exactly fits the narrative context, the outlook and even the specific vocabulary of the narrator of Ezra 1–6, so that the suspicion is hard to resist that he has added it to his *Vorlage* rather than that precisely this verse has coincidentally been omitted in Nehemiah. Noteworthy are the expressions *bêt yhwh 'ašer bîrûšālaim*, 'the house of the Lord (which is) in Jerusalem', which is identical with the expression in 1:5 (to be attributed to the narrator; see below), and *hitnaddebû*, 'offered willingly', which again features prominently in Ezra 1. We should further note the expression *bebô'ām lebêt yhwh*, 'when they came to the house of the Lord', which compares closely with 3:8, where it creates a slightly unusual impression. Finally, it hardly needs saying that the theme of 'rebuilding the house of God on its original site' dominates Ezra 1–6 as a whole.

In the face of these arguments, the counter-proposals of those who ascribe priority to Ezra 2 seem weak indeed, the more so when it is realized that in nearly every case the issue is defended in the interests of the wider view that 1 Esdras represents the original shape of the ending of the Chronicler's work, a case which could not stand if Neh. 7 were prior, in literary terms, to Ezra 2.[9]

---

[8] The Masoretic text of the end of Neh. 7:69 is corrupt. Most English versions combine the *šelōšîm wahamēš mē'ôt* to read 'five hundred and thirty priests' garments'. However, Hebrew usage dictates that in such a case the hundreds must stand first; cf. GK § 134i. Virtually all commentators now agree with KEIL that the words *wekesep mānîm* should be restored, so as to read 'thirty priestly garments and 500 minas of silver'. Cf. C.F. KEIL, *Biblischer Commentar über die nachexilischen Geschichtsbücher: Chronik, Esra, Nehemia und Esther* (Leipzig, 1870) *ad* Ezra 2:68–70.

[9] The question of the textual superiority of 1 Esdras in some cases is, of course, a quite separate issue. On this, see R.W. KLEIN, 'Old Readings in 1 Esdras: The List of Returnees from Babylon (Ezra 2//Nehemiah 7)', HTR 62 (1969), 99–107. His arguments are weakened, however, by his failure to deal with the strong case to the contrary in H.L. ALLRIK, '1 Esdras

Nevertheless, in view of the increasing popularity of this alternative position, some examination of the arguments must be undertaken here.

The earlier suggestions of Hölscher[10] and Noth[11] were given a brief reply by Rudolph (13–14). Now a more substantial, though not more convincing, case has been pressed by Mowinckel[12] and Pohlmann.[13] For instance, Mowinckel (30) is at a loss to understand why the Chronicler (as he supposes our editor to be) should have abbreviated at the end of Ezra 2 against his usual exaggerations elsewhere. Mowinckel's case is weakened here by the fact that he is apparently equally unable to suggest why there should be expansion in Neh. 7. Arguments of this sort are unlikely to be productive. In fact, however, there is a reasonable explanation for the abbreviation in Ezra, as noted already by Galling:[14] in the new context which he provided for the list, the editor may have found the reference to the Tirshatha's gifts (Neh. 7:69) awkward. This is because he probably identified the Tirshatha with Sheshbazzar. Since he has already provided a list of the vessels which Sheshbazzar brought back to Jerusalem (1:9–11), he may have felt that it would avoid confusion or misunderstanding if he amalgamated the detailed list of contributions in his *Vorlage*. Finally, appeal to the Chronicler's practice elsewhere is irrelevant on the presupposition of this article.

Mowinckel's first substantial argument (30–31), however, centres on certain difficulties which he feels about Neh. 7:69–71. In cases where these are purely textual in character, they are not strictly relevant for our present purpose. Mowinckel's main contention, however, is that v. 69 is a later interpolation or gloss in its present context. Now here, he may possibly be right: his arguments certainly carry weight, and it is a suggestion worthy of consideration. What must be emphasized, however, is that this in no way proves, as he seems to suppose, that Nehemiah must therefore be secondary to Ezra. First, the removal of Neh. 7:69 still does not give us a text that could have come directly from Ezra 2. Secondly, it leaves unexplained the remainder of the abbreviation and the fact that the plus in Ezra 2:68 is alone so coincidentally suitable to its setting in Ezra 1–6. Finally, Mowinckel has not considered what is surely the most likely suggestion, namely that if Neh. 7:69 is indeed an addition it was made by the editor of Neh. 7 to the antecedent source on which he was drawing, and so it

---

According to Codex B and Codex A as Appearing in Zerubbabel's List in 1 Esdras 5_{8-23}', ZAW 66 (1954), 272–92.

[10] G. HÖLSCHER, 'Die Bücher Esra und Nehemia', in E. KAUTZSCH (ed.), Die heilige Schrift des Alten Testaments (4th edn; edited by A. BERTHOLET; Tübingen, 1923), vol. II, 491–562.

[11] M. NOTH, Überlieferungsgeschichtliche Studien I (Halle, 1943), 128–9.

[12] S. MOWINCKEL, Studien zu dem Buche Ezra-Nehemia, I: Die nachchronistische Redaktion des Buches. Die Listen (Oslo, 1964), 29–45.

[13] K.-F. POHLMANN, Studien zum dritten Esra: Ein Beitrag zur Frage nach dem ursprünglichen Schluß des chronistischen Geschichtswerkes (FRLANT, 104; Göttingen, 1970), 57–64.

[14] GALLING, Studien, 104–5.

could have already been made before it was borrowed in Ezra 2. Mowinckel has not argued that it must be a very much later gloss. The figures of Neh. 7:69 would then still serve the argument advanced above that Ezra 2 has 'rounded up' those of his *Vorlage*,[15] whereas if Mowinckel's position were adopted we should be left with no apparent reason for the drastic reduction in figures between Ezra 2 and Neh. 7.

Mowinckel's second argument (32-3) need not detain us. It concerns Ezra 2:70 and Neh. 7:72a. Both passages, Mowinckel agrees, have suffered some textual damage in the course of transmission, so that it would be hazardous in the extreme to base any conclusions upon them. Furthermore, part of Mowinckel's case for the secondary status of Neh. 7:72 is dependent on a dismissal of contrary evidence from 1 Esdras in a manner which I have suggested elsewhere is unjustified.[16]

Mowinckel's third main argument (33-5) is an attempt to establish that Ezra 3:1 fits its context better than Neh. 7:72b. He certainly succeeds in making a plausible suggestion as to how the editor of the Ezra material understood his text. However, so much background which the text itself leaves unsaid has to be supplied by Mowinckel that one is tempted to wonder whether an author composing freely would not have expressed himself more clearly. Moreover, Mowinckel fails to observe the uncharacteristic dating system as analysed above. On the other hand, his attempt to prove the secondary nature of Neh. 7:72b completely ignores the fact that in all probability this originally stood in the Ezra Memoir (as we may call it here for the sake of convenience only). If, as Torrey,[17] Rudolph, and others have argued, it originally followed Ezra 8,[18] then both the date and the reference to the people of Israel being 'in their towns' fit perfectly after the account of the journey from Babylon in Ezra 8 with arrival in Jerusalem in the fifth month (Ezra 7:8-9).

Mowinckel's final[19] argument (40-5) concerns the original setting of the list. At first, he discusses whether the list is likely to have been an original part of the

---

[15] MOWINCKEL in fact proposes 35 instead of 30 priests' garments and he deletes the (five) hundreds. His arguments seem highly speculative to me, but even if they were correct the figures in Ezra could still be round numbers based upon the new totals of 102 and 4,200.

[16] H.G.M. WILLIAMSON, Israel in the Books of Chronicles (Cambridge, 1977), 32-3.

[17] C.C. TORREY, The Composition and Historical Value of Ezra-Nehemiah (BZAW, 2; Giessen, 1896), 29-34; Ezra Studies (Chicago, 1910), 252-84.

[18] MOWINCKEL's adherence to the priority of 1 Esdras demands that he argue that it originally followed Ezra 10, where admittedly the transition would not be so smooth. For further arguments against the priority of 1 Esdras, cf. Israel in the Books of Chronicles, 12-36, and R. HANHART, 'Zu Text und Textgeschichte des ersten Esrabuches', Proceedings of the Sixth World Congress of Jewish Studies (Jerusalem, 1977), 201-12.

[19] MOWINCKEL's lengthy interaction (36-40) with R. KITTEL, Zur Frage der Entstehung des Judentums (Leipzig, 1917, unavailable to me), goes beyond our immediate concern and appears in any case to be indecisive. Note should be made, however, of his concession (40) that the author of Ezra 1-6 'hat natürlich Neh 8 gekannt; diese Szene schwebte ihm als Vorbild vor, als er sein Ezr 3 konzipierte'.

Nehemiah Memoir. This, however, is an irrelevancy, since as already seen, the contrary view not only allows, but actually demands, that editorial activity should already have taken place before the material was borrowed by Ezra 2. More importantly, however, Mowinckel argues that the list, as preserved in the temple archives, must have stopped at Ezra 2:68. Thereafter narrative style is resumed, and this is inappropriate in a list. Since the narrative is, not unnaturally, more suitable from a historical point of view to Ezra 2–3 than to Neh. 7–8, the latter must be dependent upon the former.

This argument too, however, is not compelling. The major narrative item in Ezra 2 is found in v. 68, but this fact has already been seen to support the view that Ezra 2 borrowed from Neh. 7. In the latter chapter, the 'narrative' element concerns only a record of donations to the temple treasury.[20] The evidence of the remainder of Ezra-Nehemiah shows with what care such details were preserved. Since the list itself is already to be regarded as a compilation of several originally discrete elements,[21] there seems no reason to doubt that this concluding passage could have been added to it either while it was in the archive or by the editor responsible for the present text of Neh. 7. Indeed, we have already noted the possibility, advanced by Mowinckel himself, that Neh. 7:69 may be just such an isolated addition.

Although Pohlmann presents his case in a fresh way, his arguments are of a generally similar type to those of Mowinckel, and so need not be treated here at length. We should observe, however, that when he argues for the greater suitability of Ezra 2 to its present context, he fails to note (a) that this comes precisely in the closing verses of the chapter where, as seen above, the material is most likely to be editorial adaptation of Neh. 7, and (b) that if Ezra 2:69 were part of the narrator's own link between Ezra 1 and 3, it is strange that he did not integrate it better with the list of temple vessels in 1:9–11. It looks much more as though he is here dependent upon earlier material and allowed it to serve, albeit somewhat uneasily, in place of a narrative account of the return of which, as we will see later, no record appears to have survived for his use.

We may thus conclude this part of our examination by reaffirming that Ezra 2 with 3:1 is dependent upon Neh. 7 in its present form. The implications of this conclusion for the composition of these books as a whole can hardly be overestimated. Since Neh. 7–8 is the point at which the originally independent ac-

---

[20] Neh. 7:72a is, in my opinion, to be regarded as a part of the original Nehemiah Memoir. It links closely with Neh. 11:1 (immediately after the long interruption of the Memoir by Neh. 8–10) and may have originally formed part of the introduction to the narrative with which that chapter begins.

[21] Notice, for instance, that the long list of lay people switches without warning from those enrolled by family association (Ezra 2:3–20) to those enrolled by place of domicile (vv. 21–35), though no reason is apparent for this different principle of arrangement. Again, vv. 21–35 are further subdivided into a list introduced by $'anšê$, 'the men of', and one introduced by $b^enê$, 'the sons of', even though in such a passage these terms are synonymous. The composite nature of this list is acknowledged by most commentators.

counts concerning Ezra and Nehemiah have been most clearly interwoven, it follows that the editor responsible for Ezra 2 already knew Ezra 7–10 and Nehemiah in substantially its present shape.[22] Earlier scholars were indeed aware of this logical conclusion,[23] but made little of it because of their presupposition that Ezra 1–6 was the work of the Chronicler. In other words, for them the combined narratives about Ezra and Nehemiah were simply another of the Chronicler's sources, and there was nothing further to be said with regard to Ezra 1–6. If, however, we discount this presupposition it will follow automatically that Ezra 1–6 must be an independent composition from a date later than the combining of the Ezra and Nehemiah material. The purpose and provenance of such a composition will be broached at the end of this article. Before that, however, we must proceed to test the hypothesis against the other chapters which make up this literary unit. It will be our aim to demonstrate that the whole account can be explained on the basis of a later author writing up a narrative directly out of a number of primary sources to which he had access. At no point is it necessary to postulate an 'intermediate' editor who might have come between the sources themselves and the final author.

B. Ezra 1

At first sight, Ezra 1 contains two items of early material, the decree of Cyrus (vv. 2–4) and the inventory of temple vessels (vv. 9–11a). The remainder of the chapter is connective narrative.

The origins of the decree of Cyrus are, of course, disputed. Even now that the earlier scepticism towards all the documents in Ezra 1–6 has been largely overcome because of our increased knowledge of Persian policy towards their subjects[24] and of the epistolary conventions of the period,[25] many scholars still

---

[22] The series of tortuous conjectures which RUDOLPH has to postulate (15) in order to escape this conclusion shows all too clearly that he appreciated this conclusion and its implications but was unwilling to face them, because they would have been so damaging to his view of the Chronicler's editorial work (see also on 4:24).

[23] E. g. E. MEYER, Die Entstehung des Judenthums: Eine historische Untersuchung (Halle, 1896), 99.

[24] The most helpful survey is still R. DE VAUX, 'Les décrets de Cyrus et de Darius sur la reconstruction du temple', RB 46 (1937), 29–57 = Bible et Orient (Paris, 1967), 83–113 (ET The Bible and the Ancient Near East [London, 1971], 63–96).

[25] Cf. P. S. ALEXANDER, 'Remarks on Aramaic Epistolography in the Persian Period', JSS 23 (1978), 155–70; P.-E. DION, 'Les types épistolaires hébréo-araméens jusqu'au temps de Bar-Kokhbah', RB 96 (1979), 544–79; J. A. FITZMYER, 'Aramaic Epistolography', A Wandering Aramean: Collected Aramaic Essays (SBLMS, 25; Missoula, 1979), 183–204; L. V. HENSLEY, 'The Official Persian Documents in the Book of Ezra' (unpublished dissertation, University of Liverpool, 1977).

16. The Composition of Ezra 1–6

believe that this particular decree, which is written in Hebrew rather than Aramaic, is likely to be the Chronicler's own work, based on the written memorandum of 6:3–5. This view would not be incompatible with our approach to the composition of these chapters as a whole, though it would leave unanswered the question how our author knew about the return of Jews from Babylon during the reign of Cyrus, since this is not mentioned in Ezra 6 or in any other source known to us. Even 5:14 implies only the return of Sheshbazzar the governor. In fact, however, two points of tension between the decree and its surrounding narrative suggest that it was nevertheless an independent piece.[26] Examination of these will reveal a pattern of editorial activity which will become increasingly familiar as we proceed.

First, the form of the decree is that of a message in oral form. As regularly with this form,[27] it is introduced by the messenger formula, 'Thus says PN', continues with a report in the perfect tense describing the present, new situation (v. 2), and concludes with an imperative section which offers the choice of decision to the one addressed (vv. 3–4). Many examples of this form are to be found both in the Old Testament and elsewhere (e.g. Gen. 45:9; Num. 22:5–6; 2 Kgs 19:3–4).[28]

Needless to say, a message is normally intended for an individual or single group of people. Here, however, the author has introduced it in v. 1 as a royal proclamation, announced, presumably by heralds, over a wide area. Although this was a common enough practice in the ancient world,[29] we have little knowledge of the nature of such proclamations,[30] since they are usually reported only indirectly (e.g. 2 Chr. 24:9; Ezra 10:7). Where the content is recorded, however, it included imperative material alone; cf. Exod. 36:6; Neh. 8:15; Dan. 3:4–6.[31] Had our author been composing freely at this point, we might have expected him to follow this pattern, rather than himself adapting the form of an oral message for no apparent reason. It thus looks as though what was originally intended as a moderately localized announcement, probably to the leaders of the Jewish community, has been expanded by the new setting in which the narrator has placed it by his composition of v. 1 into a more universal proclamation.

---

[26] This conclusion still does not settle the historical question, though it is an important positive contribution to that debate. Most of the frequently voiced objections to the possibility of the decree being original have been answered by E. J. BICKERMAN, 'The Edict of Cyrus in Ezra 1', Studies in Jewish and Christian History, Part One (Leiden, 1976), 72–108.

[27] Cf. C. WESTERMANN, Grundformen prophetischer Rede (BEvT, 31; 2nd edn; Munich, 1964), 70–82 (ET Basic Forms of Prophetic Speech [London, 1967], 100–15).

[28] A note of the person addressed is hardly ever included within the message itself. GALLING's objection (Studien, 66) to the decree on these grounds is thus unjustified.

[29] Cf. BICKERMAN, Studies, 74–6.

[30] BICKERMAN's attempt (Studies, 108) to relate the form of the decree to the Roman *edictum* is unconvincing.

[31] 2 Chron. 30:5–9 is not comparable, since here the Chronicler has merely put a Levitical sermon into the mouths of the king's messengers.

The second point of tension between the decree and the narrative relates to verses 4 and 6. Both verses refer to gifts given to support the Jews who were returning to Jerusalem. Furthermore, it is clear that in verse 6 the gifts came from gentile neighbours, $s^eb̄ibōṭêhem$. Had the writer intended fellow-Jews, he would have used a word like ^aḥêhem, 'their brethren'.[32]

The position in v. 4 is less straightforward, however, because of a textual difficulty. The Revised Version renders the first part of the verse as follows: 'And whosoever is left, in any place where he sojourneth, let the men of his place help him with silver ...'. On this view, $^,an̂sê\ m^eqōmô$, 'the men of his place', is taken as the subject of the verb, with $w^ek̄ol-hanniš^,ār$, 'and whosoever is left', as a *casus pendens* linked to the resumptive verbal suffix in $y^enaśś^e,ûhû$.[33] This has given rise to the widespread interpretation that some of the Jews were too poor to go, but after receiving aid from their neighbours they too joined the return.

Older commentators found no difficulty with this; after all, verse 6 has already been seen to lend some support to this approach. More recently, however, it has (rightly, in my view) been found historically improbable that Cyrus should have commanded such assistance. This has then been used to justify the prior assumption that this cannot be an essentially accurate copy of an original decree.

Before this is conceded, however, we must inquire whether the verse has been correctly understood. In the approach outlined above, two difficulties attend the interpretation of the first words of the verse, $w^ek̄ol-hanniš^,ār$. First, if it is thought to have the technical sense of 'the remnant', that is to say in this context the Jewish community in Babylon who were about to return to Judah, then the progression of thought from v. 3 to v. 4 is harsh. On this view, the two verses would be referring to the same group of people, whereas v. 4 is more naturally understood as introducing a separate group. Secondly, $hanniš^,ār$ is never, in fact, used on its own to mean 'the remnant'. That specific sense is always made clear by other elements in the immediate context (see, for instance, Neh. 1:3), but these are lacking here.

When the word $niš^,ār$ occurs on its own, as here, we expect it to have the neutral meaning of 'the rest, remainder; that which remains after a part has been removed'.[34] May it not have this sense here too? The previous verse has spoken of such of the Jews as were willing to undertake the journey back to Jerusalem, and following the introductory question, $mî$-$b̄āk̄em$, they are addressed in the

---

[32] Cf. RUDOLPH, 220.

[33] For the pi'el of $nś^,$ = 'help', cf. 1 Kgs. 9:11; Ezra 8:36; Est. 9:3. M. D. GOLDMAN's conjecture, in 'The True Meaning of Ezra 1, 4', ABR 1 (1951), 58, that it means 'to impose a levy' is without parallel and rests on a probable misunderstanding of the earlier part of the verse.

[34] Cf. H. WILDBERGER, in THAT, vol. II, 844–55. Since I believe that sense can be made of the text at this point, there is no need to consider the conjectural emendations of BEWER, 12 (on which see RUDOLPH, 2), and H. L. GINSBERG, 'Ezra 1₄' JBL 79 (1960), 167–9.

third person singular – 'let him go up ... and let him build'. Following this, the opening words of v. 4 continue quite naturally, 'And those who remain behind (collective singular followed by plural verb) who belong to any of the places where he (i.e. the returning Jew, still referred to in the singular) is living shall help him ...'. In other words, the rest of the Jews (*hanniš'ār*), who stayed behind in Babylon for whatever reason, were materially to aid those of their fellow Jews who returned.

This interpretation makes excellent sense in the context, and has the support of 1 Esdras and the Vulgate. One problem remains, however, namely, the words following the clause just translated, *'anšê mᵉqōmô*. Bickerman (pp. 83–7), whose general understanding of this verse is similar to that adopted here, has attempted an explanation and rendering which includes *'anšê mᵉqōmô*. However, though his grammatical analysis is correct as an explanation of the Masoretic Text it is too cumbersome to allow us to believe that it represents the original text. It may therefore be suggested instead that *'anšê mᵉqōmô* be regarded as either an explanatory gloss or a 'double reading'[35] for the whole of the earlier phrase. As often with legal jargon, the opening phrase of the verse is cumbersome, and not readily intelligible. *'anšê mᵉqōmô* may therefore have originally served as a layman's equivalent. Alternatively, the similarity between the consonants of *nš'r* and *'nšy*, with *mqwm* following in each case, suggests the possibility of the one arising as a misreading of the other. Either way, for reasons of scribal caution, both synonymous readings came to be preserved within a single text.

We may thus conclude that, rather as in the case of our form-critical discussion, there is a tension between the moderately localized intention of the decree of vv. 2–4 and the wider setting in which it has subsequently been placed. This in turn supports the view that the decree is an originally independent piece. A further small pointer in this direction may be included, finally, in the introductory *wᵉgam bᵉmiḵtāḇ*, v. 1. In itself, this statement causes no surprise: it was quite usual in the ancient world for oral messages to be backed up by written documents (e.g. 2 Kgs 19:9–14; 2 Chron. 17:9; 30:1; *AP* 32).[36] Moreover, the word *mktb* is generally used elsewhere for the authoritative written form of something which the context shows was also orally proclaimed; cf. Exod. 32:16; Deut. 10:4; Isa. 38:9; 2 Chron. 35:4 with reference back to 8:14; and possibly 2 Chron. 21:12. Thus the author of Ezra 1 has left a syntactically loosely related allusion to the written source he was following.[37]

---

[35] For this phenomenon, cf. S. TALMON, 'Double Readings in the Massoretic Text', Textus 1 (1960), 144–84.

[36] A. COWLEY, Aramaic Papyri of the Fifth Century B.C. (Oxford, 1923). For further examples, cf. BICKERMAN, Studies, 105–8, and K.A. KITCHEN, Ancient Orient and Old Testament (London, 1966), 135–8.

[37] This seems more likely than the suggestion of BICKERMAN, who is followed by J.M. MYERS, Ezra-Nehemiah (AB; Garden City, 1965), 6, that the reference is to the decree being publicly placarded for all to read, for, as noted above, it was originally addressed to a more restricted audience.

If this conclusion be accepted, then we may observe that the surrounding narrative demands no historical knowledge beyond what could be deduced from the decree itself and the other sources which we know were available to him. If the date (v. 1) was not preserved in some heading or other filing note to the decree itself, he could have deduced it from 6:3. Most of the remainder of v. 1 is a theological introduction to the decree (resumed also in v. 5), reflecting on such passages as Isa. 41:2, 25; 44:28; 45:1, 13; Jer. 51:1 and 11. The reference to 'a proclamation throughout all his kingdom' is part of that universalizing of the terms of the decree already noted and is a consequence of the theological interpretation.

The wording of vv. 5–6 is so close to that of 2–4 that there can be no doubt that the narrator, knowing from his source in chapter 2 that a number of Jews did return, simply wrote up their response on the basis of the decree itself. The more specific definition of the people is that common in the writer's day. Verse 6 introduces a further theological embellishment. The point of tension already noted between this verse and v. 4 derives from the author's evident concern to present the return as a second Exodus. The motif of the 'despoiling of the Egyptians' is prominent in the Exodus accounts; cf. Exod. 3:21–2; 11:2; 12:35–6; Ps. 105:37. That our author has this motif in mind is rendered probable by a change which he has introduced between the decree and its fulfilment, namely the addition of the word $k^e l\hat{e}$, 'vessels of'. 'Vessels of silver and vessels of gold' are referred to specifically in each of the three Exodus passages just listed.

Thus vv. 1 and 5–6 can all be explained as a direct 'write-up' of vv. 2–4, given the theological presupposition of a single, united return under God's inspiration, reminiscent of the first Exodus.

The same conclusion emerges with even greater clarity in vv. 7–11, which may accordingly be treated more briefly. There is widespread agreement[38] that the list of temple vessels is based on an antecedent source. Indications which favour this conclusion include the use of the Aramaic word $k^e p\bar{o}r$, 'bowl', in v. 10, the uncertain loan-word and hapax legomenon, $^{\prime a}gart\bar{a}l$, 'dish' (?), in v. 9, the absence of the definite article in 'all (the) vessels' (v. 11), which suggests the clipped style of a summary list, and the confused condition of the list itself (see the commentaries). In addition, the Persian loan-word $gizb\bar{a}r$, 'treasurer' (v. 8), another hapax legomenon in Biblical Hebrew, and the use of the well-attested Persian name Mithredath[39] suggest the likelihood that the original introduction to the inventory has been rewritten. It is thus a reasonable conjecture that the list has been translated from Aramaic and that, as in similar instances known to us,[40]

---

[38] See particularly K. GALLING, 'Das Protokoll über die Rückgabe der Tempelgeräte', Studien, 78–88.

[39] Cf. F. JUSTI, Iranisches Namenbuch (Marburg, 1895), 209–13.

[40] Cf. J.D. WHITEHEAD, 'Some Distinctive Features of the Language of the Aramaic Arsames Correspondence', JNES 37 (1978), 119–40.

it included a fair sprinkling of words of Persian origin. In view of its contents, preservation in the temple archives is understandable.

Close parallels for such a list are provided by AP 61 and 63, though both are badly damaged.[41] It probably began 'Memorandum' (*zkrn*), followed by a summary statement that Mithredath the treasurer handed over certain vessels to Sheshbazzar, and then the date (cf. AP 61, l. 12). Thus AP 61 starts: 'Memorandum: cups of bronze ... Ḥanan son of Haggai into the hand of (*lyd*)...'.[42] With the help of Ezra 5:14, which comes from one of the Aramaic sources available to our author, and whose wording is more than coincidentally close to that of the present passage, the author could without difficulty have composed the whole of vv. 7–8 out of this heading.

The only element which cannot obviously be explained in this way is the unparalleled description of Sheshbazzar as 'the prince of Judah'. The significance of this title has never been satisfactorily explained, no suggestion having ever been able to account for its unique occurrence in this passage where a more regular term, such as 'governor' (cf. 5:14), would appear to serve equally well. The difficulty is compounded by the fact that he is not mentioned in the royal genealogy in 1 Chron. 3,[43] which appears to aim at comprehensiveness for this period, while the designation *nāśîʾ*, 'prince', need not necessarily indicate royalty (e.g. Gen. 23:6; Exod. 22:27; Lev. 4:22; Num. 1:16; Josh. 9:15).

This difficulty can, I suggest, be resolved in the light of our author's method already seen in this chapter. We have noted that his purpose is, in part, to write up his sources as a 'second Exodus'. This concern is continued in the present paragraph: already in his prophecy of the departure from Babylon, which includes several striking allusions to the first Exodus,[44] Deutero-Isaiah had introduced an additional reference to those who would be carrying with them 'the vessels of the Lord'. While not an overt part of the descriptions of the Exodus itself, it is probable that this element had come to be associated with it in the hopes for return and restoration.

With such a purpose in view, our author's thoughts at this point will have naturally turned to the account of the journey through the wilderness, as recorded particularly in Numbers. It is a well-known characteristic of that narrative that there are lists of those who were 'princes' of the various tribes (Num. 2:3–31; 7:1–83; 34:18–28). Furthermore, at Num. 7:84–6 they are associated

---

[41] See also E. SACHAU, Aramäische Papyrus und Ostraka aus einer jüdischen Militär-Kolonie zu Elephantine: Tafeln (Leipzig, 1911), pl. 55 and 53 (reverse).

[42] We cannot here go into the many difficulties raised by the text of the list itself. It will have been followed by the final summary (v. 11a), and was probably signed in the presence of witnesses.

[43] The suggestion that he should be identified with the Shenazzar of 1 Chron. 3:18 must now be abandoned; cf. P.-R. BERGER, 'Zu den Namen שׁשׁבצר und שנאצר', ZAW 83 (1971), 98–100.

[44] Cf. B.W. ANDERSON, 'Exodus Typology in Second Isaiah', in B.W. ANDERSON and W. HARRELSON (eds.), Israel's Prophetic Heritage (London, 1962), 177–95.

with a number of gold and silver vessels given for the dedication of the altar; this may have attracted our author's attention in the context of his own comparable source. The title 'prince of Judah' was thus supplied by our author as part of his typological interpretation of the return from Babylon[45] and so does not demand access to any earlier information otherwise unknown to us.

The final sentence of Ezra 1 (v. 11b) will also be a free composition by our author. Lacking indication to the contrary, he simply presented the return as a single undertaking, but did so in language which, once again, was evocative of the Exodus. The passive verb $hē'ălôṯ$, 'were brought up', is indicative of divine activity and echoes the descriptions of the Exodus. There, as here, it is followed by the 'from... to' formula, in contrast to $hôṣî'$ 'to bring out'.[46] The statement 'brought up from Babylon to Jerusalem' thus becomes the counterpart of 'brought up out of the land of Egypt, unto the land ...' (Exod. 33:1).

The brevity of our author's narrative here is revealing. Several scholars have thought that he must originally have had a fuller account of so momentous an event, and that it has subsequently been lost.[47] On our understanding, however, no such account existed. It is not the type of event which would leave a legacy of official documents of the sort to which it already appears our author had access. Writing long after the events in question, he respected the silence of his sources, but interpreted that which he deduced must have taken place.

In Ezra 1, we therefore conclude, all the material can be adequately accounted for on our hypothesis of a single author supplying an interpretative narrative framework for two official documents to which he had access, and whose content is of such a kind as to render their archival preservation highly plausible.

---

[45] Since it fits in with other aspects of our author's methods, this explanation is to be preferred to that which links the title with the prince of Ezek. 40–48: cf. L. ROST, 'Erwägungen zum Kyroserlaß', in A. KUSCHKE (ed.), Verbannung und Heimkehr (Tübingen, 1961), 301–7. In addition, it is probable that the prince there is regarded as a Davidic figure, as he is elsewhere in Ezekiel (cf. 7:27; 12:10, 12; 19:1; 21:30; 34:24; 37:25, and J.D. LEVENSON, Theology of the Program of Restoration of Ezekiel 40–48 [Missoula, 1976], 57–73). This rules out the identification with Sheshbazzar, contra H. GESE, Der Verfassungsentwurf des Ezechiel (Tübingen, 1957), 118. Finally, in Ezekiel the prince is a pan-Israelite figure, whereas in Ezra 1 he is closer to the presentation in Numbers by being linked more narrowly with the tribe of Judah (compare v. 5 with v. 8).

[46] Cf. Gen. 50:24; Exod. 3:8, 17; 33:1, and J. WIJNGAARDS, 'הוציא and העלה, a twofold approach to the Exodus', VT 15 (1965), 91–102.

[47] Indeed, TORREY, Ezra Studies, 115–39, went so far as to reconstruct the missing text, based largely on 1 Esdras. He is criticized by J.A. BEWER, 'The Gap between Ezra, Chapters 1 and 2', AJSL 36 (1919–20), 18–26, though BEWER also believes that there is a gap.

C. Ezra 4:6–6:22

We move next to the long section written in Aramaic, though in fact introduced and concluded in Hebrew. It has usually been believed that this material went through some intermediate stage of redaction before being incorporated into the present form of the text. Schaeder, for instance, developed a suggestion of Klostermann to the effect that the Aramaic material (which, he argued, began originally at 4:7) was an edited version of an original memoir by Tabeel. It was written to Artaxerxes to urge the Jewish case for rebuilding the walls. It thus included first the accusations of the community's opponents before countering them with the portrayal in Ezra 5–6 of the more favourable attitude adopted by earlier Persian kings. When the Chronicler (as Schaeder thinks) incorporated this Memoir into its present setting, he omitted material not relevant to his narrative (thus obliterating all trace of the Memoir's original purpose), and also added one or two sections, such as 5:1–2.[48]

More generally, however, commentators have maintained that the Aramaic material was a separate source in correct chronological order (i.e. with 4:6–23 following 5:1–6:18).[49] In taking up this source, the 'Chronicler' rearranged the material along thematic rather than chronological lines and added the concluding verses of chapter 6 in Hebrew. Rudolph has further correctly observed that, if it be assumed that the Chronicler himself did not write in Aramaic, 4:24, which clearly belongs to the latest redactional phase, must also have been written in Hebrew at first.

The only evidence that seems to have been advanced in favour of this majority view is that of language. However, it cannot be assumed that an author of our period could not write Aramaic if he so chose. Indeed, once it is observed that the bulk of the section is taken up with citations from letters in Aramaic, and that the narrative in which they are set frequently draws on the very wording of the documents themselves, there must be a strong presupposition in favour of the simpler view that the final author has worked directly from the original sources, as in chapter 1. Analysis will show that some long-standing difficulties raised by this passage may be explained by this approach.

---

[48] Cf. H. H. SCHAEDER, Iranische Beiträge I (Halle, 1930), 14–27; Esra der Schreiber (Tübingen, 1930), 27f. After gaining initial popularity, this theory has attracted increasing criticism; cf. DE VAUX, 'Décrets', 99–101 = 'Decrees', 80–2; RUDOLPH, 37–41; H. H. ROWLEY, 'Nehemiah's Mission and its Background', Men of God (London and Edinburgh, 1963), 211–45 (223–5); J. LIVER, 'The Problem of the Order of the Kings of Persia in the Books of Ezra and Nehemiah' (Hebrew), Studies in Bible and Judean Desert Scrolls (Jerusalem, 1971), 263–76.

[49] DE VAUX, 'Decrees', 81–2, goes so far as to assert that there is 'unanimous agreement' that 'the section which runs from Ezra 4:8 to 6:18 is wholly derived from a single Aramaic source'. See also EISSFELDT, Introduction, 543.

(i) Ezra 4:6–24

The bulk of this section is made up of references to or citation of letters unfavourable to the Jews addressed to Xerxes and Artaxerxes. It is thus out of chronological order with regard to its literary setting which relates both before (4:5) and after to the reign of Darius I. However, the fact that 4:5 has already brought the narrative down to the reign of Darius suggests that we should not quickly conclude that the author blundered owing to insufficient historical knowledge.

According to the conclusion of our discussion of chapter 2, Ezra 1–6 is to be regarded as a separate composition written later than the formation of the remainder of Ezra-Nehemiah. Now, if our author had copies of these letters in front of him, there was no place in his composition where he could include them in their fully correct chronological order, since the events in question come down to a point later than the start of the Ezra material.[50] Faced with this dilemma, he looked for a point where he could insert them in such a way that they would contribute positively to his theme. He believed that they would serve as justification for the seemingly harsh rejection of the offer of help in 4:1–3 and for his designation of those who offered as 'adversaries of Judah and Benjamin' (4:1. Comparison of vv. 2 and 10 links the two groups together).

There are then two ways in which we may understand 4:24, and both are compatible with our overall understanding of the composition of these chapters. The first supposes that the author here made clear what he was doing by use of a literary device known as 'repetitive resumption'. This is a device whereby – in the days before brackets or footnotes – an author could mark the resumption of a narrative flow which had been broken by the insertion of some digressionary material. It is done by repeating the substance of the sentence before the insertion with generally similar wording. A particularly clear example is furnished by 2 Chron. 12, because we can there see by comparison with 1 Kgs 14:25–8 that the Chronicler has himself added vv. 2b–8. The resumption is marked by the repetition of v. 2a in v. 9. Many other examples are now generally recognized.[51]

---

[50] Whenever we date Ezra's journey to Jerusalem, no one will doubt that an author of our period will have assumed that it was in the seventh year of Artaxerxes I. It is therefore probable that 4:12 was understood as a reference to Ezra and his companions.

[51] Cf. C. KUHL, 'Die "Wiederaufnahme" – ein literarkritisches Prinzip?', ZAW 66 (1952), 1–11; B. LANG, 'A Neglected Method in Ezekiel Research: Editorial Criticism', VT 29 (1979), 39–44. That longer passages than KUHL or LANG discuss may be involved is shown by I. L. SEELIGMANN, 'Hebräische Erzählung und biblische Geschichtsschreibung', ThZ 18 (1962), 305–25 (314–24); S. TALMON and M. FISHBANE, 'The Structuring of Biblical Books', ASTI 10 (1975–76), 129–53; H. G. M. WILLIAMSON, 'The Origins of the Twenty-four Priestly Courses', VTSup 30 (1979), 251–68 (265) (see above 126–40); H. VAN DYKE PARUNAK, 'Oral Typesetting: Some Uses of Biblical Structure', Biblica 62 (1981), 153–68 (160–2).

It will be noted in the passage under discussion that 4:24 resumes 4:5;[52] it could thus be regarded as an editorial device rather than a step forward in the narrative.[53]

The second way of understanding 4:24 takes $bē^ɔdayin$ as meaning 'then' in the sense 'the next thing that happened'. The particular merit of this view is that $b^eṭēlaṯ$, 'ceased', and $h^awāṯ\ bāṭ^elāʾ$, 'it remained at a standstill', can then be readily taken as the direct continuation and consequence of $ûbaṭṭīlû$, 'and they made them cease', in the preceding verse.

The results of this view for our estimation of the editor's historical knowledge of the period are grave. It would mean that he thought that the order of the first Achaemenid kings was Cyrus, Xerxes (Ahasuerus), Artaxerxes, Darius – the latter being the king during whose reign the second temple was built. Nevertheless, a desire to salvage the editor's historical reputation should not by itself weigh too heavily with us in view of his date considerably later than the events in question.

Despite its obvious advantages, this understanding of 4:24 also has difficulties to face. Chief amongst these is the very clear statement that it refers to the temple while the preceding exchange of letters deals explicitly with the walls of Jerusalem. We have no reason to suppose that the editor would have been confused about so obvious a distinction as this. Secondly, whatever other problems surround Ezra 6:14 (see further below), it does at least suggest that the editor knew that Artaxerxes came after, not before, the Darius who issued a decree concerning the temple, this being clearly, therefore, the Darius of Ezra 5–6. Thirdly, we know from Josephus that a knowledge of the correct order of the early Achaemenid kings was preserved in Jerusalem until much later times. Whether our editor had access to this material is unknown to us, but at least the possibility that he did must be conceded.

As indicated earlier, either understanding of 4:24 outlined here fits well with our general hypothesis regarding the composition of Ezra 1–6. It is either an editorial literary device, or a brief narrative statement based on the wording of 4:23 and the chronology supplied by Haggai. A final decision on the issue is thus not essential for our immediate purposes, though on balance it seems that the first view faces fewer difficulties than the second.

Turning now to the substance of the paragraph, we find nothing that requires us to postulate editorial activity between the text of the letters and the final author. Verse 6 merely summarizes the contents of a letter which (as is clearly the case with v. 7) we may suppose lay in front of the author but whose contents

---

[52] This is noted by S. TALMON, 'Ezra and Nehemiah', in K. CRIM (ed.), The Interpreter's Dictionary of the Bible, Supplementary Volume (Nashville, 1976), 317–28.

[53] Though $bē^ɔdayin$ may have sequential significance, it need not if other factors indicate otherwise; cf. KEIL ad loc. RUDOLPH's textual conjectures are therefore unnecessary.

he chose not to reveal in detail. This was possibly because it showed up the Jews in a genuinely bad light,[54] unlike the patently absurd accusations of vv. 12–16.

The second half of v. 7 shows that our author had access to a text of the letter which he again summarizes. Analogy with other such letters suggests that it would originally have been drafted in Aramaic. It is thus unlikely that we should render the concluding words of the verse by 'and translated into Aramaic'. Rather, $^{\supset a}rāmît$ is a scribal note referring forward to the following verses, exactly as at Dan. 2:4. The preceding words then mean literally 'and the writing of the copy was written in Aramaic, but translated'. In the context, 'translated' must mean from Aramaic into Hebrew. This accounts for the verse's Aramaisms, such as the use of ^{c}al meaning 'to', and it explains why our author continued to use Hebrew in his narrative up to this point 'The writing' ($k^{e}\underline{t}\bar{a}\underline{b}$) refers to the script of the letter; contrast its use at Est. 1:22 with the use of $lāšôn$ there for 'language'. The author makes this comment because he apparently considered it noteworthy that a document in Hebrew should be written in the Aramaic square script rather than the old Hebrew script. As well as furnishing interesting evidence on the time of the transition to the Aramaic script (assuming that the date proposed for our author is correct; see below), it also shows clearly that the author was working directly from the document itself.

The third letter to which our author refers was written in Aramaic, and since he is about to cite it extensively, he switches to the Aramaic language for the brief introduction in v. 8. Its content, of course, comes from the letter's heading. After $k^{e}n\bar{e}m\bar{a}^{\supset}$, 'as follows', we expect the text of the letter itself, but this does not come until vv. 11–16. Instead, we have in vv. 9–10 a fuller list of the names of those who sent the letter. Since it is known from numerous contemporary examples that Aramaic letters could include subscripts, summaries of contents, and addresses, all separate from the main text of the letter, it is plausible to suppose that our author has worked in some of this information here, again indicating that he was working directly from the original document. Aware that the result was not as smooth as could be wished,[55] he then added v. 11a as a

---

[54] Just prior to Xerxes' accession, Egypt rebelled against her Persian overlord, obliging Xerxes to pass through Palestine during 485 B.C.; cf. A. T. OLMSTEAD, History of the Persian Empire (Chicago, 1948), 227–8 and 234–6. If this explains the archaeological evidence for disturbances at a number of sites at this time (cf. G.E. WRIGHT, Shechem [London, 1965], 167–69), it would be tempting to link the accusation against the Jews with these events, though their specific cause remains unknown; cf. A.F. RAINEY, 'The Satrapy "Beyond the River"', AJBA 1/2 (1969), 51–78.

[55] In the Masoretic Text this is made even worse by the inclusion of $^{\supset e}\underline{d}ayin$ at the start of v. 9, after which we expect a verb. RV and RSV supply 'wrote', but this makes the passage into a doublet of v. 8 for no apparent reason. Others tacitly omit the word (e.g. NEB and NIV), while A. BERTHOLET, Die Bücher Esra und Nehemia (KHAT; Tübingen and Leipzig, 1902), 15, regards it as a confused doublet of $dyny^{\supset}$, and RUDOLPH emends it to $dî \, ^{\supset}innûn$, 'They (the senders) were'. On the approach adopted above, we do not expect anything here. It may therefore be tentatively suggested that, owing to the identical openings of vv. 8 and 9,

recapitulation to avoid ambiguity, and did no more in v. 11b than summarize the letter's formal heading, since he had already included the substance of the heading in his introduction.

The final letter, vv. 17–22, is given only a three-word introduction by our author. In v. 23 he states that its commands were carried out, but the lack of detail indicates that he had no other source for this account. The concluding words, 'by force and power', merely add to the negative portrayal of the community's enemies which the whole section has been designed to illustrate.

(ii) Ezra 5:1–6:18

The author's method of composition through the remainder of the Aramaic section continues unchanged. He here has two primary sources in the form of a letter from Tattenai to Darius (5:6–17) and the reply of Darius, which included the copy of the edict of Cyrus (6:3–12).[56] (The possibility of a third source for 6:15 is suggested below.) Moderately extensive as it is, the narrative framework which makes up the rest of this section can then all be explained without difficulty. Since the letters were in Aramaic, he continued to use the same language for his own composition.

(a) 5:1–2 is based on a knowledge of the books of Haggai and Zechariah. (They will also have supplied the dates in 4:5 and 24.) Thus Zerubbabel and Jeshua are mentioned here by name, but not later. In the letters themselves the Jews deal collectively with Tattenai, following the terms of Cyrus's permission to them. It would not have assisted their case to refer to Zerubbabel, since he is not mentioned in either 1:2–4 or 6:3–5. Our author's narrative thus follows closely the pattern of his sources.

(b) 5:3–4 is a narrative summary constructed directly out of Tattenai's own first-hand account in the letter which follows. The verbal parallels are so exact (compare 3a with 6a, 3b with 9b and 4 with 10a) that it would be absurd to look further for any source. Indeed, it may well be that the impossible first person plural $^{a}marnā^{\gamma}$ in v. 4, which most commentators emend to the expected third person, is to be explained by the author's failure on this occasion to make the necessary change to narrative form when copying from Tattenai's own account in v. 9.

(c) 5:5. While this verse does not in the same way arise verbally out of the following letter or its reply (though its reference to 'the elders of the Jews' clearly does), yet it is a not unreasonable inference from their contents. It is thus an exaggeration on Rudolph's part to say that it gives us information not

---

it came to be misplaced in the course of transmission from the start of v. 8, where it fits naturally and where its loss has created a certain abruptness.

[56] The authenticity of these letters, as with those of chapter 4, has here to be assumed. The many arguments in favour of this have been frequently rehearsed, and are now generally accepted.

otherwise available to us, as though some alternative source or first-hand knowledge underlay it. It is editorial in composition, commenting theologically on the narrative just recorded.

(d) 5:6 is a narrative heading to the letter, written up on the basis of the letter's own address. This explains why the address in the letter itself (v. 7b) is shorter than we should otherwise have expected: material already included here has been omitted there in order to avoid unnecessary repetition.

(e) 6:1–2. The position here is similar. The substance of this narrative must have been included in Darius's reply which follows (and cf. 5:17). Its inclusion here, and consequent omission from the transcript of the letter, helps account for the otherwise rough juxtaposition of vv. 3–5 and 6–12. The full heading to the letter, which of course stood before v. 3, left no doubt that the decree of Cyrus was a citation within the body of the letter, followed by the transition word $k^{e^c}an$ (v. 6), with repetition of the names of the addressees; cf. 7:25 for a partial parallel. Though our author's compositional method has slightly obscured this, there is no justification for inventing a completely new heading before v. 6, such as 'Then King Darius issued this order' (NEB).

(f) 6:13–14 records the prompt execution of Darius's orders, a reasonable inference by the author. Again he largely uses the vocabulary of the letter itself; cf. the names and titles in v. 13, $'osparnā'$ $'^abadû$ ('acted with all diligence'), which comes directly from the last two words of the letter, and the title 'the elders of the Jews' (v. 14; see above). The theological outlook of v. 14b[57] can hardly be divorced from that of v. 22, which undoubtedly comes from the final editor, while the reference to Haggai and Zechariah refers back to 5:1 as an *inclusio* around the work of temple building. Finally, confirmation of this position may be found in the additional observation that absolutely nothing is recounted of the many aspects of the rebuilding of the temple which we would have expected had further sources been available. The absence of such information, as with the 'gap' between chapters 1 and 2 noted earlier, is suggestive of a later author working with only the sources which he cites so fully.

(g) 6:15–18. The account of the dedication of the temple is written in our author's characteristic style and reflects his outlook. Again, there is no need to postulate the use of a source for most of this: reflection on the dedication of the first temple (1 Kgs 8; 2 Chron. 5–7) in the light of the practices of the author's own day (see further section E below) combined with general probability are sufficient to explain the material found here.

The only point not immediately covered by these considerations is the date of the completion of the temple (6:15). This, it may be granted, could well have been preserved in an inscription or temple record known to the author. Inscribed

---

[57] The curious reference to Artaxerxes has been variously explained. If our author wrote with knowledge of Ezra 7 ff., as argued here, he may have included it in anticipation of 7:15–24 and 27.

bricks are well known from buildings of the Achaemenid period,[58] and this might help explain the otherwise awkward repetition of $d^e n\bar{a}h$, 'this', in vv. 15–17.

At the same time, however, if 1 Esdras is correct in reading the twenty-third rather than the third of Adar, the date could have been calculated by the author on quite other grounds. The twenty-third day of Adar 'may be due to a desire to have what may be regarded as a liturgically apt date. Adar is the twelfth month, and if the dedication festival was an eight-day festival then the new year could be celebrated afterwards'.[59]

(iii) Ezra 6:19–22

Ezra 5:1–6:18 has centred exclusively around the building of the second temple, and for reasons already noted the author phrased his narrative joins between the primary sources in Aramaic. For this final paragraph of his composition, however, he reverts to Hebrew, the language with which he began. Apart from the fact that he may have considered it more fitting to round off his narrative in the traditional language of his people, he probably also wished to set this paragraph aside slightly from the account of the temple building itself. The concluding note about the Lord changing the attitude of the ruling king[60] towards the Jews so that he supported them so exactly matches the theological outlook of 1:1 (and others have noted similarities between this paragraph and the end of Ezra 3) that these verses should be regarded as a concluding statement to Ezra 1–6 as a whole, not just to the events of 520–515 B.C. The switch in languages is thus not to be regarded as in any way indicative of a source division. The same author remains responsible throughout. (It hardly needs saying that no source was required for the author to know how to describe a celebration of the Passover; see further section E below.)

Many problems relating to Ezra 4:6–6:22 undoubtedly remain. Our survey of compositional technique is nevertheless sufficient to show an author using the same methods, and sharing the same outlook, as the one responsible for Ezra 1–2. Someone already familiar with Ezra 7–10 and Nehemiah in its present form has here worked at a later time with only some official records and knowledge of earlier Biblical texts to reconstruct the history of the building of the second temple.

---

[58] Cf. DE VAUX, 'Decrees', 69 for references.

[59] L. H. BROCKINGTON, Ezra, Nehemiah and Esther (The Century Bible, N.S., London, 1969), 85; see also J. MORGENSTERN, VT 5 (1955), 63.

[60] The reference must be to Darius, though R. A. BOWMAN, IB III, 621f., surprisingly thinks that Artaxerxes is intended. No fully satisfactory explanation has been offered as to why he is called 'the king of Assyria'. Perhaps the phrase must be regarded as a stereotyped description of a foreign ruler, since Babylon inherited the Assyrian empire, and Persia the Babylonian. Although it was eventually Babylon which came to have this symbolic value (e.g. 1 Pet. 5:13; Rev. 14:18; 18:2), Neh. 9:32 lends some support to the view that in this earlier period that position was held by Assyria.

D. Ezra 3:1–4:5

The last part of Ezra 1–6 to be examined is 3:1–4:5. This passage is different from those already considered in that no official documents appear to be cited. The question of the method of composition must thus be approached rather differently.

Apart from a few extremely radical proposals,[61] most treatments of this section have fallen under one of two headings. On the one hand, there are those who understand its form as that of straightforward historical narrative and who simply read off the historical setting as being identical with the literary setting. On the other hand, there are those who take more seriously the apparent links with Haggai and Zech. 1–8, particularly as regards the leadership of the community. They therefore ascribe the whole account to 520 B.C., parallel with chapters 5–6. It is thus regarded as a Hebrew source complementary to the later Aramaic one.[62]

A decisive step towards breaking this *impasse* was taken, in my view, by Talmon[63] when he identified 4:4–5 as a 'summary notation'. He defines this literary device as one which 'recapitulate(s) the contents, and thus also delineate(s) the extent of a preceding textual unit'. (He cites as other examples Ezra 6:13–14; Neh. 12:26 and 13:29b–31.) On this view, the reference in 4:4 to the people of the land making the Jews afraid to build does not mark a new step in the historical narrative, but rather recapitulates the earlier statement of 3:3, while 4:5b implies that no work at all was done on the temple until the second year of Darius. In other words, 4:4–5 will be the author's way of explaining that 3:1–6 refers to an altar dedication in the reign of Cyrus, that for fear of the peoples of the land no building was undertaken at that time, and that 3:7–4:3 describes the start of the work in the time of Darius.

Turning now to the substance of the narrative we find that there is virtually nothing which demands the use of a source other than those which we already know lay at his disposal. Two possible exceptions to this apparently sweeping claim will be discussed later. Rather, what we have here is a more extended example of the same narrative technique already noted as the author's own in the verses for which he himself was responsible in chapter 1, namely a typological comparison between the events he describes and similar ones earlier in Israel's history. In chapter 1, he drew on the Exodus accounts; here, he draws comparisons, both by direct verbal allusion and more generally, with the building of the

---

[61] E. g. J. GOETTSBERGER, 'Über das III. Kapitel des Ezrabuches', Journal of the Society for Oriental Research 10 (1926), 270–80.

[62] Cf. EISSFELDT, Introduction, 543: 'It must here be observed that the source postulated for i, 1–iv, 5 overlaps substantially in material this extract from a source in iv, 6–vi, 18'.

[63] S. TALMON, IDBS, 322.

first temple under Solomon. Not every example is equally striking, but since some are beyond doubt it is reasonable to include also more distant parallels.

The gathering of the necessary materials in 3:7 reminds us at once of 1 Chron. 22:2-4 and 2 Chron. 2:7-15. The verbal parallels are sufficiently striking to demonstrate that there is a conscious allusion to the earlier description, and that it is not just due to historical necessity. They include the shipment by sea to Joppa (cf. 2 Chron. 2:15), the payment of food, drink, and oil (cf. 2 Chron. 2:9), and the bracketing together of the Sidonians and the Tyrians (cf. 1 Chron. 22:4).

The date for the start of the work in v. 8 takes this typological comparison further, for Solomon also began to build 'in the second month'; cf. 2 Chron. 3:2. It has generally been assumed that 'the second year' refers to the time after the Jews' return from the exile, but the qualifying phrase 'of their coming to the house of God at Jerusalem' suggests otherwise. Our editor speaks directly of coming 'from Babylon to Jerusalem' (1:11) when it is his intention to refer simply to the return from exile. Comparison of 3:8 with 2:68, where the same words occur, suggests by contrast that he retains this fuller expression for those times when the community took some decisive new initiative with regard to the temple cult. One such step was the altar dedication in the reign of Cyrus described in 3:1-6. In the context of 3:7, however, v. 8 is best understood to mean a second initiative and that they therefore began the actual building two years after they first turned their attention seriously to the question of the building by starting to collect the necessary materials. Now, since the building itself took some five years (compare 6:15 with 4:24 and 5:1), the whole operation took seven years. This is the same time that Solomon took to build the first temple (1 Kgs 6:38).

Still in v. 8, the appointment of Levites 'to have the oversight of the work of the house of the Lord' uses exactly the same phrase as 1 Chron. 23:4, where David is making arrangements for the building of the first temple.

The religious celebration which accompanies the foundation laying in vv. 10-11 closely echoes the description of the dedication of Solomon's temple; see especially 2 Chron. 5:11ff. and 7:6 for some particularly striking verbal parallels.

To this dependence upon the account of the building of the first temple we may add the influence of other material to which we know the author had access. Ezra 3:1, we have already seen, was drawn, with only essential contextual changes, from Neh. 7:72b-8:1, while many of the details concerning the religious practices in the following verses will simply be those of the writer's own day, based on the Pentateuch, and projected back into an earlier time. Ezra 3:12-13 is no doubt based, as has long been recognized, on Hag. 2:3. From Haggai too, of course, comes much of the outline of the narrative: the delay until the reign of Darius in commencing the building, the prominence of the foundation laying (cf. Hag. 2:18), and so on. This had to be combined by the author, however, with the contradictory assertion of Ezra 5:16 which suggested that some early work was done on the temple site. He compromised (possibly with some further knowledge; see below) by having the altar built and dedicated immediately after the initial return.

It is instructive to note how various details of the narrative are also dependent upon other texts. Thus 3:10 refers to 'the Levites, the sons of Asaph'. In the author's own day, all the temple singers were classed as Levites, but they were divided into three families. At the same time, the list of the singers in 2:41 mentions only the sons of Asaph amongst those who returned home (though it does not appear to regard them as Levites). Regarding both elements as historically determinative, it is not difficult to see how the author then arrived at his construction of this passage.

Similarly, the entry into Levitical service at the age of twenty (3:8) compares with 1 Chron. 23:24 and 27, but contrasts with 23:3 and Num. 4:3. Here again, the practices of the writer's own day (see further below) have influenced his reading of earlier texts.

Enough has been said to offer by way of summary the suggestion that the author's aim in this passage is to write a typological account of the founding of the second temple. For this purpose he has juxtaposed events from the reigns of Cyrus (3:1–6) and Darius (3:7ff.). This second half of his account is thus avowedly parallel with chapters 5–6. With the same purpose as in chapter 1, though with a different method, he has thus presented in this passage a highly theological interpretation of the events which he is later to record in a more matter-of-fact style on the basis of his sources.

The possibility of two exceptions to this conclusion was alluded to above. The first is the apparently surprising reference to Esarhaddon in 4:2. Nowhere else in the Old Testament is he said to have been responsible for settling foreigners in Israel; 2 Kgs 17 refers only to a much earlier settlement by Sargon II. This evidence of a later settlement is thus unlikely to be pure fabrication. It finds support in Isa. 7:8, whose reference to sixty-five years may well bring us down to Esarhaddon's reign.[64] Similarly, the historical texts recording the events of his reign[65] testify to his successful campaigns in the west and so suggest a plausible setting for a policy of resettlement.

Ezra 4:1–3 is thus probably based on some earlier source. It may be tentatively suggested that this was one of the two letters which the author only summarized in 4:6–7. The self-designation of another group in 4:10 favours the view that the information in 4:2b could have been similarly preserved, while the whole incident might have been recounted as part of a historical retrospect on Judaean-Samarian relations in the body of the letter (cf. 4:15). It is not difficult to see how the substance of 4:1–3 could have contributed to such an accusation, nor why the admitted foreign origins of the group in question led our author,

---

[64] Cf. R.E. CLEMENTS, Isaiah 1–39 (NCB; Grand Rapids and London, 1980), 85.
[65] ANET, 289–94.

writing much later under the impact of the more exclusive attitudes which then prevailed, to rewrite the account as he has and to justify it so elaborately in the rest of chapter 4.

The second possibility of an additional source relates to the involvement of Zerubbabel and Jeshua in the restoration of the altar in 3:1–6. The tension which this establishes with 5:16 suggests some external constraint, and it may be significant that only here are the leaders listed in the order Jeshua–Zerubbabel. On the other hand, the author may have been attracted by their prominence in the later rebuilding and have wanted a member of the Davidic family to be involved from the start. Similarly Jeshua may be listed first because of the religious nature of the ceremony. Finally, the author will have believed that they were at least present at the time on the basis of a 'flat' historical reading of 2:1–2. It is thus prudent not to decide too hastily in this particular instance. Either way, it is not damaging to our overall hypothesis.

E. Provenance and Purpose

We come finally to attempt a closer determination of the circle and date to which our author belonged. Clearly, our conclusions must be based primarily upon those parts of his work which we have attributed directly to his own hand. These are not, as it has turned out, very extensive. It should further be noted that considerable difficulties always confront attempts to identify authors and dates of historical narratives in antiquity if, as in the present case, the account does not come down to the author's own day. The somewhat speculative nature of this final step in our discussion is thus fully acknowledged. Nevertheless, there are a few clues in the relevant passages which at least enable us to hazard a suggestion which adequately accounts for the phenomena.

On the one hand, some connection with the Books of Chronicles seems likely. As Braun has observed (see above), this is most striking in chapter 3, where much of the comparison with the building of the first temple is explicitly dependent on the Chronicler's version.

On the other hand, the differences between the two works are so great that a simple identification of the author of each remains impossible, in my judgement. The spirit of the continuation of chapter 3 in 4:1–3, for instance, is utterly foreign to the outlook of the Chronicler. This and other evidence has been presented elsewhere[66] and need not be reiterated here.

In seeking to explain this curious state of affairs, attention may be drawn to the hypothesis that approximately one generation after their composition the

---

[66] *Israel in the Books of Chronicles*, 7–82; *1 and 2 Chronicles* (NCB; Grand Rapids and London, 1982).

Books of Chronicles were subjected to a light redaction by someone of decidedly pro-priestly leanings. His hand is most clearly to be seen in parts of 1 Chron. 23–27, though other passages too may be attributed to him.[67] I have argued that late in the Achaemenid period the secession of a number of the more 'open-minded' priests from Jerusalem to join with other groups at Shechem to found what later became known as the Samaritan community led to a radical reorganization of the priesthood in Jerusalem.

Inevitably, those who remained in Jerusalem will have been more rigorously exclusive than those who departed. The Chronicler's mediating position had been rejected, and attitudes had begun to polarize. To identify the author of Ezra 1–6 with this group would explain both his links with Chronicles and yet his distance from its essential outlook. His purpose in writing will have been, of course, to justify the Jerusalem temple of his day and its cult as the legitimate successors of pre-exilic Israel; hence his extensive drawing of typological comparisons with earlier periods of Israel's history, and the considerable body of evidence, which it has not been possible to present here, testifying to his concern to draw lines of continuity between the first and second temple communities.[68] He will have stood in particular amongst the successors of Ezra and Nehemiah themselves, and thus have had an interest in providing an introduction to the account of their work[69] which endeavoured to link it with the Books of Chronicles. His polemical rejection of northern participation in Ezra 4 is also partly explained on this view.

One or two points of detail strongly support this identification, and further clarify it by showing that the author came a little later than the pro-priestly reviser of Chronicles himself. First, we have already noted that the entry of Levites into service at the age of twenty (Ezra 3:8) is found in 1 Chron. 23:24b and 27. The Chronicler himself in the same chapter (v. 3) puts the age at 30. Now 1 Chron. 23:24b and 27 are clearly recognized not just as belonging to the later pro-priestly revision, but in fact as being subsequent glosses to it.[70] (The reviser

---

[67] Cf. 'The Origins of the Twenty-four Priestly Courses: a Study of 1 Chronicles xxiii-xxvii', VTSup 30 (1979), 251–68 (see above, 126–40), and the Commentary referred to in the previous note.

[68] For just one example with reference to Ezra 1, cf. P. R. ACKROYD, 'The Temple Vessels – A Continuity Theme', VTSup 23 (1972), 166–81.

[69] It should, perhaps, be mentioned that the opening words of Ezra 7:1 ('Now after these things') will also have been added by our author. It is not clear whether he was fully aware of the large interval of time which he thus bridged; for him, the journey of Ezra was the next important event in the development of his community after the dedication of the second temple; cf. GUNNEWEG, 'Zur Interpretation der Bücher Esra-Nehemia', 155. Syntactically, the phrase is not closely integrated into the following sentence.

[70] Cf. 'The Origins', 257f., especially n. 19. It is perhaps worth pointing out that all the conclusions worked out in that article were complete long before I turned my attention to Ezra 1–6, and that the identification suggested here for the author of the latter occurred to me only after I had independently completed my basic analysis of these chapters.

himself does not deal with this issue at all.) Inasmuch as Ezra 3:8 agrees with them, a development slightly beyond the position of the pro-priestly redaction is suggested.

Secondly, the ascription in Ezra 6:18 of the priestly and Levitical divisions to 'the book of Moses' (though no direct justification for this is to be found in the Pentateuch) could not come from the Chronicler, for he consistently makes David responsible for them. The pro-priestly redactor loosens this close association with David throughout his annotations to 1 Chron. 23-27 and although at no point does he go so far as Ezra 6:18, he comes close to it on occasions; cf. 1 Chron. 24:1-2.[71] This too suits a slight development from the pro-priestly redactor of Chronicles, though it moves within the same circles.

Finally, it is difficult not to suppose that the account of the celebration of the Passover in Ezra 6:19-22 has been written with a sidelong glance at the Chronicler's accounts of the Passovers of Hezekiah and Josiah (2 Chron. 30 and 35), both of which also followed temple restorations of a sort.[72] However, there is an important difference in that on the earlier occasion the priests came in for a measure of criticism by comparison with the Levites because 'they had not sanctified themselves in sufficient number' (2 Chron. 30:3; cf. 29:34), whereas here the preparedness of the priests is emphasized first (Ezra 6:20). This may be taken as an indication of where the author's sympathies lay.

If the pro-priestly reviser of Chronicles has been correctly dated at the very end of the Achaemenid period, it follows that the author of Ezra 1-6 came early in the Hellenistic period. It is an attractive speculation, therefore, to suppose that his composition was intended in part as counter-propaganda to the building at this time of the first Samaritan temple on Mount Gerizim.[73]

---

[71] In view of the comparatively late date of our author and the gradual shifting back of responsibility for the priestly courses from David to Moses, I have difficulty in following HOUTMAN here when (together with other evidence) he suggests that 'the book of Moses' is not the Pentateuch, but some other work unknown to us; cf. C. HOUTMAN, 'Ezra and the Law', OTS 21 (1981), 91-115. More likely we see a reflection here of the development of the far-reaching methods of Biblical interpretation which we know continued long after the close of the Biblical period.

[72] The points of similarity are analysed by J.B. SEGAL, The Hebrew Passover from the Earliest Times to A.D. 70 (London, 1963).

[73] Cf. R.J. BULL and G.E. WRIGHT, 'Newly Discovered Temples on Mt. Gerizim in Jordan', HTR 58 (1965), 234-7; R.J. BULL, 'The Excavation of Tell er-Ras on Mt. Gerizim', BA 31 (1968), 58-72. Josephus, Ant. xi. 306ff. (especially 324), also dates the building of this temple to the early Hellenistic period, but his account is so self-contradictory on a number of points that its evidence cannot be accepted at face value; cf. H.H. ROWLEY, 'Sanballat and the Samaritan Temple', Men of God (London and Edinburgh, 1963), 246-76; S. MOWINCKEL, Studien zu dem Buche Ezra-Nehemia, II: Die Nehemia Denkschrift (Oslo, 1964), 104-18; H.G. KIPPENBERG, Garizim und Synagoge: Traditionsgeschichtliche Untersuchungen zur samaritanischen Religion der aramäischen Periode (RVV, 30; Berlin, 1971), 50-57; R.J. COGGINS, Samaritans and Jews: The Origins of Samaritanism Reconsidered (Oxford, 1975), 93-9.

F. Concluding Summary

In this article we have sought to establish that a single author was responsible for Ezra 1–6. Ezra 7–Neh. 13 already lay before him in substantially its present form. Further, he had at his disposal a number of primary sources of such a nature as could well have been preserved in an official archive, and he also knew several other relevant works which are now found in the Old Testament. There is nothing in Ezra 1–6 which cannot be explained on this minimal assumption. Indeed, the consistent editorial handling of primary sources throughout these chapters precludes any intermediate stage in the composition. The author cannot be identified with the Chronicler. Rather, he may be a member of the circle which had earlier subjected the Books of Chronicles to pro-priestly redaction. If so, he probably worked within a few decades of the introduction of Hellenistic rule into Palestine with the purpose of justifying the legitimacy of the Jerusalem temple and its cult after a possible split in its priesthood, the establishment of the Samaritan community and the first moves to build a temple on Mount Gerizim.

17. The Belief System of the Book of Nehemiah

Two reservations need to be expressed about the title prescribed for this article. In the first place, it is superficially curious to focus attention on the book of Nehemiah in isolation from Ezra. In the view of the overwhelming majority of scholars, the separation of this single work into two books is to be ascribed to the activity of later translators only, and it overlooks the deliberate editorial intent to fuse together the roles of the two eponymous reformers, not least in the climactic chapters 8–10.[1] It is true that in recent years one or two voices have been raised in support of the view that these two books were written in separation from one another from the start,[2] but it may be doubted whether this opinion will attract widespread support. While it is, of course, possible to proceed from a literary point of view by selecting any given stretch of writing for analysis, we shall need to be careful, therefore, before we extrapolate from an artificially determined selection towards wider historical conclusions of a sort which this volume is interested to investigate.[3]

In the second place, even greater difficulties attend the use of the language of belief systems in relation to a text, and especially a text as complex as that of Nehemiah. Only people can have a belief system, and there are well-known pitfalls in seeking to move direct from text to history.[4] Even assuming that this

---

[1] For a summary introduction to the arguments in support of this position, see my Ezra, Nehemiah (WBC, 16; Waco, 1985), xxi–xxiii.

[2] See J.C. VANDERKAM, 'Ezra-Nehemiah or Ezra and Nehemiah?', in E. ULRICH et al. (eds.), Priests, Prophets and Scribes: Essays on the Formation and Heritage of Second Temple Judaism in Honour of Joseph Blenkinsopp (JSOTSup, 149; Sheffield, 1992), 55–75; D. KRAEMER, 'On the Relationship of the Books of Ezra and Nehemiah', JSOT 59 (1993), 73–92, reprinted in J.C. EXUM (ed.), The Historical Books: A Sheffield Reader (Sheffield, 1997), 303–21. To these must now be added B. BECKING's contribution to the volume in which this article first appeared: B. BECKING and M.C.A. KORPEL (eds.), The Crisis of Israelite Religion: Transformation of Religious Tradition in Exilic and Post-Exilic Times (OTS, 42; Leiden, 1999).

[3] One mitigating factor in the present instance may be that the language of belief systems is adopted from the field of cultural anthropology (see BECKING's article), a field which has also provided the model of cultural revitalization. It has been suggested elsewhere that this model may help explain the superficially curious ordering of material in the book of Nehemiah; see K.D. TOLLEFSON and H.G.M. WILLIAMSON, 'Nehemiah as Cultural Revitalization: An Anthropological Perspective', JSOT 56 (1992), 41–68, reprinted in EXUM (ed.), The Historical Books, 322–48.

[4] While the depth of these 'pits' varies from one text to another, they are not absent even from a text which stands as close to history as the Nehemiah Memoir. Though in exaggerated

hurdle can be overcome, we shall need to be clear whose belief systems we are investigating, whether those of Nehemiah himself, or those of the authors of the other sources which have gone into the make-up of the book, or those of the final editor of the work which we now have. In terms of literary study, the work of the final editor is usually the most straightforward to approach, but in terms of our present concern it seems to me to be the most elusive. Since, moreover, it is strongly tied to the question of the relationship between the books of Ezra and Nehemiah already mentioned, I shall have least to say about it. Finally, it remains almost completely unknown to what extent the belief systems reflected in the work of these various authors were shared by others or were regarded as normative by the community at the time.

With these caveats in mind, it seems clear that we must start by separating carefully between the first-person account of Nehemiah himself and the remainder of the material in the book. As I have sought to emphasize elsewhere, for every major achievement for which Nehemiah himself claims credit, there is within the book an alternative account of the same event in which the people as a whole are shown acting in concert under priestly leadership.[5] If this is true, it should be of considerable help to us. Comparison and contrast should add historical depth to the analysis and enable at least one step to be taken towards the disentanglement of core beliefs from individual agendas. It would be too crude simply to distinguish between lay and priestly outlooks. On the one hand Nehemiah was hardly a typical layman of the province; his agenda, at least at the start of his ministry, was strongly influenced by his role as a servant of imperial policy.[6] On the other hand, the remaining material is not simply 'in house' priestly, but rather reflective of the community under priestly leadership; it is thus likely to present what we might call the public face of the priesthood.[7]

---

form, the point is well made by D.J.A. CLINES, 'The Nehemiah Memoir: The Perils of Autobiography', in What Does Eve Do to Help? and Other Readerly Questions to the Old Testament (JSOTSup, 94; Sheffield, 1990), 124–64. By 'taking account of the genre and associated conventions of this kind of writing', J. BLENKINSOPP arrives at rather more conservative conclusions; see 'The Nehemiah Autobiographical Memoir', in: S.E. BALENTINE and J. BARTON (eds.), Language, Theology, and the Bible: Essays in Honour of James Barr (Oxford, 1994), 199–212.

[5] See Ezra, Nehemiah, *passim*, and especially 'Post-Exilic Historiography', in R.E. FRIEDMAN and H.G.M. WILLIAMSON (eds.), The Future of Biblical Studies: The Hebrew Scriptures (Semeia Studies; Atlanta, 1987), 189–207 (above, 199–211). This account of the material still seems preferable to me to the alternative suggestion of D.R. DANIELS to uncover 'a third source in which Ezra and Nehemiah both appear and which spans Neh 8:1–11:24; perhaps also 12:27–30; and less certainly 11:25–12:26; 12:44–13:3'; see D.R. DANIELS, 'The Composition of the Ezra-Nehemiah Narrative', in Idem et al. (eds.), Ernten, was man sät: Festschrift für Klaus Koch zu seinem 65. Geburtstag (Neukirchen-Vluyn, 1991), 311–28.

[6] This point has been rightly emphasized by K.G. HOGLUND, Achaemenid Imperial Administration in Syria-Palestine and the Missions of Ezra and Nehemiah (SBLDS, 125; Atlanta, 1992), whose work on Nehemiah in this regard seems more convincing than that on Ezra.

[7] This aspect of the book of Nehemiah is perhaps overlooked by KRAEMER (above, n. 2) in his attempt to drive a priestly versus lay wedge between the books of Ezra and Nehemiah.

A. The Nehemiah Memoir

In order to clarify these areas of overlap, we need to attend first to some features of Nehemiah's own account which are suggestive of a strongly lay type of belief system. Assuming we may afford his account any credence at all, the fact that he had previously been in service at the heart of the imperial court, and so was not much influenced by the Palestinian priesthood, tends to accentuate these features, though they may nevertheless have been shared to some degree also by others in the land whose normal contacts were outside the restrictive circle of the temple personnel themselves.

A number of points deserve mention under this heading. In the first place, Nehemiah seems to have drawn in an unsophisticated manner on the previous national history.[8] Throughout Neh. 4:1–14 (English versions, 7–20), for instance, there are numerous points of contact with the laws for, and descriptions of, the so-called 'holy war' as represented particularly in Deuteronomic texts.[9] Kellermann[10] lists the following series of connections: the enemy band together against Jerusalem; the people pray before arming themselves; the human resources for defence are slender; the forces are a conscript militia rather than a standing army; the leader proclaims God's involvement in the battle[11] and calls for faith and fearlessness; the enemy is discouraged; and the trumpet blast is the signal for battle. It is true that some of these elements do not serve quite the same function as in the earlier, classical texts, but that is only to be expected. This is the language of the laity drawing a general analogy between the present situation and some well-known stories from his people's national history. His aim is simply to encourage them by a straightforward appeal to past victories, not to engage in scribal exegesis.

The same point can be made even more forcefully in the case of Nehemiah's appeal to the example of Solomon in connection with mixed marriages:

'Was it not on account of such women that Solomon, king of Israel, sinned? Among the many nations there was no king like him; he was loved by God, and God made him king over all Israel; yet even he was led into sin by foreign wives.' (Neh. 13:26)

---

[8] I have deliberately omitted reference to 13:1–3 under this heading because there are serious doubts as to whether it was part of Nehemiah's own first-person account; see, for instance, A. H. J. GUNNEWEG, Nehemia (KAT, 19/2; Gütersloh, 1987), 163–4.

[9] See the standard collection and analysis of motifs in G. VON RAD, Der Heilige Krieg im alten Israel (AThANT, 20; Zürich, 1951) = Holy War in Ancient Israel (Grand Rapids, 1991). The subject has been frequently discussed since; we need note here only the continuing literary use of this material well after our period, as analysed, for instance, by A. RUFFING, Jahwekrieg als Weltmetapher: Studien zu Jahwekriegstexten des chronistischen Sondergutes (SBB, 24; Stuttgart, 1992).

[10] U. KELLERMANN, Nehemia: Quellen, Überlieferung und Geschichte (BZAW, 102; Berlin, 1967), 18; see too BLENKINSOPP, 'Nehemiah Autobiographical Memoir', 205.

[11] Note especially the stereotypical words of encouragement, 'our God will fight for us', in 4:14 [20]; cf. Exod. 14:14; Deut. 1:30; 3:22; 20:4; Josh. 10:14, 42; 23:10.

This appeal can be contrasted with the exegetically far more elaborate approach of Ezra in Ezra 9:1–2,[12] where a number of legal texts are combined in order to seek legitimation for the drastic policy of divorce. It is true that Nehemiah appeals to one of the same scriptural passages as does Ezra (Neh. 13:25; Ezra 9:2, 12; cf. Deut. 7:3), but the sophistication of Ezra's legal argumentation is lacking, whereas conversely Nehemiah's simplistic appeal to the negative example of Solomon, which seems to be his trump rhetorical card, is absent from Ezra. For a lay person, a simple reference to a well-known story is more effective, for being more readily intelligible, than legalistic niceties.

Secondly, this same uncomplicated approach to religion is reflected in one of Nehemiah's few references to the temple itself. In an obscure incident, Nehemiah rebuffs the devious Shemaiah's attempt to lure him into the sanctuary with the simple words 'Should a man in my position run away? Or who in my state would enter the temple[13] and live?' (Neh. 6:11). While it is true that we should be cautious before drawing far-reaching conclusions from this brief episode in which no more than the minimum response by Nehemiah is expected or required, the attitude which he adopts seems nevertheless to be just what one might expect from a layman, and it finds many parallels even today in the attitudes adopted towards sacred space. He knows that the temple is off limits for him, and that is the end of the matter. Priestly distinctions between the sacred and the profane or the varying degrees of holiness are not his concern.

Thirdly, a typically lay approach is also taken by Nehemiah with regard to some of the fundamental institutions of religion in the reforms which he undertook during his second term as governor. His attitude towards the sabbath in Neh. 13:15–21 is a good example. It is probable that by this time sabbath observance was a distinguishing feature of Jewish culture, and thus important in terms of the community's sense of self-identity. Nehemiah's concern in putting an end to the abuse of trading on the sabbath was thus likely motivated by political as much as religious concerns in so far as these can be separated. Certainly, his methods, including ensuring forcefully that foreign traders should not benefit by Jewish cessation of work, demonstrate his appreciation that more than just Jewish observance was at stake, and indeed, the fact that he set some of his own men, and later the Levites, to work on the sabbath to discourage trade testifies that outward observance overrode other considerations in his calculations. It is, furthermore, noteworthy that no theological reasoning is supplied by way of motivation, but

---

[12] For varying analyses, see J. MILGROM, Cult and Conscience: The ASHAM and the Priestly Doctrine of Repentance (SJLA, 18; Leiden 1976), 71–3; M. FISHBANE, Biblical Interpretation in Ancient Israel (Oxford, 1985), 114–23; J. BLENKINSOPP, Ezra-Nehemiah: A Commentary (OTL; London, 1988), 174–7; and my Ezra, Nehemiah, 130–32.

[13] The reference to 'doors' and the climactic parallelism in Shemaiah's 'poetic' oracle in verse 10 clearly indicate that הֵיכָל here refers to the sanctuary proper, not just to the temple precincts in general, contra A.L. IVRY, 'Nehemiah 6, 10: Politics and the Temple', JSJ 3 (1972), 35–45.

rather another appeal to the nation's past history (verse 18; cf. Jer. 17:27; Ezek. 20:12-24). In Nehemiah's understanding, therefore, the sabbath was more a symbol than a dogma, and he responds to defend it accordingly.

Moving back through chapter 13, we may suggest that the same can be said of what at first sight look like more technically cultic concerns. First, he ejects Tobiah and his belongings from one of the temple chambers and restores its use as a repository for the temple vessels, grain offering and incense (13:4-9). Secondly, on discovery that the Levites had had to go back to agricultural labour because they were inadequately supported, he recalls them, arranges for payment of the tithes to be reinstated, and sets up a committee to look after the accounts (13:10-13). In these cases too, it may be suggested, the concern is predominantly with the externals of the cult as symbol. There is nothing in the text to suggest that in the case of the expulsion of Tobiah Nehemiah was motivated by anything other than a sense of outrage that a former opponent had used his family connections to establish himself in the temple, while his concern for the Levites is very much that of the supportive outsider, seeking to ensure that the cult was adequately financed and administered. I am reminded of a story, for whose truth I cannot vouch, concerning the late Sir Winston Churchill. Asked whether he supported the Church of England, he is said to have replied, 'Yes, I support the Church like a flying buttress – holding it up from the outside!' While Nehemiah is certainly portrayed as a man of faith, it would be entirely consistent for him to have viewed the temple and its service as worthy of support in the national interest, but not something about whose inner workings he need bother. That could be safely left to the professionals.

Finally, where did God fit into Nehemiah's belief system? In brief, Nehemiah's God is the one who above all protects his people's interests, both collectively and individually. Collectively, he will give his people success in their enterprise of reasserting Jewish independence and self-respect (2:20; 6:16) and not allow shame to overcome them again (3:36-37 [4:4-5]); he will protect them (4:3 [9]), frustrate the plans of the enemy (4:9 [15]) and fight for them (4: 14 [20]) in times of peril; he is expected to uphold the social cohesion of the community (5:13; 13:25); and his help of his people is recognized by the surrounding nations (6:16). In short, he is portrayed as a God who can be relied upon to act positively in the present as he has in the past. It is not that the lessons of past judgment are completely overlooked, but rather they can be simply learnt in terms of avoiding one or two basic errors into which the previous generations had fallen (cf. 13:18, 26). This seems to reflect the uncomplicated faith of an optimistic nationalist who is confident that God is 'on our side'.

The same outlook characterizes his relationship with the individual, principally Nehemiah himself, of course. God's good hand rests on him to prosper his undertakings (2:8, 18), and he prompts Nehemiah to act in certain ways which are always successful (2:12; 7:5). Conversely, the correct attitude to adopt towards God is to fear him (5:9, 15; 7:2; cf. 4:8 [14], הַנּוֹרָא).

Nehemiah's prayers, including the series of 'remember' formulae, are indicative of this same pragmatic approach to religion: they reflect a belief that God is available to prosper the undertakings of his servants (2:4; 4:3 [9]; 6:9), to reward the good (5:19; 13:14, 22, 31), to punish the wicked (13:29), and to frustrate the plans of those who would oppose them (3:36-37 [4:4-5]; 6:14).

The one apparent exception to this consistent picture is Nehemiah's more extended prayer in Neh. 1:5-11. Many commentators, of course, have argued on a variety of grounds that this prayer was not an original part of the Nehemiah Memoir, but was added by a later editor.[14] If that is correct, it should not be further considered here. But even on the assumption that it is to be ascribed to Nehemiah himself, it in fact serves to strengthen the picture which has emerged above. Although it certainly fits in general terms within the corpus of post-exilic prose prayers, it has several distinctive features, not least form-critically. It has frequently been compared, for instance, with the communal laments, but it lacks the most characteristic feature of that genre – the complaint in its various forms – and it also switches uncharacteristically between first-person singular and plural address. Equally, while many of the elements of which the prayer is comprised have parallels elsewhere, the manner in which they are here combined is unprecedented. In short, the prayer looks like the work of someone imitating a familiar pattern and using stereotypical phraseology, but without a full understanding of the genre's inner dynamic. That does not make it any the less powerful from a religious point of view, but its idiosyncrasies are nevertheless suggestive of lay authorship.

To sum up, Nehemiah's belief system may be characterized as pragmatic and uncomplicated. His overriding concern is for a strong sense of Jewish identity within an accepted imperial framework. The religious history of his people is what has forged that identity, and the paraphernalia of temple, cultic personnel and practices serve the wider goal by offering points of cohesion and focus; their inner workings and theological underpinning are of little interest. He assumes that God's concerns and values coincide with his own, and he acts accordingly. He appears untroubled by the theological problems which the experience of exile raises for others but adopts a simple and straightforward view of religious continuity. While there is no doubting his firm personal faith, it is the faith of a politician for whom the institutions of religion serve and undergird the wider national interests.

---

[14] Earlier discussions are usefully summarized by KELLERMANN, Nehemia, 9-11, with bibliography. More recent commentators continue to adopt differing positions for much the same reasons as their predecessors. My own approach is based on my understanding that the Nehemiah Memoir developed in two stages. At its base lies a report by Nehemiah to the king on his first year in office. Much later, this was reworked by Nehemiah himself, partly in order to claim the credit for a number of reforms which had been undertaken in subsequent years. On this showing, there is no reason why the prayer should not have been part of the Memoir in this revised form; for brief justification, see my Ezra and Nehemiah (Sheffield, 1987), 15-19; Ezra, Nehemiah, xxiv-xxviii *et passim*.

B. Other Material in the Book of Nehemiah

When we turn by way of comparison and contrast to the remaining material in the book, we find ourselves in a somewhat different world. As has already been mentioned, each of the achievements for which Nehemiah claims personal credit finds a parallel in which the people act collectively under priestly and/or levitical leadership, and so we shall look at these passages next. In some cases, the parallel makes little difference for our purposes, so that there is no need to delay over the details. The account of the wall-building in 3:1–32 is a case in point.[15] Since it lacks the rubrics with which it was presumably once accompanied, we cannot speculate as to whether it reflected similar or different motivations for the undertaking of the task by comparison with those urged by Nehemiah. Much the same could be said of the alternative account of the dedication of the wall into which, I have argued elsewhere,[16] has been spliced Nehemiah's own version of the same event (12:27–43).

Somewhat more informative is the alternative account of the repopulation of Jerusalem in 11:1–20.[17] For Nehemiah himself, the whole issue is set within a firmly defensive context (7:1–4), and this may be associated with the imperial policy of militarization which Hoglund suggests Nehemiah was sent to implement.[18] Interestingly, there are some military overtones in the list in 11:3–20 itself, to which Kellermann has drawn attention,[19] and it is not impossible that these are to be related to Nehemiah's concern in some way. However, the introduction to the list in 11:1–2 sets the whole issue in a different light. Lots are cast to choose a tenth of the province's population to settle in 'the holy city', and

---

[15] That this list was not originally compiled by Nehemiah himself seems clear from the facts that its standpoint is that of the task completed, with the 'doors, bolts and bars' of the gates all in place, whereas in Nehemiah's own account this point had explicitly still not been reached by 6:1 (but cf. 7:1), that it is in the third person, unlike Nehemiah's consistently first-person narrative, and that it refers to the local leaders as אַדִּירִים (3:5), a word never encountered in Nehemiah's own lists of leaders (e.g. 2:16). This conclusion does not, of course, rule out the probability that Nehemiah made use of the list for purposes of his own when compiling his memoir.

[16] See Ezra, Nehemiah, 369–71.

[17] That none of this material, including the first two verses, derives from even a rewritten form of the Nehemiah Memoir seems now to be agreed. It is not in his first-person style, and indeed makes no reference to him; several matters of Hebrew style contrast sharply with his, and the basis for deciding who will move to the city differs from his (cf. 7:4–5). For the details, see KELLERMANN, Nehemia, 41–4, with earlier literature; more recently, GUNNEWEG, Nehemia, 140–1; BLENKINSOPP, Ezra-Nehemiah, 322–3; DANIELS, 'Composition', 327.

[18] HOGLUND, Achaemenid Imperial Administration, esp. 208–26.

[19] U. KELLERMANN, 'Die Listen in Nehemia 11 eine Dokumentation aus den letzten Jahren des Reiches Juda?', ZDPV 82 (1966), 209–27. While accepting fully the importance of this feature of the list, I have argued that the dating conclusions which KELLERMANN draws are unjustified; cf. Ezra, Nehemiah, 347–8.

those who thus 'volunteered' are blessed by the people. There are links here with the closing section of the previous chapter, notably the emphasis on tithing and the casting of lots,[20] so that the process is transformed into a sacral act, a tithe for the holy city paralleling the earlier tithe of produce for the holy place. In this small instance, then, we seem to have a mirror image of Nehemiah's belief system. If for him religion was the servant of politics, here a political undertaking has to be justified in the first place as an act of the priestly cult and presented on its terms. It is a priestly outlook which dominates the whole of life.

Finally in this section we need to attend to the pledge in Neh. 10:29-40 [28-39], to some of whose clauses reference has just been made, though it will be found to contain few surprises. The following relevant points are well known and so require little discussion. First, the specific clauses of the pledge have close parallels in the substance of the reforms of Nehemiah in chapters 5 and 13. While the historical consequences to be drawn from this observation remain open for debate, the fact of the overlap is clear, so justifying comparison. Secondly, the general clauses of the pledge specify in their introduction that the people will live in obedience to the law of God as mediated through Moses (10:29-30 [28-29]) and at their close that they will not neglect the house of God (10:40[39]b). These, then, are the overriding principles which should govern life, and it is clear that once again this outlook makes primary what Nehemiah regarded as secondary. Thirdly, however, in order to implement these general pledges in terms of specific practice in the present, some sophisticated exegesis of the law of Moses is needed, and this is precisely what we find, as Clines in particular has well explained.[21] As we saw, Nehemiah's appeals to earlier scripture were for the most part unsophisticated and never extended beyond the haggadic. Here, by contrast, the law is supreme as regulator, not just illustrator, so that the whole text breathes more the atmosphere of halakah. Concomitantly, it is only to be expected that the procedures concerning cultic regulation are much more detailed than anything which we find in Nehemiah's writing; it is an insider's view, unlike his as an outsider.

To conclude on these alternative accounts of Nehemiah's achievements, we find not so much a contradictory as a complementary belief system. Many of the fundamentals, and all the specifics, are the same, from which we may deduce that we are here close to what was deemed to be central to the community's belief system, but there are distinctions of no small moment in the relative weight to be put upon each. It could well be that Nehemiah's priorities were personal, both in the sense that he was clearly very much of an individual in character and more importantly that he alone was charged with a particular

---

[20] See T.C. ESKENAZI, In An Age of Prose: A Literary Approach to Ezra-Nehemiah (SBLMS, 36; Atlanta, 1988), 111-5.

[21] D.J.A. CLINES, 'Nehemiah 10 as an Example of Early Jewish Biblical Exegesis', JSOT 21 (1981), 111-7.

mission by the Persian king which obliged him to adopt several of the local population's standards and values as a tactic to motivate them to co-operate with him. Where differences are to be perceived between these two blocks of material in the book, therefore, it is likely, as was to be expected, that it is what I have called the alternative account which was more typical and widespread. With that provisional conclusion in mind, I turn finally to inquire briefly whether there is any support for it to be found in the work of the book's final redactor.

C. The Final Redactor

Although, as I indicated at the start of this paper, the question of the redactor's viewpoint cannot be fully discussed apart from a consideration also of the book of Ezra, there are perhaps three observations which may be drawn from what I take to be his activity in the book of Nehemiah itself.

First, it is quite obvious that he is responsible for much of the arrangement of the material in the second half of the book. At the start of this section we have in chapter 8 the delayed account of Ezra's reading from the book of the law of Moses, while at its close, from 12:44 to the end, the concern focuses, whether by way of his own composition (probably) at the start of this passage or by way of his use of the final part of the Nehemiah Memoir, on the regular support for the temple cult.[22] These two matters, it will be recalled, were similarly the subject of the opening and closing general statements of intent in the pledge at the end of chapter 10. The values of that pledge are thus given narrative support by the broader framework which has been supplied for it. While it remains the case that the dramatic climax of the book is to be found in the account of the dedication of the wall, where appropriately material from the two major sources has uniquely been woven together, theologically the editor has left a clear marker that the centre of his concern is to be found in the terms of the pledge. Law and temple are thus at the heart of his belief system, and the intricate processes of Ezra's exegesis whereby the latter may be related to the former are accepted. In this sense, Nehemiah's belief system may be said to be corrected, or at least recontextualized, by the redactor.

Secondly, a major concern of the redactor seems to surface in what is most probably a paragraph of his own composition following the account of the dedication of the walls (Neh. 12:44–47).[23] Rather than lingering over the

---

[22] Of course, there are some matters in chapter 13 which go beyond this narrow definition, something which was inevitable given the redactor's method of generally following the material found in his sources in extensive blocks. Despite this, concern for the temple is the major motif even in these verses.

[23] For this literary-critical judgement, together with the devices whereby he has joined

triumphalism of that particular occasion, he hurries straight on to emphasize that regular support for the temple cult was immediately arranged ('On that day'). At least two factors point to the idealized, if not utopian, nature of this paragraph. In the first place, chapter 13 shows how quickly the portrayal of uninterrupted financial contributions and faithful service has to be qualified, and in the second place the implication of verse 47 that this situation had obtained since the first days of the return from exile is contradicted both by the preceding narrative and by the implication of the present paragraph that it was only now that these new arrangements were put in place. But such pedantry misses the point. The redactor's concern is to draw attention to the fact that no reform movement can be said to have succeeded unless it is followed by 'routinization' – the translation of the values of the reform into a new 'steady state' in the regular life of the community. By this device, therefore, he demonstrates clearly what he thinks should be the lasting effects of the events he has recorded. That they focus on the daily service of the temple cult reinforces what we have already seen to be the cornerstone of his belief system.

Finally, it will not have escaped attention that nothing has been said so far of Nehemiah 9, the great prayer of national confession and lament. The origins of this prayer are uncertain, but it clearly derives from circles which are somewhat at variance with the prevailing outlook of most of the remainder of Ezra and Nehemiah, not least in its closing paragraph.[24] While much discussion could be devoted to this, the important question for us in the present context concerns its role in the final form of the book and hence the light it sheds on the redactor's belief system.

That it stands appropriately as a confession following the reading of the law in chapter 8 and before the covenant renewal in chapter 10 is widely agreed.[25] Of greater interest, however, is the fact that the redactor has chosen for this confession a lengthy historical recital. From one point of view, this connects with Nehemiah's own use of his people's past history as a primary medium for establishing present identity. From another point of view, however, the understanding of that history and hence the outlook of this prayer differ sharply from his simple and optimistic presentation. The structure and intercessory focus of the prayer betray an understanding of the present as a continuation of the social, political and religious conditions which had obtained in the land since the time of the Babylonian conquest.[26] It is a mistake to assimilate it to the prevailing

---

this material with the extracts from the Nehemiah Memoir in chapter 13, so inviting a reading of them as part of the process of routinization, see Ezra, Nehemiah, 380–4.

[24] For arguments against pressing this point too far, see J.G. McCONVILLE, 'Ezra-Nehemiah and the Fulfilment of Prophecy', VT 36 (1986), 205–24. Even he, however, recognizes that Nehemiah 9 goes rather further than other passages in these books.

[25] See, for instance, KELLERMANN, Nehemia, 90–92; D.J. McCARTHY, 'Covenant and Law in Chronicles-Nehemiah', CBQ 44 (1982), 25–44.

[26] For the details of this, see my 'Structure and Historiography in Nehemiah 9', in

biblical pattern of exile and restoration; the stance is rather one in which the nation has lost its sovereignty as a result of persistent rebellion against God and now looks to regain its freedom by confession and intercession. It is remarkable that in a work which is so predominantly shaped by the pattern of return from Babylon[27] there is retained this powerful voice of the community which had never been exiled from the land. It suggests that for the redactor who chose to include the prayer, the community's identity was forged not just by past history but also by the continuity of habitation in the land.

In conclusion, it has been possible to detect more than one belief system in the book of Nehemiah, and we have noted elements of similarity and difference between them. Without wishing to press the differences to the point of suggesting that they are incompatible, it is nevertheless apparent that the initially dominant, not to say strident, voice of Nehemiah himself has been significantly modified by the book's final editor in the direction of what I take to be the more widely adopted outlook of the community both at the time and subsequently.

D. ASSAF (ed.), Proceedings of the Ninth World Congress of Jewish Studies, Panel Sessions: Bible Studies and Ancient Near East (Jerusalem, 1988), 117–31 (below, 282–93).

[27] By this I refer principally, of course, to the first return in Ezra 1–2, to Ezra's return in Ezra 7–8, and to Nehemiah's in Neh. 1–2. This motif thus opens each of the major blocks of narrative in the book.

18. Structure and Historiography in Nehemiah 9

Nehemiah 9 relates how, shortly after Ezra's presentation of the law and the celebration of the Feast of Tabernacles, the people of Israel assembled on the twenty-fourth day of the seventh month and were led by the Levites in a long prayer of confession and lament. Whilst there is no good reason to doubt that the chapter is in the literary setting which the editor/author of Ezra-Nehemiah intended for it,[1] it is also probable that this does not coincide with its original historical setting. Not being able to enter into detail about such matters on the present occasion, I would simply venture the suggestion that the narrative introduction (verses 1–5a) is based on an extract from the Ezra source, and may have originally stood between Ezra 10:15 and 16, and that the prayer is of independent origin.[2] At all events, the absence of Ezra from this chapter,[3] the

---

[1] See recently B.S. CHILDS, Introduction to the Old Testament as Scripture (London, 1979), 624–38; A.H.J. GUNNENWEG, 'Zur Interpretation der Bücher Esra-Nehemia – zugleich ein Beitrag zur Methode der Exegese', VTSup 32 (1981), 146–61; D.J.A. CLINES, Ezra, Nehemiah, Esther (NCB; Grand Rapids and London, 1984), 11–12. Contrast the repeated earlier attempts to suggest that the present order is the result either of simple error in the course of textual transmission or at best of late and totally secondary redactional activity; e.g., C.C.TORREY, The Composition and Historical Value of Ezra-Nehemiah (BZAW, 2; Giessen, 1896), 29–34; idem., Ezra Studies (Chicago, 1910), 252–84; W. RUDOLPH, Esra und Nehemia (HAT; Tübingen, 1949), xxii; R.A. BOWMAN, IB, vol. 3, 560; P.P. SAYDON, 'Literary Criticism of the Old Testament: Old Problems and New Ways of Solution', in J. COPPENS, A. DESCAMPS AND É. MASSAUX (eds), Sacra Pagina I, (BETL, 12–13; Gembloux, 1959), 316–24.

[2] For a full discussion of these and related matters, see my Ezra, Nehemiah (WBC; Waco, 1985), 300 ff.

[3] The LXX introduces Ezra at v. 6, and on this basis some commentators have suggested restoring ויאמר עזרא into the admittedly corrupt v. 5. This is implausible, however. i. The evidence of the LXX is worthless, both because it does not relate to this verse, and because it is clearly a secondary addition by someone who thought that because of the present sequence of chapters Ezra must have been present. ii. The restoration is not particularly appropriate in the context. Comparison with Chapter 8 shows that if Ezra were leading the confession he would have featured prominently in the introductory narrative whereas in fact the emphasis throughout is on the Levites, who we therefore expect will lead the prayer. iii. It is normal, and probably correct, to ease the difficulties of v. 5 by restoring ברוך אתה יהוה אלהינו at the start of the prayer. If אתה was spelt defectively, as in v. 6, the consonantal text would be almost identical with the preceding clause, ברכו את־יהוה אלהיכם. Loss by parablepsis is thus plausible, but becomes less likely if ויאמר עזרא is added between the two similar clauses. The alternative proposal of B. STADE, Geschichte des Volkes Israel II (Berlin, 1888), 178, followed by A. BERTHOLET, Die Bücher Esra und Nehemia (KHAT;

18. Structure and Historiography in Nehemiah 9

lack of specific connection between the prayer and the historical circumstances, and the contrast which is thus established between it and the prayers of Ezra 9 and Neh. 1, pose difficulties for the suggestion of Torrey[4] and others that the whole chapter was once part of the Ezra Memoir. These difficulties will be reinforced below. It is thus preferable to treat the prayer separately in the first instance. Ideally, one should then move directly to a discussion of its purpose in Ezra-Nehemiah as a whole freed from the distraction of its hypothetical association with the intermediate stage represented by the Ezra material, but this second stage of discussion will have to be left to another occasion (cf. n. 2).

In order to establish a foothold for our study, it is worth pausing at the outset to ask after the formal type or genre of this prayer.[5] Though it has no precise parallel of which I am aware, it combines five elements which are otherwise familiar in a way that makes this whole passage into a most powerful expression of confession:

1. In a helpful study of Neh. 9, Gilbert[6] has observed that its overall structure is confession followed by prayer, with a link being forged by ועתה at the start of v. 32. Denying that we should look to prophecy[7] or the Psalter (e. g. Pss. 38; 51; 106; 130) for analogies, he draws attention rather to a number of brief examples of this pattern in both individual and collective confessions in the historical books.[8] This suggests that we are dealing here with a form of confession which was rooted deep in Israelite life, though elaborated here under the influence of the cult and of the Law, which has begun to replace God himself as the party against whom sin has been committed.

2. Despite Gilbert's comments, it would be churlish to deny all contact with the Psalter, for the extended historical retrospect invites comparison with a

---

Tübingen and Leipzig, 1902), 73, and H. H. SCHAEDER, Esra der Schreiber (BHT, 5; Tübingen, 1930), 9, that the words were omitted from the MT because such a confession should have been made by the high priest (Lev. 16:21) is misguided. The resultant text takes the confession further away from the high priest: Ezra at least belonged to the high priestly family (Ezra 7: 1–5), whereas the Levites did not.

[4] TORREY, Ezra Studies, 252–84.

[5] Space precludes attention to the question of poetry and prose in Neh. 9 except to say that none of the standard approaches to this issue can do justice to the whole of the passage; e. g., contrast verses 6–7 and 15a–b with 19, and for the general problem compare the provocative remarks of J. L. KUGEL, The Idea of Biblical Poetry (New Haven and London, 1981), especially Chapter 2. Despite the problems, it is helpful to use the language of poetic analysis (such as stanza) and, for convenience, to base our discussion on the line divisions set out in BHS; this does not, however, imply acceptance of other related aspects of Rudolph's analysis in this connection, such as the deletion of v. 22; cf. Esra und Nehemia, 157 and 160.

[6] M. GILBERT, 'La place de la Loi dans la prière de Néhémie 9', in M. CARREZ, J. DORÉ and P. GRELOT (eds.), De la Tôrah au Messie. Mélanges Henri Cazelles (Paris, 1981), 307–16.

[7] Contra H. GUNKEL, Einleitung in die Psalmen, ed. J. BEGRICH (Göttingen, 1933), 131–32.

[8] Cf. Num. 22:34; 1 Sam. 15:24–25; 2 Sam. 24:10; Exod. 10:16–17 (all individual) and Num. 21:7 (without ועתה); Exod. 32:31–32; Judg. 10:15 and 1 Sam. 12:10 (collective).

number of the Psalms.⁹ When this is undertaken, however, the particular similarity of Neh. 9 with Ps. 106 is often observed, for both have a hymnic introduction followed by historical recollection as a vehicle for confession and as a ground on which to base an appeal for mercy. Thus, when we press past historical recital as such to inquire after its purpose on each occasion, it is immediately to the fact of confession in Neh. 9 that we are again drawn.

3. Next, we should observe that Neh. 9 is included by von Rad among the group of texts which he categorizes as 'Doxologies of Judgement.'¹⁰ These texts are characterized in particular by the formula of confession אתה צדיק, and this is found in v. 33 of Neh. 9.¹¹ Its function is to acknowledge, as an act of worship,¹² that God is justified in his judgement on the worshipper. As von Rad's name for this type of prayer makes clear, it constitutes the most exalted, because most objective, form of confession possible.

4. Fourth, it is not without significance that the prayer is introduced in hymnic style, if the usual reconstruction of its opening is accepted (see above, n. 3). After an imperative call to praise God is found in the narrative introduction (קומו ברכו), the prayer itself then opens with a blessing construed in the passive mood (ברוך אתה) and it continues with a jussive (ויברכו). Though there is no formal connection with what follows, such as the use of the causal particle כי, it is clear that the whole of the following historical retrospect is intended to serve as a substantiation in narrative style.

This introduction, we should immediately observe, again reinforces the effectiveness of the confession by setting it in a context of praise. More than that, however, it separates Neh. 9 from most of the other doxologies of judgement (e.g. Ezra 9; Dan. 9) and draws it closer instead not only to Ps. 106, as already noted, but in particular to the doxologies in the book of Amos (4:13; 5:8–9; 9:5–6). According to Crenshaw, these doxologies 'seem to have been used on special days of penitence and confession' during the exilic or early post-exilic period.¹³ If he is right, there is no reason why, in view of the present literary setting of Neh. 9, our author should not have used material drawn directly from its original setting in the cult.

---

⁹ Cf. J. KÜHLEWEIN, Geschichte in den Psalmen (Stuttgart, 1973), 120–25: F.C. FENSHAM, 'Neh. 9 and Pss. 105, 106, 135 and 136. Post-exilic Historical Traditions in Poetic Form', JNSL 9 (1981), 35–51; idem., The Books of Ezra and Nehemiah (NICOT; Grand Rapids, 1982), 223 ff.

¹⁰ Cf. G. VON RAD, 'Gerichtsdoxologie', Gesammelte Studien zum Alten Testament, vol. 2 (Munich, 1973), 245–54.

¹¹ Its occurrence in v. 8 serves a completely different purpose.

¹² We should note the collocation of confession and worship in the introduction at v. 3 (מתודים ומשתחוים ליהוה). This will be especially pertinent if CLINES (192) is right in his suggestion that these words explicitly introduce the first part of the prayer (vv. 5b–31) whilst ויזעקו בקול גדול אל־יהוה (v. 4) introduces the second part (vv. 32–37).

¹³ J.L. CRENSHAW, Hymnic Affirmation of Divine Justice (SBLDS, 24; Missoula, 1975), 143.

5. Finally, the closing verses of the chapter have regularly been compared with the Psalms of communal lament, a form which in this late period came not infrequently to be associated in particular with confession.[14]

We may thus conclude this first part of our discussion with the suggestion that the prayer of Neh. 9 is in origin an independent piece from the post-exilic period. Its historical recital is steeped in the traditions of the people, but its use of these especially for the purpose of national confession makes this passage unusual at the very least. Though it is only a relatively brief portion of text, it thus has a significance all of its own within the total complex of post-exilic historiography. Attention to its literary structure will provide us with further important material which may help us appreciate its attitude towards both history and the future.

Since I am well aware that abstract discussions of literary structure are almost impossible to follow in oral form, I shall here confine myself to working stanza by stanza through the prayer, focusing only on the major points that need to be made and omitting much supplementary detail. In particular, we shall try to note the links which the writer forges between one period of history and another, links which inevitably come to expression in the use of literary devices, but which are based upon a clear conception of the character of God and of his ways with Israel. Finally, we shall need to observe how much of this is recapitulated with particular effect in the prayer's closing petition.

The first three stanzas are relatively straightforward; they deal with creation (v. 6), Abraham (vv. 7–8) and the Exodus (vv. 9–11). It is true that other commentators always include more material in this final section, but this is mistaken. Apart from other considerations which will emerge later, the limits of the stanza are carefully defined at its opening, v. 9a. That line introduces the sufferings in Egypt and God's deliverance at the Red Sea; these two topics are then amplified in the remainder of vv. 9b–11, whilst the substance of v. 12 belongs for equally cogent reasons with what follows.

The first stanza starts with an uncompromising statement of the incomparability of God: אתה־הוא יהוה לבדך. This is explained by reference to creation – so that nothing in heaven or on earth can challenge God's supremacy – and to the fact that the 'host of heaven' (whatever that may be) worships him.

The second stanza, vv. 7–8, starts with the same words as the first – אתה הוא יהוה – but now only as the subject of the following verbs relating to the election and deliverance of Abraham, the change in his name and the making of a covenant with him. There is a studied emphasis here on the fact that it was the creator God who chose Abraham. This stanza also adds something, however, to the description of that God: his dealings with Abraham lead inexorably to the

---

[14] Cf. C. WESTERMANN, 'Struktur und Geschichte der Klage im Alten Testament', ZAW 66 (1954), 44–80 (74f.) = Praise and Lament in the Psalms (Edinburgh, 1981), 165–213 (206).

covenant, whose substance is the promise of the land. And in this connection, emphasis falls on the close of v. 8, that God kept his promise כי צדיק אתה. Since 'righteous' conduct in relation to speech involves complete faithfulness and truth, it follows that God is not only the creator, but one whose character is such that he must fulfil what he has promised. At the same time, the elaboration of the promise of the land in these verses draws into prominence the major focus for the rest of the prayer.[15]

The third stanza, vv. 9–11, deals with God's deliverance of his people from Egypt. Embedded in the heart of this description is another brief formula, comparable with those which we have noted already and which again epitomizes what this section reveals of the character of God: ותעש־לך שם כהיום הזה. God's abiding reputation, therefore, is not just that of mighty creator (v. 6) or gracious promise maker (vv. 7–8) but of saviour who has acted in concrete terms to put his word into effect. This is the third and last stanza of the prayer to speak without qualification of God's achievements for his people; from now on they will be qualified by the accounts of rebellion. This high point is therefore singled out by the phrase כהיום הזה, a confession which contrasts sharply with the evil plight of the people היום in vv. 32 and 36.

The fourth stanza deals with the period of the wilderness wanderings and comprises the whole of vv. 12–21. The commentators have completely failed to observe the careful structure of this long but unified section, and in consequence they have often divided the passage wrongly. Whilst keeping to the theme of the wilderness wanderings, the author abandons strict adherence to the biblical sequence of events in order to present the following scheme:

a. God's gracious provision of
  i. guidance on the journey (the cloud and fire, v. 12);
  ii. good laws for guidance in all aspects of their lives (vv. 13–14);
  iii. material provision for life in the wilderness (v. 15a);
  iv. renewal of the promise of the land (v. 15b).
b. The people's ungrateful rebellion, rejecting both God's laws and his provision in their desire to return to Egypt[16] (vv. 16–18).
c. God's continuing mercy, so that he did not remove the provision made previously, namely
  i. the cloud and fire (v. 19);

---

[15] GILBERT (310) notes 13 occurrences of 'the land' in this prayer and fourteen of the verb 'to give' with God as its subject. See also P.R. ACKROYD, 'God and People in the Chronicler's Presentation of Ezra', in J. COPPENS (ed.), La Notion biblique de Dieu (Louvain, 1976), 145–62.

[16] It is widely believed, and probably correct, that we should emend במרים in v. 17 to במצרים. This is favoured not only by some MS and versional evidence but also in particular by the passage's close dependence on Num. 14:4. A further link with Egypt is established by the use of הזיד in v. 16, a verb which is used only rarely with the sense required here of 'to act arrogantly' but which is used of the Egyptians in v. 10.

ii. his spirit 'to instruct them' (להשכילם,[17] v. 20a);
iii. material provision for life in the wilderness (vv. 20b-21).

It will be noticed at once that only the last of the original group of four points (i.e. a.iv, the renewal of the promise of the land) is not recapitulated in the second group. This is because it is to be made the subject in its own right of the whole of the next section, a fact underlined by the frequent repetition in vv. 22-25 of the key words of v. 15b, namely הארץ, ירש and נתן.

This observation is of importance for two reasons; first, it has the effect of giving renewed emphasis to the theme of the land,[18] clearly regarded now as the goal of God's other more temporally limited gifts. Second, this literary device of merging two stanzas by making the last expected element of one into the complete subject of the next is something which we shall find happening again between the next two stanzas. Since on that occasion it is of particular importance for an understanding of the prayer as a whole, it is reassuring to have this confirmation that this is a conscious part of the writer's artistry and not just the result of chance.

At the heart of this long stanza in v. 17, sandwiched between descriptions of the people's rebellion, we find the words ואתה אלוה סליחות חנון ורחום ארך אפים ורב[19] (חסד). This, then, is the key statement in this section, revealing a further aspect of God's character over those already noted in the first three stanzas. Its appropriateness needs no amplification. It is immediately followed by ולא עזבתם. This is unexplained at first, but these words are repeated in v. 19 to introduce the description of the ways in which God's grace and mercy continued to be shown despite the people's rebelliousness. This phrase too will recur later to particular effect.

The fifth and penultimate stanza of the prayer, vv. 22-31, concludes the survey of Israel's history. It deals with entry into, and life in, the land. In broad terms, its structure corresponds with that of the previous section, for it too starts with a passage that speaks exclusively of God's goodness in providing for his people (vv. 22-25),[20] a central passage which includes much talk of rejection

---

[17] Elsewhere this may be used to express the results of the study and practice of God's law; see, for example, Deut. 29:8, Josh. 1:7-8 and 1 Kgs 2:3.

[18] See n. 15 above. A similar emphasis is apparent in v. 17a, where the story of the people's refusal to enter the land from Kadesh is singled out as a major example of their faithlessness.

[19] The *wāw* before חסד should be deleted with Q, many MSS and the ancient versions.

[20] In the interests of his strophic analysis, RUDOLPH deletes v. 22 as a later addition and seeks to justify this with the argument that it anticipates v. 24. This is unwarranted, however. Stylistically, there is nothing to distinguish v. 22 from its context; for instance, the three key words already noted (ירש, נתן and ארץ) all occur in it. Nor is it out of place thematically: it speaks only of the conquest of the Trans-Jordanian territories, achieved, in the biblical perspective, under Moses. Then follows (v. 23) a note about the increase in the Israelite population, with an emphasis on the word הבנים/בניהם (vv. 23 and 24). This is most appropriate as an introduction to the entry into the land proper (v. 24) because of the biblical

and rebellion and a conclusion which ends on a renewed note of God's continuing mercy. Indeed, the final words of all, כי אל חנון ורחום אתה, provide the brief statement of that aspect of God's character which the whole section reveals. Its similarity with the previous stanza is no accident, and it is underlined by the repetition of ולא עזבתם in v. 31.

Within this broad similarity, however, there is one point of crucial distinction concerning the shape of the passage which deals with the people's rebellion and God's response to it. Accepting the deuteronomic presentation of history, the writer could not speak of a single rebellion, but wished rather to expose the cyclical view which is so clear in the book of Judges. Appropriately, therefore, he presents us with three (or rather two and a half) cycles on the pattern: rebellion, handing over to a foreign power, cry for help, and response by God in mercy and deliverance; cf. vv. 26–27, 28, and 29–31. That the writer intends his description to be understood in cyclical terms is apparent from the use of comparable phraseology in each cycle; for instance, compare ותתנם ביד צריהם in v. 27, ותעזבם ביד איביהם in v. 28 and ותתנם ביד עמי הארצת in v. 30, and note the repetition of ואתה משמים תשמע in vv. 27 and 28, which links the first two cycles, of the theme of prophetic witness and of divine warning in the first and third cycles (vv. 26 and 29–30), and so on.

Within these three cycles, however, there is to be observed an intensification of the severity of God's judgement. Verse 28b is clearly more forceful in this regard than v. 27a, and despite initial appearances v. 30c is probably the strongest of all. Coming at the end of the historical survey, it is best understood as referring to the Babylonian conquest, and this seems to be confirmed by the phrase לא עשיתם כלה which follows immediately in the next verse.[21] The long historical recital thus ends at the nadir of Israel's fortunes, but also, as we have already observed, with a concluding statement in v. 31b of the continuing gracious character of God preceded by the words ולא עזבתם which we saw in the previous stanza introduced a description of the persistence of God's provision despite rebellion building up to the gift of the land itself.

At this point, it is necessary to observe that although we have spoken of three cycles in this fifth stanza, the third cycle is in fact broken off half-way through. Rebellion and handing over to a foreign power are not followed by the expected elements of cry to God and deliverance. The reason for this should by now be apparent; just as the last expected element of the fourth stanza was made the subject of the fifth, so here the element of cry for help becomes the subject of the sixth in vv. 32–37. There is, however, an important and obvious difference. Not considering that the restoration from the severe judgement of the Babylonian conquest was yet complete, our author could not record the completion of this final cycle in historical terms. Rather in a most effective and powerful move

---

emphasis that it was not the generation of Moses but that of their children who should take the land (Num. 14:29–33; Deut. 1:35–39).

[21] Note also the contrast with Ezra 9:14.

from the point of view of intercession, he catches himself and his contemporaries up into the historical continuum by actualizing the cry for help in words of confession, petition and lament which arise from their present situation. The result is that there is a confidence underlying the lament which most commentators have overlooked. The description of land and people in bondage is not a cry of despair. It is rather a holding up to God of the situation which now exists in the light of all that the past has revealed of his character and of his promise of the land in the expectation that he will not fail once again to 'hear from heaven' and to respond with deliverance.

This understanding is reinforced by the further observation that many of the key words and themes of the historical survey are recapitulated in this concluding stanza. They cannot all be itemized here, but suffice it to mention by way of illustration the obvious prominence of the land and its produce which had formed the basis of the covenant with Abraham, the goal of the Exodus and the purpose of the conquest; the repetition in vv. 32–33 of those key phrases which had earlier described the character of God; the bitter contrast between עד היום הזה in v. 32[22] and כהיום הזה in v. 10; and finally the very end of the prayer – ובצרה גדולה אנחנו – where we cannot fail to catch an echo of v. 27 in which there is a fourfold play on what our author in all probability took to be the same word group: ותתנם ביד צריהם ויצרו להם ובעת צרתם יצעקו אליך ואתה משמים תשמע וכרחמיך הרבים תתן להם מושיעים ויושיעום מיד צריהם.

Reflection on this analysis prompts a number of concluding observations about the distinctive nature of this brief but impressive account of Israel's history.

First, it should be clear by now to what an extent it is distinct from the prevailing ideology of the books of Ezra and Nehemiah as a whole.[23] This is most especially marked with regard to the books' attitude toward the Persian kings. Their benevolence towards the Jews and their initiative in the restoration under divine prompting are a key unifying element of both the major sources and the redaction of these works.[24] Moreover, because of this, although the books of Ezra and Nehemiah anticipate the need for change within the Judaean community, there is no indication that their authors were concerned for broader political change or upheaval.

Nothing could be further, however, from the atmosphere of the closing stanza of our prayer. Here, the current political status of being a subservient province in a larger empire is regarded as oppressive. Indeed, as we have seen, it is compared with the periods of divine chastisement in the pre-exilic period. More than that, however, it has become clear that, in this writer's view, inherent in the

---

[22] The use of היום in v. 36 is comparable.

[23] I am not convinced by ACKROYD's harmonizing attempt (cf. n. 15 above) to circumvent this conclusion.

[24] See, for example, Ezra 1:1–2; 3:7; 4:3; 6:1 ff.; 6:14, 22; 7:27–28; 9:9; Neh. 2:8, 18, and cf. S. JAPHET, 'Sheshbazzar and Zerubbabel – Against the Background of the Historical and Religious Tendencies of Ezra-Nehemiah', ZAW 94 (1982), 66–98, esp. 72–76.

promise of the land was the fact of a life of natural sovereignty in that land, free from any external interference. Moreover, as already indicated, the whole prayer is constructed as an elaborate confession. This, however, is just what the writer's historical perspective has led us to think will invoke God's salvation understood as political intervention. There can be no doubt, therefore, that he anticipates an imminent and dramatic upheaval in the prevailing circumstances.

Since this prayer is most often compared with Ezra 9, and indeed often attributed to the same source, let one citation from each serve to exemplify this contrast. In Neh. 9:35–36 there is a play on the root עבד; because the fathers 'did not serve you' (לא עבדוך), therefore הנה אנחנו היום עבדים; this is then followed by a line emphasizing that God's gift of the land was intended to enable his people to 'eat its fruit and its good fare' but now, it is repeated, הנה אנחנו עבדים עליה. The addition of the last word draws out the poignancy of the situation, and the writer then goes on to state that the land's produce piles up to the benefit of 'the kings whom you have set (נתתה!) over us because of our sins'. The contrast with Ezra 9:9 could hardly be more complete, for there too Ezra confesses כי עבדים אנחנו, but he then immediately qualifies this with an acknowledgement that God has not abandoned them, but has rather shown his favour to them precisely through the good will of the Persian kings in their treatment of the Jews.

Second, however, it is necessary also to draw a distinction between Neh. 9 and the messianic outlook of a prophet such as Haggai. His view, and that of the wider circle which he doubtless represented, was certainly that God would intervene dramatically in the near future, but the focus of his attention is on Zerubbabel the signet ring (Hag. 2:23) and branch (Zech. 6: 12).[25] In line with such hopes, attention is directed towards the temple and Jerusalem, but little or nothing is said regarding the land at large. By contrast, Neh. 9 gives no indication of messianic or royal expectation *sensu stricto*: the promises to David are not mentioned in the historical survey whilst in the lament the kings are merely set alongside the other components of the pre-exilic population as those who sinned and so brought down God's judgement. People and land rather than king and royal appurtenances lie at the heart of this prayer's concerns.

Third, for similar reasons and more, Neh. 9 cannot be closely compared with the thought world of the Chronicler. Although it is true that the two works correspond to a certain degree in their chronological sweep, there is little else that they have in common. As is well known, the major emphases of this prayer, such as Abraham, Exodus, Moses and the conquest of the land are of notoriously little significance to the Chronicler,[26] for whatever reason, whilst his major interests, such as David, the dynasty and the temple receive no mention here.

---

[25] In other respects, Zech. 1–8 is even further removed from Neh. 9 than Haggai. However, on Zech 1:2–6, cf. n. 40 below.

[26] Whilst the Chronicler's lack of attention to these themes is observed by many, there is less agreement as to the reason. Differing, but reasonably representative treatments may be

Fourth, then, should we look to the deuteronomists for this author's inspiration? Undoubtedly there are a number of points of close contact which have been observed in the past. Welch[27] in particular pointed out how many of the distinctive characteristics of deuteronomic thought and style are echoed here whilst we noted earlier the adoption by this writer of the typically deuteronomic fourfold cycle of Israel's life in the land. Influence from this quarter can thus scarcely be denied.

At the same time, however, Neh. 9 is hardly likely to be a product of the deuteronomists as such unless we are to stretch that already elastic designation to breaking point. On the one hand, other traditions of Israelite historiography have also fed into this prayer as is clear in particular from the sections which cover the same ground as the Pentateuch.[28] It would thus be misleading to speak of deuteronomic influence as though it were mediated directly and in isolation. For the period prior to the conquest it was one element among several in what was probably already the Pentateuch in substantially its present shape. For the life in the land, the deuteronomic history was apparently the only full and consecutive account then available, so that obviously its influence will have been paramount.

On the other hand, difficult as it may be to define deuteronomic ideology since current opinion would reckon with it developing over a period of time,[29] there are some omissions from Neh. 9 which again suggest at the least that its relationship with the deuteronomists is looser than at first appears. Enough has already been said of the failure to mention the temple and the Davidic dynasty, but it is worth recalling here their importance not only in the thought but also in the literary structure of the deuteronomic history.[30] We should also add, however, the striking fact on which only Welch has really dwelt, that captivity, exile

---

found in A.-M. BRUNET, 'La théologie du Chroniste. Théocratie et messianisme', in J. COPPENS, A. DESCAMPS and É. MASSAUX (eds.), Sacra Pagina I (BETL, 12–13; Gembloux, 1959), 384–97; S. JAPHET, 'Conquest and Settlement in Chronicles', JBL 98 (1979), 205–18; R. NORTH, 'Theology of the Chronicler', JBL 82 (1963), 369–81; G. VON RAD, Das Geschichtsbild des Chronistischen Werkes (BWANT, 54; Stuttgart, 1930), 64–80; H.G.M. WILLIAMSON, Israel in the Books of Chronicles (Cambridge, 1977), 61–66.

[27] A.C. WELCH, 'The Source of Nehemiah ix', ZAW 47 (1929), 130–37, and Post-Exilic Judaism (Edinburgh and London, 1935), 27–30.

[28] See the full list of biblical citations and allusions in J.M. MYERS, Ezra. Nehemiah (AB; Garden City, 1965), 167–69, and compare them with the standard critical divisions of the Pentateuch. To give a single example, there can be little doubt that Neh. 9:7 draws on Gen. 17:5, generally ascribed to P.

[29] For surveys, cf. J.R. PORTER, 'Old Testament Historiography', in G.W. ANDERSON (ed.), Tradition and Interpretation (Oxford, 1979), 125–62; P.R. ACKROYD, 'The Historical Literature', in D.A. KNIGHT and G.M. TUCKER (eds.), The Hebrew Bible and its Modern Interpreters (Philadelphia and Chico, 1985), 297–323.

[30] Cf. M. NOTH, Überlieferungsgeschichtliche Studien 1 (Halle, 1943), 5–6 = The Deuteronomistic History (JSOTSup, 15; Sheffield, 1981), 5–6; D.J. MCCARTHY, 'II Samuel 7 and the Structure of the Deuteronomic History', JBL 84 (1965), 131–38.

and return receive no mention in Neh. 9 even though they have come to prominence in what many regard as a late redactional layer of the deuteronomic history.[31] The perspective remains throughout on life in one form or another in the land, again in marked contrast with Ezra 9:7-15.[32]

At this point, our difficulties become acute. Welch endeavoured to explain the ethos of Neh. 9 by attributing it to a northern liturgy dating after the fall of Samaria but before the fall of Jerusalem. Other scholars have rightly not followed him in this, detecting in the dependence on the Pentateuch as a whole and in the characteristic use of the word תורה in, for instance, vv. 26 and 29,[33] signs that this prayer must belong to the post-exilic period. But in that case, just where does it fit?

The very fact that this question can be posed should warn us first against too simplistic a portrayal of the varieties of opinion within the post-exilic community. The situation is sometimes presented as though there were but two groups whose ideologies can be precisely delineated.[34] We must be careful, however, not to overlook minority opinions which fall outside such major groupings and which were yet sufficiently influential as to have left such clear traces in the biblical texts.

In seeking to formulate a positive proposal concerning Neh. 9, the evidence outlined above can lead us to think only in terms of the Judaean community which was never exiled to Babylon but which continued to inhabit the decimated land during the period of the exile and after. That such a community existed is today doubted by no one.[35] More than that is difficult to say for certain. It seems probable, however, that an important clue to their ideological stance is preserved in the polemic of Ezek. 11:15 and 33:24, where those left in

---

[31] R.E. FRIEDMAN, The Exile and Biblical Narrative (HSM, 22; Chico, 1981); cf. R.D. NELSON, The Double Redaction of the Deuteronomistic History (JSOTSup, 18; Sheffield, 1981); A.D.H. MAYES, The Story of Israel between Settlement and Exile (London, 1983).

[32] In this particular respect, the prayer of Neh. 1:5-11 also belongs with Ezra 9 against Neh. 9.

[33] For fuller details, cf. GILBERT.

[34] Despite differences between them, both PLÖGER and HANSON err in this direction, on account of which a number of critical voices have been raised against them in recent years; cf. O. PLÖGER, Theokratie und Eschatologie (WMANT, 2; 2nd ed. Neukirchen, 1962) = Theocracy and Eschatology (Oxford, 1968); P.D. HANSON, The Dawn of Apocalyptic (Philadelphia, 1975). A similar comment might also be made about the quite different approach of O.H. STECK, 'Das Problem theologischer Strömungen in nachexilischer Zeit', EvTh 28 (1968), 445-58. Whilst his observations approach ours in some respects, they are vitiated by his overhasty association of Neh. 9 with Ezra 9 and Neh. 1.

[35] Cf. E. JANSSEN, Juda in der Exilszeit (FRLANT, 69; Göttingen, 1956); P.R. ACKROYD, Exile and Restoration (London, 1968), 20-31; B. ODED in J.H. HAYES and J.M. MILLER (eds.), Israelite and Judaean History (London, 1977), 476-80; E. STERN, Material Culture of the Land of the Bible in the Persian Period (Warminster and Jerusalem, 1982), 47ff. For the influence of this on the redaction-history of Jeremiah, see most recently C.R. SEITZ, 'The Crisis of Interpretation over the Meaning and Purpose of the Exile', VT 35 (1985), 78-97.

the land saw the exile as a judgement on those deported and as a vindication of their own situation.[36] Two points indicate the close proximity of Neh. 9 to this group. One is the appeal to Abraham in each case as the recipient of the promise of the land and of the later generations' close association with him.[37] The other is the striking repetition in both the quotations of this group's claims in Ezekiel of the vocabulary already noted as receiving especial emphasis in Neh. 9's handling of the promise of the land (i.e. נתן, ירש and ארץ). Equally, the omissions from Neh. 9 receive a reasonable explanation on this theory. If it is true, as seems likely, that it was generally the poorer members of society who remained in the land, their lack of interest in the monarchy would not be surprising. Equally, if they are indeed to be associated with the עמ/גוי־הארץ(ות) of the remainder of Ezra-Nehemiah,[38] then in view of their exclusion from participation in the temple cult it was inevitable that they should have developed a liturgy that did not focus upon the Jerusalem sanctuary.

Finally, the particular but not exclusive influence of the deuteronomists on Neh. 9 would also be intelligible on this hypothesis. I have suggested elsewhere[39] that the development of the deuteronomistic history and of the school generally assumed to have been associated with it may not have been quite so unilinear as our canonical texts suggest. It would be probable, for instance, that different emphases would develop in Jerusalem and in Babylon amongst those who nevertheless shared a broadly similar outlook.[40] If it is true that Neh. 9 is the product of the later heirs of one such group, then it may help to explain why the returning exiles were so deeply suspicious of them and why their polemic is often so sharp: as in so many walks of life, it is those who in reality are closest to us who are perceived as posing the greatest threat.

---

[36] See further S. JAPHET, 'People and Land in the Restoration Period', in G. STRECKER (ed.), Das Land Israel in biblischer Zeit (Göttingen, 1983), 103–25.

[37] Cf. Neh. 9:7–8 and its setting described above within the prayer as a whole on the one hand, and Ezek. 33:24 on the other. The fact that the exilic community responded with claims of their own in relation to Abraham (e.g. Isa. 41:8; 51:2) was only to be expected.

[38] Cf. A.H.J. GUNNEWEG, עם הארץ – A Semantic Revolution', ZAW 95 (1983), 437–40.

[39] Cf. 'The Death of Josiah and the Continuing Development of the Deuteronomistic History', VT 32 (1982), 242–48.

[40] That polarization between these later groups was not in every case as extreme as might at first appear is suggested on the one hand by the fact that Neh. 9 (like the later Samaritans) uses Pentateuchal and other material that may well have taken shape in Babylon and on the other by the preservation of Neh. 9 itself in Ezra-Nehemiah. The question may here be raised, but not pursued, whether other examples of this group's 'preaching' may not have been preserved. One thinks most obviously of passages which encourage repentance by those in the land as a step towards the return of those in exile; 2 Chron. 30:6–9 has some particularly close points of correspondence with Neh. 9, and Zech. 1:2–6 is not dissimilar; cf. R.A. MASON, 'Some Echoes of the Preaching in the Second Temple? Tradition Elements in Zechariah 1–8', ZAW 96 (1984), 221–35. Also of interest in this connection is the unsubstantiated suggestion of JAPHET, 'People and Land', 113–14, that the list in Ezra 2 (Neh. 7) combines the names of those who returned (listed by family name) with those who remained (listed by settlement) in an attempt to subsume the whole community under the single category of 'returnees'.

19. The Problem with First Esdras

The apocryphal work known in English as 1 Esdras (LXX, Esdras *a;* German, 3. Esra, following the Vulgate) continues to puzzle and divide the few scholars who give it their considered attention. The fundamental problem remains, What is it? Until that issue is solved, there is little hope of agreement on such wider issues as its purpose and major themes.

The work begins somewhat abruptly as a translation into Greek of the last two chapters of the biblical books of Chronicles, continues through into Ezra without a break (and without the overlap between the end of Chronicles and the beginning of Ezra in the Hebrew version), and concludes, again somewhat abruptly, with part of Nehemiah 8, in which Ezra reads from the book of the law to the people. The order of part of the material in Ezra is different from what is found in the canonical Ezra (and as is well known, the chronological order of the Hebrew/Aramaic text in Ezra 4 is itself not straightforward), and as well as several minor deviations from the wording of the Hebrew text it includes a substantial addition at 1 Esdr. 3:1–5:3,[1] the story of the contest of the three bodyguards at the court of Darius which is won by Zerubbabel, who thereby gains the king's permission to return to Jerusalem to rebuild the temple.

In seeking to explain the nature of this work, scholars continue to adopt one of two main positions. First, there are those who argue that the work is a fragment, a book which, either by accident or design, has lost both its beginning and its ending. (Discussion of the Gospel of Mark is an obvious parallel here.) Although it is not logically a consequence of this view, those who have adopted this position have generally maintained that 1 Esdras represents the original form of the ending of the books of Chronicles. On this view, it has to be argued that the story of the three bodyguards is a later addition and that the changed order of events at the time of the first return from the Babylonian exile is a secondary consequence of this addition. It is suggested that the material about Nehemiah was added to the work of the Chronicler only at a later stage in the work's development.

The second main group of scholars argues that 1 Esdras is complete as it stands, or else very nearly so. It is a compilation of extracts from the books of Chronicles, Ezra, and Nehemiah, which were already in their present form at the

---

[1] Chapter and verse enumeration in this essay will follow that in the Rahlfs edition, with that of the RSV in brackets following where there is a difference.

time of writing, together with other material. The book can therefore tell us nothing about the history of composition of the canonical books, although it is agreed that at some points it may serve as a valuable witness for text-critical purposes.

Clearly, if the first position is correct, then it is pointless to go on to inquire about the date, setting, and purpose of 1 Esdras; those questions would have to be addressed to the supposed fuller form of the Chronicler's work as a whole. Only if the second position is correct does it make sense to study 1 Esdras as a work in its own right.

In 1970 Pohlmann published a substantial monograph on this topic in which he sought to uphold the first position.[2] He helpfully cleared the ground of much clutter from earlier discussions, so making clear the issues on which the modern debate needs to proceed, and he made a powerful case for his preferred solution. I responded to his work in 1977 with an attempt to demonstrate that the second position is more probable.[3] While I still hold to that view, the arguments have moved forward in the years since,[4] and I should not now wish to defend every aspect of the case I made then. Some points need refinement in the light of subsequent research, while other arguments have surfaced on both sides of the debate which require examination. Though it is not possible in the space of a short article to cover every issue, it seems worthwhile to review the position in the light of this more recent work. I shall therefore first set out what I now regard as the strongest arguments in favour of the second position, examining on the way some of the points that have in the meantime been thought to challenge that opinion, and then conclude with some brief comments on the possible purpose of 1 Esdras, viewed now, of course, as a self-contained work.

(1) According to the 'revised Schürer', 'perhaps the strongest argument against 1 Esdras as simply a section of an orginal translation of the whole of the work of the Chronicler is the fact that the extant Greek of the *Paralipomena* in the LXX was composed before 150 B.C. and it is implausible that two full Greek versions of the same text were produced at so early a date'.[5] When I first advanced this argument in 1977, I also emphasised that the difficulty was compounded by the fact that both Greek versions apparently originated in Alexandria, and that so far as we can tell there was in fact an economy of effort in the task of translation,

---

[2] K.-F. POHLMANN, Studien zum dritten Esra: Ein Beitrag zur Frage nach dem ursprünglichen Schluß des chronistischen Geschichtswerkes (FRLANT, 104; Göttingen, 1970). POHLMANN includes a full bibliography.

[3] H.G.M. WILLIAMSON, Israel in the Books of Chronicles (Cambridge, 1977), 12–36.

[4] For bibliography, see C. DOGNIEZ, Bibliography of the Septuagint (1970–1993) (VTSup, 60; Leiden, 1995), 171–74.

[5] E. SCHÜRER, The History of the Jewish People in the Age of Jesus Christ (175 B.C.–A.D. 135), III.2 (rev. and ed. by G. VERMES, F. MILLAR and M. GOODMAN [Edinburgh, 1987]), 712; see too A. VAN DER KOOIJ, 'On the Ending of the Book of 1 Esdras', in C.E. Cox (ed.), VII Congress of the International Organization for Septuagint and Cognate Studies, Leuven, 1989 (Atlanta, 1991), 37–49, esp. 38.

especially of the Writings: 'A double translation of a book already paralleled for considerable sections in other canonical books produced in the same place and at about the same time does not fit into such a background'. The evidence for a second century BC Alexandrian date for the Greek of 1 Esdras has been strengthened in the meantime by Talshir's study of its distinctive vocabulary.[6] The only attempt of which I am aware to answer this argument completely misses the point.[7] Even if 1 Esdras were a witness to an alternative (and more original) 'text type' of the work of the Chronicler, this would still not explain why both so closely similar text types were translated into Greek in the same place and at the same time. The claimed analogy with the Greek and Hebrew versions of Jeremiah is beside the point, of course, since there is no evidence for a translation of both textual forms of Jeremiah into Greek at that time. If, therefore, no reason can be adduced for the production of such a translation, that 'translation' can no longer serve as a witness to a hypothetical Semitic original, of whatever text type.

(2) If 1 Esdras represents the original ending of the Chronicler's work, then in that work Nehemiah 8 must have immediately followed Ezra 10. In the story of Ezra taken on its own (as this theory presupposes), however, the logical place for Nehemiah 8 is between Ezra 8 and 9, as Torrey first argued long ago;[8] the reason for its present location is a consequence of the desire to present the work of the two reformers (Ezra and Nehemiah) as two parts of the single process of restoration under God's direction. If this is correct, then the order now found in 1 Esdras must be secondary to the combining of the accounts of Ezra and Nehemiah and therefore be the result of selective compilation, not a witness to an earlier stage in composition.

Apart from the obvious fact that it deals with Ezra, the evidence that the story in Nehemiah 8 once belonged with the rest of the Ezra account (Ezra 7–10) derives from the system of dating used. In Nehemiah's first-person account, months are always referred to by name (e.g., Chislev, Neh. 1:1; Nisan, 2:1; Elul, 6:15), whereas in the Ezra material the months are consistently numbered; it is this latter system that is used at Neh 7:73 and 8:2. The main arguments for placing the original version of Nehemiah 8 between Ezra 8 and 9 are, first, that Ezra came

---

[6] Z. TALSHIR, 'The Milieu of 1 Esdras in the Light of its Vocabulary', in A. PIETERSMA and C. COX (eds.), De Septuaginta: Studies in Honour of John William Wevers on his Sixty-fifth Birthday (Mississauga, 1984), 129–47. The evidence for the LXX of Chronicles (Paralipomena) remains as before; see L.C. ALLEN, The Greek Chronicles: The Relation of the Septuagint of I and II Chronicles to the Massoretic Text (VTSup, 25 and 27; Leiden, 1974).

[7] S.L. MCKENZIE, The Chronicler's Use of the Deuteronomistic History (HSM, 33; Atlanta, 1985), 18–20. MCKENZIE is much influenced by his teacher, F.M. CROSS, 'A Reconstruction of the Judean Restoration', JBL 94 (1975), 4–18, and by the unpublished thesis of another of CROSS's pupils, R.W. KLEIN, 'Studies in the Greek Texts of the Chronicler' (Harvard, 1966). For some critical comments on CROSS's article, see my 'Eschatology in Chronicles', TynB 28 (1977), 115–54 (120–30) (above, 166–74).

[8] C.C. TORREY, The Composition and Historical Value of Ezra-Nehemiah (BZAW, 2; Giessen, 1896), 29–34; Ezra Studies (Chicago, 1910), 252–84.

to Jerusalem specifically to present and teach the law, so that some account of his doing this is to be expected at this point, secondly and most decisively that the dates in the Ezra material fit smoothly in sequence on this view (Ezra sets out in the first month and arrives in the fifth month, Ezra 7:9; he reads the law in the seventh month, Neh. 8:2; the problem of mixed marriages comes to light in the ninth month, 10:9, and is dealt with in a period starting in the tenth month, 10:16, and concluding on the first day of the first month, 10:17, one year to the day after Ezra had 'begun to go up', 7:9), and thirdly that the confession at the start of Ezra 9 seems to presuppose knowledge of the law by the people.

Those who have argued for the view that Nehemiah 8 originally followed Ezra 10 have generally done so purely on the basis of their prior beliefs about 1 Esdras.[9] They have not, therefore, brought positive arguments to bear, but have merely sought to explain away the difficulties their view faces, namely, the odd order of events and the jumbled sequence of dates. The fact that they have to resort to special pleading at this point is a weakness in their argument.

(3) The view that 1 Esdras represents the original ending of the Chronicler's work demands that it show no knowledge of any of the Nehemiah material. Claims and counterclaims on this matter have been argued to and fro over the years with no finally satisfying conclusion being reached.[10] When working in more detail on Ezra 1–6,[11] however, I became convinced that there was a glaring example of such knowledge which I had previously overlooked. As is well known, the list of those who returned to Jerusalem after the exile is repeated in Ezra 2 and Nehemiah 7. The Ezra 2 version is, of course, included in 1 Esdras (5:7ff.). While the two lists run closely parallel for the most part, they diverge slightly in their closing verses, and that in ways which strongly suggest that the Ezra 2 version is secondary, from a literary point of view, to that in Nehemiah 7. If that is so, then it follows that Ezra 2 (and *a fortiori* 1 Esdras) must have already known the accounts of Ezra and Nehemiah in their combined form.

In the introduction to his valuable commentary on Ezra and Nehemiah, however, Joseph Blenkinsopp[12] has taken issue with this proposal (though it

---

[9] E. g., S. MOWINCKEL, Studien zu dem Buche Ezra-Nehemia. I: Die nachchronistische Redaktion des Buches. Die Listen (Oslo, 1964), 7–61; and III: Die Ezrageschichte und das Gesetz Moses (Oslo, 1965), 7–11; POHLMANN, Studien, 127–48; W. TH. IN DER SMITTEN, Esra: Quellen, Überlieferung und Geschichte (SSN, 15; Assen, 1973), 35–47; K. KOCH, 'Ezra and the Origins of Judaism', JSS 19 (1974), 173–97 (179); R. MOSIS, Untersuchungen zur Theologie des chronistischen Geschichtswerkes (FTS, 92; Freiburg, 1973), 215–20. For some further consideration of their arguments, see my Ezra-Nehemiah (WBC, 16; Waco, 1985), 284–86.

[10] See Israel, 30–35; MCKENZIE, Chronicler's Use, 22–23; A. SCHENKER, 'La Relation d'Esdras A' au texte massorétique d'Esdras-Néhémie', in G. I. NORTON and S. PISANO (eds.), Tradition of the Text: Studies offered to Dominique Barthélemy in Celebration of his 70th Birthday (OBO, 109; Freiburg and Göttingen, 1991), 218–48, esp. 243–46.

[11] 'The Composition of Ezra i–vi', JTS ns 34 (1983), 1–30 (above, 244–70).

[12] J. BLENKINSOPP, Ezra-Nehemiah: A Commentary (OTL; London, 1989), 43–44.

may be noted in passing that on other grounds he nevertheless favours the view that 1 Esdras is a secondary compilation, pp. 70–71). In my original discussion of this issue, I advanced four arguments, two of which had long been noted by others, and two of which were new, to the best of my knowledge. Blenkinsopp deals only with the first two, and then fails to recognise that what he thinks speaks in favour of his position is actually a misunderstanding of the situation regarding one of the arguments to which he does not explicitly refer but which in fact tells strongly against his conclusion. Let us take each of the points in turn.

First, in the parallel continuation of the two lists (Neh. 7:72; Ezra 3:1), material which in both books serves to introduce the subsequent narrative after the conclusion of the list,[13] there is a reference to the events taking place in the seventh month. To the argument that this is tied to its context in Nehemiah (see 8:2) but left completely in the air in Ezra, Blenkinsopp replies that the seventh month is also referred to in 3:6. That is fair so far as it goes, but there is more to be said. In the present form of Nehemiah, we know which year we are talking about from the wider context. More importantly, we have already seen that the seventh month is part of a long sequence of months which give structure to the Ezra material in what was probably its original form, and furthermore that in every case the months are identified by number. In Ezra 1–6, by contrast, we are neither given any indication of which year this month relates to nor, more importantly, is this system of dating the one usually used elsewhere. In these chapters the narrator usually relates events to a given year of the king (1:1; 4:24; 6:15) or to some other fixed occasion (3:8). If the year is not stated, as at 6:19, the context leaves no doubt as to what is meant. So the reference to the seventh month without further qualification in 3:1 (and 3:6 is no doubt drawn from there, and so has little independent value as evidence) is out of character with Ezra 1–6 as a whole but exactly what we expect both stylistically and chronologically in the Ezra material (Ezra 7–10; Neh. 8). Though not the strongest of my arguments, it still carries some weight so far as it goes.

Secondly, the parallel versions of the list end with details about the voluntary donations made to the temple, and it has generally been accepted that Ezra 2:68–69 represents a summarizing of Neh. 7:69–71 in this regard. Blenkinsopp accepts that 'the argument *could* hold for the quantity of silver minas (4,700 in Nehemiah, 5,000 in Ezra) and for vestments (97 in Nehemiah, 100 in Ezra)'.[14] In fact, the case is far stronger than Blenkinsopp's summary reveals, because the 4,700 silver minas in Nehemiah is itself a compound of 500 in 7:69, 2,200 in 7:70, and 2,000 in 7:71, while the 97 vestments are likewise made up from 30 in

---

[13] As BLENKINSOPP agrees, this point is, of course, the strongest argument for seeing one version of the list as being directly dependent on the other rather than on some common original.

[14] This involves a widely adopted textual emendation at Neh 7:69; in his commentary (281), BLENKINSOPP allows that this is 'possible', though he is reluctant to accept it.

7:69 and 67 in 7:71. It is surely more likely that these have been compounded and then rounded up in Ezra than that they have been divided inaccurately in Nehemiah. Finally, Blenkinsopp states that '61,000 gold darics is hardly a rounding out of the 41,000 in Nehemiah'. That may be so, but even here it should be recognised that the 41,000 is again a compound of 1,000 in 7:69, 20,000 in 7:70 and 20,000 in 7:71. The sum may have been got wrong (or corrupted in textual transmission at the stage when numerical notations were used), but the point still holds that amalgamation of the figures is more likely than the reverse.

Finally, Blenkinsopp insists that 'due weight must also be given to the narrative continuity before and after the list in Ezra, emphasised by the same terminology – "the house of YHWH which is in Jerusalem", "heads of ancestral houses", "votive offerings"'. (Blenkinsopp could have added the phrase בבואם לבית יהוה, 2:68, which seems to relate to the awkwardly expressed but closely comparable first clause in 3:8.) This is the point at which Blenkinsopp unwittingly undermines his own position, because he has overlooked the argument I had already advanced that all these terms come in Ezra 2:68, a verse which has no parallel in the otherwise longer ending of the list in Nehemiah 7. As I wrote and would still maintain, 'This plus, however, exactly fits the narrative context, the outlook and even the specific vocabulary of the narrator of Ezra i–vi, so that the suspicion is hard to resist that he has added it to his *Vorlage* rather than that precisely this verse has coincidentally been omitted in Nehemiah' (p. 3). Ironically, Blenkinsopp's observations merely reinforce the point.

I conclude, therefore, that the dependence of Ezra 2 on Nehemiah 7 remains overwhelmingly more probable than the reverse,[15] and reaffirm that if this is so then the author of 1 Esdras, who included Ezra 2 in his work, must have known the books of Ezra and Nehemiah in substantially the same form as they have reached us.

(4) In 1977 I accepted the possibility that both the opening and the ending of 1 Esdras might have been lost, but there was some evidence to suggest that it was nevertheless not nearly so extensive as the hypothetical original work of the Chronicler. This conclusion was rejected by McKenzie, amongst others. The whole debate has been raised to a new level of sophistication, however, in two articles by van der Kooij, who argues in considerable detail that both the start and the conclusion of the work as we now have it are as intended.

---

[15] So too B. HALPERN, 'A Historiographic Commentary on Ezra 1–6: A Chronological Narrative and Dual Chronology in Israelite Historiography', in W.H. PROPP, B. HALPERN and D.N. FREEDMAN (eds.), The Hebrew Bible and Its Interpreters (Biblical and Judaic Studies from the University of California, San Diego, I; Winona Lake, 1990), 81–142, esp. 93–96, though on slightly different grounds. It is not necessary to repeat here my examination of the unconvincing arguments of earlier scholars who have taken the opposite point of view; cf. 'Composition', 4–8.

His argument about the ending of the work is the easiest to summarise.[16] He first states the problem, namely, that the present ending of 1 Esdras is καὶ ἐπισυνήχθησαν, 'and they gathered together', which looks at first sight like a translation of a detached fragment of part of Neh 8:13: Καὶ ἐν τῇ ἡμέρᾳ τῇ δευτέρᾳ συνήχθησαν 'and on the second day there were gathered together ...'. Since this comes at the start of a new paragraph in Nehemiah 8 and continues with the subject of the verb (to go no further), it is not surprising that most scholars have supposed that 1 Esdras originally did the same. Van der Kooij next develops and strengthens my arguments against Mowinckel and Pohlmann that Josephus (who clearly used 1 Esdras) cannot help us in restoring a conjectured continuation or ending of 1 Esdras; if the ending of 1 Esdras is lost, then it must have been lost before Josephus made use of it. Crucially, van der Kooij then turns to the syntax of the closing words in their Greek form, correctly pointing out that they have always been studied from the point of view of their relationship to the Hebrew (which suggests that they are fragmentary), whereas the Greek has recast this passage in a way which joins the last two words inextricably with what precedes them. Contrary to the Hebrew text, the Greek adds a καί after the ὅτι (= כי) of the previous clause to give a 'both ... and' construction, which he renders 'not only because the teaching given them had been instilled to their mind *(sic)*, but also because they had been gathered together' (p. 45). What appears at first sight to be an isolated fragment thus becomes a second reason for the people's joyful celebration. Parallels are then adduced for this line of thought (especially 2 Macc. 2:18). There is thus neither evidence nor reason for supposing that anything followed the ending of 1 Esdras which we now have.[17]

As regards the present start of 1 Esdras, van der Kooij's arguments are more intricate, and cannot be fully summarised here.[18] The gist of his case, however, is that 1:21-22 (23-24), which has no equivalent in the Hebrew text of 2 Chronicles 35, and which refers to certain accounts of Josiah's reign that were recorded in earlier times, has exact parallels in 2 Kgs 22:11-20 and the parallel 2 Chron. 34:19-28; those accounts cannot, therefore, have been included in 1 Esdras itself. This conclusion is supported, *inter alia*, by 1:31 (33), where 'the things that are now told' refers to the celebration of Passover, with which 1 Esdras begins, whereas 'the things that he had done before' refers to earlier events in Josiah's reign which 1 Esdras does not record but which Kings and Chronicles do.

If van der Kooij is right in either of his articles (and his arguments appear persuasive to me), then the 'fragment hypothesis' of 1 Esdras will have to be abandoned.[19]

---

[16] VAN DER KOOIJ, 'Ending'.

[17] A.E. GARDNER, 'The Purpose and Date of 1 Esdras', JJS 37 (1986), 18-27, adds the further argument that 'As the message contained in the final sentence matches the start of the book, there is no need to imagine that the text is incomplete' (19).

[18] A. VAN DER KOOIJ, 'Zur Frage des Anfangs des 1. Esrabuches', ZAW 103 (1991), 239-52.

[19] Note should be taken here of the work of T.C. ESKENAZI, 'The Chronicler and the

(5) It is well known that there are considerable textual and narrative obscurities in the passages that introduce some of the letters and other documents that are included in Ezra 1–6; see in particular 4:6–11 and 6:3–6. In 1983[20] I argued in some detail that these could mostly be explained in a natural way on the assumption that the editor was working directly from the documents in question, making use for his purposes not only of the substance of the letters but also of some of the summaries of contents and addresses we know from many examples were also included on such documents separately from the main body of the text. Whether or not that particular theory is accepted, it is noteworthy that the author of 1 Esdras has a considerably simpler version at just these points. He has no equivalent for the obscure reference to a letter (not cited) dating to the time of Xerxes (Ezra 4:6), and whereas Ezra 4:7–10 seems to refer to two letters (the first of which is again not cited), the second of which is given an elaborate and frequently obscure introduction, 1 Esdr 2:12 (16) refers to only one letter whose authors are an abbreviated combination of the two sets of addressees in Ezra.[21] Finally, Ezra 6:2b–12 records a letter from Darius in which the earlier memorandum of Cyrus is cited verbatim (leading to some confusion on the part of many commentators), whereas 1 Esdras cites only the memorandum of Cyrus in the first person (6:23–25 [24–26]) before switching to a mixture of third- and first-person report (6:26–33 [27–34]) for the substance of Darius's own contribution to the letter. It seems to me to be in the highest degree improbable that the Ezra versions would have been spun out of those in 1 Esdras in these cases. The obvious explanation is that 1 Esdras has simplified what already appeared to be obscure (perhaps because he was no longer familiar with Achaemenid epistolary conventions), and that he unconsciously introduced some minor inconsistencies in the process.[22]

Composition of 1 Esdras', CBQ 48 (1986), 171–85, and In an Age of Prose: A Literary Approach to Ezra-Nehemiah (SBLMS, 36; Atlanta, 1988), 155–74. ESKENAZI advances the intriguing suggestion that 1 Esdras is an independent composition by the Chronicler in which he accommodated the theology of Ezra-Nehemiah to his own. Among the points she makes is that the narrative part of the Books of Chronicles itself has an abrupt introduction towards the end of a king's reign and an ending which seems to break off in mid-sentence, both features of 1 Esdras. I do not find ESKENAZI's hypothesis fully convincing in terms of the Chronicler himself (though it should be noted that she allows the term to be used flexibly to include also a possible circle or school), even though, as we shall see later, there are some general points of comparison which might be drawn. Clearly, the literary style revealed by the opening and close of the work could not be an argument in its own right, but it does suggest that authors of this general period may not have been as concerned as we are for completely tidy starts and finishes.

[20] 'Composition'; see also Ezra-Nehemiah.
[21] See too TALSHIR, 'Milieu', 137.
[22] *Contra* SCHENKER, 'Relation', 228–31. It is curious that SCHENKER here objects to the notion that 1 Esdras might have simplified Ezra-Nehemiah when he himself uses precisely this argument to argue that the chronology of Ezra 1–6 must be secondary to that in 1 Esdras (224–28). In fact, the chronology of 1 Esdras is so confused and internally inconsistent that it is more probably to be explained as the unconscious result of the rearrangement of material

(6) It has already been noted that defenders of the view that 1 Esdras represents the original ending of the Chronicler's work have to indulge in special pleading at certain points to uphold their case. While the point is clearly not decisive, it needs to be recognised that this extends far beyond the case of the original location of Nehemiah 8. In particular, they have to maintain that the story of the three bodyguards has been added to the work later, a hypothesis vigorously contested by In der Smitten,[23] and that the material in Ezra 1–6 has been reordered subsequently, to take account of the fact that Zerubbabel was sent to Jerusalem only in the reign of Darius, whereas Hanhart has argued that these rearrangements are part of a sustained and consistent attempt to sort out the chronological problems of Ezra 1–6, something unlikely in the case of merely a subsequent reordering of certain episodes.[24] Any case that multiplies such examples of special pleading must inevitably be weakened thereby.

If, on the basis of these considerations, we may conclude that 1 Esdras is not just a fragment of the original ending of the Chronicler's work but a composition in its own right, our original question – What is it? – gains new urgency. It is not possible within the confines of this article to attempt a full answer to this question, but a few introductory comments to pave the way for future work may be added by way of a conclusion.

First, it is important to distinguish more clearly than is often the case between theme, purpose, and form. As many commentators have observed, the theme of

---

necessitated by the introduction of the story of the three bodyguards. Since that story necessitated the presence of Zerubbabel at the court of Darius he could no longer have been a leader of the first return (Ezra 2) nor present when the altar was restored at the first (Ezra 3). It therefore seems more logical to ascribe all the consequent changes in the order of material to this one cause than to divide them between earlier and later phases of the book's composition. Similarly, 1 Esdr. 5:70–71 (73) clearly contains a chronological error within 1 Esdras's own schema, since it indicates that Zerubbabel was already active in Jerusalem during the reign of Cyrus, whereas no such problem arises at Ezra 4:4–5, on which it is based. Here too it must be concluded that the author of 1 Esdras has failed to make all the necessary adjustments consequential upon his chronological reordering and that he is therefore dependent upon Ezra at this point rather than the other way round.

[23] W. TH. IN DER SMITTEN, 'Zur Pagenerzählung im 3. Esra (3 Esr. iii 1–v 6)', VT 22 (1972), 492–95. His case will be greatly strengthened if the TALSHIRS are correct in their recent study which argues (1) that the story as we have it is a translation from Aramaic, and (2) that the link between the story and its context (5:1–6) is also a translation from a Semitic language. It is clearly more probable, on this showing, that the story was included in the earliest form of the work, not added subsequently at the 'Greek' stage either by the translator himself or by some interpolator; cf. Z. and D. TALSHIR, 'The Original Language of the Story of the Three Youths (1 Esdras 3–4)', in M. FISHBANE and E. TOV (eds.), 'Sha'arei Talmon'. Studies in the Bible, Qumran, and the Ancient Near East Presented to Shemaryahu Talmon (Winona Lake, 1992), 63*–75* (Hebrew).

[24] R. HANHART, 'Zu Text und Textgeschichte des ersten Esrabuches', in I. A. SHINAN (ed.), Proceedings of the Sixth World Congress of Jewish Studies (Jerusalem 1973) (Jerusalem, 1977), 201–12. It is a pity that SCHENKER appears to have been unaware of this article, for it is relevant to his main argument that 1 Esdras represents a consistent and more original conception of the course of the history of the immediately postexilic period.

the book focuses on the temple in Jerusalem, since most of the material included can be related to it in terms of its destruction and restoration, while the exclusion of other material which must have been available to the author (in particular that relating to Nehemiah) can also be explained on this ground. It is perhaps, however, possible to be a little more specific than this, for, as recent work has emphasised, the opening and close of the book are not so much concerned with the physical building of the temple as with the community gathered there for worship on a major festival. So a more accurate definition of the book's theme might be the restoration of the temple community.[25] This may appear to be rather a humdrum definition, but it is worth remembering that if, as many scholars now accept, the books of Chronicles and of Ezra-Nehemiah were not originally parts of a single work, 1 Esdras will in fact be the first narrative representation of the continuity between the major religious institutions of the pre- and postexilic periods that those same books taken in isolation express by other means.

It has already been mentioned, however, that theme and purpose should not be confused; in order to define a work's purpose, it is necessary also to establish its date. As Myers rightly observes, 'The purpose and date of 1 Esdras are closely related. If either could be determined independently it would not be too difficult to fix upon the other'.[26] Myers himself then uses primarily linguistic arguments to suggest a date 'some time in the second century B.C.', and noting other possibilities as well, wonders whether 1 Esdras has 'something to do with the period of Antiochus III, perhaps as a kind of apologia for the Jews who had assisted him in his successful effort to wrest Coelesyria from the Ptolemaic regime and a claim for his favour in return'.[27] Gardner, meanwhile, maintains that there are sufficient linguistic parallels with 2 Maccabees which are not attested elsewhere to suggest that the two works are contemporary and that the purpose of 1 Esdras was to comfort people living during the Maccabean crisis,[28] while Attridge first considers the possibility that 1 Esdras was designed 'to play some role in the polemics of the second century between the Jerusalem temple and it[s] rivals' (i.e., Leontopolis and 'Araq-el-Amir), but then finally con-

---

[25] The main burden of SCHENKER's article is that 1 Esdras presents the restoration in the order town-altar-temple, whereas Ezra-Nehemiah has altar-temple-town (and he judges the latter to be derivative and hence secondary). There are problems with this view, however (for instance, the material in 1 Esdr. 5:45 [46] is accepted as part of the evidence for the restoration of Jerusalem, but not, apparently, when the identical material appears at Ezra 3:1), but insofar as there are indications of an interest in 1 Esdras that stretches beyond the immediate confines of the temple, they may be accommodated by the broader definition of theme offered above.

[26] J. MYERS, I & II Esdras (AB, 42; Garden City, 1974), 8.

[27] MYERS, I & II Esdras, 13.

[28] GARDNER, 'Purpose and Date'. Like others before her, GARDNER draws attention to some possible echoes of Daniel in 1 Esdras, which might be thought to favour a slightly later date than MYERS proposes (even though he too was well aware of these echoes).

cludes that it may simply have been composed to serve didactic purposes – to convey 'to a Greek reading audience, in a succinct and entertaining form, the theological lesson of Ezra-Nehemiah, that God watches over those who piously serve him, as well as the moralistic message that truth is most powerful'.[29]

With regard to all these and other possibilities which could be cited, it needs to be realised that they are starting out from an attempt to date the present form of the Greek text and then to look for a likely purpose in the light of the historical situation thus reached. Clearly, however, if 1 Esdras is in fact the translation of an already existing Semitic work, as seems more likely,[30] then we have to move back to consider the probable date of *that* work before determining its likely purpose.[31] And here, of course, we run up against a further problem with 1 Esdras, namely, the question, scarcely ever raised, of its form or genre. So long as 1 Esdras was regarded either as an earlier version of the ending of Chronicles-Ezra-Nehemiah or as the fragment of some other extended work, this question either was not, or did not need to be, tackled. In the light of the conclusions reached above, however, it cannot be avoided.

Without wishing to press the proposal too strictly, the possibility may be raised that 1 Esdras is an early form of what has come to be known as 'rewritten Bible'. As a literary categorization, this label seems first to have been used explicitly by Geza Vermes with regard to such texts as the *Genesis Apocryphon* from Qumran,[32] and he offers as a brief definition 'a narrative that follows Scripture but includes a substantial amount of supplements and interpretative developments, its fullest example being the *Jewish Antiquities* of Josephus, and

---

[29] H.W. ATTRIDGE, 'Historiography', in M.E. STONE (ed.), Jewish Writings of the Second Temple Period: Apocrypha, Pseudepigrapha, Qumran Sectarian Writings, Philo, Josephus (Compendia Rerum Iudaicarum ad Novum Testamentum, II/2; Assen and Philadelphia, 1984), 157–84 (160).

[30] See n. 23 above.

[31] This is not to deny, of course, that a later translator can be influenced by his own circumstances in the course of his work and that in this secondary setting he too may be said to have a 'purpose' of his own. Indeed, much work on the Septuagint points to the likelihood that this was not infrequently the case. The suggestions listed above should not therefore be simply dismissed out of hand. Still, it is worth bearing in mind that all the evidence we have points to the work of translation being done in Alexandria, so that the translator's purpose should be related to whatever may be deemed to have relevance in that setting, rather than drawing on exclusively Palestinian concerns. This does not narrow the range of possibilities too sharply, however, for there is evidence from Josephus that the Judaean and Samaritan diaspora communities were fiercely loyal to their respective cult centres in Palestine and that this was an ongoing matter of dispute between them (perhaps because of the need to determine the correct destination for contributions and offerings); cf. Ant. xii.10 and xiii.74–79.

[32] G. VERMES, Scripture and Tradition in Judaism: Haggadic Studies (SP-B, 4; Leiden, 1961, 1973²), 67–126; see too G.W.E. NICKELSBURG, 'The Bible Rewritten and Expanded', in STONE (ed.), Jewish Writings, 89–156, who offers the following summary: 'literature that is very closely related to the biblical texts, expanding and paraphrasing them and implicitly commenting on them' (89).

its prototype the biblical Chronicles'.[33] The most thorough discussion to date from the point of view of method, however, is that of Alexander,[34] who examines a number of generally agreed examples, emphatically endorses the view that we are dealing here with 'a definite literary genre', and lists nine principal characteristics, all of which, he insists, must be present if any particular work is to be admitted into the genre. Clearly, there is not space here to work through each of these points in turn, but it would seem that this could legitimately be done. Although by no means as complete or extensive as some of the later and better-known examples, 1 Esdras stands as an early example in the development of the genre, though considerably later, of course, than Vermes's cited prototype of Chronicles (cautiously accepted as such by Alexander).[35]

If this characterization is correct, then it only adds to our difficulties of establishing a date and purpose, for works of this type are oriented primarily towards the biblical text rather than towards the specifics of the writer's own circumstances.[36] Indeed, we should perhaps conclude that, despite the popularity of the pastime, it is a mistake to look for a 'purpose' at all, if by that is meant a single aim arising from the writer's own day which controlled his composition in its entirety. By the same token, we shall find ourselves further than ever from settling upon a firm date, beyond the outside parameters that have already been indicated. In a way which I hope Rex Mason would enjoy and even approve, it seems that the solution of one problem merely opens up another – if anything more intractable than the first.

---

[33] SCHÜRER, History of the Jewish People in the Age of Jesus Christ, III.1, 326.

[34] P. ALEXANDER, 'Retelling the Old Testament', in D. A. CARSON and H. G. M. WILLIAMSON (eds.), It Is Written: Scripture Citing Scripture: Essays in Honour of Barnabas Lindars, SSF (Cambridge, 1988), 99–121.

[35] If it is true that Ezra 1–6 was compiled around 300 BCE (see above, n. 11), then, of course, 1 Esdras cannot be earlier than part way through the third century, even in its Semitic form.

[36] One might compare the difficulties scholars have found in arriving at even an approximately agreed date for Chronicles; see the recent survey of opinions in I. KALIMI, 'Die Abfassungszeit der Chronik – Forschungsstand und Perspektiven', ZAW 105 (1993), 223–33.

Index of Biblical Passages

Old Testament

Genesis

2:7	178
3:19	177
4	77
9:20–7	77
17:5	291
17:6	179
17:16	177–9
22:2, 14	155–6
23:4	155
23:6	255
23:9, 11	155
25:27–34	76
28:17	154
35–6	76
37:5 ff.	79
38:7, 10	114
41	79
45:9	251
46:9	111
50:24	256
33:1	256
35:30	108
35:35	158
36:6	251
36:35	158
37:17, 22, 25	178
38:2	178

Exodus

3:8	256
3:17	256
3:21–2	254
11:2	254
12:8–9	235
12:35–6	254
14:14	273
22:27	255
25:9	158
25:31, 36	178
25:40	158
26:31	158
27:2	178
28:8	178
28:30	30
31:2	108
32:16	253

Leviticus

2:13	189
4:22	255
6:5–6	234
8:8	30
9:24	154
10:1–2	133
16:21	283
23:4	238
23:37	238
23:39–43	237
23:40	238
26:8	122

Numbers

1:16	255
2:3–31	255
3:4	133
4:3	266
7:1–83	255
7:84–6	255
10:8	137
14:4	286
16:1	77
18:15	236
18:19	189
22	77
22:5–6	251
25:7 ff.	77
27:12–23	149
27:19	143
27:21	30

27:23	143	18:1 ff.	77
31:6	137	19	77
34:18–28	255		

1 Samuel

Deuteronomy

		2:12–17, 22 ff.	77
1:30	273	10:11–12	123
1:37 f.	140	18:6, 7	123
3:22	273	19:24	123
7:3	274	20:4 ff.	121
10:4	253	21:12	123
16:1–8	236	22:1–5	120
16:7	235	23:14	120
16:13–15	238	24:1	120
20:4	273	25:6, 10	123
23:4	18	27:6	120
23:18	178	29–30	121
29:8	287	29:3	82
31:2 f.	141	29:5	123
31:5	143		
31:6	143	*2 Samuel*	
31:7	143–4	3:37	178
31:8	143	5:9	116
31:14	143	5:11–25	118
31:23	142–4	7:2	147
32:30	122	7:7	179
34:9	144, 149	7:12	176, 179
		7:13	177
Joshua		7:14	177, 180, 183, 185
1	146	7:16	180
1:2 ff.	144	8:8, 11	147
1:5	143	12	77
1:6	142–3	17:22, 24–5	121
1:7–8	287	17:27	121
1:7	143	18:1–4	121–2
1:9	142–3	19:13	121
1:16–20	144	19:16 ff.	121
3:7	144	20:1	122, 124
4:14	144	23:1	123
5:10–12	234	23:8–39	115
9:15	255	23:8	130
9:27	234	24	153
10:14, 42	273		
11:23	141	*1 Kings*	
21:44	141	2:1	143
23:10	273	2:1 ff.	144, 149
		2:3	287
Judges		2:4	183
1:18, 34	77	2:10–12	145
3:15	79	2:15	178
6	154–5	3:4	150
6:34	116	3:5–15	150
13	79	3:14	183

3:16–28	150	29:13–14	243
6:38	265	30:21	178–9
8	262	51:1, 11	254
6:7	234		
6:21	158	*Ezekiel*	
8:19–20	182	11:15	292
8:21	186	20:12–24	275
8:25	183	33:24	292
8:50	160	44	234
8:51, 53	186		
9:3–9	191	*Amos*	
9:5, 6	183, 193		
9:11	252	4:13	284
10:26–9	151	5:8–9	284
11:14 ff.	77	9:5–6	284
12:16	123		
12:31	178	*Micah*	
14:25–8	258	5:1	109, 193

2 Kings

Zephaniah

8:19	190	3:5	243
14:6	232		
17	266	*Haggai*	
19:8 f.	76		
19:9–14	253	1:1	11, 13, 34, 83, 86
19:35 f.	76	1:14	34, 83, 86
19:37	179	2:2	34, 83, 86
22:4	174	2:3	265
22:11–20	300	2:4	41, 86
		2:18	265
Isaiah		2:20–23	34
		2:21	34, 83
2:3	156	2:23	290
7:8	41, 266		
7:9	243	*Zechariah*	
30:17	122		
30:29	156	1:2–6	243, 290, 293
37:38	179	1:7, 8–17	171
38:9	253	3:1–10	86
41:2	254	4:10	243
41:8	293	6:11–14	171
41:25	254	6:11	86
44:28	254	6:12	216, 290
45:1, 13	254	7:5	41
49:9, 11	110		
50:11	178	*Malachi*	
51:2	293	1:9	178
55:3	186–8		

Jeremiah

Psalms

17:19–27	234	24:3	156
17:27	275	38	283
29:7	220	51	283

310

Index of Biblical Passages

105:37	254	2:1	11
106	283–4	2:2	21, 79, 83
130	283	2:14	79, 83
132:1	187	2:41	136, 266
132:8–10	186	2:42	128
132:11–12, 17	187	2:55	37
		2:58	37
Proverbs		2:59–63	160
2:19	109	2:59	30
		2:61	29
Ruth		2:63	29–30, 34
		2:66–7	230
4:11	109	2:68–9	245–6, 298
4:19	112	2:68	246–7, 249, 265, 299
		2:69	30, 169–70, 249
Ecclesiastes		2:70	37, 132, 248
3:20	177	3:1–4:5	264–7
		3:1–6	13, 264, 266–7
Esther		3:1	245–6, 248, 265, 298
		3:2	232
1	79	3:3	41, 264
1:22	260	3:4	238
3:12	56	3:6	298
8:9	56	3:7–4:3	264
9:3	56, 252	3:7	265
		3:8	131, 246, 265–6, 268–9, 298–9
Daniel		3:10–11	265
2:4	260	3:10	266
2:48	214	3:12–13	265
3	77	3:13	168
3:2, 3	56	4	28, 74, 168
3:4–6	251	4:1–3	15, 41, 160–1, 258, 266–7
3:27	56	4:2	83, 266
6:8	56	4:4–5	41, 264
9:12–13	235	4:5	258–9, 261
		4:6–6:22	257–63
Ezra		4:6–6:18	168
1–6	160, 168, 202	4:6–24	258–61
1	250–56	4:6–11	301
1:1	13, 246, 251, 253–4, 298	4:6–7	266
1:2–4	13, 27, 250–4	4:6	16, 259
1:4	252–3	4:7–24	65
1:5–6	254	4:7–23	34, 59
1:5	246	4:7	18, 260
1:6	252	4:8–23	16–17
1:7–11	13, 224, 254–6	4:8	260
1:8	84, 216, 225–6	4:9–10	260
1:9–11	247, 249	4:10	266
1:11	216, 226, 256, 265	4:11	260–1
2	13, 15, 27, 29, 32, 37, 245–50	4:12	17, 258
2:1–2	13	4:13	35

Index of Biblical Passages

4:17–22	18, 261	7:8–9	248
4:20	35	7:9	297
4:21	19	7:10	232
4:23	259	7:12–26	27, 104, 233
4:24	246, 257–9, 261, 265, 298	7:14	42–3, 232
		7:15–20	222
5:1–6:18	261–3	7:17–20	220
5:1–2	257, 261	7:17	42
5:1	265	7:19	37
5:2	86	7:21–4	36, 42
5:3–17	172	7:21	216, 228
5:3–5	262	7:22	223
5:3–4	261	7:24	35–7, 223
5:3	55	7:25–6	42
5:4	15	7:25	262
5:5	261	7:26	8, 232
5:6–17	261	8	224, 248
5:6–12	262	8:1–14	104
5:6, 7	262	8:3	168
5:8	217–18	8:14	79
5:9	261	8:20	36
5:10	15, 30	8:25–7	225, 229
5:14	11, 13, 34, 84, 216–17, 251, 255	8:27	169–70, 225
		8:31	246
5:16	13, 265, 267	8:33	29
5:17	215, 262	8:34	225
6:1–2	262	8:36	56, 228–9, 252
6:1	215	9–10	28
6:2–12	301	9	234
6:2	216	9:1–2	43, 238, 274
6:3–12	261	9:9	290
6:3–6	301	9:12	274
6:3–5	13, 251	10:3	203, 232
6:3	254	10:6	87
6:4	217–18	10:7	251
6:6–7	172	10:9	246, 297
6:7	34	10:15	282
6:9–10	220–1	10:16–17	246, 297
6:9	223	10:16	43, 282
6:10	223		
6:13–14	262, 264	*Nehemiah*	
6:14	210, 259	1:1–3	65
6:15–18	262	1:1	216, 296
6:15	246, 265, 298	1:3	252
6:18	232, 236, 269	1:5–11	276, 292
6:19–22	263, 269	2	224
6:19	246, 298	2:1	296
6:21	41	2:4	276
6:22	262	2:6	19, 207
7:1–5	283	2:7–8	38
7:1	74, 211, 268	2:7	56, 228
7:6	232	2:8–9	228
7:7	5, 29	2:8	275

2:9	56, 230	6:15	65, 211, 296
2:10	18, 49	6:16	275
2:12	275	6:17–19	18, 20
2:13–15	64	6:18	203
2:13	65	7	13, 27, 29, 32, 37
2:14	70	7:1–4	277
2:16–18	20	7:2	275
2:16	204, 277	7:4–6	20
2:17	65	7:4–5	204, 277
2:18	275	7:4	70
2:20	275	7:5	29, 275
3	14–15, 68, 202	7:6–72	245
3:1–32	64, 277	7:7, 19	79, 83
3:1	85, 87, 203	7:44	136
3:4	29	7:45	128
3:5	203, 205, 277	7:57, 60	37
3:6	68, 71	7:69–71	245–7, 298–9
3:8	66–7, 70–2	7:69	29, 170, 247–9
3:11	71	7:70	169, 246
3:13	67, 69, 71	7:71	170
3:21	29	7:72–8:1	245, 265
3:30	203	7:72	37, 246, 248, 298
3:34	67	7:73	296
3:35	18	8–10	208–9
3:36–7	275–6	8	104, 234, 296–7
4	38	8:1	232
4:1–14	273	8:2	232, 245–6, 296–7, 298
4:3	275–6	8:3, 5, 7, 8	232
4:8	204, 275	8:9	34, 232
4:9	275	8:13–15	237
4:13	204	8:13	232, 300
4:14	273, 275	8:14	232
4:15–17	20	8:15	238, 251
5	20, 205	8:16–17	237
5:1	36	8:16	238
5:2–5	35	8:18	232
5:4	20, 35, 37	9	233, 280, 282–93
5:5, 7, 8	36	9:1–5	282
5:9	36, 275	9:1	211
5:13	275	9:3	232, 284
5:14–19	60–3, 206, 216	9:4	284
5:14–18	38, 230	9:6	285
5:14–15	20	9:7–8	285–6
5:14	19, 38, 55, 82–3	9:7	291
5:15	12, 34, 220, 275	9:9–11	286
5:19	206, 276	9:12–21	286–7
6:1	203–4, 277	9:16	286
6:2	15	9:17	286–7
6:5	220	9:22–31	209, 287–8
6:7	173	9:22–5	287
6:9	276	9:26–7	288
6:10, 11	274	9:27	289
6:14	204, 206, 276	9:28, 29–31	288

Index of Biblical Passages

9:32–7	209, 288–9	13:4	87, 211
9:32	263, 283, 286	13:6–7	224
9:33	284	13:10–14	205
9:35–6	290	13:10–13	53, 275
9:36	286	13:14	187, 206, 276
10	233	13:15–22	205–6
10:2–28	205	13:15–21	274
10:2	34	13:15	211
10:17	79, 83	13:18	275
10:29–40	278	13:19	220
10:29	37, 232	13:22	206, 276
10:30–1	234	13:23–31	206
10:30	205, 232	13:23–30	205
10:31–40	234	13:23–8	28
10:31	205	13:23	211
10:32–9	53	13:25	274–5
10:32	205	13:26	273, 275
10:35	205, 232, 234–5	13:28	23, 85
10:36–7	205	13:29–31	264
10:37	232	13:29	276
10:38–9, 40	205	13:30	127
11	27	13:31	205–6, 276
11:1–20	277		
11:1–2	204	*1 Chronicles*	
11:1	249	1–9	95, 101, 106, 114, 120, 167–8
11:3–20	277		
11:3–19	136	1:7–13	150
11:19	128	2:2–8	107
11:24	39	2:3–4:23	106–14
11:25–36	31	2:3–8	111, 114
12:10–11	75, 86	2:3	113–14
12:11	85	2:9	112–13
12:22	6, 75, 80, 85–8	2:10–17	107–8, 112–13
12:23	85	2:18–24	108, 113
12:25	128	2:18–19	111
12:26	60, 211, 264	2:20	107
12:27–43	203, 277	2:21–3	111
12:31–9	64, 67	2:24	109–11
12:32, 33	80	2:25–33	107, 112–13
12:35	137	2:34–41	111, 113
12:38	71–2	2:42–50	107, 112
12:39	68, 71	2:50–2	107–8, 110
12:41	137	2:52, 53–5	111
12:44–7	279–80	2:55	111–12
12:44	211	3	111, 113
12:47	210	3:1–16	107
13	20	3:1, 4, 5	113
13:1–3	273	3:18	84, 255
13:1	211, 232	3:19–24	106, 111
13:3	232	3:19–21	167
13:4–14	206	3:19	12, 33, 58, 83
13:4–9	275	3:22	168
13:4–8	18	4:1–23	114

4:1	111, 138	14	118, 241
4:2–4	107, 110	14:7	116
4:4	110	14:8	192
4:5–7	108, 110	15–16	129
4:8–23	111	15:4	136
4:21–3	106	15:5–10	137
4:39	192	15:11	137–8
5:1–2	106	15:12, 14, 15	137
5:3	138	15:16 ff.	136
5:20	117	15:21, 24	136
6:1–81	111	15:25 ff.	137
6:31–2	158	15:26	117
6:31 ff.	136	15:28	137
7:6–12	111	16:4 ff.	136
8:1–40	111	16:10, 11	192
9:1–18	136	16:37	138
9:17 ff.	128	16:38	136
9:19	128	16:39	157
10:13–14	151, 192	16:40	232
10:14	189	17	147, 151–2
11:1–9	119	17:6	179
11:1–3	118	17:10	180, 192
11:4–9	118	17:11–14	177
11:6	82	17:11	176, 178–9
11:7	116	17:12–13	181
11:10	118–19	17:12	177, 184
11:10–47	115, 119	17:13	183, 189
11:11–47	118	17:14	180, 184, 189
11:11	130	17:16–27	180
11:13 f.	120	17:17, 23, 24	184
11:15 ff.	120	17:25	192
12:1–23	115–25	17:27	184
12:1	117–18	18–20	147
12:9	116, 121	18:1	192
12:15	121–2	18:8	146, 152
12:16	121	18:11	152
12:17	116, 124	20:4	192
12:18	116, 118, 121	21	153
12:19	116–18, 121–2, 125	21:3	192
12:20	121	21:20	154
12:21	116	21:22–5	155
12:22	121	21:26–22:1	154
12:23	115–16, 118	21:29	157
12:24–38	119	22:1–10	142
12:24 ff.	115	22:1	146
12:25	116	22:2–4	265
12:34	117	22:2, 3 f.	146
12:35	116	22:5	146, 185
12:39–41	119	22:6	143
12:39	117	22:6 ff.	141, 144–5
13–16	151	22:7–8	147
13:1–5	151	22:8	152
13:2	132	22:9–10	147, 177, 181

Index of Biblical Passages

22:9	141, 181	28:11–18	147
22:10	182, 184	28:20	142–3
22:12–13	143, 182	29:1–2	146, 185
22:13	143	29:1	182
22:14–19	183	29:2–9	146
22:15	146	29:7	168–70
22:17	117	29:8	135
22:18	141	29:11	189
22:18–19	147	29:23	144, 189
22:19	147	29:24	144
23–27	126–40, 268–9	29:25	145
23:1–2	96		
23:2	127, 132, 137	*2 Chronicles*	
23:3–6	127–8, 131–2, 134	1	241
23:3	266, 268	1:1	145
23:4	265	1:2–6	150
23:6–24	131, 138	1:3–6	157
23:13–14	131	1:4	147
23:24	266, 268	1:5	108
23:25–32	131–2	1:12	183
23:27	266, 268	1:14–17	151
24:1–19	132–3	2:6	146
24:1–2	236, 269	2:7–15	265
24:2	133	2:7, 13–14	158
24:5	132	2:14	146, 158
24:7–18	126–7, 140	2:16	146
24:7	139	3:1	146, 155–6
24:20–31	133, 138	3:2	265
25:1–31	129–31, 138	3:14	158
25:1–6	136	5–7	262
25:4	130	5:1	146, 152
25:5	116	5:2–6:11	151
25:8	131–2	5:2–14	148
26:1–19	128–9	5:5	157
26:12	133	5:11 ff.	265
26:13	131–2	5:12	136
26:20–32	133–4	6:7–9	147
26:21	135	6:9	177
27	134	6:11	148
28:1	96, 127, 135, 137	6:15–17	187
28:2–8	141	6:15	183
28:2–3, 4–10	147	6:16	182–3
28:5–6	177, 182	6:41–42	148, 186
28:5	189	7:1–3	148
28:6–7	181	7:1	154, 188, 192
28:7–10	182	7:6	148, 265
28:7–8	143	7:8–19	234
28:7	182–5	7:12–22	191–4
28:8	185	7:13–15	191–2
28:8 ff.	144	7:17–18	182, 193
28:9	143, 182	7:17	183
28:10	142–3, 182	7:19–22	193–4
28:11–19	157	7:19	185

Index of Biblical Passages

8:12–15	148	28	194
8:14	135, 253	28:16, 23	117
8:16	160	29:1	110
9:8	189	29:5–11	243
10:16	122	29:13–14	136
11:5–10	98	29:23–30	145
11:12	116	29:34	269
11:16	192	29:35	160
11:22–3	98	30	234
12:1	194	30:1	253
12:2–8, 9	258	30:3	236, 269
12:6–7	192	30:5–9	251
12:6	194	30:5	236
12:12	192	30:6–9	160, 192, 243, 293
13:4–12	159	30:10	232
13:5–8	188–9	30:11	192
13:5	177, 183	30:25	132
13:13–18	194	31:3, 4	232
14:10	117	31:17	131
15:2	194, 243	32:3, 8	117
15:4, 15	192	32:20	192
16:7–10, 12	194	32:21	82, 179
16:9	243	32:24, 26	192
17:9	232, 253	32:30	97–8
18:31	117	32:32	187
19:2	117	33:12, 13	192
19:7	243	33:14	71
19:9	143	33:19, 23	192
20:2–4	194	34:7	192
20:4	192	34:9	174
20:13–23	194	34:14, 15	232
20:20	195, 243	34:19–28	300
21:1–4	98	34:19, 30	232
21:7	177, 183, 190	35	234, 269
21:12	253	35:4	135, 253
22:7	178	35:6	236
23:3	177, 183, 190	35:8	132
23:18	135, 232, 236	35:12	232, 236
24:9	251	35:13	235
24:20	116, 124	35:15	136
25:4	232	35:20–5	98
25:8	117	35:20–4	97
26:6	98	35:26	187, 232, 236
26:7	117	36:12–16	194
26:9	69	36:12, 13	192
26:10	98	36:22	149
26:13, 15	117		

Apocrypha

1 Esdras

1:21–2, 31	300
2	74
2:12	301
3:1–5:6	13
3:1–5:3	294
5:7 ff.	297
5:45	303
5:70–1	302
6:23–5, 26–33	301
8:1	74

Baruch

2:2	235

1 Maccabees

2:1	126, 139

2 Maccabees

2:18	300

New Testament

Luke

1:5–9	126

1 Peter

5:13	263

Revelation

14:18	263
18:2	263

Index of Modern Authors

Abel, F.-M. 139
Ackroyd, P.R. 84, 100, 103, 122, 139, 148–9, 159, 164, 171, 174–5, 200, 208, 241, 244, 268, 286, 289, 291–2
Adinolfi, M. 187
Aharoni, Y. 12, 51, 53–4, 59, 83
Ahlemann, F. 200
Ahlström, G.W. 42
Aistleitner, J. 67
Albright, W.F. 31, 47, 50–1, 58, 84, 86, 112, 170
Alexander, P.S. 250, 305
Allan, J. 169
Allen, L.C. 99, 110, 296
Allrik, H.L. 31, 226, 245–6
Alt, A. 6–7, 11, 13, 17, 19, 26–7, 30, 33–4, 37, 46–50, 55, 59–60, 64, 70
Anderson, A.A. 187
Anderson, B.W. 188, 255
Anderson, G.A. 45
Anderson, G.W. 102, 291
Assaf, D. 281
Attridge, H.W. 303–4
Auld, A.G. 97
Avigad, N. 6, 11–12, 16, 33, 48, 50–1, 53–9, 61, 64, 66, 70–1, 73
Avi-Yonah, M. 65–6, 126

Baker, D.L. 163
Balentine, S.E. 272
Baltzer, K. 117, 209
Barag, D. 8, 21–3, 44–5, 53, 89
Barton, J. 272
Batten, L.W. 84, 216, 245
Baumgartner, W. 169
Becking, B. 271
Bedford, P.R. 26, 37, 40
Beeston, A.F.L. 66
Beltz, W. 106
Bengtson, H. 82
Bentzen, A. 172
Benveniste, E. 227–8
Benzinger, I. 108, 130, 176

Berger, P.-R. 13, 84, 255
Berlin, M. 132
Bernard, P. 213–14
Bertholet, A. 103, 200, 204, 223, 247, 260, 282
Betlyon, J.W. 44, 50, 57
Betz, O. 136
Beuken, W.A.M. 171–3, 187–8
Bewer, J.A. 245, 252, 256
Beyse, K.-M. 84, 171–2
Bianchi, F. 40
Bickerman, E.J. 13, 78, 251, 253
Biella, J.C. 67
Blenkinsopp, J. 26, 29, 39–40, 43, 160, 272–4, 277, 297–9
Bloch, H. 77–80
Bloch, R. 241
Boer, P.A.H. de 122
Bogoljubov, M.N. 213
Botterweck, G.J. 174, 177, 181
Bowman, R.A. 213–16, 218–19, 225, 263, 282
Braun, R.L. 100, 102, 146, 152, 175, 182–3, 185, 242, 245, 267
Bream, H.N. 98
Bresciani, E. 55
Briant, P. 221, 227, 230
Bright, J. 21, 84, 162
Brockington, L.H. 84, 87–8, 263
Bromiley, G.W. 67
Broshi, M. 69
Bruce, F.F. 126, 163
Brunet, A.-M. 113, 174, 181, 186, 291
Bull, R.J. 24, 269
Burn, A.R. 16, 214
Burrows, M. 67
Bussche, H. Van den 179
Butler, T.C. 138

Cahill, N. 212
Cameron, G.G. 61, 212–13, 215, 227
Caquot, A. 177, 182, 187, 189
Carradice, I. 212

Index of Modern Authors

Carrez, M. 209, 283
Carson, D.A. 305
Carter, C.E. 31-2
Cassuto, U. 108
Cazelles, H. 102, 202
Childs, B.S. 211, 282
Clements, R.E. 40, 266
Clines, D.J.A. 38, 102, 217, 234-5, 237-8, 272, 278, 282, 284
Cody, A. 126
Coggins, R.J. 24, 137, 210, 269
Collins, M.F. 159
Cook, J.M. 4, 14, 16, 46, 49, 214
Coppens, J. 174, 282, 286, 291
Cowley, A. 3, 17, 21, 43, 49, 56, 79, 155, 212, 253
Cox, C.E. 295-6
Crenshaw, J.L. 284
Crim, K. 259
Croft, S.J.L. 102
Cross, F.M. 12, 17, 22, 47, 49, 51-2, 54-5, 83, 85-7, 98, 102-3, 138, 155, 166-8, 170, 173, 200, 214, 217, 233, 239-40, 296
Crowfoot, J.W. 68
Curtis, E.L. 106, 113, 116-17, 121, 130, 132, 139, 147, 176, 193

Dandamaev, M. 221
Daniels, D.R. 272, 277
Davies, G.I. 58
Davies, P.R. 26, 41
Davies, W.D. 48, 199-200
Debevoise, N.C. 78
Degen, R. 213, 225
Delaunay, J.A. 213-14, 216, 218-19
Delitzsch, F. 109
Demsky, A. 106
Descamps, A. 282, 291
Destinon, J. von 78
De Vries, S.J. 158
Díaz, R.M. 58
Dillard, R.B. 100, 150
Dion, P.-E. 26, 29, 38, 99, 153, 250
Dogniez, C. 295
Doré, J. 209, 283
Driver, G.R. 19, 110, 212, 227
Driver, S.R. 99, 117
Dumbrell, W.J. 19
Durham, J.I. 143

Ehrlich, A.B. 68
Eissfeldt, O. 67, 95, 188, 244, 257, 264

Emerton, J.A. 19, 155, 173, 245
Eph'al, I. 44
Eppstein, V. 123
Eskenazi, T.C. 26, 28, 31, 36, 278, 300-1
Evans, C.D. 15, 30
Ewald, H. 130
Exum, J.C. 271

Feldman, L.H. 74, 78
Fensham, F.C. 11, 284
Finkelstein, L. 48, 199, 200
Fishbane, M. 234-8, 241, 258, 274, 302
Fisher, L.R. 117
Fitzgerald, G.M. 68
Fitzmyer, J.A. 55-6, 250
Flanagan, J.W. 159
Fohrer, G. 110
Frank, H.T. 106
Freedman, D.N. 83, 102, 138, 166-8, 170, 173, 182, 299
Frei, P. 223
Fretheim, T.E. 187
Friedman, R.E. 157, 201, 272, 292
Fritz, V. 106
Frye, R.N. 4, 16, 43, 49

Gadd, C.J. 74
Galling, K. 15, 30, 81, 83-5, 101, 136, 164, 171-2, 177, 245, 247, 251, 254
Gamberoni, J. 155
Garbini, G. 51
Gardner, A.E. 300, 303
Gardner, P. 168
Garrett, J.L. 126
Gärtner, B. 161
Gerleman, G. 99
Gershevitch, I. 4, 14, 16, 46, 212-15, 219, 222, 227
Gese, H. 30, 136, 256
Geva, H. 64, 66, 71-3
Ghul, M.A. 66
Gibson, J.C.L. 55, 155
Gignoux, Ph. 213
Gilbert, M. 209, 283, 286, 292
Ginsberg, H.L. 252
Goettsberger, J. 120, 152, 185, 264
Goldman, M.D. 252
Goldstein, J.A. 139
Goodman, M. 295
Goulder, M.D. 149
Grabbe, L.L. 25, 36, 44-5
Grafman, R. 71, 73
Greenfield, J. 45, 55-7, 83, 215

Grelot, P. 3, 209, 283
Grønbaek, J.H. 123
Gröndahl, F. 112
Gunkel, H. 283
Gunn, D.M. 124
Gunneweg, A.H.J. 102, 126, 211, 216, 220, 244, 268, 273, 277, 282, 293

Hackens, T. 45
Hallo, W.W. 15
Hallock, R.T. 61, 212, 214–15, 219–20, 222, 224, 226–7, 229–30
Halpern, B. 28, 299
Hamburger, H. 170
Hänel, J. 95–6, 119, 128, 130–1, 136, 139, 149, 154, 181
Hanhart, R. 248, 302
Hanson, P.D. 165, 190, 208, 210, 292
Haran, M. 102
Harrelson, W. 188, 255
Harrison, R.K. 167, 173
Hatch, E. 80, 82
Hauer, C.E. 118
Haupt, P. 130
Hayes, J.H. 11, 13–14, 33, 55, 199, 292
Heider, G.C. 156
Heim, R.D. 98
Hengel, M. 136
Hensley, L.V. 250
Herr, L.G. 58
Herzfeld, E.E. 169, 212, 219
Hill, G.F. 169
Hinnells, J.R. 213
Hinz, W. 213–17, 219–20, 222, 225, 227, 229
Hoffner, H.A. 117
Hoglund, K.G. 24, 33–4, 41, 43, 272, 277
Hölscher, G. 30, 77–8, 103, 200, 247
Horsley, R.A. 26
Houtman, C. 115, 233–7, 269

Im, T.-S. 102, 151
In der Smitten, W.Th. 5, 19, 104, 173, 200, 209, 233, 297, 302
Ishida, T. 201
Ivry, A.L. 274

Janssen, E. 292
Japhet, S. 7, 15, 32, 35, 100, 102, 116, 120, 153, 167, 173–5, 179, 182–3, 185–6, 189–90, 192–3, 200, 242, 289, 291, 293
Jastrow, M. 219

Jeremias, J. 126
Johnson, M.D. 113, 167
Jongkees, J.H. 168–9
Justi, F. 79, 254

Kaiser, O. 102
Kalimi, I. 305
Kamioka, K. 213–14
Kapelrud, A.S. 202
Kaufman, S.A. 54
Kaufman, Y. 127
Kautzsch, E. 30, 103, 130, 200, 247
Keil, C.F. 94, 109, 121–2, 167, 177–8, 189, 246, 259
Kellermann, U. 18–19, 68, 103–4, 173, 200–1, 205, 209, 233, 273, 276–7, 280
Kent, R.G. 3, 169
Kenyon, K. 64, 66, 68, 71–2
Kilian, R. 156
Kippenberg, H.G. 10, 24, 35, 89, 140, 157, 159, 201, 269
Kitchen, K.A. 253
Kittel, R. 94, 130, 248
Klein, R.W. 233, 246, 296
Klein, S. 112
Kline, M.G. 145
Klostermann, A. 257
Knibb, M. 210
Knight, D.A. 291
Koch, H. 220–3, 229
Koch, K. 200, 223, 297
Kooij, A. van der 295, 299–300
Korpel, M.C.A. 271
Kraeling, E.G. 212, 217
Kraemer, D. 271–2
Kreissig, H. 26, 35, 37
Kropat, A. 116
Kugel, J.L. 283
Kuhl, C. 258
Kühlewein, J. 284
Kuhrt, A. 216
Kuschke, A. 171, 256
Kutscher, E.Y. 11, 54, 217

Lang, B. 258
Lapp, N.L. 57
Lapp, P.W. 51, 53, 57, 86
LaSor, W.S. 67, 69
Lemaire, A. 12, 29, 33, 40, 45, 58, 155, 214
Lemke, W.E. 99, 107, 147, 152–3, 179–80, 190, 233, 239
Leuze, O. 46

Index of Modern Authors

Levenson, J.D. 256
Levine, B.A. 213–14
Lewis, D.M. 214–16, 227, 229
Liddell, H.G. 82
Lindblom, J. 123
Lipiński, E. 57–8
Liver, J. 127, 135, 139, 257
Lloyd, A.B. 14
Lohfink, N. 142–5
Lohse, E. 163
Lozachmeur, H. 214
Luria, B.Z. 124

Maass, F. 171
McCarter, P.K. 99, 239
McCarthy, D.J. 142–4, 209, 280, 291
McConville, J.G. 280
McCown, C.C. 18
Macdonald, J. 157
McEvenue, S.E. 6, 33, 55
Mackenzie, D.N. 220
McKenzie, S.L. 153, 239–40, 296–7, 299
Madsen, A.A. 106, 113, 116–17, 121, 130, 132, 139, 147, 176, 193
Malamat, A. 74
Marcus, R. 74, 76–7, 80–2, 85
Mason, R. 173, 210, 243, 293
Massaux, É. 282, 291
Mathias, D. 242–3
Mattingly, H. 169
Mayes, A.D.H. 292
Mazar, B. 18, 87
Meillet, A. 169
Mendelsohn, I. 106
Mendenhall, G.E. 181
Mettinger, T.N.D. 180
Meyer, E. 170, 250
Meyers, E.M. 8, 12, 22, 33, 58–9
Michaeli, F. 69–70, 106, 113, 174
Micheel, R. 153, 242
Mildenberg, L. 21, 56
Milgrom, J. 274
Milik, J.T. 126
Millar, F. 295
Miller, J.M. 11, 13–14, 33, 55, 199, 292
Miller, P.D. 33, 115, 117, 155, 233
Möhlenbrink, K. 145, 149
Moore, C.A. 98
Morgenstern, J. 81, 86, 263
Mørkholm, O. 21, 56
Mosis, R. 100, 103, 115, 118–19, 141, 151, 158, 174–5, 182–3, 185, 210, 241, 297
Moucharte, G. 45

Mowinckel, S. 19, 82, 85–7, 103–4, 200, 205, 208, 233, 246–9, 269, 297, 300
Müller, W.W. 66
Myers, J.M. 67, 84–5, 87–8, 100, 112, 115, 120, 130, 139, 144, 184, 193, 200, 215, 253, 291, 303

Naamani, I.T. 218
Naveh, J. 18, 45, 51–2, 54–7, 83, 155, 213, 216, 225
Neill, S.C. 153
Nelson, R.D. 292
Neusner, J. 78
Newsome, J.D. 102, 124, 138, 166–8, 170, 172–3, 181–2, 242
Nickelsburg, G.W.E. 304
Nicole, E. 153
Nikel, J. 245
Noe, S.P. 168–9
Noordtzij, A. 174, 177
North, R. 60–1, 98, 174, 291
Norton, G.I. 297
Noth, M. 74, 79, 93–105, 106–7, 110, 112, 115, 118, 120, 123–4, 137, 148, 152, 164, 167, 200, 241, 247, 291

Oded, B. 292
Oesterley, W.O.E. 94
Olmstead, A.T. 4, 89, 172, 260
Olyan, S.M. 45

Parker, S.B. 123
Payne Smith, R. 219
Perichanian, A.G. 28
Petersen, D.L. 102, 124, 129–30, 138, 242
Petit, T. 229
Pfeiffer, R.H. 163
Phillips, A. 210
Pietersma, A. 296
Pisano, S. 297
Plöger, O. 162–6, 175, 188, 194, 208, 210, 292
Pohlmann, K.-F. 103, 162, 168, 200, 208, 246–7, 249, 295, 297, 300
Polzin, R. 61, 116, 200
Porten, B. 3, 56, 83, 222
Porter, J.R. 85, 102, 143, 149, 291
Postgate, J.N. 57
Poulssen, N. 184
Praetorius, F. 112
Pritchard, J.B. 47
Propp, W.H. 28, 299

Rabin, C. 126
Rabinowitz, I. 19
Rad, G. von 95-6, 103, 120, 124, 128, 148-9, 163-4, 174, 177, 191, 193, 241-3, 273, 284, 291
Rahmani, L.Y. 21, 56, 83
Rainey, A. 14, 46, 117, 260
Redpath, H.A. 80, 82
Reed, W.L. 106
Rehm, M. 99, 147, 152
Reicke, B. 163
Reid, P.V. 179
Rendsburg, G. 20
Rendtorff, R. 233
Richards, K.H. 26, 28, 31, 36
Richardson, H.N. 51
Robert, Ph. de 179
Robinson, E.S.G. 169
Robinson, T.H. 94
Rofé, A. 151
Rogerson, J.W. 94
Römer, T. 32
Romerowski, S. 153
Rost, L. 256
Rothstein, J.W. 95-6, 106, 118-19, 128, 130-1, 136, 139, 149, 154, 181
Rouse, R. 153
Rowland, C.C. 210
Rowley, H.H. 83, 88, 202, 257, 269
Rudavsky, O. 218
Rudman, S. 162
Rudolph, W. 60, 68, 83-5, 87-8, 93-4, 96, 100-1, 104, 107-8, 110, 114-15, 118, 120, 128, 130-1, 133, 135-7, 139, 144, 147, 152, 154, 163-4, 167, 170-1, 173, 175, 177-8, 183-4, 188-9, 193, 200, 202, 208, 210, 216, 223, 236, 245, 247-8, 250, 252, 257, 259-61, 282-3, 287
Ruffing, A. 273
Ryckmans, J. 66

Sachau, E. 255
Saebø, M. 102
Safrai, S. 139
Saller, S.J. 50
Sancisi-Weerdenburg, H. 216
Sanders, J.A. 155
Sapin, J. 32
Sauer, G. 171
Saydon, P.P. 282
Schaeder, H.H. 200, 257, 283
Schalit, A. 78, 81, 85

Schemann, F.A.C. 78
Schenker, A. 297, 301-3
Schmidt, E.F. 169, 212-13, 215, 219
Schmidt, L. 123
Schmidt, P. 136
Schneider, H. 200
Schottroff, L. 10
Schottroff, W. 10, 187
Schramm, B. 41
Schreckenberg, H. 78
Schultz, C. 15, 30
Schürer, E. 126, 139, 295, 305
Schwartz, D.R. 44
Schwartz, M. 222
Schwyzer, E. 169-70
Scott, R. 82
Seeligmann, I.L. 125, 179, 181, 183-4, 241-2, 258
Segal, J.B. 213, 216-17, 269
Seitz, C.R. 292
Sellers, O.R. 83
Sellin, E. 30, 50
Seybold, K. 171
Shaheen, N. 72
Shaked, Sh. 213, 216, 225
Shear, T.L. 168
Shinan, I.A. 302
Shutt, R.J.H. 78
Simon, M. 180
Simons, J. 64
Smend, R. 245
Smith, J.M.P. 115
Smith, M. 6, 13, 33, 55, 60, 81, 89
Smith, P.A. 41
Smith-Christopher, D.L. 26
Snaith, N.H. 85
Soggin, J.A. 9
Speiser, E.A. 178
Stade, B. 282
Stager, L.E. 218, 220
Stark, J.K. 112
Steck, O.H. 292
Steindler, G.M. 126
Stern, E. 3, 6, 15, 17, 21, 33, 47-51, 56, 59, 61, 218, 292
Stern, M. 139-40
Stinespring, W.F. 174
Stoebe, H.J. 123
Stone, M.E. 304
Strecker, G. 15, 32, 293
Sturdy, J. 123
Sukenik, E.L. 50-1
Sumner, W.M. 214

Index of Modern Authors 323

Tadmor, H. 44, 74
Tafazzoli, A. 213
Talmon, S. 126, 138, 179, 200, 253, 258-9, 264
Talshir, D. 302
Talshir, Z. 296, 301-2
Täubler, E. 78
Thackeray, H.St.J. 74, 77, 79
Theis, J. 245
Throntveit, M.A. 102, 159, 202, 242
Tollefson, K.D. 26, 271
Torczyner, H. 130
Torrey, C.C. 5, 82, 104, 148, 152, 200, 202, 223, 248, 256, 282-3, 296
Tov, E. 99, 235, 302
Trumbull, H.C. 189
Tucker, G.M. 291
Tuland, C.G. 68-9, 75, 80, 84, 87
Tuplin, C. 212, 214, 229
Tushingham, A.D. 64

Ulrich, E.C. 99, 153, 239, 271

VanderKam, J.C. 44, 271
Van Dyke Parunak, H. 258
Vardaman, E.J. 126
Vaux, R. de 13, 59, 106, 126, 134, 139, 220, 250, 257, 263
Veenhof, K.R. 215
Vermes, G. 295, 304-5
Vincent, L.-H. 50
Vogelsang, W. 213
Volz, P. 188

Waggoner, N.M. 21, 56
Washington, H.C. 28

Waterman, L. 171
Watzinger, C. 50
Weill, J. 79
Weinberg, J.P. 26-39, 42, 223
Weiss, I.H. 79
Welch, A.C. 95, 102, 120, 127-8, 130-1, 133, 136, 166-7, 291-2
Wellhausen, J. 94, 99, 106, 109-10, 191
Welten, P. 69, 98, 100-1, 116-17, 124, 138, 148-9, 151
Wenham, G.J. 145-6
Westermann, C. 242, 251, 285
Wette, W.M.L. de 94
White, J.B. 15
Whitehead, J.D. 254
Widengren, G. 11, 22, 33, 55, 199
Whitelam, K.W. 8-10
Wijngaards, J. 256
Wikgren, A. 74, 77
Wildberger, H. 252
Willi, T. 94, 97, 100-1, 118, 137, 148, 154, 174, 179, 194, 240-1
Wilson, R.R. 112
Winter, P. 126
Wiseman, D.J. 74
Wolff, H.W. 106
Wright, G.E. 24, 47, 260, 269
Wright, J.S. 84

Yadin, Y. 126, 134
Yamauchi, E.M. 20
Yardeni, A. 56

Zakovitch, Y. 151
Zeron, A. 121-2
Ziegler, K.-H. 78

Subject Index

Abijah 188–9
Abraham 285, 293
Ahzai 16, 21, 55, 59
Akkadian 55, 57, 214, 216, 218–19
Alexander the Great 86–88
Alexandria 295
Amasai 121–2
Amestris 16
Ammon(ite) 18, 58
Arachosia 214, 216, 227
Aramaic 51, 55–7, 60–1, 78, 117, 213–20, 227, 254, 256, 260, 263, 302
'Araq el-Emir 18, 303
Ark 147, 151, 159, 186
Arsames 16, 19, 227–8
Artaxerxes 4, 22, 49, 79, 81, 168, 210–11, 257–9, 262
Artaxerxes I 17–18, 27, 29, 35, 37, 65, 82, 172, 214, 220
Artaxerxes II 22, 29, 81–2, 84, 87–9
Artaxerxes III Ochus 22, 44, 81–2, 84, 87–9
Asaph 136, 266
Assyria(ns) 17, 263

Baal 155
Babylon 8, 11, 13, 32, 42, 224, 227, 251, 281
Babylonian Chronicle 74
Bagohi 21–2, 81–4
Bagoses 21–2, 24, 44, 74–5, 79, 81–4, 89, 140
Behistun inscription 56
Bethany 51
Beth-hakkerem 15
Beth-zur 15, 83
Beyond the River 6, 11, 14, 17–18, 20, 46
Bezalel 158
Bigvai 21
broad wall, the 70–1
bullae 11–12, 33, 52–5

Cambyses 14
Churchill, Sir Winston 275

citizen-temple community 27–8, 30–1, 35–7, 39–40, 43, 45
coins 8, 21–2, 44–5, 47, 50, 52–3, 56–7, 83, 168–70
Croesus of Lydia 168
Ctesias 16
Cyrus 13–15, 27, 29–30, 210, 226, 251–2, 261–2, 264
Cyrus Cylinder 221

Daric 30, 168–70
Darius 4, 210–11, 259, 261, 263–4
Darius I 13–14, 29–30, 46, 88, 168–72, 220–2, 258
Darius II 84, 88
Darius III 88
Darius the Persian 6, 88
Deuteronomistic History 93, 239–43
Diodorus Siculus 82
doxologies of judgement 284
Drachma 30, 170
Dung Gate 67–70

Edomites 15
Egypt(ian) 14, 16, 22, 49, 89, 227, 260
Elamite 61, 214–15, 219
Elephantine 3, 17, 21–2, 43, 47, 49, 56, 79, 81–5, 89
Eliashib 80, 85–7, 203
Elnathan 12, 14, 16, 33, 54–5, 57, 59
Ephraim Gate 70–1
Esarhaddon 41, 266
Ethan 136
Exodus 254–6
Ezra 5, 8, 16, 20, 23, 29, 35, 42–3, 81, 222, 225, 229–30, 233, 258, 282
Ezra Memoir 104, 248, 283, 296–7

fathers' house 28, 32
Fish Gate 71

gatekeepers 30, 128–9, 136
Genesis Apocryphon 304
Gerizim 152, 154, 157, 160, 269–70

Gershom 133
Gibeon 47-8, 51, 150, 154, 158-9
Gideon 154
gloss 110

Hananiah 84
haoma ceremony 213
Hebron 15, 118-20
Heman 136
Herodotus 3, 76, 169
Hezekiah 69, 159-60, 175
Hezekiah the governor 56
Hezekiah's tunnel 97
high priest 8, 21-2, 24, 27, 30, 34, 44-5, 75, 80, 84-7, 172-4, 211, 283
Hinnom Valley 69-70
holy war 273
Huramabi 158
Hyrcania 22-3, 89

immediate retribution 191-2
India 227
installation 141-2

Jaddua 86
jar handles 16, 47, 52-3
Jeduthun 136
Jehoiarib 139
Jehoshaphat 69
Jericho 15, 23, 51
Jerusalem 15, 18, 38, 47-8, 51-2, 64-73, 118-19, 140, 156, 161, 164, 204, 259, 268
Jeshanah 68
Jeshua 30, 86, 171, 261, 267
Jesus 22, 24, 44, 74, 81, 84-5, 87
Jewish Quarter, the 64
Joannes 22, 44, 74-5, 80, 84-7, 140
Johanan the priest 8, 21, 44, 53, 80-1, 84-7
Joiakim 211
Josephus 3, 21, 23-4, 74-89, 168, 259, 300, 304
Joshua 141-5
Josiah, death of 97

Kandahar 227
Keilah 15
Khirbet Beit Lei 155
Kidron Valley 70
Kimhi 115
Kohathites 133

Lachish 15
Leontopolis 303
Letter of Aristeas 77
Levites 30, 127-8, 131, 133-8, 265-6, 269, 282
Levitical sermons 242-3
Lod, Hadid and Ono 15, 32
Lord of Hosts 173
lot-casting 204

Machpelah, cave of 155
Mannuya 230
Mareshah 15
Mechilta 79
Megabyzos 16-17, 49
Meshelemiah 128
Midrash Rabba 79
Migdol Papyrus 55-6
Mishneh Gate 68, 71
Mithredath 226, 254-5
Mizpah 15
Molek 156
Moriah 155-6
Moṣah 52
Moses 158

Nebuchadnezzar 14
Nehemiah 6, 16-21, 23, 27, 29, 33, 37-9, 44, 46, 48-9, 59-63, 64-72, 82, 85, 210, 271-81
Nehemiah Memoir 5, 87, 103-4, 201, 205-8, 249, 271, 273-6
Nicolas of Damascus 77

Obed-edom 128-9, 136
Oholiab 158
Old Persian 3, 169, 215-16, 219, 227-8
Ophel 64, 66, 70-2
Ostanes 83

Palaeo-Hebrew 51, 57
Palmyrene 112
Parnaka 62, 220
Pelusium 76
Pentateuch 94-5, 149, 232-3
Persepolis 169, 212-15, 227
Persepolis texts 61, 212-31
Phoenicia(n) 22, 112
Piraeus 170
Pollux 169
Pool of Siloam 72
priests 131-3, 137, 140
prince of Judah 255-6

Qumran 139
4QSam[a] 98, 239–40

Rabshakeh 82
Ramat Raḥel 12, 16, 21, 33, 51, 53–5, 58–9
repetitive resumption 138, 258
rewritten Bible 304–5
routinization 280

Sabaean 66
sabbath 274–5
Samaria 6, 11, 13, 16–17, 20, 24, 27, 33–4, 41, 46–9, 57, 59–60, 81–3, 85, 292
Samaria Papyri 83, 214
Samaritans 23, 140, 152, 154, 157, 159–60, 164, 207, 268–70
Sanballat 17–18, 23, 49, 57, 87
Sardis 168, 227
Sargon II 266
seals 11–12, 17, 33, 45, 47–55, 57–9, 61
Sennacherib 76
Shechem 23–4, 47–8, 51, 140, 157, 159, 161, 207, 268
Shelomith 12, 14, 33, 54, 58–9
Shenazzar 84
Sheshbazzar 11, 13–14, 34, 46, 48, 55, 59, 84, 217, 225–6, 247, 251, 254
Shiloh 159
Shiqmona 52
Shishak 192
singers, Levitical 30, 96, 129–31, 136, 266
Solon 20
source citation formulae 97
Succession Narrative 121, 124
summary notation 264
Susa 224
Syriac 54

Tabeel 18
tabernacle 108, 154, 157–8
Tabernacles 237–8
Tattenai 15, 30, 34, 172, 261
tax(ation) 35–7, 52–3
Tel Gamma 83
temple 39–40, 42–3, 53, 141, 146–7, 150–61, 164, 185, 203, 210, 220, 259, 262–70, 273, 275, 303
Temple Scroll 233
temple servants 36–7
Tennes 22–3, 89
Tirshatha 29, 34, 247
Tobiah 18, 44, 59, 275
Tower of the Furnaces 71
typology 154, 158
Tyropoeon 67, 69–70

Udjahorresnet 14, 43
Ugaritic 67, 112
Uzziah 69

Valley Gate 67, 69, 71–2

Wâdī ed-Dâliyeh 3, 17, 49, 57
Western hill 64, 66, 69–72

Xerxes 4, 16, 214, 258, 260

Yeḥezqiyah 21, 44
Yeho'ezer 16, 21, 55, 59

Zerubbabel 11–14, 16, 34, 46, 48, 55, 58–9, 83, 86, 166–7, 170–2, 210, 261, 267, 290, 294, 302
Ziklag 119
Zoroastrianism 222

www.ingramcontent.com/pod-product-compliance
Lightning Source LLC
Chambersburg PA
CBHW052146300426
44115CB00011B/1536